PLANETARY URBANISM
The Transformative Power of Cities

Sabine Kraft, Anna Aichinger, Zhen Zhang, ed.

ARCH+ Verlag Aachen

Content / Inhalt

Planetary Urbanism
The Transformative Power of Cities

URBANISATION AND ENVIRONMENTAL PROTECTION

BASIC DATA OF COMPETITION

Entries
125 contributions

Participants
386 participants in different teams
from 31 countries

Prizes
4 prizes, 1. Category
7 prizes, 2. Category
7 prizes, 3. Category

Prize Sum
24,000 Euro

Preliminary Review Group
Sandra Giegler – design
Sabine Kraft – architecture, urban design
Joachim Krausse – cultural Science, design Theory
Philipp Schneider – architecture
Angelika Schnell – architecture,
architectural Theory
Nicole Opel – architecture

International Jury
Gita Goven – one of South Africa's foremost sustainability thinkers, CEO of ARG Design and a founding partner of communiTgrow
Ursula Kleefisch-Jobst – Managing Curator at the M:AI Museum for Architecture and the Art of Engineering in North Rhine-Westphalia
Sabine Kraft – architect, urbanist and publicist, associate editor of ARCH+ since 1984
Joachim Krausse – philosopher and cultural scientist, Professor for Design Theory at Anhalt University of Applied Sciences Dessau
Edurado Lopéz Moreno – Director of Research and Capacity Development at UN-HABITAT, the United Nations Human Settlements Programme
Paul Mijksenaar – designer and partner of Mijksenaar wayfinding experts, Professor at Delft University of Technology
Philipp Oswalt – architect and publicist, Professor for Architectural Theory and Designing at University Kassel
Benno Pilardeaux – earth scientist, head of Media and Public Relations of the German Advisory Council on Global Change (WBGU)
Saskia Sassen – sociologist and economist, Professor of Sociology and Chair of The Committee on Global Thought at Columbia University

We are delighted to present to you the outcomes of the international competition "PLANETARY URBANISM – CRITIQUE OF THE PRESENT IN THE MEDIUM OF INFORMATION DESIGN" within this catalogue. In times of rapid urbanisation, innovative approaches and creative ideas are essential to successfully master the great social and spatial challenges. We want to congratulate the participants on their multi-faceted, intellectually challenging and aesthetically convincing contributions!

Urbanisation and environmental protection are closely intertwined. The growing interdependence of global habitats makes worldwide collaborative action necessary. In this context, environmental foreign policy, as an important future field of diplomacy, is continually gaining in significance.

The Federal Foreign Office has been active in international environmental protection for several years. In the course of environmental foreign policy and climate diplomacy, the Federal Foreign Office is supporting projects worldwide that sharpen the awareness for international environment and climate protection. It is our goal to actively support the transformation towards a sustainable, low-carbon way of life and economic activity. The competition "PLANETARY URBANISM" is one of the projects supported by us. The competition puts the global urbanisation process into the context of social, ecological and economic questions, it provides an exceptional platform to develop diverse ideas and solutions for urgent questions. The increasingly significant medium of information design, also crucial in political education, helps to convey complex circumstances in an understandable way.

Wir freuen uns, Ihnen mit diesem Katalog die Ergebnisse des internationalen Wettbewerbs "PLANETARY URBANISM – KRITIK DER GEGENWART IM MEDIUM DES INFORMATION DESIGN" zu präsentieren. In Zeiten rasanter Urbanisierung sind innovative Ansätze und kreative Ideen unerlässlich, um die großen sozialen und räumlichen Herausforderungen erfolgreich zu meistern. Die Teilnehmenden möchten wir zu ihren facettenreichen, intellektuell herausfordernden und ästhetischen Beiträgen beglückwünschen!

Urbanisierung und Umweltschutz sind eng miteinander verknüpft. Die wachsende gegenseitige Abhängigkeit von weltweiten Lebensräumen macht ein weltweites gemeinschaftliches Handeln notwendig. In diesem Zusammenhang nimmt auch die Bedeutung der Umweltaußenpolitik als wichtiges Zukunftsfeld der Diplomatie stetig zu.

Das Auswärtige Amt ist seit mehreren Jahren im internationalen Umweltschutz aktiv. Im Rahmen der Umweltaußenpolitik und Klimadiplomatie unterstützt das Auswärtige Amt weltweit Projekte, die das Bewusstsein für den internationalen Schutz der Umwelt und des Klimas schärfen. Unser Ziel ist es, die Transformation hin zu einer nachhaltigen, kohlenstoffarmen Lebens- und Wirtschaftsweise aktiv zu unterstützen. Der Wettbewerb "PLANETARY URBANISM" ist eines der von uns geförderten Projekte. Der Wettbewerb stellt den globalen Verstädterungsprozess in den Kontext von sozialen, ökologischen und ökonomischen Fragen, er bietet eine außergewöhnliche Plattform, um vielfältige Ideen und Lösungen für drängende Fragen zu entwickeln. Das auch in der Politikvermittlung zunehmend bedeutsame Medium des Information Design hilft komplexe Sachverhalte in verständlicher Form zu transportieren.

Berlin, im April 2016

Thomas H. Meister
Referatsleiter Klima- und Umwelt-Außenpolitik sowie nachhaltige Wirtschaft
Auswärtiges Amt

THE TRANSFORMATIVE POWER OF CITIES

Sabine Kraft, Anna Aichinger, Zhen Zhang

In 2015 the journal ARCH+ launched a second international competition entitled "Planetary Urbanism – Critique of the Present" sponsored by the German Federal Foreign Office and in consultation with the German Advisory Council on Global Change (WBGU). Because the first competition "Out of Balance – Critique of the Present" was such a success in terms of the number of participants, its international reach and the quality of the submissions[1], the competition's modus operandi was maintained. In the framework of the given theme, the location and terms of reference could be chosen freely, as long as they were based on empirical evidence. Again, the visual representation was to be in the medium of information design. The competition was enhanced by the option of submitting proposals, likewise on an empirical basis, for the improvement of the analysed situation – in the sense of a realisable utopia – and with "Planetary Urbanism" a more specific topic was set which, as it transpired, is infinitely more difficult to handle.[2] What motivated us to do so?

"The 21st century will be the century of cities: Urban environments will become the main organisational form for almost all human societies"[3] and almost all the future issues of humanity will be decided in the cities. The unstoppable progress of global urbanisation however raises more questions than we can currently answer. Does the process of urbanisation manifest itself in characteristic attributes, recognisable patterns in different parts of the world? Are the environmental effects comparable? Are the causes of migration comparable? And what are the downsides of the urbanisation process, i.e., what happens to the rural regions left behind? Urbanisation overturns all traditional structures, but is it in fact a process that is open to general analysis, which can be conceptually defined, or does it come in diverse singular movements that can only be interpreted empirically?

"The momentum of the surge in urbanisation affects first and foremost countries in Asia and Africa and almost 90 percent of the urban population growth up to 2050 is expected to occur on these two continents. By then, an estimated three quarters of the global urban population will be living there."[4] What kinds of structures are being formed? Can they in fact still be described as cities, or is the city breaking up in a process of ongoing change into an urban landscape that consumes land, in which the conventional geographical relationship of centre and periphery no longer applies and the differentiation between city and countryside disappears? And above all: How can the changing reality of life in these urban entities be described?

One of the main reasons for the choice of topic was the hope of gaining insight, by means of an open international competition, into the social reality of life in the cities of the global South. Can we, who still live with a traditional grasp of the city in regulated, well-protected conditions that we take for granted until they no longer function, even begin to imagine a life without basic public services, without a social safety net? Can the social situation in the rapidly expanding megacities of the developing and emerging nations in fact be compared with life in the historic cities that owe their growth to industrialisation in the 19th century?

Urbanisation involves a tremendous transformative power – in respect of the "external" circumstances and physical changes in the environment as well as inwardly, with regard to humankind's life processes and models. Cities have always transformed the lives of their inhabitants, even if not as rapidly as they do today. Daily life itself should be the indicator and measure of change.[5] But this evades scientific analysis. Daily life cannot be described without the people who live it,

Die Zeitschrift ARCH+ hat 2015 unter dem Titel "Planetary Urbanism" einen zweiten internationalen Wettbewerb zur Kritik der Gegenwart ausgeschrieben, gesponsert vom Auswärtigen Amt der Bundesrepublik Deutschland und beraten durch den Wissenschaftlichen Beirat der Bundesregierung Globale Umweltveränderung (WBGU). Da "Out of Balance", der erste Kritik der Gegenwart-Wettbewerb, zu einem großen Erfolg wurde sowohl im Hinblick auf die Zahl der Teilnehmer und die internationale Verbreitung als auch die Qualität der eingereichten Arbeiten[1], wurde das Procedere des Wettbewerbs beibehalten. Im Rahmen des gestellten Themas konnten der Ort und die Aufgabenstellung auf empirisch belegter Grundlage frei gewählt werden. Die Darstellung sollte wieder im Medium des Information Design erfolgen. Erweitert wurde die Ausschreibung um die Möglichkeit, ebenfalls auf empirischer Grundlage auch Vorschläge zur Verbesserung der analysierten Situation einzureichen – im Sinne einer Realutopie – und es wurde mit "Planetary Urbanism" ein spezifischeres Thema gestellt, das, wie sich zeigte, ungleich schwierigerer zu bearbeiten ist.[2] Was hat uns dazu bewogen?

"Das 21. Jahrhundert wird das Jahrhundert der Städte sein: Urbane Räume werden zur zentralen Organisationsform nahezu aller menschlichen Gesellschaften"[3] und nahezu alle Zukunftsfragen der Menschheit werden in den Städten entschieden werden. Die unaufhaltsam voranschreitende Verstädterung der Welt wirft jedoch mehr Fragen auf, als es derzeit Antworten gibt. Zeigen sich im Prozess der Urbanisierung in den verschiedenen Teilen der Welt charakteristische Merkmale, wiedererkennbare Muster? Sind die Auswirkungen auf die Umwelt vergleichbar? Sind die Ursachen für die Migration vergleichbar und wie sieht die Kehrseite des Urbanisierungsprozesses aus: Was geschieht eigentlich auf dem verlassenen "Land"? Urbanisierung wälzt alle überkommenen Strukturen um, aber ist sie überhaupt ein Prozess, der einer allgemeinen Analyse zugänglich ist, der sich auf den "Begriff bringen" lässt oder zerfällt er in diverse Einzelbewegungen, die nur noch empirisch nachgezeichnet werden können?

"Die Wucht des Urbanisierungsschubs betrifft vor allem Länder in Asien und Afrika. Knapp 90 % des Wachstums der urbanen Bevölkerung bis 2050 werden in diesen beiden Kontinenten erwartet. Dann werden dort voraussichtlich nahezu drei Viertel der globalen Stadtbevölkerung leben."[4] Was sind das für Gebilde, die entstehen, lassen sie sich überhaupt noch mit dem Begriff Stadt fassen oder ist die Stadt dabei, sich in einen Prozess fortwährender Veränderungen aufzulösen, in eine Land konsumierende urbane Landschaft, in der das überkommene geographische Verhältnis von Zentrum und Peripherie nicht mehr gilt und die Unterscheidung zwischen Stadt und Land verschwindet? Und vor allem: Wie kann die sich verändernde Lebenswirklichkeit in diesen urbanen Gebilden beschrieben werden?

Einer der Hauptgründe für die Themenstellung war wohl die Hoffnung, über einen international ausgeschriebenen Wettbewerb Einblick in die soziale Lebenswirklichkeit in den Städten des globalen Südens zu bekommen. Können wir, die wir noch mit einem klassischen Verständnis von Stadt in verregelten, mehrfach abgesicherten Verhältnissen leben, die ihrer Selbstverständlichkeit erst dann entkleidet werden, wenn es mal nicht funktioniert, uns auch nur annäherungsweise ein Leben ohne öffentliche Grundversorgung, ohne soziales Netz vorstellen? Lässt sich die soziale Situation in den schnellwachsenden Metropolen der Entwicklungs- und Schwellenländer überhaupt vergleichen mit dem Leben in den historischen Städten, die ihr Wachstum der Industrialisierung bereits im 19. Jahrhundert verdanken?

Urbanisierung beinhaltet eine gewaltige transformative Kraft – sowohl was die "äußeren" Umstände und physische Veränderungen in der Umwelt betrifft, wie auch nach innen gewandt im Hinblick auf die Lebensabläufe und -modelle der Menschen. Städte haben seit jeher das Leben ihrer Bewohner verändert, wenn auch nicht in so kurzen Zeiträumen wie heute. Das Alltagsleben selbst sollte der Indikator für und Maßstab von Veränderungen sein.[5] Es entzieht sich jedoch der

without their emotions and their states of mind. This lends itself more to artistic forms of expression, e.g. the poetic exaltation of everyday banality, documentary films, etc., than to analysis. But it is possible to scientifically analyse the framework conditions within which urban daily life evolves, which have changed with the development of the cities and continue to do so. Here, a fascinating story about daily urban live is to be written.

Submissions for the competition were received from 125 teams with a total of 386 participants from 31 countries. Did these entries meet our expectations and our hopes for the competition? Despite some big surprises regarding the selected topics, no, not at first glance – the panels did not reflect the diversity of urban life. But on closer examination it became clear that many of the submissions accomplish precisely what they were supposed to: they demonstrate, based on concrete empirical examples, the framework conditions that change as a result of the urbanisation process and which account for the transformation of urban life. In order to present the highly heterogeneous projects in this issue, these framework conditions have been categorised and utilised as a structural concept:

GLOBALISATION, OR THE LOCAL EFFECTS OF ECONOMIC INTERDEPENDENCE

The living conditions in cities are strongly affected by the global economy, by the (extremely imbalanced) interrelationships between production, consumption and waste disposal on an international level. Highly disparate local framework conditions evolve in the states and cities of the former industrial nations and those of the Global South. So, the world of consumption that informs daily life in the historic cities is inconceivable without the production and import of goods from low-wage countries. It is not possible to know the conditions in which these goods were produced just by looking at them; the flipside of consumption remains invisible.[6] By contrast, in the cities of the global South the industrialised nations' outsourcing of production and especially industrial pollution, the outsourcing of waste disposal and catastrophic working conditions yield living conditions that can only be controlled to a certain extent on a local level. The export of subsidised agricultural products in particular to the developing and emerging nations destroys the foundations for the subsistence of local small businesses and peasant farmers, who are forced to migrate. For both reasons – capital export and the outsorcing of industry, and the import of cheap goods – globalisation is one of the major forces driving the urbanisation process. Three projects serve as examples of the competition entries compiled in this section:

The Promised Land:
Rising demand of palm oil since the 1970s has led to local environmental degradation. Where it is produced is however not always where it is consumed. Malaysia is only using a fraction of the produced oil for its own purposes, while half of all supermarket products are enriched with palm oil mostly imported from Malaysia.

New Tribal Territories:
Odisha, India, is a trading hub becoming a production and extraction site for international investors. The consequences are deforestation, destruction of agricultural surfaces, and deprivation of the living space of the local indigenous population.

Urbanism of Disassembly:
After their lifetime contribution to contemporary urbanisation, most of the obsolete ships end up on the beach of Alang, India. The project tracks how the shipbreaking business finds its way to the Global South, where a higher profit can be expected due to the geographical conditions, cheap labour and lax environmental laws.

THE INTERCONNECTED CITY, OR THE INFLUENCE OF SCIENCE AND TECHNOLOGY

There is no doubt that the achievements of technology with the emergence of the modern age have had the most profound influence on life in the cities. The transformation of the rhythm of life as a result of independence from the natural day/night cycle, its hastening due to the new modes of locomotion and communication and timesaving in the physical reproduction of life are well documented. The digitalisation of all spheres of life is having a similarly incisive effect on daily life. The accelerated interconnection of increasing volumes of data results in the creation of a digital image of the city tailored to each individual's wishes and requirements, which may be navigated at will. The superimposition of an electronic network on the physical world creates new relationships of proximity and distance and displaces traditional time patterns. New practices in spatial use, daily routines and communication patterns evolve, raising new questions concerning manipulation[7] and the protection of privacy. If, as Lefebvre states, the transformation of everyday life implies revolution, then this has taken place here.[8]

wissenschaftlichen Analyse. Der Alltag lässt sich nicht ohne die Menschen, die ihn leben, ohne ihre Gefühle und Befindlichkeiten beschreiben. Er ist eher künstlerischen Ausdrucksformen zugänglich, z.B. in der poetischen Überhöhung der Banalität des Tagtäglichen, in filmischen Dokumentationen etc. Was aber sehr wohl der wissenschaftlichen Analyse zugänglich ist, sind die Rahmenbedingungen, innerhalb derer sich der städtische Alltag entfaltet, die sich mit der Entwicklung der Städte verändert haben und ständig weiter verändern. Hier wäre eine spannende Geschichte des städtischen Alltags zu schreiben.

Es wurden Wettbewerbsbeiträge von 125 Teams mit insgesamt 386 Teilnehmern aus 31 Ländern eingereicht. Haben diese Arbeiten unsere Erwartungen und die mit dem Wettbewerb verbundenen Hoffnungen erfüllt? Trotz großer Überraschungen, was die gewählten Themen betrifft, nein, auf den ersten Blick nicht, es kam uns auf den Tafeln nicht die Vielfalt des urbanen Lebens entgegen. Erst bei näherer Analyse zeigte sich, dass viele Arbeiten genau das leisten, worauf es ankommt: Am konkreten empirischen Beispiel die Rahmenbedingungen aufzuzeigen, die sich infolge des Urbanisierungsprozesses verändern und denen die Transformation des städtischen Lebens geschuldet ist. Für die Präsentation der sehr heterogenen Arbeiten in dieser Ausgabe wurden diese Rahmenbedingungen kategorisiert und als Gliederungskonzept verwendet:

GLOBALISIERUNG ODER DIE LOKALEN EFFEKTE ÖKONOMISCHER VERFLECHTUNG

Die Lebensverhältnisse in den Städten werden stark durch die globale Ökonomie, die Verflechtung von Produktion, Konsumtion und Entsorgung im internationalen Maßstab bestimmt – und das geschieht in einem sehr asymmetrischen Verhältnis. Es entstehen in den Ländern und Städten der ehemaligen Industriestaaten und denjenigen des globalen Südens sehr unterschiedliche lokale Rahmenbedingungen. So ist die das Alltagsleben in den historischen Städten prägende Konsumwelt ohne die Produktion in Billiglohnländern und den Import der Waren nicht denkbar. Man sieht es den Waren jedoch nicht an, unter welchen Bedingungen sie hergestellt werden, die Kehrseite des Konsums bleibt unsichtbar.[6] Demgegenüber zeitigen die Auslagerung der Produktion, vor allem auch der umweltbelastenden Industrie, die Auslagerung der Müllentsorgung und die katastrophalen Arbeitsverhältnisse in den Städten des globalen Südens Lebensbedingungen, die lokal nur sehr bedingt beeinflussbar sind. Der Export insbesondere von subventionierten Agrarprodukten in die Entwicklungs- und Schwellenländer zerstört die Subsistenzgrundlage des heimischen Kleingewerbes und der Kleinbauern, sie sind zur Migration gezwungen. Globalisierung ist aus beiden Gründen, Kapitalexport und Auslagerung von Industrie sowie Import von Billigprodukten, eine der maßgeblichen Kräfte, die den Urbanisierungsprozess vorantreiben.

Drei Arbeiten sollen als Beispiel für die in diesem Kapitel versammelten Wettbewerbsbeiträge dienen:

The Promised Land:
Die steigende Nachfrage nach Palmöl seit den 1970er Jahren hat zu einer örtlichen Umweltzerstörung geführt. Wo es hergestellt wird, ist jedoch nicht immer dort, wo es auch verbraucht wird. Ein Land wie Malaysia verbraucht nur einen Bruchteil des produzierten Öls für eigene Zwecke, während ca. die Hälfte aller Supermarktprodukte in Malaysia mit Palmöl angereichert sind, das aus Malaysia importiert wurde.

New Tribal Territories:
Odisha in Indien ist ein Umschlagplatz, der zu einem Produktions- und Abbaugebiet für internationale Investoren wird. Die Konsequenzen sind Waldrodung, Zerstörung der landwirtschaftlichen Nutzflächen sowie Raub des Lebensraums der indigenen Bevölkerung.

Urbanism of Disassembly:
Nach ihrem langjährigen Beitrag zur gegenwärtigen Urbanisierung enden überalterte Schiffe am Strand von Alang, Indien. Das Projekt zeigt auf, wie die Schiffsverschrottungsaktivitäten ihren Weg in den globalen Süden fanden. Dessen einzigartige geografische Lage, die billigen Arbeitskräfte und die nicht oder kaum vorhandenen Umweltschutzkontrollen bedeuten höhere Gewinne.

DIE VERNETZTE STADT ODER DER EINFLUSS VON WISSENSCHAFT UND TECHNIK

Es steht außer Frage, dass die Errungenschaften der Technik mit Beginn der Moderne das Leben in den Städten am tiefgreifendsten beeinflusst haben. Die Veränderung des Lebensrhythmus durch die Unabhängigkeit vom natürlichen Tag-/Nachtzyklus, seine Beschleunigung durch die neuen Modi der Fortbewegung und Kommunikation und die Zeitersparnis in der physischen Reproduktion des Lebens sind gut dokumentiert. Ähnlich einschneidend in den Alltag wirkt sich die Digitalisierung aller Lebensbereiche aus. Durch die forciert vorangetriebene Vernet-

Under the banner of the Smart City, managing the city by all-round networking – including the personal consumption figures of the municipal infrastructure, from basic provisions to transport systems – is advocated so that functional processes can be better modified to meet changing needs and requirements and to establish a sustainable urban metabolism. Without wishing to go into the security concerns and ideological implications in greater depth, a Smart City cannot exist without "smart" residents, who adapt their day-to-day lives.

Manila – Ground Constellations:
In Metro Manila, Philippines, private developments leave the city structure fragmented, streets networks chaotic, and public transportation underfinanced. The project derives a pattern through existing situations to facilitate orientation in the chaotic urban conditions.

Syrbia:
In the real world, the bodies of the Syrian refugees are in crisis; thanks to the transcendent Internet, their spirit is with friends and family back home in Syria. Through WiFi-spots in Belgrade they find home in a non-place – "Syrbia", born from a tangible Serbia and a virtual Syria.

Subversive Tehran:
In Tehran, public spaces are not the real stage of everyday life. There is an invisible counterpart of the city behind the facades, where subversive activities take place. These places are connected to the digital world, through which part of the participatory nature of the city is re-established.

Just Trust Us – Or Take This:
Cities are becoming "smart" and "intelligent". Usually, we accept the conditions of service as a mere annoyance. The price that we pay is loss of sovereignty and privacy. Is action without data supply even an option in the interconnected digital city?

NEOLIBERAL CITY POLITICS, OR THE ORGANISATION OF COEXISTENCE

Since the 19th century the traditional functions of the urban infrastructure, such as water supply and sanitation, electricity supply, district heating, waste disposal and processing, the provision of public transport networks and services, road construction, housing construction, the provision of local supply facilities, the design and maintenance of the public sphere, the provision of parks and recreation areas, etc., have fallen to the municipalities, who meet these responsibilities through local government and the foundation of municipally owned companies. As the neoliberal paradigm shift has shown, this form of management is not immutable: the question of what the local community – meaning the community of urban citizens – is responsible for, what its range of duties are, how many community services are realised by the local community and its members and in which form, is subject to political decisions. Supposedly in the name of efficiency, public tasks have been "outsourced" to private providers or investors, right through to the sale of municipal housing stock and real estate. Regardless of the fact that the municipalities thereby voluntarily curtail their sphere of influence and management options regarding the equalisation of social disparities, this outsourcing means less access to once public services for the urban poor, especially so in developing and emerging nations, that their living conditions deteriorate through privatisation and incidences of exclusion rise.

One central aspect of neoliberal urban policy, not only in the historic metropolises, is the redevelopment of the city to accommodate the return of the better-off to the inner cities. The spatial structure of the city, i.e. the living conditions – the location and condition of housing – and the access to public space are the factors that exert the greatest influence on daily life. The gentrification of former working class neighbourhoods, the demolition of so-called slums in good locations, the construction of new housing on expensive inner city land and the commodification of public space have strengthened the tendency towards social segregation and pushed not only the urban poor, but also the lower middle classes, to the peripheries. After barely forty years of neoliberal economic management, the social divide has grown significantly.

Medellín – Human Right on Water:
Medellín's public multi-utility company has increasingly behaved like a privately owned operation, thus systematically disconnecting low-income households from the city's water network. A guaranteed human right until recently, the water circulation has run dry in many parts of the city.

Dwellings:
In 2006, the city of Dresden sold its entire communal housing to a private real estate firm. It thereby redeemed its horrendous debts, but at the expense of giving up control over its own housing policies.

---

zung von immer mehr Daten entsteht ein digitales Abbild der Stadt, in dem zugeschnitten auf die jeweilige Persönlichkeit nach Wunsch und Erfordernis navigiert werden kann. Die Überlagerung des physischen Raums mit einem elektronischen Netzwerk schafft neue Nähe- und Distanzbeziehungen und verschiebt überkommene Zeitmuster. Es bilden sich neue Praktiken des Raumgebrauchs, Alltagsroutinen und Kommunikationsmuster heraus – und es entstehen neue Fragen der Manipulation[7] und des Schutzes der Persönlichkeit. Wenn nach Lefebvre die Veränderung des Alltags eine Revolution bedeutet, hier hat sie stattgefunden.[8]

Unter dem Begriff der Smart City wird in der Bewirtschaftung der Stadt die Vernetzung aller, auch der persönlichen Verbrauchsdaten der kommunalen Infrastruktur von der Grundversorgung bis zu den Verkehrssystemen propagiert, um Funktionsabläufe besser an wechselnde Bedarfe und Anforderungen anpassen zu können und einen nachhaltigen städtischen Metabolismus zu etablieren. Ohne hier auf die Sicherheitsbedenken und ideologischen Implikationen näher eingehen zu wollen, eine Smart City wird es ohne den "smarten" Bewohner, der seinen Alltag anpasst, nicht geben.

Manila – Ground Constellations:
In Metro-Manila auf den Philippinen hinterlassen private Bauprojekte eine fragmentierte Stadtstruktur, ein chaotisches Straßennetz und unterfinanzierte öffentliche Verkehrsmittel. Das Projekt leitet ein Organisationssystem von bestehenden Situationen her, um in den chaotischen städtischen Bedingungen zu orientieren.

Syrbia:
"Syrbien" ist ein Nichtort, geboren aus einem wirklichen Serbien und einem virtuellen Syrien. In der realen Welt stecken die Körper der syrischen Flüchtlinge in einer Krise; dank des transzendenten Internets ist ihr Geist bei ihren Freunden und ihrer Familie zu Hause in Syrien. Mittels WLAN-Punkten in Belgrad finden sie ihren Ort, ihr Daheim, in einem Nichtort – "Syrbien".

Subversive Tehran:
In Teheran sind öffentliche Räume nicht die wirkliche Bühne des täglichen Lebens. Es gibt ein unsichtbares Gegenstück zu der Stadt, in der subversive Aktivitäten stattfinden. Diese Räume sind mit der digitalen Welt verbunden, die virtuell Teile des partizipatorischen Wesens der Stadt wieder herstellt.

Just Trust Us – Or Take This:
Städte werden "smart" und "intelligent". Meistens akzeptieren wir die Geschäftsbedingungen der Dienste und betrachten sie als lästiges Häkchen, das es zu setzen gilt. Der Preis, den wir dafür zahlen, ist der Verlust von Souveränität und Privatsphäre. Gibt es überhaupt ein Handeln ohne Datenabgabe in der vernetzten digitalen Stadt?

NEOLIBERALE STADTPOLITIK ODER DIE ORGANISATION DES ZUSAMMENLEBENS
Seit dem 19. Jahrhundert sind die klassischen Aufgaben der städtischen Infrastruktur wie Wasserversorgung und Kanalisation, Elektrizitätsversorgung, Fernwärme, Abfallbeseitigung und -verarbeitung, Bereitstellung öffentlicher Verkehrsnetze und -betriebe, Straßenbau, Wohnungsbau, Bereitstellung von Wohnfolgeeinrichtungen, Gestaltung und Pflege des öffentlichen Raums, Anlage von Park- und Erholungsflächen etc. den Kommunen zugewachsen und wurden von ihnen durch die kommunale Verwaltung und die Gründung eigener städtischer Betriebe erfüllt. Wie sich mit dem neoliberalen Paradigmenwechsel zeigte, ist dies keine unveränderliche Form der Bewirtschaftung: Die Frage, wofür das Gemeinwesen – und das heißt die Gemeinschaft der Stadtbewohner – zuständig ist, was seine Aufgabenbereiche sind, wie viel an Leistungen vom Gemeinwesen für die Gemeinschaft und den Einzelnen in welcher Form erbracht wird, unterliegt politischen Entscheidungen. Unter dem vorgeblichen Kriterium der Effizienz wurden öffentliche Aufgaben an private Anbieter oder Investoren "ausgelagert" bis hin zum Verkauf kommunaler Wohnungsbestände und Liegenschaften. Abgesehen davon, dass die Kommunen dadurch freiwillig ihren Handlungsspielraum und ihre Steuerungsmöglichkeiten im Ausgleich sozialer Disparitäten beschneiden, hat diese Auslagerung zur Folge, dass ehemals öffentliche Leistungen für die städtisch Armen besonders auch in den Entwicklungs- und Schwellenländern schwerer zugänglich sind, dass ihre Lebenssituation sich durch Privatisierung verschlechtert und die Ausgrenzungen zunehmen.

Ein zentraler Aspekt neoliberaler Stadtpolitik nicht nur in den historischen Metropolen betrifft unmittelbar den Umbau der Stadt entsprechend der Rückwanderungstendenz der Bessergestellten in die Innenstädte. Die räumliche Struktur der Stadt, d.h. die Wohnverhältnisse – Lage und Beschaffenheit der Wohnungen – und die Zugänglichkeit des öffentlichen Raums sind die Faktoren, die den größten Einfluss auf das Alltagsleben ausüben. Die Gentrifizierung ehemaliger Arbeiterviertel, der Abriss von "Slums" in guter Lage, der Wohnungsneubau auf

World Metropols: About Wages and Prices: In our society, is everyone remunerated appropriate to his or her performance? A worldwide comparison of the striking income differentials sheds a not-so-liberal light on neoliberalism, usually understood as operating globally and universally valid.

INFORMAL STRUCTURES, OR SELF-ORGANISATION AS A SURVIVAL STRATEGY

Where there are no or only inadequate community services, or when these services do not reach certain groups, informal structures, i.e. forms of self-help and self-organisation, evolve. These are typical for the unplanned urbanisation processes found in developing and emerging nations. Because of the creative potential that flourishes in them, informal structures are often readily glorified as a political strategy in the context of a bottom-up urbanism. Such idealisations should not blind us to the fact that this form of self-help results from the brutal need to survive and that coping with everyday life absorbs all the strength that would be needed for the structural improvement of living conditions. Additionally, self-organised provisions are often more expensive than public sector provisions.[9] An effective political strategy would exploit the existing creative potential to manage the community without relieving the local authorities of their social obligations.

Informal structures are however a phenomenon that is no longer restricted to the developing and emerging nations. In historical industrial cities too, informal citizens' engagement has become indispensable in countering the neoliberal curtailment of public services.

Information Overload:
In 2012, 2013 and 2014 the research group walked through Karail Basti, Dhaka's biggest informal settlement, debated with its inhabitants and asked questions concerning the everyday struggle for living space, basic provision and employment. The resulting map is approximating the reality of life of Karail's inhabitants, who have to manage without any stately support.

Lima – Co-produced City:
Planned in the 1950s, Lima's formal social housing projects have been modified by their residents over the years, taking on a similar character to informal settlements. The research questions the conception of social housing as a planned artefact, and suggests a process-oriented typology, potentially leading to a "co-produced" city.

THE URBAN METABOLISM, OR THE RELATIONSHIP WITH NATURE AND THE ENVIRONMENT

Since the 1970s the agricultural cultivation of gardens and open spaces that played an important role in the postwar era has declined: it was deemed "no longer necessary". Representative green areas replaced private kitchen gardens and allotments and roadside fruit trees were no longer harvested. Active engagement with the environment and nature gave way to a more visual relationship with nature. These days, as so often in the course of urban history, the relationship with nature has reached the opposite extreme. This shift finds its most radical expression in so-called urban farming.

But the "ecological turn" is no longer just about the integration of more nature in the city; in the management of the community it is about a fundamental redefinition of the relationship to nature, about an environmentally friendly urban metabolism. This applies not only to the economical use of resources, to water provision and waste water management, waste prevention and recovery, to material recycling and the resolution of traffic problems, but also – although they are not metabolic functions in the strict biological sense – to pollution, air quality, light pollution and all aspects of energy conservation and CO_2 reduction.
This change has far-reaching repercussions for the organisation of day-to-day life in cities as regards both the services provided by local government and the daily routines of their inhabitants.

Alongside the many entries that deal with the individual aspects of the urban metabolism, the following two submissions integrate these aspects in a realisable utopia:

Re-Generator:
How can building systems ensure that the rapid growth of cities does not happen at the expense of their surrounding ecosystems? A permeable housing structure, organised like a network of cells and elevated above ground, leaves the wetlands of Hangzhou in their natural state.

Hybrid Practices in the Venice Lagoon:
The ecosystem of the Venice lagoon was sorely afflicted by construction and decade-long industrial production. Today, the city and its lagoon system could profit from economic scenarios that combine traditional knowledge with sustainable technologies.

teuren innerstädtischen Grundstücken und die Kommodifizierung des öffentlichen Raums haben die Tendenz zur sozialen Segregation verstärkt und nicht nur die städtisch Armen, sondern auch die untere Mittelschicht an die Ränder verdrängt. Nach knapp 40 Jahren neoliberalen Wirtschaftens hat die soziale Spaltung der Gesellschaft deutlich zugenommen.

Medellín – Human Right on Water: Medellíns öffentliches Versorgungsunternehmen hat sich in den letzten Jahren zunehmend wie ein Privatunternehmen verhalten und so Haushalte mit niedrigem Einkommen systematisch aus dem städtischen Wassernetz ausgegliedert. Eben noch ein garantiertes Menschenrecht, ist die Wasserzirkulation in vielen Teilen der Stadt versiegt.

Dwellings: Die Stadt Dresden verkaufte im Jahr 2006 ihren gesamten kommunalen Wohnungsbestand an einen privaten Immobilienkonzern. Sie tilgte damit zwar ihre horrenden Schulden, aber mit dem Preis, die Kontrolle über ihre eigene Wohnungspolitik aufzugeben.

World Metropols: About Wages and Prices: Wird in unserem Gesellschaftssystem jeder der eigenen Leistung angemessen entlohnt? Eine weltweite Gegenüberstellung der frappierenden Einkommensunterschiede lässt den Neoliberalismus, der sich als global agierend und universal gültig versteht, schließlich doch nicht so liberal erscheinen.

INFORMELLE STRUKTUREN ODER SELBSTORGANISATION ALS ÜBERLEBENSSTRATEGIE

Wo es keine oder nur unzureichende Leistungen des Gemeinwesens gibt bzw. diese Leistungen bestimmte Gruppen nicht erreichen, bilden sich informelle Strukturen, d.h. Formen der Selbsthilfe und Selbstorganisation. Sie sind typisch für die ungeplanten Urbanisierungsprozesse in den Entwicklungs- und Schwellenländern. Informelle Strukturen werden wegen des kreativen Potentials, das sich in ihnen entfaltet, gern als politische Strategie im Kontext eines Bottom-up Urbanismus verklärt. Solche Idealisierungen sollten nicht darüber hinwegtäuschen, dass diese Form der Selbsthilfe aus der brutalen Notwendigkeit des Überlebens resultiert und dass die Bewältigung des Alltags alle Kraft absorbiert, die für strukturelle Verbesserungen der Lebenssituation benötigt würde. Außerdem ist die in Eigenregie betriebene Versorgung häufig teurer, als es die öffentlichen Leistungen sind.[9] Eine sinnvolle politische Strategie würde das vorhandene kreative Potential in der Verwaltung des Gemeinwesens nutzen, ohne die Kommunen aus der sozialen Verantwortung zu entlassen.

Informelle Strukturen sind jedoch nicht mehr nur ein Phänomen der Entwicklungs- und Schwellenländer. Auch in den historischen Industriestädten ist informelles bürgerschaftliches Engagement parallel zur neoliberalen Einschränkung der öffentlichen Leistungen unverzichtbar geworden.

Information Overload:
In den Jahren 2012, 2013 und 2014 ging die Forschungsgruppe durch Karail Basti, Dhakas größte informelle Siedlung, diskutierte mit seinen Bewohnern und stellte Fragen zu dem alltäglichen Kampf um Wohnraum, grundlegende Versorgung und Arbeit. Die entstandene Karte ist eine Annäherung an die Lebensrealität der Bewohner Karails, die gänzlich ohne staatliche Unterstützung auskommen müssen.

Lima – Co-produced City:
Die in den 1950er Jahren geplanten Sozialwohnungsbauten Limas wurden im Laufe der Jahre von ihren Bewohnern modifiziert und wurden so informellen Siedlungen immer ähnlicher. Die Studie hinterfragt das Konzept des Sozialwohnungsbaus als geplantes Artefakt und schlägt eine prozessorientierte Typologie vor, die den Weg zu einer "ko-produzierten" Stadt ebnen könnte.

DER STÄDTISCHE STOFFWECHSEL ODER DAS VERHÄLTNIS ZU NATUR UND UMWELT

Seit den 70er Jahren war die agrarische Bewirtschaftung von Gärten und Freiflächen, die in der Not der Nachkriegszeit eine wichtige Rolle spielte, rückläufig – "man hatte es nicht mehr nötig". Private Nutzgärten und Mietergärten wurden durch repräsentatives Grün ersetzt, Obstbäume an den Straßen nicht mehr abgeerntet. Der aktive Umgang mit Raum und Natur wich einem eher optischen Naturbezug. Heute, wie so oft im Verlauf der Stadtgeschichte, hat sich das Verhältnis zur Natur diametral verkehrt. Im sogenannten Urban Farming findet dieser Wechsel seinen radikalsten Ausdruck.

Aber mit der "ökologischen Wende" geht es nicht mehr nur um eine Integration von mehr Natur in die Stadt, sondern in der Bewirtschaftung des Gemeinwe-

MIGRATION, OR THE PROMISE OF A BETTER LIFE

The inexorable advance of the urbanisation process is fuelled by migration. Worldwide, around 60 million people are "on the move". Migration is rarely voluntary; instead, it reflects the extreme inequality in living conditions, both in comparison with the former industrial nations and internally in the developing and emerging nations. Migration is a phenomenon first and foremost of the Global South. It has three main causes: firstly, the typical rural-urban migration. This results from the fact that the agricultural way of life no longer sustains families, which, along with environmental catastrophes, the harbingers of climate change, is chiefly due to the local effects of a global economy, such as cheap exports, seed monopolies, land acquisitions, etc. Furthermore, as a consequence of industrialisation, which is also experiencing dramatic growth in the Global South, cities have always been associated with the promise of work and a better life. Secondly, migrant labour, i.e., the migration of a family member often for an unlimited time, motivated by the desire to improve the family's local living conditions. The better earning opportunities in the cities come at the cost of catastrophic public services and indescribable housing conditions. China's economic miracle is based on domestic migration, Dubai's construction boom on the import of Asian workers. In Europe too, seasonal migration is on the rise with the import of cheap labour in the building sector, agriculture and the service industries. Thirdly, the exodus from crisis areas and war zones – ongoing conflicts without hope of resolution – in order to apply for temporary or permanent asylum.

A number of the competition entries addressed this controversial issue, although due to the currently rapid development of the refugee situation, some of the data has already become outdated. Our focus here was on the documentation of the method of analysis, which remains valid irrespective of the provisional data.

States of Refuge:
The built environment is an integral part of the "state of refuge". Aside from the refugee route itself, characterised by diverse spatial borders, on arriving in Austria, asylum seekers are again confronted by built spaces of inclusion and exclusion. The project calls attention to the effects of spatial design and planning – or the lack of it – and argues for a proactive inclusion of architectural issues in the asylum discourse.

City Pixels – Migrant Workers in China:
The booming Chinese cities are made through the collective effort of a backstage group whose existence is widely ignored – the migrant workers. They have made great contributions, but they have to accept unfair treatment. The project uses a graphic metaphor to draw attention to this acute issue of injustice.

1 Sabine Kraft, ed., Out of Balance, Aachen: ARCH+ Verlag, 2013
2 See the competition outline in this issue, "The Future will be Decided in the Cities", p. 12
3 WBGU – German Advisory Council on Global Change (2016), "The century of the cities"; in: WBGU, ed., Humanity on the Move – Unlocking the Transformative Power of Cities, Berlin: WBGU
4 Ibid.
5 In the French discourse initiated by Henri Lefebvre and Paul-Henry de Chombart de Lauwe everyday life becomes the main reference point for empirically founded socio-spatial theories based on the close connection between ethnology and the social sciences; cf. Sabine Kraft: "Die soziale Wirklichkeit des Wohnens", in: ARCH+ 218, Wohnerfahrungen, November 2014. Cf. also the significance of everyday life according to Henri Lefebvre, Christian Schmid: "Planetary Urbanisation: Henri Lefebvre and the Right to the City", in this issue, p. 26
6 Cf. Philipp Oswalt: "Outsourcing. Zur Architektur globaler Ungleichheit und ihrem Nutzen", in: ARCH+ 206/207, Politische Empirie, July 2012, p. 136 et seqq.
7 The term "persuasive computing" describes techniques of manipulation designed to steer human behaviour in the desired direction and marks the transition from computer programming to the programming of the human race. Cf. Roberto V. Zicari, in: "Digitale Demokratie statt Datendiktatur", www.spektrum.de/news/wie-algorithmen-und-big-data-unsere-zukunft-bestimmen/1375933
8 Cf. Christian Schmidt, loc. sit., p. 32
9 Cf. Elisa T. Bertuzzo's analysis of the costs of self-organisation, in "On the Myth of Informal Urbanisation: Karail Basti, Dhaka", in this issue, p. 110 et seqq.

Translated from German by Rebecca Williams

---

sens um eine grundsätzliche Neudefinition des Verhältnisses zur Umwelt, um einen umweltverträglichen, städtischen Metabolismus. Das betrifft nicht nur den sparsamen Umgang mit Ressourcen, die Wasserver- und Abwasserentsorgung, Müllvermeidung und -aufbereitung, Wertstoffrecycling, die Lösung der Verkehrsprobleme, sondern auch, obwohl das in der streng biologischen Analogie keine Stoffwechselfunktionen sind, die Schadstoffbelastung, Luftqualität, Lichtverschmutzung und alle Aspekte des Energiesparens und der CO2-Reduktion. Für die Organisation des städtischen Alltags hat dieser Wandel weitreichende Auswirkungen, sowohl was die Leistungen der kommunalen Verwaltung betrifft wie auch die alltäglichen Routinen der Bewohner.

Neben den vielen Arbeiten, die sich mit den Einzelaspekten des städtischen Metabolismus beschäftigen, sollen hier zwei Arbeiten genannt werden, die diese Aspekte zu einer Realutopie integrieren:

Re-Generator:
Wie können Bausysteme dazu beitragen, dass das rasche Wachstum von Städten nicht auf Kosten der umliegenden Ökosysteme geht? Eine als aufgeständertes Netzwerk von Zellen organisierte, wasserdurchlässige Wohnstruktur belässt das Marschland in Hangzhou in seinem natürlichen Zustand.

Hybrid Practices in the Venice Lagoon:
Das Ökosystem der Lagune von Venedig wurde durch bauliche Eingriffe und jahrzehntelange industrielle Produktion stark beeinträchtigt. Heute können die Stadt und ihr Lagunensystem von Wirtschaftsszenarien profitieren, die traditionelles Wissen mit nachhaltigen Technologien verbinden.

MIGRATION ODER DAS VERSPRECHEN EINES BESSEREN LEBENS

Der unaufhaltsam voranschreitende Urbanisierungsprozess speist sich aus Migration. Weltweit sind ca. 60 Millionen Menschen "unterwegs". Migration erfolgt selten freiwillig, sondern spiegelt die extrem ungleichen Lebensbedingungen im Vergleich zu den ehemaligen Industrienationen, aber auch intern in den Entwicklungs- und Schwellenländern wider. Migration ist vor allem ein Phänomen des globalen Südens. Es gibt drei Hauptursachen: Erstens die typische Land-Stadt-Wanderung. Sie resultiert daraus, dass die agrarische Lebensweise die Familien nicht mehr ernährt, was neben Umweltkatastrophen, den Vorboten des Klimawandels, vor allem auf die lokalen Effekte globaler Ökonomie wie Billigexporte, Saatgutmonopole, Landaufkäufe etc. zurückzuführen ist. Außerdem bergen Städte durch die Industrialisierung, die auch im globalen Süden eine rasante Entwicklung nimmt, seit jeher das Versprechen auf Arbeit und ein besseres Leben. Zweitens die Wanderarbeit als Migration eines Familienmitglieds auf – häufig unbegrenzte – Zeit. Die Motivation liegt in der lokalen Verbesserung der Lebensverhältnisse der Familie. Die besseren Verdienstmöglichkeiten in der Stadt werden durch eine katastrophale Versorgung und unbeschreibliche Wohnsituationen erkauft. Chinas Wirtschaftswunder basiert auf heimischen Wanderarbeitern, Dubais Bauboom auf dem Import asiatischer Arbeitskräfte. Auch in Europa nimmt die saisonale Wanderarbeit mit dem Import von Billigarbeitskräften im Bausektor, in der Landwirtschaft und dem Dienstleistungsgewerbe wieder zu. Drittens die Flucht aus Krisen- und Kriegsgebieten, die auf nicht lösbaren Dauerkonflikten basieren, um Asyl – auf Zeit oder Dauer – zu beantragen.

Einige der eingereichten Wettbewerbsbeiträge haben sich diesem brisanten Thema gewidmet, wobei aufgrund der rasanten aktuellen Entwicklung in der Flüchtlingsfrage die Daten teilweise bereits überholt sind. Worauf es uns hier ankam, war die Analysemethode, die unabhängig von den temporären Daten aktuell bleibt, zu dokumentieren.

States of Refuge:
Die gebaute Umgebung ist ein maßgeblicher Bestandteil des "Zustands der Flucht". Neben dem Fluchtweg an sich sind Asylsuchende an ihrem Ankunftsort in Österreich erneut mit gebauten Räumen der Ein- und Ausgrenzung konfrontiert. Das Projekt zeigt die Auswirkungen räumlichen Handelns und Planens – oder dessen Abwesenheit – auf und argumentiert für ein proaktives Eintreten von Fragestellungen der Architektur in den Asyldiskurs.

City Pixels – Migrant Workers in China:
Die boomenden chinesischen Städte entstehen durch die gemeinsame Anstrengung einer hinter der Bühne stehenden, in ihrer Existenz weitgehend ignorierten Gruppe – die Wanderarbeiter. Sie haben unschätzbare Beiträge geleistet, müssen jedoch ungerechte Behandlung akzeptieren. Das Projekt verwendet eine grafische Metapher, um die Aufmerksamkeit auf dieses akute Problem der Ungerechtigkeit zu lenken.

NEW ORLEANS

NEW YORK

AARAU

BERLIN

DRESDEN

NAPLES

ATLANTA

MADRID

LONDON

HALLE

MIAMI

MEXICO CITY

SÃO PAULO

MEDELLÍN

BUENOS AIRES

LIMA

III. INFORMAL VS REGULATED

RIO DE JANEIRO

LOCATIONS
OF PUBLISHED
PROJECTS

● CITIES
■ COUNTRIES

V. URBAN METABOLISM

ACCRA

CAIRO

DUR

10

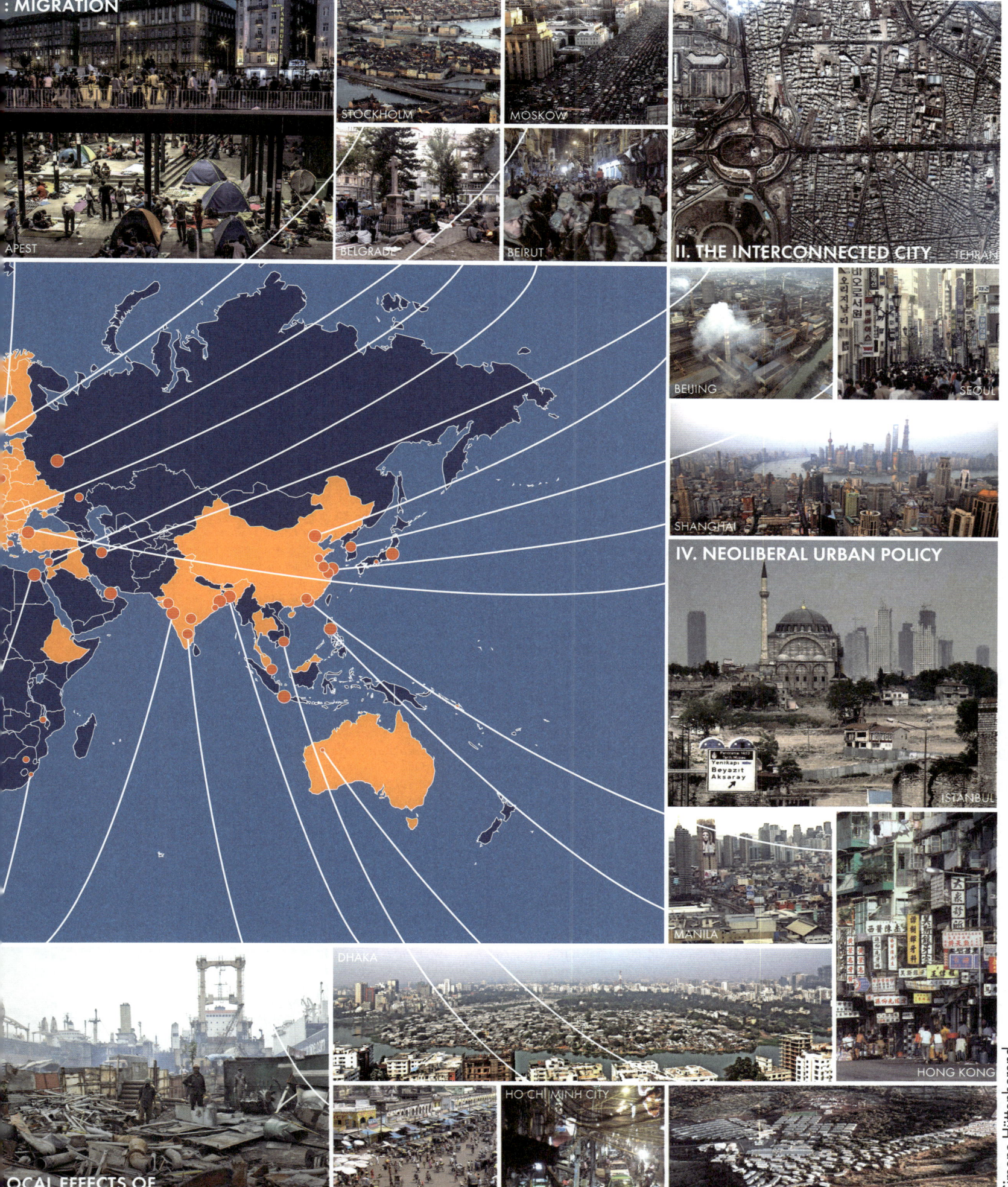

: MIGRATION

STOCKHOLM

MOSKOW

II. THE INTERCONNECTED CITY

APEST

BELGRADE

BEIRUT

TEHRAN

BEIJING

SEOUL

SHANGHAI

IV. NEOLIBERAL URBAN POLICY

Yenikapı
Beyazıt
Aksaray

ISTANBUL

MANILA

HONG KONG

DHAKA

OCAL EFFECTS OF
OBALISATION

ALANG

BENGALURU

HO CHI MINH CITY

PILBARA

© Simone Hüttenberend

11

THE FUTURE WILL BE DECIDED IN THE CITIES Sabine Kraft

The following text was part of the outline of the competition "Planetary Urbanism – Critique of the Present in the Medium of Information Design" which was launched in 2014. A selection of entries are shown in this issue.

The Topic

Hastened by industrialisation, the progressive urbanisation of our world has profoundly transformed the planet and continues to do so. The impacts of these changes have not yet been grasped in full, and an end to this process is not foreseeable.

Cities were always centres of innovation and the driving force of developments, throughout all epochs and cultures. The organisation of life in cities formed the starting point for the development of structures based on the division of labour and hence the release of creative potentials that benefited science, technology and the arts, for the accumulation of capital, increasing prosperity and the refinement of life. With few exceptions, cities were also the stages on which the struggles for more social equality and for societal progress played out. Cities are likely humankind's greatest cultural achievement and, in this respect, a marker of the Anthropocene period, the geological age defined by human activity.

While the development of the (European) city over the course of its two-and-a-half thousand year history features umpteen radical departures, within which the forms of the reproduction of urban life have fundamentally changed, cities nevertheless remained insular structures up to the nineteenth century. By contrast, the degree of urbanisation that we are witnessing today is unprecedented. The further development of the Anthropocene period ought to be closely linked with whether or how we can organise or 'manage' the urbanisation that emanates from this process, and which revolutionises the established conditions no longer merely on a local, regional or national level, but which has long-since become a global phenomenon with far-reaching geological and geopolitical repercussions.

Virtually all the questions concerning the future of humankind are related to the urbanisation of the world, or come about as its consequence:
• The predicted growth in the population to more than 9 billion by 2050 will have to be mastered primarily in the cities.
• Cities functionalise the countryside and subject it to the postulate of their provision and transform agricultural structures. At the level at which urbanisation is progressing, a traditional agricultural subsistence is made more difficult – to say nothing of the looming battle over who will use agricultural reserve areas.
• The material and energy exchange processes of cities and agglomerations impinge on nature and the environment to a far greater extent than rural forms of settlement. Sustainability in the sense of a circular economy is first and foremost also a question of urban metabolism.
• The consumption of energy and resources in cities, the waste products and emissions of their non-sustainable metabolisms, fuel climate change; conversely, cities, above all some of the newer megacities, will be most affected by climate change.
• Besides the energy supply, the availability of water is the most pressing problem for the future. The rising standard of living in cities is increasing agricultural water consumption, whereby the cities themselves are contributing significantly in many ways to the shortage of resources.
• The migration from rural to urban areas driven by the prospect of better living conditions has become a global migration movement, rendering traditional models of national limits or territorial administration unions superfluous and seemingly historically obsolete.
• The extreme social disparities on a global level are reflected in the cities, especially in the booming cities of the southern hemisphere and in the Asian region. A large proportion of the population lacks infrastructure, healthcare, access to educa-

Thema

Die im Gefolge der Industrialisierung beschleunigt voranschreitende Verstädterung unserer Welt brachte und bringt tiefgreifende Überformungen des Planeten mit sich, die bisher weder in ihren Auswirkungen voll erfasst werden können, noch ist ein Ende dieses Prozesses absehbar.

Städte waren immer Orte der Innovation und treibende Kraft von Entwicklungen – quer durch alle Epochen und Kulturen. Die Organisation des Lebens in Städten schuf den Ausgangspunkt für die Herausbildung arbeitsteiliger Strukturen und damit die Freisetzung schöpferischer Potentiale, die Wissenschaft, Technik und den Künsten zu Gute kamen, für die Akkumulation von Kapital, einen wachsenden Wohlstand und eine Verfeinerung des Lebens. Städte waren (bis auf wenige Ausnahmen) auch die Orte, wo die Kämpfe um mehr soziale Gerechtigkeit und gesellschaftlichen Fortschritt ausgetragen wurden. Städte sind die wahrscheinlich größte kulturelle Leistung der Menschen und insofern ein zentrales Kennzeichen des Anthropozäns, des vom Menschen bestimmten geologischen Zeitalters.

Die Entwicklung der (europäischen) Stadt weist im Verlauf ihrer zweieinhalbtausendjährigen Geschichte mehrere Umbrüche auf, innerhalb derer sich die Formen der Reproduktion des städtischen Lebens grundlegend gewandelt haben, doch blieben Städte bis ins 19. Jahrhundert insuläre Strukturen. Demgegenüber ist das Ausmaß der Verstädterung, wie wir sie heute erleben, beispiellos. Die weitere Entwicklung des Anthropozäns dürfte eng daran geknüpft sein, ob bzw. wie es gelingt, diesen Urbanisierungsprozess zu gestalten, den Sog zu "managen", der von diesem Prozess ausgeht, und der die bestehenden Verhältnisse nicht mehr nur im lokalen, regionalen oder nationalen Maßstab umwälzt, sondern der längst ein planetarisches Phänomen geworden ist, ein Phänomen mit weitreichenden geologischen und geopolitischen Auswirkungen.

So gut wie alle Zukunftsfragen der Menschheit sind mit der Verstädterung der Welt verbunden bzw. entstehen durch sie:
• *Das bis 2050 prognostizierte Bevölkerungswachstum auf mehr als 9 Milliarden Menschen wird vor allem in den Städten zu bewältigen sein.*
• *Städte funktionalisieren und unterwerfen das Land ihrem Versorgungspostulat und wälzen überkommene agrarische Strukturen um. In dem Maße, wie die Verstädterung voranschreitet, wird eine traditionelle landwirtschaftliche Subsistenz erschwert – ganz abgesehen von dem sich abzeichnenden globalen Verteilungskampf um die Nutzung agrarischer Reserveflächen.*
• *Die materiell-energetischen Austauschprozesse von Städten und Ballungsräumen greifen sehr viel tiefer als ländliche Siedlungsformen in die Natur bzw. Umwelt ein. Nachhaltigkeit im Sinne einer Kreislaufwirtschaft ist vor allem auch eine Frage des städtischen Metabolismus.*
• *Die Energie- und Ressourcennutzung von Städten, die Ausssscheidungsprodukte und Emissionen ihres nicht-nachhaltigen Stoffwechsels treiben den Klimawandel an, umgekehrt werden Städte, vor allem ein Teil der neueren Megacities, am stärksten vom Klimawandel betroffen sein.*
• *Neben der Energieversorgung stellt die Wasserverfügbarkeit das drängendste Zukunftsproblem dar. Der steigende Lebensstandard in den Städten treibt den agrarischen Wasserverbrauch in die Höhe, wobei die Städte selbst auf vielerlei Weise nicht unerheblich zur Verknappung der Ressourcen beitragen.*
• *Die von der Suche nach besseren Lebensverhältnissen geleitete Stadt-Land-Wanderung ist zu einer globalen Migrationsbewegung geworden, der gegenüber die überkommenen Modelle nationaler Eingrenzung oder territorialer Zweckverbände hilflos bleiben und historisch überholt erscheinen.*
• *Das im Weltmaßstab extreme soziale Gefälle spiegelt sich in den Städten wider, vor allem in den explodierenden Städten der südlichen Halbkugel und im asiatischen Raum. Es fehlt für einen großen Teil der Bevölkerung an Infrastruktur, Gesundheitsversorgung, Zugang zu Bildung, angemessenen Wohnverhältnissen und einer lebensfreundlichen Umgebung.*
• *Ausschlaggebend für die Versorgung in den Städten wird sein, wie sich das*

tion, adequate living conditions and a hospitable environment.

• How the relationship between the individual and the community is regulated will be key to maintaining provisions in the cities. The model of increasing isolation, the fully equipped individual and the private household pushes not only social, but also ecological and economic limits.

• The difficult conditions for migrants starting out in a city make imagination and resourcefulness essential to survival. As long as the political will exists, this holds great promise for the development of new solutions to the challenges of urban coexistence.

• Cities are where new models of political participation must be developed and put to the test – models that facilitate the distribution of societal wealth according to the changing circumstances.

We are living in an age of radical change characterised by the interleaving and rapid development of two processes in particular. As such, the unstoppable process of urbanisation corresponds with the unstoppable process of the digitalisation of all functional aspects and spheres of life. While urbanisation fundamentally changes material structures, i.e., the physical world around us, digitalisation creates an intangible metastructure, so to say a 'world beyond the world', the influence of which often remains invisible. Everyday urban life plays out in these two worlds; maintaining the physical existence of the city is no longer conceivable without background digital regulation, whether the organisation of the urban infrastructure with transport, energy and water management, the work of the municipal authorities in diverse offices and law enforcement, business dealings with the circulation of goods, money and services or private communication structures and social networks.

Reference to the quantitative dimensions of the urbanisation process is by now commonplace in literature concerning the city. But what does this urbanisation of the world mean, and what are its consequences? The image of the city that we create for ourselves is an ideal one with a linear history; urban planning is largely based on ideal concepts handed down from the past. How does a city or an agglomeration function today and what, or how much, do we in fact know about this? How do the electronic and physical worlds intersect and which tendencies are found in both? Are there any explanatory models that still cover the organisational structures of both city and agglomeration, or do these drift apart in their development, depending on whether or to what degree they are networked, whether they are growing or shrinking, how many inhabitants they have, whether the per capita income is rising or falling, whether they have a sustainable approach to, e.g., transport or waste management, the geographical or climate zone they are located in or the nature of their environs, etc. These and similar questions form the point of departure for the competition.

Information Design

Today, the difficulty of empirically describing reality no longer lies in a lack of information, but, to the contrary, in the constantly growing amount of data that makes it difficult to draw an overall picture of society and to distinguish between what is important and what is unimportant. Today we have access to an inestimable wealth of data, much of it automatically generated: statistics, personal data, photos, documents, etc. Hardly anything seems able to elude this universal visibility in the digital age. At the same time, the present is increasingly opaque. There is precise data for more and more questions of detail, but it is getting harder to find orientation and gain an overview of the present; the quantitative description of phenomena is getting denser, but understanding of the underlying relations and processes seems to be waning. Considering that all societal activity depends on information, the wealth of data poses a real dilemma; we can indeed speak of a "digital opacity". Automated processing with the aid of programmes that autonomously view, order, and evaluate data in no way automatically creates transparency. A situation arises in which political activity is not empirically verifiable and is dissolved in politically exploitable contradictions.

Information design is more than a collection of data: information design uses data to create statements that provide insights into societal circumstances. Information design reveals connections behind the surface of the phenomena. Information design provides orientation. It creates a hierarchy of information based on relevance and content. It reduces complexity, thereby creating an overview.

Information design is not neutral. The shaping of information is influenced by the interest in knowledge. An enlightening, emancipatory information design reveals facts that are repressed, not spoken of, or forgotten, but that are nonetheless essential for understanding the present. And it thereby influences the perspective of societal activity. The image of the world we make for ourselves determines how we act.

Translated from German by Rebecca Williams

Verhältnis des Einzelnen zum Gemeinwesen regelt. Das Modell fortschreitender Vereinzelung, individueller Komplettausstattung und des privaten Haushalts stößt nicht nur an soziale, sondern auch an ökologische und ökonomische Grenzen.

• *Die schwierigen Anfangsbedingungen der Migranten in der Stadt machen Phantasie und Einfallsreichtum zur Überlebensvoraussetzung. Darin liegt – sofern es politisch gewollt wird – eine große Chance für die Entwicklung neuer Lösungen des städtischen Miteinanders.*

• *Die Städte sind der Ort, wo neue Modelle der politischen Teilnahme entwickelt und erprobt werden müssen, Modelle, die es erlauben, die Verteilung des gesellschaftlichen Reichtums entsprechend sich verändernder Verhältnisse auszuhandeln.*

Wir leben in einer Umbruchzeit, die durch die Verschränkung und rasante Entwicklung vor allem zweier Prozesse gekennzeichnet ist. So korrespondiert der unaufhaltsame Prozess der Urbanisierung mit dem unaufhaltsamen Prozess der Digitalisierung aller Funktions- und Lebensbereiche. Während die Urbanisierung die materiellen Strukturen, d.h. die uns physisch umgebende Welt, grundlegend verändert, erschafft die Digitalisierung eine immaterielle Metastruktur, gewissermaßen "eine Welt über der Welt", deren prägender Effekt vielfach unsichtbar bleibt. Das alltägliche städtische Leben spielt sich in diesen zwei Welten ab, die Aufrechterhaltung der physischen Existenz der Stadt ist ohne die digitale Steuerung im Hintergrund nicht mehr denkbar, sei es der Betrieb der städtischen Infrastruktur mit Verkehr, Energie- und Wasserversorgung und Entsorgung, sei es die Arbeit der städtischen Verwaltung mit den diversen Ämtern und den Ordnungskräften, sei es das Geschäftsleben mit der Waren- und Geldzirkulation und den Dienstleistungen oder seien es die privaten Kommunikationsstrukturen und sozialen Netze.

Der Verweis auf die quantitativen Dimensionen des Urbanisierungsprozesses ist im Schrifttum zur Stadt mittlerweile ein Allgemeinplatz. Aber was bedeutet diese Verstädterung der Welt und was folgt daraus? Das Bild, das wir uns von der Stadt machen, ist ein idealtypisches, das historische Züge trägt, die Stadtplanung orientiert sich größtenteils an idealen Konzepten, die aus der Historie überkommen sind. Wie funktionieren Stadt und/oder Agglomerationsräume heute, was bzw. wie viel wissen wir tatsächlich darüber? Wie verschränken sich die elektronische und die physische Welt, welche Tendenzen lassen sich für beides aufspüren? Gibt es überhaupt noch gemeinsame Erklärungsmodelle für die Organisationsstruktur Stadt/Agglomerationsraum oder driften sie in ihrer Entwicklung auseinander, je nachdem, ob bzw. wie weit sie vernetzt sind, ob sie wachsen oder schrumpfen, wie viel Einwohner sie haben, ob das Pro-Kopf-Einkommen steigt oder fällt, ob sie z.B. den Verkehr oder die Abfallwirtschaft nachhaltig gestalten, in welcher geografischen bzw. klimatischen Zone sie liegen, wie das Umland beschaffen ist etc. Solche und ähnliche Fragestellungen bilden den Ausgangspunkt des Wettbewerbs.

Information Design

Die Schwierigkeit einer empirischen Beschreibung von Realität liegt heute nicht mehr in einem Mangel an Informationen, sondern umgekehrt in der beständig anwachsenden Menge an Daten, die es erschwert, ein Gesamtbild der Gesellschaft zu zeichnen und zwischen Wichtigem und Unwichtigem zu unterscheiden. Wir haben heute Zugang zu einer unübersehbaren Fülle von Daten, die häufig automatisch generiert werden: Statistiken, Personendaten, Fotos, Dokumente usw. Kaum etwas scheint sich dieser Allsichtbarkeit im digitalen Zeitalter entziehen zu können. Zugleich wird die Gegenwart zunehmend undurchschaubarer. Während es für mehr und mehr Detailfragen präzise Daten gibt, wird es schwieriger, sich Orientierung und Überblick über die Gegenwart zu verschaffen, während sich die quantitative Beschreibung von Phänomenen verdichtet, scheint das Verständnis für grundlegende Relationen und Prozesse zu schwinden. Die Datenfülle ist in Anbetracht der Informationsabhängigkeit allen gesellschaftlichen Handelns ein echtes Dilemma, man kann durchaus von einer "digitalen Unübersichtlichkeit" sprechen. Die automatisierte Verarbeitung mit Hilfe von Programmen, die selbsttätig Daten sichten, einordnen und bewerten, erzeugt eben keineswegs automatisch Transparenz. Es entsteht eine Situation, in der politisches Handeln empirisch nicht überprüfbar ist und in politisch ausschlachtbare Widersprüchlichkeiten aufgelöst wird.

Information Design ist mehr als eine Ansammlung von Daten: Information Design erzeugt mittels der Daten Aussagen, die Einsichten in gesellschaftliche Verhältnisse geben. Information Design zeigt unter der Oberfläche der Phänomene Zusammenhänge auf. Information Design vermittelt Orientierung. Es hierarchisiert Information in Hinsicht auf Relevanz und Aussage. Es reduziert Komplexität und schafft damit Überblick.

Information Design ist nicht neutral. Die Gestaltung von Information ist beeinflusst vom Erkenntnisinteresse. Ein aufklärerisches, emanzipatives Information Design legt Tatsachen offen, die verdrängt, verschwiegen oder vergessen, aber gleichwohl wesentlich für das Verständnis der Gegenwart sind. Und sie beeinflusst damit perspektivisch das gesellschaftliche Handeln. Das Bild, das wir uns von der Welt machen, ist maßgeblich dafür, wie wir handeln.

13

THE RIGHT TO THE CITY David Harvey

[...] The city, the noted urban sociologist Robert Park once wrote, is "man's most consistent and on the whole, his most successful attempt to remake the world he lives in more after his heart's desire. But, if the city is the world which man created, it is the world in which he is henceforth condemned to live. Thus, indirectly, and without any clear sense of the nature of his task, in making the city man has remade himself."[1] If Park is correct, then the question of what kind of city we want cannot be divorced from the question of what kind of people we want to be, what kinds of social relations we seek, what relations to nature we cherish, what style of life we desire, what aesthetic values we hold. The right to the city is, therefore, far more than a right of individual or group access to the resources that the city embodies: it is a right to change and reinvent the city more after our hearts' desire. It is, moreover, a collective rather than an individual right, since reinventing the city inevitably depends upon the exercise of a collective power over the processes of urbanization. The freedom to make and remake ourselves and our cities is, I want to argue, one of the most precious yet most neglected of our human rights. How best then to exercise that right?

Since, as Park avers, we have hitherto lacked any clear sense of the nature of our task, it is useful first to reflect on how we have been made and remade throughout history by an urban process impelled onwards by powerful social forces. The astonishing pace and scale of urbanization over the last hundred years means, for example, that we have been remade several times over without knowing why or how. Has this dramatic urbanization contributed to human well-being? Has it made us into better people, or left us dangling in a world of anomie and alienation, anger and frustration? Have we become mere monads tossed around in an urban sea? These were the sorts of questions that preoccupied all manner of nineteenth century commentators, such as Friedrich Engels and Georg Simmel, who offered perceptive critiques of the urban personas then emerging in response to rapid urbanization.[2] These days it is not hard to enumerate all manner of urban discontents and anxieties, as well as excitements, in the midst of even more rapid urban transformations. Yet we somehow seem to lack the stomach for systematic critique. The maelstrom of change overwhelms us even as obvious questions loom. What, for example, are we to make of the immense concentrations of wealth, privilege, and consumerism in almost all the cities of the world in the midst of what even the United Nations depicts as an exploding "planet of slums"?[3]

To claim the right to the city in the sense I mean it here is to claim some kind of shaping power over the processes of urbanization, over the ways in which our cities are made and remade, and to do so in a fundamental and radical way. From their very inception, cities have arisen through the geographical and social concentration of a surplus product. Urbanization has always been, therefore, a class phenomenon of some sort, since surpluses have been extracted from somewhere and from somebody, while control over the use of the surplus typically lies in the hands of a few (such as a religious oligarchy, or a warrior poet with imperial ambitions). This general situation persists under capitalism, of course, but in this case there is a rather different dynamic at work. Capitalism rests, as Marx tells us, upon the perpetual search for surplus value (profit). But to produce surplus value capitalists have to produce a surplus product. This means that capitalism is perpetually

[...] Der berühmte amerikanische Stadtsoziologe Robert Park schrieb einmal, die Stadt sei "der konsequenteste und insgesamt erfolgreichste Versuch des Menschen, die Welt, in der er lebt, nach seinen eigenen Vorstellungen umzugestalten. Doch wenn die Stadt die vom Menschen erschaffene Welt ist, dann ist sie auch die Welt, in der er fortan zu leben verdammt ist. Folglich hat sich der Mensch, auf indirektem Wege und ohne deutliches Bewusstsein für die Natur seiner Aufgabe, in der Erschaffung der Stadt selbst neu erschaffen."[1] Wenn Park Recht hat, kann die Frage, in welcher Art von Stadt wir leben wollen, nicht von der Frage getrennt werden, welche Art von Menschen wir sein wollen, welche Arten von sozialen Beziehungen wir anstreben, welches Verhältnis zur Natur wir pflegen, welchen Lebensstil wir uns wünschen, an welchen ästhetischen Werten wir festhalten. Das Recht auf Stadt ist also weit mehr als das Recht auf individuellen oder gemeinschaftlichen Zugriff auf die Ressourcen, welche die Stadt verkörpert: Es ist das Recht, die Stadt nach unseren eigenen Wünschen zu verändern und neu zu erfinden. Darüber hinaus ist es ein kollektives anstelle eines individuellen Rechts, da das Neuerfinden der Stadt unvermeidlich von der Ausübung einer kollektiven Macht über die Urbanisierungsprozesse abhängt. Die Freiheit, uns selbst und unsere Städte zu erschaffen und immer wieder neu zu erschaffen, ist meiner Ansicht nach eins der kostbarsten und dennoch am meisten vernachlässigten unserer Menschenrechte. Wie sollen wir dieses Recht also am besten in Anspruch nehmen?

Da wir, wie Park betont, bisher nur ein vages Verständnis von der Natur unserer Aufgabe besitzen, ist es sinnvoll, zunächst darüber nachzudenken, wie wir im Verlauf der Geschichte durch einen von machtvollen gesellschaftlichen Kräften vorangetriebenen urbanen Prozess erschaffen und erneuert worden sind. Das erstaunliche Tempo und Ausmaß der Urbanisierung in den letzten hundert Jahren bedeutet beispielsweise, dass wir bereits mehrere Male neu erschaffen wurden, ohne zu wissen, weshalb oder wie. Hat diese dramatische Urbanisierung einen Beitrag zum menschlichen Wohlbefinden geleistet? Hat sie uns zu besseren Menschen gemacht, oder uns in einer Welt der Anomie und Entfremdung, der Wut und Enttäuschung hängengelassen? Sind wir zu Monaden geworden, die in einem urbanen Meer umhergespült werden? Fragen dieser Art beschäftigten alle möglichen Autoren des 19. Jahrhunderts, etwa Friedrich Engels und Georg Simmel, die scharfsinnig die stereotypen urbanen Rollen kritisierten, die damals in Reaktion auf die rasante Urbanisierung entstanden.[2] Heutzutage ist es nicht schwer, angesichts einer sogar noch rasanteren Transformation der Städte die verschiedensten Formen des urbanen Unbehagens, der Angst, aber auch der Erregung aufzulisten. Doch aus irgendeinem Grund scheint uns der Mut zu einer systematischen Kritik zu fehlen. Der Sog des Wandels überwältigt uns, obgleich sich offensichtliche Probleme anbahnen. Was sollen wir etwa von der immensen Konzentration von Wohlstand, Privilegien und Konsumgütern in nahezu allen Städten der Erde halten, einer Erde, die selbst die Vereinten Nationen mittlerweile als Planeten der explodierenden Slums bezeichnen?[3]

Das Recht auf Stadt in dem Sinne zu beanspruchen, der mir hier vorschwebt, bedeutet, grundsätzlich und radikal die Macht einzufordern, Urbanisierungsprozesse zu gestalten und mitzuentscheiden, wenn es darum geht, auf welche Art und Weise unsere Städte erschaffen und erneuert werden sollen. Seit ihren Anfängen sind Städte durch die geografische und gesellschaftliche Konzentration von Mehrprodukten entstanden. Die Urbanisierung war also schon immer gewissermaßen ein Klassenphänomen, da Überschüsse irgendwo irgendwem entzogen wurden, während die Kontrolle über ihre Verwendung typischerweise in den Händen weniger lag (etwa einer religiösen Oligarchie oder eines Kriegers mit imperialen Ambitionen). An dieser allgemeinen Situation ändert sich im Kapitalismus selbstverständlich nichts, allerdings ist nun eine ganz andere Dynamik im Gang. Wie Marx uns erklärt, beruht der Kapitalismus auf dem ständigen Streben nach Mehrwert

producing the surplus product that urbanization requires. The reverse relation also holds. Capitalism needs urbanization to absorb the surplus products it perpetually produces. In this way an inner connection emerges between the development of capitalism and urbanization. Hardly surprisingly, therefore, the logistical curves of growth of capitalist output over time are broadly paralleled by the logistical curves of urbanization of the world's population. [...]

In what ways, then, has capitalist urbanization been driven by the need [...] to expand the terrain of profitable capitalist activity? I argue here that it plays a particularly active role (along with other phenomena such as military expenditures) in absorbing the surplus product that capitalists are perpetually producing in their search for surplus value.[4]

Consider, first, the case of Second Empire Paris. The crisis of 1848 was one of the first clear crises of unemployed surplus capital and surplus labor side-by-side, and it was Europe-wide. It struck particularly hard in Paris, and the result was an abortive revolution on the part of unemployed workers and those bourgeois utopians who saw a social republic as the antidote to capitalist greed and inequality. The republican bourgeoisie violently repressed the revolutionaries but failed to resolve the crisis. The result was the ascent to power of Louis Bonaparte, who engineered a coup in 1851 and proclaimed himself emperor in 1852. To survive politically, the authoritarian emperor resorted to widespread political repression of alternative political movements, but he also knew that he had to deal with the capital surplus absorption problem, and this he did by announcing a vast program of infrastructural investment both at home and abroad. Abroad this meant the construction of railroads throughout Europe and down into the Orient, as well as support for grand works such as the Suez Canal. At home it meant consolidating the railway network, building ports and harbors, draining marshes, and the like. But above all it entailed the reconfiguration of the urban infrastructure of Paris. Bonaparte brought Haussmann to Paris to take charge of the public works in 1853.

Haussmann clearly understood that his mission was to help solve the surplus capital and unemployment problem by way of urbanization. The rebuilding of Paris absorbed huge quantities of labor and capital by the standards of the time and, coupled with authoritarian suppression of the aspirations of the Parisian labor force, was a primary vehicle of social stabilization. Haussmann drew upon the utopian plans (by Fourierists and Saint-Simonians) for reshaping Paris that had been debated in the 1840s, but with one big difference: he transformed the scale at which the urban process was imagined. When the architect Hittorf showed Haussmann his plans for a new boulevard, Haussmann threw them back at him, saying "not wide enough ... you have it 40 meters wide and I want it 120." Haussmann thought of the city on a grander scale, annexed the suburbs, and redesigned whole neighborhoods (such as Les Halles) rather than just bits and pieces of the urban fabric. He changed the city wholesale rather than piecemeal. To do this, he needed new financial institutions and debt instruments constructed on Saint-Simonian lines (the Crédit Mobilier and Immobilier). What he did in effect was to help resolve the capital surplus disposal problem by setting up a Keynesian system of debt-financed infrastructural urban improvements.

(Profit). Doch um Mehrwert zu erzeugen, müssen Kapitalisten ein Mehrprodukt erzeugen. Das bedeutet, dass der Kapitalismus fortwährend das Mehrprodukt erzeugt, das die Urbanisierung benötigt. Umgekehrt gilt dasselbe. Der Kapitalismus benötigt die Urbanisierung, um das Mehrprodukt zu absorbieren, das er fortwährend erzeugt. Auf diese Weise entsteht ein innerer Zusammenhang zwischen der Entwicklung des Kapitalismus und der Urbanisierung. Daher überrascht es kaum, dass die logistischen Wachstumskurven der kapitalistischen Produktion historisch weitgehend parallel zu den logistischen Kurven der Verstädterung der Weltbevölkerung verlaufen. [...]

Inwiefern können wir also sagen, dass die kapitalistische Urbanisierung von dem Bedürfnis angetrieben wurde, [...] das Terrain für profitable kapitalistische Aktivitäten auszuweiten? Die These, die ich hier vertreten möchte, lautet, dass sie (zusammen mit anderen Faktoren wie etwa den Rüstungsausgaben) bei der Absorption des Mehrprodukts, das Kapitalisten in ihrem Streben nach Mehrwert permanent produzieren, eine besonders wichtige Rolle spielt.[4]

Betrachten wir zunächst die Situation im Paris des Zweiten Kaiserreichs. Die Krise von 1848 war eine der ersten Krisen, die eindeutig durch ungenutzte Überschüsse an Kapital und Arbeitskräften ausgelöst wurde, und sie erstreckte sich über ganz Europa. In Paris schlug sie besonders hart zu, was eine gescheiterte Revolution der unbeschäftigten Arbeiter und bürgerlicher Utopisten hervorrief, die eine sozialistische Republik als Mittel gegen kapitalistische Habgier und Ungleichheit ansahen. Die Bourgeoisie drängte die Revolutionäre gewaltsam zurück, konnte die Krise aber nicht meistern. Nach einem Staatsstreich 1851 regiert ab 1852 Napoleon III. Um sein politisches Überleben zu sichern, setzte der autoritäre Kaiser auf die umfassende Unterdrückung alternativer politischer Bewegungen. Er wusste allerdings auch, dass er sich des Problems der Absorption des Kapitalüberschusses annehmen musste, weshalb er enorme Infrastrukturmaßnahmen im In- und Ausland ankündigte. Im Ausland betraf dies die Errichtung neuer Bahnstrecken durch ganz Europa und bis in den Orient sowie die Unterstützung großer Bauvorhaben wie dem Suezkanal. Im Inland ging es um den Zusammenschluss des Eisenbahnnetzes, neue Häfen, das Trockenlegen von Sumpfgebieten und Ähnliches. Vor allem beinhaltete das Programm jedoch die Umgestaltung der städtischen Infrastruktur von Paris. 1853 holte Napoleon III. den Politiker und Stadtplaner Georges-Eugène Haussmann nach Paris, um ihm die Leitung der Bauvorhaben anzuvertrauen.

Haussmann verstand sofort, dass seine Aufgabe darin bestand, das Problem der Arbeitslosigkeit und das der Kapitalüberschüsse durch Urbanisierung zu lösen. Der Umbau von Paris absorbierte nach damaligem Maßstab dann auch ungeheure Mengen an Arbeitskraft und Kapital und war, neben der autoritären Unterdrückung der Pariser Arbeiterschaft, eines der wichtigsten Instrumente der sozialen Stabilisierung. Haussmann stützte sich auf die Pläne zur Umgestaltung von Paris, über welche die Anhänger utopischer Sozialisten wie Charles Fourier und Henri de Saint-Simon bereits in den vierziger Jahren des 19. Jahrhunderts diskutiert hatten – allerdings mit einem großen Unterschied: Er dachte in ganz anderen Dimensionen. Als der Architekt Jakob Ignaz Hittorff Haussmann seine Entwürfe für einen neuen Boulevard zeigte, warf dieser ihm die Skizzen mit den Worten vor die Füße: "Das ist nicht groß genug ... Bei Ihnen ist er 40 Meter breit, aber ich will 120!" Haussmann stellte sich die Metropole in einem größeren Maßstab vor, er gemeindete Vororte ein und gestaltete ganze Viertel neu (etwa Les Halles), statt nur hier und dort Veränderungen in der Struktur der Stadt vorzunehmen. Er transformierte die Stadt umfassend, nicht stückchenweise. Dafür benötigte er neue Finanzinstitutionen und Finanzierungsinstrumente, die nach den Plänen der Saint-Simonisten entworfen wurden (Crédit Mobilier und Immobilier). Faktisch trug er dazu bei, das Problem des Kapitalüberschusses zu lösen, indem er ein keynesianisches Programm der schuldenfinanzierten Stadterneuerung auflegte.

The system worked very well for some fifteen years, and it entailed not only a transformation of urban infrastructures but the construction of a whole new urban way of life and the construction of a new kind of urban persona. Paris became "the city of light," the great center of consumption, tourism and pleasure – the cafés, the department stores, the fashion industry, the grand expositions all changed the urban way of life in ways that could absorb vast surpluses through crass consumerism (which offended traditionalists and excluded workers alike). But then, in 1868, the overextended and increasingly speculative financial system and credit structures on which this was based crashed. Haussmann was forced from power. In desperation, Napoleon III went to war against Bismarck's Germany, and lost. In the vacuum that followed arose the Paris Commune, one of the greatest revolutionary episodes in capitalist urban history. The Commune was wrought in part out of a nostalgia for the urban world that Haussmann had destroyed (shades of the 1848 Revolution) and the desire to take back their city on the part of those dispossessed by Haussmann's works. But the Commune also articulated conflictual forward-looking visions of alternative socialist (as opposed to monopoly capitalist) modernities that pitted ideals of centralized hierarchical control (the Jacobin current) against decentralized anarchist visions of popular control (led by the Proudhonists). In 1872, in the midst of intense recriminations over who was at fault for the loss of the Commune, there occurred the radical political break between the Marxists and the anarchists that, to this day, still unfortunately divides so much of the left opposition to capitalism.[5]

Fast-forward now to the United States in 1942. The capital surplus disposal problem that had seemed so intractable in the 1930s (and the unemployment that went with it) was temporarily resolved by the huge mobilization for the war effort. But everyone was fearful as to what would happen after the war. Politically the situation was dangerous. The federal government was in effect running a nationalized economy (and was doing so very efficiently), and the United States was in alliance with the communist Soviet Union in the war against fascism. Strong social movements with socialist inclinations had emerged in response to the depression of the 1930s, and sympathizers were integrated into the war effort. We all know the subsequent history of the politics of McCarthyism and the Cold War (abundant signs of which were there in 1942). As under Louis Bonaparte, a hefty dose of political repression was evidently called for by the ruling classes of the time to reassert their power. But what of the capital surplus disposal problem?

In 1942 there appeared a lengthy evaluation of Haussmann's efforts in an architectural journal. It documented in detail what he had done that was so compelling and attempted an analysis of his mistakes. The article was by none other than Robert Moses, who after World War II did to the whole New York metropolitan region what Haussmann had done to Paris.[6] That is, Moses changed the scale of thinking about the urban process and – through the system of (debt-financed) highways and infrastructural transformations, through suburbanization, and through the total re-engineering not just of the city but of the whole metropolitan region – he defined a way to absorb the surplus product and thereby resolve the capital surplus absorption problem. This process, when taken nation-wide, as it was in all the major metropolitan centers of the United States (yet another transformation of scale), played a crucial role in the stabilization of global capitalism after World War II (this was a period when the United States could afford to power the whole global noncommunist economy through running trade deficits).

The suburbanization of the United States was not merely a matter of new infrastructures. As in Second Empire Paris, it entailed a radical transformation in lifestyles and produced a whole new way of life in which new products – from suburban tract housing to refrigerators and air conditioners, as well as two cars in the driveway and an enormous increase in the consumption of oil – all played their

Dieses System funktionierte etwa 15 Jahre lang und führte nicht nur zu einer Transformation der urbanen Infrastruktur, sondern auch zur Entstehung einer völlig neuen urbanen Lebensart und völlig neuer urbaner Typen. Paris wurde zur "Stadt der Lichter", zum wichtigsten Zentrum für Konsum, Tourismus und Vergnügen – die Cafés, die Kaufhäuser, die Modeindustrie und die großen Messen veränderten das städtische Leben derart, dass im Zuge eines geradezu haarsträubenden Konsumismus (der die Traditionalisten erzürnte und die Arbeiter ausschloss) gigantische Überschüsse absorbiert wurden. 1868 brachen dann jedoch das überforderte und zunehmend spekulative Bankensystem und die Finanzierungsstrukturen zusammen, auf denen all das zuvor basiert hatte. Haussmann wurde die Macht entzogen. In seiner Verzweiflung zog Napoleon III. gegen Bismarcks Deutschland in den Krieg – und verlor. In dem darauffolgenden Vakuum erhob sich die Pariser Kommune, eine der bedeutendsten revolutionären Episoden in der kapitalistischen Stadtgeschichte. Die Kommune speiste sich einerseits aus der Sehnsucht nach der urbanen Welt, die Haussmann zerstört hatte (die langen Schatten der Revolution von 1848), andererseits wollten jene Bewohner, die Haussmanns Projekten hatten Platz machen müssen, ihre Stadt zurückerobern. Gleichzeitig kamen in den Ereignissen aber auch konkurrierende Visionen einer sozialistischen (im Gegensatz zur monopolkapitalistischen) Moderne zum Ausdruck; man stritt darüber, ob man den Weg der zentralisierten hierarchischen (die jakobinische Position) oder jenen der dezentralisierten Kontrolle durch das Volk einschlagen sollte, der von den Anarchisten (angeführt von den Proudhonisten) propagiert wurde. In den hitzigen Auseinandersetzungen beschuldigten sich die Parteien gegenseitig, für die Niederlage der Kommune verantwortlich zu sein, und so kam es 1872 zu jenem radikalen politischen Bruch zwischen Marxisten und Anarchisten, der große Teile der linken Opposition gegen den Kapitalismus bedauerlicherweise bis heute spaltet.[5]

Machen wir nun einen Sprung in die Vereinigten Staaten des Jahres 1942. Das Problem der Absorption des Kapitalüberschusses, das (wie die es begleitende Arbeitslosigkeit) in den dreißiger Jahren nicht zu bewältigen schien, wurde durch die große Mobilisierung von Ressourcen für die Kriegsanstrengungen vorübergehend gelöst. Allerdings sorgte man sich darum, was nach dem Krieg geschehen würde. Die politische Situation war gefährlich. Die Regierung betrieb faktisch eine verstaatlichte Wirtschaft (und zwar äußerst effektiv), und die Vereinigten Staaten waren mit der kommunistischen Sowjetunion im Kampf gegen den Faschismus verbündet. In Reaktion auf die Depression in den Dreißigern waren starke soziale Bewegungen mit sozialistischen Neigungen entstanden, deren Sympathisanten in die Kriegsanstrengungen einbezogen wurden. Wir alle kennen den darauf folgenden Verlauf der Geschichte: die Politik des McCarthyismus und den Kalten Krieg (wofür es schon 1942 eine ganze Reihe von Anzeichen gab). Wie bereits unter Napoleon III. waren die herrschenden Klassen jener Zeit offenkundig in einem hohen Maße auf politische Unterdrückung angewiesen, um ihre Macht zu behaupten. Doch was war mit dem Problem der Absorption des Kapitalüberschusses?

1942 erschien in einem Architekturmagazin eine ausführliche Einschätzung der Bemühungen Haussmanns. Detailliert wurde darin dargelegt, was an seinem Werk so ansprechend war, und versucht, seine Fehler zu analysieren. Der Verfasser des Artikels war kein Geringerer als Robert Moses, der nach dem Zweiten Weltkrieg in der gesamten Metropolregion New York das umsetzte, was Haussmann in Paris getan hatte.[6] Das heißt, Moses änderte den Maßstab des Denkens über den urbanen Prozess, und so gelang es ihm – durch ein System (schuldenfinanzierter) Highways und Infrastrukturmaßnahmen, durch Suburbanisierung und einen kompletten Umbau nicht nur der Stadt, sondern aller Teile der Metropolregion –, das Mehrprodukt zu binden und damit das Problem der Absorption des Kapitalüberschusses zu lösen. Dieser Prozess erfasste alle wichtigen Großstädte der Vereinigten Staaten (eine weitere Transformation des Maßstabs) und spielte eine bedeutende Rolle in der Stabilisierung des globalen Kapitalismus nach dem Zweiten Weltkrieg (einer Zeit, als die Vereinigten Staaten es sich leisten konnten, weltweit die nichtkommunistische Wirtschaft anzutreiben, indem sie ein riesiges Handelsdefizit in Kauf nahmen).

Bei der Suburbanisierung in den USA ging es nicht nur um neue Infrastruktur. Wie der Umbau von Paris im Zweiten Kaiserreich hatte sie auch eine radikale Umgestaltung der Lebensstile zur Folge und brachte eine völlig neue Art zu leben hervor, in der neue Produkte – von vorstädtischen Reihenhaussiedlungen über Kühlschränke und Klimaanlagen bis hin zu zwei Autos in der Einfahrt sowie ein enormer Anstieg des Ölverbrauchs – ihren Teil zur Absorption des Überschusses

part in the absorption of the surplus. Suburbanization (alongside militarization) thus played a critical role in helping to absorb the surplus in the post-war years. But it did so at the cost of hollowing out the central cities and leaving them bereft of a sustainable economic basis, thus producing the so-called "urban crisis" of the 1960s, defined by revolts of impacted minorities (chiefly African-American) in the inner cities, who were denied access to the new prosperity.

Not only were the central cities in revolt. Traditionalists increasingly rallied around Jane Jacobs and sought to counter the brutal modernism of Moses's large-scale projects with a different kind of urban aesthetic that focused on local neighborhood development, and on the historical preservation, and ultimately gentrification, of older areas. But by then the suburbs had been built, and the radical transformation in lifestyle that this betokened had all manner of social consequences, leading feminists, for example, to proclaim the suburb and its lifestyle as the locus of all their primary discontents. As had happened to Haussmann, a crisis began to unfold such that Moses fell from grace, and his solutions came to be seen as inappropriate and unacceptable towards the end of the 1960s. And if the Haussmannization of Paris had a role in explaining the dynamics of the Paris Commune, so the soulless qualities of suburban living played a critical role in the dramatic movements of 1968 in the United States, as discontented white middle-class students went into a phase of revolt, seeking alliances with other marginalized groups and rallying against US imperialism to create a movement to build another kind of world, including a different kind of urban experience (though, again, anarchistic and libertarian currents were pitted against demands for hierarchical and centralized alternatives).[7]

Along with the '68 revolt came a financial crisis. It was partly global (with the collapse of the Bretton Woods agreements), but it also originated within the credit institutions that had powered the property boom in the preceding decades. This crisis gathered momentum at the end of the 1960s, until the whole capitalist system crashed into a major global crisis, led by the bursting of the global property market bubble in 1973, followed by the fiscal bankruptcy of New York City in 1975. The dark days of the 1970s had arrived, and the question then was how to rescue capitalism from its own contradictions. In this, if history was to be any guide, the urban process was bound to play a significant role. As William Tabb showed, the working through of the New York fiscal crisis of 1975, orchestrated by an uneasy alliance between state powers and financial institutions, pioneered a neoliberal answer to this question: the class power of capital was to be protected at the expense of working-class standards of living, while the market was deregulated to do its work. But the question then was how to revive the capacity to absorb the surpluses that capitalism must produce if it was to survive.[8]

Fast-forward once again to our current conjuncture. International capitalism was on a roller-coaster of regional crises and crashes (East and Southeast Asia in 1997–98, Russia in 1998, Argentina in 2001, and so on) until it experienced a global crash in 2008. What has been the role of urbanization in this history? In the United States it was accepted wisdom until 2008 that the housing market was an important stabilizer of the economy, particularly after the high-tech crash of the late 1990s. The property market absorbed a great deal of the surplus capital directly through new construction (of both inner-city and suburban housing and new office spaces), while the rapid inflation of housing asset prices, backed by a profligate wave of mortgage refinancing at historically low rates of interest, boosted the internal US market for consumer goods and services. The global market was stabilized partly through US urban expansion and speculation in property markets, as the US ran huge trade deficits with the rest of the world, borrowing around $2 billion a day to fuel its insatiable consumerism and the debt-financed wars in Afghanistan and Iraq during the first decade of the twenty-first century.

beitrugen. Die Suburbanisierung spielte also (neben der Militarisierung) in den Nachkriegsjahren eine wichtige Rolle dabei, den Kapitalüberschuss aufzunehmen. Der Preis dafür war jedoch die Aushöhlung der Stadtzentren, die einer nachhaltigen ökonomischen Grundlage beraubt wurden. Dadurch kam es zu der sogenannten "urbanen Krise" der sechziger Jahre, in deren Zuge von dieser Entwicklung betroffene Minderheiten (hauptsächlich Afroamerikaner) in den Innenstädten revoltierten. Der Zugang zum neuen Wohlstand war ihnen verwehrt geblieben.

Nicht nur die Stadtzentren begehrten auf. Traditionalisten folgten zunehmend der kanadischen Aktivistin und Architekturkritikerin Jane Jacobs und bemühten sich darum, dem schonungslosen Modernismus der Großprojekte von Moses eine andere Art von urbaner Ästhetik entgegenzusetzen, die ihr Augenmerk auf die Entwicklung lokaler Nachbarschaften sowie die Erhaltung und letztendlich Gentrifizierung älterer Gegenden richtete. Die Vorstädte waren zu diesem Zeitpunkt allerdings längst gebaut, und die mit ihnen einhergehende radikale Transformation des Lebensstils hatte bereits allerlei gesellschaftliche Auswirkungen. So erklärten etwa führende Feministinnen, ihre Unzufriedenheit richte sich hauptsächlich gegen die Vorstadt und die mit ihr verbundene Gestaltung des Lebens. Wie im Fall Haussmann kam es zur Krise, und Moses fiel in Ungnade. Gegen Ende der sechziger Jahre erschienen seine Ansätze inadäquat und unannehmbar. Ebenso wie die Unternehmungen Haussmanns die Dynamik der Pariser Kommune erklären helfen, trug die Seelenlosigkeit des vorstädtischen Lebens zu den dramatischen Ereignissen in den USA im Jahr 1968 bei, als unzufriedene weiße Studenten aus der Mittelschicht zu revoltieren begannen, sich mit marginalisierten Gruppen verbündeten und gegen den US-Imperialismus demonstrierten, um eine Bewegung für eine andere Welt ins Leben zu rufen. Dazu gehörte auch eine andere Art urbaner Erfahrung (obgleich die anarchistischen und libertären Strömungen wieder gegen Forderungen nach hierarchischen und zentralisierten Alternativen ausgespielt wurden).[7]

Mit der Revolte von Achtundsechzig ging eine Finanzkrise einher. Sie hatte zum Teil globale Ursachen (den Zusammenbruch des Bretton-Woods-Systems), rührte aber auch von den Kreditinstituten her, die den Immobilienboom der vorangegangenen Jahrzehnte befeuert hatten. Ende der sechziger Jahre nahmen die Schwierigkeiten zu, bis das gesamte kapitalistische System in eine Krise stürzte. Sie begann damit, dass 1973 die Blase auf dem weltweiten Immobilienmarkt platzte. Dem folgte der Bankrott der Stadt New York im Jahr 1975. Die dunklen Tage der siebziger Jahre waren angebrochen, und die Frage lautete nun, wie man den Kapitalismus vor seinen eigenen Widersprüchen retten konnte. Wenn die Geschichte in irgendeiner Weise als Orientierungshilfe dienen sollte, musste der urbane Prozess dabei eine bedeutende Rolle spielen. Wie der Ökonom William Tabb aufzeigte, ebnete die Lösung der New Yorker Finanzkrise, die schließlich durch eine schwierige Allianz aus staatlichen Stellen und privaten Finanzinstituten gemeistert wurde, den Weg für eine neoliberale Antwort auf diese Frage: Die Klassenmacht des Kapitals wurde auf Kosten des Lebensstandards der Arbeiterklasse bewahrt, während der Markt dereguliert wurde, um seine Arbeit zu tun. Allerdings ergab sich nun die Frage, wie man die Fähigkeit erneuern konnte, die Überschüsse zu absorbieren, die der Kapitalismus produzieren muss, so er denn überleben soll.[8]

Machen wir noch einmal einen Sprung und betrachten unsere gegenwärtige Lage. Bis es 2008 zum weltweiten Crash kam, befand sich der internationale Kapitalismus auf einer Berg-und-Tal-Fahrt, die von regionalen Krisen und Zusammenbrüchen geprägt war (Ost- und Südostasien 1997-98, Russland 1998, Argentinien 2001 etc.). Welche Rolle spielte die Urbanisierung in dieser Geschichte? In den Vereinigten Staaten galt es bis 2008 als anerkannte Lehrmeinung, dass der Immobilienmarkt ein wichtiger Stabilisator der Wirtschaft sei, insbesondere nach dem Platzen der Dotcom-Blase in den späten neunziger Jahren. Durch neue Bauprojekte (im Bereich des innerstädtischen und vorstädtischen Wohnungsbaus sowie durch neue Bürogebäude) floss ihm ein großer Teil des überschüssigen Kapitals direkt zu, während die rasante Inflation der Immobilienpreise, getrieben von einer Welle der leichtfertigen Hypothekenrefinanzierung zu historisch niedrigen Zinssätzen, den US-Binnenmarkt für Konsumgüter und Dienstleistungen ankurbelte. Der Weltmarkt wurde zumindest teilweise durch die urbane Expansion und die Immobilienspekulationen in den Vereinigten Staaten stabilisiert. Gleichzeitig stieg allerdings das US-Handelsdefizit gegenüber dem Rest der Welt immer weiter an. Um ihren unersättlichen Konsum und die schuldenfinanzierten Kriege in Afghanistan und im Irak bezahlen zu können, mussten sich die Amerikaner in der ersten Dekade des 21. Jahrhunderts etwa zwei Milliarden Dollar pro Tag leihen.

But the urban process underwent another transformation of scale. In short, it went global. So we cannot focus merely on the US. Property market booms in Britain, Ireland, and Spain, as well as in many other countries, helped power the capitalist dynamic in ways that broadly paralleled that in the US. The urbanization of China over the last twenty years [...] has been of a radically different character, with a heavy focus on building infrastructures. Its pace picked up enormously after a brief recession in 1997 or so. More than a hundred cities have passed the 1 million population mark in the last twenty years, and small villages, like Shenzhen, have become huge metropolises of 6 to 10 million people. Industrialization was at first concentrated in the special economic zones, but then rapidly diffused outwards to any municipality willing to absorb the surplus capital from abroad and plough back the earnings into rapid expansion. Vast infrastructural projects, such as dams and highways – again, all debt-financed – are transforming the landscape.[9] Equally vast shopping malls, science parks, airports, container ports, pleasure palaces of all kinds, and all manner of newly minted cultural institutions, along with gated communities and golf courses, dot the Chinese landscape in the midst of over-crowded urban dormitories for the massive labor reserves being mobilized from the impoverished rural regions that supply the migrant labor. As we shall see, the consequences of this urbanization process for the global economy and for the absorption of surplus capital have been huge.

But China is only one epicenter for an urbanization process that has now become genuinely global, in part through the astonishing global integration of financial markets that use their flexibility to debt-finance urban projects from Dubai to São Paulo and from Madrid and Mumbai to Hong Kong and London. The Chinese central bank, for example, has been active in the secondary mortgage market in the US, while Goldman Sachs has been involved in the surging property markets in Mumbai and Hong Kong capital has been invested in Baltimore. Almost every city in the world has witnessed a building boom for the rich – often of a distressingly similar character – in the midst of a flood of impoverished migrants converging on cities as a rural peasantry is dispossessed through the industrialization and commercialization of agriculture. [...]

But this urbanization boom has depended, as did all the others before it, on the construction of new financial institutions and arrangements to organize the credit required to sustain it. Financial innovations set in train in the 1980s, particularly the securitization and packaging of local mortgages for sale to investors world-wide, and the setting up of new financial institutions to facilitate a secondary mortgage market and to hold collateralized debt obligations, has played a crucial role. The benefits of this were legion: it spread risk and permitted surplus savings pools easier access to surplus housing demand, and also, by virtue of its coordinations, it brought aggregate interest rates down (while generating immense fortunes for the financial intermediaries who worked these wonders). But spreading risk does not eliminate risk. Furthermore, the fact that risk can be spread so widely encourages even riskier local behaviors, because the risk can be transferred elsewhere. Without adequate risk-assessment controls, the mortgage market got out of hand, and what happened to the Péreire Brothers in 1867–68 and to the fiscal profligacy of New York City in the early 1970s was then repeated in the sub-prime mortgage and housing asset-value crisis of 2008. The crisis was concentrated in the first instance in and around US cities (though similar signs could be seen in Britain), with particularly serious implications for lowincome African-Americans and single head-of-household women in the inner cities. It also affected those who, unable to afford the skyrocketing housing prices in the urban centers, particularly in the US southwest, moved to the semi-periphery of metropolitan areas to take up

Der Maßstab des urbanen Prozesses erfuhr noch eine weitere Veränderung: Er wurde global. Wir dürfen uns also nicht allein auf die USA konzentrieren. Immobilienbooms in England, Irland, Spanien und vielen anderen Ländern trieben dort die kapitalistische Dynamik auf ähnliche Weise an wie in den Vereinigten Staaten. [...] die Entwicklung in China (war) während der letzten zwanzig Jahre eine radikal andere. Dort widmete man sich in erster Linie dem Aufbau der Infrastruktur. Nach einer kurzen Rezession in den Jahren 1997 und 1998 legte die Urbanisierung dann enorm an Geschwindigkeit zu. Mehr als 100 chinesische Städte haben in den letzten 20 Jahren die Marke von einer Million Einwohnern überschritten, und aus kleinen Dörfern wie Shenzhen sind riesige Metropolen mit sechs bis zehn Millionen Einwohnern geworden. Zunächst wurden die Sonderwirtschaftszonen industrialisiert, anschließend alle Gemeinden, die bereit waren, den ausländischen Kapitalüberschuss zu absorbieren und die Gewinne in die rasche Expansion zu reinvestieren. Gigantische Infrastrukturprojekte wie Staudämme und Schnellstraßen – wiederum allesamt schuldenfinanziert – verwandeln die Landschaft.[9] Zudem übersäen riesige Einkaufszentren, Forschungsparks, Flug- und Containerhäfen, Vergnügungsstätten aller Art sowie neu ins Leben gerufene Kulturinstitutionen, geschlossene Wohnanlagen und Golfplätze die chinesische Landschaft. Sie finden sich neben überfüllten städtischen Wohnheimen für die zahlreichen aus den verarmten ländlichen Regionen stammenden Menschen, welche die Arbeitskräftereserve bilden und sich als Wanderarbeiter verdingen. Wie wir noch sehen werden, waren die Auswirkungen dieses Urbanisierungsprozesses auf die Weltwirtschaft und auf die Absorption des Kapitalüberschusses enorm.

Gleichwohl ist China nur ein Epizentrum dieser Entwicklung, die inzwischen überall zu beobachten ist. Ein Grund dafür ist die erstaunliche weltweite Integration der Finanzmärkte, die ihre Flexibilität nutzen, um von Dubai bis São Paulo, von Madrid und Mumbai bis Hongkong und London urbane Projekte durch Schulden zu finanzieren. So beteiligte sich etwa die chinesische Volksbank (also die Zentralbank der Volksrepublik) am sekundären Hypothekenmarkt in den USA, Goldman Sachs war auf dem sich rasant entwickelnden Immobilienmarkt in Mumbai aktiv und Kapital aus Hongkong wurde in Baltimore im US-Bundesstaat Maryland investiert. Nahezu jede Stadt auf dem Planeten hat – oft mit den gleichen negativen Folgen – einen Bauboom erlebt, der von und für die reiche Oberschicht initiiert wurde. Gleichzeitig kommen Massen verarmter Migranten in den Städten zusammen, da sich die ländlichen Kleinbauern aufgrund der Industrialisierung und Kommerzialisierung der Landwirtschaft ihrer Lebensgrundlage beraubt sehen. [...]

Wie alle anderen vor ihm, beruhte auch dieser Urbanisierungsboom auf der Konstruktion neuer Finanzinstitutionen und -regelungen, um so die für seine Aufrechterhaltung benötigten Kredite verfügbar zu machen. Eine entscheidende Rolle spielten dabei innovative Finanzinstrumente, die in den achtziger Jahren entwickelt wurden. Dazu gehören insbesondere das Verbriefen und das Zusammenlegen mehrerer lokaler Hypotheken, die anschließend als Pakete an Investoren rund um den Globus verkauft werden, sowie die Gründung neuer Finanzinstitutionen, um die Schaffung eines sekundären Hypothekenmarkts zu begünstigen und sogenannte collateralized debt obligations (CDOs) einzuführen. Mit diesem Vorgehen waren einige Vorteile verbunden: Es streute das Risiko, und bisher nicht verwendete Spareinlagen konnten leichter für Überschüsse bei der Wohnungsnachfrage verwendet werden. Durch Koordinierungsleistungen senkte es außerdem die Gesamtzinssätze (während es riesige Vermögen für die Finanzvermittler erwirtschaftete, die diese Wunder bewirkten). Die Verteilung eines Risikos schafft es jedoch nicht aus der Welt. Zudem fördert die Möglichkeit, es so breit zu streuen, risikobereites Verhalten auf lokaler Ebene, da das Risiko gewissermaßen ausgelagert werden kann. Ohne angemessene Kontrollen der Risikobewertung lief der Hypothekenmarkt aus dem Ruder, und was 1867-68 den Brüdern Émile und Isaac Péreire und in den frühen siebziger Jahren aufgrund ihres verschwenderischen Umgangs mit den eigenen Finanzen der Stadt New York passiert war, wiederholte sich in der Krise der Subprime-Hypotheken* und der Immobilienvermögenswerte von 2008. Das Zentrum der Krise bildeten zunächst amerikanische Städte und deren Umland (obgleich in Großbritannien ähnliche Entwicklungen erkennbar waren). Besonders hart traf es einkommensschwache Afroamerikaner und alleinerziehende Frauen in den Innenstädten. Auch diejenigen, die an den Rand der Metropolregionen gezogen waren, weil sie sich die sprunghaft ansteigenden Immobilienpreise in den Stadtzentren, insbesondere im Südwesten der USA, nicht mehr leisten konnten, hatten mit Problemen zu kämpfen: Zu anfänglich niedrigen Kreditzinssätzen waren sie in Reihenhäuser gezogen, die gebaut worden waren, weil man auf steigende Preise spekuliert hatte. Nach kurzer Zeit sahen sie sich je-

* Als subprime mortgages werden Hypotheken für Kreditnehmer mit geringer Bonität bezeichnet; Anm. d. Übers.

speculatively built tract housing at initially easy credit rates, but who then faced escalating commuting costs with rising oil prices and soaring mortgage payments as market-interest rates kicked in. This crisis, with vicious local impacts on urban life and infrastructures (whole neighborhoods in cities like Cleveland, Baltimore, and Detroit have been devastated by the foreclosure wave), threatened the whole architecture of the global financial system, and triggered a major recession to boot. The parallels with the 1970s are, to put it mildly, uncanny [...].

As in all the preceding phases, this most recent radical expansion of the urban process has brought with it incredible transformations in lifestyles. Quality of urban life has become a commodity for those with money, as has the city itself in a world where consumerism, tourism, cultural and knowledge-based industries, as well as perpetual resort to the economy of the spectacle, have become major aspects of urban political economy, even in India and China. The postmodernist penchant for encouraging the formation of market niches, both in urban lifestyle choices and in consumer habits, and cultural forms, surrounds the contemporary urban experience with an aura of freedom of choice in the market, provided you have the money and can protect yourself from the privatization of wealth redistribution through burgeoning criminal activity and predatory fraudulent practices (which have everywhere escalated). Shopping malls, multiplexes, and box stores proliferate (the production of each has become big business), as do fast-food and artisanal market places, boutique cultures and, as Sharon Zukin slyly notes, "pacification by cappuccino." Even the incoherent, bland, and monotonous suburban tract development that continues to dominate in many areas, now gets its antidote in a "new urbanism" movement that touts the sale of community and a boutique lifestyle as a developer product to fulfill urban dreams. This is a world in which the neoliberal ethic of intense possessive individualism can become the template for human personality socialization. The impact is increasing individualistic isolation, anxiety, and neurosis in the midst of one of the greatest social achievements (at least judging by its enormous scale and all-embracing character) ever constructed in human history for the realization of our hearts' desire.

But the fissures within the system are also all too evident. We increasingly live in divided, fragmented, and conflict-prone cities. How we view the world and define possibilities depends on which side of the tracks we are on and on what kinds of consumerism we have access to. In the past decades, the neoliberal turn has restored class power to rich elites.[11] In a single year several hedge fund managers in New York raked in $3 billion in personal remuneration, and Wall Street bonuses have soared for individuals over the last few years from around $5 million towards the $50 million mark for top players (putting real estate prices in Manhattan out of sight). Fourteen billionaires have emerged in Mexico since the neoliberal turn in the late 1980s, and Mexico now boasts the richest man on earth, Carlos Slim, at the same time as the incomes of the poor in that country have either stagnated or diminished. As of the end of 2009 (after the worst of the crash was over), there were 115 billionaires in China, 101 in Russia, 55 in India, 52 in Germany, 32 in Britain, and 30 in Brazil, in addition to the 413 in the United States.[12] The results of this increasing polarization in the distribution of wealth and power are indelibly etched into the spatial forms of our cities, which increasingly become cities of fortified fragments, of gated communities and privatized public spaces kept under constant surveillance. The neoliberal protection of private property rights and their values becomes a hegemonic form of politics, even for the lower middle class. [...]

Surplus absorption through urban transformation has, however, an even darker aspect. It has entailed repeated bouts of urban restructuring through "creative destruction." This nearly always has a class dimension, since it is usually the poor, the underprivileged, and those marginalized from political power that suffer first and foremost from this process. Violence is required to achieve the new urban world on the wreckage of the old. Haussmann tore through the old Parisian impoverished quarters, using powers of expropriation for supposedly public benefit,

doch aufgrund der steigenden Ölpreise mit zusätzlichen Pendelkosten konfrontiert. Als die Marktzinssätze wirksam wurden, schnellten zudem die Hypothekenraten in die Höhe. Diese Krise, die verheerende Auswirkungen auf das urbane Leben und die Infrastruktur in den lokalen Nachbarschaften hatte (in Städten wie Cleveland, Baltimore und Detroit verwaisten infolge der vielen Zwangsvollstreckungen ganze Stadtviertel), bedrohte das globale Finanzsystem als solches und löste obendrein eine schwere Rezession aus. Die Parallelen zu den siebziger Jahren sind, um es milde auszudrücken, unheimlich [...].

Wie in allen vorangegangenen Phasen der Urbanisierung hat diese jüngste, massive Ausweitung des urbanen Prozesses einen unvorstellbaren Wandel des Lebensstils mit sich gebracht. In einer Welt, in der Konsumismus, Tourismus, Kultur- und Wissensindustrien und eine ständige Flucht in die Ökonomie des Spektakels zu wesentlichen Aspekten der urbanen politischen Ökonomie geworden sind, ist städtische Lebensqualität, wie auch die Stadt selbst, zu einer Konsumware für Menschen mit Geld geworden; das gilt sogar für China und Indien. Die postmoderne Neigung, hinsichtlich der Wahl des urbanen Lebensstils, der Kaufgewohnheiten sowie kultureller Formen die Schaffung von Marktnischen zu unterstützen, verleiht der heutigen städtischen Erfahrung eine Aura der Entscheidungsfreiheit am Markt – sofern man das nötige Geld hat und sich vor der Privatisierung der Vermögensumverteilung durch boomende kriminelle Aktivitäten und rücksichtslose betrügerische Methoden (die sich überall ausgebreitet haben) schützen kann. Einkaufszentren, Multiplex-Kinos und riesige Supermärkte sprießen aus dem Boden (ihr Bau ist zu einem großen Geschäft geworden), ebenso Filialen von Fast-Food-Ketten, Kunsthandwerksmärkte und Boutiquen. Hinzu kommt ein Phänomen, das die Soziologin Sharon Zukin treffend als "Befriedung durch Cappuccino" bezeichnet hat. Selbst gegen die Zersiedelung durch den massenhaften Bau langweiliger Reihenhäuser in den Vorstädten, der in vielen Gebieten nach wie vor das Bild bestimmt, wird als Gegengift ein "neuer Urbanismus" angeboten, der Gemeinschaftsgefühl und Boutiquen-Lifestyle als Produkte bewirbt, die urbane Träume zu erfüllen helfen. Es handelt sich um eine Welt, in der die neoliberale Ethik eines habgierigen Individualismus zur Schablone für die Sozialisation der menschlichen Persönlichkeit werden kann. Die Auswirkungen sind zunehmende individuelle Isolation, Ängste und Neurosen, und all das trotz der größten gesellschaftlichen Leistungen (zumindest wenn man sie nach ihrem enormen Ausmaß und allumfassenden Charakter beurteilt), die im Laufe der Menschheitsgeschichte vollbracht wurden, um uns der Verwirklichung unserer Herzenswünsche näher zu bringen.

Doch die Risse im System sind deutlich zu erkennen. Immer mehr Menschen leben in gespaltenen, fragmentierten und konfliktanfälligen Städten. Wie wir die Welt sehen und Chancen definieren, hängt davon ab, in welchem Viertel wir leben und welche Art von Konsum wir uns leisten können. In den vergangenen Jahrzehnten hat die neoliberale Wende den reichen Eliten die Klassenmacht zurückgegeben.11 In einem einzigen Jahr haben einige Hedgefonds-Manager in New York drei Milliarden US-Dollar an Vergütungen eingestrichen. Die Boni an der Wall Street sind in den letzten Jahren in die Höhe geschnellt, für Spitzenverdiener von etwa fünf Millionen auf fast fünfzig Millionen US-Dollar (in der Folge sind die Immobilienpreise in Manhattan ins Unermessliche gestiegen). In Mexiko sind seit der neoliberalen Wende in den späten achtziger Jahren 14 Menschen zu Milliardären geworden, und das Land rühmt sich heute des reichsten Mannes auf Erden, Carlos Slim, während die Einkommen der Armen im gleichen Zeitraum stagnierten oder fielen. Ende 2009 (nachdem der schlimmste Teil des Crashs vorüber war) gab es zusätzlich zu den 413 Milliardären in den Vereinigten Staaten 115 in China, 101 in Russland, 55 in Indien, 52 in Deutschland, 32 in Großbritannien und 30 in Brasilien.12 Die Folgen dieser sich verschärfenden Polarisierung bei der Verteilung von Reichtum und Macht haben die räumliche Gestaltung unserer Städte unauslöschlich geprägt. Es entstehen immer mehr verschanzte Fragmente, geschlossene Wohnanlagen und öffentliche Räume unter ständiger privater Überwachung. Der neoliberale Schutz von privaten Eigentumsrechten und deren Werten wird zu einer hegemonialen Form der Politik, selbst für die untere Mittelklasse. [...]

Die Absorption des Überschusses durch urbane Transformation hat allerdings eine noch dunklere Seite als die der Isolation und Fragmentierung. Sie hat wiederholt die Umgestaltung städtischer Räume durch Prozesse der "schöpferischen Zerstörung" nach sich gezogen. Dies hat so gut wie immer mit den Verhältnissen zwischen den Klassen zu tun, da für gewöhnlich in erster Linie die Armen, Unterprivilegierten und von der politischen Macht Ausgeschlossenen darunter leiden. Um die neue städtische Welt auf den Trümmern der alten zu errichten, muss Gewalt angewendet werden. Haussmann nahm die alten, verarmten Viertel von Paris auseinander, wandte seine Befugnisse zur Zwangsenteignung im Namen eines angeblich öffentlichen Interesses an und tat all dies im Namen der Stadtverschönerung, Umweltsanierung und urbanen Erneuerung. Absichtlich sorgte er

and did so in the name of civic improvement, environmental restoration, and urban renovation. He deliberately engineered the removal of much of the working class and other unruly elements, along with insalubrious industries, from Paris's city center, where they constituted a threat to public order, public health and, of course, political power. He created an urban form where it was believed (incorrectly, as it turned out, in 1871) sufficient levels of surveillance and military control were possible so as to ensure that revolutionary movements could easily be controlled by military power. But, as Engels pointed out in 1872,

In reality, the bourgeoisie has only one method of solving the housing question after its fashion – that is to say, of solving it in such a way that the solution perpetually renews the question anew. This method is called "Haussmann" [...] The breeding places of disease, the infamous holes and cellars in which the capitalist mode of production confines our workers night after night, are not abolished; they are merely shifted elsewhere! The same economic necessity that produced them in the first place, produces them in the next place.[14]

Actually it took more than a hundred years to complete the bourgeois conquest of central Paris, with the consequences that we have seen in recent years of uprisings and mayhem in those isolated suburbs within which the marginalized immigrants and the unemployed workers and youth are increasingly trapped. The sad point here, of course, is that the processes Engels described recur again and again in capitalist urban history. Robert Moses "took a meat axe to the Bronx" (in his infamous words), and long and loud were the lamentations of neighborhood groups and movements, which eventually coalesced around the rhetoric of Jane Jacobs, at the unimaginable destruction not only of valued urban fabric but also of whole communities of residents and their longestablished networks of social integration.[15] But in the New York and Parisian case, once the brutal power of state expropriations had been successfully resisted and contained by the agitations of '68, a far more insidious and cancerous process of transformation occurred through fiscal disciplining of democratic urban governments, land markets, property speculation, and the sorting of land to those uses that generated the highest possible financial rate of return under the land's "highest and best use." Engels understood all too well what this process was about too:

The growth of the big modern cities gives the land in certain areas, particularly in those areas which are centrally situated, an artificially and colossally increasing value; the buildings erected on these areas depress this value instead of increasing it, because they no longer belong to the changed circumstances. They are pulled down and replaced by others. This takes place above all with workers' houses which are situated centrally and whose rents, even with the greatest overcrowding, can never, or only very slowly, increase above a certain maximum. They are pulled down and in their stead shops, warehouses and public building are erected.[16]

It is depressing to think that all of this was written in 1872, for Engels's description applies directly to contemporary urban processes in much of Asia (Delhi, Seoul, Mumbai) as well as to the contemporary gentrification of, say, Harlem and Brooklyn in New York. A process of displacement and dispossession, in short, also lies at the core of the urban process under capitalism. This is the mirror image of capital absorption through urban redevelopment. Consider the case of Mumbai, where there are 6 million people considered officially as slum-dwellers settled on land for the most part without legal title (the places where they live are left blank on all maps of the city). With the attempt to turn Mumbai into a global financial center to rival Shanghai, the property development boom gathers pace and the land the slum-dwellers occupy appears increasingly valuable. The value of the land in Dharavi, one of the most prominent slums in Mumbai, is put at $2 billion, and the pressure to clear the slum (for environmental and social reasons that mask the land grab) is mounting daily. Financial powers, backed by the state, push for forcible slum clearance, in some cases violently taking possession of a terrain occupied for a whole generation by the slum-dwellers. Capital accumulation on the land through real estate activity booms as land is acquired at almost no cost. [...] dispossession (though less brutal and more legalistic) can be found in the US, through the abuse of rights of eminent domain to displace long-term residents in reasonable housing in favor of higher-order land uses (such as condominiums and box stores). Challenged in the US Supreme Court, the liberal justices carried the day against the conservatives in saying it was perfectly constitutional for local jurisdictions to behave in this way in order to increase their property tax base.

dafür, dass ein großer Teil der Arbeiterklasse und anderer widerspenstiger Elemente zusammen mit gesundheitsschädlichen Industriezweigen aus dem Pariser Stadtzentrum entfernt wurden, wo sie eine Bedrohung für die öffentliche Ordnung, die Gesundheit und natürlich die politische Macht darstellten. Er erschuf eine Stadtform, von der man annahm (fälschlicherweise, wie sich 1871 herausstellte), in ihr seien Überwachung und militärische Kontrolle in ausreichendem Umfang möglich, um sicherzugehen, dass revolutionäre Bewegungen mithilfe von militärischer Macht leicht kontrolliert werden könnten. Wie Engels jedoch 1872 betonte:

In Wirklichkeit hat die Bourgeoisie nur eine Methode, die Wohnungsfrage in ihrer Art zu lösen – das heißt, sie so zu lösen, daß die Lösung die Frage immer wieder von neuem erzeugt. Diese Methode heißt: "Haussmann". [...] Die Brutstätten der Seuchen, die infamsten Höhlen und Löcher, worin die kapitalistische Produktionsweise unsre Arbeiter Nacht für Nacht einsperrt, sie werden nicht beseitigt, sie werden nur – verlegt! Dieselbe ökonomische Notwendigkeit, die sie am ersten Ort erzeugte, erzeugt sie auch am zweiten.[14]

Tatsächlich dauerte es über ein Jahrhundert, bis die bürgerliche Eroberung des Pariser Zentrums abgeschlossen war. Die Konsequenzen dieser Entwicklung haben wir in den letzten Jahren während der Aufstände und des Chaos in den isolierten Vorstädten beobachten können, in denen die ins Abseits gedrängten Immigranten sowie die beschäftigungslosen Arbeiter und Jugendlichen zunehmend gefangen sind. Das Traurige daran ist natürlich, dass die von Engels beschriebenen Prozesse in der kapitalistischen Stadtgeschichte wieder und wieder stattfinden. Robert Moses ist (um es mit seinen eigenen berüchtigten Worten auszudrücken) "mit der Axt durch die Bronx" gezogen. Er löste damit langanhaltende und lautstarke Klagen von Stadtteilgruppen und Bewegungen aus, die sich gegen die unvorstellbare Zerstörung nicht nur wertvoller städtischer Bausubstanz, sondern auch ganzer Anwohnergemeinschaften mit ihren fest etablierten Netzwerken sozialer Integration wandten und schließlich den Worten von Jane Jacobs folgten.15 Allerdings kam es sowohl in Paris als auch in New York nach dem erfolgreichen Widerstand der Achtundsechziger-Bewegung gegen die brutale Macht staatlicher Enteignung zu einem viel hinterhältigeren, geschwürartig wuchernden Transformationsprozess durch fiskalische Disziplinierung demokratischer städtischer Regierungen, Grundstücksmärkte und Immobilienspekulation. Zudem wurden Grundstücke "bestmöglich verwendet", um die höchste Rendite zu erzielen. Auch Engels verstand nur zu gut, worum es bei diesem Prozess ging:

Die Ausdehnung der modernen großen Städte gibt in gewissen, besonders in den zentral gelegenen Strichen derselben dem Grund und Boden einen künstlichen, oft kolossal steigenden Wert; die darauf errichteten Gebäude, statt diesen Wert zu erhöhn, drücken ihn vielmehr herab, weil sie den veränderten Verhältnissen nicht mehr entsprechen; man reißt sie nieder und ersetzt sie durch andre. Dies geschieht vor allem mit zentral gelegenen Arbeiterwohnungen, deren Miete, selbst bei der größten Überfüllung, nie oder doch nur äußerst langsam über ein gewisses Maximum hinausgehn kann. Man reißt sie nieder und baut Läden, Warenlager, öffentliche Gebäude an ihrer Stelle.[16]

Es ist deprimierend, wenn man bedenkt, dass all dies im Jahr 1872 geschrieben wurde. Schließlich lässt sich Engels' Beschreibung direkt auf die heutigen urbanen Prozesse in einem großen Teil Asiens (Delhi, Seoul, Mumbai) sowie auf die gegenwärtige Gentrifizierung von beispielsweise Harlem und Brooklyn in New York übertragen. Kurz gesagt ist der urbane Prozess unter den Bedingungen des Kapitalismus im Kern auch ein Prozess der Verdrängung und Enteignung. Er ist das Spiegelbild der Kapitalabsorption durch städtische Neugestaltung. Betrachten wir etwa das Beispiel Mumbai. Sechs Millionen Einwohner gelten offiziell als Slumbewohner. Sie lassen sich auf Grundstücken nieder, zumeist ohne einen Rechtsanspruch auf diese vorweisen zu können (die Gegenden, in denen sie leben, sind auf allen Stadtplänen frei gelassen). Mit dem Versuch, Mumbai in ein globales Finanzzentrum zu verwandeln, das es mit Schanghai aufnehmen kann, schreitet die Grundstückserschließung voran, und das von den Slumbewohnern bewohnte Land erscheint immer wertvoller. Der Bodenwert von Dharavi, einem der bekanntesten Slums Mumbais, wird auf zwei Milliarden US-Dollar geschätzt, und täglich steigt der Druck, den Slum (angeblich aus ökologischen und sozialen Gründen, die den Landraub maskieren) abzureißen. Mächtige Finanzunternehmen, die von staatlicher Seite unterstützt werden, drängen auf die Zwangsräumung der Armensiedlungen und reißen in manchen Fällen gewaltsam Boden an sich, der seit einer ganzen Generation von Slumbewohnern besiedelt wird. Die Kapitalakkumulation durch Immobilienaktivitäten auf den Grundstücken floriert, da das Land zu niedrigsten Preisen erworben wird. [...]

Ähnliche Beispiele für Zwangsenteignungen (obgleich weniger brutal und eher in einem legalen Rahmen) finden sich auch in den USA, dann nämlich, wenn das Recht des Staates auf Enteignung missbraucht wird, um langjährige Bewohner aus bezahlbaren Wohnungen zu vertreiben und die Grundstücke für eine lukrativere Bodennutzung (etwa für Eigentumswohnungen und Einkaufszentren) zu verwenden. Als dieses Vorgehen vor dem Obersten Gerichtshof der Vereinigten Staaten angefoch-

In Seoul in the 1990s, the construction companies and developers hired goon squads of sumo-wrestler types to invade whole neighborhoods and smash down with sledgehammers not only the housing but also all the possessions of those who had built their own housing on the hillsides of the city in the 1950s, on what by the 1990s had become highvalue land. Most of those hillsides are now covered with high-rise towers that show no trace of the brutal processes of land clearance that permitted their construction. In China millions are being dispossessed of the spaces they have long occupied. Lacking private property rights, they can be simply removed from the land by the state by fiat, offered a minor cash payment to help them on their way (before the land is turned over to developers at a high rate of profit). In some instances people move willingly, but widespread resistance is also reported, the usual response to which is brutal repression by the Communist Party. In the Chinese case, it is often populations on the rural margins who are displaced, illustrating the significance of Lefebvre's argument, presciently laid out in the 1960s, that the clear distinction that once existed between the urban and the rural was gradually fading into a set of porous spaces of uneven geographical development under the hegemonic command of capital and the state. [...]

Urbanization, we may conclude, has played a crucial role in the absorption of capital surpluses and has done so at ever-increasing geographical scales, but at the price of burgeoning processes of creative destruction that entail the dispossession of the urban masses of any right to the city whatsoever. Periodically this ends in revolt, as in Paris in 1871, when the dispossessed rose up seeking to reclaim the city they had lost. The urban social movements of 1968, from Paris and Bangkok to Mexico City and Chicago, likewise sought to define a different way of urban living from that which was being imposed upon them by capitalist developers and the state. If, as seems likely, the fiscal difficulties in the current conjuncture mount and the hitherto successful neoliberal, postmodernist, and consumerist phase of capitalist absorption of the surplus through urbanization is at an end, and if a broader crisis ensues, then the question arises: Where is our '68 or, even more dramatically, our version of the Commune?

By analogy with transformations in the fiscal system, the political answer is bound to be much more complex in our times precisely because the urban process is now global in scope and wracked with all manner of fissures, insecurities, and uneven geographical developments. But cracks in the system are, as Leonard Cohen once sang, "what lets the light in." Signs of revolt are everywhere (the unrest in China and India is chronic, civil wars rage in Africa, Latin America is in ferment, autonomy movements are emerging all over the place, and even in the US the political signs suggest that most of the population is saying "enough is enough" with respect to rabid inequalities). Any of these revolts could suddenly become contagious. Unlike the fiscal system, however, the urban and peri-urban social movements of opposition, of which there are many around the world, are not tightly coupled at all. Indeed, many have no connection to each other. It is unlikely, therefore, that a single spark will, as the Weather Underground once dreamed, spark a prairie fire. It will take something far more systematic than that. But if these various oppositional movements did somehow come together – coalesce, for example, around the slogan of the right to the city – then what should they demand?

The answer to the last question is simple enough: greater democratic control over the production and use of the surplus. Since the urban process is a major channel of use, then the right to the city is constituted by establishing democratic control over the deployment of the surpluses through urbanization. To have a surplus product is not a bad thing: indeed, in many situations a surplus is crucial to adequate survival. Throughout capitalist history, some of the surplus value created has been taxed away by the state, and in social-democratic phases that proportion rose significantly, putting much of the surplus under state control. The whole neoliberal project over the last thirty years has been oriented towards privatization of control over the surplus. The data for all OECD countries show, however, that the share of gross

ten wurde, waren die liberalen Richter mit ihrer Argumentation den konservativen überlegen. Sie erklärten es für völlig verfassungsgemäß, wenn die örtlichen Behörden auf diese Weise verfahren, um damit ihre Grundsteuerbasis aufzubessern.

In den neunziger Jahren engagierten Bauunternehmer in Seoul Schlägertrupps, die aus Männern mit Sumoringer-Statur bestanden, um ganze Stadtviertel zu terrorisieren. Mit Vorschlaghämmern zerschmetterten sie nicht nur die Wohnungen, sondern auch das gesamte Hab und Gut der Menschen, die in den fünfziger Jahren ihre eigenen Behausungen auf den Hängen der Stadt errichtet hatten, welche in den Neunzigern zu Grundstücken von hohem Wert wurden. Heute sind die meisten dieser Hügel mit Hochhäusern bebaut, die keine Spuren der brutalen Durchführung der Landräumung mehr aufweisen, die ihre Errichtung erst ermöglichte. In China werden Millionen aus den Orten vertrieben, in denen sie lange Zeit gelebt haben. Da sie über keinerlei Eigentumsrechte verfügen, können sie durch den Staat einfach per Anordnung vom Land vertrieben werden, und bekommen als Unterstützung bloß eine geringe Summe Bargeld in die Hand gedrückt (bevor das Land mit hohem Profit an Bauunternehmer übergeben wird). In manchen Fällen ziehen die Menschen freiwillig um, aber es gibt auch Berichte über weitverbreiteten Widerstand, den die Kommunistische Partei normalerweise mit brutaler Unterdrückung beantwortet. Im Falle Chinas trifft die Vertreibung häufig die Bevölkerung in den ländlichen Randgebieten. Das belegt die Bedeutung von Lefebvres in den sechziger Jahren vorausschauend geäußertem Argument, dem zufolge die einst klare Unterscheidung zwischen dem Urbanen und dem Ländlichen unter der hegemonialen Herrschaft von Kapital und Staat nach und nach zu einer Reihe durchlässiger Räume verschwimmt, die sich ungleich entwickeln. [...]

Die Urbanisierung, so können wir festhalten, spielt eine bedeutende Rolle bei der Absorption der Kapitalüberschüsse, und zwar in einem immer größeren geografischen Maßstab. Der Preis sind jedoch aufblühende Prozesse schöpferischer Zerstörung, die den urbanen Massen jegliches Recht auf Stadt nehmen. Dies führt regelmäßig zu Aufständen, wie etwa 1871 in Paris, als sich die Enteigneten erhoben, um die Stadt zurückzufordern, die sie verloren hatten. Die urbanensozialen Bewegungen, die 1968 in Paris, Bangkok, Mexiko- Stadt oder auch in Chicago entstanden, wollten ebenfalls eine Art des urbanen Lebens entwickeln, die sich von der unterschied, die ihnen von kapitalistischen Bauunternehmern und dem Staat aufgezwungen wurde. Wenn, wie es aller Wahrscheinlichkeit nach der Fall sein wird, die gegenwärtigen finanziellen Turbulenzen zunehmen, die bislang erfolgreiche neoliberale, postmoderne und konsumistische Phase der kapitalistischen Absorption des Überschusses durch Urbanisierung am Ende ist und eine größere Krise folgt, dann stellt sich die Frage: Wo bleibt unser Achtundsechzig? Oder, um es noch dramatischer zu formulieren: Was ist mit unserer Version der Pariser Kommune?

Analog zu den Transformationen im Finanzsystem ist auch die politische Antwort heute zwangsläufig viel komplexer, eben weil der urbane Prozess sich weltweit ausgedehnt hat und von allen möglichen Rissen, Unsicherheiten und ungleichen Entwicklungen in verschiedenen Regionen durchzogen ist. Doch Risse im System sind, wie Leonard Cohen einst sang, die Stellen, an denen "das Licht hereinfällt". Anzeichen für Revolten finden sich in allen Teilen der Welt (in China und Indien sind Unruhen mittlerweile an der Tagesordnung, in Afrika toben Bürgerkriege, in Lateinamerika gärt es, autonome Bewegungen entstehen dort überall, und selbst in den Vereinigten Staaten gibt es politische Anzeichen dafür, dass der Großteil der Bevölkerung den sich verschärfenden Ungleichheiten mit der Einstellung "Das Maß ist voll!" begegnet). Jede dieser Revolten könnte plötzlich ansteckend wirken. Im Gegensatz zum Finanzsystem besteht aber zwischen den urbanen und periurbanen sozialen Oppositionsbewegungen, von denen es rund um den Globus eine Menge gibt, kein fester Zusammenhang. Tatsächlich existiert zwischen vielen von ihnen überhaupt keine Verbindung. Daher ist es unwahrscheinlich, dass ein einziger Funke ein Präriefeuer entzünden kann, wie es sich einst die linksradikale Organisation Weather Underground aus den USA erträumte. Dafür wird etwas viel Systematischeres nötig sein. Sollten diese verschiedenen oppositionellen Bewegungen dennoch irgendwie zueinanderfinden – wenn sie zum Beispiel das Recht auf Stadt zu einem gemeinsamen Anliegen machten –, wie müssten dann ihre Forderungen lauten?

Die Antwort auf diese letzte Frage ist recht einfach: größere demokratische Kontrolle über die Produktion und Nutzung des Kapitalüberschusses. Da der Kapitalüberschuss zu einem großen Teil für den urbanen Prozess verwendet wird, gründet das Recht auf Stadt darauf, dass die Verteilung der durch die Urbanisierung entstandenen Überschüsse einer demokratischen Kontrolle unterworfen wird. Über ein Mehrprodukt zu verfügen ist nichts Schlechtes: In vielen Situationen ist ein Überschuss sogar für ein auskömmliches Überleben entscheidend. In der Geschichte des Kapitalismus hat sich der Staat durch Steuern stets etwas von

output taken by the state has been roughly constant since the 1970s. The main achievement of the neoliberal assault, then, has been to prevent the state share expanding in the way it did in the 1960s. One further response has been to create new systems of governance that integrate state and corporate interests and, through the application of money power, assure that control over the disbursement of the surplus through the state apparatus favors corporate capital and the upper classes in the shaping of the urban process. Increasing the share of the surplus under state control will only work if the state itself is both reformed and brought back under popular democratic control.

Increasingly, we see the right to the city falling into the hands of private or quasi-private interests. In New York City, for example, we have a billionaire mayor, Michael Bloomberg, who is reshaping the city along lines favorable to the developers, to Wall Street and transnational capitalist class elements, while continuing to sell the city as an optimal location for high-value businesses and a fantastic destination for tourists, thus turning Manhattan in effect into one vast gated community for the rich. (His developmental slogan, ironically, has been "Building Like Moses with Jane Jacobs in Mind."[21]) In Seattle a billionaire like Paul Allen calls the shots, and in Mexico City the wealthiest man in the world, Carlos Slim, has the downtown streets re-cobbled to suit the tourist gaze. And it is not only affluent individuals who exercise direct power. In the town of New Haven, strapped for any resources for urban reinvestment of its own, it is Yale University, one of the wealthiest universities in the world, that is redesigning much of the urban fabric to suit its needs. Johns Hopkins is doing the same for East Baltimore, and Columbia University plans to do so for areas of New York (sparking neighborhood resistance movements in both cases, as has the attempted land-grab in Dharavi). The actually existing right to the city, as it is now constituted, is far too narrowly confined, in most cases in the hands of a small political and economic elite who are in a position to shape the city more and more after their own particular needs and hearts' desire.

But let us look at this situation more structurally. In January every year an estimate is published of the total of Wall Street bonuses earned for all the hard work the financiers engaged in during the previous year. In 2007, a disastrous year for financial markets by any measure (though by no means as bad as the year that followed), the bonuses added up to $33.2 billion, only 2 percent less than the year before (not a bad rate of remuneration for messing up the world's financial system). In mid-summer of 2007, the Federal Reserve and the European Central Bank pumped billions of short-term credit into the financial system to ensure its stability, and the Federal Reserve dramatically lowered interest rates as the year progressed every time the Wall Street markets threatened to fall precipitously. Meanwhile, some 2 or perhaps 3 million people – mainly a mix of single-woman-headed households, African-Americans in central cities, and marginalized white populations in the urban semi-periphery – have been or are about to be rendered homeless by foreclosures. Many city neighborhoods and even whole peri-urban communities in the United States were boarded up and vandalized, wrecked by the predatory lending practices of the financial institutions. This population received no bonuses. Indeed, since foreclosure means forgiveness of debt, and that is regarded as income, many of those foreclosed on face a hefty income tax bill for money they never had in their possession. This awful asymmetry poses the following question: Why did the Federal Reserve and the US Treasury not extend medium-term liquidity help to the households threatened with foreclosure until mortgage restructuring at reasonable rates could resolve much of the problem? The ferocity of the credit crisis would have been mitigated, and impoverished people and the neighborhoods they inhabited would have been protected. Furthermore, the global financial system would not have teetered on the brink of total insolvency, as happened a year later. To be sure, this would have extended the mission of the Federal Reserve beyond its normal remit, and gone against the neoliberal ideological rule that, in the event of a conflict between the well-being of financial institutions and that of the people, then the people should be left to one side. It would also have gone against capitalist class preferences with respect to income distribution and neoliberal notions of

dem erzeugten Mehrwert angeeignet. In den Phasen, in denen sozialdemokratische Parteien regierten, stieg dieser Anteil erheblich an, so dass der Staat einen Großteil des Überschusses kontrollierte. Das ganze neoliberale Projekt der letzten 30 Jahre ist darauf ausgerichtet, die Kontrolle des Überschusses zu privatisieren. Die Zahlen für die OECD-Länder zeigen jedoch, dass der vom Staat beanspruchte Anteil an der Bruttoproduktion seit den siebziger Jahren nahezu gleich geblieben ist. Der Haupterfolg des neoliberalen Angriffs war also die Verhinderung einer Ausdehnung des Staatsanteils, wie sie in den sechziger Jahren erfolgte. Außerdem wurden neue Formen des Regierens entwickelt, die Staats- und Firmeninteressen miteinander verflechten. Dank der Macht des Geldes können sie sicherstellen, dass die Kontrolle des Staatsapparats über die Ausgabe des Überschusses das Unternehmenskapital und die Oberschicht bei der Gestaltung des urbanen Prozesses begünstigt. Den Anteil des staatlich kontrollierten Überschusses zu erhöhen bringt also nur etwas, wenn der Staat selbst reformiert und wieder der demokratischen Kontrolle des Volkes unterstellt wird.

Wir beobachten vermehrt, wie das Recht auf Stadt in die Hände von privaten oder quasiprivaten Interessen fällt. In New York bekleidet zum Beispiel der Milliardär Michael Bloomberg das Amt des Bürgermeisters. Er gestaltet die Stadt im Sinne der Bauunternehmer, der Wall Street sowie der transnationalen kapitalistischen Klassenelemente um, und vermarktet sie zugleich weiterhin als optimalen Standort für erfolgreiche Unternehmen und als hervorragendes Reiseziel für Touristen. Faktisch verwandelt er Manhattan damit in eine riesige geschlossene Wohnanlage für die Reichen. (Der Wahlspruch für seine Stadtentwicklung lautet ironischerweise: "Bauen wie Moses, aber mit Jane Jacobs im Hinterkopf".[21]) In Seattle hat der Milliardär Paul Allen das Sagen, und in Mexiko-Stadt lässt Carlos Slim die Straßen in der Innenstadt wieder mit Kopfsteinen pflastern, um sie für die Touristen ansehnlicher zu machen. Und nicht nur wohlhabendeEinzelpersonen üben direkte Macht aus. Die Stadt New Haven im US-Bundesstaat Connecticut etwa verfügt selbst nicht über die nötigen Ressourcen für Reinvestitionen im urbanen Bereich, und daher kann die Yale University, eine der reichsten Universitäten der Welt, weite Teile der Stadt nach ihren Bedürfnissen formen. Die Johns Hopkins University führt dasselbe in East Baltimore durch, und die Columbia University hat ähnliche Pläne für bestimmte Gegenden von New York (wie auch infolge des versuchten Landraubs in Dharavi sind in beiden Fällen in den betroffenen Nachbarschaften Widerstandsbewegungen entstanden). Das bestehende Recht auf Stadt, so wie es gegenwärtig beschaffen ist, ist viel zu eng begrenzt und liegt in den meisten Fällen in den Händen einer kleinen politischen und wirtschaftlichen Elite, die in der Lage ist, die Stadt mehr und mehr nach ihren eigenen speziellen Bedürfnissen und Wünschen zu gestalten.

Betrachten wir die Situation etwas struktureller: Im Januar jedes Jahres wird eine Schätzung veröffentlicht, auf welche Summe sich die Boni belaufen, die an der Wall Street für all die harte Arbeit vergeben wurden, die die Finanzexperten im vorangegangenen Jahr geleistet haben. 2007, einem in jeder Hinsicht katastrophalen Jahr für die Finanzmärkte (wenn auch keinesfalls so schlimm wie 2008), summierten sich die Boni auf 33,2 Milliarden US-Dollar. Das waren nur zwei Prozent weniger als 2006 – kein schlechter Vergütungssatz dafür, das Weltfinanzsystem in den Sand zu setzen. Im Sommer 2007 stellten die US-Notenbank und die Europäische Zentralbank Milliarden in Form kurzfristiger Kredite bereit, um die Stabilität des Finanzsystems zu sichern, und die US-Notenbank setzte die Zinssätze im Laufe des Jahres jedes Mal dramatisch herab, wenn die Wall-Street-Märkte jäh zu fallen drohten. Zur selben Zeit wurden zwei oder sogar drei Millionen Menschen – hauptsächlich alleinerziehende Mütter mit ihren Kindern, Afroamerikaner in den Stadtzentren und die marginalisierte weiße Bevölkerung in der urbanen Halbperipherie – durch Zwangsvollstreckungen obdachlos oder stehen kurz davor, es zu werden. Die räuberischen Kreditvergabepraktiken der Finanzinstitute führten dazu, dass in den Vereinigten Staaten viele Stadtviertel und sogar ganze Gemeinden im Umkreis von Städten verwaisten und nun zerfallen. Dieser Teil der Bevölkerung erhielt keine Boni: Im Gegenteil, da Zwangsvollstreckung Schuldenerlass bedeutet, und Schuldenerlass als Einnahme angesehen wird, werden viele, die ihr Wohneigentum verloren haben, mit einem saftigen Einkommenssteuerbescheid für Geld konfrontiert, das sie niemals besessen haben. Diese fürchterliche Schieflage lässt die folgende Frage aufkommen: Warum haben die Notenbank und das Finanzministerium der USA die mittelfristigen Liquiditätshilfen nicht auch den von Zwangsvollstreckung bedrohten Haushalten zukommen lassen, bis das Problem dadurch hätte gelöst werden können, dass die Hypotheken zu vertretbaren Zinssätzen zurückgezahlt würden? Die Kreditkrise hätte weniger grausame Folgen gehabt, verarmte Menschen und ihre Stadtviertel wären geschützt worden und außerdem hätte sich das globale Finanzsystem ein Jahr darauf nicht am Rande des völligen Zusammenbruchs bewegt. Das hätte den Aufgabenbereich der Notenbank freilich über das Übliche hinaus erweitert und gegen die neoliberale, ideologische Vorschrift verstoßen, dass bei einem Konflikt zwischen dem Wohlergehen

personal responsibility. But just look at the price that was paid for observing such rules and the senseless creative destruction that resulted from it. Surely something can and should be done to reverse these political choices?

But we have yet to see a coherent oppositional movement to all of this in the twenty-first century. There is, of course, a multitude of diverse urban struggles and urban social movements (in the broadest sense of that term, including movements in the rural hinterlands) already in existence. Urban innovations with respect to environmental sustainability, cultural incorporation of immigrants, and urban design of public housing spaces are observable around the world in abundance. But they have yet to converge on the singular aim of gaining greater control over the uses of the surplus (let alone over the conditions of its production). One step, though by no means final, towards unification of these struggles is to focus sharply on those moments of creative destruction where the economy of wealth-accumulation piggybacks violently on the economy of dispossession, and there proclaim on behalf of the dispossessed their right to the city – their right to change the world, to change life, and to reinvent the city more after their hearts' desire. That collective right, as both a working slogan and a political ideal, brings us back to the age-old question of who it is that commands the inner connection between urbanization and surplus production and use. Perhaps, after all, Lefebvre was right, more than forty years ago, to insist that the revolution in our times has to be urban – or nothing.

1 Robert Park, On Social Control and Collective Behavior, Chicago: Chicago University Press, 1967: 3.
2 Friedrich Engels, The Condition of the Working-Class in England in 1844, London: Penguin Classics, 2009; Georg Simmel, "The Metropolis and Mental Life," in David Levine, ed., On Individualism and Social Forms, Chicago: Chicago University Press, 1971.
3 Mike Davis, Planet of Slums, London: Verso, 2006.
4 For a fuller account of these ideas see David Harvey, The Enigma of Capital, and The Crises of Capitalism, London: Profile Books, 2010.
5 This account is based on David Harvey, Paris, Capital of Modernity, New York: Routledge, 2003.
6 Robert Moses, "What Happened to Haussmann," Architectural Forum 77 (July 1942): 57–66; Robert Caro, The Power Broker: Robert Moses and the Fall of New York, New York: Knopf, 1974.
7 Henri Lefebvre, The Urban Revolution, Minneapolis: University of Minnesota Press, 2003.
8 William Tabb, The Long Default: New York City and the Urban Fiscal Crisis, New York: Monthly Review Press, 1982; David Harvey, A Brief History of Neoliberalism, Oxford: OUP, 2005.
9 Thomas Campanella, The Concrete Dragon: China's Urban Revolution and What it Means for the World, Princeton, NJ: Princeton Architectural Press, 2008.
10 do not apply
11 Harvey, A Brief History of Neoliberalism; Thomas Edsall, The New Politics of Inequality, New York: Norton, 1985.
12 Jim Yardley and Vikas Bajaj, "Billionaires' Ascent Helps India, and Vice Versa," New York Times, July 27, 2011.
13 do not apply
14 Friedrich Engels, The Housing Question, New York: International Publishers (1935): 74–7.
15 Marshall Berman, All That Is Solid Melts Into Air, London: Penguin, 1988.
16 Friedrich Engels, The Housing Question: 23.
17-20 do not apply
21 Scott Larson, "Building Like Moses with Jane Jacobs in Mind," PhD dissertation, Earth and Environmental Sciences Program, City University of New York, 2010.

Excerpt of :
David Harvey, Rebel Cities. From the Right to the City to the Urban Revolution from the 1. Chapter: The Right to the City
First published by Verso 2012
© David Harvey 2012.
ISBN: 978-1-84467-882-2

von Finanzinstituten und dem der Menschen die Menschen vernachlässigt werden sollten. Es hätte ebenfalls gegen die Bevorzugung einkommensstarker Klassen im Kapitalismus und gegen neoliberale Vorstellungen von Eigenverantwortung verstoßen. Doch sollten wir uns den Preis vergegenwärtigen, der für das Einhalten solcher Vorschriften und die daraus resultierende sinnlose schöpferische Zerstörung gezahlt wurde. Kann und sollte nicht etwas getan werden, um diese politischen Entscheidungen rückgängig zumachen?

Im 21. Jahrhundert warten wir allerdings nach wie vor auf eine vereinigte oppositionelle Bewegung, die sich gegen all das richtet. Natürlich gibt es bereits eine Vielzahl verschiedener städtischer Kämpfe und urbaner sozialer Bewegungen (urban im weitesten Sinne, wozu auch Bewegungen in ländlichen Einzugsgebieten gehören). Weltweit lassen sich städtische Innovationen in Bezug auf ökologische Nachhaltigkeit, kulturelle Eingliederung von Immigranten und die urbane Gestaltung des sozialen Wohnungsbaus in Hülle und Fülle beobachten. Auf das Ziel, größere Kontrolle über die Verwendung des Überschusses zu erlangen, müssen sie sich jedoch erst noch einigen (von seinen Produktionsbedingungen ganz zu schweigen). Ein Schritt, wenn auch bei Weitem nicht der letzte, in Richtung einer Vereinigung dieser Bemühungen besteht darin, sich auf die Momente der schöpferischen Zerstörung zu konzentrieren, in denen die Ökonomie der Vermögensakkumulation stark abhängig ist von einer Ökonomie der Enteignung, und dort das Recht auf Stadt im Namen der Enteigneten zu proklamieren – ihr Recht darauf, die Welt und das Leben zu verändern und die Stadt auf eine Art neu zu erfinden, die eher ihren Wünschen entspricht. Dieses kollektive Recht, als Leitspruch für die Zusammenarbeit und auch als politisches Ideal, führt uns zurück zu der alten Frage, wer über den inneren Zusammenhang zwischen Urbanisierung und Überschussproduktion und -verwendung verfügt. Vielleicht hatte Lefebvre vor über 40 Jahren in der Tat recht, als er darauf beharrte, dass die Revolution unserer Zeit in jedem Fall eine urbane sein muss.

1 Robert Park, On Social Control and Collective Behavior, Chicago: Chicago University Press, 1967, S. 3.
2 Friedrich Engels, Die Lage der arbeitenden Klasse in England, MEW, Bd. 2, Berlin: Dietz, 1972 [1845]; Georg Simmel, Die Großstädte und das Geistesleben, Frankfurt am Main: Suhrkamp, 2006 [1903].
3 Mike Davis, Planet der Slums, deutsch von Ingrid Scherf, Berlin, Hamburg: Assoziation A, 2007.
4 Eine umfassendere Darstellung dieser Gedanken finden Sie in David Harvey, Das Rätsel des Kapitals entschlüsseln: Den Kapitalismus und seine Krisen überwinden, deutsch von Christian Frings, Hamburg: VSA, 2011.
5 Diese Darstellung basiert auf David Harvey, Paris, Capital of Modernity, New York: Routledge, 2003.
6 Robert Moses, "What Happened to Haussmann", Architectural Forum 77 (Juli 1942), S. 57-66; Robert Caro, The Power Broker: Robert Moses and the Fall of New York, New York: Knopf, 1974.
7 Henri Lefebvre, Die Revolution der Städte.
8 William Tabb, The Long Default: New York City and the Urban Fiscal Crisis, New York: Monthly Review Press, 1982; David Harvey, Kleine Geschichte des Neoliberalismus, deutsch von Niels Kadritzke, Zürich: Rotpunktverlag, 2007.
9 Thomas Campanella, The Concrete Dragon: China's Urban Revolution and What it Means for the World, Princeton, NJ: Princeton Architectural Press, 2008.
10 entfällt
11 David Harvey, Kleine Geschichte des Neoliberalismus; Thomas Edsall, The New Politics of Inequality, New York: Norton, 1985.
12 Jim Yardley und Vikas Bajaj, "Billionaires' Ascent Helps India, and Vice Versa", New York Times, 27. Juli 2011.
13 entfällt
14 Friedrich Engels, Zur Wohnungsfrage, Berlin: Dietz, 1988 [1872], S. 92-95.
15 Marshall Berman, All That Is Solid Melts Into Air, London: Penguin, 1988.
16 Friedrich Engels, Zur Wohnungsfrage, S. 27.
17-20 entfällt
21 Scott Larson, "Building Like Moses with Jane Jacobs in Mind", PhD Dissertation, Earth and Environmental Sciences Program, City University of New York, 2010.

Textauszug aus:
David Harvey, Rebellische Städte. Vom Recht auf Stadt zur urbanen Revolution aus dem 1. Kapitel: Das Recht auf Stadt
Aus dem Englischen von Yasemin Dinçer.
© David Harvey 2012.
© der deutschen Ausgabe Suhrkamp Verlag Berlin 2013
ISBN 978-3-518-12657-8

WORLD MAP OF URBANISATION

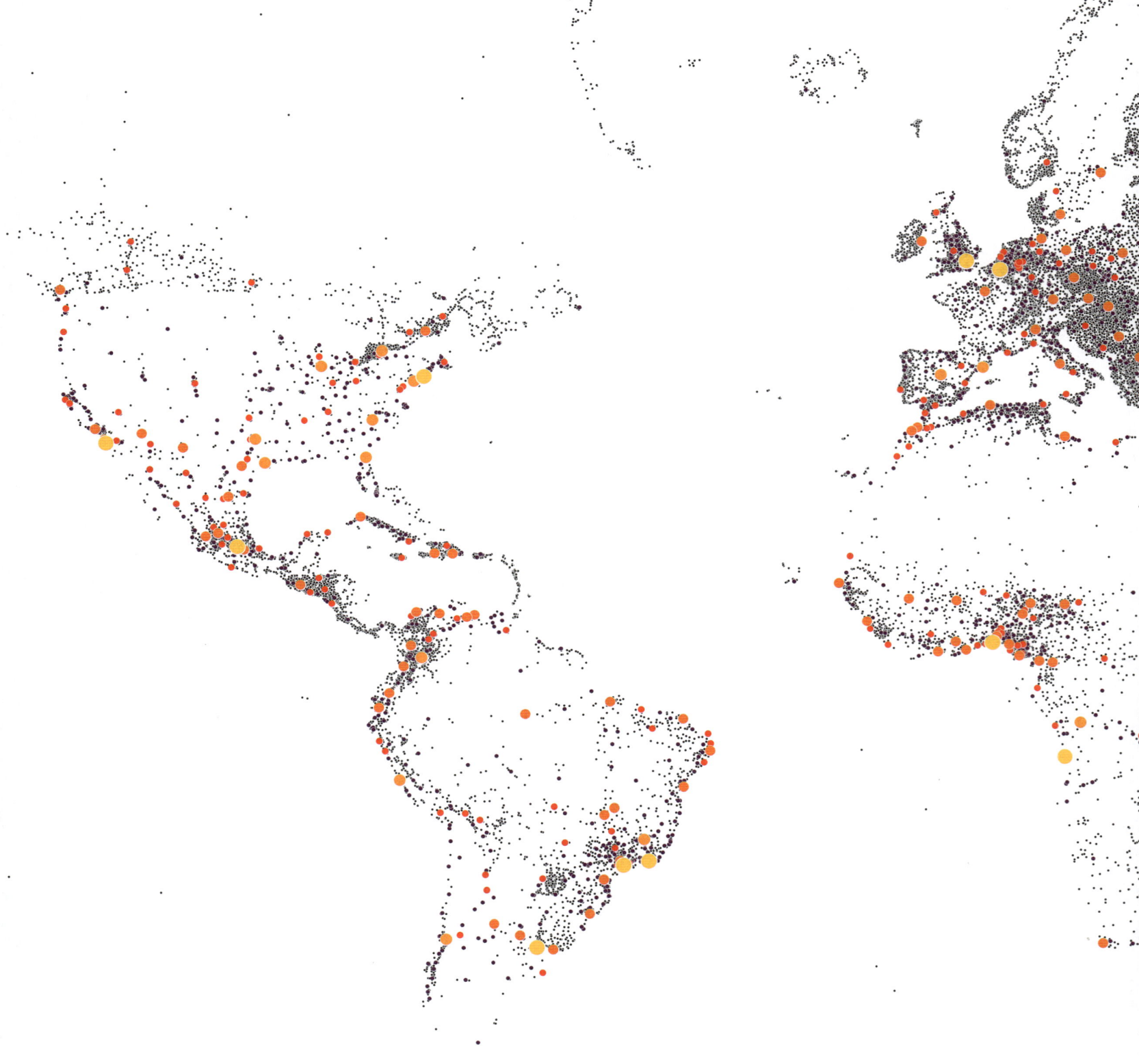

Cities with a population of
- · less than 100,000
- · 100,001 - 500,000
- 500,001 - 1,000,000
- 1,000,001 - 5,000,000
- 5,000,001 - 1,000,000
- more than 10,000,000

Agglomerations with more than 10 million inhabitants, 2014

01. Tokyo	37,877,000	07. Osaka	20,123,000
02. Delhi	24,953,000	08. Beijing	19,520,000
03. Shanghai	22,991,000	09. New York	18,591,000
04. Mexico City	20,991,000	10. Cairo	18,419,000
05. São Paulo	20,831,000	11. Dhaka	16,982,000
06. Bombay	20,741,000	12. Karachi	16,126,000

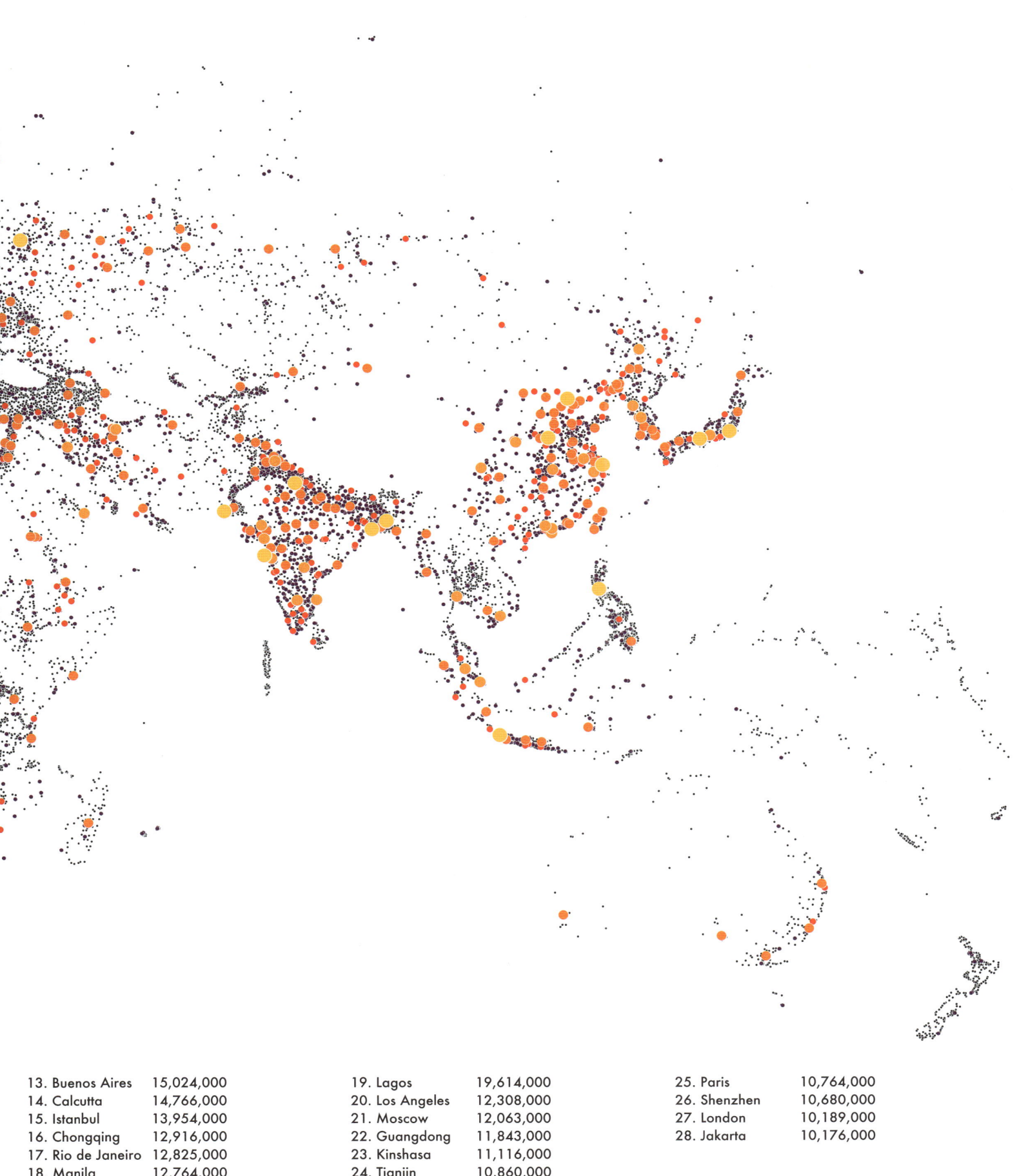

13. Buenos Aires	15,024,000	19. Lagos	19,614,000	25. Paris	10,764,000
14. Calcutta	14,766,000	20. Los Angeles	12,308,000	26. Shenzhen	10,680,000
15. Istanbul	13,954,000	21. Moscow	12,063,000	27. London	10,189,000
16. Chongqing	12,916,000	22. Guangdong	11,843,000	28. Jakarta	10,176,000
17. Rio de Janeiro	12,825,000	23. Kinshasa	11,116,000		
18. Manila	12,764,000	24. Tianjin	10,860,000		

(United Nations, Department of Economic and Social Affairs, Population Division (2015). World Urbanization Prospects: The 2014 Revision, (ST/ESA/SER.A/366).)

© Simone Hüttenberend

PLANETARY URBANIZATION: HENRI LEFEBVRE UND DAS RECHT AUF DIE STADT Christian Schmid

The phrase "the right to the City" has been making a comeback as a rallying cry in recent years. In cities of the North and the South alike, it is used by urban social movements, by political alliances, by international organizations, and also at academic conferences. The renaissance of the slogan is remarkable, as it hearkens back to the late 1960s, a specific moment in the history of urbanization. At the time, it was coined by French philosopher Henri Lefebvre in response to the urban crisis of that period. However, the situation then was quite different from the one today. The resurgence of this rallying cry therefore raises some important questions: Are we experiencing a new urban crisis? What are its specific traits and characteristics? What distinguishes it from earlier phases of urbanization? In order to clarify these questions, it is useful to return to the original conception of the term and explore its (potential) meanings for urbanization today.

1) STRUGGLES FOR THE CITY

The crisis of the city

Lefebvre's concept of the "right to the city" is based on his investigation of urbanization in France during the 1960s (Stanek, 2011). Like most of the Western industrialized nations, France was marked by the ascent of Fordism and the expansion of the Keynesian welfare state. This development was accompanied by massive migration from rural to urban areas and a fundamental change in spatial structures: Functionalist urban planning led to a massive restructuring of inner city areas; the margins of the cities were dominated by mass production of social housing as well as by an extensive proliferation of single-family detached housing units.

These urban transformations also entailed a fundamental modernization of everyday life. Contemporary critics conceptualized this specific aspect of urbanization as a "crisis of the city". What constituted this crisis? At the time, there were different answers: for example, Jane Jacobs (1969 [1961]) criticized the loss of public space in North American cities; Alexander Mitscherlich (1965) complained about the "inhospitality" of the cities in the post-war period; the Situationists polemicized against the destruction of city quarters caused by functional urbanism (1976). For Lefebvre, this crisis consisted primarily of a tendency towards the homogenization of lifestyles and an engineering and colonization of daily life. In middle-class suburbs and in working-class housing estates, analogous conditions prevailed – the monotony of the labour process, the order of functionalized and bureaucratized cities, and the normative constraints of the modernized urban everyday life (Lefebvre, 1996).

The right to the city

The "crisis of the city" was also an important departure point for the manifold social movements of the late 1960s. They were not only aimed against Western imperialism and the Vietnam War, or against various forms of discrimination and marginalization. They were also directed against alienation in daily life, against the modernization of cities and the destruction of their specific qualities, and against exclusion from urban life. They were struggles for a different city.

Der Slogan "Das Recht auf die Stadt" ist in den letzten Jahren erneut zu hören. An verschiedensten Orten, in den Städten des Nordens wie des Südens, wird er von urbanen Bewegungen, politischen Allianzen, internationalen Organisationen und auch wissenschaftlichen Konferenzen eingesetzt. Die Renaissance dieses Slogans ist erstaunlich, geht er doch in die späten 1960er Jahre zurück, und damit auf einen spezifischen historischen Moment der Urbanisierung. Damals hatte ihn der französische Philosoph Henri Lefebvre geprägt, als eine Antwort auf die urbane Krise jener Jahre. Die Situation war allerdings sehr verschieden von heute. Das Wiederauftauchen dieses Slogans wirft deshalb einige wichtige Fragen auf: Gibt es heute eine neue urbane Krise? Was sind ihre Eigenschaften und Besonderheiten? Was sind die Unterschiede zu früheren Phasen der Urbanisierung? Zur Klärung dieser Fragen ist es hilfreich, auf die ursprüngliche Konzeption dieses Begriffs zurückzukommen und seine (möglichen) Bedeutungen für die heutige Urbanisierung auszuloten.

1) KÄMPFE UM DIE STADT

Die Krise der Stadt

Lefebvres Konzept des "Rechts auf die Stadt" beruht auf einer spezifischen urbanen Erfahrung, die dieser im Frankreich der 1960er Jahre untersucht hat (vgl. hierzu Stanek 2011). Wie die meisten westlichen Industrieländer war auch Frankreich damals vom Aufstieg des Fordismus und vom Ausbau des keynesianischen Wohlfahrtsstaates geprägt. Diese Entwicklung war mit einer massiven Migration von ländlichen zu städtischen Gebieten und einer grundlegenden urbanen Transformation verbunden: Der funktionalistische Städtebau führte zu einer tiefgreifenden Restrukturierung der Innenstädte, und an den Rändern der Agglomerationen dominierten einerseits der Massenwohnungsbau und anderseits die großflächige Erstellung von Einfamilienhäusern.

Diese urbanen Transformationen brachten auch eine grundlegende Modernisierung der Alltagswelt mit sich. Die zeitgenössische Kritik fasste dieses spezifische Moment der Urbanisierung als "Krise der Stadt". Worin bestand diese Krise? Darauf gab es damals unterschiedliche Antworten: So kritisierte beispielsweise Jane Jacobs (1969 [1961]) den Verlust des öffentlichen Raumes in den nordamerikanischen Städten, Alexander Mitscherlich (1965) beklagte die "Unwirtlichkeit" der Städte der Nachkriegszeit, und die Situationisten polemisierten gegen die Zerstörung der Quartiere durch den funktionalen Urbanismus (1976). Für Lefebvre bestand die städtische Krise vor allem in der Tendenz zur Homogenisierung der Lebensbedingungen und in der Konditionierung und Kolonisierung des Alltagslebens, der Monotonie des Arbeitsprozesses und der erdrückenden Ordnung der bürokratisierten Konsumgesellschaft: Ob in den Vorstädten der Mittelklassen oder im Massenwohnungsbau der Arbeiterfamilien, in beiden Fällen herrschten die Enge und die normierenden Zwänge der fordistischen Kleinfamilie, die durch die dominante Form des funktionalen Städtebaus noch verstärkt wurden (Lefebvre 1968: 111; Lefebvre 1970b: 128).

Lefebvre regarded these events, especially those of May 1968 in Paris, as parallels to those of the Paris Commune of 1871. Programmatically, he demanded a "right to the city": the right not to be displaced into a space produced for the specific purpose of discrimination. "In these difficult conditions, at the heart of a society which cannot completely oppose them and yet obstructs them, rights which define civilization […] find their way. These rights which are not well recognized, progressively become customary before being inscribed into formalized codes. They would change reality if they entered into social practice: right to work, to training and education, to health, housing, leisure, to life. Among these rights in the making features the right to the city, not to the ancient city, but to urban life, to renewed centrality, to places of encounter and exchange, to life rhythms and time uses, enabling the full and complete usage of these moments and places, etc.)" (Lefebvre, 1996: 178).

Thus, Lefebvre's concern was not to propose a new comprehensive slogan demanding the right to the basic needs. It was about something more – a specific urban quality, which had hitherto been neglected in public debate: access to the resources of the city for all segments of the population, and the possibility of experimenting with and realizing alternative ways of life. Regarding the discussion of Lefebvre's conception of the right to the city, compare e.g. Schmid 2005, Wastl-Walter et al. 2005, Purcell 2008, Holm/Gebhardt 2011, Brenner/Marcuse/Mayer 2012.

Demands for a new and renewed urban life were raised repeatedly during subsequent years in many places and in multiple forms. For many of these urban actions, urban movements, and also urban revolts, documentation is fragmentary; their history has yet to be written. Despite the many differences, there are obvious similarities among these urban struggles: they can be understood, in the most general sense, as struggles against social exclusion and marginalization, and they articulate a demand for centrality, for access to the material and immaterial resources of a city. In this sense, they address the spatial dialectics of centre and periphery, and of appropriation and domination.

2) COMPLETE URBANIZATION AND THE SPECIFICITY OF THE URBAN

Complete urbanization

Against the background of these manifold urban struggles, the crucial question is how the urban dialectic can be conceptualized. Tellingly, Lefebvre's first major statement of his emergent urban ideas and concepts, entitled Le droit à la ville [The right to the city], was presented in the "mythical" year 1968 (Lefebvre 1996/1968). Only two years later, however, he subjected this first approach to a fundamental review and extension in another major book, La revolution urbaine [The urban revolution] (Lefebvre 2003/1970). The main critique in this latter work concerns precisely the notion of the "city" itself: his search for the urban had led Lefebvre to a radical shift in his perspective, from the analysis of a form, the city, to a process – urbanization.

The point of departure of this new understanding of the urban is Lefebvre's famous thesis of the complete urbanization of society. This thesis states that contemporary social reality can no longer be grasped with the categories "city" and "countryside", but must be analyzed in terms of an emerging urban society. The epistemological shift involved here cannot be overestimated. Lefebvre's theory constitutes a radical break with the traditional Western conception of the city. For the classic definitions of this notion were based on the assumption that the city is a clearly identifiable unit that provides the environment for a distinctively "urban" way of life.

Against these definitions, Lefebvre's thesis of complete urbanization points towards a long-term conception of urban transformation. As Friedrich Engels in The condition of the working class in England (2009 [1844]) had already recognized, the Industrial Revolution marked the beginning of a massive migration from rural areas to the cities in conjunction with the spatial concentration of factories and workers under industrial capitalism. Lefebvre proceeds to conceptualize the process of industrialization in a general sense as the extension of the industrial logic to society as a whole. Industrialization and urbanization, he states, form a highly complex and conflictual unit. Industrialization supplies the conditions and means of urbanization, while urbanization results from the spread of industrial production across the entire globe. From this point of view, Lefebvre derives his understanding of urbanization as a reshaping and colonization of rural areas by an urban fabric as well as a fundamental transformation of historic cities (Lefebvre 1972a: 9f.).

Das Recht auf die Stadt

Die "Krise der Stadt" bildete auch einen wichtigen Ausgangspunkt der vielfältigen Bewegungen der späten 1960er Jahre, die sich nicht nur gegen den westlichen Imperialismus und den Krieg in Vietnam richteten, sondern auch gegen verschiedenste Formen von Diskriminierung und Ausgrenzung. Sie wandten sich auch gegen eine fremdbestimmte Alltagswelt, gegen die Modernisierung der Städte, gegen die Vertreibung aus den Innenstädten und den Ausschluss vom städtischen Leben, gegen den Verlust der städtischen Qualitäten: Es waren auch Kämpfe für eine andere Stadt.

Lefebvre sah in diesen Ereignissen und im speziellen im Pariser Mai 68 Parallelen zur Commune von 1871. Programmatisch forderte er ein "Recht auf die Stadt": das Recht, nicht in einen Raum abgedrängt zu werden, der bloß zum Zweck der Diskriminierung produziert wurde. Er stellt dieses Recht den anderen Rechten gleich, welche die urbane Zivilisation definieren: das Recht auf Arbeit, Ausbildung, Gesundheit, Wohnung, Freizeit, auf das Leben. Das Recht auf die Stadt bezieht sich dabei nicht einfach auf die Wiederherstellung der alten Stadtzentren, sondern auf Teilhabe am urbanen Leben, auf eine erneuerte Zentralität, auf Orte des Zusammentreffens und des Austausches, auf Lebensrhythmen und eine Verwendung der Zeit, die einen vollen und ganzen Gebrauch dieser Orte erlauben. Es lässt sich nur als das Recht auf ein transformiertes, erneuertes urbanes Leben formulieren (Lefebvre 1968: 146).

Es ging Lefebvre also nicht darum, das Recht auf die bekannten Grundbedürfnisse einzufordern, und dafür einen übergeordneten konzeptionellen und begrifflichen Rahmen zu schaffen. Er forderte vielmehr eine Erweiterung dieser Rechte um einen Aspekt, der bislang in der öffentlichen Debatte vernachlässigt blieb: die spezifisch städtischen Qualitäten, der Zugang zu den Ressourcen der Stadt für alle Teile der Bevölkerung, die Möglichkeit, alternative Lebensentwürfe ausprobieren und realisieren zu können. Für eine Diskussion von Lefebvres Konzeption des Rechts auf die Stadt vgl. z.B. auch Schmid 2005, Wastl-Walter et al. 2005, Purcell 2008, Holm/Gebhardt 2011, Brenner/Marcuse/Mayer 2012.

Forderungen nach einem neuen und erneuerten urbanen Leben wurden in den folgenden Jahren an den verschiedensten Orten und in vielfältigen Formen immer wieder erhoben. Viele dieser urbanen Aktionen, urbanen Bewegungen und auch urbanen Revolten sind nur wenig dokumentiert; ihre Geschichte muss noch geschrieben werden. Trotz der großen Unterschiede lassen alle diese städtischen Kämpfe klare Gemeinsamkeiten erkennen: Sie wenden sich im weitesten Sinne gegen soziale Ausgrenzung und Ausschluss, sie beinhalten eine Thematisierung der räumlichen Dialektik von Zentrum und Peripherie und von Aneignung und Domination. Es sind Kämpfe um die Zentralität, um den Zugang zu den materiellen und immateriellen Ressourcen einer Stadt.

2) DIE VOLLSTÄNDIGE URBANISIERUNG UND DIE BESONDERHEIT DES STÄDTISCHEN

Die vollständige Urbanisierung

Vor dem Hintergrund dieser vielfältigen Auseinandersetzungen um die Stadt fragt es sich, wie sich die städtische Dialektik theoretisch fassen lässt. Die ersten Ideen und Konzepte seiner Theorie zur Stadt präsentierte Lefebvre unter dem Titel Le droit à la ville im "mythischen" Jahr 1968. Bereits zwei Jahre später entwickelte er diese erste Annäherung mit La révolution urbaine weiter und unterzog sie zugleich einer fundamentalen Kritik: Er erkannte, dass das Urbane nicht mehr länger als Form zu begreifen, sondern als Prozess zu analysieren ist. Damit verschob sich der Fokus der Analyse von der "Stadt" auf die "Urbanisierung".

Der Ausgangspunkt dieser Neukonzeption findet sich in der berühmten These der vollständigen Urbanisierung der Gesellschaft, die er an den Anfang seines Buches zur urbanen Revolution stellt. Sie besagt, dass sich die heutige soziale Wirklichkeit nicht mehr mit den Kategorien von "Stadt" und "Land" erfassen lässt, sondern dass sie mit Begriffen der entstehenden urbanen Gesellschaft analysiert werden muss. Der epistemologische Wechsel, der damit verbunden ist, kann gar nicht groß genug eingeschätzt werden: Lefebvres Theorie bedeutet einen radikalen Bruch mit dem traditionellen westlichen Verständnis der Stadt. Denn die klassischen Definitionen von Urbanität gingen immer von der Stadt als klar identifizierbarer Einheit aus, die eine distinkte urbane Lebensweise begründet.

Demgegenüber verweist Lefebvres These der vollständigen Urbanisierung auf eine langfristige Konzeption urbaner Transformation: Wie bereits Friedrich Engels erkannt hatte, begann mit der industriellen Revolution eine massive Migration von den ländlichen Gebieten in die Städte – ein Resultat der durch die industrielle Logik bewirkten Konzentration von Produktionsmitteln und Arbeits-

As a consequence, urbanization affects the whole planet: In one of his last texts (1989), Lefebvre outlined the possibility that the city loses itself in a planetary metamorphosis. The recently formulated concept of planetary urbanization (cf. Brenner/Schmid 2011 and 2015, Merrifield, 2013) is addressing and more closely examining precisely this process of the expansion of urban areas into the remotest corners of the world.

One crucial consequence of the planetary urban transformation is the dissolution of the city itself: for Lefebvre, the city can no longer be understood as an object or as a definable unit. It is instead an historical category that is disappearing as urbanization progresses. The question thus arises as to how the urban can still be theoretically grasped under conditions in which society as a whole has been urbanized. Lefebvre's inquiry into this question yields three core concepts: mediation, centrality, and difference (see also Schmid, 2005; Kipfer et al., 2008).

The urban level: mediation

In a first approximation, Lefebvre identifies the urban as a specific level or order of social reality. It is an intermediary and mediating level situated between two others – on the one hand, the private level, the proximate order, everyday life, and dwelling; on the other hand, the global level, the distant order, the world market, the state, knowledge, institutions, and ideologies. This intermediate level has a decisive function: it serves as a relay and as mediation, connecting the global and the private levels.

In urbanized society, however, the urban level is in danger of being whittled away between the global and the private levels. On the one hand, industrialization and the logic of the global market produce a universal rationale shaped by technology, and thus a tendency towards homogenization. The unique traits of the place and its location thus seem to disappear. On the other hand, space is parceled out and submitted to a corporate, individual logic. In this attack from "above" and "below", the city is threatened with attrition. The result is the dissolution of urban units, which disintegrate into countless disconnected fragments, leading in turn to the proliferation of overflowing, apparently indistinguishable urban landscapes. Thus, the complete urbanization of society tends to eliminate the urban level of mediation. (Lefebvre 1970a: 103f)

However, it is only in the most extreme thesis of the disappearance of the city that the importance of the urban becomes visible for Lefebvre. In this context, he suggests, the city must be seen as a social resource. It constitutes an essential device for the organization of society, it brings together diverse elements of society, and thus it becomes productive.

The urban form: centrality

These considerations enable Lefebvre to arrive at a new definition of the city – the city as a centre. In this sense, the city creates a condition in which heterogeneous elements no longer exist in isolation. As a place of encounter, communication, and information, the city is also a place in which constraints and normality are dissolved, and are joined by the elements of the playful and unpredictable. For Lefebvre, the space-time vector converges to zero in urban space; every point can become a focal point that attracts all, a privileged place upon which everything converges (Lefebvre, 2003: 39).

Centrality therefore does not refer to a concrete geographic situation, but to a pure form. Its logic represents the synchronicity of objects and people that can be assembled around a given point. What is it that comes together in urban space? Centrality as a form does not entail a concrete content, but merely defines the possibility of an encounter. It constitutes itself both as an act of thought and as a social act. Mentally, it is the synchronicity of events, of perceptions, and of the elements of a whole. Socially, it amounts to the convergence and combination of goods and activities. Centrality can thus also be understood as a totality of differences (Lefebvre, 2003: 39).

Urban space-time: difference

This leads to the third marker of the urban – the city is a place of difference. Differences are points of active connection and should be clearly distinguished from particularities that remain isolated from one another. Particularities are derived from nature, location, and natural resources; they are bound to local conditions and are thus derived from rural society. They are isolated, external, and can easily revert into antagonisms. However, in the course of history, such particularities come into mutual contact. Out of their confrontation arises a mutual "understanding" and thus difference. The instant of confrontation is always a decisive one. Trans-

---

kräften (vgl. Engels 1971). Lefebvre fasst nun den Prozess der Industrialisierung in einem allgemeinen Sinne, als Ausdehnung der industriellen Rationalität auf die gesamte Gesellschaft. Industrialisierung und Urbanisierung bilden demnach eine hoch komplexe und konfliktgeladene Einheit: Die Industrialisierung liefert die Bedingungen und die Mittel zur Urbanisierung, und die Urbanisierung ist die Konsequenz der sich über den ganzen Globus ausbreitenden industriellen Produktion. Ausgehend von dieser Bestimmung versteht Lefebvre Urbanisierung als Überformung und Kolonisierung der ländlichen Gebiete durch ein urbanes Gewebe und zugleich als grundlegende Transformation der historischen Städte (Lefebvre 1972a: 9f.).

In der Konsequenz erfasst die Urbanisierung den ganzen Planeten: In einem seiner letzten Texte skizzierte Lefebvre (1989) die Möglichkeit, dass sich die Stadt in einer planetaren Metamorphose verliert. Mit dem jüngst formulierten Konzept der planetaren Urbanisierung (vgl. Brenner/Schmid 2011 und 2015, Merrifield 2013) wird genau dieser Prozess der Ausdehnung der urbanen Gebiete in die hintersten Winkel der Welt thematisiert und genauer untersucht.

Eine wichtige Konsequenz dieser planetaren urbanen Transformation liegt darin, dass sich die Stadt auflöst. Sie lässt sich nicht mehr als Objekt, als abgrenzbare Einheit erfassen, sie ist vielmehr eine historische Kategorie, die mit dem Urbanisierungsprozess verschwindet. Damit stellt sich aber das Problem, wie sich das Städtische in einer urbanisierten Gesellschaft noch theoretisch konzipieren lässt. Lefebvres Suche förderte drei zentrale Begriffe zu Tage: Mediation, Zentralität, Differenz (vgl. im Folgenden Schmid 2005 und Kipfer et al. 2008).

Die urbane Ebene: Mediation

In einer ersten Annäherung identifiziert Lefebvre das Städtische als eine spezifische Ebene oder Ordnung der gesellschaftlichen Wirklichkeit. Sie ist eine mittlere und vermittelnde Ebene, die sich zwischen zwei anderen situiert: der privaten Ebene, der nahen Ordnung, dem Alltagsleben, dem Wohnen einerseits; der globalen Ebene, der fernen Ordnung, dem Weltmarkt, dem Staat, dem Wissen, den Institutionen und den Ideologien anderseits. Dieser Zwischenebene kommt eine entscheidende Bedeutung zu: Sie dient als Relais, als Mediation, als Vermittlung zwischen der globalen und der privaten Ebene.

In der urbanisierten Gesellschaft droht die urbane Ebene jedoch zwischen der globalen und der privaten zerrieben zu werden. Auf der einen Seite bringen die Industrialisierung und die Logik des Weltmarktes eine universelle, durch die Technik bestimmte Rationalität hervor, und damit eine homogenisierende Tendenz – die Eigenheiten des Ortes und der Lage scheinen zu verschwinden. Auf der anderen Seite wird der Raum parzelliert und einer privatwirtschaftlichen, individuellen Logik unterworfen. In diesem doppelten Angriff von "oben" und von "unten" kommt es zur Auflösung der städtischen Einheiten, sie zerfallen in zahllose zusammenhangslose Fragmente. Es entstehen ausufernde Stadtlandschaften, die sich kaum mehr zu unterscheiden scheinen. Mit der vollständigen Urbanisierung der Gesellschaft geht somit gerade die Ebene der Mediation verloren (Lefebvre 1970a: 103f).

In der extremsten These des Verschwindens der Stadt wird jedoch für Lefebvre erst die Bedeutung des Städtischen sichtbar: Die Stadt ist als gesellschaftliche Ressource zu begreifen. Sie bildet ein wesentliches Dispositiv für die Organisation der Gesellschaft, sie führt unterschiedlichste Elemente der Gesellschaft zusammen und wird so produktiv.

Die urbane Form: Zentralität

Ausgehend von diesen Überlegungen findet Lefebvre eine neue Definition der Stadt: Die Stadt ist ein Zentrum. Sie schafft eine Situation, in der unterschiedliche Dinge nicht länger getrennt voneinander existieren. Als Ort der Begegnung, der Kommunikation und der Information ist sie auch ein Ort, an dem sich Zwänge und Normalitäten auflösen und das spielerische Moment und das Unvorhersehbare hinzutreten. Für Lefebvre strebt der Raum-Zeit-Vektor im urbanen Raum gegen null; jeder Punkt kann zum Brennpunkt werden, der alles auf sich zieht, zum privilegierten Ort, an dem alles konvergiert (Lefebvre 1972a: 46).

Zentralität beschreibt hier also nicht eine konkrete geographische Situation, sondern eine reine Form. Ihre Logik steht für die Gleichzeitigkeit der Dinge und Menschen, die sich um einen Punkt zusammenbringen lassen. Was kommt zusammen im urbanen Raum? Die Zentralität als Form sagt nichts aus über den Inhalt, sie definiert lediglich die Möglichkeit eines Zusammentreffens. Sie konstituiert sich sowohl als Akt des Denkens wie auch als sozialer Akt. Mental ist sie die

formed by the confrontation, the elements no longer assert themselves in isolation from one another. Instead, they can only present and re-present themselves in and through their interactions (Lefebvre 1970a: 64f).

Therefore, the specific quality of urban space arises from the simultaneous presence of very different worlds and value-systems, of ethnic, cultural, and social groups, activities, and knowledge. Urban space creates the possibility of bringing together these different elements and making them productive. At the same time, however, they have a constant tendency to separate themselves from one another. The decisive question therefore is how these differences are experienced and lived in actual everyday life.

As Kipfer (2008) reminds us, there is an important distinction between minimal and maximal difference. Minimal or induced difference tends towards formal identity, which fragments everyday life and pushes social groups into the periphery. Maximal or produced difference implies a fundamental social transformation.

In a Lefebvrian framework, the city can thus be defined as a place where differences encounter, acknowledge, and explore one another, and affirm or cancel out one another. (Lefebvre 1972a: 105). Distances in space and time are replaced with opposites, contrasts and superimpositions, and with the coexistence of multiple realities. Lefebvre's positive conception of the urban as differential space-time should be understood as referring to a concrete utopia (Stanek 2011). It points towards a possibility, a promise, not an already achieved reality. It must constantly be produced and reproduced (Lefebvre, 2003: 38).

3) THE PRODUCTION OF URBAN SPACE

The three dimensions of the production of space
As has become clear, Lefebvre opened up a new pathway towards defining the urban in La révolution urbaine. First of all, it constitutes the level of mediation between the global and the private. Secondly, its form is centrality, assembly, encounter, and interaction. Finally, the urban is characterized by difference; it is a place where differences come together and generate something new. This leads to the question of how these different aspects are related to each other, and how they are socially produced. It gives rise to a new radical shift in analytical perspective. It requires a more general term and a more general theory – the term "space" and the theory of production of space, which Lefebvre elaborated in La production de l'espace [The production of space] in 1974 (Lefebvre 1991).

This theory rests on the assumption that the production of space can be split analytically into three dialectically linked dimensions or processes. These dimensions – which Lefebvre also refers to as "formants" or "moments" in the production of space – are defined in duplicate: The first is the triad of "spatial practices", "representations of space", and "spaces of representation"; the second is the "perceived", "conceived", and "lived" space. This duplicate string of terms points to a twofold approach to space: a phenomenological approach on the one hand, and a linguistic or semiotic approach on the other (Schmid, 2005, 2008, 2010).

Urban practice
Space has, first of all, a perceptible component that can be grasped with the five senses. It relates directly to the materiality of the elements that constitute a space. Spatial practice combines these elements into a spatial order, an order of synchronicity. Urban space is therefore a place of material interaction and of physical encounter. This practical aspect of mediation, centrality, and difference can be seen as the superimposition and interlacing of networks of production and of communication channels, as a combination of social networks in everyday life, as places of encounter and exchange that are amenable to surprises and innovations.

This means that urban space can be empirically observed. What is happening in the streets? Who is present, who encounters whom? What resources are available, and who has access to them? Primarily, what is meant here is the physical presence of people in urban space. Very often, in urban research only the residents of an urban area are considered. But urban space also includes those who work there, visitors, street vendors, and diverse types of places. Shops, restaurants, meeting places, and venues for cultural and social exchange set the stage for urban life.

Opportunities for social interaction are, however, unequally distributed across urban space. In certain places, urban resources are concentrated, while in other areas they are thinly scattered and diffuse. The question of access to these

Gleichzeitigkeit der Ereignisse, der Wahrnehmungen, der Elemente eines Ganzen. Sozial bedeutet sie das Zusammentreffen und die Vereinigung von Gütern und Tätigkeiten. Die Zentralität lässt sich somit auch als eine Gesamtheit von Differenzen verstehen (Lefebvre 1968: 89).

Die urbane Raum-Zeit: Differenz
Damit ergibt sich die dritte Bestimmung des Städtischen: Die Stadt ist ein Ort der Differenz. Differenzen sind klar von Eigenheiten zu unterscheiden: Sie sind aktive Bezugselemente, während Eigenheiten gegeneinander isoliert bleiben. Die Eigenheiten kommen von der Natur, der Lage, den natürlichen Ressourcen. Sie sind an lokale Bedingungen gebunden und beziehen sich entsprechend noch auf die rurale Gesellschaft. Sie sind isoliert, äußerlich und können leicht in Antagonismus gegenüber anderen Eigenheiten umschlagen. Im Verlaufe der Geschichte treten sie aber miteinander in Kontakt. Aus ihrer Konfrontation entsteht ein "Verständnis" füreinander und damit die Differenz. Der Moment der Konfrontation ist immer konflikthaft. Transformiert durch die Auseinandersetzung behaupten sich die Elemente nicht mehr getrennt voneinander. Stattdessen können sie sich nur in ihren gegenseitigen Verhältnissen präsentieren und re-präsentieren (Lefebvre 1970a: 64f).

Entscheidend ist deshalb, wie diese Differenzen im konkreten Alltag erlebt und gelebt werden. Die spezifische Qualität des urbanen Raumes entsteht erst durch die gleichzeitige Präsenz von ganz unterschiedlichen Welten und Wertvorstellungen, von ethnischen, kulturellen und sozialen Gruppen, Aktivitäten und Kenntnissen. Der urbane Raum schafft die Möglichkeit, all diese unterschiedlichen Elemente zusammenzubringen und fruchtbar werden zu lassen. Zugleich besteht jedoch immer auch die Tendenz, dass sie sich gegeneinander abschotten und voneinander separieren.

Wie Kipfer (2008) betont, gibt es deshalb eine wichtige Unterscheidung zwischen minimaler und maximaler Differenz. Die minimale oder induzierte Differenz tendiert zur formalen Identität, sie bringt eine vermeintliche Vielfalt und Individualität hervor, die aber nur Variationen des Gleichen darstellen, wie die unterschiedlichen Formen von Einfamilienhäuschen in einer ansonsten monotonen suburbanen Siedlung, oder die inszenierten Formen von Heterogenität in vielen gentrifizierten Gebieten. Solche minimalen Differenzen verstärken aber letztlich nur die Fragmentierungen des Alltagslebens und die Tendenzen zur sozialen Segregation. Maximale oder produzierte Differenz beinhaltet demgegenüber Konfrontationen und Auseinandersetzungen, und sie führt zu einer grundlegenden sozialen Transformation.

Die Stadt lässt sich demnach als Ort definieren, an dem die Unterschiede sich kennen, anerkennen und erproben, sich bestätigen oder aufheben (Lefebvre 1972a: 105). An die Stelle von Raum-Zeit-Distanzen treten Gegensätze, Kontraste, Überlagerungen und das Nebeneinander verschiedener Wirklichkeiten. Lefebvres positive Konzeption des Urbanen als differentielle Raum-Zeit ist dabei als konkrete Utopie zu verstehen: Sie zeigt eine Möglichkeit, ein Versprechen, nicht eine bereits erfüllte Wirklichkeit. Sie muss ständig produziert und reproduziert werden.

3) DIE PRODUKTION DES URBANEN RAUMES

Die drei Dimensionen der Produktion des Raumes
Wie deutlich wurde, öffnete Lefebvre in La révolution urbaine einen neuen Weg zur Definition des Urbanen: Es konstituiert erstens die Ebene der Vermittlung zwischen dem Globalen und dem Privaten. Seine Form ist zweitens die Zentralität, das Zusammentreffen, die Begegnung, die Interaktion. Drittens ist das Urbane durch die Differenz gekennzeichnet, es ist ein Ort, an dem Unterschiede aufeinander prallen und dadurch Neues generieren. Allerdings fragt es sich, wie diese unterschiedlichen Kategorien miteinander zusammenhängen. Die Klärung dieser Frage erfordert einen allgemeineren Begriff, der sie umfasst und auf einer übergeordneten Ebene abbildet. Dieser Begriff ist der "Raum": Lefebvre stellte fest, dass die urbane Frage das Auftauchen einer neuen Problematik enthüllt hätte – die Problematik des Raumes, die diejenige des Urbanen und des Alltäglichen einschließe (Lefebvre 1974: 107). Die neue oder erweiterte Theorie kündigt Lefebvre bereits in La révolution urbaine an, und vier Jahre später legte er mit La production de l'espace schließlich eine umfassende Analyse dazu vor.

Damit kommt es erneut zu einem radikalen Wechsel der analytischen Perspektive: Es geht darum, zu zeigen, wie der (urbane) Raum produziert wird. Im Zentrum dieser Theorie steht die Vorstellung, dass sich die Produktion des Raumes analytisch in drei dialektisch miteinander verbundene Dimensionen oder Pro-

resources is immediately linked to their distribution. The struggle for the right to remain within urban space has always been among the central questions provoked by urban revitalization programs, gentrification, or projects for slum improvement.

Due to the huge expansion of urban areas today, though, this issue is no longer confined to the traditional urban core areas. The classic model of urbanity based on the examples of metropolises such as Berlin, Paris, or Chicago has long been overtaken by worldwide urbanization processes. In the overflowing cityscapes of the North and the South, manifold new forms of centrality have evolved. In order to make some progress in this direction, it would be necessary to demarcate new definitions of "urbanity" or "urban quality" based on the effects of interaction processes in urban space. For the mere presence of different social groups and networks is not sufficient for the emergence of an urban culture. What matters, rather, is the way they interact and the quality of these interaction processes. Differences must always be understood dynamically. Is the outcome an open exchange, or are differences curtailed and domesticated? Such questions also pertain to the immaterial conditions of communication – the rules and norms governing urban spaces. This brings us to the second moment in the production of urban space – the conception of space.

The definition of the urban

As Lefebvre noted, a space cannot be perceived without having first been conceived in the mind. A conceived space is therefore a depiction that reflects and defines a space and thus also represents it. The combination of individual elements into a whole that is subsequently regarded as space requires a mental effort. Constructions or conceptions of space are supported by social conventions that define which elements are related to one another and which ones are excluded – conventions that are not immutable, but often contested, and which are negotiated in discursive (political) practice. This is a social production process that is connected to the production of knowledge and power structures. In a broader sense, the representations of space also include social rules and ethics.

Our conception of the "city" therefore depends on society's definition of the urban and thus on the idea of the city, the design, the map, the concept, or the scientific theory that attempts to define and demarcate the urban. Such definitions of the city always contain mechanisms of inclusion and exclusion and thus become battlegrounds for a variety of strategies and interests. All kinds of political and economic actors, urban specialists, and intellectuals intervene in this field, and urban movements may also have considerable impact.

These definitions do not mark the end point; they immediately translate into political questions, for they are directly connected to rules and norms that define who and what is admissible or prohibited and what is included or excluded in urban space. Often, implicit distinctions, and invisible boundaries play important roles here that are hidden to the outside observer.

The urban experience

The third dimension in the production of space is what Lefebvre calls "spaces of representation". These are spaces that signify "something". They refer not to space itself, but to a third, other aspect – for instance, a divine power, logos, the state, or the male or female principle. This dimension of the production of space refers to the process of signification, which is expressed in (material) symbolism. The production of significance imparts symbolic meaning to spaces and thus turns them into spaces of representation. This aspect of space is encountered or experienced by people in their everyday life, which is why Lefebvre also calls it "espace vécu", a space that is lived or experienced. A lived, practical experience cannot be fully grasped by theoretical analysis. "Something" always remains, an ineffable residue that defies analysis and that can only be expressed by artistic means.

The city is thus always also a concrete, practical experience, a place of its residents who use it and appropriate it in their everyday practices. The nature of a "city" is something that its inhabitants learn from infancy – and something they combine with their memories. It is therefore crucial in this context which experiences are inscribed in space and in the collective consciousness. Such experiences contain both collective and individual aspects; they include positive and negative values; they may be banal and commonplace or spectacular and far-reaching. Struggles for the city themselves are constitutive elements of such urban experiences. They facilitate concrete processes of appropriation and the recognition that urban spaces can be used in different ways than were previously envisaged. Thus, urban "moments" such as May 1968 in Paris are crucial reference points whose effects persist many years later, influencing contemporary debates and urban practices in distinctive ways.

zesse aufspalten lässt. Diese Dimensionen – Lefebvre nennt sie auch Formanten oder Momente der Produktion des Raumes – sind doppelt bestimmt und dementsprechend auch doppelt benannt: erstens die Triade von "räumlicher Praxis", "Repräsentation des Raumes" und "Räumen der Repräsentation", zweitens dem "wahrgenommenen", "konzipierten" und "gelebten" Raum. Diese doppelte Reihe von Begriffen weist auf einen zweifachen Zugang zum Raum hin: einerseits einen phänomenologischen, andererseits einen linguistischen bzw. semiotischen (vgl. hierzu auch Schmid 2005, und 2008).

Die urbane Praxis

Raum hat zunächst einen wahrnehmbaren Aspekt, der sich mit den fünf Sinnen erfassen lässt. Dieser bezieht sich direkt auf die Materialität der Elemente, die einen Raum konstituieren. Die räumliche Praxis verknüpft diese Elemente zu einer räumlichen Ordnung, einer Ordnung des Gleichzeitigen. Der urbane Raum ist deshalb ein Raum der materiellen Interaktion und des physischen Zusammentreffens. Dieser praktische Aspekt der Mediation, der Zentralität und der Differenz lässt sich als Überlagerung und Verknotung von Produktionsnetzwerken und Kommunikationskanälen verstehen, als Verbindung von sozialen Netzen des Alltagslebens, als Orte der Begegnung und des Austausches, die offen sind für Überraschungen und Innovationen.

Damit ist der urbane Raum der konkreten Beobachtung zugänglich: Was passiert auf den Strassen? Welche Ressourcen gibt es und wer hat Zugang dazu? Wer ist präsent, wer begegnet sich? Zuallererst geht es hier um die physische Präsenz der Menschen im urbanen Raum. Sehr oft werden diese auf die Bewohnerinnen und Bewohner eines Quartiers reduziert. Aber zu einem städtischen Raum gehören auch die Arbeitenden, die Besucher, die Straßenhändler, und die entsprechenden Orte: Läden, Restaurants, Treffpunkte, Orte des kulturellen und sozialen Austauschs bilden den Rahmen, in dem sich urbanes Leben abspielen kann.

Die Möglichkeiten der Interaktion sind jedoch ungleich über den städtischen Raum verteilt. An gewissen Orten gibt es Konzentrationen von städtischen Ressourcen, an anderen Ausdünnung und Zerstreuung. Direkt damit verknüpft ist die Frage des Zugangs zu diesen Ressourcen. Der Kampf um das Recht, im städtischen Raum bleiben zu können, ist seit jeher eine der zentralen Fragen der urbanen Bewegungen, ob es um Aufwertungsprogramme und Gentrifizierung oder um Programme zur "Slumsanierung" geht.

Mit der planetaren Urbanisierung hat sich der Fokus der urbanen Frage verschoben. Das klassische Modell der Urbanität, das westliche Metropolen wie Berlin, Paris oder Chicago zum Vorbild nahm, ist von der Urbanisierung längst überholt worden. In den ausufernden urbanen Landschaften des Nordens und Südens haben sich vielfältige neue Formen der Urbanität herausgebildet. Um diese erfassen zu können, braucht es eine neue Definition von "Urbanität", die sich insbesondere auf die Qualität von Interaktionsprozessen im städtischen Raum bezieht. Denn das Vorhandensein von unterschiedlichen Menschen und Handlungszusammenhängen allein ist nicht ausreichend für eine urbane Kultur. Entscheidend ist vielmehr, welche Qualität die Interaktionsprozesse annehmen, und auf welche Weise sie ineinander greifen. Differenzen müssen dynamisch begriffen werden: Kommt es zu einem offenen Austausch, oder werden die Unterschiede eingegrenzt und domestiziert? Damit sind auch die immateriellen Bedingungen der Kommunikation angesprochen, die Regeln und Normen, die in den urbanen Räumen herrschen. Dies führt zum zweiten Moment der Produktion des urbanen Raumes: Der Konzeption des Raumes.

Die Definition des Städtischen

Wie Lefebvre feststellte, lässt sich ein Raum nicht wahrnehmen, ohne dass er zuvor gedanklich konzipiert worden wäre. Ein konzipierter Raum ist mithin eine Darstellung, die einen Raum abbildet und definiert und ihn damit auch repräsentiert. Das Zusammenbringen von einzelnen Elementen zu einem Ganzen, das dann als Raum betrachtet wird, setzt eine gedankliche Leistung voraus. Konstruktionen oder Konzeptionen des Raumes stützen sich auf gesellschaftlichen Konventionen ab, die festlegen, welche Elemente zueinander in Beziehung gesetzt und welche ausgeschlossen werden, Konventionen, die nicht unabänderlich sind, sondern oft umstritten und umkämpft, und die im diskursiven (politischen) Einsatz ausgehandelt werden. Es handelt sich um einen gesellschaftlichen Produktionsprozess, der mit der Produktion von Wissen verbunden und mit Machtstrukturen verknüpft ist. In einem weiten Sinne umfassen die Repräsentationen des Raumes auch gesellschaftliche Regeln und eine Ethik.

Das, was wir als "Stadt" verstehen, ist also abhängig von der gesellschaftlichen Definition des Städtischen und damit auch vom Bild der Stadt, dem Entwurf, der Karte, dem Konzept oder der wissenschaftlichen Theorie, die versucht, das Städtische zu definieren und festzulegen. Solche Stadtdefinitionen beinhalten immer entsprechende Einschluss- und Ausschlussmechanismen und werden somit zum

Urbanization and urbanity

The theory of production of space therefore includes, at core, a three-dimensional production process – firstly, material production; secondly, the production of knowledge; thirdly, the production of meaning. These three dimensions of the production of space form a contradictory, dialectic unity. The determination is a threefold one; space is only produced through the interaction among all three elements.

Space is the result of production processes that take place in time. This basic presupposition leads to a dynamic conception of urban space as being constantly produced and reproduced. Urban qualities do not appear automatically as the result of urbanization. Urbanization lays the groundwork for generating urban situations, but the latter are created only as the result of multiple actions. This also implies a constant struggle over the content of the urban. Concrete, "lived" urbanity is the outcome of continuous conflicts and contestations. "The city" is not a general category, but a concrete, historical one that is perpetually being renewed and redefined – both in theory and in practice.

From this point of view, the "right to the city" may be redefined as the "right to (urban) space" – that is, as the right to participate at the transformation of space and to control investment into space (Lefebvre, 1978: 317).

4) THE NEW METROPOLITAN MAINSTREAM AND THE COMMODIFICATION OF THE URBAN

The rediscovery of the urban

Based on the theoretical reflections sketched above, it is possible to decipher some key aspects of global urbanization during the last few decades. While urbanization has accelerated and generalized, there is also strong, albeit diffuse, evidence in many places that urban spaces are being reclaimed. During the course of the 1970s and 1980s, these "urban values" were increasingly embraced by broader social strata. This marked the beginning of a long history of a "rediscovery of the urban", a trend which is sometimes also labeled an "urban renaissance" (Porter and Shaw, 2008).

This rediscovery of the urban was also closely intertwined with the dynamics of globalization, which has been closely associated with new forms of centrality and agglomeration. Two aspects are essential here. On the one hand, centrality plays a key role for global economic control and command functions and for certain forms of innovation, especially those that require a wide variety and multiplicity of inputs for the development and creation of complex products. On the other hand, metropolitan centres became privileged spaces for the new urban elites that had formed under the neoliberal development model (Sassen, 1996; Scott, 1998).

Lefebvre already recognized the first signs of this development. He observed that the metropolitan centres are becoming high-grade consumer products, and indeed manage to survive due to their simultaneous role as places of consumption and as consumable places. The old centres thus fully enter the relations of exchange and exchange value, not without remaining use value at the same time. Thereby the decision-making centre and the consumption centre, the decision-making power and consumption capacity coincide. Based on this strategic convergence, an exorbitant centrality is created on the terrain through their alliance: The urban cores are turned into citadels of power, while their population becomes an elite (Lefebvre, 1996: 73; Lefebvre, 2003: 79).

Lefebvre's clear-sighted analysis sketched a development whose full effects are only today becoming widespread – the global city model has now become generalized, as "metropolitan" values, cultures and lifestyles are widely accepted and sought after. A corresponding set of urban strategies and policies have come to form the new general guidelines of urban development – the metropolitan has become mainstream.

The new metropolitan mainstream

The term "new metropolitan mainstream" was developed to decipher a broad range of phenomena that have recently emerged in cities around the world. Initially, this mainstream is articulated as a norm that defines what is to be regarded as urban or metropolitan while also presenting certain standards and processes for urban planning and design. The promotion of "soft" location factors, of "quality of life" for elites, and of a prestigious blend of cultural amenities and offerings for luxury consumption is today part of the standard policy repertoire for attracting capital investment and highly qualified workers. Accordingly, many contemporary cities both in the global North and in the global South have been equipped with skyscrapers, flagship projects, and "star" architecture. The "standard metropolitan architecture" is becoming the new fuel of global urbanization.

Einsatzfeld unterschiedlicher Strategien und Interessen. In dieses Feld intervenieren unterschiedlichste politische und ökonomische Akteure, städtische Spezialisten, Intellektuelle, und auch städtische Bewegungen können einen erheblichen Einfluss haben.

Bei diesen Definitionen bleibt es nicht stehen, sie werden unmittelbar zu politischen Fragen, denn sie sind direkt mit Regeln, Normen und Zwängen verbunden, die festlegen, wer und was im urbanen Raum zugelassen oder verboten ist, eingeschlossen oder ausgeschlossen wird. Hier spielen oft auch implizite Regeln, Unterscheidungen und unsichtbare Grenzen eine wichtige Rolle, die sich Außenstehenden oft nicht erschließen.

Die urbane Erfahrung

Die dritte Dimension der Produktion des Raumes nennt Lefebvre "Räume der Repräsentation". Es handelt sich hierbei um Räume, die "etwas" bezeichnen. Sie verweisen nicht auf den Raum selbst, sondern auf etwas anderes, drittes: eine göttliche Macht, den Logos, den Staat, das männliche oder das weibliche Prinzip. Diese Dimension der Produktion des Raumes bezieht sich auf den Bedeutungsprozess, der sich an einer (materiellen) Symbolik festmacht: Die Bedeutungsproduktion belegt Räume mit einem symbolischen Gehalt und macht sie so zu Räumen der Repräsentation. Dieser Aspekt des Raumes wird von den Menschen in ihrer Alltagspraxis erlebt oder erfahren, und Lefebvre nennt ihn deshalb auch "espace vécu", den erlebten oder gelebten Raum. Das Erlebte, die praktische Erfahrung, lässt sich durch die theoretische Analyse nicht ausschöpfen. Es bleibt immer ein Mehr: ein unaussprechliches und unanalysierbares Residuum, das sich nur mit künstlerischen Mitteln ausdrücken lässt.

Die Stadt ist also immer auch eine konkrete, praktische Erfahrung, ein Ort der Bewohnerinnen und Bewohner, die ihn benützen und ihn sich in ihren Alltagspraktiken aneignen. Was eine "Stadt" ist, lernen sie von Kindheit an – und verbinden es auch mit ihren Erinnerungen. Hier ist deshalb entscheidend, welche Erlebnisse und Erfahrungen sich in den Raum und ins kollektive Gedächtnis einschreiben. Sie haben sowohl kollektive wie individuelle Momente, sie enthalten positive und negative Werte, sie können banal und alltäglich sein oder auch spektakulär und einschneidend. Die Auseinandersetzungen um die Stadt sind selbst konstitutiver Bestandteil solcher städtischer Erfahrungen. Sie ermöglichen konkrete Aneignungsprozesse, und damit die Erfahrung, dass urbane Räume auch anders gestaltet und genutzt werden können, als bislang vorgesehen. So sind urbane Momente wie der Pariser Mai 1968 entscheidende Referenzpunkte, die noch Jahre später nachwirken, und nicht nur die Diskussion, sondern gerade auch die urbane Praxis beeinflussen.

Urbanisierung und Urbanität

Die Theorie der Produktion des Raumes umfasst im Kern also einen dreidimensionalen Produktionsprozess: erstens die materielle Produktion, zweitens die Produktion von Wissen, drittens die Produktion von Bedeutungen. Die drei Dimensionen der Produktion des Raumes bilden eine widersprüchliche dialektische Einheit. Es handelt sich um eine dreifache Determination: Erst im Zusammenspiel aller drei Pole entsteht Raum.

Aus diesen Überlegungen ergibt sich ein dynamisches Verständnis des urbanen Raumes, der ständig produziert und reproduziert wird: Der Raum ist das Resultat von aktiven Produktionsprozessen, die sich in der Zeit abspielen. Es wird deutlich, dass sich die urbanen Qualitäten nicht automatisch als Resultat des Urbanisierungsprozesses ergeben. Die Urbanisierung legt die Basis zur Generierung von urbanen Situationen, aber sie werden nur als Resultat von vielfältigen Aktionen erzeugt. Dies impliziert auch eine ständige Auseinandersetzung um den Inhalt des Urbanen. Konkrete, "gelebte" Urbanität ist das Ergebnis von ständigen Debatten und Kämpfen. "Die Stadt" ist nicht eine allgemeine, sondern eine konkrete, historische Kategorie, die – in Theorie und Praxis – laufend erneuert und neu definiert wird.

Aus dieser Sicht lässt sich das "Recht auf die Stadt" nochmals neu definieren: als das "Recht auf den (urbanen) Raum", und damit auch das Recht, an der Transformation und Erneuerung des urbanen Raumes teilzuhaben (vgl. Lefebvre 1978: 317).

Processes of gentrification and displacement have spread tremendously in recent years while also becoming more differentiated. Private and public strategies are increasingly intertwined, with urban policies now actively promoting gentrification and the attendant displacement of marginalized populations. The various forms of urban upgrading are now increasingly spreading on a global scale, into the cities of the South, into suburban areas, and even into smaller cities. Fourth, these trends also entail a significant rescaling of urban development. Processes of gentrification and displacement are no longer limited to individual neighbourhoods; rather, entire intra-urban areas and even large parts of metropolitan regions are upgraded and transformed into zones of reproduction for metropolitan elites. A massive increase of land and real estate prices and the accompanying housing crisis have already imposed heavy restrictions on access to these areas for less privileged parts of the population.

Centralization and peripheralization

Another aspect of centralization must be mentioned in this context – displacement and exclusion from centrality. The dialectics of centre and periphery must today be reconsidered. It has long ceased to be determined in geographic terms, and neither does it always follow the logistical principles that are the basis of transportation infrastructure (Veltz, 1996). Rather, centrality today implies the availability of manifold possibilities and access to social resources. Conversely, peripheralization stands for dispersion, demarcation, and exclusion from urban life. This was already problematized in the debates on world cities and global cities in the 1980s and 1990s – it inspired the metaphor of "citadel and ghetto" (Friedmann and Wolff 1982), the "dialectics of centrality and marginality" (Sassen, 1996), and also the concept of the "quartered city" (Marcuse, 1989). Today, this dialectics is articulated in a new form insofar as the less controlled, relatively non-commercialized interstitial spaces within the metropolitan cores are now almost completely disappearing.

From a general point of view, this is a manifestation of the fundamental contradiction within the dialectic of the urban. On the one hand, the social potential of urban space lies precisely in its capacity to facilitate contacts and mutual interaction between the various parts of society. On the other hand, access to urban resources is increasingly controlled and appropriated by global metropolitan elites. This not only limits access to urban space but also imposes limits on its social productivity. In this process, urban space loses some of its essential elements, but especially its most important characteristic – the possibility of unexpected, unplanned encounters and interactions.

The commodification of the urban

Such processes should be regarded as elements of long-term tendencies in capitalist urbanization. Urbanization leads not only to the dissolution of historic forms of the city and to urban sprawl, but also to the formation of new centralities. Centrality is always ambivalent in this context, since on the one hand it creates possibilities for unexpected encounters, while conversely, it is also susceptible to economic exploitation. This ambivalence brings us to yet another process – the commodification of urban life.

This development, of course, is not a new one. The city has long been the place where the market has installed itself and flourished, and it also constitutes the privileged arena in which the world of commodities unfolds – as Walter Benjamin (1995) analyzed so brilliantly for the late 19th century metropolis of Paris. What is new, however, is the systematic economic exploitation of urban space. The city itself, urban life, becomes a commodity. This process can be described as the commodification of the urban (Kipfer and Schmid 2004; Kipfer et al., 2008).

As Lefebvre noted, this strategy goes far beyond simply selling space, bit by bit. Space itself, and not only the land and real estate, becomes exchange value. As a consequence, urban space becomes the very general object of production, and hence of the formation of surplus value: "The deployment of the world of commodities now affects not only objects but their containers, it is no longer limited to content, to objects in space. More recently, space itself has begun to be bought and sold. Not the earth, the soil, but social space, produced as such, with this purpose, this finality (so to speak)" (Lefebvre, 2003: 154).

The commodification of the urban has not yet been grasped adequately in all of its dimensions and implications. This process encompasses not only the sale of parcels of land, and the reservation of exclusive locations for certain population groups. At stake, more generally, is the process by which urban space as such is exploited. The entire space is sold – including the people living in it, as well as the social resources and the economic effects produced by them. Urban life itself is implicated in the economic process of valorization and is thereby transformed. This means that the qualities of urban space – difference, encounter, creativity – become part of the economic logic and of systematic exploitation of productivity gains.

4) DER NEUE METROPOLITANE MAINSTREAM UND DIE KOMMODIFIZIERUNG DES STÄDTISCHEN

Die Wiederentdeckung des Städtischen

Ausgehend von den oben skizzierten theoretischen Überlegungen lässt sich die Entwicklung der Urbanisierung in den letzten Jahrzehnten neu bestimmen. Während sich der Urbanisierungsprozess immer weiter verallgemeinerte, kam es zugleich zu einem diffusen, aber kontinuierlichen Prozess der Wiederaneignung urbaner Räume. Im Verlaufe der 1970er und 1980er Jahre rückten diese "urbanen" Werte in vielen Städten immer mehr ins gesellschaftliche Zentrum und wurden von breiteren sozialen Schichten aufgegriffen. Damit kam es zu einer langen Geschichte der "Wiederentdeckung des Städtischen".

Diese Wiederentdeckung des Städtischen war auch stark durch ökonomische Aspekte von Globalisierung und Neoliberalisierung bestimmt, die zu neuen Formen der räumlichen Agglomerierung und einer erneuerten Bedeutung der Zentralität führten. Im Wesentlichen geht es dabei um zwei Aspekte: Einerseits spielt die Zentralität bei der Herstellung von globalen ökonomischen Kontroll- und Leitungsfunktionen sowie bei Innovationsprozessen eine zentrale Rolle, insbesondere bei solchen, die zur Entwicklung und Herstellung von komplexen Produkten vielfältige Inputs benötigen. Andererseits wurden die metropolitanen Zentren zu privilegierten Reproduktionsräumen der neuen urbanen Eliten, die sich im Verlauf des neoliberalen Entwicklungsmodells herausgebildet hatten. Damit wurde auch die "andere Seite" der Zentralität sichtbar: Das Wiederauftauchen der Stadt als Entscheidungs- und Kontrollzentrum (vgl. hierzu z.B. Sassen 1996).

Lefebvre hat die ersten Ansätze dieser Entwicklung bereits erkannt. Er sah, dass die Zentren zum hochwertigen Produkt des Konsums werden und dank dieser doppelten Rolle überleben: als Orte des Konsums und als konsumierbare Orte. So treten die alten Zentren vollständig in den Tausch und den Tauschwert ein, nicht ohne gleichzeitig Gebrauchswert zu bleiben. Dabei vereinigen sich das Entscheidungszentrum und das Konsumzentrum, Entscheidungsmacht und Konsumfähigkeit fallen zusammen. Basierend auf ihrer strategischen Konvergenz schafft ihre Allianz auf dem Terrain eine exorbitante Zentralität: Die Metropolen werden zu Bollwerken der Macht, ihre Bevölkerung wird zur Elite (Lefebvre 1968: 21, 124; Lefebvre 1972a: 87; Lefebvre 1974: 383f.).

Mit dieser klarsichtigen Analyse hat Lefebvre eine Entwicklung skizziert, die erst heute ihre volle Tragweite entfaltet: "Metropolitane" Werte, Kulturen und Lebensstile sind zu einem allgemein akzeptierten Maßstab geworden, und die entsprechenden Strategien und Politiken bilden die neuen Leitlinien der Stadtentwicklung – das Metropolitane wird zum Mainstream.

Der neue metropolitane Mainstream

Mit dem Begriff "neuer metropolitaner Mainstream" wird ein ganzes Bündel von Phänomenen zusammengefasst, die sich in den letzten Jahren in vielen Städten der Welt entwickelt haben (vgl. Schmid/Weiss 2004). Zunächst präsentiert er sich als eine Norm, die nicht nur definiert, was als urban oder metropolitan zu gelten hat, sondern auch bestimmte Standards und Verfahren festlegt, nach denen Städte geplant und gebaut werden. Die Förderung von "weichen" Standortfaktoren, von "Lebensqualität" für die Eliten und einem prestigeträchtigen Kultur- und Konsumangebot gehören heute zum Standardrepertoire, um Kapital und hochqualifizierte Arbeitskräfte anzulocken. Entsprechend werden heute viele Städte, im Norden wie im Süden, mit Wolkenkratzern, flagship projects und Stararchitektur ausstaffiert. Die "standard metropolitan architecture" wird zum neuen Einheitsbrei der globalen Urbanisierung.

Diese Prozesse haben sich in den letzten Jahren enorm ausgeweitet und zugleich ausdifferenziert. So greifen heute privatwirtschaftliche und staatliche Strategien immer stärker ineinander, wobei die Politik mit Maßnahmen zur Aufwertung von Quartieren oft ganz gezielt Gentrifizierungsprozesse und die damit verbundene Verdrängung bestimmter Bevölkerungsgruppen vorantreibt. Die verschiedenen Formen der urbanen Aufwertung verbreiten sich heute in globalem Maßstab, in die Städte des Südens, in die urbane Peripherie und auch in kleinere Städte. Damit ist auch ein Maßstabssprung verbunden: Nicht mehr nur einzelne Quartiere sind von diesen Prozessen betroffen, sondern ganze innerstädtische Gebiete und sogar große Teile von Metropolitanregionen werden aufgewertet und zum Reproduktionsraum für die metropolitanen Eliten transformiert. Eine enorme

5) THE URBAN AS CONCRETE UTOPIA

Theory and practice

Forty years ago, Lefebvre observed the rise of a new problematique and introduced the slogan "the right to the city". Obviously, the situation today is no longer the same, and we are living in a completely different urban world. Nevertheless, it is precisely in this situation that this call is heard anew, in the "global West" as well as in the "global South". In this context, the call for a right to the city also acquires new importance and a new content. Three tendencies are particularly noticeable here.

First, the focus today is once again on basic needs such as access to shelter, food, clean water, health, and education. This is due largely to the massive urbanization of the global South, but also due to increasing levels of socioeconomic polarization in major parts of the world.

Second, the call for a right to the city also represents a response to the withdrawal of the (national) state from many areas of social life. Significant tasks are today delegated to the regional or local levels. This has not only imparted new importance to the local, but has also caused increased fragmentation, segregation, and inequality. The various alliances that have coalesced around the rallying cry of the right to the city demand – and, through their practice, in fact constitute – a new unity in the splintered and fragmented urban regions.

Third, such alliances also today facilitate the formation of new collective moments. Even if many alliances appear, at first glance, to be pursuing a rather pragmatic course (see Mayer, this volume), they contain the potential to reframe the urban question, to discover new, self-determined definitions of the urban in the sprawling urban landscapes, and to open up possibilities for conceiving and living different forms of urban life.

As Lefebvre indicates, the point of departure of critical social theory should always be everyday life, the banal, the ordinary. Changing everyday life: this is the real revolution! (Lefebvre 1972b: 51). Everyday life is today marked by urbanization, and we must therefore study its potential. With complete urbanization, the city is becoming virtually omnipresent, and any point has the potential to become central and be transformed into a place of encounter, difference, and innovation. This means viewing urbanization from a different point of view. Urbanization creates the possibility of an urban society. But it must be realized. There is no automatism involved. This is precisely the historic lesson that Lefebvre is communicating.

Over a decade ago, John Friedmann (1993: 139) stated in his text The Right to the City that "a city can truly be called a city only when its streets belong to the people." More recently, David Harvey's influential text with the same title defined the right to the city as the right to control the urbanization process and to institute new modes of urbanization (Harvey, 2008: 40). Although he was writing in an earlier moment, Lefebvre's analysis actually went one step further by postulating a generalized form of self-management (autogestion généralisée) as the basis and expression of that right (Lefebvre, 2003: 150). Ultimately, this means the rearticulation, in a radically new context, of the long-standing demand for the right to self-determination – a right that is indispensible for the creation of a different society.

Possible urban worlds

It should be clear that the right to the city must include more than merely the right to exist and to satisfy basic needs. This "more", this additional aspect, is precisely what defines urban society. The urban is a constant reinvention, it may assume very diverse forms, and the purpose here is not to propose yet another range of normative models. This, however, implies viewing the contemporary urban crisis as an opportunity to imagine alternatives and to create new possible urban worlds. (cf. Harvey 1996 and INURA 1998).

Thus, the same old issues are at stake, albeit in a new context: What is a city, and what does urban living mean? Who is to determine the urban future? Lefebvre opened up a new pathway towards understanding urbanization. In his analysis, urban society is not an already achieved reality, but a potential, an open horizon. The quality of this analysis is that it transcends mere criticisms of urbanization, and proceeds to explore its inherent possibilities and potentials. However, they can only be realized through a fundamental social transformation – an urban revolution.

This text is an abbreviated and slightly supplemented version of "Henri Lefebvre, the right to the city and the new metropolitan mainstream", in: Neil Brenner, Peter Marcuse, Margit Mayer (Eds.): "Cities for People, not for Profit: Critical Urban Theory and the Right to the City", Routledge, New York, 2012, p. 42–62.

Translated from German by Christopher Findlay

Bodenpreissteigerung und die damit zusammenhängende Wohnungsnot haben in vielen Metropolen heute den Zugang zur gesamten Region für weniger privilegierte Bevölkerungsgruppen bereits stark eingeschränkt.

Zentralisierung und Peripherisierung

Zentralisierungsprozesse haben also auch eine Kehrseite, die sich in Verdrängungsprozessen und dem Ausschluss von der Zentralität zeigt. Die Dialektik von Zentrum und Peripherie muss heute neu gedacht werden: Sie ist schon lange nicht mehr geographisch determiniert, und sie folgt auch nicht mehr in allen Fällen den logistischen Prinzipien, die den Transportnetzen zugrunde liegen. Zentralität steht heute vielmehr für die Verfügbarkeit von vielfältigen Möglichkeiten und den Zugang zu sozialen Ressourcen. Demgegenüber steht Peripherisierung für die Zerstreuung, die Abgrenzung, den Ausschluss vom städtischen Leben. Dies ist schon seit längerem in den Debatten zur World City und zur Global City thematisiert worden: In der Figur von "Zitadelle und Ghetto" (Friedmann/Wolff 1982), in der "Dialektik von Zentralität und Marginalität" (Sassen 1996), oder auch in der Figur der "vielfach geteilten Stadt" (Marcuse 1989). Heute erreicht diese Dialektik eine neue Qualität, indem Aufwertungs- und Gentrification-Prozesse und damit verbunden auch entsprechende Verdrängungsprozesse immer weitere innerstädtische Gebiete erfassen. Die wenig kontrollierten und kommerzialisierten Zwischenräume und Ritzen innerhalb der metropolitanen Kerne drohen zusehends zu verschwinden.

Aus einem allgemeinen Blickwinkel betrachtet, manifestiert dies den grundlegenden Widerspruch innerhalb der Dialektik des Städtischen: Auf der einen Seite liegt die Produktivität des urbanen Raumes darin, die unterschiedlichsten Elemente der Gesellschaft in Kontakt und gegenseitige Reaktion zu bringen. Auf der anderen Seite werden die urbanen Ressourcen zunehmend durch die globalen Eliten kontrolliert und angeeignet. Dies beschränkt den Zugang und begrenzt zugleich die Produktivität des Urbanen. Der urbane Raum verliert in diesem Prozess wesentliche seiner Elemente, insbesondere aber seine wichtigste Eigenschaft: die Möglichkeit zu unverhofften und ungeplanten Begegnungen und Interaktionen.

Die Kommodifizierung des Urbanen

Diese Prozesse sind als Teil der langfristigen Tendenzen kapitalistischer Urbanisierung zu betrachten: Urbanisierung führt nicht nur zur Auflösung der historischen Formen der Stadt und zur Ausdehnung von urbanen Gebieten, sondern auch zur Herausbildung von neuen Zentralitäten. Zentralität ist dabei immer ambivalent: Einerseits öffnet sie die Möglichkeiten zu unverhofftem Zusammentreffen, andererseits lässt sie sich aber auch ökonomisch ausbeuten. Damit ist ein weiterer Prozess angesprochen: Das Hineinziehen des urbanen Lebens in den ökonomischen Verwertungsprozess.

Auch dies ist selbstverständlich kein neuer Prozess: Schon lange ist die Stadt der Ort, wo sich der Markt installiert und entwickelt hat, und sie bildet auch die privilegierte Bühne, auf der sich die Welt der Ware entfaltet – wie es schon Walter Benjamin (1982) für die Metropole Paris Ende des 19. Jahrhunderts beschrieben hat. Neu jedoch ist die systematische ökonomische Verwertung des urbanen Raumes. Die Stadt selbst, das urbane Leben, wird zur Ware. Dieser Prozess lässt sich als Kommodifizierung des Urbanen bezeichnen (Kipfer/Schmid 2004, Kipfer et al. 2008).

Wie Lefebvre feststellte, reicht die Strategie dabei sehr viel weiter als der einfache Verkauf eines "Stücks Raum" nach dem anderen. Denn der Raum selbst, und nicht mehr nur der Grund und Boden, wird zum Tauschwert. Der Raum wird zum globalen Objekt der Produktion und damit zur Schaffung von Mehrwert: "Die Entfaltung der Welt der Ware ergreift das die Objekte enthaltende Gefäß. Sie beschränkt sich nicht mehr auf die Inhalte, auf die Objekte im Raum. Seit kurzem wird sogar der Raum gekauft und verkauft. Nicht der Grund, der Boden, sondern der soziale Raum als solcher, das Produkt als solches [...]" (Lefebvre 1972a: 164).

Dieser Prozess der Kommodifizierung des Städtischen wurde bisher in seinen Dimensionen und Konsequenzen nicht wirklich erfasst. Er bedeutet nämlich nicht nur den Verkauf oder die Nutzung von kleineren oder größeren Grundstücken, oder die Reservierung von exklusiven Lagen für bestimmte Bevölkerungsgruppen, sondern es geht um den Prozess der Verwertung des urbanen Raumes als solchen. Der ganze Raum wird verkauft – d.h. mitsamt den Menschen, die ihn bevölkern, mitsamt den sozialen Ressourcen und den dadurch erzeugten Effekten. Das urbane Leben selbst wird in den Verwertungsprozess hineingezogen und dabei transformiert. Dies bedeutet also, dass die Qualitäten des urbanen Raumes, Differenz, Begegnung, Kreativität, Teil werden von ökonomischen Dispositiven und systematischer Ausschöpfung von Produktivitätsgewinnen.

5) DAS STÄDTISCHE ALS KONKRETE UTOPIE

Das Recht auf die Stadt heute

Vor vierzig Jahren beobachtete Lefebvre das Auftauchen einer neuen Problematik, und lancierte den Slogan "Recht auf die Stadt". Offensichtlich herrscht heute nicht mehr die gleiche Situation, wir leben in einer völlig anderen urbanen Welt. Dennoch kehrt gerade in dieser Situation dieser Ruf zurück, er ertönt in den Städten Süd- und Nordamerikas, und er erschallt auch wieder in Europa, in London, Hamburg, Berlin. In diesem Kontext gewinnt er zugleich eine neue Bedeutung und einen neuen Inhalt. Dabei springen vor allem drei Tendenzen ins Auge:

Erstens stehen heute wieder verstärkt grundlegende Lebensbedürfnisse im Vordergrund, wie Zugang zu sauberem Wasser, Wohnung, Gesundheit, Bildung. Dies hat wesentlich mit der massiven Urbanisierung in Lateinamerika, Afrika und Teilen Asiens zu tun, aber auch mit der zunehmenden sozio-ökonomischen Polarisierung in weiten Teilen der Welt.

Zweitens bedeutet dies auch eine Reaktion auf den Rückzug des (nationalen) Staates aus vielen Bereichen des sozialen Lebens. Wesentliche Aufgaben werden heute auf die regionale bzw. lokale Ebene delegiert. Dies hat nicht nur zu einer neuen Bedeutung des Lokalen, sondern auch zu verstärkter Fragmentierung, Segregation und Ungleichheit geführt. Die verschiedenen Allianzen, die sich unter dem Slogan "Recht auf die Stadt" formiert haben, fordern und konstituieren durch ihre Praxis heute eine neue Einheit in den zersplitterten und fragmentierten urbanen Regionen.

Drittens ermöglichen solche Allianzen auch neue kollektive Momente. Auch wenn viele Allianzen zunächst eine eher pragmatische Linie verfolgen, haben sie das Potential, einen neuen Blick auf die urbane Frage zu werfen und in den ausufernden Stadtlandschaften neue, selbstbestimmte Definitionen des Urbanen zu finden, Freiräume zu schaffen, um andere Entwürfe des Urbanen zu denken und zu leben.

Wie Lefebvre betonte, sollte dabei der Ausgangspunkt immer der Alltag sein, das Banale, das Gewöhnliche. Den Alltag verändern: Das ist eine Revolution! (Lefebvre 1972b: 51). Dieser Alltag ist heute durch die vollständige Urbanisierung geprägt, mit der das Städtische virtuell allgegenwärtig geworden ist. Potenziell kann jeder Punkt zentral werden, zu einem Ort der Auseinandersetzung, der Differenz, der Kreativität. Das bedeutet, Urbanisierung mit anderen Augen zu betrachten: Die Urbanisierung bringt die Möglichkeit zu einer urbanen Gesellschaft hervor. Aber diese Möglichkeit muss realisiert werden, es gibt keinen Automatismus. Gerade darin liegt die historische Lektion, die uns Lefebvre übermittelt.

Bereits vor über einem Jahrzehnt hat John Friedmann in seinem Text "The right to the city" konstatiert: "a city can truly be called a city only when its streets belong to the people" (Friedmann 1993: 139). Und David Harvey (2008: 40) definierte in seinem weit rezipierten Text mit dem gleichen Titel das Recht auf die Stadt als Recht, den Urbanisierungsprozess zu kontrollieren und neue Formen der Urbanisierung einzuführen. Lefebvre ging sogar noch einen Schritt weiter und forderte die allgemeine Selbstverwaltung (Lefebvre 1972a: 160). Letztlich wird damit unter neuen Vorzeichen ein altes Selbstbestimmungsrecht eingefordert, das erst eine andere Gesellschaft ermöglichen kann.

Mögliche urbane Welten

Das Recht auf die Stadt muss in jedem Fall mehr bedeuten als das klassische Existenzrecht und die Befriedigung der Grundbedürfnisse. Es ist gerade dieses Mehr, dieses Andere, das letztlich eine urbane Gesellschaft kennzeichnet. Das Urbane ist immer wieder eine Neuerfindung und kann sehr verschiedene Formen annehmen. Deshalb kann es nicht darum gehen, hier erneut normative Modelle vorzugeben. Das heißt aber auch, die heutige urbane Krise als Chance zu sehen, Alternativen zu denken und neue mögliche urbane Welten zu kreieren (vgl. Harvey 1996 und INURA 1998).

Damit stehen die alten Fragen unter neuen Vorzeichen erneut zur Diskussion: Was ist eine Stadt, und was bedeutet urbanes Leben? Wer soll über die urbane Zukunft entscheiden? Lefebvre hat einen neuen Weg zum Verständnis der Urbanisierung eröffnet: Er analysierte die urbane Gesellschaft nicht als bereits erfüllte Wirklichkeit, sondern als Möglichkeit, als offenen Horizont. Die besondere Qualität dieser Analyse liegt gerade darin, dass sie nicht bei einer Kritik der Urbanisierung stehenbleibt, sondern die in ihr enthaltenen Möglichkeiten und Potentiale auslotet. Sie können aber nur durch einen grundlegenden sozialen Wandel realisiert werden – eine urbane Revolution.

Dieser Text ist die stark gekürzte und leicht ergänzte Fassung von "Henri Lefebvre und das Recht auf die Stadt", publiziert in: Holm, A. and Gebhardt, D. (Hrsg.): Initiativen für ein Recht auf die Stadt. Theorie und Praxis städtischer Aneignungen. VSA Verlag, Hamburg, 2011, 25–51.

References

- Benjamin, Walter (1982): Paris, die Hauptstadt des XIX. Jahrhunderts. In: W. Benjamin, Gesammelte Schriften, Band V1. Suhrkamp, Frankfurt a.M. S.45-59.
- Brenner, Neil / Marcuse Peter / Mayer Margit (Hrsg.) (2012): Cities for people, not for profit: critical urban theory and the right to the city. Routledge, New York.
- Brenner, Neil / Schmid, Christian (2015): Towards a new epistemology of the urban? In: City 19/2–3, 151–182.
- Brenner, Neil / Schmid, Christian (2011): Planetary urbanization. In: M.Gandy (ed.): Urban constellations. Jovis Verlag, Berlin, 10–13.
- Engels, Friedrich (1971): Die Lage der arbeitenden Klasse in England. Dietz, Berlin; (2009) The Condition of the Working Class in England. London: Penguin.
- Friedmann, John (1993): The right to the city. In: M. Morse and J. Hardoy (Hrsg.): Rethinking the Latin American city. Johns Hopkins University Press, Baltimore, S. 135–151.
- Friedmann, John / Wolff, Goetz (1982): World city formation: an agenda for research and action. In: International Journal of Urban and Regional Research, 6/1, S. 309–344.
- Harvey, David (2008): The right to the city. In: New Left Review 53 (September/October), S. 23–40.
- Harvey, David (1996): Justice, nature and the geography of difference. Blackwell, Cambridge, Ma.
- Holm, Andrej / Gebhardt, D. (Hrsg.) (2011): Initiativen für ein Recht auf die Stadt. Theorie und Praxis städtischer Aneignungen. VSA Verlag, Hamburg.
- INURA (Hrsg.) (1998): Possible Urban Worlds. Urban strategies at the end of the 20th century. Birkhäuser, Basel.
- Jacobs, Jane (1969 [1961]): Tod und Leben großer amerikanischer Städte. Bauwelt Fundamente 4, Ullstein, Berlin u.a.
- Kipfer, Stefan (1998): Urban politics in the 1990s: notes on Toronto. In: INURA: Possible Urban Worlds. Birkhäuser, Basel, S. 172–179.
- Kipfer, Stefan / Schmid, Christian / Goonewardena, Kanishka / Milgrom, Richard (2008): Globalizing Lefebvre? In: K. Goonewardena et al. (Hrsg.): Space, difference, everyday life: reading Henri Lefebvre. Routledge, New York, S. 285–305.
- Kipfer, Stefan / Schmid, Christian (2004): Right to the City / Bourgeois Urbanism. Research agenda prepared for the International Network of Urban Research and Action, March, 2004, Toronto.
- Lefebvre, Henri (1968): Le droit à la ville. Anthropos, Paris; (1996) (1996) 'Right to the City', in E. Kofman and E. Lebas (eds) Writings on Cities: Henri Lefebvre, pp. 63–184. Oxford UK and Cambridge Ma.: Blackwell.
- Lefebvre, Henri (1970a): Le manifeste différentialiste. Gallimard, Paris.
- Lefebvre, Henri (1970b): Du rural à l'urbain. Anthropos, Paris.
- Lefebvre, Henri (1972a): Die Revolution der Städte. List, München, (2003) The Urban Revolution. University of Minnesota Press, Minneapolis.
- Lefebvre, Henri (1972b): Das Alltagsleben in der modernen Welt. Suhrkamp, Frankf. a.M.
- Lefebvre, Henri (1974): La production de l'espace. Anthropos, Paris; (1991) The Production of Space. Oxford: Blackwell.
- Lefebvre, Henri (1978): De l'État, tome IV: les contradictions de l'État moderne. Union Générale d'Editions, Paris.
- Merrifield, Andy (2013): The urban question under planetary urbanization. In: International Journal for Urban and Regional Research, 37/3, 909-922.
- Marcuse, P. (1989): Dual City: a muddy metaphor for a quartered city, in International Journal of Urban and Regional Research 13/4, pp. 697–708.
- Mitscherlich, Alexander (1965): Die Unwirtlichkeit unserer Städte. Anstiftung zum Unfrieden. Suhrkamp, Frankfurt a.M.
- Purcell, Mark (2008): Recapturing democracy: Neoliberalization and the struggle for alternative urban futures. Routledge, New York.
- Sassen, Saskia (1996): Metropolen des Weltmarktes. Die neue Rolle der Global Cities. Campus, Frankfurt a.M.
- Schmid, Christian (2005): Stadt, Raum und Gesellschaft: Henri Lefebvre und die Theorie der Produktion des Raumes. Stuttgart: Franz Steiner Verlag.
- Schmid, Christian (2008): Henri Lefebvre's theory of the production of space: Towards a three-dimensional dialectic. In Space, difference, everyday life: Reading Henri Lefebvre, ed. K. Goonewardena et al., 27–45. New York: Routledge.
- Schmid, Christian / Weiss, Daniel (2004): The new metropolitan mainstream. In: INURA / R. Palosicia (Hrsg.): The contested metropolis: Six cities at the beginning of the 21st century, Birkhäuser, Basel, S. 252–260.
- Situationistische Internationale (1976): Situationistische Internationale 1958–1969. Gesammelte Ausgaben des Organs der Situationistischen Internationale, Bd.1. MaD Verlag, Hamburg.
- Stanek, Lukasz (2011): Henri Lefebvre on space: architecture, urban research, and the production of theory: University of Minnesota Press, Minneapolis.
- Wastl-Walter, Doris / Staeheli, Lynn A. / Dowler, Lorraine (Hrsg.) (2005): "Rights to the city". IGU Geography Publication Series, Vol. III, Rom.

THE TRANSITORY CENTURY WBGU

What kind of homes should people live in? Where can they settle? How close may their neighbours encroach on them?

These questions are as old as our civilization, but in the 21st century they are being asked in a new way. Because this century is characterized by a *contradiction dynamic* that eclipses much of our previous experience of social change: rapidly growing populations in many developing countries versus shrinking populations in some industrialized countries; the enrichment of tiny elites versus the ongoing economic marginalization of the majority; guarded luxury real estate surrounded by squalid, poor neighbourhoods in many megacities; improved access to basic supplies and services for billions of Earth dwellers, while at the same time their long-term life-support systems are being destroyed by resource looting, climate change and environmental pollution.

Theoretically, the globalized economy generates unprecedented possibilities for prosperity for each and every one of us, yet only a minority of the world's population has the prerequisites, the skill and, in particular, the luck to take advantage of these opportunities. The global precariat still comprises over 700 million people living on less than 2 US dollars a day. Furthermore, over 4 billion people have to get by on less than 10 dollars a day. At the same time, the number of billionaires is growing at breathtaking speed. As a result, in the late modern age humanity is fanning out into countless factions, spread apart by the ultra centrifuge of accelerated 'progress', which is still being driven by the massive use of fossil fuels and is becoming more and more dominated by electronic information technology.

Nothing stands still on our planet any more, and above all, hardly anyone stays in the same place. In the Europe of the 19th century, many people who first saw the light of the world in their parents' home were also laid to rest there. Today, however, anyone who grows up in a residential block, hut or villa is highly unlikely to die there. He or she will move many times during their lifetime – from house to house, from countryside to city, from village to metropolis, from home country to neighbouring country, from continent to continent. Places of residence, workplaces, holiday destinations and retirement homes are increasingly becoming stations on the road from cradle to grave, and even these episodic lodgings only serve as points of reference for the hyper-mobile individual, who is constantly commuting, travelling, roving, fleeing. These relocations of humanity are driven by the pursuit of happiness and self-fulfilment, by human curiosity, by the efficiency logic of global value chains, or by the harsh laws of poverty, violence and social disintegration. A *civilization of accelerated movement* has emerged from the culture of immobility.

Highly diverse pull and push factors are at work, as well as strong centrifugal and centripetal forces. In the course of thousands of years, such forces have brought people together and dispersed them again, created and concentrated settlements and caused them to fray, triggered, steered, inhibited and finally stopped migrations by individuals or entire peoples. In certain historical phases, the different forces push in the same direction; in others they are in conflict with each other. In the latter case, 'trapped communities' can emerge, i.e. groups of people whose will to migrate is politically, economically or ecologically blocked.

One decisive contributory influence behind the emergence of today's modern period, with its extremely rapid settlement dynamics, was what happened in the 17th to 19th centuries, initially in England, Scotland and Wales. Particularly during the Enclosure Movement, there was an extensive privatization and restructuring of rural areas, which led to a dramatic increase in agricultural production. The resultant population growth created not least an army of young, displaced workers, who headed for the expanding cities of the Industrial Revolution from the late 18th century onwards.

Wie sollen sich die Menschen behausen, wo können sie sich niederlassen, wie nahe dürfen ihnen die Nachbarn rücken?

Diese Fragen sind so alt wie unsere Zivilisation, doch im 21. Jahrhundert werden sie auf neue Weise gestellt. Denn dieses Jahrhundert ist geprägt von einer Widerspruchsdynamik, die viele bisherige Erfahrungen sozialen Wandels in den Schatten stellt: Vielerorts rapide wachsende Bevölkerungen in den Entwicklungsländern und mancherorts schrumpfende Populationen in den Industrieländern, Bereicherung winziger Eliten und fortschreitende ökonomische Marginalisierung der Mehrheit, bewachte Luxusimmobilien umringt von menschenunwürdigen Quartieren in zahlreichen Megastädten, verbesserte Elementarversorgung von Milliarden Erdenbürgern bei gleichzeitiger Zerstörung ihrer langfristigen Lebensgrundlagen durch Ressourcenplünderung, Klimawandel und Umweltverschmutzung.

Die globalisierte Wirtschaft schafft im Prinzip unerhörte Wohlstandsmöglichkeiten für jeden und jede, doch hat nur eine Minderheit der Weltbevölkerung die Voraussetzungen, das Geschick und insbesondere das Glück, diese Chancen wahrzunehmen. Das globale Prekariat umfasst noch immer über 700 Mio. Menschen, die von weniger als 2 US-$ am Tag leben. Zudem müssen mehr als 4 Mrd. Menschen mit weniger als 10 US-$ pro Tag auskommen. Gleichzeitig wächst die Zahl der Milliardäre in atemberaubendem Tempo. Somit fächert sich die Menschheit in der späten Moderne in unzählige Fraktionen auf, auseinandergespreizt von der Ultra-Zentrifuge des beschleunigten "Fortschritts", der immer noch vom massiven Einsatz fossiler Brennstoffe angetrieben und immer stärker von der elektronischen Informationstechnologie dominiert wird.

Nichts steht mehr still auf unserem Planeten, und vor allem, fast keiner bleibt, wo er einmal war. Viele, die im Europa des 19. Jahrhunderts im Elternhaus das Licht der Welt erblickten, wurden dort auch zur letzten Ruhe gebettet. Wer dagegen heute in einem Wohnblock, einer Hütte oder einer Villa aufwächst, dürfte kaum dort sterben. Er oder sie werden im Laufe des Lebens viele Male umziehen – von Haus zu Haus, vom Land in die Stadt, vom Dorf in die Metropole, vom Heimatstaat zum Nachbarstaat, von Kontinent zu Kontinent. Wohnorte, Arbeitsplätze, Urlaubsziele und Alterssitze werden immer mehr zu Zwischenstationen auf dem Pfad zwischen Wiege und Bahre, und selbst diese episodischen Quartiere dienen nur als Referenzpunkte für das hypermobile Individuum, das unablässig pendelt, reist, vagabundiert, flüchtet. Diese Umzüge der Menschheit sind angetrieben vom Streben nach Glück und Selbstverwirklichung, von menschlicher Neugier, von der Effizienzlogik globaler Wertschöpfungsketten oder aber von den rohen Gesetzen von Not, Gewalt und Gesellschaftszerfall. Aus der Kultur der Sesshaftigkeit ist eine Zivilisation der beschleunigten Bewegung *hervorgegangen.*

Am Werk sind höchst unterschiedliche Zug- und Schubfaktoren, genauso wie starke Zentrifugal- und Zentripetalkräfte. Solche Antriebe haben im Laufe der Jahrtausende die Menschen zusammengeführt und wieder zerstreut, Siedlungen geschaffen, verdichtet und zerfranst, Wanderungen von Einzelnen oder ganzen Völkern ausgelöst, gelenkt, gehemmt und schließlich unterbunden. In gewissen historischen Phasen wirken die verschiedenen Antriebe gleichgerichtet, in anderen Phasen liegen sie im Widerstreit. Im letzteren Falle können etwa "Trapped Communities" entstehen, also Menschengruppen, deren Migrationswillen politisch, ökonomisch oder ökologisch blockiert ist.

Beim Werden der Hochmoderne mit ihrer sich heute überschlagenden Siedlungsdynamik war mitentscheidend, was im 17. bis 19. Jahrhundert zunächst in England, Schottland und Wales geschah: Insbesondere im Rahmen des "Enclosure Movement" kam es zu einer weitgehenden Privatisierung und Neugestaltung des ländlichen Raums, welche die agrarische Produktion dramatisch steigerte.

This development turned the historical, demographic relationship between city and countryside on its head: in 1600 about 80% of the British population were still living in the country; in 1900, by contrast, about 80% were city residents. The population growth was accommodated by both a denser settlement of the urban cores and the planned extension and design of the suburbs (workers' settlements, social housing, garden colonies, etc.).

This process ran its course in a similar way in all classic industrialized countries, but in some cases resulted in intolerable humanitarian conditions, so that after the 1870s – and even more so after the First World War – architects, economists, moral philosophers and politicians began to think intensively about how these conditions might be improved. Among other things, the vision of the 'functional segregation' of urban residential, working and recreational areas was concisely laid down in the Athens Charter, which was the result of a Mediterranean cruise organized in the summer of 1933 by the avant-garde urban planners association Congrès Internationaux d'Architecture Moderne (CIAM) and dominated by Le Corbusier's powerful personality. The idea was to replace the overcrowded historical cities by settlements based on a modular system ('unités d'habitations') that expanded linearly or concentrically into the surrounding countryside.

The Charter's ideas were bold, but naive and often lacking a 'human scale'. This was shown when the basic idea was implemented in many cities in the post-war period, but often in a modified or distorted form. In this context, a special pair of factors was of great importance in Europe: first, the large-scale destruction of old city districts in the Second World War, and second, the triumph of the automobile, particularly as a result of the availability of cheap oil for geostrategic reasons from the 1950s onwards. Post-war Germany in particular, where virtually all the major cities had been bombed to rubble, was very open to visions of 'modernism' and developed it further to fit into the misguided perspective of the 'car-friendly city'. After 1960 there was a strong development towards urban sprawl, both in the USA and in the entire western world, which put functional segregation into practice at enormous environmental cost, though largely in ways that were very different from those dreamt of by the CIAM protagonists. The resulting mixed structures of grown, planned and economically opportune neighbourhoods were not yet influenced, let alone characterized, by the guiding concept of sustainability.

However, in the last decades of the 20th century, and especially after the fall of the Berlin Wall, this guiding concept gained outstanding importance in public discourse in the highly developed industrialized countries. This led not least to a discussion on problematic aspects of the contemporary design of urban and rural spaces – from landscape destruction to the acceleration of climate change by greenhouse-gas emissions in the construction and transport sectors. In addition, planners, architects and cultural scientists agreed that the spatial reintegration of the various urban services – from accommodation to active participation in policy-making processes – was urgently required for the recovery of identity and quality of life. Today, these two largely parallel movements are united in the general call for a renewed *densification and limitation* of city areas.

This would suggest that the Athens Charter has now been rejected, although the challenges of settlements in the 21st century are much too complex to draw any final conclusions on urban development. First, there is so-called globalization, i.e. the conquest of the entire planet by a highly networked, market-economy-based production-consumption system, which is kept going and further accelerated by the intensive use of fossil energy sources. However, the course of this development is asynchronous; countries like China are rapidly catching up with the western industrialized countries, while countries in central Africa are currently only just preparing to leave the pre-modern stage. Accordingly, some regions of the world are today re-enacting different phases of European and American urban history, even if these are only touched upon and greatly speeded up. In this respect, strong centring and suburbanization forces are at work world-wide, resulting not only in primary and secondary densification processes, but also in different kinds of functional segregation. The only difference is that everything is taking place on a scale that dwarfs the historical models, as illustrated by such examples as Mexico City, Lagos and Manila on the one hand, and Brasilia, Islamabad and Songdo on the other. In modern reality, everything that is described using the generic term

Das dadurch ausgelöste Bevölkerungswachstum schuf nicht zuletzt ein Heer von jungen, "freigesetzten" Arbeitskräften, die ab dem späten 18. Jahrhundert in die expandierenden Städte der industriellen Revolution strebten.

Diese Entwicklung stellte das historische demographische Stadt-Land-Verhältnis auf den Kopf, denn um 1600 lebten noch etwa 80 % der Briten auf dem Land, um 1900 dagegen ca. 80 % in der Stadt. Der menschliche Zuwachs wurde sowohl durch verstärkte Belegung der urbanen Kerne als auch durch planerische Erweiterung und Gestaltung der Stadtränder (Arbeitersiedlungen, sozialer Wohnungsbau, Gartenkolonien usw.) untergebracht.

Dieser Prozess lief auf ähnliche Weise in allen klassischen Industrieländern ab, führte jedoch zu teilweise unerträglichen humanitären Verhältnissen, über deren Verbesserung Architektinnen, Ökonomen, Moralphilosophinnen und Politiker seit den 1870er Jahren und zunehmend nach dem Ende des Ersten Weltkriegs intensiv nachzudenken begannen. So entstand u.a. die Vision der "funktionalen Entflechtung" von Wohnen, Arbeiten und Erholen, die in der "Charta von Athen" prägnant festgehalten wurde. Letztere resultierte aus einer Kreuzfahrt im Mittelmeer im Sommer 1933, welche die avantgardistische Stadtplanervereinigung Congrès Internationaux d'Architecture Moderne (CIAM) durchführte und die von Le Corbusier's mächtiger Persönlichkeit dominiert wurde. Die überfüllten historischen Städte sollten nunmehr durch Siedlungen aus dem Baukasten ("Unités d'Habitations") ersetzt werden, welche linear oder auch konzentrisch ins Umland vorstießen.

Die Vorstellungen der Charta waren kühn, aber naiv und oft ohne "menschliches Maß". Dies zeigte sich, als in der Nachkriegszeit das zugrundeliegende Denken in zahlreichen Städten umgesetzt wurde, allerdings häufig in abgewandelter bzw. verzerrter Form. Dabei war in Europa ein spezielles Faktorenpaar von großer Bedeutung, nämlich erstens die großflächige Zerstörung alter Stadtviertel durch den Zweiten Weltkrieg und zweitens der Siegeszug des Automobils, insbesondere aufgrund der geostrategisch bedingten Verfügbarkeit von billigem Erdöl ab den 1950er Jahren. Gerade Nachkriegsdeutschland, wo nahezu alle Großstädte zu Schutt bombardiert waren, rezipierte die Visionen des "Modernismus" bereitwillig und entwickelte sie zur Fehlperspektive von der "autogerechten Stadt" fort. Ab 1960 kam es in den USA und der ganzen westlichen Welt zu einer starken Suburbanisierungsdynamik (Urban Sprawl), welche die funktionale Entflechtung unter gewaltigen Umweltkosten realisierte, allerdings weitgehend anders, als von den CIAM-Protagonisten erträumt. Die so hervorgebrachten Mischstrukturen aus gewachsenen, geplanten und wirtschaftlich opportunen Quartieren waren noch nicht vom Leitbild der Nachhaltigkeit beeinflusst oder gar geprägt.

In den letzten Dekaden des 20. Jahrhunderts und insbesondere nach dem Fall der Berliner Mauer erhielt jenes Leitbild in den hochentwickelten Industrieländern jedoch eine herausragende Bedeutung im öffentlichen Diskurs. Dadurch wurden nicht zuletzt problematische Aspekte der zeitgenössischen Gestaltung urbaner und ruraler Räume thematisiert, von der Landschaftszerstörung bis hin zur Beschleunigung des Klimawandels durch Treibhausgasemissionen aus Bausektor und Transportwesen. Zudem setzte sich bei Planerinnen, Architekten und Kulturwissenschaftlerinnen die Auffassung durch, dass für die Wiedergewinnung von Identität und Lebensqualität die räumliche Re-Integration der verschiedenen städtischen Leistungen (von der Unterbringung bis zur aktiven Beteiligung an politischen Gestaltungsprozessen) dringend geboten wären. Diese beiden, weitgehend parallelen Strömungen vereinigen sich heute in der allgemeinen Forderung nach erneuter Verdichtung und Begrenzung der Stadtareale.

Damit scheint die Charta von Athen verworfen, doch die Herausforderungen des Siedlungswesens im 21. Jahrhundert sind viel zu komplex, um endgültige städtebauliche Schlüsse zu ziehen. Da ist zunächst die sogenannte Globalisierung, also die Eroberung des ganzen Planeten durch ein hochgradig vernetztes, marktwirtschaftlich organisiertes Produktions-Konsumptions-System, das durch intensiven Einsatz fossiler Energieträger in Gang gehalten und weiter beschleunigt wird. Diese Entwicklung verläuft jedoch asynchron, wobei Länder wie China rasch zu den westlichen Industriestaaten aufschließen, während Länder in Zentralafrika sich gerade anschicken, das prämoderne Stadium zu verlassen. Entsprechend werden in manchen Regionen der Erde heute auch verschiedene Phasen der europäisch-amerikanischen Stadtgeschichte nachgestellt, wenngleich nur in Andeutungen und zumeist im Zeitraffer. Insofern sind weltweit sowohl starke Zentrierungs- als auch Suburbanisierungskräfte am Werk, so dass es ebenso zu primären und sekundären Verdichtungen als auch zu funktionalen Entmischungen unterschiedlicher Art kommt. Nur dass sich alles in Größenordnungen abspielt, welche die historischen Vorbilder in den Schatten stellen, wie die Beispiele Mexiko-Stadt, Lagos und Manila auf der einen Seite und die Exempel Brasilia, Islamabad und Songdo auf der anderen Seite illustrieren. Was alles mit dem Oberbegriff "Urbanisierung" bezeichnet wird, ist in moderner Wirklichkeit ein fragmentiertes, hektisches, zeitver-

'urbanization' is a fragmented, hectic, time-delayed pulsating of the global urban fabric – with a basic tendency towards expansion. For, overall, the world's population is still growing at a dramatic rate.

One can either helplessly take note of this development or try to exert a positive influence on it, even try to shape it. However, anyone who concentrates solely on 'densification' will fall short. To do a better job, it is necessary to understand 21st-century settlement dynamics in its entirety, while reducing its complexity to a level that can be analysed and developed into a strategy. This is precisely what the WBGU has set out to do in its flagship report. Accordingly, it introduces a three-level analysis which distinguishes between the fundamental *forces, forms* and *values* of the overall system..

Let us begin with the forms, meaning the large archetypal patterns of today's urban reality. The WBGU identifies the following as basic forms: (1) the *historically grown, 'mature' city,* (2) *publicly or privately planned urbanization (most of which today is rapidly expanding),* and (3) the *informal settlement,* whose variants range from precarious shelters for refugees to illegally built villas for oligarchs and nomenklatura. It goes without saying that there are countless nuances and transitions within these basic patterns; moreover, as a rule, the three archetypes – similar to the aggregate states of a substance – appear together within an urban municipality and mix to form heterogeneous structures. Luxury neighbourhoods and slums can often be found in immediate proximity, sometimes only separated by rough concrete walls.

But what are the forces that create the basic patterns and their mixtures? Among the many active factors, the WBGU identifies the great 'master builders of the city', namely (1) *time,* (2) *power* and (3) *need* as fundamental forces. Initially, this is a metaphorical way of describing urban complexity, but it does offer significant heuristic potential. Of course, each category of master builders can be broken down into various types – for example 'time' into maturing, decay, acceleration or rupture; 'power' into actor groups like the state, elites, investors, revolutionary innovators or civil-society networks; and 'need' into hunger, violence, overpopulation or displacement. When a settlement entity and its rural hinterland are evolving, redeveloping and declining, there are usually constellations of actors at work with alternating common and conflicting interests.

The cities of the past were the cradles of human culture, the forums of political discourse, the engines of scientific and economic progress, the venues of social integration. Can these achievements be repeated in the transitory 21st century with its tumultuous urbanization dynamics?

Again the WBGU concentrates on three qualities of human settlements which deserve and require special efforts, namely (1) *Eigenart* (a German word meaning 'character'), i.e. the unmistakeable individual manifestations of the physical and cultural living environments created by urban societies, (2) *inclusion,* i.e. enabling citizens to use and further develop their city as equals, and (3) *sustaining of the natural life-support systems,* i.e. forming and operating the urban substance in harmony with local, regional and global ecological guard rails. The WBGU regards these qualities as urban basic and target values which fit together to form a 'normative compass'.

setztes Pulsieren des globalen Stadtgefüges mit expansiver Grundtendenz. Denn insgesamt wächst die Weltbevölkerung immer noch dramatisch.

Man kann diese Entwicklung hilflos zur Kenntnis nehmen oder aber versuchen, sie positiv zu beeinflussen, ja, sie zu gestalten. Wer dabei allerdings allein auf "Verdichtung" setzt, wird zu kurz springen. Wer es besser machen will, muss die Siedlungsdynamik des 21. Jahrhunderts in ihrer Gesamtheit begreifen, ihre Komplexität jedoch auf ein analyse- und strategiefähiges Maß reduzieren. Eben dies hat sich der WBGU in seinem Hauptgutachten zum Ziel gesetzt. Dementsprechend führt der Beirat eine Drei-Ebenen-Betrachtung ein, die zwischen den fundamentalen Kräften, Formen *und* Werten *des Gesamtsystems unterscheidet.*

Beginnen wir mit den Formen, womit die großen archetypischen Muster der heutigen urbanen Realität gemeint sind. Der WBGU identifiziert als Grundform (1) die historisch gewachsene, sozusagen gereifte Stadt, *(2) die* öffentlich oder privat geplante, heute zumeist rasch expandierende Urbanisation *und (3) die* informelle Siedlung, *deren Varianten von prekären Behausungen für Flüchtlinge bis zu gesetzeswidrig errichteten Villen für Oligarchien und Nomenklatura reichen. Es versteht sich von selbst, dass es innerhalb dieser Grundmuster unzählige Abstufungen und Übergänge gibt; zudem treten die drei Archetypen – ähnlich wie Aggregatszustände einer Substanz – in der Regel gemeinsam innerhalb einer Stadtkommune auf und fügen sich zu heterogenen Gebilden. Oft finden sich Luxusquartiere und Slums in unmittelbarer Nachbarschaft, manchmal nur durch rohe Betonmauern voneinander getrennt.*

Doch was sind die Kräfte, welche die Grundmuster und ihre Mixturen hervorbringen? Unter den vielen Wirkfaktoren identifiziert der Beirat die großen "Baumeisterinnen der Stadt", nämlich (1) die Zeit, *(2) die* Macht *und (3) die* Not *als fundamentale Kräfte. Dies ist zunächst einmal ein metaphorischer Zugang zur urbanen Komplexität, der jedoch erhebliches heuristisches Potenzial besitzt. Natürlich lässt sich jede Baumeisterkategorie in diverse Typen zerlegen – etwa "die Zeit" in Reifung, Zerfall, Beschleunigung oder Ruptur, "die Macht" in Akteursgruppen wie Staat, Eliten, Investoren, revolutionäre Innovatoren oder zivilgesellschaftliche Netzwerke, "die Not" schließlich in Hunger, Gewalt, Überbevölkerung oder Vertreibung. Beim Werden, Umgestalten und Vergehen eines Siedlungsgebildes und seines ländlichen Rückraums sind zumeist Akteurskonstellationen mit abwechselnd gemeinsamen und widerstrebenden Interessen am Werk.*

Die Städte der Vergangenheit waren die Wiege der menschlichen Kultur, die Foren der politischen Diskurse, die Motoren des wissenschaftlichen und wirtschaftlichen Fortschritts, die Stätten der sozialen Integration. Können diese Leistungen auch im transitorischen 21. Jahrhundert mit seiner tumultartigen Urbanisierungsdynamik erbracht werden?

Wiederum konzentriert sich der Beirat auf drei Qualitäten des Siedlungswesens, die besondere Anstrengungen verdienen und erfordern, nämlich (1) die Eigenart, *also die unverwechselbaren individuellen Ausprägungen der von Stadtgesellschaften hervorgebrachten, physischen und kulturellen Lebensumwelten, (2) die* Teilhabe, *also die Ermöglichung der gleichberechtigten Nutzung und Fortentwicklung der Stadt durch ihre Bürgerinnen und (3) die* Erhaltung der natürlichen Lebensgrundlagen, *also Formung und Betrieb der urbanen Substanz im Einklang mit lokalen, regionalen und globalen ökologischen Leitplanken. Der WBGU sieht diese Qualitäten als urbane Grund- und Zielwerte an, welche sich zu einem "normativen Kompass" fügen.*

Damit ist der Drei-Ebenen-Ansatz umrissen, der das Gutachten strukturiert und die Basis für Systemanalysen und Interventionsoptionen darstellt. Anhand der Abbildung kann dies exemplifiziert werden: Macht und Not können zum Beispiel den massiven Aufbau von seelenlosen Planstädten vorantreiben, die möglicherweise ressourceneffizienter sind als historische Quartiere. Andererseits können in funktionalen,

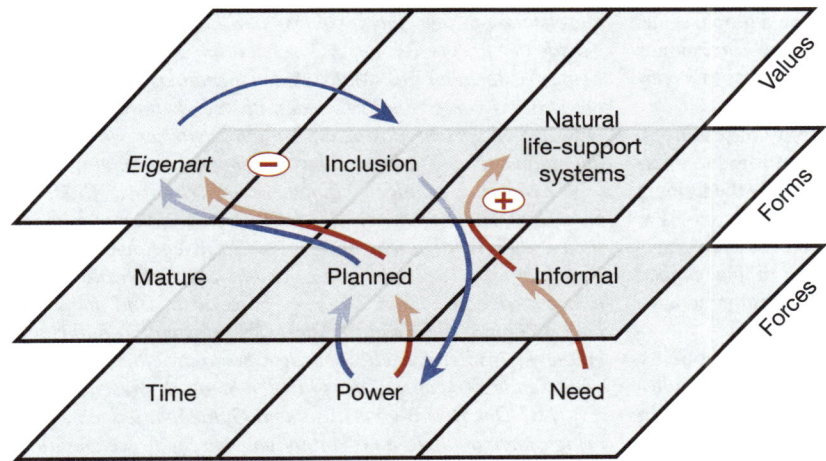

Chart of dominating global settlement patterns (forms), their drivers (forces) and their challenges regarding the "normative compass" of the WBGU (values). Source: WBGU

Schema dominierender globaler Siedlungsmuster (Formen), deren Treiber (Kräfte) und deren Herausforderungen in Bezug auf den "normativen Kompass" des WBGU (Werte). Quelle: WBGU

This is the outline of the three-level approach that structures the report and provides the basis for systems analyses and intervention options. This can be exemplified by the Figure. Power and need can, for example, expedite the massive construction of soulless, planned cities that are possibly more resource-efficient than historical city districts. On the other hand, a distinct sense of togetherness and uniqueness can rarely develop in functional, quickly built new cities that are designed on the drawing board. If, however, state control is weakened by external circumstances (such as the collapse of communism in central and eastern Europe after 1989), this can also open up opportunities for citizens to 'reconquer' the urban space, which strengthens the efficacy of civil society and with it the Eigenart of the respective city. The corresponding double causal network is characterized in the illustration by red/blue arrows and the +/- signs. The importance of feedback is also highlighted in this way. Proactive urban policy could use this systems perspective for orientation in order to recognize and implement effective measures for enhancing the desired qualities.

The WBGU's systems analysis also shows that there are no universal templates for the transformation towards sustainability in the highly diverse urban societies of, for example, Copenhagen, Mumbai, Kigali and Guangzhou. But, at the same time, predictable global systemic risks and regional problem centres – which should be of great importance, for example, for decision-makers in the field of international cooperation – can develop from the sum of local urbanization processes. Global settlement dynamics over the next three decades are therefore likely to influence the decision on whether critical planetary guard rails can be observed.

The poorer half of the soon-to-be 9-10 billion people on Earth are living in informal settlements, but also in mature cities, in developing countries and emerging economies, and their quality of life is massively impaired by local environmental degradation. Social exclusion and inequality, as well as the related local, national and transnational potential for instability, are on the increase in many urban formations and in very many societies. In the cities of Asia, and to a lesser extent in Africa, the approx. 2 billion people who will rise to the global middle classes by 2030/2040 will demand inclusion rights and could thus become engines of urban modernization. However, where these rights are not granted to them, there is a risk of political upheavals. [...]

The WBGU's preferred way of shaping people's settlement areas *progressively as well as consistently* can already be clearly seen in the 2007 'Leipzig Charter'. The Leipzig Charter is more than a negative response to the long-discredited Athens Charter – it formulates a bright, guiding concept for the renaissance of the European city in the spirit of integration. In essence, the postulates of the Charter – i.e. "the city must be attractive"; "get the people on board"; "good governance in the city"; "climate-change mitigation is also an urban task" – precisely target the WBGU's demands for Eigenart, inclusion and the sustaining of natural life-support systems. However, in the WBGU's opinion the Leipzig Charter does not go far enough in at least two respects:

First, the corresponding discussions concentrate on the European city, which is largely already the product of the above-mentioned, centuries-old dynamics and where informal settlements play a marginal role in every respect. However, the future of urban civilization – indeed our entire civilization – will be decided on the *global stage* and in particular in the societies of the developing countries and emerging economies, where the majority of people currently relocating are to be found. In this respect, the Leipzig Charter must be reformulated on a global scale. How can humanity find again a guiding concept of urbanity that also corresponds to the cultural diversity of city drafts, i.e. that does not feel euro-centric but nevertheless discreetly shows the achievements of occidental cities?

Second, planetary crises – such as global warming, the scarcity of resources, social disparity and displacement – demand much faster and more profound interventions by public and private decision-makers than those proposed by the Leipzig Charter. This is why *the transformation* of modernity in its existential crisis is at the top of the global agenda. And only if the most important urban centres can marshal the strength for this transformation can it succeed worldwide. In this respect, the Leipzig Charter should be updated into a social contract for the comprehensive renewal of the global settlement system.

[...] In its report, however, the WBGU goes further and almost implicitly brings a notion into play which could help overcome the contemporary contradictions of the urban discourse: this refers to the vision of *polycentric integration*. In order to be able to understand this vision, we must return to the opposing forces of urban formation that were discussed at the beginning.

am Reißbrett entworfenen und zügig erbauten Neustädten nur selten distinkte Wir-Gefühle und Eigenheiten entstehen. Wird jedoch der staatliche Durchgriff durch äußere Umstände geschwächt (wie beim Zusammenbruch des Spät-Kommunismus in Mittel- und Osteuropa nach 1989), dann ergeben sich auch Chancen für die "Rückeroberung" des urbanen Raums durch die Bürger. Dies stärkt die Wirkmacht der Zivilgesellschaft und damit die Eigenart der jeweiligen Stadt. Das entsprechende doppelte Kausalgeflecht ist in der Abbildung durch rote/blaue Pfeile sowie durch die Zeichen +/- charakterisiert. Auf diese Weise wird auch die Bedeutung von Rückkopplungen hervorgehoben. Proaktive Stadtpolitik könnte sich an dieser Systembetrachtung orientieren, um effektive Maßnahmen zur Verbesserung der gewünschten Qualitäten zu erkennen und zu implementieren.

Die WBGU-Systemanalyse zeigt auch, dass es keine universellen Schablonen für die Transformation zur Nachhaltigkeit in den höchst unterschiedlichen Stadtgesellschaften etwa von Kopenhagen, Mumbai, Kigali und Guangzhou gibt. Doch zugleich können aus der Summe lokaler Urbanisierungsprozesse vorhersehbar globale Systemrisiken und regionale Problemzentren entstehen, die etwa für Entscheidungsträger im Feld der internationalen Kooperation von großer Bedeutung sein sollten. So dürfte die weltweite Siedlungsdynamik in den kommenden drei Dekaden mit darüber entscheiden, ob kritische planetarische Leitplanken eingehalten werden können.

Die Lebensqualität jener ärmeren Hälfte der bald 9-10 Mrd. Menschen, die in informellen Siedlungen, aber auch in reifen Städten der Entwicklungs- und Schwellenländer lebt, wird durch lokale Umweltdegradierung massiv beeinträchtigt. Soziale Exklusion und Ungleichheit sowie damit verbundene lokale, nationale, aber auch transnationale Instabilitätspotenziale nehmen in vielen Stadtformationen und in sehr vielen Gesellschaften zu. In den Städten Asiens und in geringerem Maße auch Afrikas werden die gut 2 Mrd. Menschen, die bis 2030/2040 in die globalen Mittelschichten aufsteigen, Teilhaberechte einfordern und könnten so zu Motoren urbaner Modernisierung werden. Wo ihnen diese Rechte nicht zuerkannt werden, drohen jedoch politische Verwerfungen. [...]

Die vom WBGU favorisierte Art, den Siedlungsraum der Menschen im Fortschritt beständig zu gestalten, scheint bereits deutlich in der "Charta von Leipzig" aus dem Jahre 2007 auf. Die Leipzig-Charta ist mehr als ein negativer Reflex auf die längst diskreditierte Athen-Charta – sie formuliert ein helles Leitbild für die Renaissance der europäischen Stadt im Geiste der Integration. Im Kern zielen die Postulate der Charta, nämlich "Die Stadt muss schön sein"; "Bürger mitnehmen"; "Gutes Regieren in der Stadt"; "Klimaschutz ist auch städtische Aufgabe", genau auf die WBGU-Forderungen nach Eigenart, Teilhabe und Erhaltung der natürlichen Lebensgrundlagen. Allerdings geht die Leipzig-Charta aus Sicht des Beirats in mindestens zweierlei Hinsicht noch nicht weit genug:

Erstens konzentrieren sich die entsprechenden Überlegungen auf die europäische Stadt, die zumeist schon das Produkt der oben beschriebenen Dynamiken durch die Jahrhunderte ist und bei der informelle Siedlungen eine in jeder Hinsicht marginale Rolle spielen. Die Zukunft der urbanen und auch unserer ganzen Zivilisation wird jedoch auf dem globalen Schauplatz und insbesondere in den Gesellschaften der Entwicklungs- und Schwellenländer entschieden werden, wo gerade der größte Teil der Menschheit im Umzug begriffen ist. Insofern muss die Leipzig-Charta im Welt-Maßstab neu formuliert werden. Wie findet die Menschheit ein Leitbild von Urbanität wieder, das der kulturellen Diversität auch der Stadtentwürfe entspricht, das also nicht eurozentrisch wirkt und die Errungenschaften abendländischer Städte gleichwohl schonend zur Geltung bringt?

Zweitens verlangen planetarische Krisen wie Erderwärmung, Ressourcenknappheit, soziale Disparität und Vertreibung viel raschere und tiefere Interventionen durch öffentliche und private Entscheiderinnen als die Leipzig-Charta vorschlägt. Auf der globalen Agenda steht mithin die Transformation der in die Existenzkrise geratenen Moderne ganz oben. Und nur wenn die wichtigsten urbanen Zentren die Kraft für diese Transformation aufbringen, kann sie weltweit gelingen. Insofern ist die Leipzig-Charta zu einem Gesellschaftsvertrag für die umfassende Erneuerung des globalen Siedlungswesens fortzuschreiben.

[...] Der Beirat geht in seinem Gutachten jedoch noch darüber hinaus und bringt, eher implizit, eine Vorstellung ins Spiel, welche die zeitgenössischen Widersprüche des Stadtdiskurses überwinden helfen könnte: Gemeint ist die Vision von der polyzentrischen Integration. Um sie verstehen zu können, müssen wir zu den gegensätzlichen Kräften der Stadtformung zurückkehren, die eingangs angesprochen wurden:

Zweifellos sind Metropolen wie London, Shanghai oder Johannesburg heute mächtige Attraktoren, welche dem weiteren Hinterland Ressourcen entziehen, eine

There is no doubt that, today, metropolises like London, Shanghai or Johannesburg are powerful attractors that draw resources from the broad hinterland, generate a considerable rural exodus, and expand with a growing number of suburbs and satellite settlements. The periphery, or 'urban fringe', becomes the decisive growth zone, while the centres are more often than not economically 'segregated' – and demographically and culturally depleted as a result. It is evident that there are limits to this growth – humanitarian, structural and ecological. Otherwise it would be conceivable that by the end of the 21st century there might only be about a hundred 'super cities' remaining, embedded in the global wasteland of the devalued rural areas, competing with each other for capital, talent and luxury.

But this is neither desirable nor realistic. Strong forces – such as the rapid digitization of society and the substitution of fossil fuels by renewable energy – can in fact counteract the megatrend of continuous agglomeration. A city like Hong Kong, with its enormous collection of skyscrapers, comes close to being a caricature of the 'modernistic' ideal of urbanization. Yet this structure is only viable if it constantly sucks in oil and metals, food and fibres from all over the world, digests it all on the spot, and disposes of it as metabolic residues in the surrounding area. It is impossible to imagine a less sustainable urban perspective. However, electronic communications and renewable energy from the sun, wind, waves and biomass can and should bring space back into the urban equation.

In order not to fall into the trap of 'functional segregation' again, and to make it possible to implement the urban qualities Eigenart, inclusion, and sustaining of the natural life-support systems, the ever deepening urban-rural gap must be further reduced and space created for a comprehensive polycentric perspective. This means, in a sentence, the creation of numerous networked cores of all sizes, where the generic services of the city can be combined in critical density. The polycentric renaissance of the Ruhr area is probably the best example here, but there are also many other regions and districts where this leitmotif is already operating – e.g. Emilia Romagna in Italy, the San Francisco Bay Area in the USA, Randstad in the Netherlands, the Pearl River Delta (Guangzhou) in China or the metropolitan region of Lima and Callao in Peru.

[...] A more profound look into cultural history reveals that polycentric structures of settlement, the economy and governance have successfully advanced extraordinary creativity and productivity in some societies. Outstanding historical illustrations include Greek antiquity, which thrived in the Polis network and spanned the entire Mediterranean region and parts of the Orient, and the Renaissance, born in the cities of northern and central Italy, which pointed the way to modernity from the 14th century onwards. Also significant in this context was the multinuclear organization of the Holy Roman Empire of the German Nation before and especially after the Thirty Years War, where numerous small states and free cities became epicentres of progress. In an historic moment, when the ability of nation states to control and convince is on the wane, it might be useful to recall this 'post-Westphalian' perspective – where cities were the central places of human organization and quality of life.

Furthermore, an analysis of the present day puts the polycentric vision to a test that is related to specific crises of today. Also Germany, whose fateful 'shrinkage' and 'ageing' already seemed inevitable, has recently been directly confronted with the challenges arising from the growing influx of migrants from the Middle East and Africa. If we do not want to advocate the partitioning off of national territories in disregard of human rights (e.g. Article 16a(1) of the German constitution: 'Persons persecuted on political grounds shall have the right of asylum') and humanitarian principles, we must give serious consideration to sustainable concepts for receiving and integrating millions of refugees. Initial observations and analyses suggest that – whenever they have a choice – migrants try to settle mainly in and around major cities, a fact that applies both to the migrants' countries of origin (e.g. Syria or Ethiopia) and to the host countries (e.g. Germany or Sweden). However, there are many indications that a polycentric urban organization could significantly increase a society's capabilities to absorb and integrate refugees and job-seekers. This should not least be a priority research topic.

Excerpt of: WBGU – German Advisory Council of Global Change (2016): Humanity on the Move. Unlocking the Transformative Power of Cities. Summary. Berlin: WBGU.

Translated from German: Bob Calverhouse

---

betrāchtliche Landflucht erzeugen und sich mit einer wachsenden Zahl von Vororten und Satellitensiedlungen verbreitern. Die Peripherie, der sogenannte "Urban Fringe", wird dabei zur entscheidenden Wachstumszone, während die Zentren nicht selten ökonomisch "entmischt" und dadurch demographisch und kulturell ausgedünnt werden. Dass auch dieses Wachstum Grenzen hat – humanitärer, struktureller und ökologischer Art – ist offensichtlich. Ansonsten wäre es denkbar, dass am Ende des 21. Jahrhunderts lediglich eine Hundertschaft von "Super-Städten", eingebettet in die globale Brache des entwerteten ländlichen Raumes, miteinander um Kapital, Talent und Luxus konkurrierten.

Dies ist jedoch weder erstrebenswert noch realistisch: Dem Megatrend der fortwährenden Agglomeration können nämlich starke Kräfte entgegenwirken, wie zum Beispiel die rapide Digitalisierung der Gesellschaft und die Substitution von fossiler durch erneuerbare Energie. Eine Stadt wie Hongkong kommt dem "modernistischen" Wunschbild einer Urbanisation, die zu gewaltigen Hochhäusern aufgetürmt ist, karikaturhaft nahe. Dieses Gebilde ist aber nur lebensfähig, wenn es unablässig Erdöl und Metalle, Fasern und Lebensmittel aus der ganzen Welt aufsaugt, sie vor Ort verdaut und als metabolische Rückstände ins Umland entsorgt. Weniger nachhaltig kann eine urbane Perspektive nicht sein. Mit der elektronischen Kommunikation und den Energiequellen aus Sonne, Wind, Wellen und Biomasse kann und muss jedoch die Fläche wieder ins urbane Spiel zurückkehren.

Um dabei nicht wieder in die Falle der "funktionalen Entflechtung" zu tappen und die Verwirklichung der urbanen Qualitäten Eigenart und Teilhabe sowie die Erhaltung der natürlichen Lebensgrundlagen zu ermöglichen, muss das immer steiler werdende Stadt-Land-Gefälle wieder reduziert und Raum für eine umfassende polyzentrische Perspektive geschaffen werden. Letztere besagt, in einem Satz ausgedrückt, die Schaffung zahlreicher vernetzter Kerne aller Größenordnungen, wo die generischen Leistungen der Stadt in kritischer Dichte vereinigt werden können. Die polyzentrische Renaissance des Ruhrgebiets dürfte hier die Probe aufs Exempel sein, aber es gibt auch viele weitere Regionen und Distrikte, wie die Emilia Romagna in Italien, die San Francisco Bay Area in den USA, Randstad in den Niederlanden, das Perlflussdelta (Guangzhou) in China oder die Metropolregion Lima/Callao in Peru, wo besagtes Leitmotiv schon wirksam ist.

[...] Ein tieferer Blick in die Kulturgeschichte macht deutlich, dass polyzentrische Strukturen von Siedlung, Wirtschaft und Gouvernanz außerordentliche Kreativität und Produktivität von Gesellschaften befördern konnten. Als herausragende historische Illustrationen seien die im Polis-Verbund aufblühende griechische Antike genannt, die den gesamten Mittelmeerraum und Teile des Orients umspannte, sowie die in den ober- und mittelitalienischen Städten geborene Renaissance, welche ab dem 14. Jahrhundert der Moderne den Weg wies. Bedeutsam in diesem Zusammenhang ist auch die vielkernige Organisation des Heiligen Römischen Reiches Deutscher Nation vor und insbesondere nach dem Dreißigjährigen Krieg, wo zahlreiche Kleinstaaten und reichsfreie Städte zu Epizentren des Fortschritts wurden. In einem historischen Moment, da die Nationalstaaten an Steuerungs- und Überzeugungsfähigkeit nachlassen, sei diese "post-westfälische" Perspektive – mit den Städten als zentralen Orten menschlicher Organisation und Lebensqualität – in Erinnerung gebracht.

Der Blick auf die Gegenwart stellt die polyzentrische Vision zudem auf einen Prüfstand, der mit besonderen aktuellen Krisen zu tun hat: Auch Deutschland, dessen schicksalhafte "Schrumpfung" und "Überalterung" schon beschlossen schien, ist seit kurzem unmittelbar mit den Herausforderungen konfrontiert, die sich aus dem wachsenden Zustrom von Migranten aus dem Mittleren Osten und Afrika ergeben. Falls man nicht der nationalen Abschottung unter Missachtung von Menschenrechten (etwa Art. 16a Abs. 1 GG: "Politisch Verfolgte genießen Asylrecht") und der Humanität das Wort reden will, muss man ernsthaft über nachhaltige Konzepte zur Aufnahme und Integration von Millionen von Flüchtlingen nachsinnen. Erste Beobachtungen und Analysen deuten darauf hin, dass sich die Migrantinnen – falls sie überhaupt eine Wahl haben – vorwiegend im Umfeld von größeren Städten anzusiedeln versuchen. Dies gilt übrigens sowohl für die Ursprungsländer der Migration (wie Syrien oder Äthiopien) als auch für die Aufnahmeländer (wie Deutschland oder Schweden). Vieles spricht jedoch dafür, dass die polyzentrische Organisation des Urbanen die Fähigkeiten einer Gesellschaft zur Absorption und Integration von Flüchtlingen und Arbeitssuchenden deutlich erhöhen könnte. Dies sollte nicht zuletzt ein Forschungsthema ersten Ranges werden.

Auszug aus: WBGU – Wissenschaftlicher Beirat der Bundesregierung Globale Umweltveränderungen (2016): Der Umzug der Menschheit: Die transformative Kraft der Städte. Zusammenfassung. Berlin: WBGU.

I. LOCAL EFFECTS

The situation in cities, above all those in the developing and emerging nations, is characterised by the intertwining of economies on a global scale, by the export of capital to low-wage nations, by the exploitation of raw materials, extractive agriculture and land grabbing on the one hand and the export of goods, monopolies and the linking of export policies and development aid on the other. Job distribution, working conditions, immigration or shrinkage, pollution and environmental destruction are local effects of global economic activity that cannot be managed solely on a local level.

OF GLOBALISATION

Die Situation in den Städten, vor allem in den Städten der Entwicklungs- und Schwellenländer wird durch die Verflechtung der Wirtschaft im globalen Maßstab, durch Kapitalexport in Billiglohnländer, durch Ausbeutung von Rohstoffen, extraktive Landwirtschaft und Landgrabbing auf der einen Seite, durch Warenexport, Monopole und die Kopplung von Exportpolitik und Entwicklungshilfe auf der anderen Seite geprägt. Die Verteilung von Arbeitsplätzen, Arbeitsbedingungen, Zuwanderung bzw. Schrumpfung, Schadstoffbelastungen und Umweltzerstörungen sind lokale Effekte globalen Wirtschaftens, die allein auf lokaler Ebene nicht zu steuern sind.

THE KINGS GIANTS

Sarah Ann Sutter, Wolfgang Gruber, Carolin Lahode, Ina Nikolova

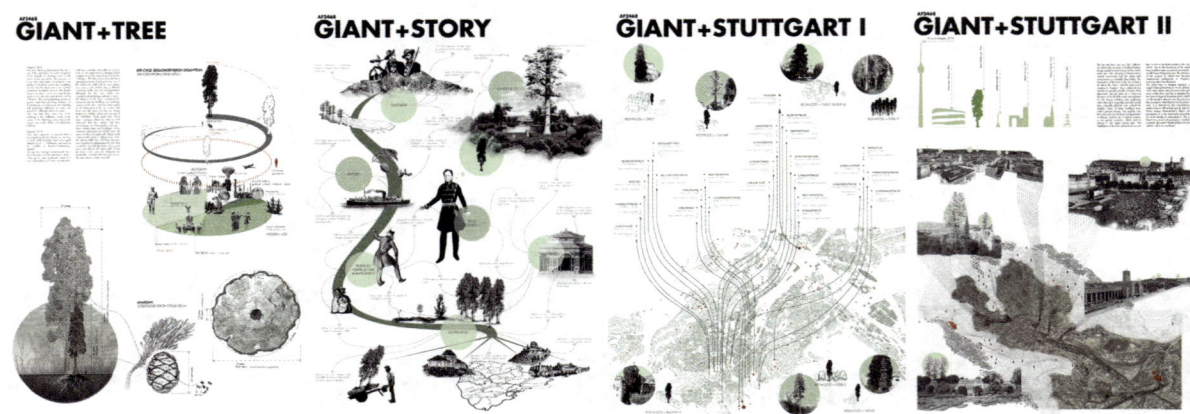

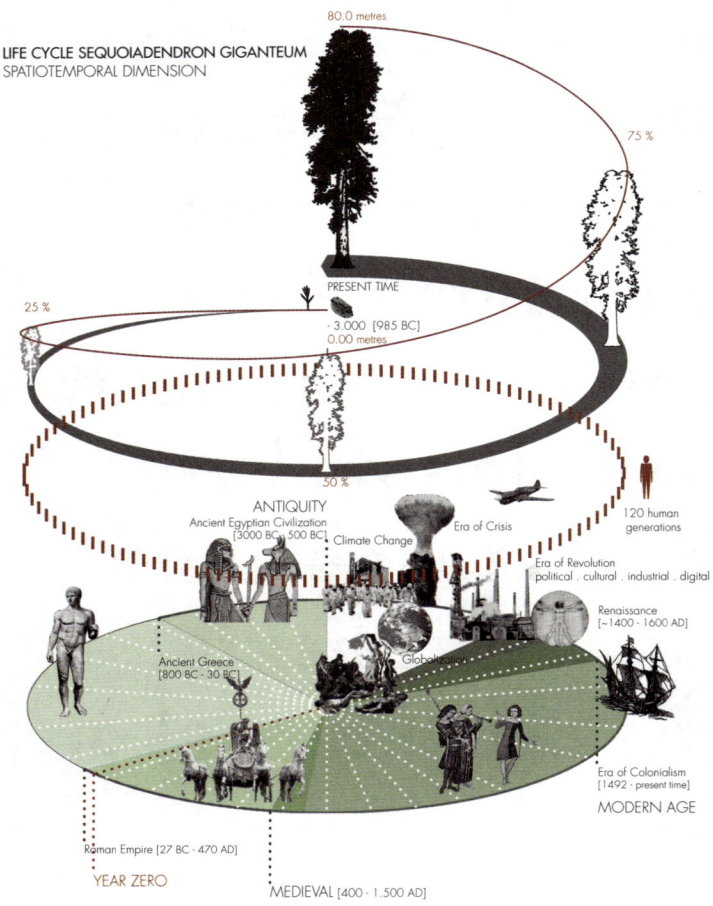

Stuttgart 1863

Ever since King Wilhelm I. heard of the discovery of the giant trees, he dreamt of planting some of the Giants in his own parks. He instructed the royal building and gardening authorities to order one pound of Californian redwood seeds and already one year later there were over 5000 seedlings breeding in the Wilhelma, which, in the course of the following years, were spread across the whole of Baden-Württemberg.

Stuttgart 2015

To date scientists were able to count a total of 120 giant trees in Stuttgart which originate from the seeds acquired for the Wilhelma – today, all of them are natural monuments. Every tree is connected differently to the city, and each city treats each tree in a different way. Sometimes the buildings maintain a respectful distance to the trees; sometimes the redwoods and the buildings stand extremely close to each other. At times a tree stands at an intersection in the city center. Some redwoods are being treated as exhibits. These mute colossuses are fixed points in the city – more definite than most buildings.

Some American redwoods are 3000 years old and more than 80 meters tall. How will urban development address this phenomenon or what would the city look like today if the giant trees were already 80 meters tall? Would the trees, in this case, be Stuttgart's true landmarks, instead of the television tower, the main station, or the city hall?

Not all of the trees were planted by the King's building and gardening authorities, because authorities mistakenly ordered a greater amount of seeds than originally planned. Many of these seedlings were sold to private buyers. This explains why the redwoods can be found at representative places, such as city or church squares, or on private property, which used to belong to the upper social class. The initiators of the project in 1864 thus helped to shape the city and became unintentional participants in ongoing urban development.

The giant trees of Stuttgart represent a unique urban phenomenon. Apart from the fact, that the import of giant trees can be understood as an event of migration, it is the exceptions which lend a city its particularity in our globalised world, where cities become more and more alike. It is defined by the extraordinary stories it has to tell and its specific places. These unique characteristics shape our perception of a city and make it possible for us to identify it, understand it, like it, hate it, to perceive it as random, or clearly structured. Or simply to make it our "home".

•

Stuttgart 1863

Seit König Wilhelm I. von der Entdeckung der Riesenbäume in Nordamerika erfuhr, träumte er davon, die Giganten auch in seinen Gärten anzupflanzen. Er beauftragte die königliche Bau- und Gartendirektion, ein Pfund Samen des kalifornischen Mammutbaumes zu bestellen, und ein Jahr später konnten bereits 5000 Jungpflanzen der sogenann-

The giant sequoia's global footprint, traced through the centuries.

Der über die Jahrhunderte nachgezeichnete globale Fußabdruck des Mammutbaums.

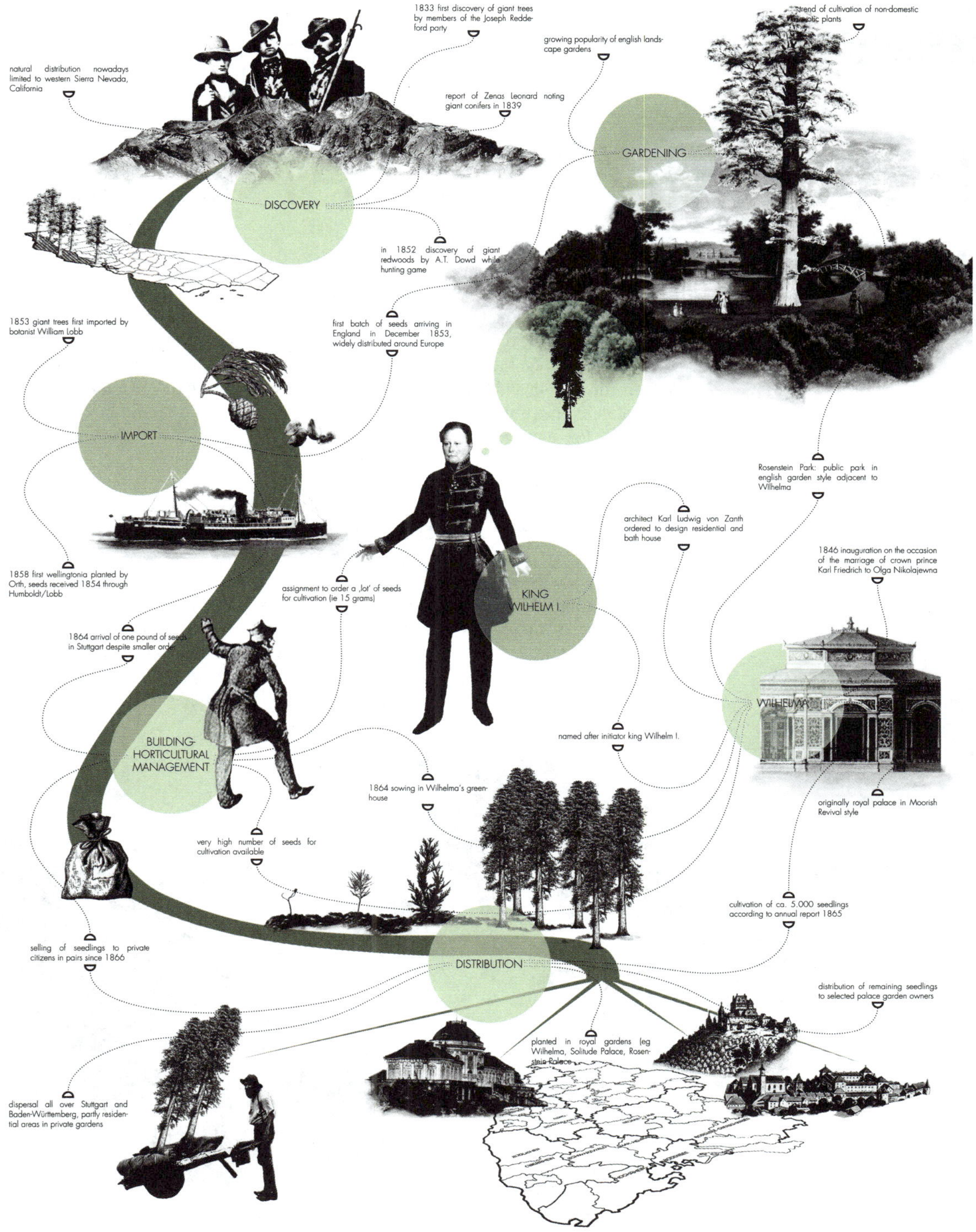

natural distribution nowadays limited to western Sierra Nevada, California

1833 first discovery of giant trees by members of the Joseph Reddeford party

growing popularity of english landscape gardens

trend of cultivation of non-domestic exotic plants

report of Zenas Leonard noting giant conifers in 1839

GARDENING

DISCOVERY

in 1852 discovery of giant redwoods by A.T. Dowd while hunting game

1853 giant trees first imported by botanist William Lobb

first batch of seeds arriving in England in December 1853, widely distributed around Europe

IMPORT

Rosenstein Park: public park in english garden style adjacent to Wilhelma

architect Karl Ludwig von Zanth ordered to design residential and bath house

1846 inauguration on the occasion of the marriage of crown prince Karl Friedrich to Olga Nikolajewna

1858 first wellingtonia planted by Orth, seeds received 1854 through Humboldt/Lobb

assignment to order a ,lot' of seeds for cultivation (ie 15 grams)

KING WILHELM I.

1864 arrival of one pound of seeds in Stuttgart despite smaller order

named after initiator king Wilhelm I.

WILHELMA

originally royal palace in Moorish Revival style

BUILDING-HORTICULTURAL MANAGEMENT

1864 sowing in Wilhelma's green-house

very high number of seeds for cultivation available

cultivation of ca. 5.000 seedlings according to annual report 1865

distribution of remaining seedlings to selected palace garden owners

selling of seedlings to private citizens in pairs since 1866

DISTRIBUTION

planted in royal gardens (eg Wilhelma, Solitude Palace, Rosen-stein-Palace)

dispersal all over Stuttgart and Baden-Württemberg, partly residen-tial areas in private gardens

---

ten Wilhelma-Saat gezüchtet werden, die in den darauffolgenden Jahren in ganz Baden-Württemberg verteilt wurden.

Stuttgart 2015

Bis dato wurden insgesamt 120 Mammutbäume der Wilhelma-Saat in Stuttgart erfasst – heute alle Naturdenkmäler. Jeder Baum ist anders mit der Stadt vernetzt, und die Stadt geht anders mit jedem Baum um. Mal hält die Bebauung ehrerbietig Abstand, mal stehen Bäume und Häuser eng beieinander. Oder der Baum steht an einer Kreuzung mitten in der Stadt. Manche Bäume werden wie Exponate behandelt. Die stummen Riesen sind Fixpunkte der Stadt – mehr noch als manche Bauten.

Einige der Mammutbäume in Amerika sind heute über 3000 Jahre alt und über 80 m hoch. Wie wird die Entwicklung der Stadt mit diesem Phänomen umgehen oder wie würde die Stadt heutzutage aussehen, wenn die Mammutbäume bereits 80 m hoch wären? Wären die Bäume dann die wahren Landmarken Stuttgarts und nicht der Fernsehturm, der Hauptbahnhof oder das Rathaus?

Nicht alle Bäume wurden von der königlichen Bau- und Gartendirektion angepflanzt – da eine größere Menge an Samen bestellt wurde als geplant, wurden viele Jungpflanzen privat weiterverkauft. Dementsprechend stehen die Mammutbäume entweder an repräsentativen öffentlichen Orten oder auf damaligen Privatgrundstücken der gehobenen Gesellschaftsschicht. Durch ihre punktuellen Eingriffe wurden die Akteure aus dem Jahr 1864 ungewollt zu Teilnehmern an der Stadtentwicklung.

Bei den Stuttgarter Mammutbäumen handelt es sich um ein einmaliges städtebauliches Phänomen. Abgesehen davon, dass das Importieren von Mammutbäumen als ein Migrationsereignis verstanden werden kann, bleibt in unserer globalisierten Welt, in der sich die Großstädte immer mehr ähneln, ihre Einzigartigkeit erhalten. Es sind die außerordentlichen Geschichten, die eine Stadt erzählt, ihre besonderen Orte, die ihren Charakter festigen. Das prägt unsere Wahrnehmung einer Stadt, ermöglicht es uns, uns mit ihr zu identifizieren, sie zu verstehen, zu mögen, zu hassen, als chaotisch oder übersichtlich zu empfinden. Oder schlicht sie zu unserer "Heimat" zu machen.

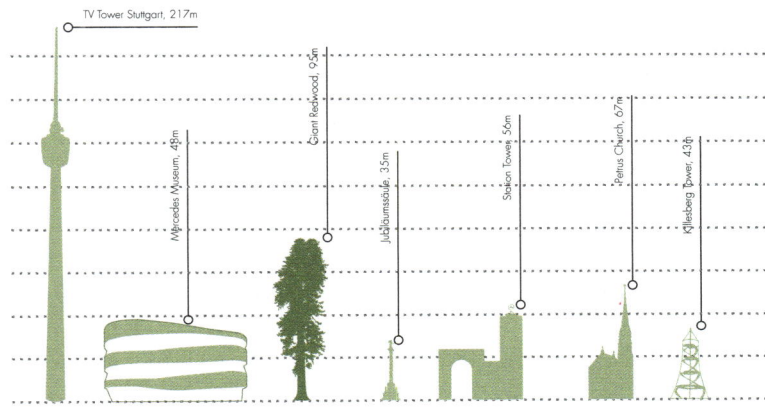

TV Tower Stuttgart, 217m

Mercedes Museum, 48m

Giant Redwood, 95m

Jubiläumssäule, 35m

Station Tower, 56m

Petrus Church, 67m

Killesberg Tower, 43m

THE PROMISED LAND Ira Leifried, Louisa Höppner

Palm oil is mainly used to manufacture food products, cosmetics, soaps, fuel for cars or power plants. Rising demand since the 1970s has led to dramatic growth and to cultivation on large-scale monocultural plantations.

Production and circulation of products is no longer limited to a region or country, but integrated in a complex global process, partly showing grotesque features; e.g. when a country like Malaysia is only using a fraction of the produced oil for its own purposes, while half of all supermarket products imported by Malaysia are enriched with palm oil.

The project aims at raising awareness of environmental degradation due to palm oil production in tropical rain forests against the background of worldwide palm oil consumption through supermarket products and responsibility of consumers.

•

Palmöl wird hauptsächlich für Lebensmittel, Kosmetikprodukte, Seifen, Kraftstoffe für den motorisierten Verkehr und in Biogasanlagen eingesetzt. Die steigende Nachfrage seit den 1970er Jahren hat zu einem dramatischen Wachstum und dem Anbau auf großflächigen monokulturellen Plantagen geführt.

Produktion und Vertrieb der Produkte beschränken sich nicht mehr auf ein Land oder eine Region, sondern sind in einen komplexen globalen Prozess integriert, der teilweise groteske Züge aufweist, wenn z.B. ein Land wie Malaysia nur einen Bruchteil des produzierten Öls selbst verbraucht, während die Hälfte aller Supermarktprodukte, die Malaysia importiert, mit Palmöl angereichert sind.

Anliegen des Projekts ist es, auf die Umweltzerstörung durch die Palmölproduktion in tropischen Regenwäldern vor dem Hintergrund des weltweiten Palmölkonsums in Supermarktprodukten und die Verantwortung der Konsumenten aufmerksam zu machen.

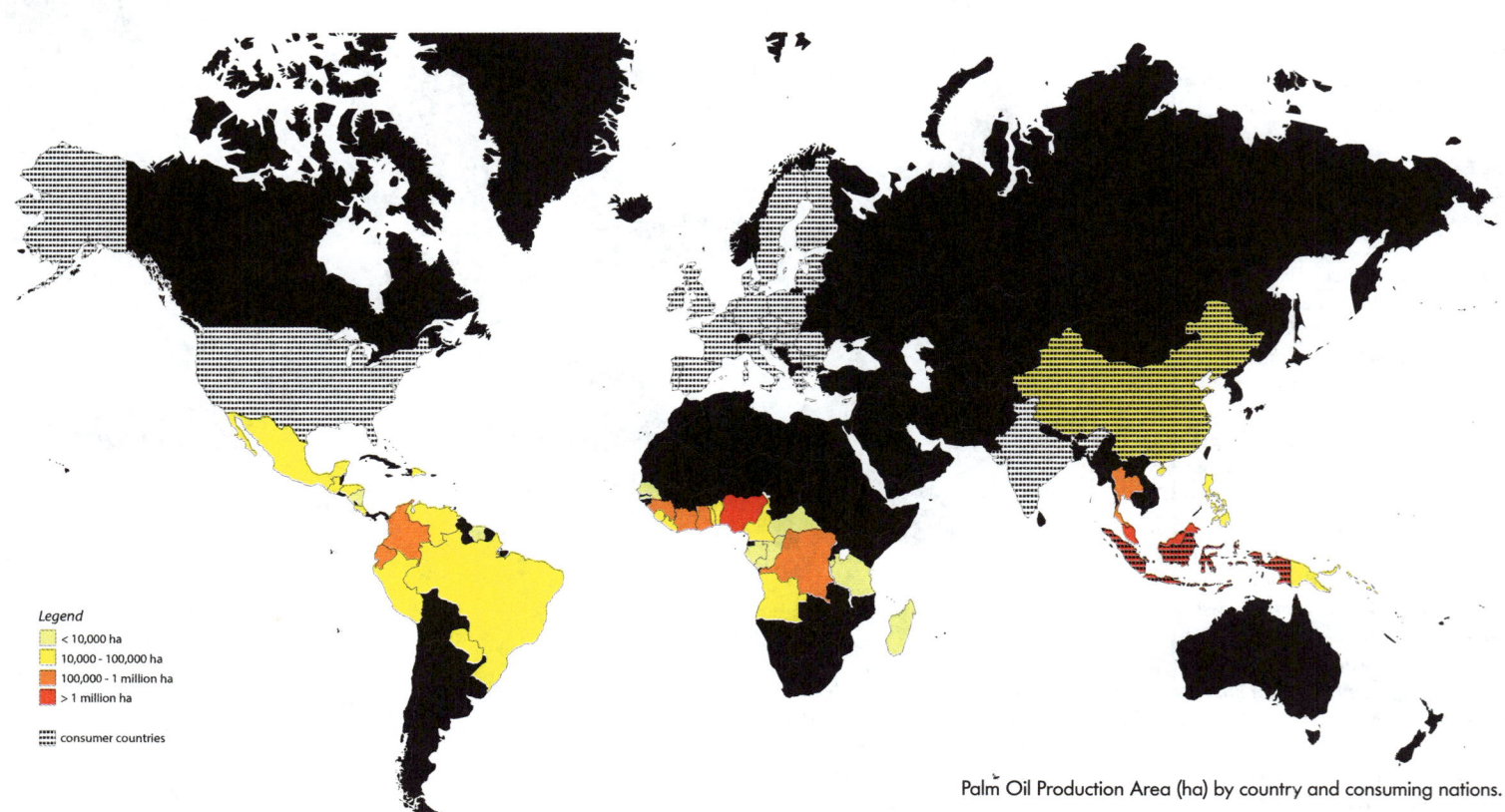

Legend

▨	< 10,000 ha
▨	10,000 - 100,000 ha
▨	100,000 - 1 million ha
▨	> 1 million ha
▦	consumer countries

Palm Oil Production Area (ha) by country and consuming nations.

Palm Oil & Production worldwide

In June 2015, french ecology minister Segolène Royal said in an interview with the french television that people should stop eating a famous hazelnut-chocolate spread because the harvest of one of its ingredients leads to deforestation of tropical rainforests. Segolène Royals foreay refers to palm oil, one of the main ingredients in about half of all packaged foods.

Nowadays palm oil is contained in thousand of everyday products. More than 90 percent of the produced oil is used to manufacture food products, cosmetics, soaps, fuel for cars or power plants.

Palm oil is a type of vegetable oil and can be derived from the palm fruit. Oil palms can only be cultivated in the tropics and there have been produced around 54 million tonnes of palm oil in 2011.

Rising demand for vegetable oils since the 1970s has led to a cultivation shift on to large-scale plantations which has stimulated dramatic area growth in the last decade. Globally, oil palm area increased by 43% from approximately 6 million ha in 1990 to 10.2 million ha in 2002.

Today 85% of the worldwide palmoil is produced in Malaysia and Indonesia. With around 31 million tonnes Indonesia is the number one ranked country in palm oil production with more than 9 million hectares of cultivation areas [Fig.01]. 26 million hectares are projected for Indonesia for 2025.

Palm oil plantations worldwide take up more than 16.4 million hectares which is nearly half the area of Germany (around 35,7 million ha). Other producer countries include Brazil, Columbia, Ecuador, Nigeria, the Ivory Coast, Honduras, and Papua New Guinea [Fig.02] which hope to increase their market share in the upcoming years.

India, China, Indonesia and Europe are the main consumers of palm oil. It is estimated that the average EU citizen consumes up to 60.0 kg of palm oil per year. [Fig.03]

Most companies disguise labelling their products as containing palm oil and instead refer to it as „vegetable oil and fat" and it has only been since the beginning of 2015 that german law requires to explicitly label palm oil in the product ingredient list.

One way for consumers to protect the rainforests would be to avoid palm oil and to buy palm oil free products.

New York, USA
$2bn

Miami, USA
$2,5bn

New Orleans, USA
$1,8bn

Guayaquil, Ecuador
$3,1bn

Tianjin, China
$2,2bn

Guangzhou, China
$13,2bn

Shenzhen, China
$3,1bn

Ho Chi Minh City, Vietnam
$1,9bn

Mumbai, India
$6,4bn

Kolkata, India
$3,3bn

Cities with the 10 highest annual flood costs ($) by 2050.

Palm Oil & Climate Change

Current forest conversion by plantation companies contributes to climate change. Tropical peatland forests store more carbon per unit than any other ecosystem in the world. Therefore we must transform the palm oil industry in order to stop this development.

Climate change and global warming may affect especially coastal settlements during the next 30 years, which are particularly vulnerable to impacts of climate change, such as sea level rise and extreme storms.

The visualistion [Fig.11] shows which cities in the world will have to deal with a projected increase in flood costs by 2050. Countries as China, India and the United States will have to invest more than 2 billion dollar on average for each big coastal city in order to protect their citizens from flooding and climate change impacts.

Producing palm oil without causing further deforestation or peatland destruction is possible if steps towards a responsible production are taken. The demand for palm oil is huge and rising, therefore the only way to maintain economic performance while halting the damage to the environment and farming communities is a sustainable agriculture.

Plantation developers could improve yields and plant on degraded land. It has been shown that by improving yields (through strategies such as tree breeding and better management practices) and expanding only onto land with low carbon storage, worldwide demand for palm oil could be met until 2020 without destroying further forests or peatlands. The governements could formulate biodiesel policies which explicitly regulate the amount and the sources of vegetable oils in biofuels.

Moreover the palm oil related businesses will have to ensure that non of their raw materials contribute to tropical dforestation or destruction of peatland swamps.

But still the strongest possibility to change something lies in consumers hands: businesses normally pay attention to the individuals' purchases and their feedback on products. In order to protect their brand and the image of the company they are willing to change the companies policies based on critique by consumers. If consumers exerted their influence and bought and supported those companies, which are already working with palm oil from sustainable sources, there is a good chance that oil palms will only be planted in a sustainable manner in a few years.

improving yields

better management practices

environmental laws

biofuel policies

consumer power

[Fig.12] Solutions and proposals towards a sustainable production

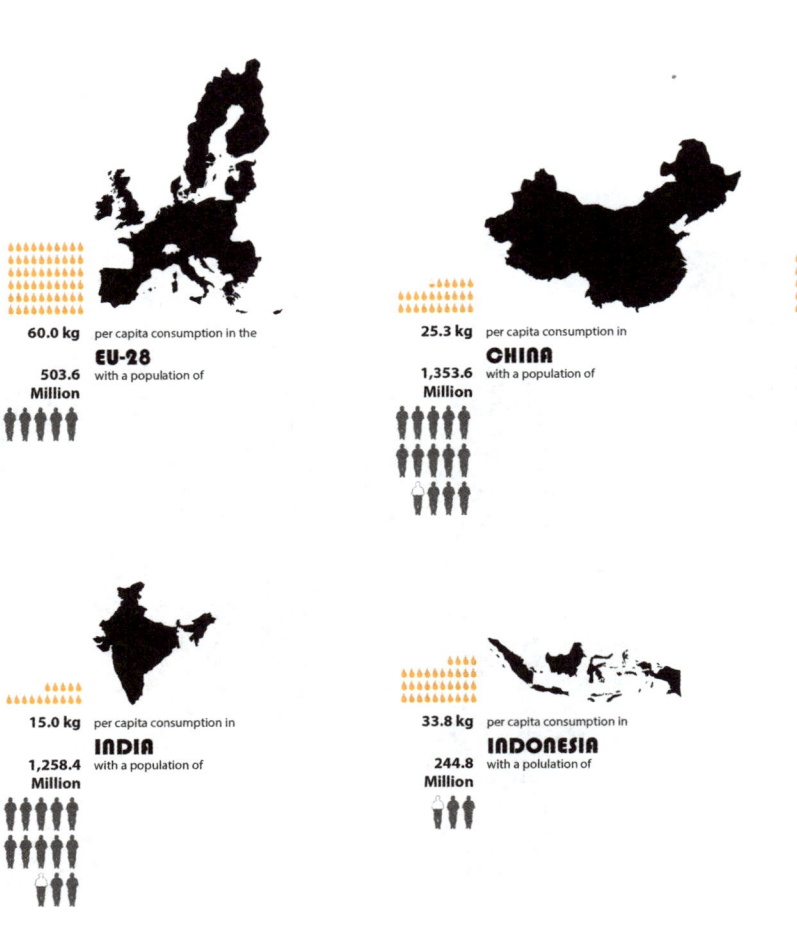

60.0 kg per capita consumption in the
EU-28
503.6 Million with a population of

25.3 kg per capita consumption in
CHINA
1,353.6 Million with a population of

55.3 kg per capita consumption in the
USA
315.8 Million with a population of

15.0 kg per capita consumption in
INDIA
1,258.4 Million with a population of

33.8 kg per capita consumption in
INDONESIA
244.8 Million with a polulation of

Legend:
1.0 kg per capita consumption in
COUNTRY
100.00 Million with a population of

DEM GOO

SUPERMARKET

TRANSPORT

MANUFACTURE OF FOOD PRODUCTS, COSEMETICS, DETERGENTS & CANDLES

CHEMICAL PROCESSING

[Fig. 03] per capita consumption (palmoil) in chosen countries

Palm Oil & Tropical Deforestation

The palm oil industry is linked to major issues such as deforestation, habitat degradation, climate change, indigenius right abuses and animal cruelty. In some regions, oil palm cultivation has caused deforestation of tropical rainforests and peatlands. This means that land, which has once been covered by primary forest (forest that has never been touched by man) was cleared in order to cultivated with oil palm plantations.
With an expected groth of the world population up to 9 billion people by the year 2060 there will also be an increasing demand of energy and food which will result in a rising demand for vegetable oils like palm oil.[Fig.04]

Because of its high yields (amount of oil produced per hectare per year) in comparison with other vegetable oils and its relatively low labor costs it is the least expensive oil on the market today. [Fig.05] Replacing palm oil by other vegetable oils would mean that much larger amounts of land would need to be used since palm trees produce 4-10 times more oil than other crops per unit. But this development has it's price: Malaysia has the world's highest rate of forest loss between 2000 and 2012. [Fig.06]] (Indonesia ranked 3rd in forest loss) When the tropical forests and peatlands as storage of carbon dioxide (CO_2) get lost, carbon is released into the atmosphere, which drives global warming.

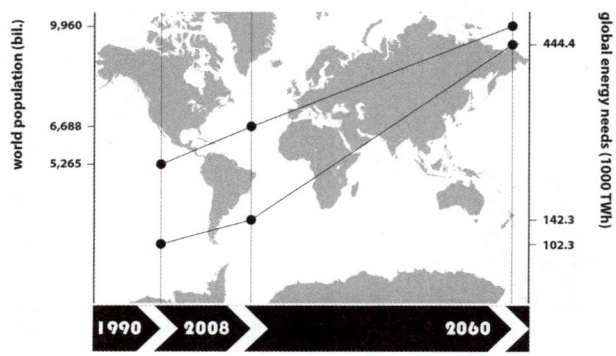

[Fig.04] development and proposed world population and global energy needs by 2060

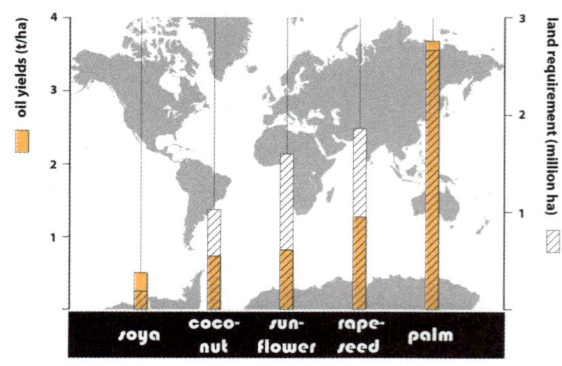

[Fig.05] oil yields and land requirements

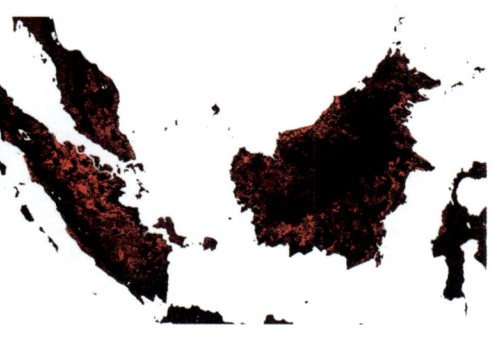

[Fig.06] deforestation (red) in Indonesia and Malaysia from 2000-2013

ca. 1500

ca. 300

ca. 7300

ca. 400

- 17%

critically endangered species and loss of biodiversity

food conflicts

methan and carbon dioxide emissions

fuel consumption

use of pesticides

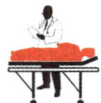

diseases

water pollution

land conflicts

land clearing without permits and displacement of indigenous people

[Fig.07] negative impacts caused by palm oil plantations

RAIN FOREST AND PEATLANDS

TROPICAL DEFORESTATION

PALM PLANTATIONS

PALM OIL MILLS

[Fig.10] palm oil supply chain

Palm Oil & Social Impacts

Moreover the clearing of tropical rainforests leads to various environmental and social problems:

The rapid expansion of oil palm plantations in Indonesia and Malaysia continues to lead to hundreds of disputes and conflicts over land and between communities and companies or local government. The sumatran orangutan, tiger, rhino and the pygmy elephants are facing their extinction within a few years due to habitat loss and are ranked as critically endangered. Other problems are an increase of human- wildlife conflicts, as populations of wild animals are squeezed into smaller fragments of natural habitat, reduced biodiversity in plantations or harvesting of endangered animal species for food or pet trade. Impacts also include soil erosion (because of drainage and fires) and increase a flooding risk and salt water intrusion, which will cause problems in the future. The oil palm monocultures require the use of pesticides which enter the water bodies as chemical run off (pollution) and can harm aquatic biodiversity. People exposed to a high level of pollution (caused by the oil palm plantations) suffer from diseases in asthma, bronchitis and other respiratory illnesses. [Fig.07] Furthermore transnational corporations and large landowners establish larger and larger landholdings st the expense of small farmers.

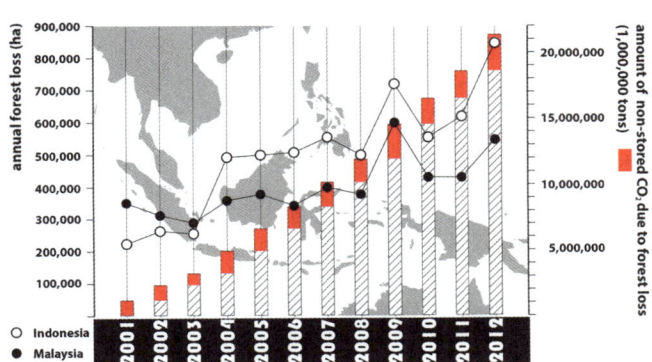

[Fig.08] annual forest loss and amount of non-stored CO$_2$ due to forest loss

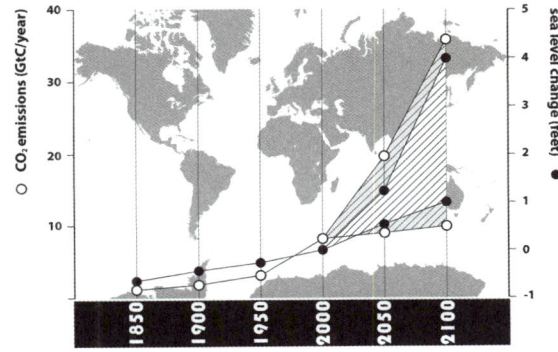

[Fig.09] CO$_2$ emissions and expected sea level change

NEW TRIBAL TERRITORIES Elizabeth Yarina

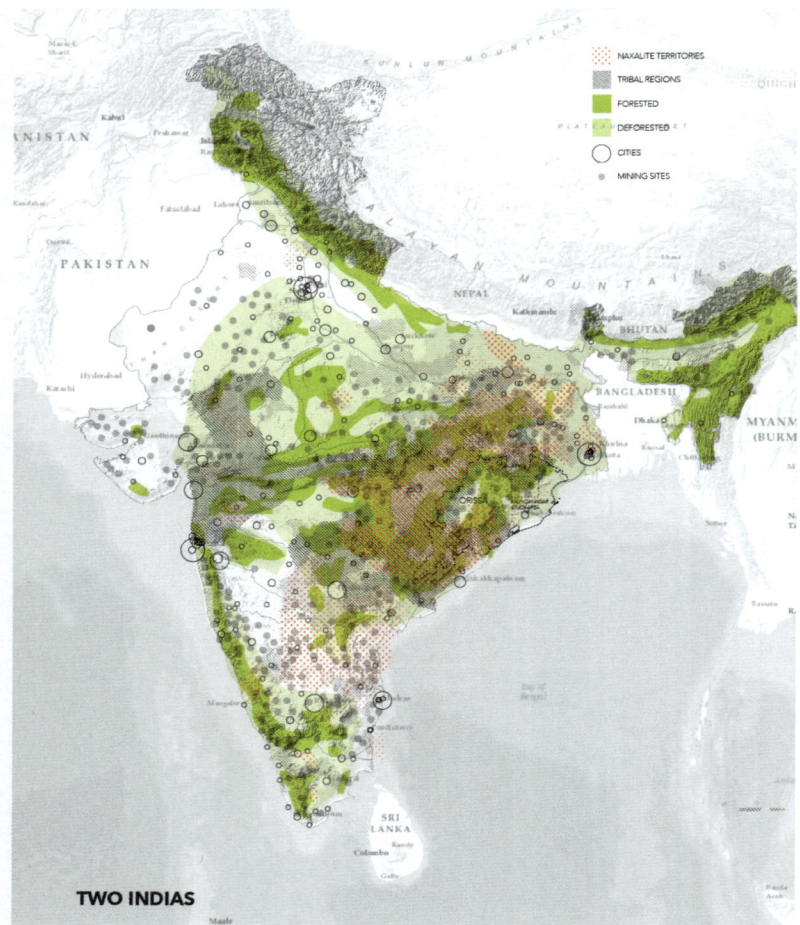

TWO INDIAS

The cartography shows tribal territories (orange) and areas of deforestation (green) in India.

Modernisation processes come along with the often illusive hope for improved living standards and participation in the global community. But for indigenous people (Adivasi) in the Indian federal state of Odisha, who today make up about 23% of the population, it comes at a steep cost.[1]

The 1865 "Colonial Forest Act", which seized any land covered with trees to serve the needs of the colonial elite, marked the beginning of a long history of displacements of Adivasi from their tribal territories. Adivasi were no longer permitted to collect forest produce, farm forest land, or hunt forest game. Thus they were robbed of their traditional livelihood, based on shifting agriculture, hunting and gathering, and resource consumption through marking specific forest stands or species as sacred.[2] Since 1947, the year of the Indian independence act, the governmental territorial administration granted land tenure to established agricultural villages only, while the semi-nomadic Adivasi remained nearly entirely landless.

Today, Odisha is a trading hub for the resource-rich hinterland[3] and the rapidly urbanising Indian cities. This leads to the promotion of land as a production and extraction site for international investors[4], with dozens of industrial projects realised within special economic zones and by legislated development incentives. Deforestation and the creation of mines, factories, large-scale dams and reservoirs destroy agricultural surfaces and living space, and push indigenous people into precarious wage labour in urban areas. The militant uprisings of the Naxalites, a Maoist anti-industrial movement, and the proliferation of anti-industrialisation protests in Odisha[5], reflect this imbalance between local and global interests.

The project conceives of alternative modes of modernisation that create a dialogue between local and global economies and ways of life. Through deforestation and increased agricultural productivity, Adivasi are to take back control over their territories. The combination of industrial production as well as agriculture and craftsmanship in tune with local circumstances provides livelihoods for industrial workers and Adivasi. Within the framework of such "hybrid economies" the landscape, shaped by industrial activities, is re-forested and converted to yield larger crops, mediate toxicity of industrial activities and accommodate growing (migratory) populations. Housing, development of settlements, and forest product industries become a part of the forest.

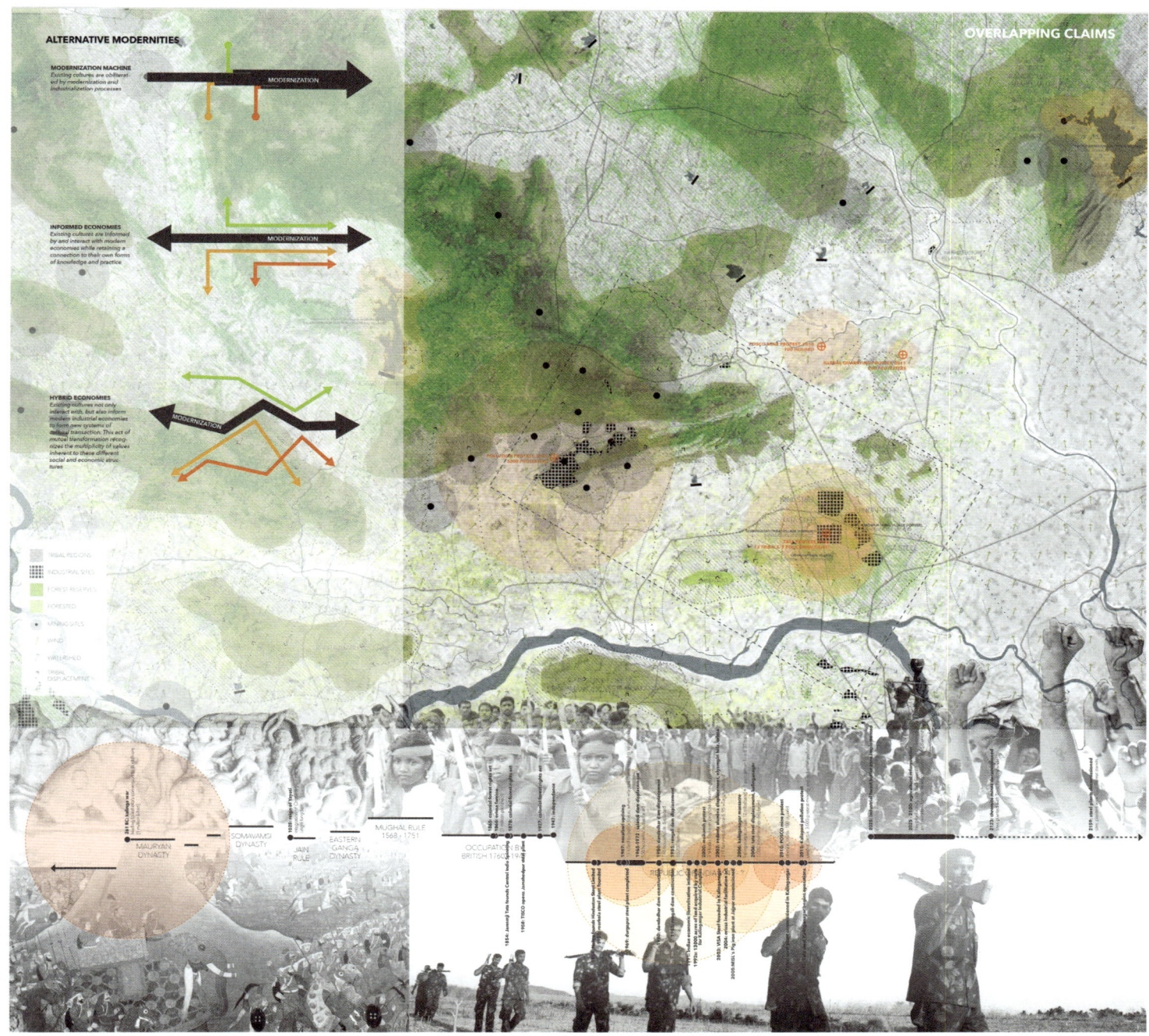

Modernisation has led to overlapping claims on Adivasi land, armed conflict and obliteration of Adivasi culture. An alternative mode of modernisation is to be formulated.

Der Modernisierungsprozess geht einher mit der häufig trügerischen Hoffnung auf gehobene Lebensstandards und Teilhabe an der Weltgemeinschaft. Von den indigenen Einwohnern (Adivasi) des indischen Bundestaats Odisha, die heute ca. 23 % der Bevölkerung ausmachen, forderte er einen hohen Preis.[1]

Der "Colonial Forest Act" von 1865, der alle bewaldeten Areale Indiens den britischen Kolonialherren unterstellte, markierte den Anfang einer langen Geschichte von Vertreibungen der Adivasi aus ihren Stammesgebieten. Den Adivasi wurde es untersagt, Waldland zu bewirtschaften, Waldtiere zu jagen oder Waldfrüchte zu sammeln. Dadurch wurden sie ihrer traditionellen Lebensgrundlage beraubt, die auf Wanderfeldbau, Jagen und Sammeln,

und Ressourcenverbrauch durch Heiligsprechung bestimmter Forstbestände oder Waldtierarten basierte.[2] Ab 1947, dem Jahr der indischen Unabhängigkeit, erkannte die staatliche Gebietsverwaltung Landbesitz lediglich etablierten Bauerndörfern zu, während die semi-nomadischen Adivasi fast gänzlich ohne Landbesitz blieben.

Odisha ist heute Umschlagplatz des rohstoffreichen Hinterlandes[3] und der schnell wachsenden Städte Indiens. Dies führt zur globalen Vermarktung von Land als Produktions- und Abbaugebiet für internationale Investoren[4], und zur Realisierung dutzender industrieller Projekte in Sonderwirtschaftszonen und durch staatliche Entwicklungsanreize. Waldrodung und Bau von Minen, Fabriken und großmaßstäblichen Staudämmen und Reservoirs zer-

stören landwirtschaftliche Nutzflächen und Lebensraum und drängen Indigene in prekäre Lohnarbeit in verstädterte Gebiete. Die bewaffneten Aufstände der Naxaliten, einer industriefeindlichen, maoistischen Bewegung, und die Verbreitung von Anti-Industrialisierungsprotesten in Odisha[5], spiegeln dieses Ungleichgewicht zwischen lokalen und globalen Interessen wider.

Das Projekt formuliert den Anspruch, alternative Modi von Modernisierung zu entwickeln, die einen Dialog zwischen lokalen und globalen Lebens- und Wirtschaftsweisen aufbauen. Durch Aufforstung und Steigerung landwirtschaftlicher Produktivität sol-

len die Adivasi Kontrolle über ihr Land zurückgewinnen. Die Kombination von industrieller Produktion und auf lokale Verhältnisse abgestimmte Landwirtschaft und Handwerkstechnik bietet eine Lebensgrundlage für Industriearbeiter und Adivasi. Im Rahmen dieser "hybriden Wirtschaftsweise" wird die von industriellen Aktivitäten geprägte Landschaft bewaldet und umgenutzt, um höhere Ernteerträge zu erzielen, die Toxizität industrieller Aktivität auszugleichen und die wachsende (nomadische) Bevölkerung zu beherbergen. Wohnraum, Siedlungsentwicklung und Forstwirtschaft werden so ein Teil des Waldes.

SECTIONAL ECOSYSTEMS: PAST, PRESENT AND FUTURE

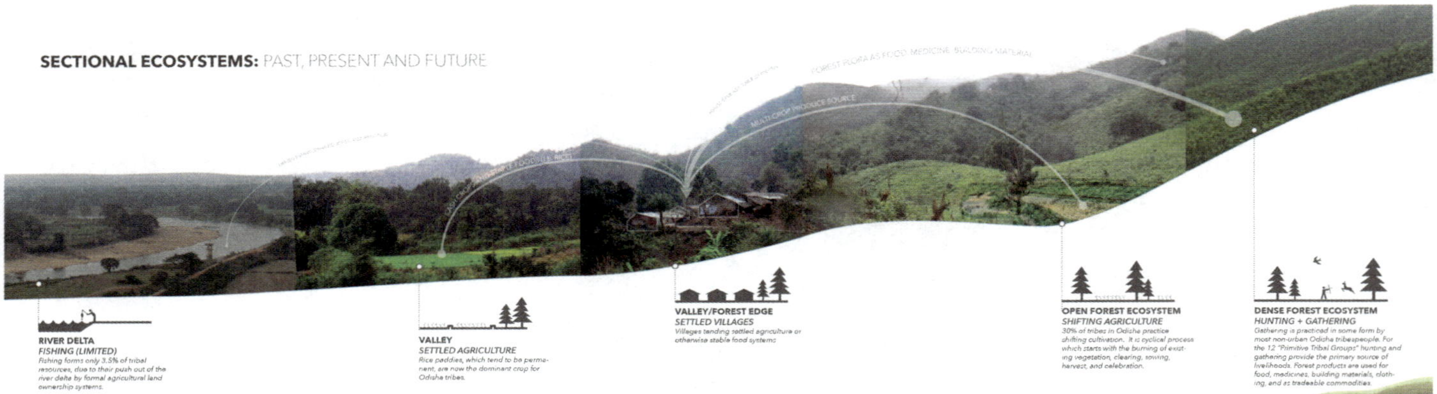

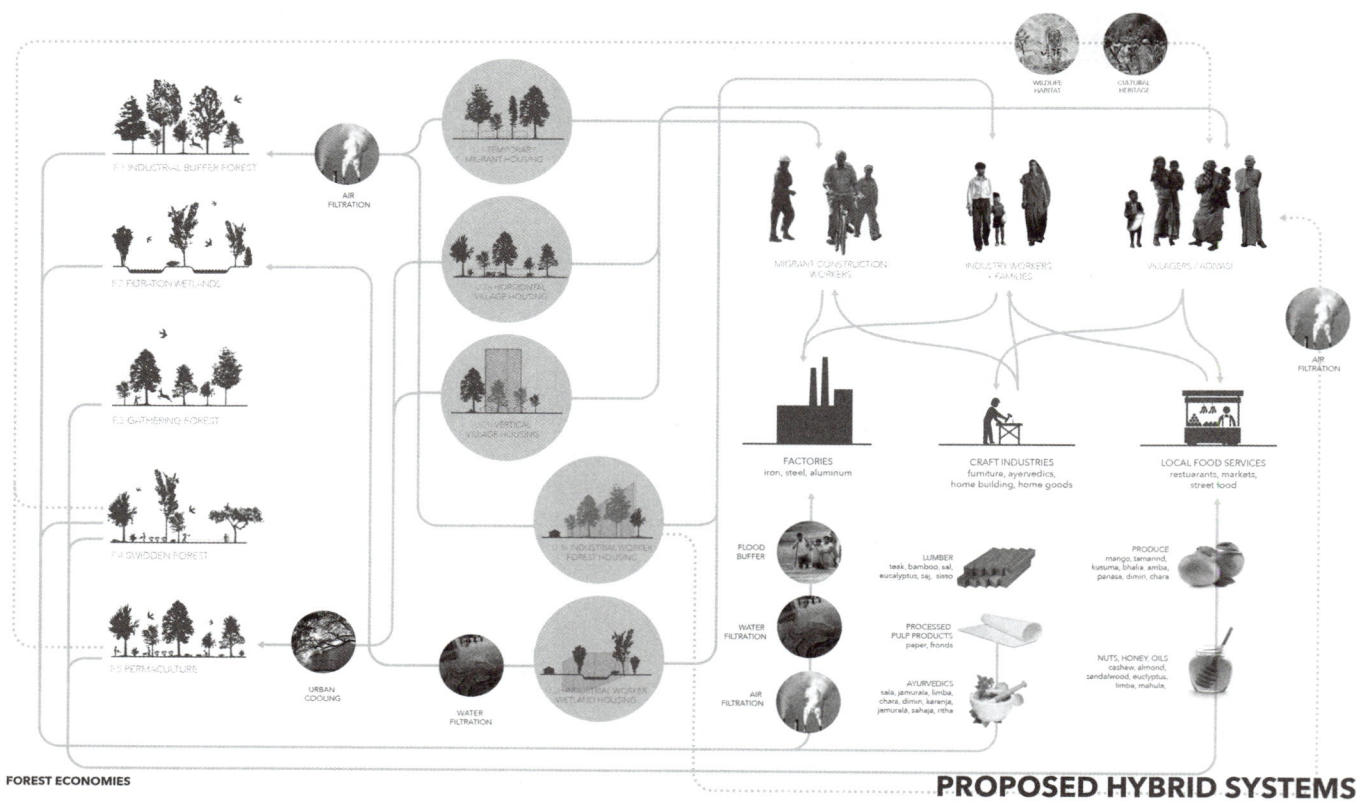

RIVER DELTA
FISHING (LIMITED)
Fishing forms only 3.5% of tribal resources, due to their push out of the river delta by formal agricultural land ownership systems.
VALLEY
SETTLED AGRICULTURE
Rice paddies, which tend to be permanent, are now the dominant crop for Odisha tribes.
VALLEY/FOREST EDGE
SETTLED VILLAGES
Villages tending settled agriculture or otherwise stable food systems
OPEN FOREST ECOSYSTEM
SHIFTING AGRICULTURE
30% of tribes in Odisha practice shifting cultivation. It is cyclical process which starts with the burning of existing vegetation, clearing, sowing, harvest, and celebration.
DENSE FOREST ECOSYSTEM
HUNTING + GATHERING
Gathering is practiced in some form by most non-urban Odisha tribespeople. For the 12 "Primitive Tribal Groups" hunting and gathering provide the primary source of livelihoods. Forest products are used for food, medicines, building materials, clothing, and as tradeable commodities.

TRIBAL LAND USE SECTION

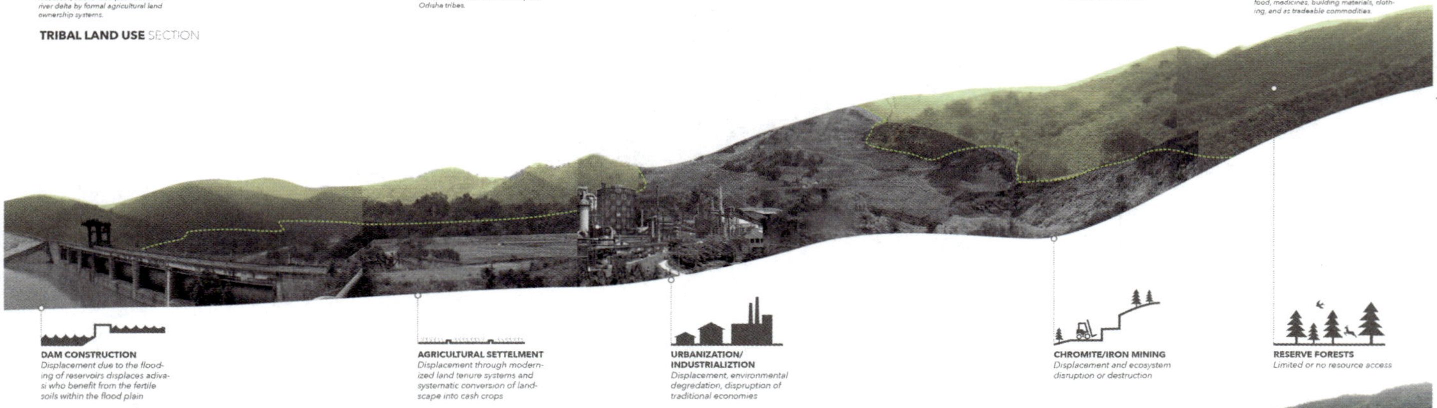

DAM CONSTRUCTION
Displacement due to the flooding of reservoirs displaces adivasi who benefit from the fertile soils within the flood plain
AGRICULTURAL SETTELMENT
Displacement through modernized land tenure systems and systematic conversion of landscape into cash crops
URBANIZATION/ INDUSTRIALIZTION
Displacement, environmental degredation, disprupton of traditional economies
CHROMITE/IRON MINING
Displacement and ecosystem disruption or destruction
RESERVE FORESTS
Limited or no resource access

"MODERN" LAND USE SECTION

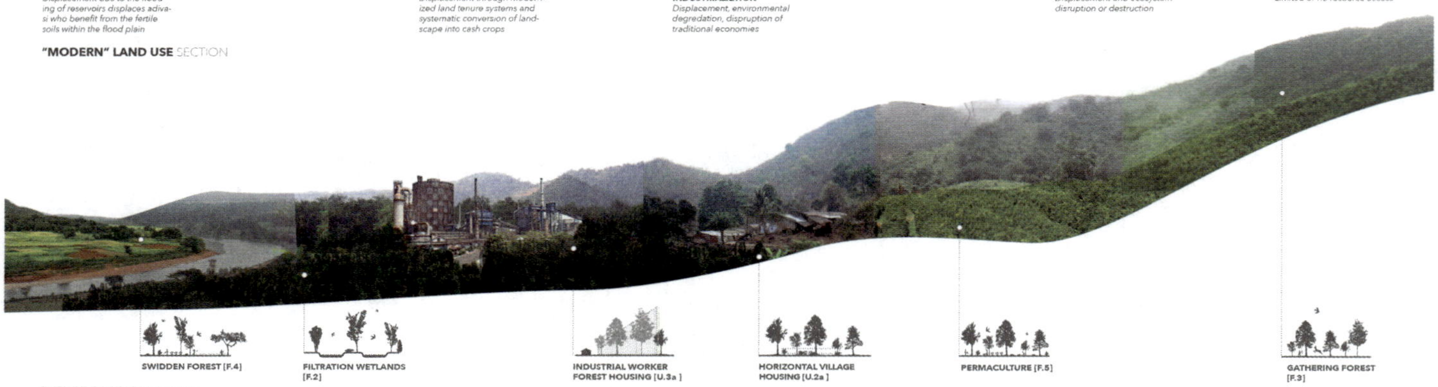

SWIDDEN FOREST [F.4]
FILTRATION WETLANDS [F.2]
INDUSTRIAL WORKER FOREST HOUSING [U.3a]
HORIZONTAL VILLAGE HOUSING [U.2a]
PERMACULTURE [F.5]
GATHERING FOREST [F.3]

FUTURE FORESTS SECTION

INDUSTRIAL BUFFER FOREST
FILTRATION WETLANDS
GATHERING FOREST
SWIDDEN FOREST
PERMACULTURE
AIR FILTRATION
URBAN COOLING
WATER FILTRATION
TEMPORARY MIGRANT HOUSING
HORIZONTAL VILLAGE HOUSING
VERTICAL VILLAGE HOUSING
INDUSTRIAL WORKER FOREST HOUSING
INDUSTRIAL WORKER WETLAND HOUSING
WILDLIFE HABITAT
CULTURAL HERITAGE
MIGRANT CONSTRUCTION WORKERS
INDUSTRY WORKERS + FAMILIES
VILLAGERS / ADIVASI
AIR FILTRATION
FACTORIES
iron, steel, aluminum
CRAFT INDUSTRIES
furniture, ayervedics, home building, home goods
LOCAL FOOD SERVICES
restuarants, markets, street food
FLOOD BUFFER
WATER FILTRATION
AIR FILTRATION
LUMBER
teak, bamboo, sal, eucalyptus, saj, sisso
PROCESSED PULP PRODUCTS
paper, fronds
AYURVEDICS
sala, jamurala, limba, chara, dimin, karanja, jamurala, sahaja, ritha
PRODUCE
mango, tamarind, kusuma, bhalia, amba, panasa, dimin, chara
NUTS, HONEY, OILS
cashew, almond, sandalwood, euclyptus, limba, mahula,

FOREST ECONOMIES

PROPOSED HYBRID SYSTEMS

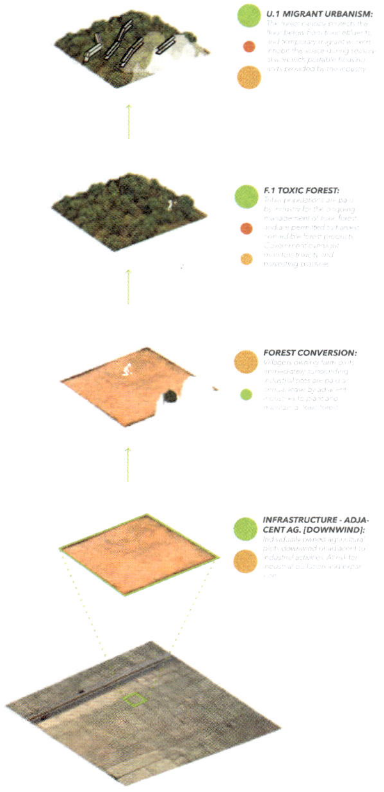

IA INFRASTRUCTURAL TOXICITY

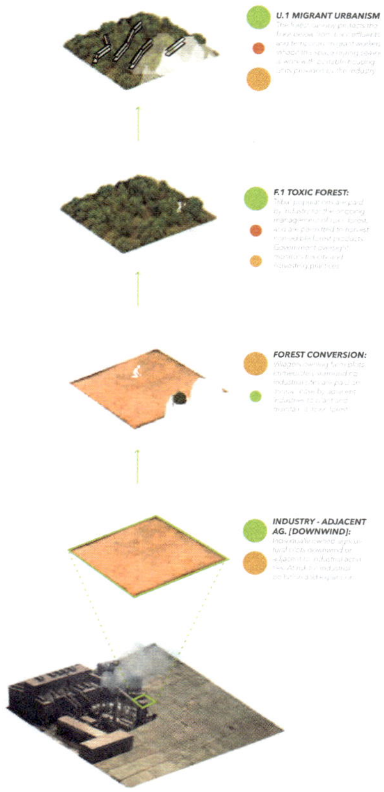

TA AIRBORNE TOXICITY

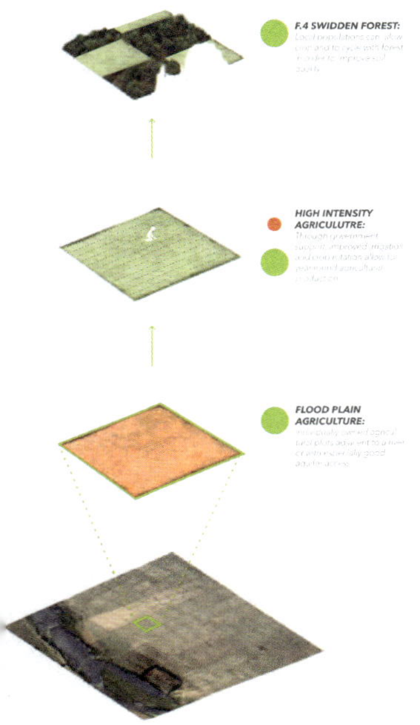

- **U.1 MIGRANT URBANISM:**
- **F.1 TOXIC FOREST:**
- **FOREST CONVERSION:**
- **INFRASTRUCTURE - ADJACENT AG. [DOWNWIND]:**

- **U.1 MIGRANT URBANISM:**
- **F.1 TOXIC FOREST:**
- **FOREST CONVERSION:**
- **INDUSTRY - ADJACENT AG. [DOWNWIND]:**

RA RIVER ADJACENT

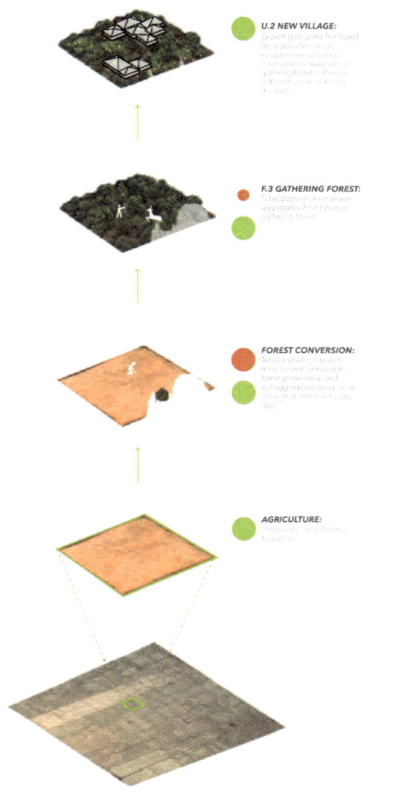

AA AGRICULTURE ADJACENT

- **F.4 SWIDDEN FOREST:**
- **HIGH INTENSITY AGRICULUTRE:**
- **FLOOD PLAIN AGRICULTURE:**

- **U.2 NEW VILLAGE:**
- **F.3 GATHERING FOREST:**
- **FOREST CONVERSION:**
- **AGRICULTURE:**

SCENARIO 01 *FILTRATION WETLANDS*

FOREST AND VILLAGE EXPANSION

SCENARIO 02 *MIGRANT HOUSING AND VILLAGE BUFFER*

SCENARIO 03 *EXISTING VILLAGE EXPANSION*

FUTURE SCENARIOS

51

Local Effects of Globalisation

PILBARA – COUNTRY, COLONY AND URBANISATION

Ben De Nardi
Michael Davis
Linus Tan
Michael Maginness
Peter Raisbeck
Peter Hogg
Linda Kennedy

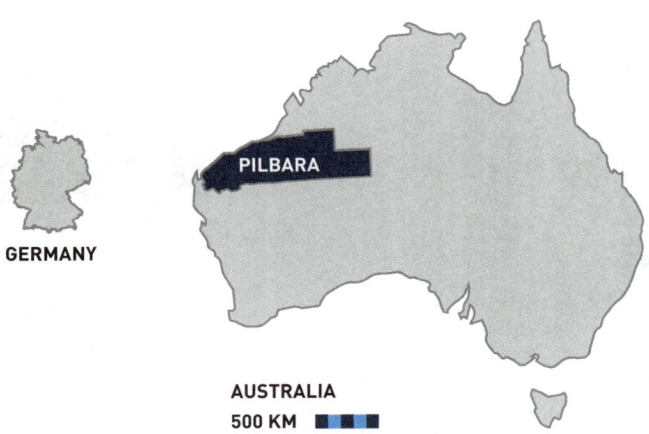

GERMANY

AUSTRALIA
500 KM

"Country": A term used by Aboriginal people of Australia to refer to their cultural connection with the land to which they belong and their place of "Dreaming". This cultural connection is based on each community's distinct traditions and lore, and is inclusive of all things in the landscape (landforms, water, air, trees, rocks, animals) and extends to the connection between the physical environment and cultural practices (knowledge, songs, stories, art) as well as all people (past, present and future), in both traditional and contemporary Aboriginal cultures.

Australia's present colonial urban development has resulted in the degradation of "Country", social disparity and cultural genocide. How can future urban development ensure respect for "Country" and culture?

Since the 1788 invasion and annexation of land and waters of 250 Aboriginal peoples, spread across the entire continent, the continuing colonial strategies of claiming land ownership – initially through the lie of "terra nullius" – have provided justification for a forced urbanisation, which solely benefits the dominant colonial culture. Aboriginal peoples were violently disconnected from "Country" by murder and massacre and mass displacement to missions and other institutions, assimilated by compulsion, the land subjugated by sheep breeding, mining and industrialisation.

The 1992 High Court Ruling in the case Mabo vs. Queensland (No. 2) gave way to the recognition of legal entitlement to land ownership for the Australian indigenous population. This legislation, however, is seriously flawed in its requirement to prove continuity of traditional laws and customs on specific areas of land. Such proof is often impossible to give. Internal migration since colonial invasion may be seen more as a survival strategy than a free decision.

Aboriginal peoples maintained strong trade relationships with other nation groups across the continent and island neighbours including Indonesia and Papua New Guinea, yet global urban connections were primarily migration-based.

In the post-war years, a downright migration boom occurred, as Australia was praised internationally as the "lucky country", open for boundless opportunity. In more recent years, Australia has restricted migration and the movement of people – a policy specifically targeted at asylum seekers – while simultaneously global economic relationships, meaning movements of commodities and capital, are accelerating, particularly with China and regarding the sale of iron ore.

The colonial process of "Country" degradation and displacement of Aboriginal peoples continues into the present, most recent examples are the "White Paper for Developing North-

"Land": Mit diesem Begriff beziehen sich die australischen Aborigenes nicht nur auf ihre Verbindung mit ihrem jeweiligen Lebensraum, sondern auch auf das, was sie ihren "Ort des Träumens" nennen. Diese kulturelle Verbindung beruht auf den besonderen Traditionen und Überlieferungen jeder Aborigines-Gemeinschaft; sie beinhaltet alle zur Landschaft zählenden Dinge (Landformen, Wasser, Luft, Bäume, Felsen, Tiere) und umfasst außerdem noch die Verbindung zwischen der physischen Umwelt und Kulturpraktiken (Wissen, Lieder, Geschichten, Kunst) sowie alle Menschen (in Vergangenheit, Gegenwart und Zukunft), nicht nur in traditionellen, sondern auch in zeitgenössischen Aborigines-Kulturen.

Die koloniale Stadtentwicklung Australiens hat zu einer Degradierung des "Landes" und zu sozialer Disparität und kulturellem Genozid geführt. Wie kann eine zukünftige Stadtentwicklung einen respektvollen Umgang mit "Land" und Kultur gewährleisten?

Seit der 1788 erfolgten Invasion und Aneignung des Landes und der Gewässer der mehr als 250 über den ganzen australischen Kontinent verteilten Aborigines-Völker haben die fortgesetzten kolonialen Strategien der Aneignung von Grund und Boden – anfangs mittels der Lüge von der "Terra nullius" – die Rechtfertigung für eine forcierte Urbanisierung zum alleinigen Nutzen der dominanten Kolonialkultur geliefert. Die Aborigines-Völker wurden mittels Mord und Massakern sowie der massenhaften Umsiedlung in Missionen und andere Institutionen gewaltsam vom "Land" getrennt und erzwungenermaßen assimiliert, das Land städtischen Ansiedlungen, Schafzucht, Bergbau und Industrialisierung unterworfen.

Die 1992 gefällte High-Court-Entscheidung im Fall Mabo vs. Queens-

land (No. 2) bereitete den Weg für eine Anerkennung des Rechtsanspruchs auf Grundbesitz für die Ureinwohner Australiens. Das entsprechende Gesetz ist allerdings realitätsfern, da es einen Beweis für die Kontinuität traditioneller Gesetze und Bräuche auf einem spezifischen Stück Land verlangt. Dieser Beweis ist häufig nicht zu erbringen. Die seit der kolonialen Invasion im Landesinneren stattfindende Migration der Aborigines scheint eher eine Überlebensstrategie als eine freie Entscheidung zu sein.

Die Aborigines-Völker pflegten rege Handelsbeziehungen mit anderen Volksgruppen auf dem Kontinent und mit den Bewohnern benachbarter Inseln, darunter Indonesien und Papua-Neuguinea, aber die globalen urbanen Verbindungen waren in erster Linie durch die Einwanderung geprägt. In den Nachkriegsjahren gab es einen regelrechten Immigrationsboom, als Australien weltweit als "das glückliche Land" gepriesen wurde, als ein Land der unbegrenzten Möglichkeiten. In jüngerer Zeit hat Australien die Einwanderung, d.h. "die Bewegung von Menschen" eingeschränkt – eine Politik, die sich vor allem gegen Asylsuchende richtet –, während gleichzeitig die globalen wirtschaftlichen Beziehungen, insbesondere zu China, d.h. die Bewegung von Waren und Kapital intensiviert wurden, vor allem was den Export von Eisenerz betrifft.

Der koloniale Prozess der Degradierung des "Landes" und der Vertreibung der Aborigines-Völker setzt sich bis in die Gegenwart fort; jüngste Beispiele sind das "White Paper for Developing Northern Australia" (2015) und andere geleakte Regierungsdokumente, die die geplante Schließung ausgewählter, entlegener Aborigines-Gemeinschaften umreißen, zunächst durch das Abschalten von Strom und Wasser, wodurch erneut eine Umsiedelung erzwun-

ern Australia" (2015) and other leaked government documents, which outline the intended closure of selected remote Aboriginal communities, initially through the discontinuation of electricity and water services, again forcing the displacement of Aboriginal peoples. The White Paper also highlights significant modifications to the landscape – e.g. through large scale agricultural developments in the Pilbara region. Because almost 85% of Australia's population reside in coastal regions, the inner land is used for the future planning of Australia's urban and economic development.

"New geographies of uneven spatial development have been emerging through a contradictory interplay between rapid, explosive processes of urbanisation and various forms of stagnation, shrinkage and marginalisation, often in close proximity to one another."[1]

In the same way that the European "Terra Nullius" myth assumed the emptiness of the Australian continent – when in fact it contained a cultural, social and ecological complexity incomprehensible to colonial invaders –, the prevailing epistemology of "the Urban" falsely assumes the emptiness of central Australia; it is viewed as a homogenous landscape, romanticised as "the Outback", that exists disconnected from populated coastal regions and urban agglomerations. In reality, there are fully urbanised regions in the Pilbara, linked to planetary urbanisation.

The perceived geographical emptiness of the Pilbara masks its role as a socially relevant region within the economic processes of global capitalism. These processes generate uneven spatial developments and revive early colonial practices of land degradation and displacement of Aborigines. The operationalisation of the Pilbara exemplifies, how "the Urban" has become the central episteme[1] of our time in its global reach. The natural abundance of iron ore has ensured its integration into the rapid urbanisation of China and the operational field of the Asian megapolis.

The political and economic ramifications of Mao Tse-tung's death in 1976 and the subsequent rise of Teng Hsiao-ping to the leader of the Chinese communist party were central historical events in the urban transformation of the Pilbara. With the success of the so-called "Asian Tiger" economies, the Communist Party under Deng leadership sought to reinforce Chinese dominance in East Asia.

It pursued a path of economic reform that gradually introduced a controlled market economy to China in order to increase the wealth and technological capacity required for regional supremacy.

This process of liberalisation led to rapid urbanisation on a then globally unprecedented scale. Due to the dissolution of China's rural communes and their limited (economic) security, undocumented rural migrants flooded China's coastal cities in search of work. By the mid-1990s, China had been opened up to foreign investment, resulting in the collapse of many state owned enterprises. Competitive pricing mechanisms became the driving force restructuring the Chinese economy. Resulting unemployment created a potentially destabilising labour surplus, which could be absorbed through a policy of large scale urbanisation of debt-financed mega-projects and infrastructural investment; the Beijing Olympics are just one notable example.

In his examination of Chinese neoliberalism, David Harvey explains that "the massive infrastructural investments under way in China have entrained much of the global economy".[2] In few places is this truer than it is in Australia, and in particular Western Australia and the Pilbara, which has fulfilled the demand for natural resources of China's accelerating urbanisation. The rapid urbanisation led by deficit funded mega-projects was consolidated by the subsequent growth of a lucrative Chinese property market, encouraged by favourable relationships and loans between private developers and Chinese state banks, and by the encouragement of a "democracy of consumption".[2]

Due in part to the legacy of Maoist policies, China had been predominantly self-reliant in regards to natural resources, however, from the early 2000s onwards, with the drastic increase in the need for natural resources prompted by urbanisation, imports filled the deficit with Australia providing its primary source of metals. The Pilbara's natural abundance of iron ore and its relative proximity to the Chinese market have solidified its position as a primary supplier of the iron ore feeding Chinese urbanisation; 78.9% of Western Australian iron ore was exported to China in 2014, while almost 60% of Chinese iron ore imports came from Australia in 2014.[3]

The explosive population growth in the Pilbara and dramatic increase in the median income between 2006 and 2011 masks the reality of growing demographic and economic inequality. Increase of population and income concerned above all the non-indigenous population, while only moderate economic gains could be noted for the indigenous population. This development was accompanied by a dramatic increase in a non-resident itinerant worker population. Data reveal how scantly the neoliberal notions of market-

gen werden soll. Das White Paper fasst auch beträchtliche Veränderungen der Landschaft ins Auge – z.B. durch große landwirtschaftliche Projekte in der Pilbara-Region. Da fast 85 % der australischen Bevölkerung in den Küstenregionen lebt, wird das Landesinnere für die zukünftige Planung von Australiens städtischer und wirtschaftlicher Entwicklung herangezogen.

"Neue Geografien einer unausgeglichenen räumlichen Entwicklung haben sich herausgebildet durch ein widersprüchliches Wechselspiel zwischen rapiden, explosiven Prozessen der Urbanisierung und diversen Formen der Stagnation, des Schrumpfens und der Marginalisierung, oftmals in unmittelbarer Nähe zueinander." (Brenner & Schmidt, 2015)[1]

So wie der europäische "Terra Nullius"-Mythos von der Leere des australischen Kontinents ausging – während dieser in Wirklichkeit eine den kolonialen Invasoren unbegreifliche kulturelle, soziale und ökologische Vielfalt beherbergte –, so geht auch die vorherrschende Epistemologie des "Urbanen" von der Leere des Landesinneren aus; es wird als eine homogene, als "Outback" verklärte Landschaft betrachtet, die losgelöst von den besiedelten Küstenregionen und urbanen Ballungsräumen existiert. Tatsächlich gibt es in der Pilbara vollständig urbanisierte, mit der weltweiten Urbanisierung verknüpfte Regionen. Die scheinbare geografische Leere der Pilbara verschleiert deren Rolle als eine sozial und politisch relevante Region innerhalb der ökonomischen Prozesse des globalen Kapitalismus; diese Prozesse erzeugen unausgeglichene räumliche Entwicklungen und lassen frühe koloniale Praktiken der Degradierung des Landes und der Vertreibung der dort lebenden Aborigines wieder aufleben.

Die Operationalisierung der Pilbara veranschaulicht, wie das "Urbane" zum zentralen Epistem (Brenner & Schmidt, 2015)[1] unserer Zeit in seiner globalen Reichweite geworden ist. So hat der natürliche Reichtum an Eisenerz dazu geführt, dass die Pilbara in die rapide Urbanisierung Chinas und das Operationsgebiet der asiatischen Megapolis einbezogen worden ist.

Die politischen und ökonomischen Folgen von Mao Tse-tungs Tod im Jahr 1976 und der anschließende Aufstieg Teng Hsiao-pings zum Führer der Kommunistischen Partei Chinas waren zentrale historische Ereignisse in der urbanen Transformation der Pilbara. Angesichts des wirtschaftlichen Erfolgs der sogenannten asiatischen Tigerstaaten versuchte die Kommunistische Partei unter Tengs Führung, die chinesische Dominanz in Fernost

zu verstärken. Sie verfolgte einen Weg der Wirtschaftsreformen, der in China schrittweise eine kontrollierte Marktwirtschaft einführte, um den Reichtum und die technologische Kapazität zu steigern, die die Voraussetzungen einer regionalen Vormachtstellung waren. Dieser Prozess der Liberalisierung führte zu einer rapiden Urbanisierung in einem bis dahin weltweit beispiellosen Maßstab. Infolge der Auflösung der chinesischen Landkommunen und ihrer begrenzten (wirtschaftlichen) Sicherheit überfluteten Wanderarbeiter ohne Papiere auf der Suche nach Arbeit die chinesischen Küstenstädte. Mitte der 1990er Jahre hatte sich China für ausländische Investitoren geöffnet, was zum Bankrott vieler chinesischer Staatsbetriebe führte. Die Preisbildung unter Wettbewerbsbedingungen wurde zur treibenden Kraft der Umstrukturierung der chinesischen Wirtschaft. Die daraus resultierende Arbeitslosigkeit schuf einen politisch potenziell destabilisierenden Arbeitskräfteüberschuss, der jedoch mittels einer Politik der umfassenden Urbanisierung durch schuldenfinanzierte Megaprojekte und infrastrukturelle Investitionen aufgefangen wurde; die Olympischen Spiele von Peking sind dafür nur ein besonders bekanntes Beispiel.

In seiner Untersuchung des chinesischen Neoliberalismus erklärt David Harvey, dass "die massiven infrastrukturellen Investitionen, die in China in Gang gesetzt worden sind, die Weltwirtschaft kräftig angekurbelt haben" (Harvey 2005, 140).[2] Es gibt nur wenige Orte, wo dies mehr zutrifft, als in Australien, insbesondere in Westaustralien und in der Pilbara, die die chinesische Nachfrage nach Rohstoffen für die wachsende Urbanisierung Chinas befriedigt. Die rapide, durch defizitfinanzierte Megaprojekte vorangetriebene Urbanisierung wurde konsolidiert durch die anschließende Herausbildung eines lukrativen chinesischen Immobilienmarkts, befördert durch günstige Beziehungen und Kredite zwischen privaten Developern und chinesischen Staatsbanken und durch die Förderung einer "Demokratie des Konsums" (Harvey 2005, 133).[2]

China war in seinen natürlichen Ressourcen weitgehend autark gewesen, was zum Teil auf die frühere maoistische Politik zurückging, doch seit Anfang der 2000er Jahre, mit der durch die Urbanisierung hervorgerufenen drastischen Steigerung des Rohstoffbedarfs, erhöhten Importe das Staatsdefizit, und Australien avancierte zum Chinas bedeutendster Quelle von Rohmetallen. Der natürliche Eisenerzreichtum der Pilbara und ihre relative Nähe zum chinesischen Markt

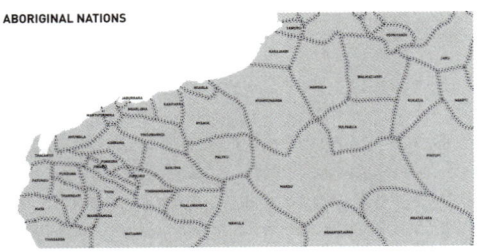

ABORIGINAL NATIONS

LANG MAYA	YINDHAWANGKA	KARAJARRI
PAYUNGU	BANJIMA	YAWURU
THALANYJI	YINDJIBARNDI	MANGALA
PURDUNA	NGARLUMA	YULPARIJA
THARRGARI	JABURRARA	NGAANYATJARRA
YINGGARDA	KARIYARRA	NGATATJARA
NHUWALA	NGARLA	PINTUPI
MARTUTHUNIRA	NYAMAL	NGARTI
KURRAMA	PALYKU	KUKATJA
PINIKURA	WAWULA	WALMATJARRI
JIWARI	NGALAWANGKA	GOONIYANDI
THIIN	NYANGUMARDA	JARU
WARRIYANGGA	MARDU	NGARTI
WATJARRI		

EXTENT OF THE PILBARA

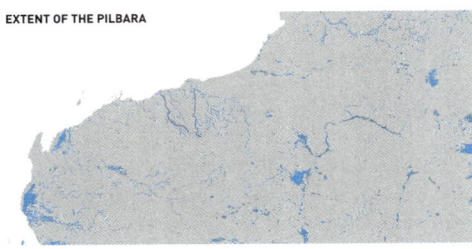

MINING TENEMENTS

- ■ EXISTING TENEMENTS
- ■ PENDING TENEMENTS

MINE LOCATIONS

- ■ LIVE MINES
- ■ ABANDONED MINES

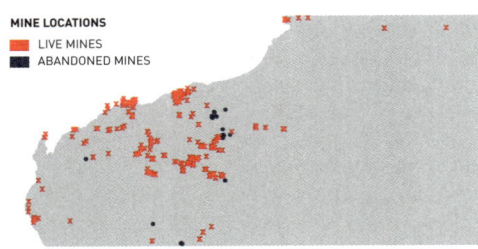

DISPLACEMENT & MIGRATION

- ■ CATTLE STATIONS
- ■ 1903 PASTORAL LEASES
- ■ ABORIGINAL MISSIONS
- ■ WESTERN DESERT GROUPS MOVEMENTS

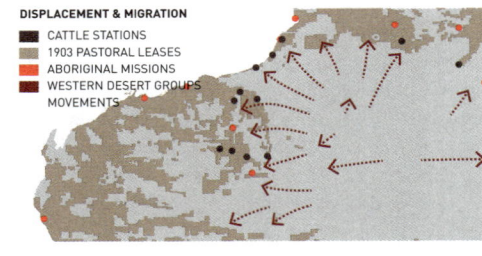

CHINA
JAPAN
ASIA
EUROPE
AUSTRALIA
DATA UNAVAILABLE

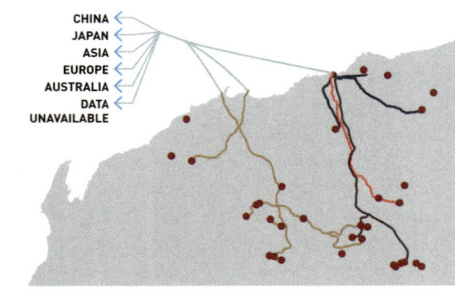

IRON ORE EXPORTS	IRON ORE EXPORTS in million tonnes	
■ ROUTE TO BHP	CHINA	199.97
■ ROUTE TO RIO TINTO	JAPAN	48.96
■ ROUTE TO FORTESCUE	OTHER ASIA	32.87
	EUPORE	5.5
■ ROAD TRANSPORT	AUSTRALIA	3.63
■ SHIPPING ROUTE	DATA UNAVAILABLE	145.74
■ MINES		

based economic development accompanying planetary urbanisation remedy social inequality that was forced on indigenous peoples by colonialisation; it further shows how the neoliberal doctrine is generating a continuation of this colonialisation. Especially the enormous difference between employment in Aboriginal and non-indigenous communities in the Pilbara, attest to the different social imperatives of people living on "Country", whose systems of cultural and social value do not correspond with the exchange value-dictated notion of work and employment. High numbers of people in these communities are not part of the accepted and officially measured labour force. The lack of socially and culturally appropriate opportunities is made visible by the tendency of people in these communities to leave the labour force entirely, as access to welfare based Community Developmental Employment Projects (CDEP) is limited.

By example of Australia's second-biggest iron ore mine, Mount Whaleback in the Pilbara region of West Australia, a traditional native land of four Aboriginal peoples, the project is criticising the colonial concept of "the Urban" and reveals its geopolitical importance. The proposal is speculative, as it should be realised after the termination of iron ore extraction in the hundred years to then follow, yet envisaging a future urban development that strategically occupies landscape degraded by global urbanisation and uses infrastructural networks already in place.

The "Whaleback Settlement" is an autonomous settlement, sealed off against existing power structures and comparable to a micro-nation, that functions after principles of self-administration of self-organised groups, public referendums facilitating consensual decision-making, and reciprocal aid.

The existing infrastructure is re-appropriated for the use of the "Whaleback Settlement". With our proposal of an adapted mine closure plan and the rehabilitation of the mine site an approximate restoration of the landscape to its pre-extraction state is inevitable; the "Whaleback Settlement" now exists within the borders of land degraded by the Whaleback Mine.

The fertile ground of such sites within the region can potentially offer a basis for similar settlements in other places. Through the decoupling of the site from the global networks of iron ore extraction, it constitutes a semi-closed system, which cooperates with other similarly occupied degraded landscapes in the region and thus establishes relationships not based on the exploitation of resources and labour power, but on mutual respect and cooperation.

haben ihre Position als Hauptlieferant des für die chinesische Urbanisierung benötigten Eisenerzes gefestigt; 2014 wurden 78,9 % des in Westaustralien geförderten Eisenerzes nach China exportiert (Dept. Mines and Petroleum, 2014), während beinahe 60 % der chinesischen Eisenerzimporte 2014 aus Australien stammten (Dept. Mines and Petroleum, 2014).[3]

Die Bevölkerungsexplosion in der Pilbara und die gewaltige Zunahme des mittleren Einkommens zwischen 2006 und 2010 verschleiern die Realität einer wachsenden sozialen und ökonomischen Ungleichheit. Die Bevölkerungs- und die Einkommenszunahme betraf vor allem die nicht indigene Bevölkerung, während für die indigene Bevölkerung nur moderate wirtschaftliche Verbesserungen zu verzeichnen waren. Diese Entwicklung ging einher mit der drastischen Zunahme einer nicht ansässigen Population von Wanderarbeitern. Die Daten offenbaren, wie wenig die die globale Urbanisierung begleitenden neoliberalen Vorstellungen von einer marktgesteuerten Wirtschaftsentwicklung in der Lage sind, die sozialen Nachteile auszugleichen, die der indigenen Bevölkerung durch die Kolonisierung aufgezwungen worden sind; sie zeigen außerdem, wie die neoliberale Doktrin eine Fortführung dieser Kolonisierung bewirkt. Vor allem der enorme Unterschied zwischen der Erwerbstätigkeit der Aborigines-Gemeinschaften und denen der nicht indigenen Bevölkerung in der Pilbara bestätigen die unterschiedlichen sozialen Imperative von Menschen, die vom "Land" leben und deren kulturelle und soziale Wertesysteme nicht mit den tauschwertbestimmten Vorstellungen von Arbeit und Beschäftigung übereinstimmen. Eine große Zahl von Mitgliedern dieser Gemeinschaften zählen nicht zur akzeptierten und amtlich erfassten Erwerbsbevölkerung. Das Fehlen sozial und kulturell angemessener Chancen wird daran ablesbar, dass viele Mitglieder dieser Gemeinschaften dazu neigen, aus dem Arbeitsleben ganz auszusteigen, da der Zugang zu wohlfahrtsstaatlichen Beschäftigungsprogrammen im Rahmen der Community Developmental Employment Projects (CDEP) eingeschränkt ist.

Am Beispiel von Australiens zweitgrößter Eisenerzmine, Mount Whaleback in der westaustralischen Pilbara-Region, der traditionellen Heimat von vier Aborigines-Völkern, kritisiert dieses Projekt das koloniale Konzept des "Urbanen" und zeigt dessen geopolitische Bedeutung auf. Dieser Vorschlag ist insofern spekulativ, als er nach Beendigung des Eisenerzabbaus während der folgenden hundert Jahre in die Tat umgesetzt werden soll, er fasst jedoch eine künftige Stadtentwicklung ins Auge, die bestehende infolge der globalen Ur-

banisierung degradierte Landschaften strategisch besetzt und die vorhandenen infrastrukturellen Netzwerke nutzt.

Das Whaleback Settlement ist eine autonome Ansiedlung, die sich gegen die bestehenden Machtstrukturen abschottet und mit einer Mikronation vergleichbar ist, die nach den Prinzipien der Selbstverwaltung im Wechsel von sich selbstorganisierenden Gruppen und allgemeinen Versammlungen mit Konsensentscheidungen und gegenseitigen Hilfeleistungen funktioniert.

Die bestehende Infrastruktur wird für die Nutzung durch das Whaleback Settlement einem neuen Zweck zugeführt. Mit der vorgeschlagenen Anpassung des Minenstilllegungsplans und der Sanierung des Minengeländes kommt es zwangsläufig zu einer annähernden Wiederherstellung der Landschaft, wie sie vor Beginn des Eisenerzabbaus gewesen war; das Whaleback Settlement wird nur innerhalb der Grenzen des von der Whaleback-Mine degradierten Landes existieren.

Die fruchtbare Natur solcher Areale in der Region liefert womöglich eine Ausgangsbasis für ähnliche Ansiedlungen an anderen Orten. Indem man das Areal von den globalen Netzwerken des Eisenerzabbaus abkoppelt, bildet es ein halb geschlossenes System, das mit ähnlich besetzten degradierten Landschaften in der Region zusammenarbeitet und dadurch Beziehungen etabliert, die nicht auf der Ausbeutung von Ressourcen und Arbeitskräften basieren, sondern auf gegenseitigem Respekt und Zusammenarbeit.

Die Grafik zeigt Wirtschaftsdaten vom Beginn des 21. Jhdt. bis in die Gegenwart. Sie stellt die reziproke Beziehung dar zwischen den gleichzeitig ablaufenden Prozessen der Urbanisierung in China und in der Pilbara vor dem Hintergrund der demografischen und sozioökonomischen Situation dreier in der Pilbara beheimateten Bevölkerungsgruppen. Quelle: Drei in diesem Zeitraum durchgeführte Volkszählungen.

Der sozioökonomische Status der indigenen und nicht indigenen Bevölkerungsgruppen wird zusammen mit den sozioökonomischen Statistiken der Aborigines-Gemeinschaften in der Pilbara visualisiert.

The graphic shows economic data ranging from the beginning of the 21st century until today. It depicts the reciprocal relationship between simultaneous processes of urbanisation in China and the Pilbara against the background of the demographic and social situation of three groups of inhabitants in the Pilbara.

The socio-economic status of the indigenous and non-indigenous population is visualised with socio-economic statistics of Aboriginal peoples in the Pilbara.

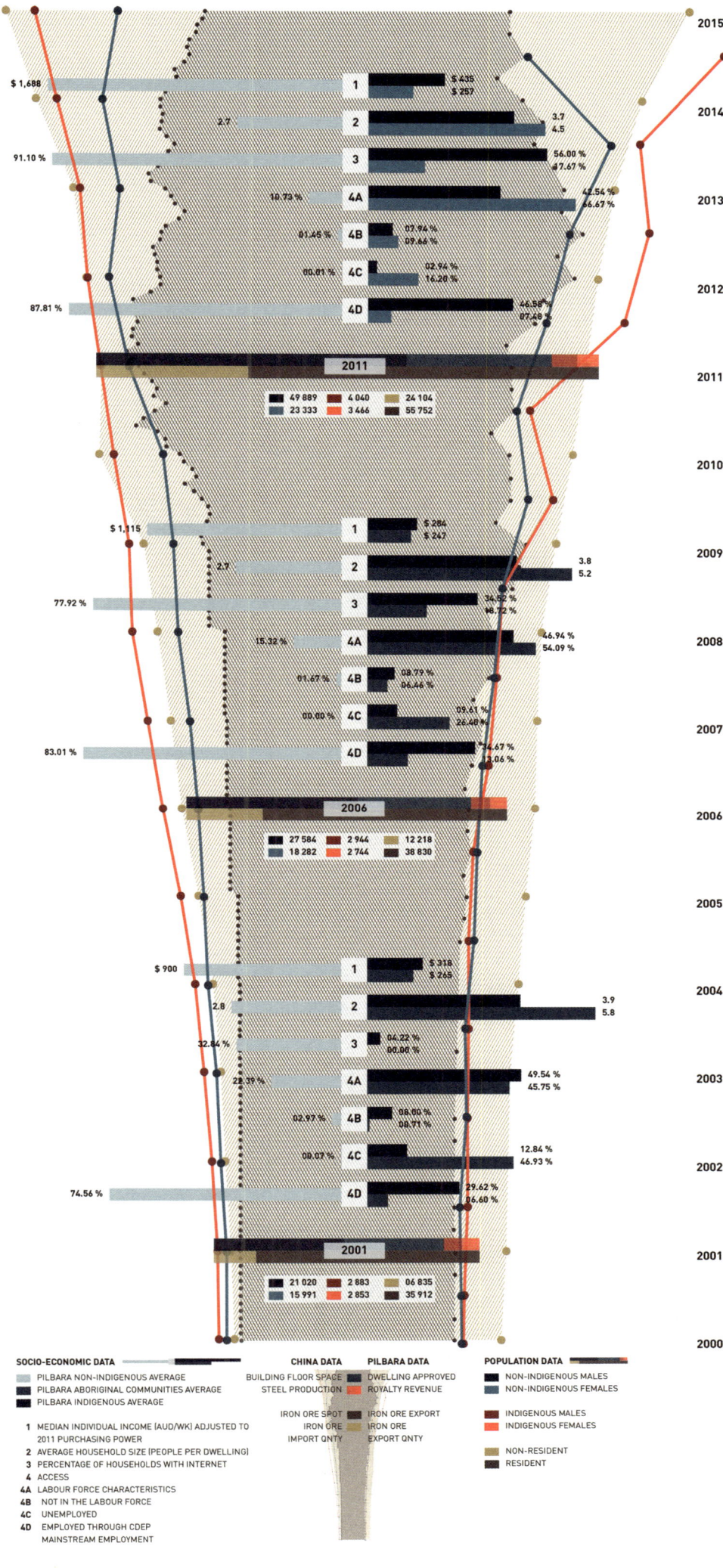

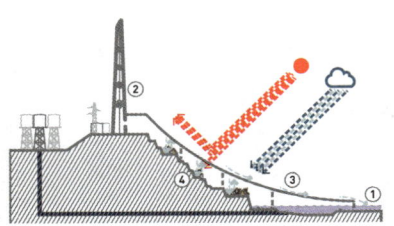 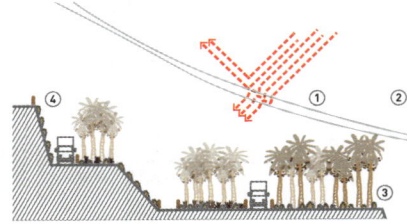 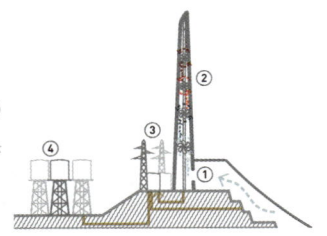

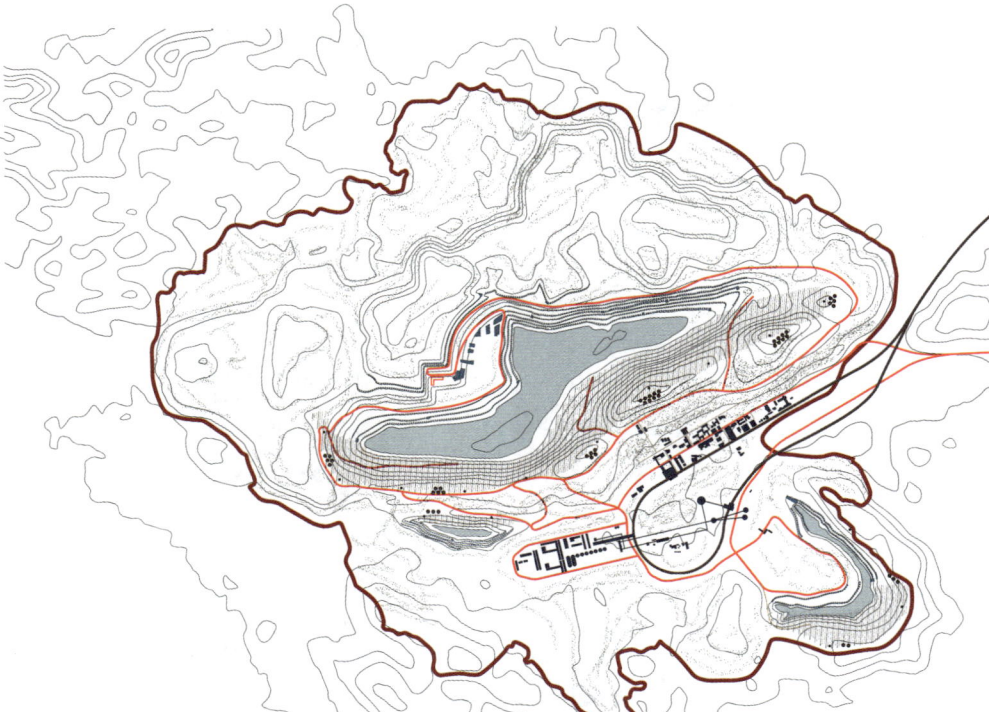

Die Ansiedlung soll in der Energieversorgung autark und in der Ernährung weitgehend autark sein. Der erste Schritt ist die Wiederherstellung des Grundwasserspiegels durch das Abschalten der Drainagepumpen, die derzeit die Mine trocken halten. Dadurch entsteht im Zentrum der Ansiedlung ein Teich. Die Terrassen an der Nordseite werden der städtische Teil der Ansiedlung, die südlichen Terrassen der landwirtschaftliche Teil sein.

Der Teich wird nicht nur Wasser für die Landwirtschaft und die Bewohner bereitstellen, sondern auch das örtliche Mikroklima stabilisieren. Dazu wird ein "Zelt" vom Teich bis zum äußeren Rand der landwirtschaftlichen Terrassen gespannt. Es erzeugt ein eigenes Mikroklima und produziert "Regen", indem es die Feuchtigkeit des Teichs absorbiert und recycelt.

Entlang des südlichen Rands der Mine werden thermische Kamine installiert, die Strom für die Ansiedlung erzeugen. Die heiße Luft wird von der Wasseroberfläche des Teichs aufsteigen, unter dem Zelt entlangströmen, durch die Kamine aufsteigen und die dort angebrachten Turbinen antreiben, die Strom für das Whaleback Settlement produzieren. Die aufsteigende Luft sorgt gleichzeitig innerhalb der Ansiedlung für eine kühle Brise.

Die Wohnterrassen, hineingebaut in die Nordseite der Mine, beschatten sich gegenseitig, was im heiß-trockenen Pilbara-Klima für angenehme Kühle sorgt. Die in die Erde gegrabenen Behausungen mildern das heiße Klima und stabilisieren die Hänge, während die flacher gelegenen Areale als öffentliche Räume fungieren. Die agrarisch genutzten Terrassen liegen auf der Südseite der Mine, wo die Sonneneinstrahlung intensiver ist. Diese Terrassen bestehen aus dem Abraum der Mine.

The settlement's energy supply should be self-sufficient, and the food supply widely self-sufficient. First steps are the recovery of ground water height by deactivating the drainage pumps that are now keeping the mine dry. Thus, a lake in the centre of the settlement is created. The terraces on the north side are to be the urban part of the settlement, southern terraces are to be the agricultural part.

The lake will not only provide food for agriculture and inhabitants, but also stabilise the local micro-climate. For this purpose a "tent" is spanned between the lake and the peripheral terraces. It creates its own micro-climate and produces "rain" by partly absorbing and recycling the lake's humidity.

Along the southern edge of the mine, thermal ducts will be installed to produce energy for the settlement. The hot air will rise from the surface of the lake, flow below the agricultural tent and propel the herein installed turbines, which produce electricity for the settlement. The rising air simultaneously creates a breeze within the settlement.

The housing terraces, constructed in the northern side of the mine, are shading each other, thus helping to keep things cool in the hot, arid Pilbara climate. The buildings, burrowed into the earth mitigate the hot climate and stabilise the slopes, while flatter areas act as common spaces. The agricultural terraces are on the southern side of the mine, where sun exposure is more permanent. The agricultural terraces are composed of the spoil from the mine.

NEW ORLEANS – PORT CITY TO GLOBAL HINTERLAND

Jacob Mitchell
Xuan Kuai
Justine Holzman
Karen May
Ran Liu
Giovanni Coakley
Chris He
Sean Williams
Maureen Jackson
Madeline Richard
Sarah Schramm
Jeff Carney

New Orleans: Port City to Global Hinterland

After 80 years of economic development for international trade and extensive river regulation, the delicate ecosystem of the lower Mississippi region, Louisiana, is on the brink of collapse. The region has lost around 4900 km² of its coastal wetlands, which equals a loss of a football field sized area every 30 minutes.[1] Historically, deltaic wetlands acted as a natural storm buffer, protecting urban agglomerations by attenuating storm surge, reducing wind speed, and absorbing flood water. The Mississippi river carries its sediment to low-lying deltaic areas, thus building up land and sustaining the entire deltaic ecosystem.

From the 1930s onwards, large-scale levee systems were constructed alongside Mississippi river to enhance flood protection and more efficiently channel trading ships.[2] Paradoxically, the very levees installed for flood protection have prevented the river from depositing sediment into the now cut-off delta, thus causing wetlands to erode more and more quickly and sink into the Gulf of Mexico.[1] Loss of land of course increases the danger of widespread flooding disaster such as Hurricane Katrina in 2005.

The ongoing development of the regions' ports into major entrepôts for global trade implies an ever-expanding shipping industry with high demand for energy and infrastructure. Pipelines and navigation channels have allowed saline water to invade and eradicate sweet-water wetlands. The MRGO (Mississippi River Gulf Outlet) channel for example, constructed to provide a shorter route between open water and New Orleans' inner port, channelled Hurricane Katrina's storm surge right into the core of Greater New Orleans.[3]

Along with environmental degradation, global shipping industry has brought about a fragmentation of regional settlement structures. In New Orleans, highly concentrated industry along the riverbanks has cut off the historic link between the river and the inner city, and has led to suburban sprawl. Street grids connecting the port with the city's commercial centres have vanished, while dockworkers no longer live in close proximity to the river, but in satellite towns further inland. Today, New Orleans is disconnected from global commerce flowing daily to and from its ports.

Decades of privileging international trade over the upkeeping of local socio-ecological systems have made the drawbacks of industrial development painfully visible. Costs are being borne exclusively by local inhabitants and environments, while benefits are being dispersed throughout the globe.
Text: Anna Aichinger

Nach 80 Jahren ökonomischer Entwicklung hin zu internationalem Handel und umfassender Flussregulierung ist das empfindliche Ökosystem der unteren Region des Mississippi, Louisiana, am Rande des Zusammenbruchs. Die Region hat ca. 4900 qkm an küstennahen Feuchtgebieten verloren, was dem Verlust einer fußballplatzgroßen Fläche alle 30 Minuten entspricht.[1] In der Vergangenheit bildeten Feuchtgebiete im Flussdelta eine natürliche Sturmabwehr; sie schützten städtische Gebiete, indem sie die anbrandenden Wogen abschwächten, die Windgeschwindigkeit reduzierten und das Flutwasser absorbierten. Der Mississippi trug seine Flusssedimente in tieferliegende Gebiete des Deltas, wo sie Landmasse bildeten und so das gesamte Ökosystem des Deltas aufrechterhielten.

Ab den 1930ern wurden großmaßstäbliche Dammsysteme entlang des Mississippi errichtet, um den Hochwasserschutz zu verbessern und Handelsschiffe effizienter zu schleusen.[2] Paradoxerweise haben eben jene als Hochwasserschutz erbauten Dämme den Fluss daran gehindert, Sedimente im nun abgetrennten Delta abzulagern, und so bewirkt, dass Feuchtgebiete immer schneller erodieren und in den Golf von Mexiko absinken.[1] Landverlust erhöht offensichtlich die Gefahr weitläufiger Hochwasserkatastrophen wie durch den Hurrikan Katrina im Jahr 2005.

Die fortlaufende Entwicklung regionaler Häfen zu führenden Umschlagplätzen für globalen Handel bringt eine kontinuierlich expandierende Handelsschifffahrt mit hoher Nachfrage nach Energie und Infrastruktur mit sich. Durch Pipelines und Schifffahrtskanäle konnte Salzwasser in Süßwasserfeuchtgebiete vordringen und diese zerstören. So hat der Mississippi River Gulf Outlet Kanal (MRGO), als kürzere Route zwischen offenem Meer und dem inneren Hafen von New Orleans errichtet, die Sturmwogen des Hurrikans Katrina direkt ins Herz von Greater New Orleans geleitet.[3]

Neben der Umweltzerstörung führt die globale Schifffahrtsindustrie zur Fragmentierung regionaler Siedlungsstrukturen. Die stark verdichtete Industrie entlang der Flussufer hat die historischen Zusammenhänge zwischen dem Fluss und der Innenstadt zerstört und zur Zersiedelung geführt. Straßennetze, die den Hafen mit den kommerziellen Zentren der Stadt verbunden haben, sind verschwunden, während Hafenarbeiter nicht mehr in der Nähe des Flusses, sondern in Satellitenstädten weiter landeinwärts leben. Heute ist die Stadt New Orleans abgekoppelt von dem globalen Handelsverkehr, der täglich durch ihre Häfen fließt.

Die jahrzehntelange Begünstigung des internationalen Handels gegenüber der Instandhaltung lokaler ökologischer Systeme haben die Nachteile industrieller Entwicklungen nur zu sichtbar gemacht. Die Kosten werden ausschließlich von der lokalen Bevölkerung und Umwelt getragen, während die Gewinne in der ganzen Welt verteilt sind.

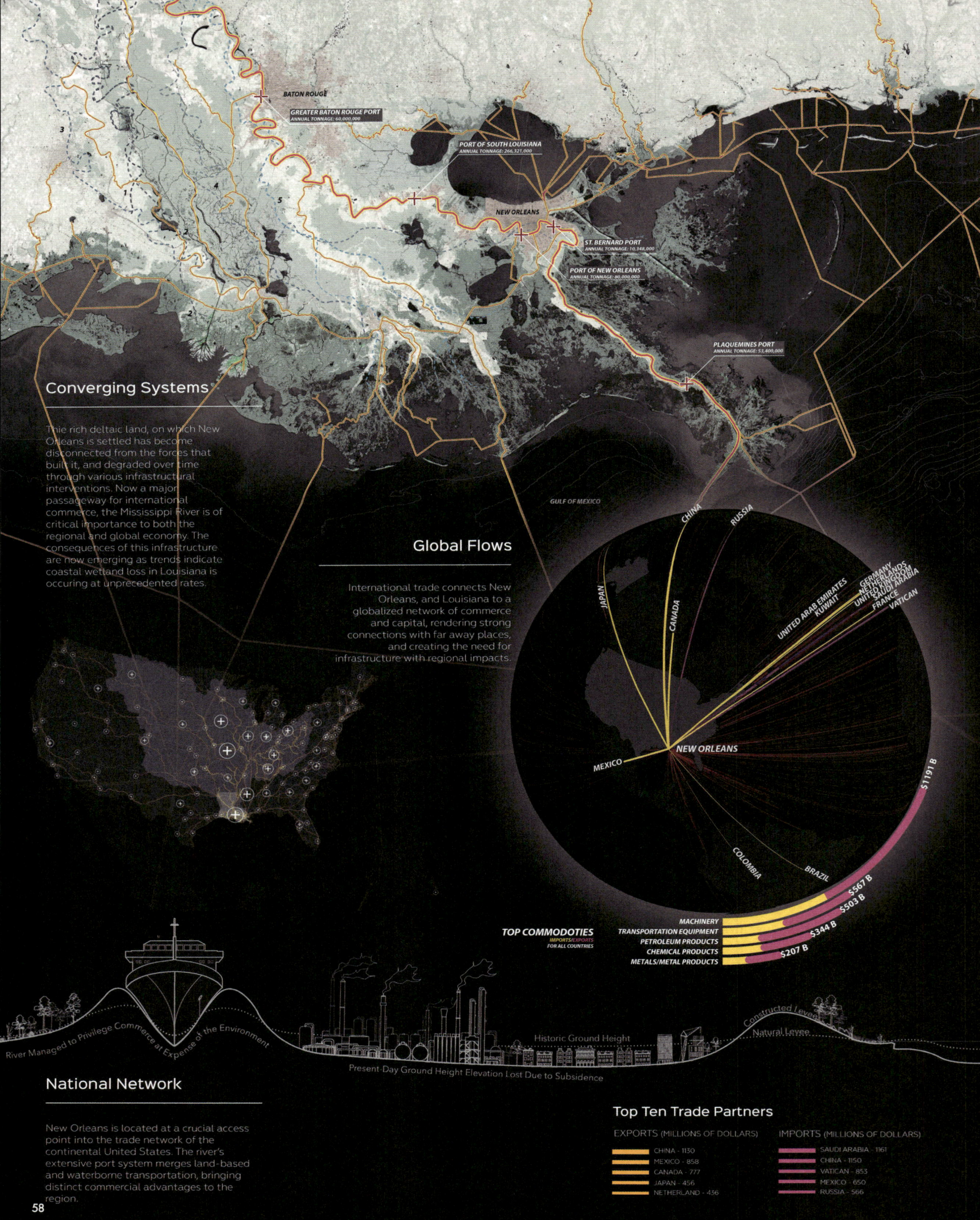

BATON ROUGE

GREATER BATON ROUGE PORT
ANNUAL TONNAGE: 60,000,000

PORT OF SOUTH LOUISIANA
ANNUAL TONNAGE: 266,327,000

NEW ORLEANS

ST. BERNARD PORT
ANNUAL TONNAGE: 10,348,000

PORT OF NEW ORLEANS
ANNUAL TONNAGE: 80,000,000

PLAQUEMINES PORT
ANNUAL TONNAGE: 53,400,000

Converging Systems

This rich deltaic land, on which New Orleans is settled has become disconnected from the forces that built it, and degraded over time through various infrastructural interventions. Now a major passageway for international commerce, the Mississippi River is of critical importance to both the regional and global economy. The consequences of this infrastructure are now emerging as trends indicate coastal wetland loss in Louisiana is occuring at unprecedented rates.

Global Flows

International trade connects New Orleans, and Louisiana to a globalized network of commerce and capital, rendering strong connections with far away places, and creating the need for infrastructure with regional impacts.

GULF OF MEXICO

JAPAN
CHINA
RUSSIA
CANADA
UNITED ARAB EMIRATES
KUWAIT
GERMANY
NETHERLANDS
UNITED KINGDOM
SAUDI ARABIA
FRANCE
VATICAN

MEXICO

NEW ORLEANS

COLOMBIA
BRAZIL

$1191 B

$567 B

$503 B

$344 B

$207 B

TOP COMMODOTIES
IMPORTS/EXPORTS
FOR ALL COUNTRIES

MACHINERY
TRANSPORTATION EQUIPMENT
PETROLEUM PRODUCTS
CHEMICAL PRODUCTS
METALS/METAL PRODUCTS

River Managed to Privilege Commerce at Expense of the Environment

Constructed level

Natural Levee

Historic Ground Height

Present-Day Ground Height Elevation Lost Due to Subsidence

National Network

New Orleans is located at a crucial access point into the trade network of the continental United States. The river's extensive port system merges land-based and waterborne transportation, bringing distinct commercial advantages to the region.

Top Ten Trade Partners

EXPORTS (MILLIONS OF DOLLARS)	IMPORTS (MILLIONS OF DOLLARS)
CHINA - 1130	SAUDI ARABIA - 1161
MEXICO - 858	CHINA - 1150
CANADA - 777	VATICAN - 853
JAPAN - 456	MEXICO - 650
NETHERLAND - 456	RUSSIA - 566

5 m
4 m
3 m
2 m
1 m
0 m
-1 m
-2 m
-3 m
-4 m
-5 m
-6 m
-7 m

2005 Hurricane Katrina

2005 Hurricane Rita

2008 Hurricane Gustav

storm surge

sea level rise

relative sea level rise

subsidence

Legend

>25% RESIDENTS EMPLOYED IN INDUSTRY

INDUSTRY REGION

Adjacency and Separation

Louisiana's port system and waterborne transportation infrastructure is part of an increasingly industrialized corridor that is driving new settlement patterns, and separating shipping and industry from traditional urban form and development planning. What emerges are two very distinct forms of urbanization; an area of highly concentrated industry along the river, and dispersed suburban sprawl.

Dispersed / Disengaged

The port system of New Orleans is a crucial part of Louisiana's economy that is managed to maintain its economic viability. As a result of economic development, industries that rely on the port system have emerged along the river banks, while individuals who work in industry reside in satellite urban areas at the periphery of the industrial spine, creating a new urban industrial form.

1   RIVER   INDUSTRY   LEVEE   MARSH

2   RIVER   INDUSTRY   RURAL   SUBURB

3   RIVER   PORT   WALL   CITY

TO HIGHER GROUND

URBANISM OF DISASSEMBLY Aditya Barve

Shipbreaking: the rise and fall of a migratory industry

Shipping is not only the backbone of modern economy, but contemporary urbanization is only made possible by the maritime movement of over 90% of commodities. After 25 to 30 years of average lifespan, these ships end up as floating liabilities spawning a global web of industrial urbanization. Most of these ships, often full of hazardous waste, end up on the beach of Alang in India, waiting to be brought down to their last material essence – steel.

Although many different methods exist for disposing of a vessel, shipbreaking is most prevalent as it is an excellent source of reusable and recyclable material. There is a clear link between economic development and shipbreaking activity in any maritime economy.[1] The industry of shipbreaking, as observed, is a migratory phenomenon. From the after-war booming years until early 70s, shipbreaking was carried out mostly on the dry docks of Western Europe and America. Soon as eastern manufacturing economies became more resource hungry, the industry followed emerging economies of Korea, Japan, China, and Taiwan, as a quick way to obtain the much-needed steel.

Alang, situated on the western shore of the Gulf of Cambay in India, is currently the berthing place for half of the world's over 700 scrapped ships every year. It was in 1984 during the economic recession, attributed to a worldwide general adoption of neo-liberal economic policies, that Alang first rose to prominence. Due to the recession and government regulations the prices of scrapping ships in the eastern shipbreaking yards skyrocketed. The yards in the Indian subcontinent offered a less expensive alternative. The method employed here is known as 'beaching'. These locations in the Indian subcontinent have world's highest tidal ranges, which means, at spring tides, ships can be driven as far up the beach as possible, over the mudflats and onto the beach, making elaborate dry-docks unnecessary.

However, it is a huge environmental challenge to dispose of these colossal objects. Often over 10,000 tons in dead weight, they contain oil residue, lead paint, asbestos, PCB (Polychlorinated biphenyl) and other hazardous and toxic material on board. Stringent environmental laws in developed countries make ship-scrapping an elaborate process of decontamination, driving the costs upwards. The cost escalation led to a process of ship breaking activities migrating to developing countries chiefly in South Asia, where lowest operational expenses could be found, due to unique geography, cheap labor and lack of environmental control.

The global flows of obsolete vessels to these sites require circumventing the legalities of OECD countries. Often these ships transfer owners, flags of registrations to circumvent legal structure in the western world that prevents the sale of toxic ships to developing world. Even though shipbreaking has been brought under scrutiny of international law of Basel and Hong Kong Convention, the situation stays shadowy.

The social-political economy of shipbreaking is complex and highlights conflicting interests, especially for a developing economy like India. In India, by recognizing shipbreaking as an industry, the state has given clear indication that it recognizes the economic importance of the shipbreaking. To learn a lesson from the rise and fall of industrial cities, Alang needs to go beyond the mono-cultural industry before it becomes just another historical site of the migratory industry. Upgrading a contaminating shipbreaking industry to poly-cultural ship recycling sectors might help Alang to turn the hazardous waste into a widely ranging economy.

•

Schiffsverschrottung: Aufstieg und Fall einer Wanderindustrie

Verschiffung ist nicht bloß das Rückgrat der modernen Wirtschaft – auch die gegenwärtige Urbanisierung wird erst durch den Überseetransport von mehr als 90 % aller Waren möglich. Nach einer durchschnittlichen Lebensdauer von 25 bis 30 Jahren enden die Schiffe als schwimmende Passiva, die ein weltweites Netz der industriellen Urbanisierung hervorbringen. Die meisten dieser Schiffe, die häufig voller Sondermüll stecken, enden am Strand von Alang in Indien, wo sie darauf warten, in ihrem zentralen Sein – Stahl – ausgeschlachtet zu werden.

Obwohl es eine Vielzahl von Entsorgungsmethoden gibt, ist die Verschrottung die gebräuchlichste, da Schiffe eine hervorragende Quelle für wiederverwendbares und recycelbares Material sind. In jeder Seeschifffahrtsökonomie gibt es eine klare Verbindung zwischen der wirtschaftlichen Entwicklung und der Aktivität des Verschrottens.[1] Die Schiffsverschrottung ist, wie sich gezeigt hat, ein Wanderphänomen. Sie wurde von den Boomjahren der Nachkriegszeit bis Anfang der 1970er Jahre zum überwiegenden Teil in westeuropäischen oder amerikanischen Trockendocks durchgeführt. Als die östlichen Fertigungsindustrien einen größeren Hunger nach Ressourcen entwickelten, wanderte die Industrie zu den im Aufstieg begriffenen Ökonomien Koreas, Japans, Chinas und Taiwans, wo sich die Verschrottung von Schiffen als ein schneller Weg erwies, an den dringend benötigten Stahl zu gelangen.

Heute ist das am Golf von Khambhat gelegene Alang der letzte Ankerplatz für die Hälfte der weltweit jährlich mehr als 700 verschrotteten Schiffe. 1984 hörte man zum ersten Mal von Alang, zur Zeit der Rezession, die auf eine weltweite Übernahme der neoliberalen Wirtschaftsdoktrin zurückgeführt wird. Wegen der Rezession und staatlichen Regulierungsmaßnahmen explodierten die Kosten für die Verschrottung von Schiffen in den fernöstlichen Demontagewerften. Ihre Konkurrenten auf dem indischen Subkontinent boten eine kostengünstigere Alternative. Die hier verwendete Methode ist als "Strandung" bekannt. An diesen Orten gibt es den weltweit höchsten Tidenhub, so dass die Schiffe bei Springflut so weit wie möglich in Richtung Festland gefahren werden können, über das Watt bis direkt auf den Strand, was technisch aufwendige Trockendocks überflüssig macht.

Allerdings bedeutet die Entsorgung dieser kolossalen Objekte eine enorme ökologische Herausforderung. Sie weisen oftmals ein Leergewicht von mehr als 10.000 Tonnen auf, haben Ölrückstände, Bleifarbe, Asbest, PCB und andere gefährliche oder toxische Stoffe an Bord. Strenge Umweltschutzauflagen machen die Schiffsverschrottung zu einem komplexen Prozess der Dekontamination und treiben die Kosten in die Höhe. Dieser Kostenanstieg führte dazu, dass sich die Verschrottungsaktivitäten in die unentwickelten Länder, vor allem nach Südasien, verlagerten. Deren einzigartige geografische Lage, die billigen Arbeitskräfte und die nicht oder kaum vorhandenen Umweltschutzkontrollen bedeuteten niedrigere Betriebskosten.

Der globale Zustrom von überalteten Schiffen zu diesen Orten setzt eine Missachtung der rechtlichen Bestimmungen der OECD-Länder voraus. Viele dieser Schiffe wechseln Eigner und Flagge, um die gesetzlichen Regelungen der westlichen Welt zu umgehen, die einen Verkauf dieser toxischen Schiffe an Entwicklungsländer verbieten. Die Situation bleibt undurchschaubar, obwohl mit den Übereinkommen von Basel und HongKong die Verschrottung von Schiffen der internationalen Rechtsaufsicht unterstellt wurde.

Die soziopolitische Ökonomie der Schiffsverschrottung ist komplex und wirft ein Schlaglicht auf kollidierende Interessen, besonders für eine aufstrebende Wirtschaft wie Indien. In Indien hat der Staat – durch seine Anerkennung der Schiffsverschrottung als Industrie – deutlich zu verstehen gegeben, dass er sich der wirtschaftlichen Bedeutung dieses Gewerbes bewusst ist.

Um eine Lektion aus dem Aufstieg und Fall der Industriestädte zu ziehen, muss Alang, damit es nicht zu einer weiteren historischen Stätte der Wanderindustrie wird, über die Monokulturwirtschaft hinausgehen. Würde die einseitige schmutzige Verschrottungsmaschinerie zur vielfältigen Schiffsrecyclingindustrie aufgewertet, könnte Alang es schaffen, den gefährlichen Abfall in eine breitgefächerte Wirtschaft umzuwandeln.

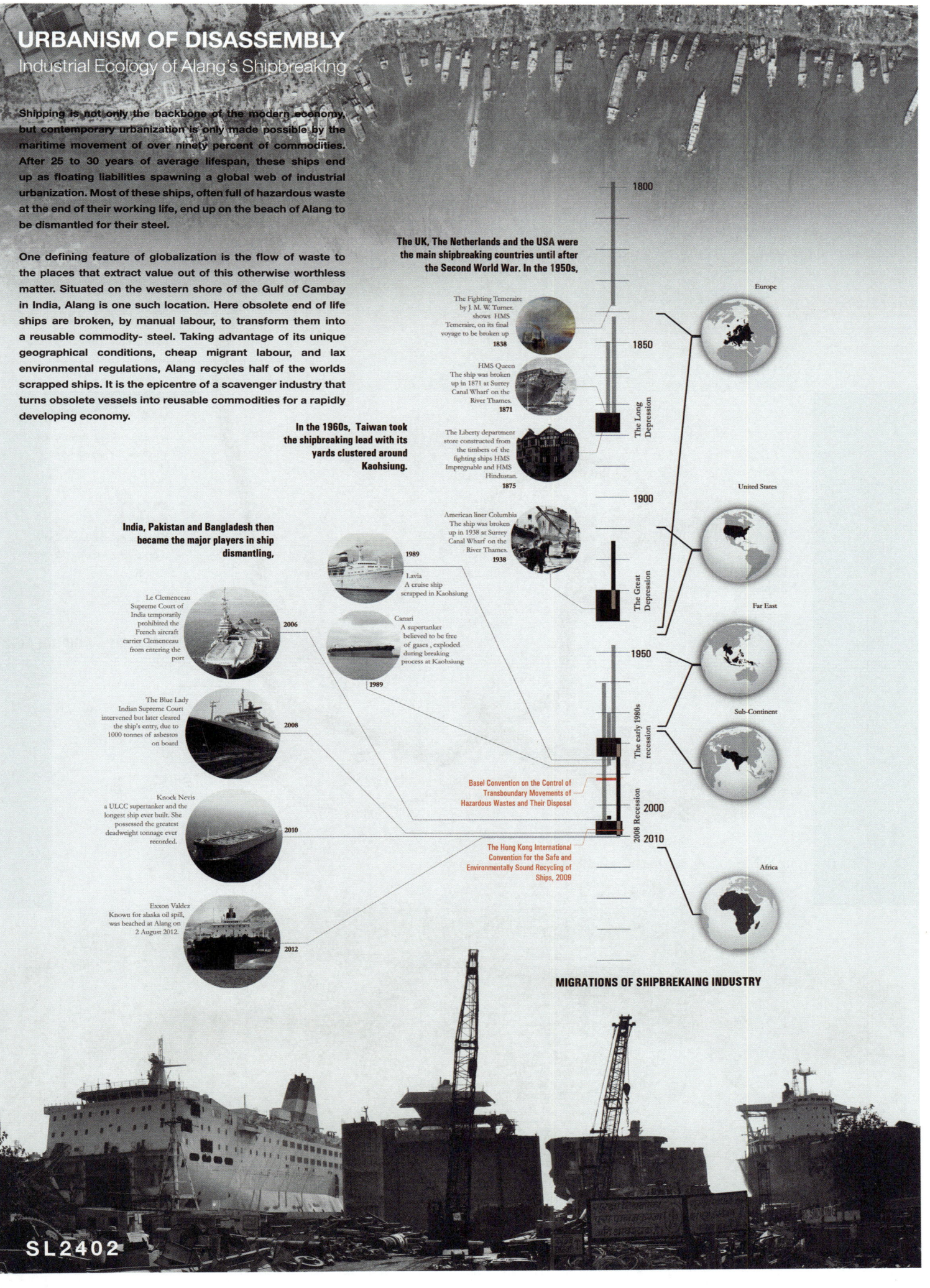

URBANISM OF DISASSEMBLY
Industrial Ecology of Alang's Shipbreaking

Shipping is not only the backbone of the modern economy, but contemporary urbanization is only made possible by the maritime movement of over ninety percent of commodities. After 25 to 30 years of average lifespan, these ships end up as floating liabilities spawning a global web of industrial urbanization. Most of these ships, often full of hazardous waste at the end of their working life, end up on the beach of Alang to be dismantled for their steel.

One defining feature of globalization is the flow of waste to the places that extract value out of this otherwise worthless matter. Situated on the western shore of the Gulf of Cambay in India, Alang is one such location. Here obsolete end of life ships are broken, by manual labour, to transform them into a reusable commodity- steel. Taking advantage of its unique geographical conditions, cheap migrant labour, and lax environmental regulations, Alang recycles half of the worlds scrapped ships. It is the epicentre of a scavenger industry that turns obsolete vessels into reusable commodities for a rapidly developing economy.

The UK, The Netherlands and the USA were the main shipbreaking countries until after the Second World War. In the 1950s,

The Fighting Temeraire by J. M. W. Turner. shows HMS Temeraire, on its final voyage to be broken up
1838

HMS Queen
The ship was broken up in 1871 at Surrey Canal Wharf on the River Thames.
1871

The Liberty department store constructed from the timbers of the fighting ships HMS Impregnable and HMS Hindustan.
1875

American liner Columbia
The ship was broken up in 1938 at Surrey Canal Wharf on the River Thames.
1938

In the 1960s, Taiwan took the shipbreaking lead with its yards clustered around Kaohsiung.

India, Pakistan and Bangladesh then became the major players in ship dismantling,

Le Clemenceau
Supreme Court of India temporarily prohibited the French aircraft carrier Clemenceau from entering the port
2006

The Blue Lady
Indian Supreme Court intervened but later cleared the ship's entry, due to 1000 tonnes of asbestos on board
2008

Knock Nevis
a ULCC supertanker and the longest ship ever built. She possessed the greatest deadweight tonnage ever recorded.
2010

Exxon Valdez
Known for alaska oil spill, was beached at Alang on 2 August 2012.
2012

1989
Lavia
A cruise ship scrapped in Kaohsiung

1989
Canari
A supertanker believed to be free of gases , exploded during breaking process at Kaohsiung

1800
1850
1900
1950
2000
2010

The Long Depression
The Great Depression
The early 1980s recession
2008 Recession

Basel Convention on the Control of Transboundary Movements of Hazardous Wastes and Their Disposal

The Hong Kong International Convention for the Safe and Environmentally Sound Recycling of Ships, 2009

Europe

United States

Far East

Sub-Continent

Africa

MIGRATIONS OF SHIPBREKAING INDUSTRY

SL2402

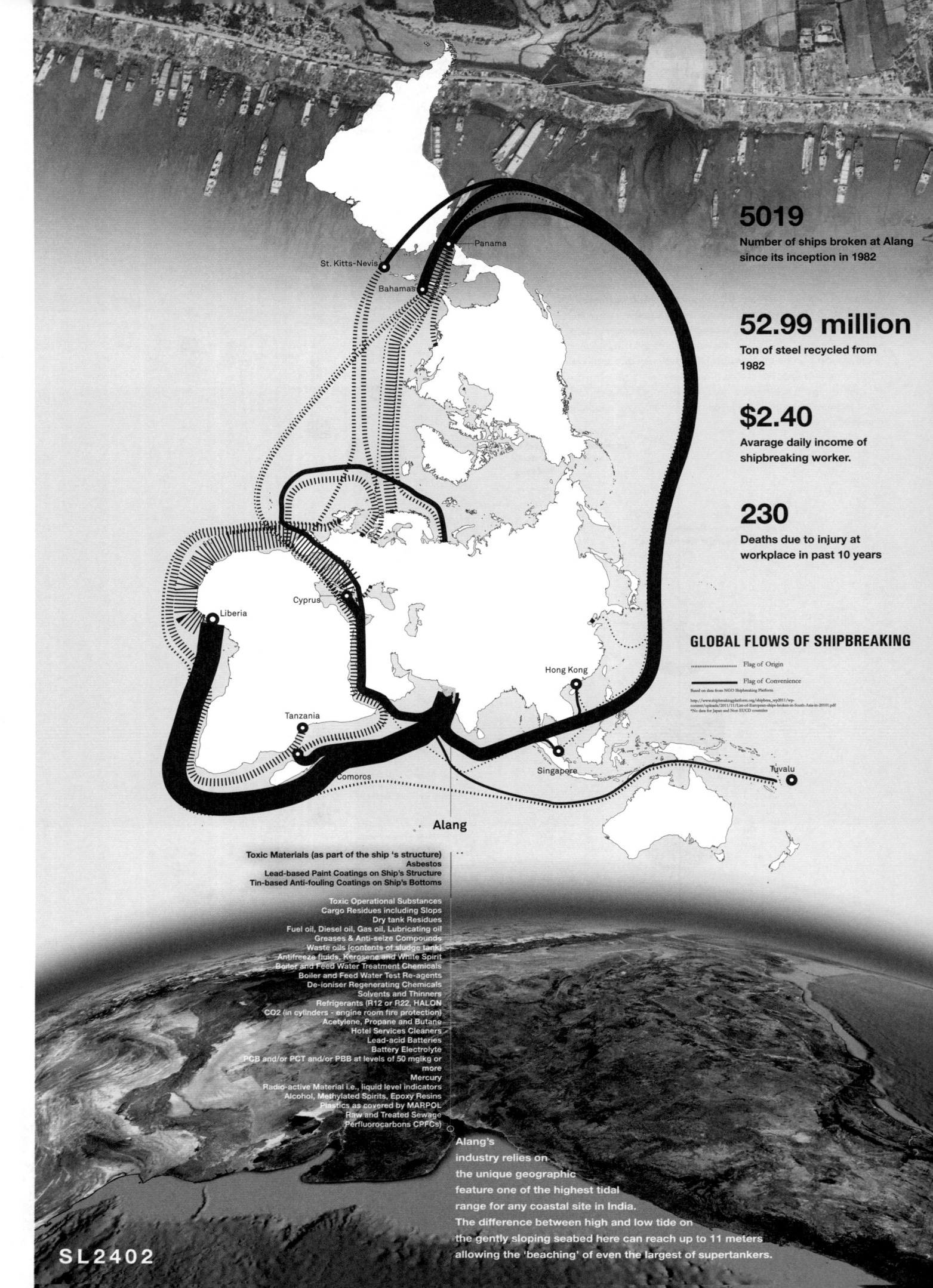

5019

Number of ships broken at Alang since its inception in 1982

52.99 million

Ton of steel recycled from 1982

$2.40

Avarage daily income of shipbreaking worker.

230

Deaths due to injury at workplace in past 10 years

Panama

St. Kitts-Nevis

Bahamas

Cyprus

Liberia

Hong Kong

Tanzania

Comoros

Singapore

Tuvalu

Alang

GLOBAL FLOWS OF SHIPBREAKING

.... Flag of Origin

━━━━ Flag of Convenience

Based on data from NGO Shipbreaking Platform

http://www.shipbreakingplatform.org/shipbrea_wp2011/wp-content/uploads/2011/11/List-of-European-ships-broken-in-South-Asia-in-20101.pdf
*No data for Japan and Non EUCD countries

Toxic Materials (as part of the ship 's structure)
Asbestos
Lead-based Paint Coatings on Ship's Structure
Tin-based Anti-fouling Coatings on Ship's Bottoms

Toxic Operational Substances
Cargo Residues including Slops
Dry tank Residues
Fuel oil, Diesel oil, Gas oil, Lubricating oil
Greases & Anti-seize Compounds
Waste oils (contents of sludge tank)
Antifreeze fluids, Kerosene and White Spirit
Boiler and Feed Water Treatment Chemicals
Boiler and Feed Water Test Re-agents
De-ioniser Regenerating Chemicals
Solvents and Thinners
Refrigerants (R12 or R22, HALON
CO_2 (in cylinders - engine room fire protection)
Acetylene, Propane and Butane
Hotel Services Cleaners
Lead-acid Batteries
Battery Electrolyte
PCB and/or PCT and/or PBB at levels of 50 mglkg or more
Mercury
Radio-active Material i.e., liquid level indicators
Alcohol, Methylated Spirits, Epoxy Resins
Plastics as covered by MARPOL
Raw and Treated Sewage
Perfluorocarbons CPFCs)

Alang's industry relies on the unique geographic feature one of the highest tidal range for any coastal site in India.
The difference between high and low tide on the gently sloping seabed here can reach up to 11 meters allowing the 'beaching' of even the largest of supertankers.

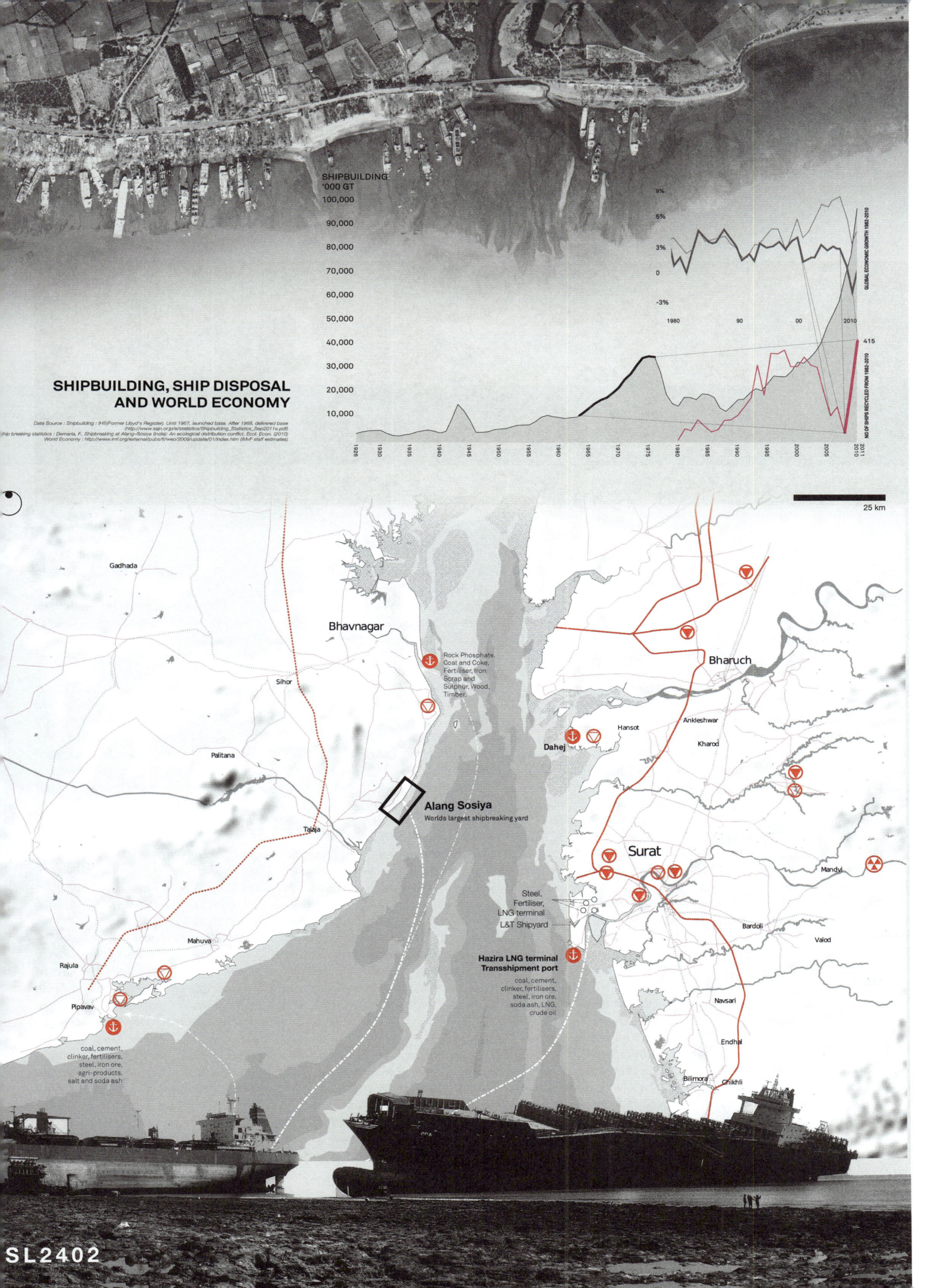

SHIPBUILDING
'000 GT

SHIPBUILDING, SHIP DISPOSAL
AND WORLD ECONOMY

Data Source : Shipbuilding : IHS(Former Lloyd's Register). Until 1967, launched base. After 1968, delivered base
(http://www.sajn.or.jp/statistics/Shipbuilding_Statistics_Sep2011e.pdf)
Ship breaking statistics : Demaria, F. Shipbreaking at Alang-Sosiya (India). An ecological distribution conflict, Ecol. Econ. (2010)
World Economy : http://www.imf.org/external/pubs/ft/weo/2009/update/01/index.htm (IMF staff estimates)

25 km

Gadhada

Bhavnagar

Rock Phosphate,
Coal and Coke,
Fertiliser, Iron
Scrap and
Sulphur, Wood,
Timber.

Bharuch

Sihor

Hansot

Ankleshwar

Palitana

Dahej

Kharod

Alang Sosiya
Worlds largest shipbreaking yard

Taiaja

Surat

Mandvi

Steel,
Fertiliser,
LNG terminal
L&T Shipyard

Bardoli

Mahuva

Valod

Rajula

**Hazira LNG terminal
Transshipment port**
coal, cement,
clinker, fertilisers,
steel, iron ore,
soda ash, LNG,
crude oil

Navsari

Pipavav

Endhal

coal, cement,
clinker, fertilisers,
steel, iron ore,
agri-products,
salt and soda ash

Bilimora

Chikhli

GLOBAL URBAN CULTURE

Leon Schubert
Yasin Altunok
Khaliun Aldar

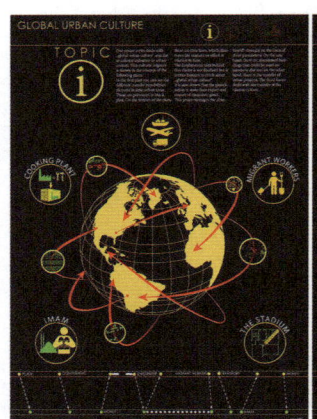 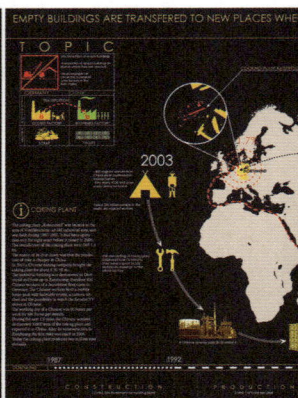 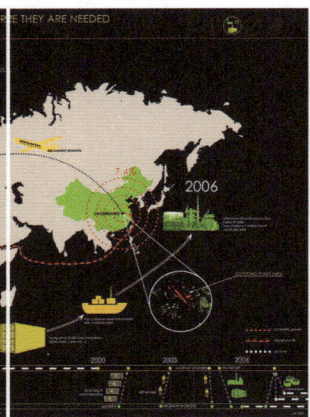 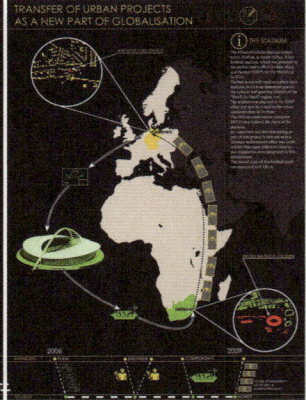 

"We might profitably conceive of the Bilbao gallery as a site, located in a number of cross-cutting spatial arrangements, as a consumption space, as networked temporally and transculturally, but as much dependent on local political will as on global circuits of recognition. This is particularly important when one considers the 'Bilbao Effect' as something materially different from the building itself."
McNeill, Donald: The "Bilbao Effect"[1]

Locality in global flux: 3 Transplants

For participants in the globalizing process, geographical distance is no longer a barrier – goods would appear wherever in demand. However, some goods exceed their usual biography of being exported, imported, and consumed; instead they are artifacts of cultures being transplanted, exercising long lasting and wide-ranging chain effects on localities and identities.

Kaiserstuhl

Since late 1990s, dozens of coking plants and steel blast furnaces were transferred to China from Germany's old industrial Ruhr valley, contributing to the burst in China's steel production in the last decades.[2] "Kaiserstuhl" is one of them.

Erected in 1992 in Ruhr valley city Dortmund, "Kaiserstuhl" was built to be the most modern coke making facility in Europe, supplying coke to a nearby blast furnace. 2000 saw the closure of the blast furnace; the coking plant was thus shut down after mere 8 years in operation. In 2006 "Kaiserstuhl" developed into a true goldmine after being sold to a prominent coking company in China, and began producing coking coal on the other side of the world.

400 Chinese migrant workers came to Germany to disassemble the giant, while Dortmund suffers from loss of jobs in a post-industrial era. China has bought technical drawings together with the factory in the hope of building more factories in China, while Germany is envisaging a post-industrial area, turning the once smoky Ruhr area into a green "Industrial Heritage Trail". While Germany has reduced its carbon emissions, cleaned its skies and is now the world's pioneer in fighting against global warming, China seems to have successfully transplanted the heart of Ruhr valley, with its steady production impulse and smoke emitting arteries.

With China's rising smog issue, the Ministry of Environmental Protection is tightening its environmental guidelines.[3] It is only a matter of time until these transplanted factories see the end of their lifespan.

Moses-Mabhida-Stadium

The "Moses-Mabhida-Stadium" was built for the World Cup South-Africa in 2010. Conceived in the renowned German architecture office Gerkan, Marg and Partner (gmp), it was realized in Durban

"Wir können uns das Bilbao-Museum gewinnbringend vorstellen als einen Platz innerhalb einer Anzahl sich kreuzender räumlicher Anordnungen, als zeitlich und transkulturell vernetzt, aber genauso abhängig vom lokalen politischen Willen wie von globalen Kreisläufen des Wiedererkennens. Das ist besonders wichtig, wenn man den 'Bilbao-Effekt' als etwas betrachtet, was sich materiell vom Gebäude selbst unterscheidet."
Donald McNeill: The "Bilbao Effect"[1]

Lokalität in globalem Fluss: 3 Transplantationen

Für die am Globalisierungsprozess Beteiligten ist geografische Entfernung keine Barriere mehr – Güter erscheinen, wo immer man ihrer bedarf. Manche Güter sprengen allerdings den Rahmen ihrer üblichen Biografie des Exportiert-, Importiert- und Konsumiertwerdens und sind stattdessen Artefakte und Kulturen, die transplantiert werden und dauerhafte und weitreichende Auswirkungen auf Lokalitäten und Identitäten haben.

Kaiserstuhl

*Seit den späten 1990er Jahren sind Dutzende von Kokereianlagen und Stahlhochöfen von Deutschlands altem Industriegebiet an der Ruhr nach China verschifft worden, wo sie maßgeblich zum chinesischen Stahlboom der vergangenen Jahrzehnte beigetragen ha-*ben[2]*; die "Kaiserstuhl"-Anlage ist eine davon.*

1992 in Dortmund eingeweiht, war "Kaiserstuhl" die modernste Kokerei Europas; sie versorgte einen nahegelegenen Hochofen mit Koks. Im Jahr 2000 wurde der Hochofen stillgelegt, und deshalb wurde auch die Kokerei dichtgemacht, nach nur acht Jahren Betrieb. Im Jahr 2006 entwickelte sich die "Kaiserstuhl"-Anlage zu einer wahren Goldgrube, nachdem sie an ein großes chinesisches Verkokungsunternehmen verkauft worden war und auf der anderen Seite der Welt Kokskohle zu produzieren begann.

Vierhundert chinesische Wanderarbeiter kamen nach Deutschland, um die gigantische Anlage zu zerlegen, zu einer Zeit, als Dortmund unter dem Arbeitsplatzverlust der postindustriellen Ära litt. China hat nicht nur die Anlage gekauft, sondern auch die dazugehörigen technischen Zeichnungen, weil man in China weitere Anlagen dieser Art zu bauen hofft, während Deutschland eine postindustrielle Landschaft ins Auge fasst und das einstmals versmogte Ruhrgebiet in einen grünen "Industrieerbe-Pfad" verwandelt. Während Deutschland seine Kohlendioxidemissionen reduziert sowie seine Luft gereinigt hat und weltweit zum Vorreiter im Kampf gegen die Erderwärmung avanciert ist, scheint China das industrielle Herz des Ruhrgebiets erfolgreich transplantiert

by various construction participants. Recent news like "Fifa corruption: Morocco won 2010 World Cup vote – not South Africa"[4] further highlight the fanatic enthusiasm to become locale for major international events. Designed by celebrity architects, such venues would hopefully give impulse to a chain effect of economic boom and cultural prosperity, finally reshaping the local identity – similar to the famous "Bilbao Effect".

Nevertheless, fates of such implants vary. Athen's 2004 Olympics legacy is criticized for a possible role in the nation's economic meltdown; Vancouver's 2010 games venues remain in use only through a $110m governmental fund trust; London's 2012 Olympics has helped improve public transport in poorer areas but the opening of Queen Elizabeth Olympic Park in 2014 was troubled with controversy.[5]

In 2013, with the termination of government's World Cup subsidy, Durban's "Moses-Mabhida-Stadium" suffered a financial loss of R34.6m ($2.41m).[6] It was decided in November 2015 that the stadium would be incorporated under Durban's International Convention Centre for potential income streams.[7]

Imam

"Imam" is an Islamic leadership position. Trained in Islamic countries like Turkey, the candidates go through long and strict education before they lead worship services in mosques all over the world. In a non-Islamic country particularly, a mosque, besides being a place for praying, is often a place for social activities and education. A mosque plus its "Imam" could be seen as a cultural educational institution transplanted into a new socio-political context; it even fulfills a potential task of diplomacy, marking the border of Islamic culture on a non-Islamic territory. In the wake of the recent Paris attacks, the diplomatic pedagogic roles of the "Imam" are gradually placed in spotlight. French Muslims' largest representative group has called for Imams to be given a certificate "like a driving licence" to preach after being tested for extremism.[8] In Belgium, classrooms are set up by an Imam to provide guidance to children as young as 9 and 10, thus to prevent them being exposed to extremist thoughts and radical worldview.[9]

The three cases of global transplantation foremost announce the flux of local identity within the fluctuating web of global rise and fall. Furthermore, these transplanted artifacts become focal locales of strategy, diplomacy, or negotiation. The various outcomes highlight their hard-to-define potential to be either a blessing or a curse; in either case locality and identity are imbedded into a constant flux.

zu haben, mitsamt dem unablässigen Produktionsimpuls und den Rauch ausstoßenden Arterien dieses Organs.

Angesichts des immer akuter werdenden Smogproblems hat das chinesische Umweltschutzministerium seine Umweltschutzrichtlinien verschärft.[3] Es ist nur eine Frage der Zeit, bis diese transplantierten Industrieanlagen ihr Lebensende erreicht haben.

Moses-Mabhida-Stadion

Das "Moses-Mabhida-Stadion" wurde für die 2010 in Südafrika abgehaltene Fußballweltmeisterschaft gebaut. Von dem renommierten deutschen Architekturbüro Gerkan, Marg und Partner (gmp) entworfen, wurde es in Durban von diversen Baufirmen aus dem Boden gestampft. Jüngere Zeitungsschlagzeilen wie "FIFA-Korruption: Nicht Südafrika, sondern Marokko gewann die Abstimmung zur Ausrichtung der WM 2010"[4] offenbaren, mit welch fanatischem Enthusiasmus man sich darum bewirbt, Schauplatz für große internationale Sportveranstaltungen zu werden. Die von Stararchitekten entworfenen Bauwerke werden, so hofft man, einen Wirtschaftsboom auslösen und kulturelle Prosperität bewirken und letztlich die lokale Identität neu definieren – dem "Bilbao-Effekt" vergleichbar.

Das Schicksal solcher Implantationen variiert jedoch von Ort zu Ort. Das Erbe der 2004 in Athen abgehaltenen Olympiade soll eine nicht unwesentliche Rolle beim Zusammenbruch der griechischen Wirtschaft gespielt haben; die Sportstätten der Spiele von Vancouver (2010) bleiben nur dank eines von der Regierung bereitgestellten Treuhandfonds von 110 Millionen Dollar in Betrieb; die Londoner Olympiade von 2012 hat den öffentlichen Nahverkehr in ärmeren Gegenden verbessert, doch die 2014 erfolgte Eröffnung des Queen Elizabeth Olympic Park war eine umstrittene Angelegenheit.[5]

Als die staatlichen WM-Subventionen 2013 ausliefen, musste Durbans "Moses-Mabhida-Stadion" einen finanziellen Verlust von 34,6 Mio. R (2,41 Mio. $) verkraften.[6] Im November 2015 beschloss man, das Stadion wegen einer erhofften Ertragsverbesserung in das International Convention Centre von Durban einzugliedern.[7]

Imam

"Imam" bezeichnet eine islamische Führungsposition. In islamischen Ländern wie der Türkei ausgebildet, durchlaufen die Kandidaten eine lange und strenge Ausbildung, bevor sie Gottesdienste in Moscheen überall auf der Welt abhalten dürfen. In einem nicht islamischen Land ist eine Moschee nicht nur eine Gebetsstätte, sondern meist auch ein Ort für soziale und pädagogische Aktivitäten. Eine Moschee und ihr Imam können als eine kulturelle Erziehungsinstitution angesehen werden, die in ein neues soziales und politisches Umfeld transplantiert worden ist; sie erfüllt sogar eine potenziell diplomatische Aufgabe, indem sie die Grenzen der islamischen Kultur auf einem nicht islamischen Territorium markiert. Im Gefolge der jüngsten Pariser Terroranschläge rücken die diplomatische und die pädagogische Rolle des Imams zunehmend in den Fokus des öffentlichen Interesses. Die größte Interessenvertretung der französischen Muslime verlangt, dass Imame eine "dem Führerschein vergleichbare" Erlaubnis zum Predigen erhalten sollen, nachdem man sie auf Extremismus getestet hat.[8] In Belgien werden von Imamen Klassen für neun- bis zehnjährige Schüler eingerichtet, um diese zu unterweisen, ohne dass sie extremistischem Gedankengut oder radikalen Ideologien ausgesetzt sind.[9]

Die drei Arten von globaler Transplantation annoncieren den Fluss lokaler Indentität innerhalb des sich unentwegt verändernden Netzes des globalen Aufstiegs und Niedergangs. Darüber hinaus werden diese transplantierten Artefakte zu Brennpunkten der Strategie, der Diplomatie oder der Verhandlung. Die verschiedenen Ergebnisse werfen ein Schlaglicht auf ihr schwer zu definierendes Potenzial als ein Segen oder ein Fluch; in beiden Fällen sind Lokalität und Identität in einen ununterbrochenen Fluss eingebettet.
Text: Zhen Zhang

T O P I C

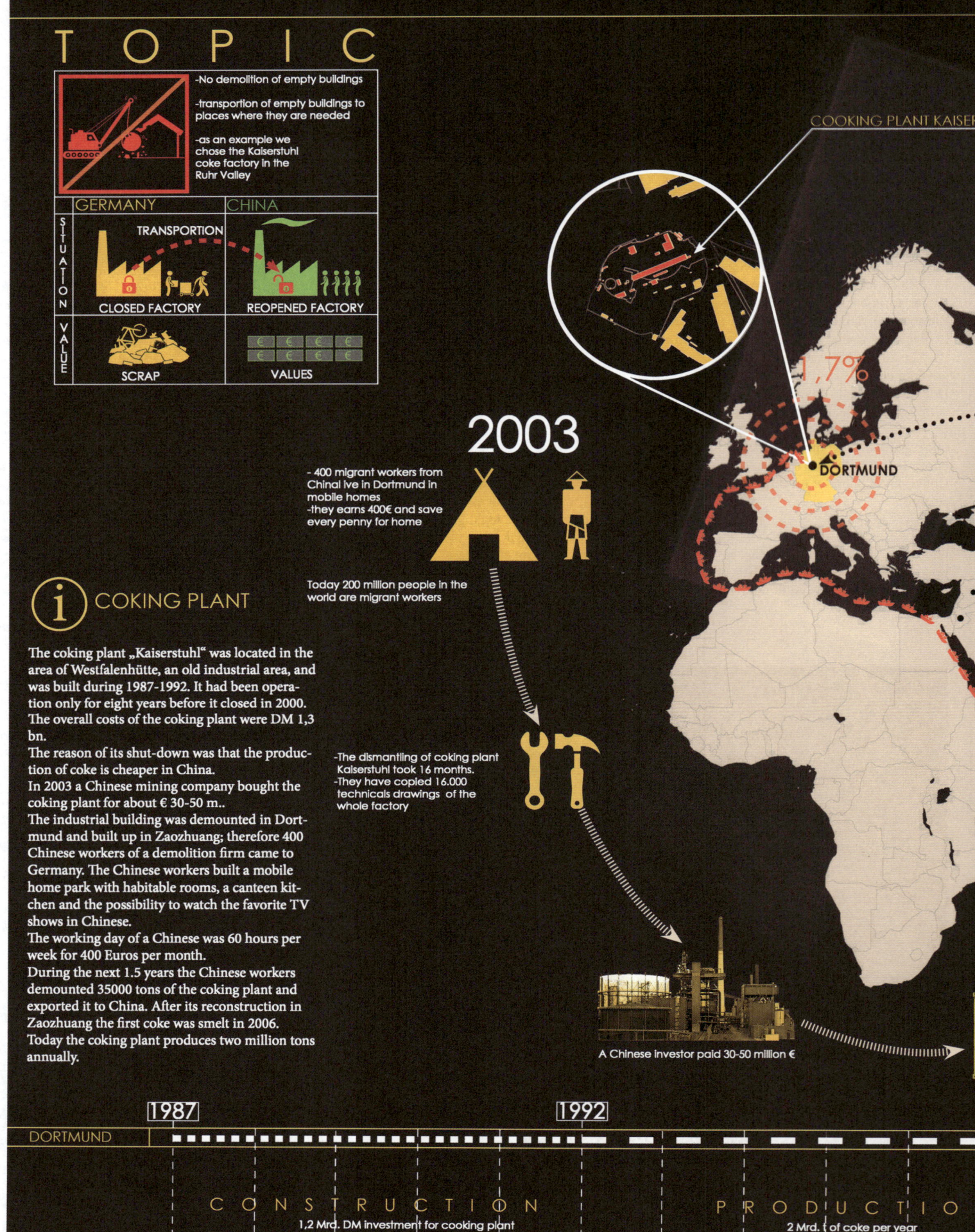

-No demolition of empty buildings

-transportion of empty buildings to places where they are needed

-as an example we chose the Kaiserstuhl coke factory in the Ruhr Valley

GERMANY

CHINA

SITUATION

TRANSPORTION

CLOSED FACTORY

REOPENED FACTORY

VALUE

SCRAP

VALUES

COOKING PLANT KAISERS

DORTMUND

1,7%

2003

- 400 migrant workers from Chinal ive in Dortmund in mobile homes
-they earns 400€ and save every penny for home

Today 200 million people in the world are migrant workers

-The dismantling of coking plant Kaiserstuhl took 16 months.
-They have copied 16.000 technicals drawings of the whole factory

(i) COKING PLANT

The coking plant „Kaiserstuhl" was located in the area of Westfalenhütte, an old industrial area, and was built during 1987-1992. It had been operation only for eight years before it closed in 2000. The overall costs of the coking plant were DM 1,3 bn.

The reason of its shut-down was that the production of coke is cheaper in China.

In 2003 a Chinese mining company bought the coking plant for about € 30-50 m..

The industrial building was demounted in Dortmund and built up in Zaozhuang; therefore 400 Chinese workers of a demolition firm came to Germany. The Chinese workers built a mobile home park with habitable rooms, a canteen kitchen and the possibility to watch the favorite TV shows in Chinese.

The working day of a Chinese was 60 hours per week for 400 Euros per month.

During the next 1.5 years the Chinese workers demounted 35000 tons of the coking plant and exported it to China. After its reconstruction in Zaozhuang the first coke was smelt in 2006. Today the coking plant produces two million tons annually.

A Chinese investor paid 30-50 million €

1987

1992

DORTMUND

C O N S T R U C T I O N

1,2 Mrd. DM investment for cooking plant

P R O D U C T I O N

2 Mrd. t of coke per year

ZAOZHUANG

THEY ARE NEEDED

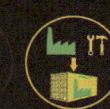

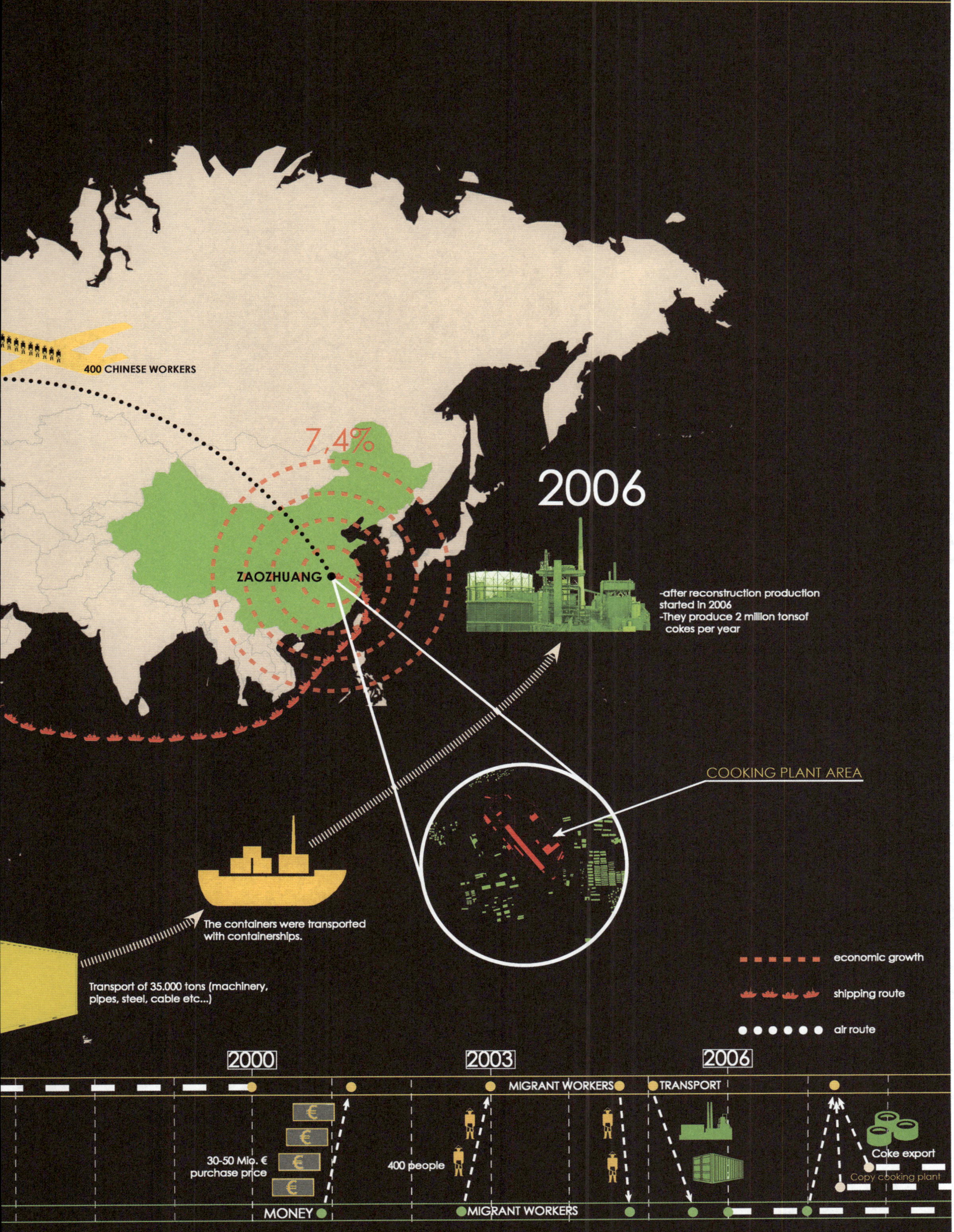

400 CHINESE WORKERS
7,4%
ZAOZHUANG
2006
-after reconstruction production started in 2006
-They produce 2 million tonsof cokes per year
COOKING PLANT AREA
The containers were transported with containerships.
Transport of 35.000 tons (machinery, pipes, steel, cable etc...)
economic growth
shipping route
air route
2000
2003
2006
MIGRANT WORKERS
TRANSPORT
30-50 Mio. € purchase price
400 people
Coke export
Copy cooking plant
MONEY
MIGRANT WORKERS

THE RUSH ON FOREIGN LAND: AN OVERVIEW OF INTERNATIONAL LAND INVESTMENTS

by Cornelius Hirsch
Felix von der Weppen
Cecil von Treu

Since the year 2000 an increasing number of international land-investments have been documented. The investors, whether private or governmental, seek large-scale land areas around the globe. They focus on long-term leases (60–99 years) and purchase to produce food and non-food commodities. Once the deals are signed and vast acres cultivated, the produced goods are generally exported and sold on the world market or transferred to the investor's country.

These land investments are primarily located in less developed countries of the Global South. Little information about the contract details is accessible to the public. Still, the impact on economic, social and ecological aspects in countries that host such investments (provider countries) seems inevitable.

The map displays the worldwide activity of investors and providers of land, linking the Top 10 Investors to the Top 10 Provider Countries.

Canada

992.196 ha

461.750 h

411.095 ha

68.000 ha

1.400.

2.2#

168.1

138.3/3 ha

117.99/ ha

USA

Brazil
1.631.074 ha

Top 10 Provider Countries

- South Sudan
- Papua New Guinea
- Indonesia
- Sudan
- DRC
- Mozambique
- Congo
- Ukraine
- Brazil
- Russian Federation

0   1   2   3   4   5 Mio. hectare

Top 10 Investor Countries

- USA
- Malaysia
- United Arab Emirates
- Singapore
- United Kingdom
- Canada
- India
- Saudi Arabia
- Jordan
- Hong Kong

0   2   4   6   8   10 Mio. hectare

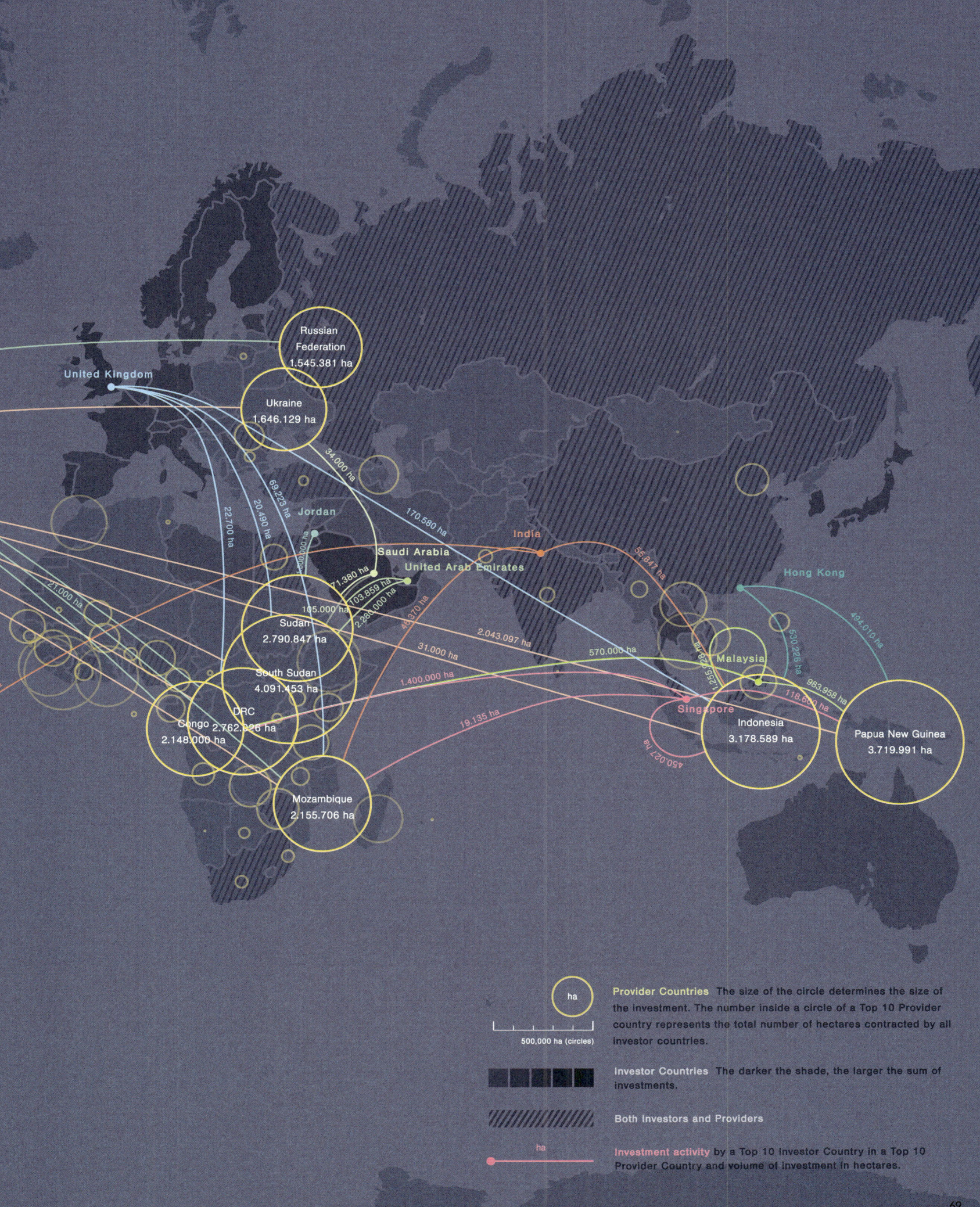

Russian
Federation
1.545.381 ha

Ukraine
1.646.129 ha

United Kingdom

34.000 ha

69.223 ha

20.490 ha

22.700 ha

Jordan

170.580 ha

India

Hong Kong

Saudi Arabia
United Arab Emirates

71.380 ha

103.859 ha

105.000 ha

2.280.000 ha

56.841 ha

484.010 ha

21.000 ha

Sudan
2.790.847 ha

2.043.097 ha

570.000 ha

530.926 ha

983.959 ha

Malaysia

South Sudan
4.091.453 ha

31.000 ha

1.400.000 ha

118.000 ha

1.255.967 ha

DRC
Congo 2.762.926 ha
2.148.000 ha

19.135 ha

Singapore

Indonesia
3.178.589 ha

Papua New Guinea
3.719.991 ha

450.027 ha

Mozambique
2.155.706 ha

ha

500,000 ha (circles)

Provider Countries The size of the circle determines the size of the investment. The number inside a circle of a Top 10 Provider country represents the total number of hectares contracted by all investor countries.

Investor Countries The darker the shade, the larger the sum of investments.

Both Investors and Providers

ha

Investment activity by a Top 10 Investor Country in a Top 10 Provider Country and volume of investment in hectares.

69

1,166
concluded deals
(reported)

&

42,861,983
hectares
(reported)

equal

1.67 x

the size
of Ecuador

The development and drivers of land investments

The number of reported investments show a rapid increase in the last two decades. Among others, the economic crises and surge of international food prices between 2003–2009 influenced the development. The price for food is driven by factors such as population growth, biofuel demand, changing consumer preferences with increasing disposable income etc. Hence, the investment in land seems a reliable and valuable asset.

It appears that the number of deals declined since 2013. The reason being the ongoing documentation of constantly evolving data availability. Therefore, many deals are not yet included in the underlying database. Nevertheless, since 2000 a total number of 1166 concluded investments (covering an area of approx. 43 million hectares) have been documented.

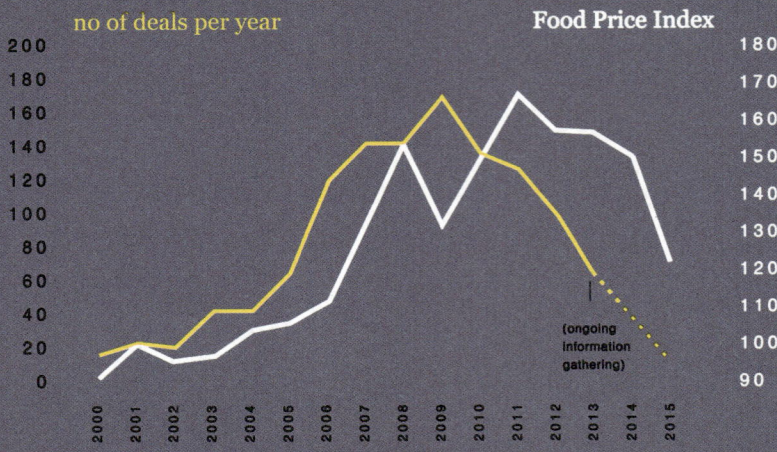

Who are the investors?

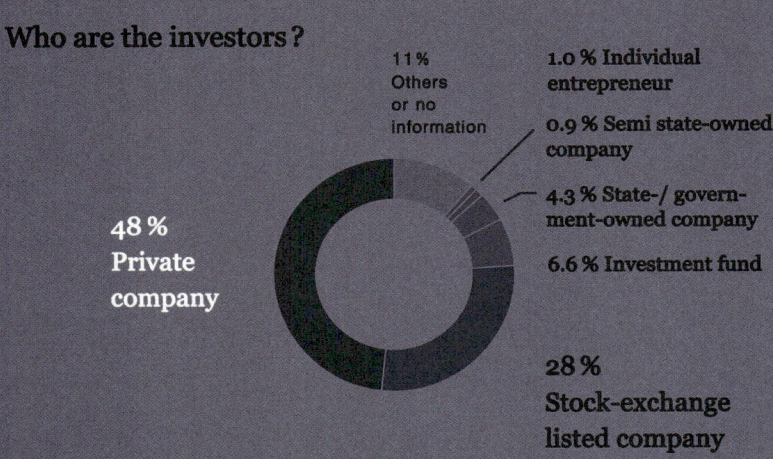

11 % Others or no information

1.0 % Individual entrepreneur

0.9 % Semi state-owned company

4.3 % State-/ government-owned company

6.6 % Investment fund

48 % Private company

28 % Stock-exchange listed company

What do the contracts look like?

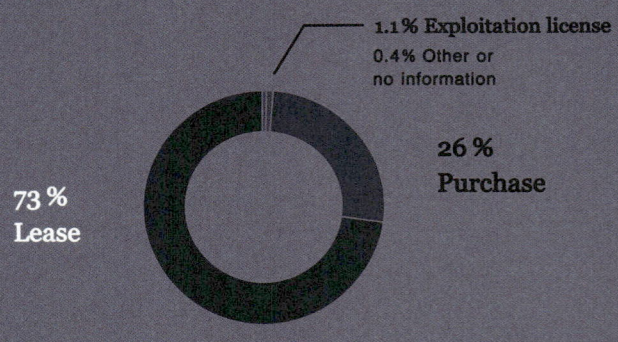

1.1 % Exploitation license
0.4 % Other or no information

26 % Purchase

73 % Lease

Which sectors are involved?

Multiple intention (28 %)

Industry, conservation and other (0.3 %)

Renewable Energy (0.7 %)

Tourism (1.3 %)

48 % Agriculture

21 % Forestry

What land-use is driving the investment?

9 % Other or no information

3 % Livestock

36 % Food crops

10 % Non-food agricultural

12 % Agricultural (unspecified)

12 % Wood and fibre including forest management

17 % Agrofuels

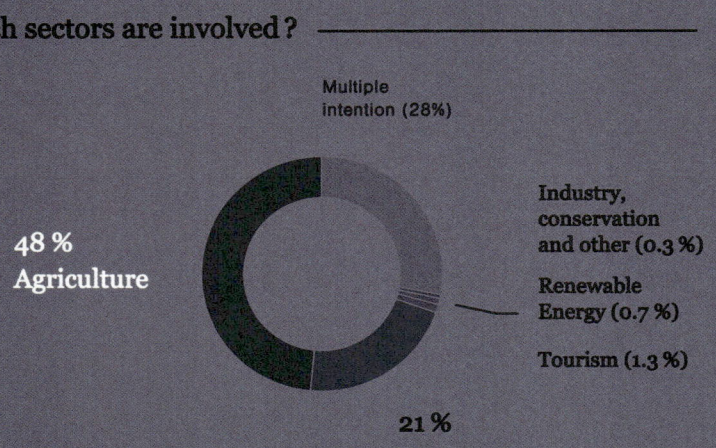

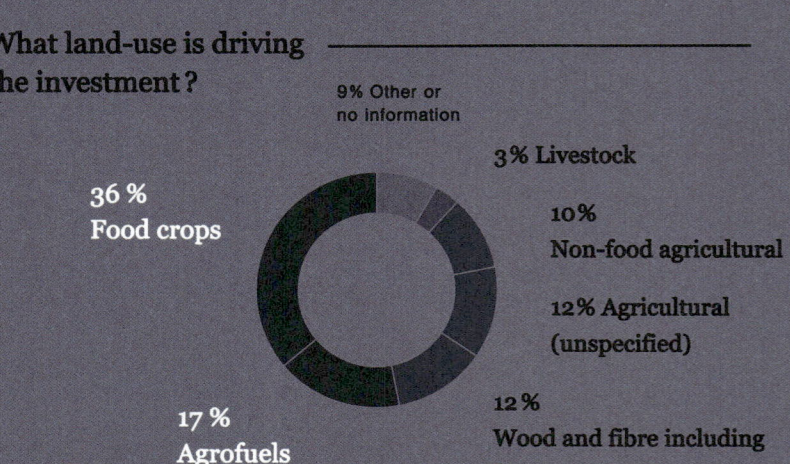

Countries with agricultural land scarcity outsource their food production

The Gulf Region is actively investing in East Africa. Due to the scarcity of arable land, many Gulf States are highly dependent on international food markets to satisfy their domestic consumption. Therefore, foreign land investments are a suitable strategy to outsource food production to countries such as the former Sudan and Ethiopia.

The palm oil hotspot –
Classic agribusinesses expand their production

South East Asia forms a hotspot for land deals. Many agribusinesses, which seek to incorporate the sector of primary commodity production, are based in the region. Moreover, palm oil takes up a big share of investment portfolios. Due to favourable climate conditions and geographic proximity, the investments are concentrated in Oceania and South East Asia.

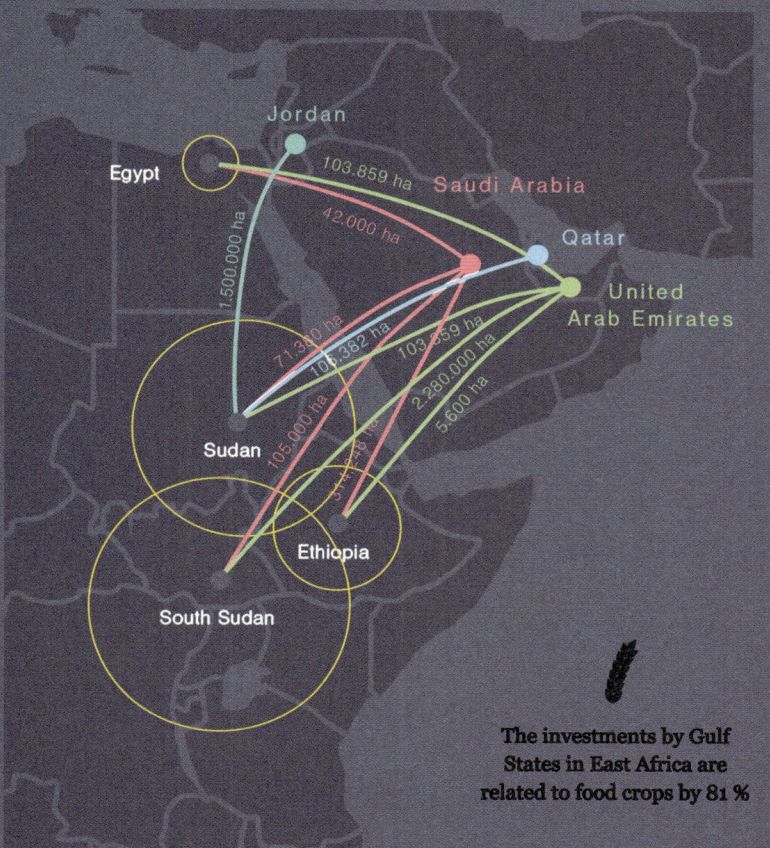

The investments by Gulf States in East Africa are related to food crops by 81 %

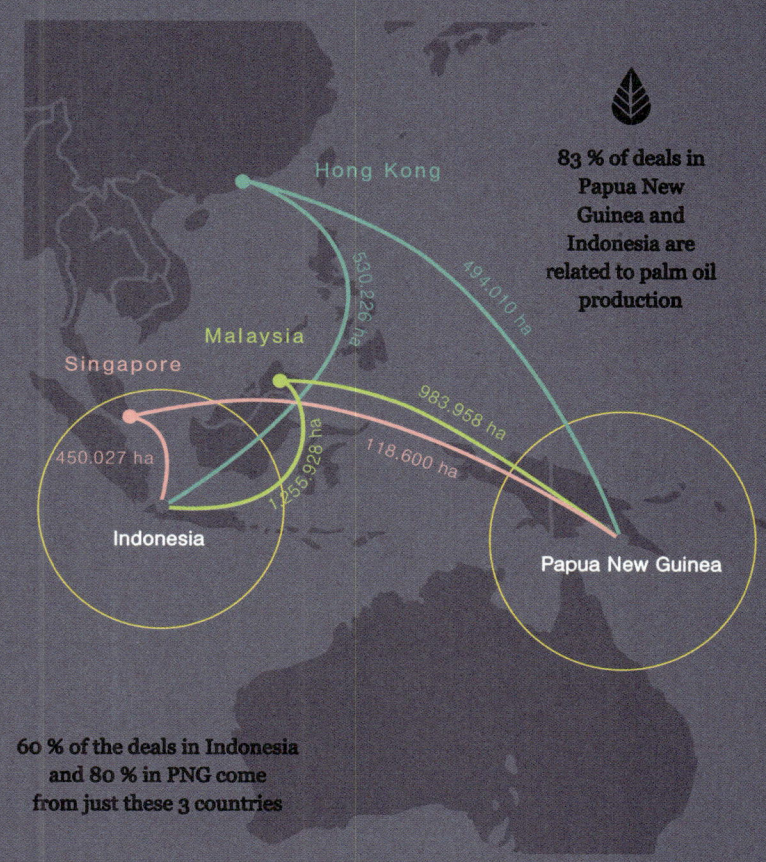

83 % of deals in Papua New Guinea and Indonesia are related to palm oil production

60 % of the deals in Indonesia and 80 % in PNG come from just these 3 countries

Financial investors seek solid investments

The UK is a good example of a diverse investing stakeholder. Here, many financial institutions and investment funds are increasingly looking for reliable and attractive investment opportunities in land all over the world. In addition, the agrofuel mandates established by the EU created incentives for private stakeholders to further engage in land investments.

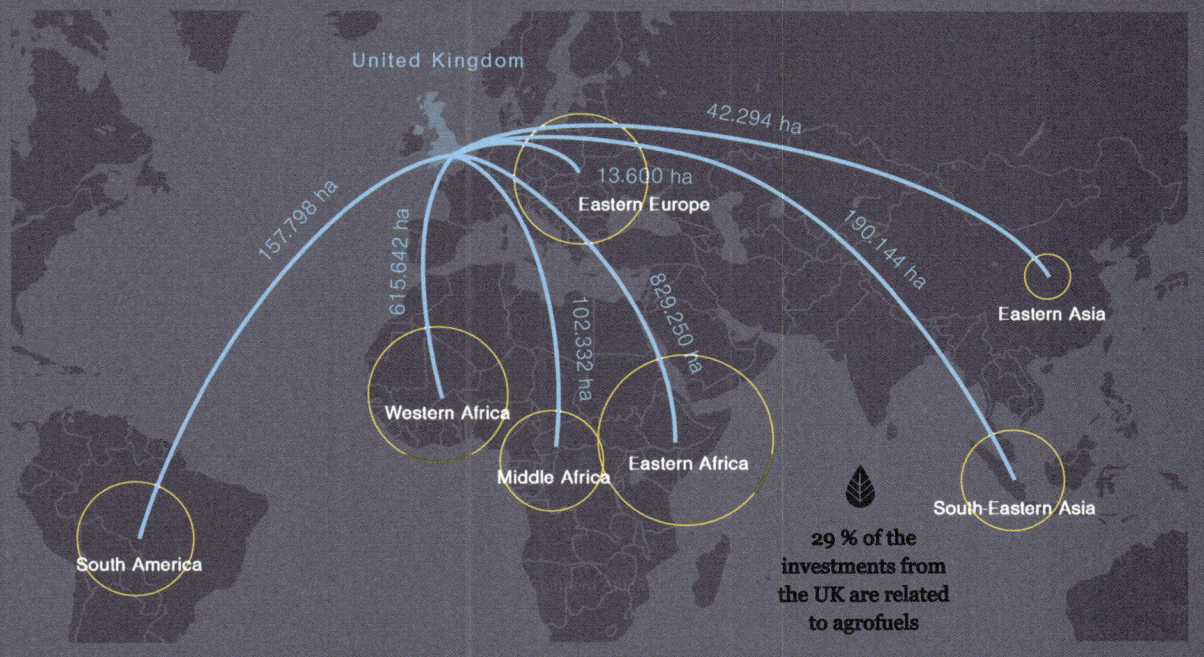

29 % of the investments from the UK are related to agrofuels

The presented figures are based on data by the Land Matrix, an initiative which monitors and documents large-scale land acquisitions. The Food Price Index is from FAO.org If you wish to get more information about the data, visit landmatrix.org. To get a better understanding of the elementary drivers behind the rush on foreign land, have a look at landmapping.org (launching June 2016).

Networks, material and electronic alike, superimpose a secondary structure on physical space that establishes new relationships of proximity and distance defined by time, rather than space. Networks that emerge from a web of social relationships also generate such a space of proximity regardless of the physical dimensions of the space and, in the case of digital networks, this happens in real time. Social behaviour constitutes an own "lived-in" space. Digital networks constitute space or a multitude of spaces. Networks generate synergy effects and have an intensifying function; their properties are not a sum of the properties of the individual components, but characterise an independent "organism".

CONNECTED CITY

Netze, materielle wie elektronische, überlagern den physischen Raum mit einer sekundären Struktur, die neue Nähe- bzw. Distanzbeziehungen herstellt, welche sich nicht räumlich, sondern zeitlich definieren.

Auch Netzwerke, die aus einem Geflecht sozialer Beziehungen entstehen, schaffen einen solchen Raum der Proximität unabhängig von den physischen Dimensionen des Raums und das geschieht, wenn es sich dabei um digitale Netzwerke handelt, in Echtzeit.

Soziales Verhalten konstituiert einen eigenen, "gelebten" Raum. Digitale Netzwerke konstituieren Raum bzw. eine Vielzahl von Räumen. Netzwerke erzeugen Synergieeffekte und haben Verstärkerfunktion, ihre Eigenschaften ergeben sich nicht als Summe der Eigenschaften der einzelnen Teile, sondern charakterisieren einen eigenständigen "Organismus".

CITY UPDATE

Eva Eiling, Britta Feemers, Sophia Pafitis

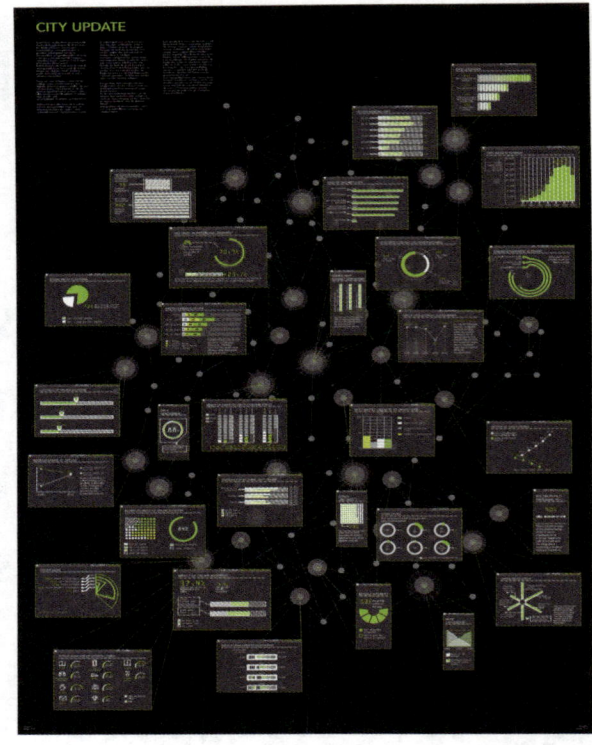

Since around 2000 the term "Smart City" has been established as a label for sustainable urban development. The loosely defined term is employed to promote the use of digital technologies to reduce urban energy consumption and environmental impacts of motorised traffic and to implement carbon neutral energy systems.

"Smart Cities" introduce new types of regulation to shape the exchange of goods, services and information, partially or entirely developed by high-tech corporations. Projects like "Songdo City" in South Korea, "Masdar" in Abu Dhabi und "PlanIT Valley" in Portugal are prime examples for modes of urban development that resonate with the belief that technological advancements, rather than e.g. municipal policies, are able to solve society's most pressing problems.

The notion of "smart" urban development "[...] appears to have originated within [high-tech] businesses, rather than with any party, group or political movement." By outsourcing municipal functions to high-tech cor-porations, the city turns into "a market, where technology corporations can sell [and test] their products and services."*

The increased use of digital technologies restructures the use of urban space and people's everyday lives. Individual daily routines are based more and more on remote access of goods, services, and social contacts. Conversely, individuals' "digital lives" are utilised by technology corporations to enhance their services according to use patterns of entire urban populations, and hence to further profit and gain market momentum.

"City Update" attempts to trace effects of digital technologies on personal everyday lives in cities, and provides information on use patterns of online social networks and online shopping in particular.

Sources

http://futurezone.at/digital-life/der-grosse-smart-city-schwindel/70.209.138

* Adam Greenfield: Against the Smart City. 2013.

Seit 2000 wird der Begriff "Smart City" als Label für nachhaltige Stadtentwicklung eingesetzt. Der unscharf umrissene Begriff wirbt für den Einsatz digitaler Technologien, um den städtischen Energieverbrauch und die Umweltauswirkungen des motorisierten Verkehrs zu reduzieren und um klimaneutrale Energiesysteme zu verwirklichen.

"Smart Cities" führen neue Formen der Regulierung ein, die den Austausch von Waren, Dienstleistungen und Information gestalten und teilweise oder vollständig durch High-Tech-Unternehmen entwickelt werden. Projekte wie "Songdo City" in Südkorea, "Masdar" in Abu Dhabi und "PlanIT Valley" in Portugal sind Musterbeispiele für Stadtentwicklungsmodi, die aus dem Glauben heraus entstanden sind, dass technologischer Fortschritt, und nicht z.B. kommunale Politik, im Stande ist, die dringendsten gesellschaftlichen Probleme zu lösen.

"Intelligente" Stadtentwicklung "[...] scheint in High-Tech-Unternehmen entstanden zu sein, anstatt in einer Partei, Gruppierung oder politischen Bewegung." Durch die Ausgliederung von Regierungsfunktionen an High-Tech-Unternehmen wird die Stadt zu einem "[...] Markt, auf dem Technologiekonzerne ihre Produkte und Dienste verkaufen können."*

Der vermehrte Einsatz digitaler Technologien strukturiert die Nutzung des Stadtraums und den Alltag der Bewohner neu. Individuelle Tagesabläufe setzen sich mehr und mehr aus Remote-Zugriffen auf Waren, Dienste und soziale Kontakte zusammen. Umgekehrt wird dieses "digitale Leben" des Einzelnen von Technologiekonzernen genutzt, um ihre Dienste in Form von Gebrauchsmustern für die gesamte städtische Bevölkerung zu optimieren, ihren Profit zu steigern und ihre Position am Markt zu stärken.

"City Update" versucht Auswirkungen digitaler Technologien auf den persönlichen Alltag von Städtern aufzuzeigen und stellt insbesondere Informationen über Gebrauchsmuster sozialer Netzwerke und Online-Shopping zur Verfügung.

Text: Anna Aichinger

FACEBOOK-FRIENDS

On average Germans had
75
Facebook-friends in 2010

On average Germans had
342
Facebook-friends in 2013

CITY / SOCIAL LIFE / NO TRUST

NO TRUST IN FACEBOOK-„FRIENDS"

think that people don't care about one another in real life.
70,9%

23,7%
You have never talked to about one third of your social media contacts.

CITY / SOCIAL LIFE / MEETING FRIENDS ONLINE

MEETING FRIENDS ONLINE

	total	14-19 years	20-29 years	30-39 years	40-49 years

- I agree
- I partly agree
- I don't really agree
- Ich don't agree

Number of respondends that agreed to the following statement: „The large amount of new social media offerings cause that I meet friends less often".

CITY / GOVERNMENT / FEAR OF SECURITY GAPS

FEAR OF SECURITY GAPS

- fear of data theft
- data transparency
- lack of security during data transfer
- lack of information during data processing
- handling data carefully
- none of them

CITY / GOVERNMENT / ONLINE-WAR

ONLINE-WAR AGAINST TERRORISM?

Gefahrenabwehr bei Terrorgefahr — 78%
Verbraucherschutz — 75%
Datenschutz — 64%

78% of respondents think, the state should influence the internet more to prevent terrorist attacks.

CITY / GOVERNMENT / ONLINE-BANKING

HOW OFTEN DO YOU USE ONLINE-BANKING

57% few times a week
13% few times a day
30% few times a month

CITY / GOVERNMENT / ELECTRONIC GOVERNMENT

USAGE OF ELECTRINIC GOVERNMENT

46% — 46% — 45% — 36% — 47%
2010 · 2011 · 2012 · 2013 · 2014

possible reason:
On July 2013 Edward Snowden published secret documents which uncovered a worldwide net of spying systems and showed that the NSA and its partner employments wanted to super-vise any kind of electronic communication.

CITY / SHOPPING / PRICE COMPARISON

PRICE COMPARISON

88%

compare prices online before buying.

CITY / SHOPPING / PRICE COMPARISON

USAGE OF SMARTPHONE TO COMPARE PRICES

- total
- women
- men

buying — calling up price information — calling up product information

---

CITY / LIFESTYLE / MOST WANTED

MOST WANTED PRODUCTS VIA SMARTPHONE

- books
- electronic cars
- tickers/ booking trips
- fashion / accesoires

CITY / SHOPPING / BOOKING TRIPS

REASONS FOR BOOKING TRIPS ONLINE

- better price comparison — 80,36% / 84,46% / 58,13%
- comfort — 58,93% / 43,38% / 58,33%
- faster — 48,02% / 58,28% / 56,33%

- 14-29 years
- 30-49 years
- 50+ years

CITY / SHOPPING / BUYING BEHAVIOR

BUYING BEHAVIOR OF ONLINE SHOPPERS

84%

- bis 29 years
- 30 - 45 Jahre
- 46 - 60 years
- über 60 years

- Online-Shoppers
- other shoppers

CITY / LIFESTYLE / CLOUD SECURITY

CLOUD SECURITY"?

73%

think that the NSA scandal in 2012 affec-ted their trust in cloud servide massively.

CITY / LIFESTYLE / HOME OFFICE

HOME OFFICE

How many hours a week do you practice home-based business?

0h — 1 10h — 11 20h — 21 40h — 41h — not possible

percentage of respondends

CITY / SHOPPING / IMPACT OF ONLINE SHOPPING

IMPACT OF ONLINE SHOPPING

37,4%
increasingly buying online

8,9%
bascally buying less

- inner cities get desolated
- jobs get lost

CITY / LIFESTYLE / MOBILE INTERNET

MOBILE INTERNET

53%
are going online on the way

DATA AB...

cas... registere... by th... polic...

NETFLIX

number of... bers wor...
number o... Germany...

E-COMMERCE IN RURAL CHINA

Pengfeng Chen, Zi Li, Yuefan Kuang

"In short, they resemble observations of a flaneur, the viewer who takes pleasure in abandoning himself to the artificial world of high capitalist civilization. One could describe this figure as the viewing-device through which Benjamin formulates his own theoretical assumptions concerning modernity, converging in a Marxist critique of commodity fetishism."
Martina Lauster, Walter Benjamin's Myth of the Flâneur

Road to Modernity: "Ganjie" – a virtual Flâneur
The scale of spatial and social disparity between urban and rural China is no second to any other country in the world. While the urban areas – cities and towns – stage all all cultural, social and economical performances; the rural areas are excluded from achievements of the fruitful modernization process in China. Surely the internet is a chance to break the geographical barrier, however, very few people in the rural areas own computers or are capable of using the internet.

"Ganjie", which literally means "going to the market" in Chinese, is aimed to change it all. As an online-trade platform, it enables local information exchange and purchase of agricultural resources among villagers. Moreover, it enables villagers to enjoy the benefits of urban development – more specifically, to enjoy urban products. The internet site is coupled with a physical establishment. An operating centre in the town is supported by service spots in villages. Local entrepreneurs are trained to run these hotspots to help villagers to get connected to the internet and provide guidance and service for online shopping.

Founded in 2013 in the rural town Suichang in Zhejiang Province, "Ganjie" had more than 2000 service spots in villages and 400 staff members by April 2015, further aiming on a national-wide campaign including 20,000 such spots in villages. Behind the high ambition is abundant media and governmental support. A former unknown town, "Suichang" is now famous for the so-called "Suichang Model" – pioneering in e-commerce in rural China. With slogans like "Going shopping on Ganjie, saving thousands in one year", "E-commerce, better village, better life", e-commerce is portrayed as patriotic entrepreneurship able to solve the poverty problem in rural China. In May 2015, an e-commerce meeting was held in Suichang; present were seven governmental officials from the Ministry of Commerce People's Republic of China. With China's GDP growth slowing down from 10.6% in 2010 to 7.3% in 2014, it is no wonder that the government would receive farmers' contribution to a new round of economic growth with applause.

The seemingly perfect plan certainly has its downside. Foremost it would mean that an already dominating consumption culture spreads further into the rural area. The current economical indigenous lifestyle of rural habitants would soon witness a soaring upgrade into a modern lifestyle, or shall we call it a high consumption society to its full extent? The invisible online trade network also has its physical counterpart, namely the logistic footprint. Delivery services are keeping up with the booming online volume, which raises spatial territorial questions.

SUICHANG MODEL
遂昌电商模式

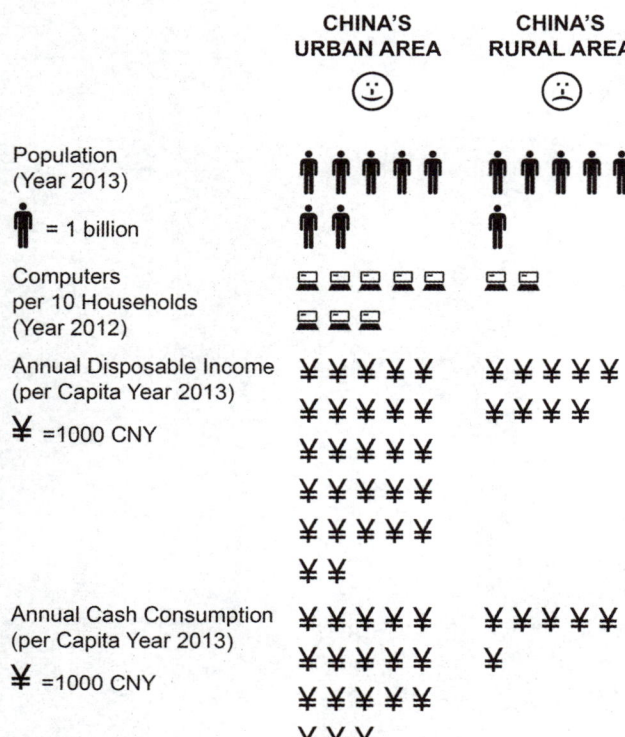

Comparison of present socio-economic conditions in urban and rural China

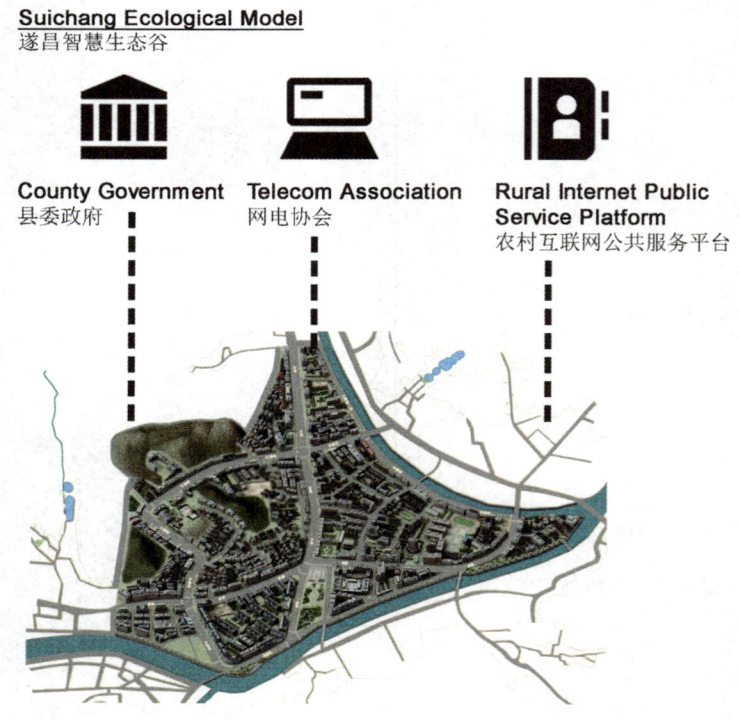

Administration and organisation of the Suichang Model

E-commerce goes rural
How does a typical household generate income?

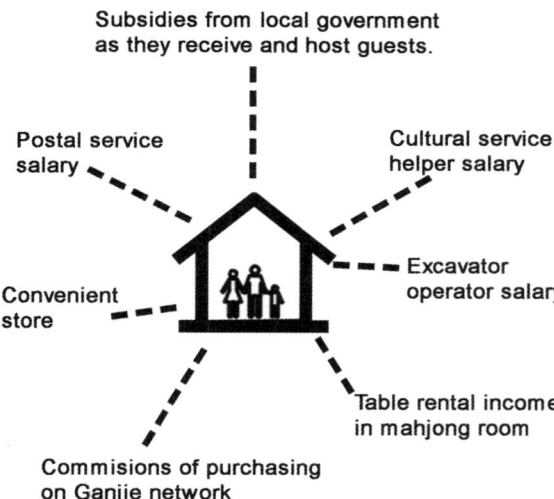

- Subsidies from local government as they receive and host guests.
- Postal service salary
- Cultural service helper salary
- Convenient store
- Excavator operator salary
- Table rental income in mahjong room
- Commisions of purchasing on Ganjie network

Production Chain Model of E-commerce Platform

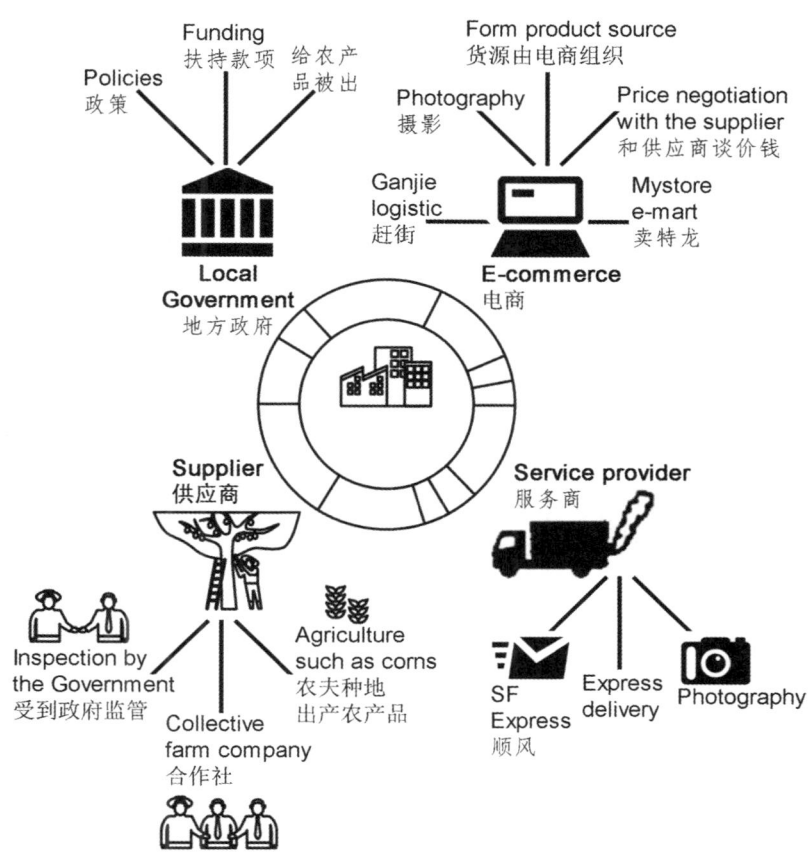

On the "Ganjie" website, articles like "The most comfortable bed ever for a 92-year-old woman" and "A first pair of women's shoes ever since 35 years" tell stories of happy shoppers in villages.

"Ganjie" would probably contribute to rural villagers' happiness for a few years, before China faces another round of social and ecological challenges as foreseeable consequences.

•

"Kurz gesagt, sie ähneln den Beobachtungen eines Flaneurs, des Betrachters, der sich mit Vergnügen der Welt der hochkapitalistischen Zivilisation hingibt. Man könnte diese Gestalt als den Betrachtungsapparat bezeichnen, durch den Benjamin seine theoretischen Annahmen über die Moderne formuliert, die auf eine marxistische Kritik des Warenfetischismus hinauslaufen."
Martina Lauster, Walter Benjamin's Myth of the Flâneur

Der Weg zur Moderne: "Ganjie" – ein virtueller Flaneur

Nirgendwo auf der Welt ist der räumliche und soziale Gegensatz zwischen Stadt und Land so stark ausgeprägt wie in China. Während die urbanen Gebiete – Groß- und Kleinstädte – mit allen kulturellen, sozialen und ökonomischen Leistungen aufwarten können, sind die ländlichen Gebiete von den Errungenschaften des fruchtbaren Modernisierungsprozesses in China ausgeschlossen. Das Internet böte sicher eine Chance, die geografische Barriere zu durchbrechen, doch nur wenige Landbewohner besitzen einen Computer oder sind in der Lage, das Internet zu nutzen.

"Ganjie" – ein chinesische Begriff, der wörtlich "auf den Markt gehen" bedeutet – soll dies alles verändern. Als eine E-Commerce-Plattform ermöglicht "Ganjie" einen lokalen Informationsaustausch zwischen Dorfbewohnern und den Kauf von landwirtschaftlichen Gerätschaften, Dünger, Saatgut und dergleichen. Darüber hinaus ermöglicht es den Dorfbewohnern, von der städtischen Entwicklung zu profitieren bzw. in den Genuss städtischer Produkte zu kommen. Die Website ist mit einer physischen Einrichtung gekoppelt. Ein Operationszentrum in der Stadt wird von Servicespots in den Dörfern unterstützt. Ortsansässige Unternehmer leiten diese Service-Hotspots, um den Dorfbewohnern zu einem Internetzugang zu verhelfen und sie in die Welt des Online-Shoppings einzuführen.

2013 in der Landstadt Suichang in der Provinz Zhejiang gegründet, hatte "Ganjie" im April 2015 mehr als 2.000 dörfliche Servicespots und 400 Mitarbeiter; das Ziel einer kürzlich gestarteten landesweiten Kampagne sind 20.000 solcher dörflichen Spots – ein ehrgeiziges Vorhaben, das nicht nur von den Medien, sondern auch von der Regierung nach Kräften unterstützt wird. Die früher unbekannte Landstadt Suichang ist heute berühmt wegen des "Suichang-Modells" – ein Pionier der E-Commerce-Entwicklung für das ländliche China.

Mit Slogans wie "Auf Ganjie shoppen gehen, in einem Jahr Tausende sparen" oder "E-Commerce – ein besseres Dorf, ein besseres Leben" wird der Internethandel als ein patriotisches Unternehmen dargestellt, das das Armutsproblem im ländlichen China lösen könnte. Im Mai 2015 wurde in Suichang eine E-Commerce-Konferenz veranstaltet, an der auch sieben Regierungsvertreter aus dem Handelsministerium der VR China teilnahmen. Angesichts der rückläufigen Entwicklung des BIP – es sank von 10,6 % im Jahr 2010 auf 7,3 % im Jahr 2014 – würde die Regierung einen Beitrag der Bauern zu einer neuen Runde des wirtschaftlichen Wachstums begrüßen.

Dieser scheinbar perfekte Plan hat jedoch auch eine Kehrseite. Er würde vor allem dazu führen, dass eine in den Städten bereits vorherrschende Konsumkultur auch auf die ländlichen Gebiete übergeht. Der gegenwärtige, noch immer traditionell geprägte wirtschaftliche Lebensstil der Landbewohner würde binnen Kurzem ein tiefgreifendes Upgrade zu einem modernen Lifestyle erleben – oder sollen wir von einer vollendeten Hochkonsumgesellschaft sprechen? Das unsichtbare E-Commerce-Netzwerk hat auch ein physisches Pendant, nämlich den logistischen Fußabdruck. Zustelldienste halten Schritt mit dem boomenden Internethandel, was räumlich-territoriale Fragen aufwirft.

Auf der "Ganjie"-Website erzählen Artikel wie "Das komfortabelste Bett, das eine 92-Jährige jemals hatte" oder "Das erste Paar Frauenschuhe seit 35 Jahren" Geschichten von zufriedenen E-Commerce-Dörflern. "Ganjie" würde vermutlich ein paar Jahre lang zur Zufriedenheit der Landbevölkerung beitragen, bis China sich mit einer neuen Runde von sozialen und ökologischen Herausforderungen konfrontiert sieht, die vorhersehbare Folgen dieser Entwicklung sind.
Text: Zhen Zhang

ANTI-PACK-AGING
Sheila Seyfert-Menzel, Katalin Gennburg

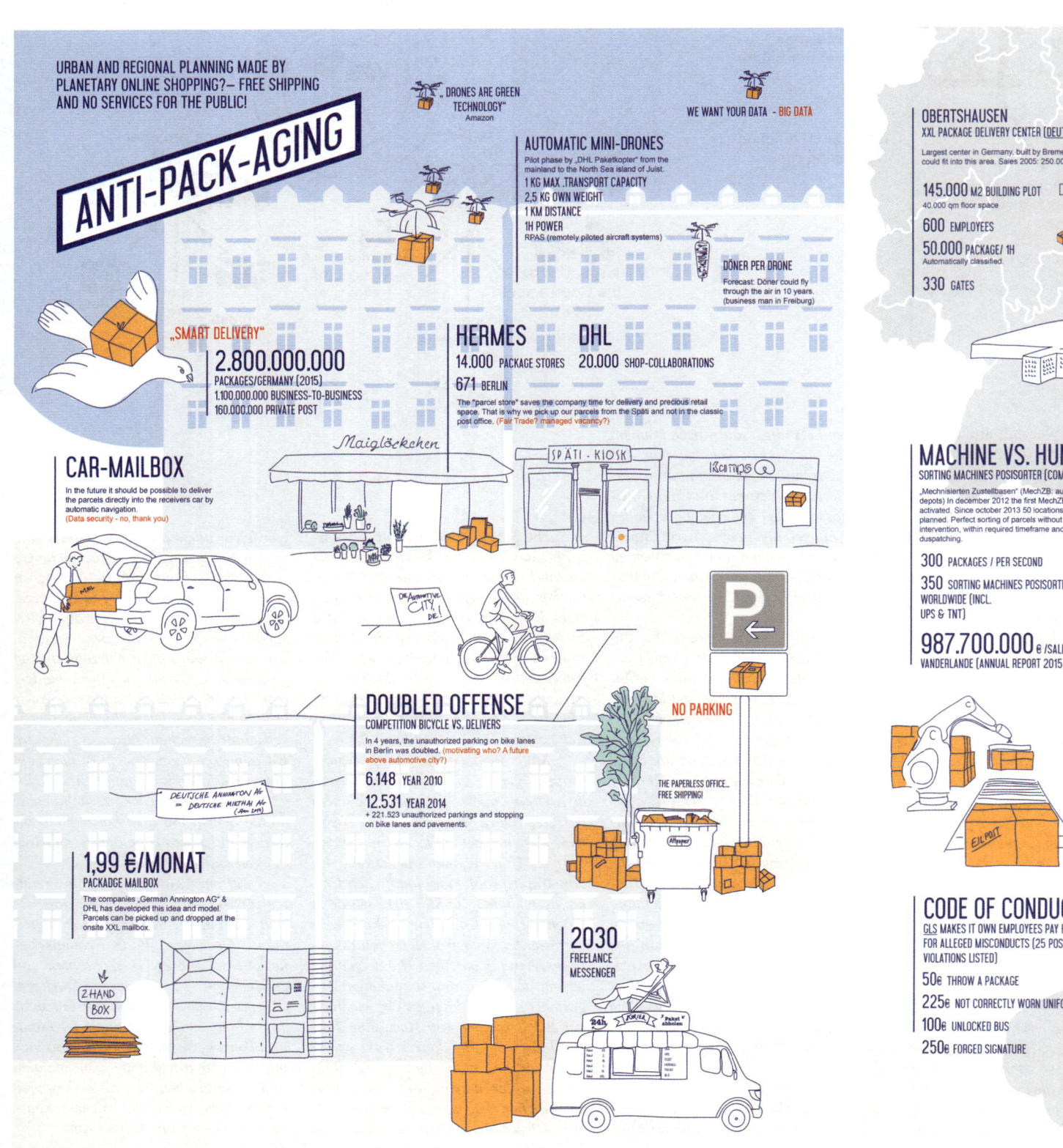

URBAN AND REGIONAL PLANNING MADE BY
PLANETARY ONLINE SHOPPING?— FREE SHIPPING
AND NO SERVICES FOR THE PUBLIC!

"DRONES ARE GREEN
TECHNOLOGY"
Amazon

WE WANT YOUR DATA - BIG DATA

ANTI-PACK-AGING

AUTOMATIC MINI-DRONES
Pilot phase by „DHL Paketkopter" from the
mainland to the North Sea island of Juist.

1 KG MAX .TRANSPORT CAPACITY
2,5 KG OWN WEIGHT
1 KM DISTANCE
1H POWER
RPAS (remotely piloted aircraft systems)

DÖNER PER DRONE
Forecast: Döner could fly
through the air in 10 years.
(business man in Freiburg)

„SMART DELIVERY"
2.800.000.000
PACKAGES/GERMANY (2015)
1.100.000.000 BUSINESS-TO-BUSINESS
160.000.000 PRIVATE POST

HERMES
14.000 PACKAGE STORES
671 BERLIN

DHL
20.000 SHOP-COLLABORATIONS

The "parcel store" saves the company time for delivery and precious retail
space. That is why we pick up our parcels from the Späti and not in the classic
post office. (Fair Trade? managed vacancy?)

Maiglöckchen

SPÄTI - KIOSK

Kamps

CAR-MAILBOX
In the future it should be possible to deliver
the parcels directly into the receivers car by
automatic navigation.
(Data security - no, thank you)

DIE Automotive
CITY !
DIE

P

NO PARKING

DOUBLED OFFENSE
COMPETITION BICYCLE VS. DELIVERS

In 4 years, the unauthorized parking on bike lanes
in Berlin was doubled. (motivating who? A future
above automotive city?)

6.148 YEAR 2010
12.531 YEAR 2014
+ 221.523 unauthorized parkings and stopping
on bike lanes and pavements.

THE PAPERLESS OFFICE...
FREE SHIPPING!

DEUTSCHE ANNINGTON AG
= DEUTSCHE MIETHAI AG
(Jüri Lietz)

1,99 €/MONAT
PACKADGE MAILBOX
The companies „German Annington AG" &
DHL has developed this idea and model.
Parcels can be picked up and dropped at the
onsite XXL mailbox.

2 HAND
BOX

2030
FREELANCE
MESSENGER

OBERTSHAUSEN
XXL PACKAGE DELIVERY CENTER (DEUTSCHE POST DHL)

Largest center in Germany, built by Bremer. 5 football fields
could fit into this area. Sales 2005: 250.000.000 €.

145.000 M2 BUILDING PLOT
40.000 qm floor space

600 EMPLOYEES

50.000 PACKAGE/ 1H
Automatically classified.

330 GATES

BREMER

MACHINE VS. HUMANS
SORTING MACHINES POSISORTER (COMPANY: VANDERLANDE)

„Mechnisierten Zustellbasen" (MechZB: automatized
depots) In december 2012 the first MechZB was
activated. Since october 2013 50 locations are
planned. Perfect sorting of parcels without manual
intervention, within required timeframe and correct
duspatching.

300 PACKAGES / PER SECOND

**350 SORTING MACHINES POSISORTERS
WORLDWIDE (INCL.
UPS & TNT)**

UPS   TNT

987.700.000 € /SALES
VANDERLANDE (ANNUAL REPORT 2015)

CODE OF CONDUCT
GLS MAKES IT OWN EMPLOYEES PAY FINES
FOR ALLEGED MISCONDUCTS (25 POSSIBLE
VIOLATIONS LISTED)

50€ THROW A PACKAGE
225€ NOT CORRECTLY WORN UNIFORM
100€ UNLOCKED BUS
250€ FORGED SIGNATURE

ŁÓD
LOGIS
DPD
5000

90.0
Logist
sorting

43.0
Automa

32
1,5
171

Her

SHO
Online st
9,7%
Online tr
34.30
39,2%
Average
year / pe
69,87
102,1

EILPOST

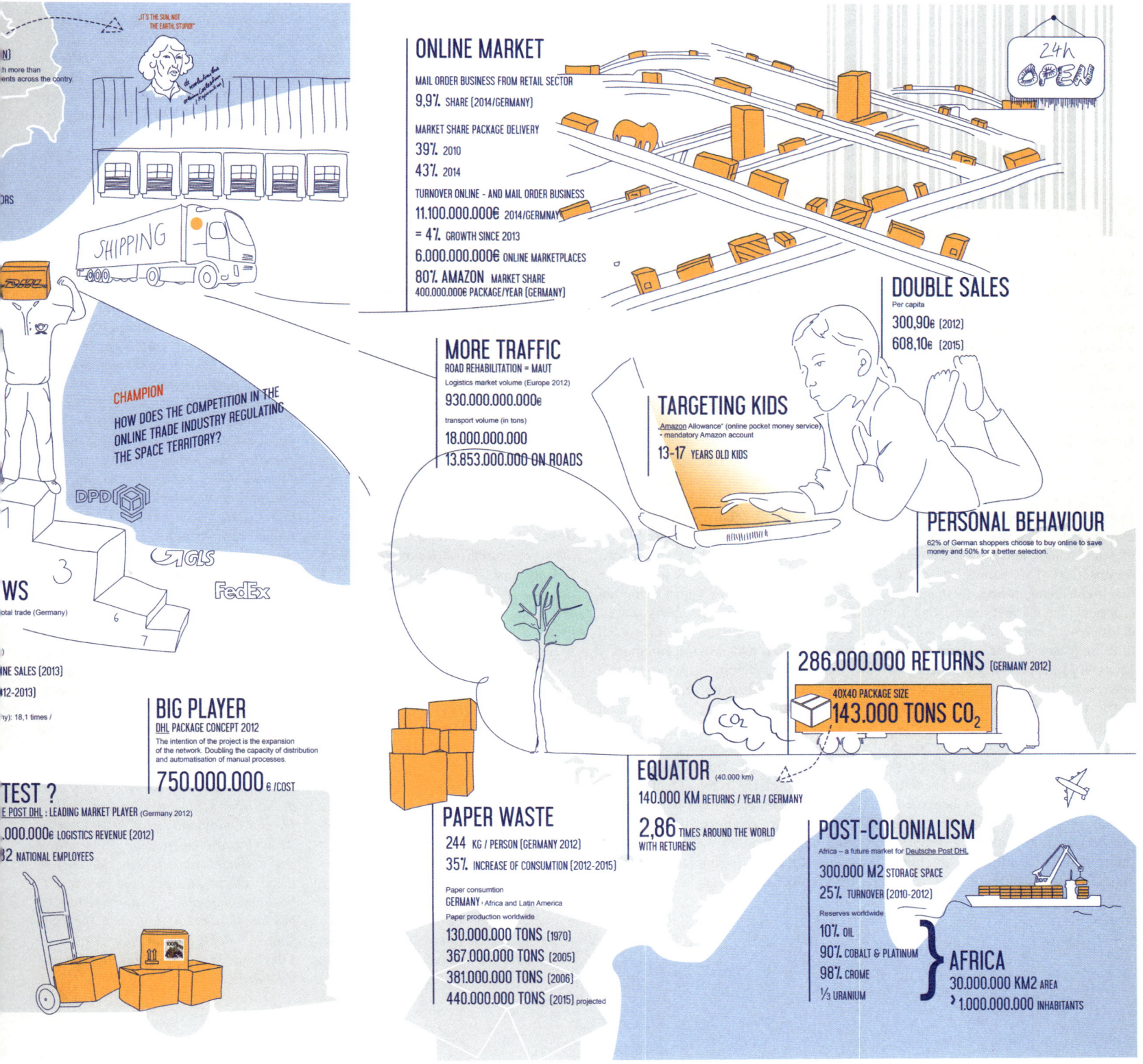

ONLINE MARKET

MAIL ORDER BUSINESS FROM RETAIL SECTOR

9,9% SHARE (2014/GERMANY)

MARKET SHARE PACKAGE DELIVERY

39% 2010

43% 2014

TURNOVER ONLINE - AND MAIL ORDER BUSINESS

11.100.000.000€ 2014/GERMNAY

= 4% GROWTH SINCE 2013

6.000.000.000€ ONLINE MARKETPLACES

80% AMAZON MARKET SHARE
400.000.000€ PACKAGE/YEAR (GERMANY)

"JT'S THE SUN, NOT THE EARTH, STUPID"

SHIPPING

CHAMPION

HOW DOES THE COMPETITION IN THE ONLINE TRADE INDUSTRY REGULATING THE SPACE TERRITORY?

DPD

GLS

FedEx

WS

total trade (Germany)

NE SALES (2013)

12-2013)

ny): 18,1 times /

BIG PLAYER

DHL PACKAGE CONCEPT 2012

The intention of the project is the expansion of the network. Doubling the capacity of distribution and automatisation of manual processes.

750.000.000 € /COST

TEST ?

E POST DHL : LEADING MARKET PLAYER (Germany 2012)

.000.000€ LOGISTICS REVENUE (2012)

2 NATIONAL EMPLOYEES

MORE TRAFFIC

ROAD REHABILITATION = MAUT

Logistics market volume (Europe 2012)

930.000.000.000€

transport volume (in tons)

18.000.000.000

13.853.000.000 ON ROADS

TARGETING KIDS

"Amazon Allowance" (online pocket money service)
• mandatory Amazon account

13-17 YEARS OLD KIDS

PAPER WASTE

244 KG / PERSON (GERMANY 2012)

35% INCREASE OF CONSUMTION (2012-2015)

Paper consumtion
GERMANY › Africa and Latin America
Paper production worldwide

130.000.000 TONS (1970)

367.000.000 TONS (2005)

381.000.000 TONS (2006)

440.000.000 TONS (2015) projected

EQUATOR (40.000 km)

140.000 KM RETURNS / YEAR / GERMANY

2,86 TIMES AROUND THE WORLD WITH RETURENS

DOUBLE SALES

Per capita

300,90€ (2012)

608,10€ (2015)

PERSONAL BEHAVIOUR

62% of German shoppers choose to buy online to save money and 50% for a better selection.

286.000.000 RETURNS (GERMANY 2012)

40X40 PACKAGE SIZE
143.000 TONS CO_2

POST-COLONIALISM

Africa – a future market for Deutsche Post DHL

300.000 M2 STORAGE SPACE

25% TURNOVER (2010-2012)

Reserves worldwide

10% OIL

90% COBALT & PLATINUM

98% CROME

1/3 URANIUM

AFRICA

30.000.000 KM2 AREA

› 1.000.000.000 INHABITANTS

24h OPEN

We are facing a new mode of consumption and circulation of products: online trade. Internet shopping is a global and increasingly transnational phenomenon. Consumption is highly affected by all kinds of online shopping possibilities, which are increasingly specified for all kinds of personal consumption desires, children included. When leaving one's data by purchasing online, one becomes an object for targeted, personalised advertisement. The digital marketplace is not only a trend anymore, but a hard-fought business. In Germany, sales per capita through online shopping have doubled between 2012 and 2015.[1]

So far, the fast growth of digital economy has been discussed above all with respect to its effects on cities, the danger of small retailers dying out, and subsequently, the changed use of urban space as well as an emptying of functions regarding public space. Urban diversity, which not least lies in the range and specialisation of small retail offers, has for quite some time been affected by monopolisation and displacement processes and is further threatened by online trade. At present, an expansion of retail chains and variety stores can be observed. This means that there is a self-enhancing process at hand: purchases via the internet reduce the physically present range of goods, which in turn increases online purchases. The necessary transport of goods leads to a massive increase of traffic; analogous traffic movements that are caused by "digital traffic".

On that point, one has to consider a peculiarity of digital purchases: Firstly, it brings with it the freedom to order without limits – 24 hours a day – and secondly, the freedom to return purchased goods within a certain time frame. This is used thoroughly. In Germany, approx. 286,000,000 returns

took place in 2012.[2] Try to imagine: By positioning 286,000,000 parcels measuring 40x40cm in one line we would get along the equator 2.86 times. If using a Deutsche Post DHL car, approximately 143,000 tons of CO_2 would be produced. Cities are effected to a high degree: the expansion of online trade and the increase of traffic through delivery services has repercussions on streets, parking spaces and (urban) infrastructure in general. With increased traffic the need for public street space is raised. But there are yet other people concerned: In the branch of delivery services and the services around this branch, massively expanding with online trade and the privatisation of the German postal service, severe competition for market shares is contended at the expense of the workers, who have to work free-lance in many cases.

The often cost-free returns, made convenient by preprints, are a central aspect within the expansion strategy of online traders. The willingness to purchase online is increasing with the decreasing risk of having to receive or keep unwanted goods. An essential aspect lies in the so-called "selective order" of more items for viewing. Here, the presence of retailers is imitated in an absurd way. Free returns are not economically viable in many cases. After the Marxian labour theory of value, value is added to the commodity by transport, which, in the case of a free return, cannot be realised via its price. An immediate consequence of this policy are the extremely bad and, above all, for the general public invisible working conditions of employees of online traders. To the extent that online traders achieve a monopoly position compared to retailers, the shopping possibilities online will increase in price. Not a lot of phantasy is needed for this scenario.

Wir sind mit einer neuen Form des Konsums und der Zirkulation von Produkten konfrontiert: dem Internethandel. Einkaufen im Internet ist ein globales und zunehmend auch ein grenzüberschreitendes Phänomen. Der Konsum wird stark von diesen digitalen Einkaufsmöglichkeiten aller Art geprägt, die immer mehr auf persönliche Konsumbedürfnisse und unterschiedliche Zielgruppen, Kinder eingeschlossen, zugeschnitten werden. Wer seine Daten per Einkauf im Netz hinterlässt, wird zum Objekt gezielter, personalisierter Werbung. Der digitale Marktplatz ist nicht mehr nur ein Trend, sondern hart umkämpftes Business. In Deutschland haben sich die Umsätze im Onlinehandel zwischen den Jahren 2012 und 2015 verdoppelt.[1]

Dieses rasante Wachstum der digitalen Wirtschaft wird bisher vor allem in seinen Auswirkungen auf die Städte diskutiert, auf die Gefahr des Absterbens des Einzelhandels hin und auf in der Folge veränderten Stadtgebrauch und eine Funktionsentleerung des öffentlichen Raums. Die städtische Vielfalt, die nicht zuletzt in der Breite und Spezialisierung des Einzelhandelsangebots liegt, ist bereits seit Längerem durch Konzentrations- und Verdrängungsprozesse beeinträchtigt und wird durch den Internethandel weiter bedroht. Was derzeit zu beobachten ist, ist die Ausbreitung von Ketten und Billigläden. Das heißt, es handelt sich um einen sich selbst verstärkenden Prozess: Der Kauf per Internet reduziert das physisch präsente Warenangebot, was wiederum den Internetkauf verstärkt.

Ein bisher wenig beleuchteter Aspekt ist die Frage der Lieferung der Online-Bestellungen. Bei dem erforderlichen Warentransport handelt es sich um eine massive Steigerung des Verkehrsaufkommens, um analoge Verkehrsbewegungen, die von "digitalem Verkehr" verursacht werden. Dazu muss man eine Besonderheit des digitalen Einkaufens berücksichtigen: Es bringt erstens die Freiheit mit sich, unbegrenzt bestellen zu können – 24 Stunden am Tag, und zweitens die bestellte Ware innerhalb einer bestimmten Frist zurücksenden zu können. Das wird weidlich genutzt. In Deutschland fanden im Jahr 2012 ungefähr 286.000.000 Rück-

sendungen statt. Man versuche sich vorzustellen: 286.000.000 Pakete der Größe 40x40 cm nebeneinander gelegt umrunden 2,86-mal den Äquator. Wenn für diese 286.000.000 Rücksendungen ein Deutsche Post DHL-Auto benutzt wird, werden 143.000 Tonnen Kohlendioxid freigesetzt.[2] Städte sind in hohem Maße betroffen: die Expansion des Onlinehandels und die Zunahme des Verkehrs durch Lieferdienste hat Auswirkungen auf Straßen, Parkplätze und die (städtische) Infrastruktur im Allgemeinen. Mit dem wachsenden Verkehrsaufkommen von Lieferdiensten steigt der Bedarf an öffentlichen Straßenflächen. Aber es gibt noch andere Betroffene: In der Branche der Lieferdienste und der Dienstleistungen rund um diese Branche, die mit dem Onlinehandel und der Privatisierung der deutschen Post massiv gewachsen sind, werden die harten Konkurrenzkämpfe um Marktanteile auf Kosten der Arbeitskräfte, die in vielen Fällen auf eigene Rechnung arbeiten müssen, ausgetragen.

Das häufig kostenlose und durch Vordrucke bequeme Retournieren der bestellten Ware ist ein zentraler Bestandteil der Expansionsstrategie des Onlinehandels. Die Bereitschaft zum Onlinekauf steigt mit dem abnehmenden Risiko, Nicht-Erwünschtes zu erhalten bzw. behalten zu müssen. Ein wesentlicher Aspekt liegt hier auch in der sogenannten "Auswahlbestellung" mehrerer Artikel zur Ansicht. Damit wird auf absurde Weise die Präsenz des Einzelhandelsangebots imitiert. Die kostenlosen Rücksendungen sind in vielen Fällen nicht kostendeckend. Nach der Marx'schen Arbeitswerttheorie wird der Ware durch den Transport Wert zugeführt, der sich im Falle des kostenlosen Rücktransports nicht über den Preis realisieren kann. Eine unmittelbare Folge dieser Politik sind die extrem schlechten und vor allem für die Öffentlichkeit nicht sichtbaren Arbeitsbedingungen der Angestellten der Onlinehäuser. In dem Maße, wie diese Onlinehäuser eine Monopolposition gegenüber dem Einzelhandel gewinnen, werden sich auch die Einkaufsmöglichkeiten im Netz verteuern. Für dieses Szenario bedarf es nicht viel Phantasie.

MANILA –
GROUND CONSTELLATIONS

Adrian Lorenzo Alfonso
Mary Pearl Robles

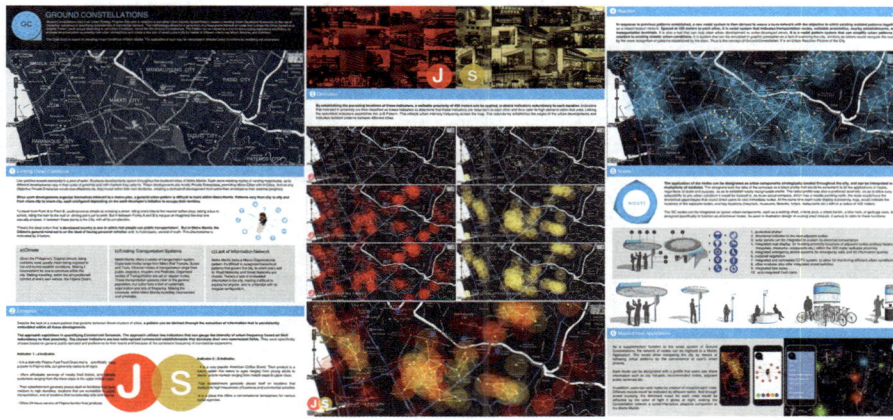

Travelling from point A to point B could be as simple as crossing a street, taking a bus to school, or driving one's car to work. But in between points A and B is the city, with all its complexities. Like pebbles carelessly tossed in a pool of water, business developments spawn throughout the clustered cities of Metro Manila. Each stone creates ripples of varying magnitudes, as developments differ in their proximity to markets they cater to. Developed mostly by private enterprises, they promote micro-cities within cities. And like any private enterprise, they cost-effectively invest within their own territories only, creating a striking contrast between areas they envelope and external peripheries. Since such developments organize themselves introvert to a macro plan, a general urban pattern is difficult to track within Metro Manila. The existing public transportation systems suffers from a lack of systematic organization and frequency, making commuting incredibly unreliable. A lack of suitable information systems makes it difficult to decipher chaotic street networks and to orient oneself in the city.

Despite the lack of a macro-organizational system governing these clusters of cities, a pattern can be derived through the extraction of information that is consistently embedded within all these developments. The project uses two widely established food chains as indicators. Linking the indicators establishes the "J+S Pattern", which reflects urban density and commercial frequency, and indicates edges of urban development as well as isolated areas. A network is created that stitches existing isolated micro-cities together and forms a close-looped nodal system, simplifying orientation in existing chaotic urban conditions. Spaced at the walkable distance of 400 meters, the nodal system indicates transportation routes and terminals, walkable proximities and nearby facilities. It is also a tool that can help steer urban development in under-developed areas. Nodes are designed as urban components (waiting sheds, benches, bike racks …) that share an emergency phone and surveillance system, as well as an easily recognizable radial profile. The network of nodes can be digitalized as a mobile application, allowing navigation through Metro Manila by means of smart phones.

Von Punkt A nach Punkt B zu gelangen, könnte so leicht sein, wie eine Straße zu überqueren oder wie mit dem Bus zur Schule oder mit dem Auto zur Arbeit zu fahren. Doch zwischen den Punkten A und B liegt die Stadt in all ihrer Vielfältigkeit. Wie gedankenlos in einen Teich geworfene Kieselsteine entstehen im Städtecluster von Metro Manila an allen Ecken und Enden Geschäftskomplexe. Jeder Stein erzeugt Wasserkräuselungen von unterschiedlicher Größe, da sich diese Komplexe hinsichtlich ihrer Nähe zu den von ihnen bedienten Märkten unterscheiden. Meist von Privatunternehmen entwickelt, bilden sie Mikrostädte innerhalb von Städten. Und wie jedes Privatunternehmen investieren sie kosteneffektiv nur innerhalb ihrer eigenen Territorien, wodurch sie einen verblüffenden Gegensatz zwischen den von ihnen umfassten Arealen und den äußeren Peripherien bewirken. Da solche Komplexe entstehen, ohne dass sie in einen Makroplan eingebunden sind, lässt sich ein allgemeines städtisches Muster in Metro Manila nur schwer ausmachen. Den bestehenden Systemen der öffentlichen Transportmittel mangelt es an systematischer Organisation und Frequenz, was den Pendelverkehr unglaublich unzuverlässig macht. Das Fehlen geeigneter Informationssysteme erschwert die Entzifferung der chaotischen Straßennetze und die Orientierung in der Stadt.

Trotz des Fehlens eines makroorganisatorischen Systems, das diesem Städtecluster eine Ordnung verleihen könnte, lässt sich über eine Heranziehung von Informationen, die auf konsistente Weise in all diese Komplexe eingebettet sind, ein Muster erstellen. Das Projekt verwendet zwei weitverbreitete Lebensmittelketten als Indikatoren. Die Verbindung dieser Indikatoren ergibt das "J+S-Muster", das die städtische Dichte und die kommerzielle Frequenz widerspiegelt und das nicht nur die Ränder der Stadtentwicklung aufzeigt, sondern auch isolierte Areale. Es wird ein Netzwerk erzeugt, das die bestehenden, voneinander isolierten Mikrostädte verbindet und ein geschlossenes System von Knotenpunkten bildet, das die Orientierung unter den bestehenden chaotischen städtischen Bedingungen erleichtert. Unterteilt in zu Fuß zurücklegbare Distanzen von jeweils 400 Metern, zeigt das Knotenpunktsystem Verkehrslinien und Endstationen sowie fußläufige Nachbarschaften und nahe gelegene Einrichtungen auf. Es ist gleichzeitig ein Werkzeug, das dabei helfen kann, die Stadtentwicklung in unterentwickelten Arealen zu steuern. Die Knotenpunkte werden als städtische Komponenten designt (Wartehäuschen, Bänke, Fahrradständer etc.), die nicht nur ein Notruftelefon und ein Überwachungssystem haben, sondern auch ein leicht erkennbares radiales Profil. Das Netzwerk von Knotenpunkten kann als mobile App digitalisiert werden, was eine per Smartphone gesteuerte Navigation durch Metro Manila ermöglicht.

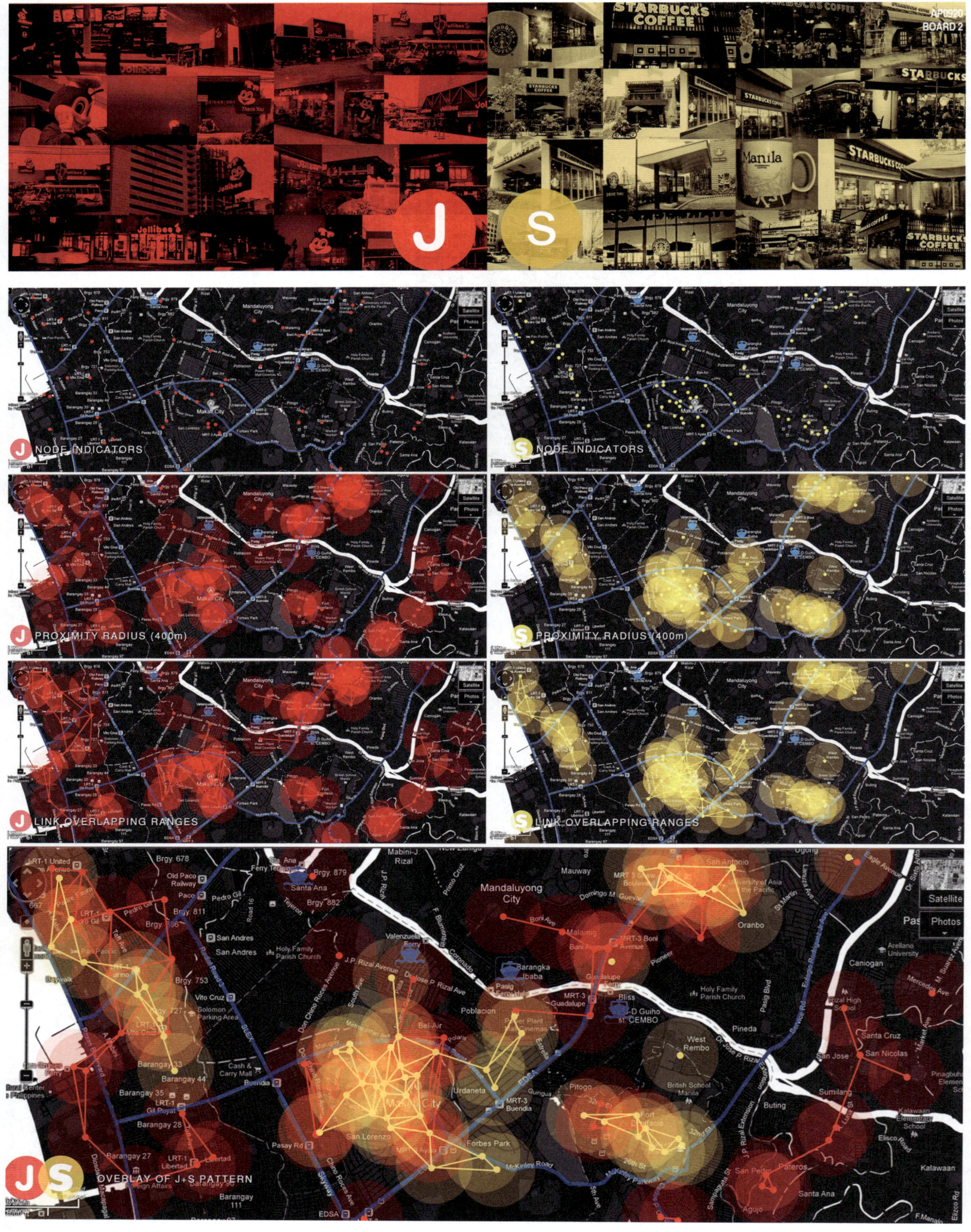

J   S

J NODE INDICATORS

S NODE INDICATORS

J PROXIMITY RADIUS (400m)

S PROXIMITY RADIUS (400m)

J LINK OVERLAPPING RANGES

S LINK OVERLAPPING RANGES

J S OVERLAY OF J+S PATTERN

Indicator 1 : J-Indicator.

- It is a distinctly Filipino Fast Food Chain that is specifically very popular to Filipino kids, but generally caters to all ages.

- offers affordable servings of mostly fried dishes, and attracts customers ranging from the lower class to the upper middle class.

- Their establishment generally places itself on locations that have medium to high densities, locations that are accessible to public transportation, and at locations that considerably safe and secure.

- Offers 24-hours service of Filipino familiar food products.

Indicator 2 : S-Indicator.

- It is a very popular American Coffee Brand. Their product is a luxury option that caters to ages ranging from young adults to above and to markets ranging from middle class to upper class.

-This establishment generally places itself on locations that medium to high frequencies of business and commercial activities.

-It is a place that offers a conversational atmosphere for various social agendas.

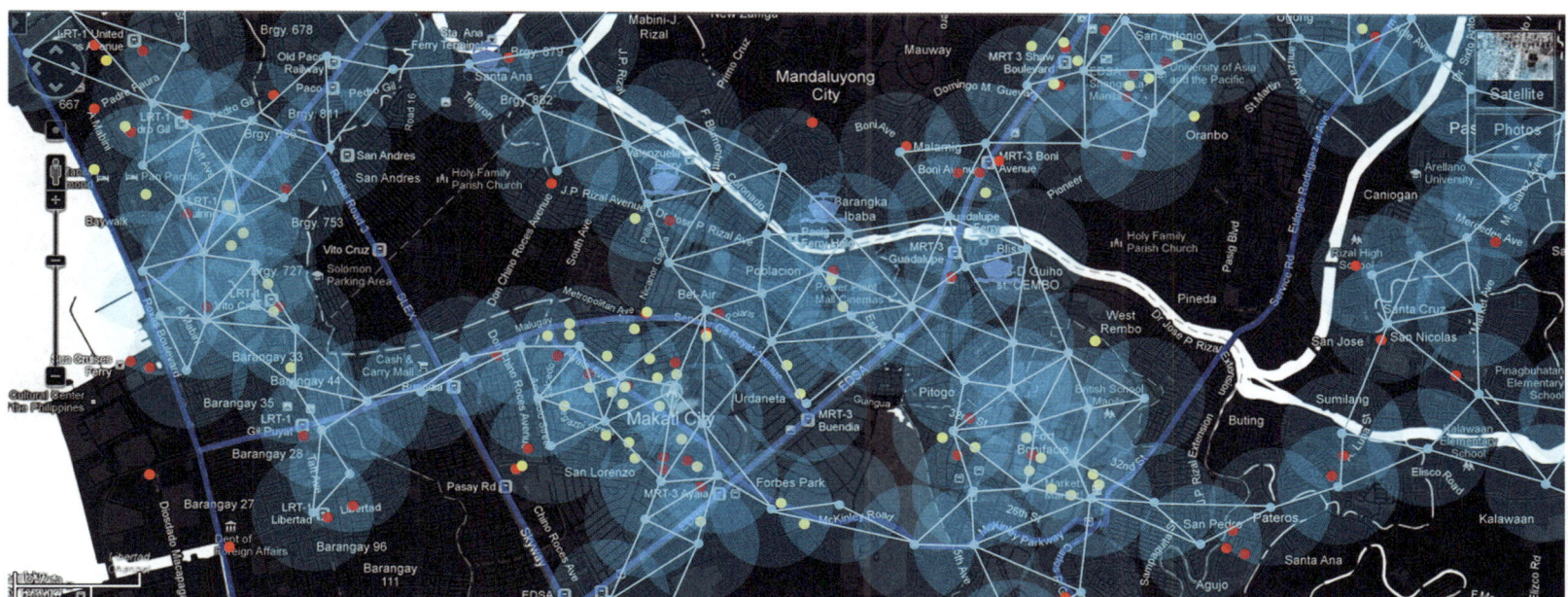

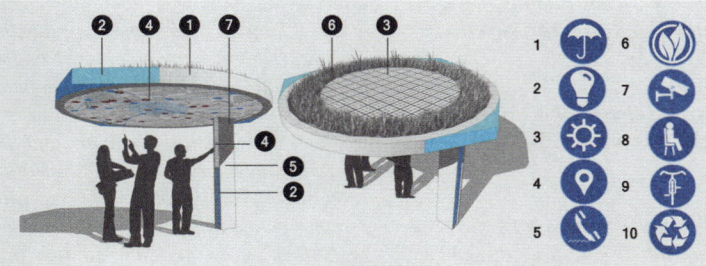

1. protective shelter
2. directional indicator to the next adjacent nodes
3. solar panels can be integrated to sustain its electrical consumption
4. integrated map display, for locating proximity locations of adjacent nodes and key locations (hospitals, museums, restaurants etc.) within the 400 meter walkable proximity
5. integrated emergency phone systems for emergency calls and for information queries
6. installed vegetation
7. integrated and concealed CCTV system, to allow for monitoring different urban conditions
8. other modules also offer integrated street benches
9. integrated bike racks
10. and integrated trash cans

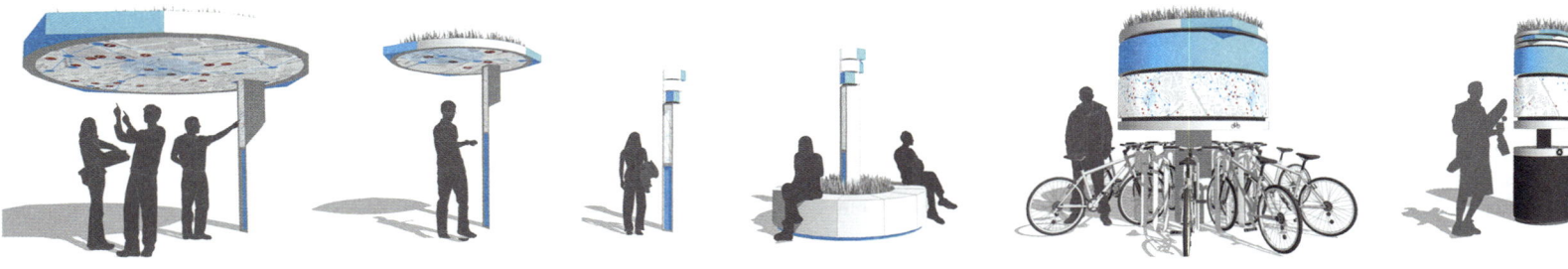

left page
An analysis of the spatial distribution of two popular commercial food chains in Manila provides a framework for orientation within the fragmented city structure.

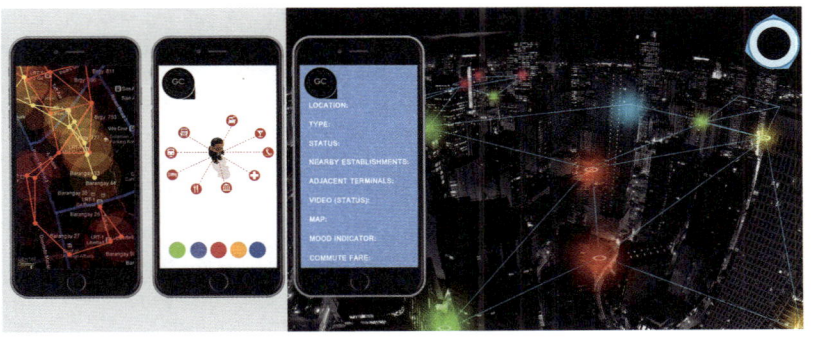

The closed-loop nodal system, spaced at the walkable distance of 400 meters, indicates transportation routes and terminals and nearby facilities. Its nodes are designed as low-threshold service facilities.

SYRBIA
Natalija Paunic
Aleksandar Bursac

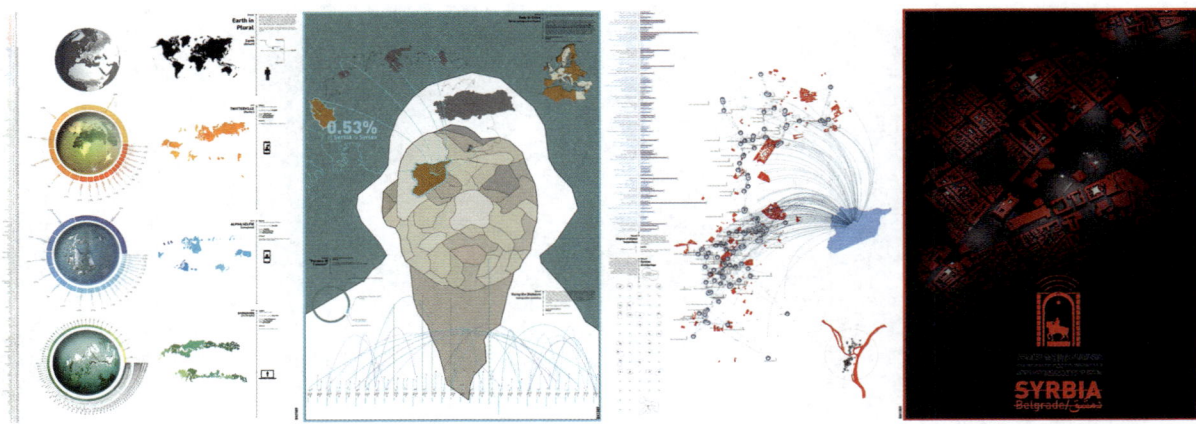

Digital/Physical Schisms: Syrbian[1] Archipelago

virtual

1. almost or nearly as described, but not completely or according to strict definition.

computing

2. not physically existing as such but made by software to appear to do so.

Life and the internet – the separation and connection of the two phenomena is a discourse that seems contemporary, but it has respectively been argued for decades.

"In the early '80s we began to live in two kinds of cities. One is the city as a material object, which is physically present and supported by physical objects. Beside that, the city as phenomenon is the city that arose with filtered media in societies that had been developed suddenly in the' 80s. It is the city as information and a virtual city as an event. In this kind of city time and space are not stable. Needless to say, these two cities have to correspond to the two sides of the same coin that can not be separated from each other. Thus, throughout the '80s, the city continued to expand as a phenomenon and gradually formed a space independent of the city as a material object."[2]

It is hard to imagine life without the internet. We hear that sentence often – and usually with a negative undertone. This sentence seems to hold a premise that tells us that the internet has taken over a part of our life. The digital layer seems to have constructed a virtual infrastructure, in which we have agreed to take part, in which we project ourselves and build another kind of nature. We can be sitting alone and yet be together by texting, or we can be sitting with people and still be checking our notifications half of the time. The internet gave us the impression of accessibility, endless possibilities and complete up-to-dateness. Many anthropologists have already argued whether these benefits have actually turned out to be our vices and problems – after heroic excitement about the brave new world, we have recently been witnessing the similar amount of criticism towards the digital features we are able, or maybe even obliged, to use.[3]

However, as extreme conditions tend to show most notable qualities, the digital mantle that shifts between roles of master and servant has been recognized as an unexpected shelter in a recent event that has drawn the attention of the citizens of Belgrade, Serbia – the extreme condition being the refugee migrations from Syria.

Digitale/Physische Schismen: Der Syrbische[1] Archipel

virtuell

1. fast oder beinahe so, wie beschrieben, jedoch nicht vollständig oder einer strengen Definition entsprechend.

computing

2. nicht als solches physisch existent, aber erscheint mittels Software so als ob.

Das Leben und das Internet – die Trennung und die Verknüpfung dieser zwei Phänomene ist ein Diskurs, der aktuell zu sein scheint, jedoch schon seit Jahrzehnten geführt wird.

"In den frühen 1980er Jahren begannen wir, in zwei Arten von Städten zu leben. Zum einen gibt es die Stadt als ein materielles Objekt, das physisch präsent ist und von physischen Objekten unterstützt wird. Zum anderen gibt es die Stadt als ein Phänomen, das mit den gefilterten Medien entstand, wie sie in den 1980er Jahren plötzlich in Gesellschaften entwickelt wurden. Das ist die Stadt als Information und eine virtuelle Stadt als ein Ereignis. In dieser Art von Stadt sind Zeit und Raum nichts Stabiles. Es versteht sich von selbst, dass diese beiden Städte den zwei nicht voneinander zu trennenden Seiten einer Münze entsprechen müssen. So expandierte die Stadt in den 1980er Jahren kontinuierlich als ein Phänomen und erzeugte nach und nach einen Raum, der von der Stadt als einem materiellen Objekt geschieden war."[2]

Es ist schwer, sich ein Leben ohne das Internet vorzustellen. Diesen Satz hört man oft – und meist mit einem negativen Unterton. Er scheint eine Prämisse zu enthalten, die besagt, dass das Internet die Kontrolle über einen Teil unseres Lebens übernommen hat. Die digitale Schicht scheint eine virtuelle Infrastruktur hervorgebracht zu haben, an der wir freiwillig partizipieren, in die wir uns hineinprojizieren und in der wir eine alternative Art von Natur erschaffen. Wir können allein dasitzen und dennoch per SMS mit anderen zusammen sein; oder wir können mit anderen zusammen sein und dennoch während der Hälfte der Zeit unsere Nachrichten checken. Das Internet gab uns den Eindruck von Zugänglichkeit, von unbegrenzten Möglichkeiten, das Gefühl, stets up-to-date zu sein. Viele Anthropologen werfen bereits die Frage auf, ob sich diese Vorzüge nicht eher als Laster oder als problematisch erwiesen haben – nach der euphorischen Begeisterung über die schöne, neue Welt erleben wir seit Kurzem eine ähnlich stark ausgeprägte Kritik an den digitalen Anwendungen, die wir benutzen können oder vielleicht auch müssen.[3]

Extreme Zustände neigen jedoch dazu, die bemerkenswertesten Eigenschaften hervorzubringen, und der digitale Schutzmantel, der mal als Herr und mal als Diener erscheint, ist bei einem noch nicht lange zurückliegenden Geschehen, das die Bürger Belgrads aufmerksam verfolgt haben, als eine unerwartete Zuflucht erkannt worden – die hier gemeinten extremen Zustände

As the immigrants have been travelling – walking, hiding, being transported by shipping containers, endangering their lives and lives of their loved ones, their bodies have experienced suffocation, stress, hunger, fatigue and pain. Yet, the agonizing path of the immigrant's body through Eurasian corridors from the Middle East towards Western Europe is not mirrored in any way by the transcendent internet communication to their friends and family back home in Syria. They wander through the city, searching for areas with free internet connection, browsing for a spot to enter the void in which we all meet, leaving our surrogate selves in the physical world (on the Earth Default[4]). This was the one way that these people could meet each other, being physically separated but spiritually connected. Skype, Facebook, emails – they travel at the speed of light, piercing in seconds through distances the body of the immigrant has endured and suffered for months. The immigrants are in search of a home away from the country they hail from. Their bodies are in crisis, so they reach out to disembodied Digital Earths[5] through unprotected WiFi points in Belgrade. They find (their place) home in a nonplace.

This nonplace in particular has been given a name – Syrbia, made by a combination of its tangible and virtual parent countries – Serbia and Syria.

It is to be anticipated that events that take place online ought to leave traces in the physical world, the one we inhabit with our bodies, even though each day less with our minds. The scale of these events and their consequences vary from completely marginal to planetary. With the body searching for its place on Earth and not being able to find it, people find home and meet in an intangible, invisible "place" that seems to layer the world with such great intensity that it manages to absorb life and all of its features. It is no longer a metaphor, it is reality greater than the one we see off screen.

Virtuality of the Syrbian Archipelago becomes imprinted on the physical reality of Belgrade. It changes the morphology of Belgrade reaching out from the digital expanse of the Archipelago that is made manifest as a physical reality through the mediation of the bodies of immigrants guided by the digital.

Syrbia is an idea, with its existence gravitating between urban structure of Belgrade and infrastructure of the omnipresent virtual communication and life. Through history, people settled areas near water, on the hills, in the valleys for protection and security. The future of settlement could be accused to depend on hotspots. The ephemeral shelters which are produced by hotspots in the city aren't immigrants' homes, they are devices for keeping the body safe while living in Syrbia.

This journey reflects on the current crisis of not only our physical surroundings, but also our very physiology when it clashes with what is commonly referred to as the digital. It is only made more so apparent in the example of the Syrian immigrants since their crisis is far more immediate in a way which accentuates this deepening schism.

The question these observations and analysis open is whether the digital can form the physical, whether the binary infrastructure can unintentionally design the urban space we inhabit?[6]

The structure of population of Serbia is currently changed by 0.53%. Parks of the capital of Serbia are overflowing with people having nowhere to sleep and nowhere to go, except to linger in the midst of Belgrade's public spaces. They are not interested in staying in Serbia, the ultimate destination on their route are countries of the European Union, so their actions in Serbia are completely temporary and collateral. The only real intention is to survive, and keep in touch through the internet – and yet their presence is notable in most parts of the city centre.

The material seems to trace the immaterial, so that new forms of ephemeral architecture and hybrid urban typologies can emerge, the melting together of place, data space and physiology into a digital-actual mixture observable as a corporeal imprinting of the virtual environments into the physical space that we inhabit.

sind die der derzeitigen Flüchtlingsmigration aus Syrien.

Während die Migranten unterwegs waren – zu Fuß, von einem Versteck zum nächsten hastend, in Frachtcontainer gepfercht, wobei sie ihr Leben und das ihrer engsten Angehörigen aufs Spiel setzten –, litten ihre Körper unter Erstickungsgefahr, Stress, Hunger, Erschöpfung und Schmerzen. Die unglaublichen Strapazen ihres Weges durch die eurasischen Korridore vom Nahen Osten nach Westeuropa spiegeln sich jedoch kein bisschen in der transzendenten Internet-Kommunikation wider, die die Migranten mit ihren Freunden und mit ihrer Familie zu Hause in Syrien pflegen. Sie wandern durch die Stadt und suchen nach Orten mit einem kostenlosen Internetzugang, halten Ausschau nach einem Hotspot, von dem aus sie in die Leere gelangen können, in der wir uns alle treffen, wobei wir unser jeweiliges Ersatz-Ich in der physischen Welt zurücklassen (auf der "Earth Default/Erde Standardeinstellung"[4]). Dies war die einzige Weise, auf die diese Menschen einander treffen konnten, physisch voneinander getrennt, aber geistig verbunden. Skype, Facebook, E-Mails – diese reisen mit Lichtgeschwindigkeit, legen in Sekunden Entfernungen zurück, die die Körper der Migranten monatelang erduldet und erlitten haben. Die Migranten sind auf der Suche nach einem Daheim, fernab des Landes, aus dem sie stammen. Ihre Körper stecken in einer Krise, und so greifen sie nach den körperlosen digitalen Erden[5], mittels ungeschützter WLAN-Punkte in Belgrad. Sie finden ihren Ort, ihr Daheim, in einem Nichtort. Dieser Nichtort hat einen Namen bekommen – Syrbien, eine Kombination aus seinem materiellen und seinem virtuellen Mutterland, Serbien und Syrien.

Es ist zu erwarten, dass Ereignisse, die online stattfinden, ihre Spuren in der physischen Welt hinterlassen, der Welt, die wir mit unseren Körpern, aber von Tag zu Tag weniger mit unserem Geist bewohnen. Die Dimension dieser Ereignisse und ihrer Folgen variiert von völlig marginal bis global. Während der Körper auf der Erde nach seinem Platz sucht, ohne diesen entdecken zu können, finden die Menschen ein Daheim und einen Treffpunkt in einem immateriellen, unsichtbaren "Ort", der die Welt so stark zu beschichten scheint, dass er das Leben und all seine Eigenschaften zu absorbieren vermag. Das ist keine Metapher mehr, sondern eine Realität, die größer ist als alles, was wir jenseits des Bildschirms sehen können.

Die Virtualität des Syrbischen Archipels prägt sich in die physische Re-

alität Belgrads ein. Sie verändert die Morphologie Belgrads, indem sie über die digitale Ausbreitung des Archipels hinausgreift, der durch die Vermittlung der vom Digitalen gelenkten Körper der Migranten eine physische Gestalt annimmt.

Syrbien ist eine Idee, ein Phänomen, dessen Existenz zwischen der städtischen Struktur Belgrads und der Infrastruktur der allgegenwärtigen virtuellen Kommunikation und des davon geprägten Lebens angesiedelt ist. Im Laufe der Geschichte haben sich Menschen immer nahe dem Wasser angesiedelt, auf Bergen, in Tälern, weil sie dort Schutz und Sicherheit fanden. Zukünftige Ansiedlungen hängen möglicherweise von Hotspots ab. Die von Hotspots in der Stadt erschaffenen ephemeren Zufluchtsorte sind kein "Daheim" der Migranten, sondern Einrichtungen, die ihrem Körper Schutz bieten, während sie in Syrbien leben.

Diese Reise spiegelt die gegenwärtige Krise wider, die nicht nur unsere physische Umgebung betrifft, sondern auch unsere Physiologie, wenn diese auf das trifft, was wir normalerweise als das Digitale bezeichnen. Das wird durch das Beispiel der syrischen Migranten nur noch offensichtlicher, da deren Krise viel unmittelbarer ist – auf eine Weise, die dieses Schisma deutlich zutage treten lässt.

Die Frage, die diese Erörterungen aufwerfen, läuft darauf hinaus, ob das Digitale das Physische formen kann, ob die binäre Infrastruktur den von uns bewohnten städtischen Raum unbeabsichtigt zu entwerfen vermag.[6]

Die Bevölkerung Serbiens hat derzeit um 0,53 % zugenommen. Die Parks der Hauptstadt Serbiens sind voller Menschen, die keinen Schlafplatz und nichts zu tun haben und sich deshalb auf den öffentlichen Plätzen Belgrads aufhalten. Sie wollen nicht in Serbien bleiben, denn das eigentliche Ziel ihrer Reise sind die Länder der Europäischen Union – vor diesem Hintergrund ist das, was sie in Serbien machen, völlig temporär und kollateral. Das Einzige, was sie wollen, ist zu überleben und über das Internet in Verbindung zu bleiben – gleichwohl ist ihre Präsenz fast überall im Stadtzentrum nicht zu übersehen.

Das Materielle scheint dem Immateriellen zu folgen, so dass neue Formen einer ephemeren Architektur und hybride städtische Typologien entstehen können, ein Verschmelzen von Ort, Datenraum und Physiologie zu einem digital-physischen Konglomerat, bei dem sich virtuelle Umgebungen körperlich in den von uns bewohnten physischen Raum einprägen.

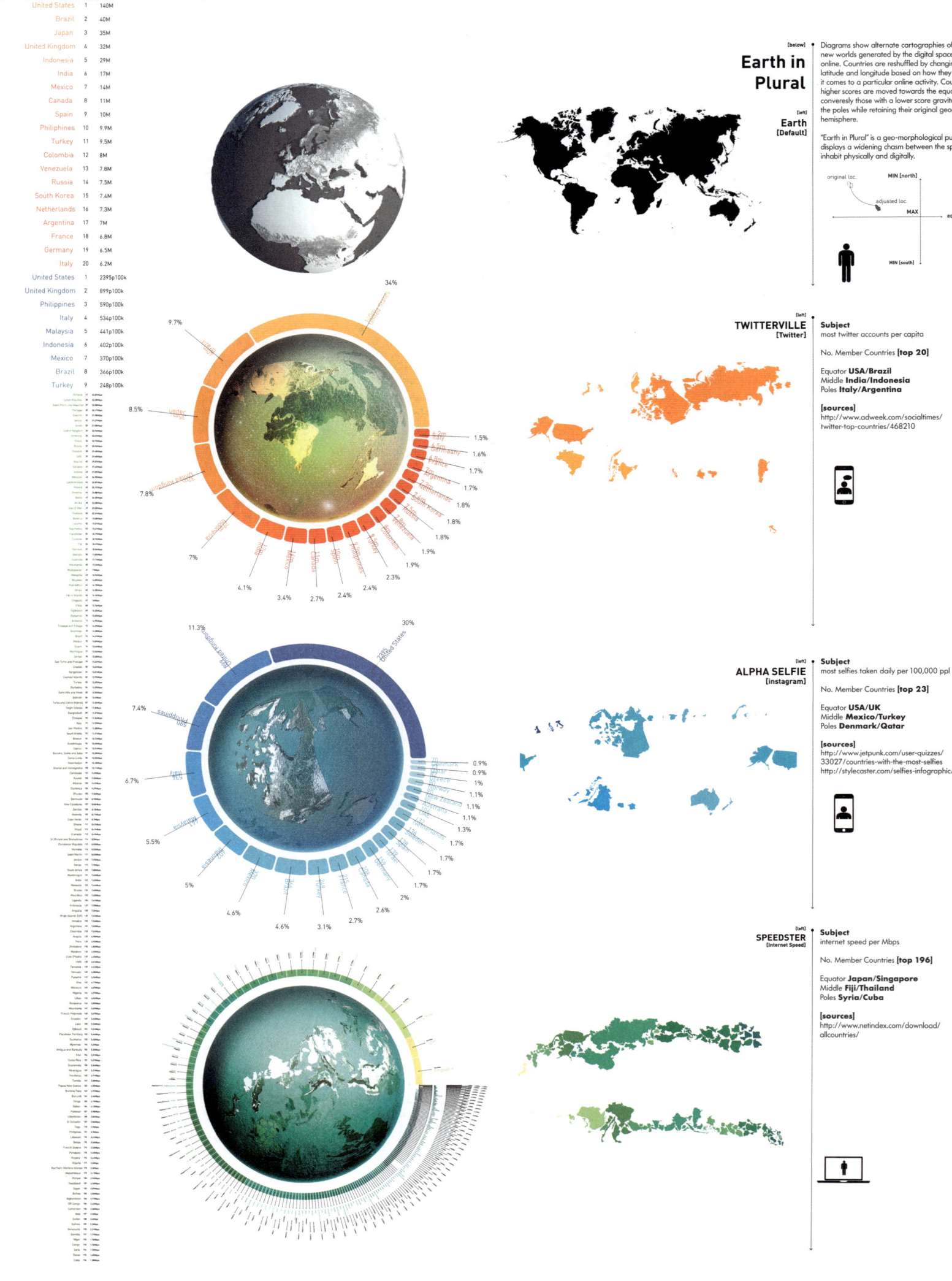

Earth in Plural

[below] Diagrams show alternate cartographies of stra
new worlds generated by the digital space we
online. Countries are reshuffled by changing the
latitude and longitude based on how they score
it comes to a particular online activity. Countrie
higher scores are moved towards the equator a
conversely those with a lower score gravitate to
the poles while retaining their original geograph
hemisphere.

"Earth in Plural" is a geo-morphological pun th
displays a widening chasm between the spaces
inhabit physically and digitally.

[Left]
Earth
[Default]

TWITTERVILLE
[Twitter]

[left]
Subject
most twitter accounts per capita

No. Member Countries [top 20]

Equator **USA/Brazil**
Middle **India/Indonesia**
Poles **Italy/Argentina**

[sources]
http://www.adweek.com/socialtimes/
twitter-top-countries/468210

ALPHA SELFIE
[instagram]

[left]
Subject
most selfies taken daily per 100,000 ppl

No. Member Countries [top 23]

Equator **USA/UK**
Middle **Mexico/Turkey**
Poles **Denmark/Qatar**

[sources]
http://www.jetpunk.com/user-quizzes/
33027/countries-with-the-most-selfies
http://stylecaster.com/selfies-infographic/

SPEEDSTER
[Internet Speed]

[left]
Subject
internet speed per Mbps

No. Member Countries [top 196]

Equator **Japan/Singapore**
Middle **Fiji/Thailand**
Poles **Syria/Cuba**

[sources]
http://www.netindex.com/download/
allcountries/

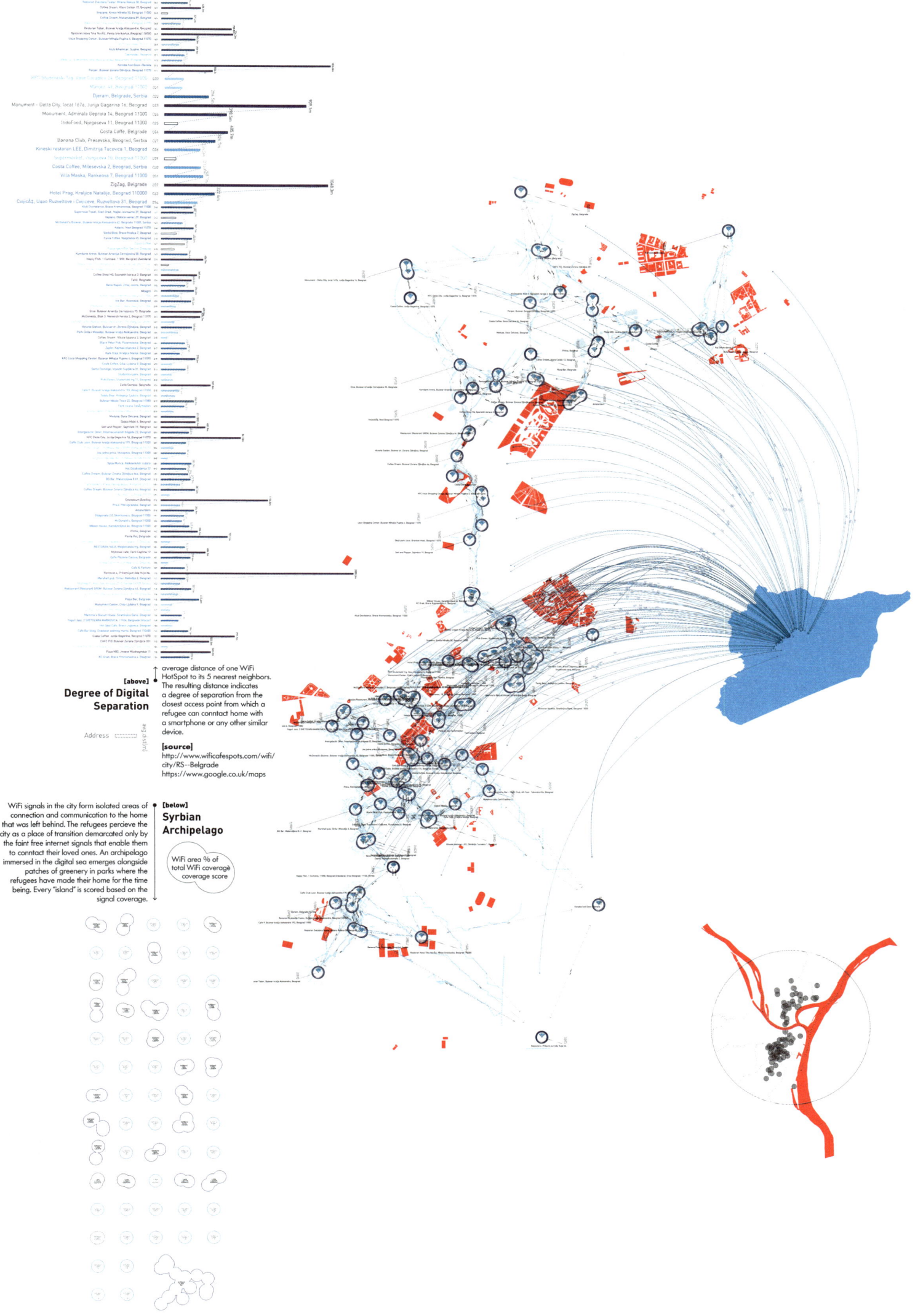

[above]
Degree of Digital Separation

Address ⬡⬡⬡

average distance of one WiFi HotSpot to its 5 nearest neighbors. The resulting distance indicates a degree of separation from the closest access point from which a refugee can conntact home with a smartphone or any other similar device.

[source]
http://www.wificafespots.com/wifi/city/RS--Belgrade
https://www.google.co.uk/maps

WiFi signals in the city form isolated areas of connection and communication to the home that was left behind. The refugees percieve the city as a place of transition demarcated only by the faint free internet signals that enable them to conntact their loved ones. An archipelago immersed in the digital sea emerges alongside patches of greenery in parks where the refugees have made their home for the time being. Every "island" is scored based on the signal coverage.

[below]
Syrbian Archipelago

WiFi area % of total WiFi coverage coverage score

SUBVERSIVE TEHRAN Ivo Pekec, Fereshteh Assadzadeh

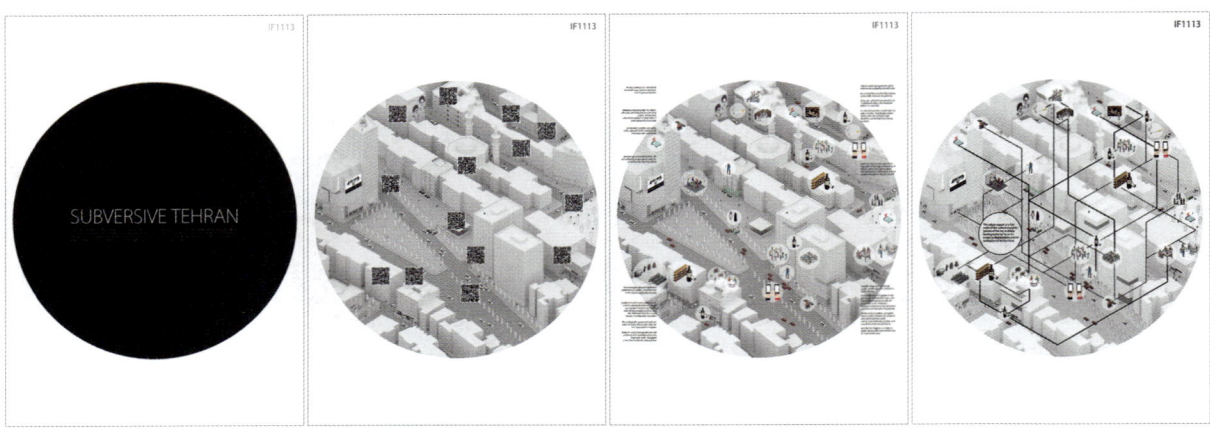

"The inferno of the living is not something that will be; if there is one, it is what is already here, the inferno where we live every day, that we form by being together. There are two ways to escape suffering it. The first is easy for many: accept the inferno and become such a part of it that you can no longer see it. The second is risky and demands constant vigilance and apprehension: seek and learn to recognize who and what, in the midst of inferno, are not inferno, then make them endure, give them space."[1]
Italo Calvino

I. Subversive Tehran: Visualizing the Invisible City

In the last century, Tehran experienced a massive population growth, becoming the third largest city in the Middle East, right after Cairo and Istanbul. Born into rapid modernization and urbanization, Tehran's well-educated youths in particular have high potential and desire to participate in the public sphere. The problem is, that a conventional public sphere is almost non-existent in Tehran.

Radical changes happened after the Islamic Revolution in 1979. Massive transformations in the social classes and crippling ideological and religious rules triggered rapid changes in the cities of Iran. The ones in power started remaking the cities according to an ideology based on an austere version

of Islam. In Tehran, a segregation of its citizens from the public spaces began as a consequence of the new restrictions. Large public spaces were taken over by pro regime forces, and slowly transformed in to"'enclosed' or 'interior spaces' of their ideological self".[2] Individuals gradually began to move the activities they used to partake in the public sphere into their more protected and safe private spaces. When someone from outside the country visits for the first time, they usually don't expect nude art galleries or rock bands practicing in apartments, but things like this are commonplace in Tehran, they simply are not visible or easily accessible.

With isometric snapshot a fictional district of Tehran, "Subversive Tehran" shows how people cease to participate in any form of activities in public spaces, find or invent alternatives to continue their activities, and how new forms of space get created in the process. The first view shows the rigid physical appearance of the city, with QR codes indicating information of invisible places; the second view makes visible the locations of the subversive spaces; the third view visualizes the network between the spaces and their connection to the digital world. Gathered through field research, interviews, historical materials as well as rumors, qualitative information is visualized to reveal the invisible city.

"Die Hölle der Lebenden ist nicht etwas, das erst noch kommen wird. Wenn es eine gibt, ist es die, die schon da ist, die Hölle, in der wir jeden Tag leben, die wir durch unser Zusammensein bilden. Es gibt zwei Arten, nicht unter ihr zu leiden. Die erste fällt vielen leicht: die Hölle zu akzeptieren und so sehr Teil von ihr zu werden, dass man sie nicht mehr sieht. Die zweite ist riskant und verlangt ständige Aufmerksamkeit und Lernbereitschaft: zu suchen und erkennen zu lernen, wer und was inmitten der Hölle nicht Hölle ist, und ihm Dauer und Raum zu geben."[1]
Italo Calvino

I. Subversive Teheran: Die unsichtbare Stadt visualisieren

Im letzten Jahrhundert erfuhr Teheran ein gewaltiges Bevölkerungswachstum. Es wuchs zur drittgrößten Stadt des Mittleren Ostens heran, direkt nach Kairo und Istanbul. In eine Welt der rasanten Modernisierung und Urbanisation hinein geboren, strebt vor allem die gebildete Jugend Teherans nach einer Beteiligung an der Öffentlichkeit. Problematisch hierbei ist, dass es eine konventionelle Öffentlichkeit in Teheran fast gar nicht gibt.

Nach der islamischen Revolution 1979 fanden radikale Änderungen statt. Massive Umwandlungen in den Gesellschaftsschichten und lähmende ideologische und religiöse Regeln lösten rasche Veränderungen in den Städten Irans aus. Gemäß einer auf einer strikten Auslegung des Islams basierenden Ideologie begannen die Machthaber mit einer Erneuerung der Städte. Als Konsequenz der neuen und einschränken-

den Regeln kam es in Teheran zu einer Segregation der Bevölkerung aus dem öffentlichen Raum. Großflächige öffentliche Räume wurden von regierungsnahen Kräften übernommen und langsam in "geschlossene und innere Räume ihres ideologischen Selbst"[2] transformiert. Bewohner begann nach und nach ihre Aktivitäten aus der Öffentlichkeit heraus in ihre geschützten und sicheren privaten Räume zu verlagern, um weiterhin an Aktivitäten teilzuhaben, die in der Öffentlichkeit unterdrückt wurden. Wenn man von außerhalb zum ersten Mal nach Teheran reist, erwartet man generell nicht, dass man auf Galerien mit Akt-Kunst oder in Wohnungen auftretende Rockbands trifft, solche Dinge sind jedoch weitverbreitet in Teheran; sie sind lediglich nicht sichtbar oder leicht zugänglich.

In drei isometrischen Schnappschüssen eines fiktionalen Bezirks in Teheran wird in "Subversive Teheran" gezeigt, wie die Menschen aufhören, an irgendwelchen Aktivitäten in öffentlichen Räumen teilzunehmen; wie sie Alternativen finden oder erfinden, um ihren Aktivitäten weiter nachzugehen; wie dabei neue Formen von Räumen entstehen. Die erste Grafik zeigt die starre physikalische Erscheinung der Stadt, in ihr eingebettet sind QR-Codes mit Informationen über die versteckten Räume. Die zweite Grafik macht die Lage der subversiven Räume sichtbar. Die dritte Grafik visualisiert das Netzwerk zwischen den Räumen und ihre Verbindung mit dem digitalen Raum. Die Daten und Informationen, die für das Projekt gesammelt wurden, sind qualitativer Natur. Sie wurden vor Ort

"The freedom to make and remake our cities and ourselves is […] one of the most precious yet most neglected of our human rights."[4]
David Harvey

II. Public Space – Counterpublics

"Public sphere", according to Jürgen Habermas, can be described when three conditions apply – a guarantee to access for all citizens, to freedom of assembly and to freedom of expressing one's opinions.[3] As spaces of everyday activities, it is believed that the idea and practice of democracy is ingrained in public spaces. They embody Henri Lefebvre's idea of the right to the city, which is further defined by David Harvey as "a collective rather than an individual right".[4]

Whose right do public spaces embody? Looking at the development of public spaces in history, it can be observed that they are inherently contradictory; in the sense that they have always been exclusive in who has been able to participate in them, they have never been truly democratic. Nancy Fraser coined the term "counterpublics"[5] to describe the spaces that are established by people excluded from the public sphere as a response to the lack of concern for the activities they might need public spaces for.

"Subversive Tehran" belongs to "counterpublics". Facing a multitude of exclusions, citizens have established spaces that have to become subversive to be able to continue existing. Activities might start in a given space, but they could rapidly change their location or even cease to exist at all, either because the authorities shut them down or because they simply are replaced by other options. These spaces are living examples of the "open source urbanism" defined by Saskia Sassen, in which cities are incomplete and can "constantly be remade" through a "myriad of interventions and little changes".[6] For the existence of such spaces, "time, and not space, should be seen as the primary context"; while "space becomes active, social, and is released from the hold of static formalism".[7] Subversion is dynamic and in constant flux; the temporal dimension is essential. This gives them certain immunity against control.

"The city is dead, long live the network."[14]
Thomas Sieverts

III. Physical Space – Virtual Space

The subversive spaces developed from being in a fixed physical space to more fluid "counterpublics" that are accessible with the right kind of information. The logical next step is the "counterpublics" developing away from a "space of places" to becoming a "space of flows".[8] Manuel Castells sees the main paradigm of contemporary society as a network that is dependent on the flow between goods, resources and, most importantly in the case of understanding "counterpublics", information.[8]

In recent years, despite attempts to censor its use[9], the use of internet cafes, private internet connections and mobile phones has allowed people to access information that was previously unattainable in the public sphere. In contrast to the physical city, the restrictions one encounters on the Internet are more easily overcome, making it a viable strategy for some types of subversive spaces.

The digital realm re-establishes parts of the participatory nature of the city in the virtual. Especially fringe groups of society, for instance the LGBT community, religious minorities, or writers affected by censorship, have found safer ways of partaking in their activities online than they could in physical spaces. Members of the Baha'i religion organize university classes online (as they are not allowed to attend regular universities in Iran) and "cyber synagogues" free the Jewish community from the struggles they experience in public.[10,11] While digital spaces allow the participation in public space that is part of the "intangible metastructure"[12] of the Internet, the digital realm does not replace physical spaces, as space forms "the material support of time-sharing social practices"[13]. It mainly opens a door of more stable and safe access to the physical "counterpublics".

Creating spaces for the activities taken away from the citizens of Tehran in the public realm can be described as a form of hacking the city, regardless of if they exist as physical "counterpublics" or if they became "spaces of flows" and shifted to the digital realm. In any case, people who use the space apply meaning to it; through their lived experience people redefine the concept of public space and democracy. In "Subversive Tehran", people manage to interact and maybe gradually collectively unveil the repressive veil that has been put over their city.

gesammelt, stammen aus Interviews und historischen Dokumenten und aus Gerüchten. Durch solche Informationen wird die unsichtbare Stadt visualisiert.

"Die Freiheit, uns selbst und unsere Städte zu erschaffen und immer wieder neu zu erschaffen, ist meiner Ansicht nach eins der kostbarsten und dennoch am meisten vernachlässigten unserer Menschenrechte."[4]
David Harvey

II. Öffentlichkeit – Gegenöffentlichkeit

Laut Jürgen Habermas kann "Öffentlichkeit" beschrieben werden als das Vorhandensein dreier Bedingungen: ein garantierter Zugang für alle Bürger, Versammlungsfreiheit und freie Meinungsäußerung.[3] Als Räume des alltäglichen Lebens beinhalten Räume die Idee und Praxis von Demokratie. Sie verkörpern Henri Lefebvres Idee über das Recht auf Stadt, die von David Harvey als "ein kollektives statt individuelles Recht" weiter definiert wurde.[4]

Wessen Recht verkörpern öffentliche Räume? Betrachtet man die historische Entwicklung öffentlicher Räume, zeigt sich, dass diese inhärent widersprüchlich sind, in dem Sinne, dass sie immer exklusiv in ihrer Zugänglichkeit waren, nie wirklich demokratisch. Nancy Fraser prägte den Begriff "counterpublics"[5] zur Beschreibung von Räumen, die von aus der Öffentlichkeit ausgeschlossenen Menschen etabliert wurden, zur Schaffung ihrer eigenen Öffentlichkeit als Antwort auf die für ihre Aktivitäten fehlenden Räume.

"Subversive Teheran" gehört zur Gegenöffentlichkeit. Angesichts einer Vielzahl von Einschränkungen haben die Bewohner Teherans Räume erschaffen, die subversiv werden müssen, um weiter zu existieren. Aktivitäten beginnen etwa in bestimmten Räumen, sie können aber schnell ihren Standort ändern oder sich völlig auflösen, entweder weil sie von den Autoritäten aufgelöst werden oder weil sie ganz einfach durch andere Optionen ersetzt werden. Solche Räume sind lebende Beispiele, die von Saskia Sassen als "Open Source Urbanismus" definiert wurden. Dabei sind die Städte unvollständig und können "sich konstant neu entwickeln", durch "eine Vielzahl von Interventionen und kleinen Veränderungen".[6] Für die Existenz solcher Räume, "sollte Zeit und nicht Raum als primärer Kontext gesehen werden"; während "Raum aktiv, sozial und aus den Fängen eines statischen Formalismus befreit wird".[7] Subversion ist dynamisch und in ständigem Fluss. Die zeitliche Dimension ist essentiell für diese Räume. Dies verleiht ihnen eine gewisse Immunität gegenüber Kontrolle.

"Die Stadt ist tot, es lebe das Netzwerk."[14]
Thomas Sieverts

III. Physischer Raum – virtueller Raum

Die subversiven Räume entwickelten sich zunächst aus fixen physischen Räumen zu beweglichen "counterpublics", die über Informationen zugänglich sind. Der konsequente nächste Schritt wäre die Entwicklung von "counterpublics"als "spaces of places" hin zu reinen "spaces of flows".[8] Manuel Castells sieht das zentrale Paradigma der heutigen Gesellschaft als ein Netzwerk, das auf dem Fluss zwischen Gütern, Ressourcen, und im Falle der "counterpublics" für das Verständnis am wichtigsten, Information, beruht.[8]

Trotz vieler Versuche, das Internet zu zensieren[9], ermöglichten in den letzten Jahren Internetcafes, private Internetzugänge und Mobiltelefone der Bevölkerung Zugang zu Informationen, die zuvor in der Öffentlichkeit unzugänglich waren. Im Gegensatz zur physischen Stadt sind die Restriktionen, mit denen man im Internet konfrontiert wird, einfacher zu umgehen, was es zu einer brauchbaren Strategie für subversive Räume macht.

Der digitale Raum stellt virtuell Teile des partizipatorischen Wesens der Stadt wieder her. Insbesondere Randgruppen der iranischen Gesellschaft, wie die Homosexuellen-Gemeinde, religiöse Minderheiten oder von Zensur betroffene Autoren, haben online sicherere Methoden gefunden, an ihren Aktivitäten teilzuhaben, als es ihnen in physischen Räumen möglich wäre. Mitglieder der Baha'i Religion etwa organisieren Universitätskurse im Internet (da ihnen der Besuch von normalen Universitäten untersagt ist); "Cyber-Synagogen" befreien die jüdische Gemeinde von den Einschränkungen, die sie in der Öffentlichkeit erfahren.[10,11] Während digitale Räume die Teilnahme im öffentlichen Raum, der Teil der "immateriellen Meta-Struktur"[12] des Internets ist, erlauben, ersetzt der digitale Raum den physischen Raum trotzdem nicht, da Raum die "materielle Grundlage für gemeinsame soziale Begegnungen bildet"[13]. Er eröffnet hauptsächlich Zugang zu stabileren und sichereren Kommunikationsmethoden, die auch eine physische Gegenöffentlichkeit entstehen lassen.

Die Schaffung von Räumen für Aktivitäten, die aus dem öffentlichen Raum weggenommen wurden, kann schlussfolgernd als eine Form von "hacking the city" beschrieben werden, unabhängig davon, ob sie als physische "counterpublics" existieren oder sich in digitale Räume verlagert haben. In jedem Fall bekommt die Öffentlichkeit Bedeutung durch die Menschen, die sie nutzen; das Konzept von öffentlichem Raum und Demokratie wird durch die gelebte Erfahrung der Bevölkerung neu definiert. In "Subversive Teheran" schafft es die Bevölkerung zu interagieren und möglicherweise den repressiven Schleier, der sich über ihre Stadt gelegt hat, nach und nach abzulegen.

Locating subversive spaces in Tehran behind the city's rigid physical appearance.

Verortung der subversiven Räume in Teheran hinter der starren physischen Erscheinung der Stadt.

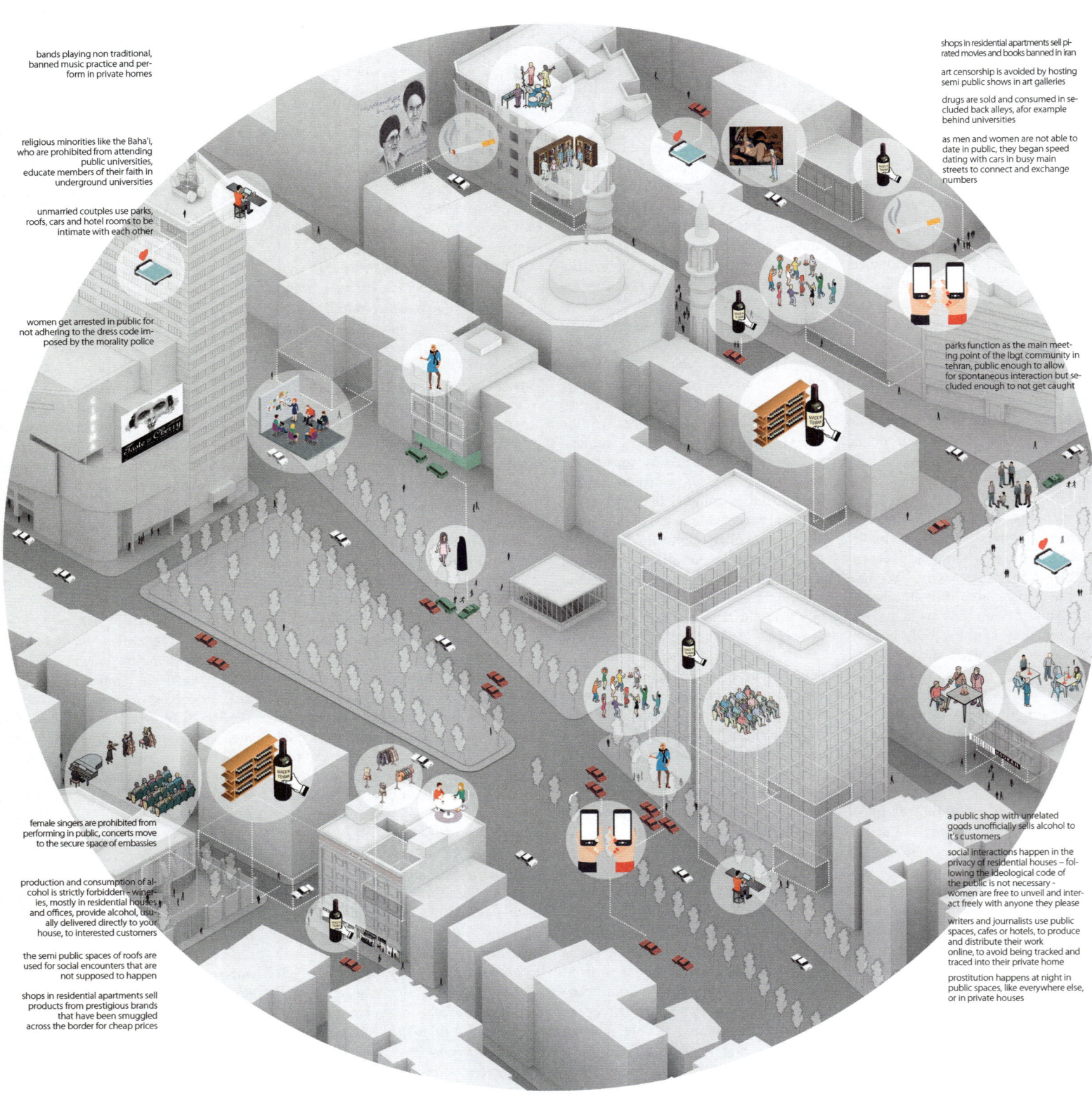

bands playing non traditional, banned music practice and perform in private homes

religious minorities like the Baha'i, who are prohibited from attending public universities, educate members of their faith in underground universities

unmarried coutples use parks, roofs, cars and hotel rooms to be intimate with each other

women get arrested in public for not adhering to the dress code imposed by the morality police

female singers are prohibited from performing in public, concerts move to the secure space of embassies

production and consumption of alcohol is strictly forbidden – wineries, mostly in residential houses and offices, provide alcohol, usually delivered directly to your house, to interested customers

the semi public spaces of roofs are used for social encounters that are not supposed to happen

shops in residential apartments sell products from prestigious brands that have been smuggled across the border for cheap prices

shops in residential apartments sell pirated movies and books banned in iran

art censorship is avoided by hosting semi public shows in art galleries

drugs are sold and consumed in secluded back alleys, afor example behind universities

as men and women are not able to date in public, they began speed dating with cars in busy main streets to connect and exchange numbers

parks function as the main meeting point of the lbgt community in tehran, public enough to allow for spontaneous interaction but secluded enough to not get caught

a public shop with unrelated goods unofficially sells alcohol to it's customers

social interactions happen in the privacy of residential houses – following the ideological code of the public is not necessary – women are free to unveil and interact freely with anyone they please

writers and journalists use public spaces, cafes or hotels, to produce and distribute their work online, to avoid being tracked and traced into their private home

prostitution happens at night in public spaces, like everywhere else, or in private houses

Visualising the network between the
subversive spaces, constituted through the
digital world.

*Visualisierung des Netzwerks der subversiven
Räumen, das sich in der digitalen Sphäre
konstituiert.*

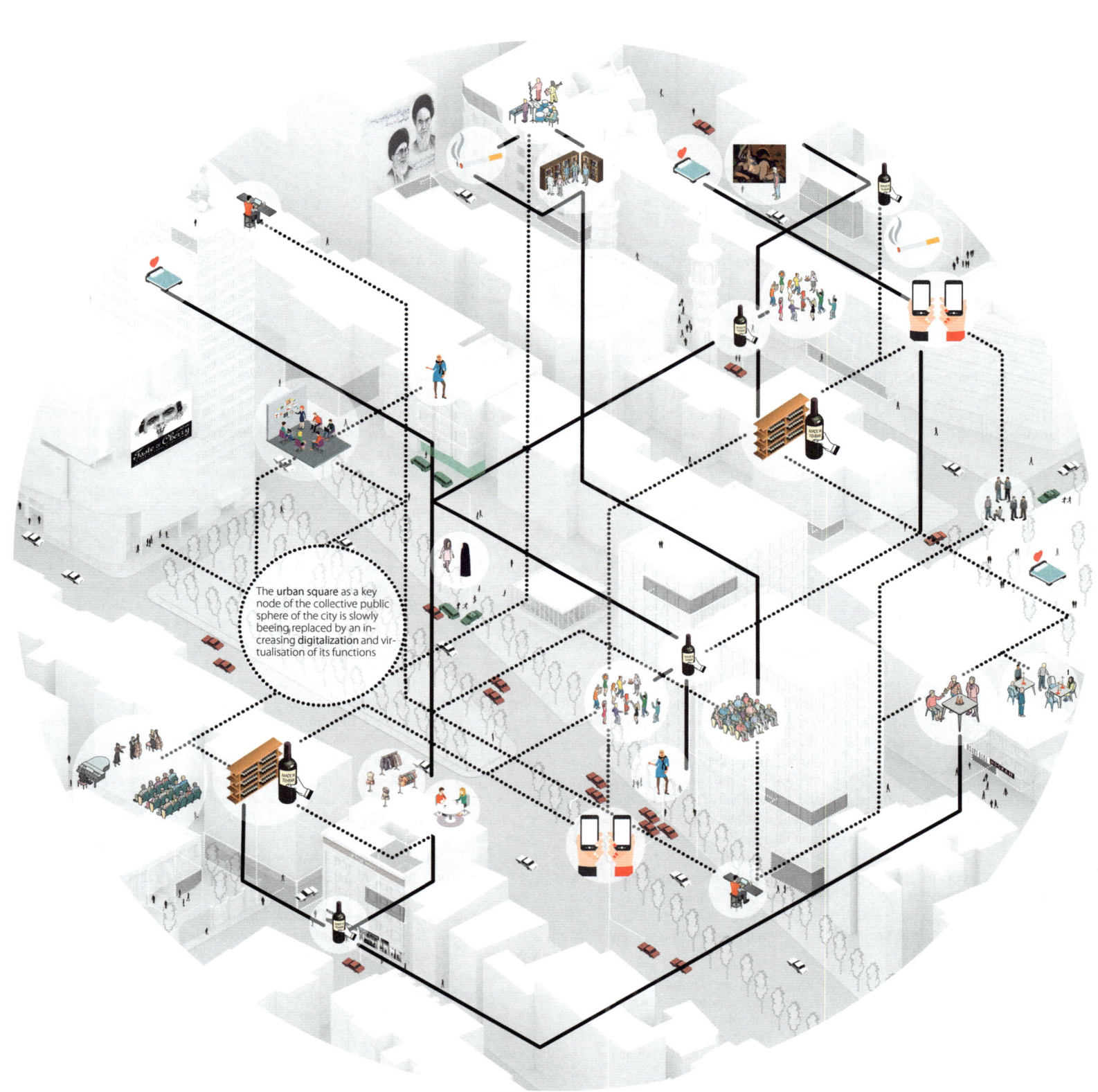

The urban square as a key
node of the collective public
sphere of the city is slowly
beeing replaced by an in-
creasing digitalization and vir-
tualisation of its functions

JUST TRUST US – OR TAKE THIS

Curie Kure, Hanna Biresch

Thesis: In the digital city the user needs to be informed entirely about technical and legal relations so that he/she can understand and accept terms of use in a sovereign way.

The digital city surrounds us, we live in it, we construct it and we design it. Cities are becoming "smart" and "intelligent". Data giants like Cisco Systems, Google, Facebook and Co. dream of inter-connected cities. In 2014, the city of Hamburg signed the "Smart City Memorandum of Understanding" together with Cisco Systems: the city is to be designed more efficiently.

One example for more efficiency is the citizen's Kiosk. The Kiosk allows citizens to spare government office visits by utilising video communication. Measuring and regulating transportation as well as street lighting will optimise life in the city. For the time being, Cisco provides this service for free. But is it largely unclear what happens to our data, who saves it and how it is passed on. So far, no detailed information has been made available to the public. The Hamburger Commissioner for Data Privacy and Freedom of Information is yet to be consulted.

The scope of the German Federal Data Protection Act (BDSG) and the Hamburger Data Protection Act (HmbDSG) is not easily comprehensible for the juridical layman. And because the application of law is not based on the location of the user, but on the location of providing businesses, knowledge of various national laws is required.

The debates on Data Privacy Laws, the NSA affairs and economic interests give rise to concern. Usually, we accept the conditions of service as a mere annoyance. Also, we prefer using one password only. Emails? No, we

don't encrypt them either. Is it possible to live in the digital city without accepting the terms of conditions?

In order to use services such as Apps, Browsers and Co., you are required to accept the terms of use, the privacy policies and the tracking instruments (e.g. cookies). Otherwise the user is being excluded.

Facebook and Google are among the most visited websites worldwide. The amount of interlinking within Facebook's or Google's clauses illustrate how exhaustive and non-linear the services' conditions are. The average user will neither understand the technical texts nor will they take the time required to read the texts. In this sense, Google is rated as an extreme example, and does not make it easy for the user: If you want to read all the terms and conditions, then you have to click through a labyrinth of conditions. Still, we click on "accept".

The price that we pay is loss of sovereignty and privacy. Without knowing what data is surrendered, how it is passed on and what it is used for, no one can act in a sovereign way. Terms of conditions should be transparent and easily understandable for the user. Is it possible to check all terms and conditions of applications used in order to protect data? Is action without data supply even an option in the interconnected digital city?

Information and transparency sensitises citizens to topics such as data acquisition and data trade. With this in mind: have fun and "Sapere aude!"[*1]

*Kant Immanuel: Response to the question: What is Enlightenment? In: Kant, Immanuel; Mendelsohn, Moses; Schiller, Friedrich: What is Enlightenment?, Thesis and Definitions, Ed. Erhard Bahr, Stuttgart 1996, p.9-17, here p.9.

These: In der digitalen Stadt muss der Nutzer besser über technische und gesetzliche Zusammenhänge aufgeklärt sein, um Nutzungsbedingungen zu verstehen und souverän akzeptieren zu können.

Die Digitale Stadt umgibt uns, wir leben in ihr, wir gestalten sie und sie gestaltet uns. Städte werden "smart" und "intelligent". Die vernetzten Städte sind das, wovon Datengiganten wie Cisco Systems, Google, Facebook und Co. träumen.

2014 hat Hamburg das "Smart City Memorandum of Understanding" mit Cisco Systems unterzeichnet: die Stadt soll effizienter gestaltet werden. Beispielsweise bietet Cisco den Bürgerkiosk an. In einer Box kann der Bürger sich Behördengänge ersparen und mittels Videoverbindung mit der Behörde sprechen. Messungen und Steuerungen des Verkehrs und der Straßenbeleuchtung sollen das Leben in der Stadt optimieren. Vorerst bietet Cisco diesen Dienst kostenlos an. Was allerdings mit den erfassten Daten passiert, wer sie speichert und weitergibt, ist unklar. Bislang stehen der Öffentlichkeit keine detaillieteren Informationen zur Verfügung. Auch die hamburgische Beauftragte für Datenschutz und Informationsfreiheit wurde noch nicht zu Rate gezogen.

Für juristische Laien ist der Inhalt des Deutschen Bundesdatenschutzgesetzes (BDSG) und des Hamburgischen Datenschutzgesetzes (HmbDSG) nicht leicht verständlich. Und da nicht das Land, in dem der Dienst genutzt wird, sondern der Firmensitz des Unternehmens entscheidet, welches Gesetz greift, muss man auch dieses Wissen mitbringen.

Die Debatten über Datenschutzgesetze, ökonomische Interessen und die NSA-Affären geben dem Bewohnern allen Grund, gewisse Fragen zu stellen. Meistens akzeptieren wir jedoch die

Bedingungen der Dienste und betrachten sie als lästiges Häkchen, das es zu setzen gilt. Wir nutzen auch gerne ein und dasselbe Passwort. Emails? Nein, die verschlüsseln wir auch nicht. Besteht die Möglichkeit in der digitalen Stadt zu leben, ohne den Bedingungen zuzustimmen?

Um Dienste wie Apps, Browser und Co. nutzen zu können, muss der Bürger Nutzungsbedingungen, Datenschutzbestimmungen und Trackinginstrumente (z.B. Cookies) akzeptieren. Andernfalls wird er ausgeschlossen.

Weltweit gehören Facebook und Google zu den meistbesuchten Websites. Die Anzahl der Verlinkungen innerhalb der Bestimmungen von Facebook und Google verdeutlicht, wie lang und nicht-linear die Bedingungen der Dienste sind. Der durchschnittliche Nutzer wird sich weder die Mühe machen, den Verlinkungen zu folgen, noch wird er die Zeit aufbringen, derer es bedarf, die Texte zu lesen. Google gilt hier als Extrembeispiel und macht es dem Nutzer nicht leicht: Will man all die Bedingungen lesen, die Google einfordert, muss man sich durch ein Labyrinth von Bestimmungen klicken. Wir klicken trotzdem auf "akzeptieren".

Der Preis, den wir dafür zahlen, ist der Verlust von Souveränität und Privatsphäre. Ohne zu wissen, welche Daten man abgibt, an welche Dritte sie weitergegeben werden und zu welchem Zweck sie genutzt werden, kann man nicht frei und souverän handeln. Für den Nutzer sollten Datenschutzbestimmungen transparent und einfach zu erschließen sein. Ist es möglich, jede Anwendung zu prüfen und persönliche Daten zu schützen? Kann es überhaupt Handeln ohne Datenabgabe in der vernetzten digitalen Stadt geben?

*Information und Transparenz sensibilisieren den Bewohner für Themen wie Datenerfassung und Datenhandel. In diesem Sinne: viel Spaß und "Sapere aude!"[*1]*

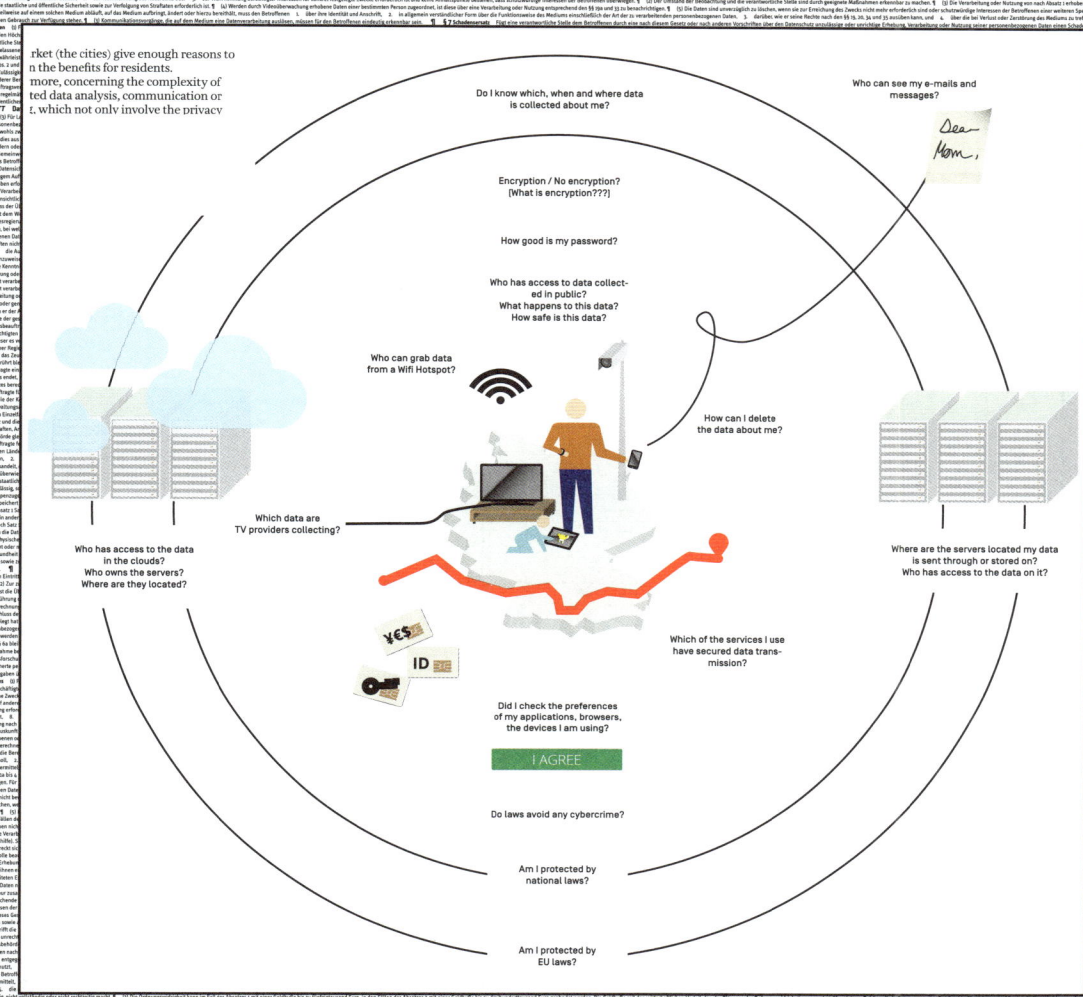

.rket (the cities) give enough reasons to
n the benefits for residents.
more, concerning the complexity of
ted data analysis, communication or
t, which not only involve the privacy

Do I know which, when and where data
is collected about me?

Who can see my e-mails and
messages?

Dear
Mom,

Encryption / No encryption?
[What is encryption???]

How good is my password?

Who has access to data collect-
ed in public?
What happens to this data?
How safe is this data?

Who can grab data
from a Wifi Hotspot?

How can I delete
the data about me?

Which data are
TV providers collecting?

Who has access to the data
in the clouds?
Who owns the servers?
Where are they located?

Where are the servers located my data
is sent through or stored on?
Who has access to the data on it?

Which of the services I use
have secured data trans-
mission?

YES
ID

Did I check the preferences
of my applications, browsers,
the devices I am using?

I AGREE

Do laws avoid any cybercrime?

Am I protected by
national laws?

Am I protected by
EU laws?

MBURG DATA PROTECTION LAWS (WITHOUT ANNOTATIONS)
MBURGISCHES DATENSCHUTZGESETZ

WHICH OF THE FOLLOWING TYPES OF SECURITY SOFTWARE DO YOU USE ON YOUR PRIVATE COMPUTER?

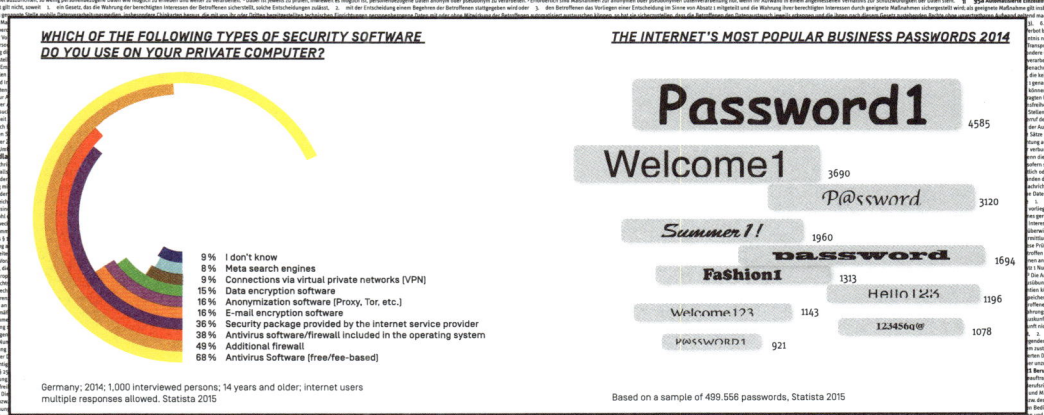

- 9 % I don't know
- 8 % Meta search engines
- 9 % Connections via virtual private networks (VPN)
- 15 % Data encryption software
- 16 % Anonymization software (Proxy, Tor, etc.)
- 16 % E-mail encryption software
- 36 % Security package provided by the internet service provider
- 38 % Antivirus software/Firewall included in the operating system
- 49 % Additional firewall
- 68 % Antivirus software (free/fee-based)

Germany; 2014; 1,000 interviewed persons; 14 years and older; internet users
multiple responses allowed. Statista 2015

THE INTERNET'S MOST POPULAR BUSINESS PASSWORDS 2014

Password1 — 4585
Welcome1 — 3690
P@ssw0rd — 3120
Summer!! — 1960
password — 1694
Fa5hion1 — 1313
Hello123 — 1196
Welcome123 — 1143
123456q@ — 1078
PASSWORD1 — 921

Based on a sample of 499.556 passwords, Statista 2015

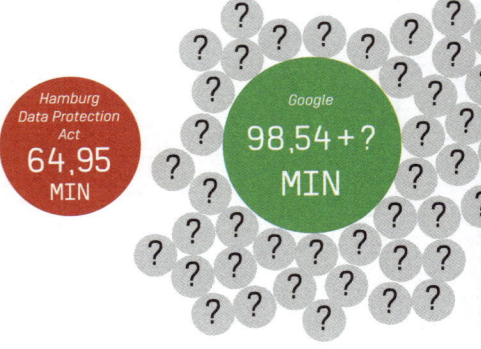

AVERAGE READING RATE AND COMPREHENSION (GERMAN LANGUGE)

Rates of reading include reading for memorization (fewer than 100 wpm);
reading for learning (100–200 wpm); reading for comprehension (200–400 wpm)

good reader		2000 CPM
average reader		1200 CPM
untrained reader		500 CPM

CPM = Characters per Minute (100 CPM = 20 Words Per Minute (WPM))

DISCOVERING "HOW IS MY PRIVACY PROTECTED"

| = 1 character

| = Linked text passage

—● = link leads to a new website

The headlines are displayed in the language that comes up automatically when visiting the website in Hamburg, Germany. Behind the headlines you find the amount of characters.

HOW LONG DOES IT TAKE TO READ THE POLICIES, INFOS AND TERMS OF USE OF ...

German Federal Data Protection Act
111,8 MIN

Hamburg Data Protection Act
64,95 MIN

Google
98,54 +? MIN

BUNDESDATENSCHUTZGESETZ 134161
German Federal Data Protection Act

HAMBURGISCHES DATENSCHUTZGESETZ (OHNE ERLÄUTERUNGEN) 77934
Hamburg Data Protection Act (without annotations)

FACEBOOK

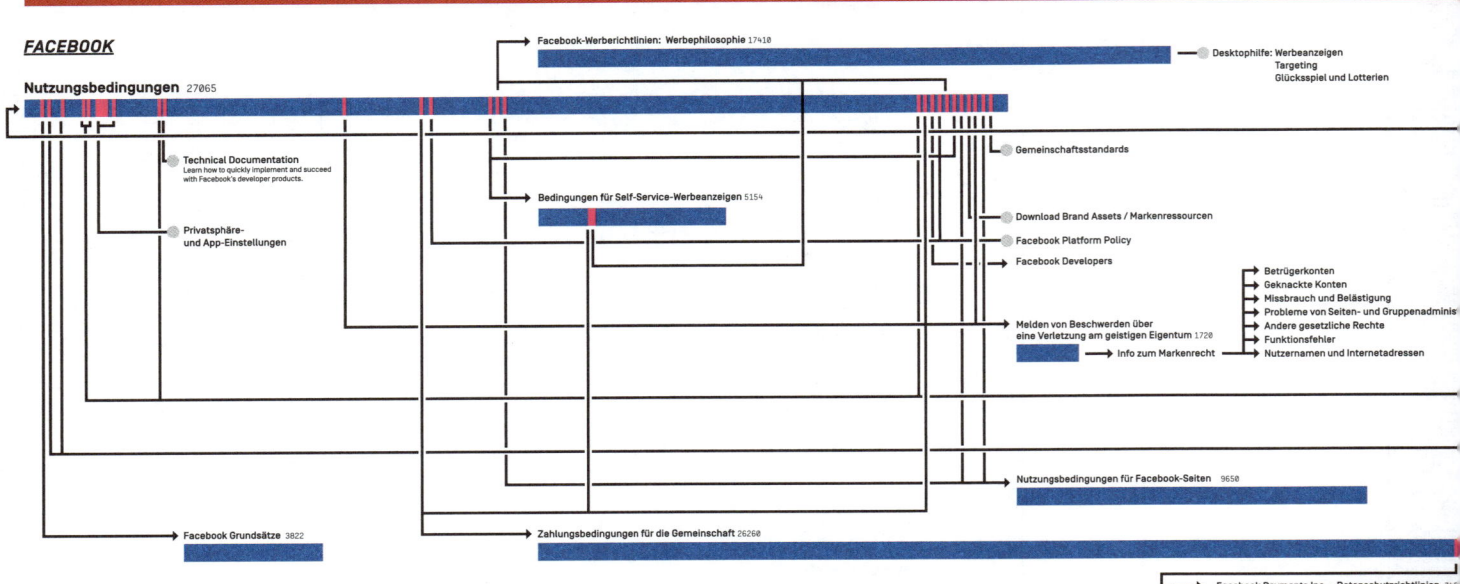

Facebook-Werberichtlinien: Werbephilosophie 17410
Desktophilfe: Werbeanzeigen / Targeting / Glücksspiel und Lotterien

Nutzungsbedingungen 27065

Technical Documentation
Learn how to quickly implement and succeed with Facebook's developer products.

Privatsphäre- und App-Einstellungen

Bedingungen für Self-Service-Werbeanzeigen 5154

Gemeinschaftsstandards

Download Brand Assets / Markenressourcen

Facebook Platform Policy

Facebook Developers

Melden von Beschwerden über eine Verletzung am geistigen Eigentum 1720
→ Info zum Markenrecht

Betrügerkonten
Geknackte Konten
Missbrauch und Belästigung
Probleme von Seiten- und Gruppenadminis
Andere gesetzliche Rechte
Funktionsfehler
Nutzernamen und Internetadressen

Nutzungsbedingungen für Facebook-Seiten 9650

Facebook Grundsätze 3822

Zahlungsbedingungen für die Gemeinschaft 26260

Facebook Payments Inc. – Datenschutzrichtlinien 745

GOOGLE

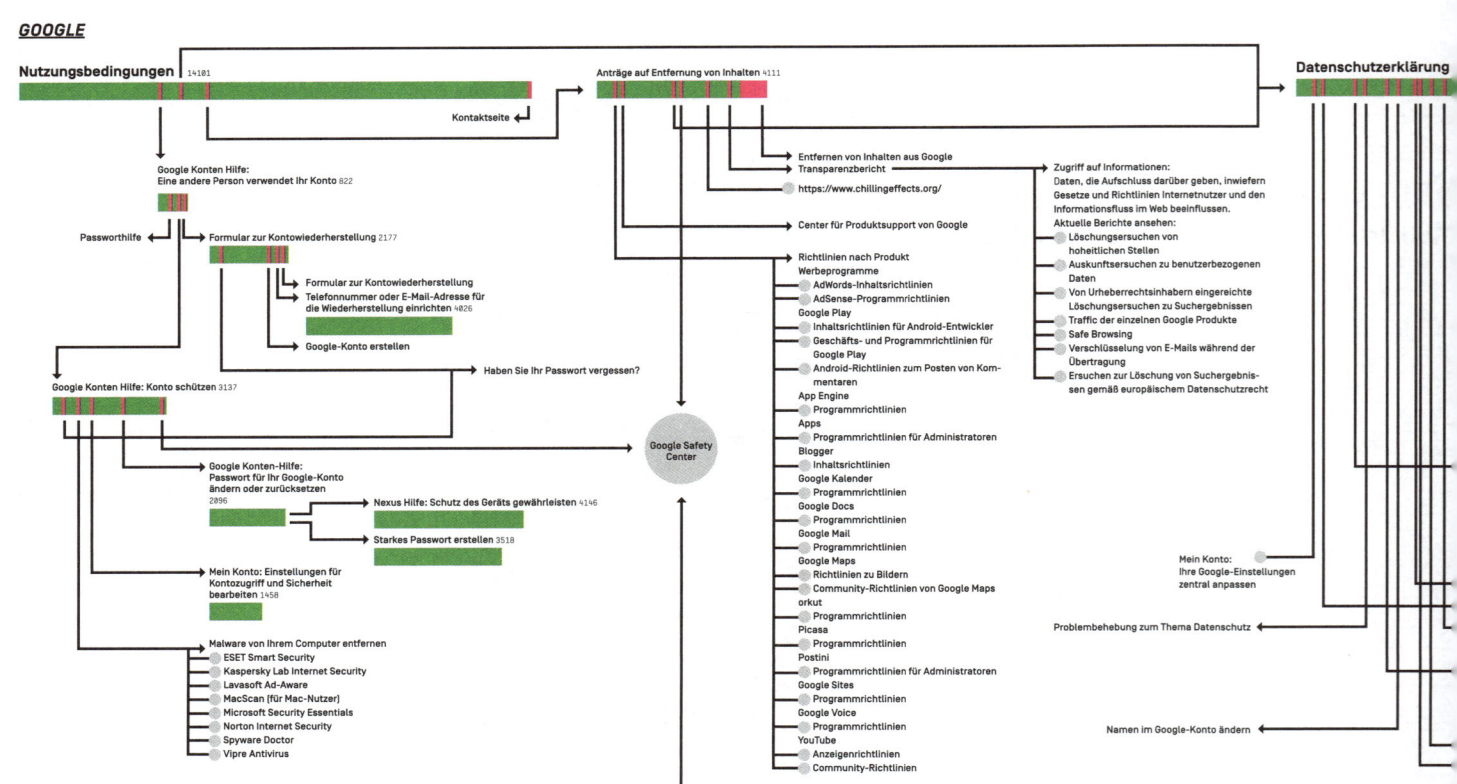

Nutzungsbedingungen 14101

Anträge auf Entfernung von Inhalten 4111

Datenschutzerklärung

Kontaktseite

Google Konten Hilfe: Eine andere Person verwendet Ihr Konto 822

Passworthilfe

Formular zur Kontowiederherstellung 2177

Formular zur Kontowiederherstellung
Telefonnummer oder E-Mail-Adresse für die Wiederherstellung einrichten 4026

Google-Konto erstellen

Haben Sie Ihr Passwort vergessen?

Google Konten Hilfe: Konto schützen 3137

Google Konten-Hilfe: Passwort für Ihr Google-Konto ändern oder zurücksetzen 2896

Nexus Hilfe: Schutz des Geräts gewährleisten 4146

Starkes Passwort erstellen 3518

Mein Konto: Einstellungen für Kontozugriff und Sicherheit bearbeiten 1458

Malware von Ihrem Computer entfernen
ESET Smart Security
Kaspersky Lab Internet Security
Lavasoft Ad-Aware
MacScan (für Mac-Nutzer)
Microsoft Security Essentials
Norton Internet Security
Spyware Doctor
Vipre Antivirus

Google Safety Center

Entfernen von Inhalten aus Google
Transparenzbericht
https://www.chillingeffects.org/
Center für Produktsupport von Google

Richtlinien nach Produkt
Werbeprogramme
AdWords-Inhaltsrichtlinien
AdSense-Programmrichtlinien
Google Play
Inhaltsrichtlinien für Android-Entwickler
Geschäfts- und Programmrichtlinien für Google Play
Android-Richtlinien zum Posten von Kommentaren
App Engine
Programmrichtlinien
Apps
Programmrichtlinien für Administratoren
Blogger
Inhaltsrichtlinien
Google Kalender
Programmrichtlinien
Google Docs
Programmrichtlinien
Google Mail
Programmrichtlinien
Google Maps
Richtlinien zu Bildern
Community-Richtlinien von Google Maps
orkut
Programmrichtlinien
Picasa
Programmrichtlinien
Postini
Programmrichtlinien für Administratoren
Google Sites
Programmrichtlinien
Google Voice
Programmrichtlinien
YouTube
Anzeigenrichtlinien
Community-Richtlinien

Zugriff auf Informationen:
Daten, die Aufschluss darüber geben, inwiefern Gesetze und Richtlinien Internetnutzer und den Informationsfluss im Web beeinflussen.
Aktuelle Berichte ansehen:
Löschungsersuchen von hoheitlichen Stellen
Auskunftsersuchen zu benutzerbezogenen Daten
Von Urheberrechtsinhabern eingereichte Löschungsersuchen zu Suchergebnissen
Traffic der einzelnen Google Produkte
Safe Browsing
Verschlüsselung von E-Mails während der Übertragung
Ersuchen zur Löschung von Suchergebnissen gemäß europäischem Datenschutzrecht

Mein Konto: Ihre Google-Einstellungen zentral anpassen

Problembehebung zum Thema Datenschutz

Namen im Google-Konto ändern

Just trust us – or take this!

The autonomous user: Is it possible to decide with sovereignty and to entirely know my rights?

Here you see counted the characters of the Terms of Use, Privacy Policies and, if available, infos about cookies (or other technologies to identify or track the user) from the two most popular websites.* If the texts were available in German language, the headlines are left in German. It is pointed out where the reader finds links to further information.

This fact reveals a first dilemma: In the two displayed extreme cases, the non-linear information rather leaves the reader uninformed and confused. One never knows if everything is read completely. Additionally, imprecise wording leaves open whether and precisely which data is collected, processed or shared with third parties. At last we criticize the amount of text taking too much time to read and understand. Distrust in governmental protection is growing

around the debates and surprises about data retention and the current rumours about the european data protection laws. This is why we also considered the lengths of The German Data Protection Law (Bundesdatenschutzgesetz) and the Hamburg data protection law.

As one conclusion we see that people not being able to understand formal language in their mother tongue German are excluded as well as those whose English is not good enough. This applies especially to children and elderly people. Even if in the Terms of Use children up to a certain age might be excluded to using that service, everyone knows how easy it is to accept anything without reading before.

*https://en.wikipedia.org/wiki/List_of_most_popular_websites based on data from Alexa Rank and SimilarWeb

Facebook

126,1 + ?
MIN

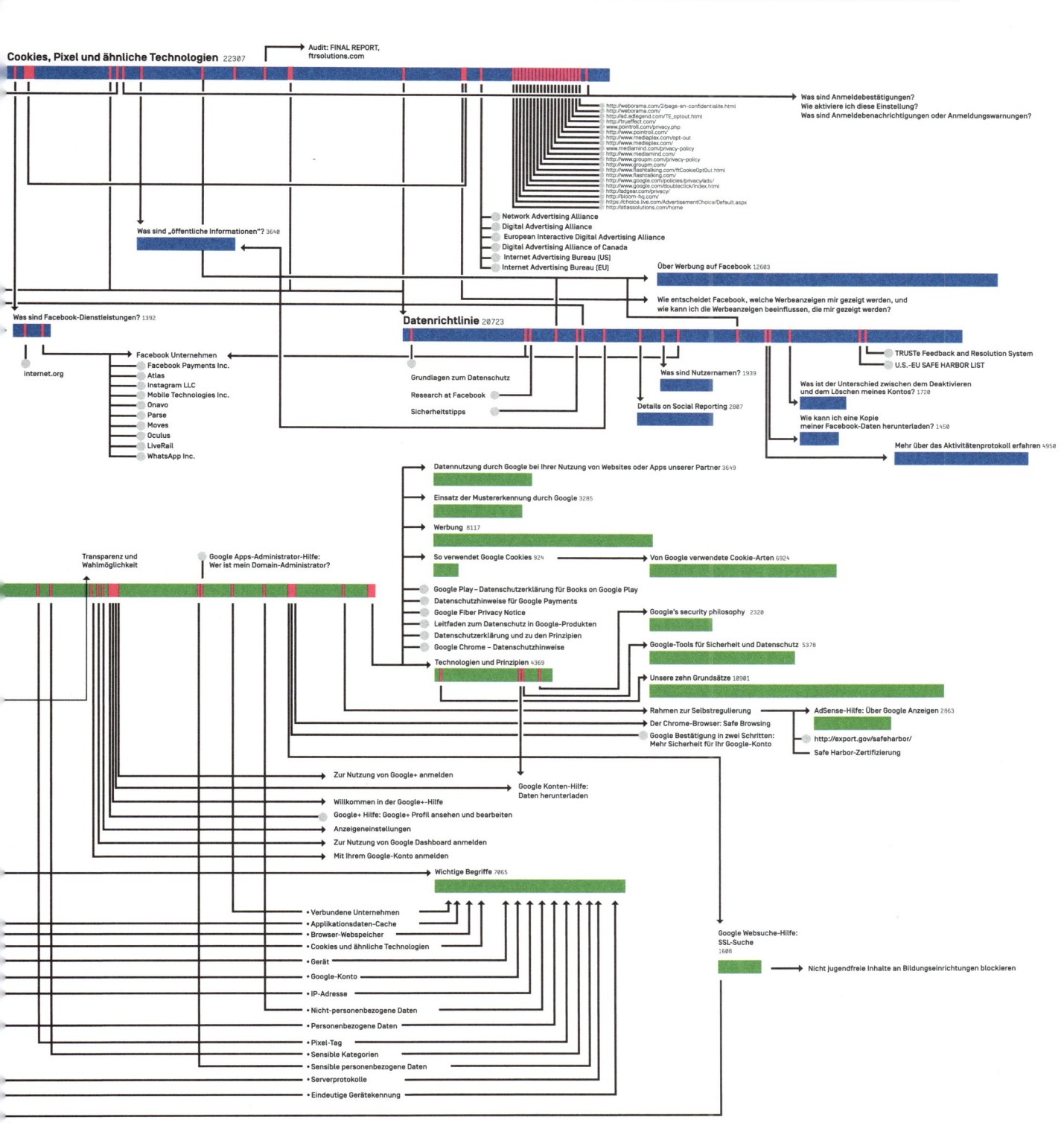

Cookies, Pixel und ähnliche Technologien 22307

Audit: FINAL REPORT, ftrsolutions.com

http://weborama.com/2/page-en-confidentialite.html
http://weborama.com/
http://ad.adlegend.com/TE_optout.html
http://trueeffect.com/
www.pointroll.com/privacy.php
www.pointroll.com/
http://www.mediaplex.com/opt-out
http://www.mediaplex.com/
http://www.mediamind.com/privacy-policy
http://www.mediamind.com/
http://www.groupm.com/privacy-policy
http://www.groupm.com/
http://www.flashtalking.com/ftCookieOptOut.html
http://www.flashtalking.com/
http://www.google.com/policies/privacy/ads/
http://www.google.com/doubleclick/index.html
http://adgear.com/privacy/
http://bloom-hq.com/
https://choice.live.com/AdvertisementChoice/Default.aspx
http://atlassolutions.com/home

Was sind Anmeldebestätigungen?
Wie aktiviere ich diese Einstellung?
Was sind Anmeldebenachrichtigungen oder Anmeldungswarnungen?

Was sind „öffentliche Informationen"? 3640

Network Advertising Alliance
Digital Advertising Alliance
European Interactive Digital Advertising Alliance
Digital Advertising Alliance of Canada
Internet Advertising Bureau [US]
Internet Advertising Bureau [EU]

Über Werbung auf Facebook 12603

Wie entscheidet Facebook, welche Werbeanzeigen mir gezeigt werden, und wie kann ich die Werbeanzeigen beeinflussen, die mir gezeigt werden?

Was sind Facebook-Dienstleistungen? 1392

internet.org

Facebook Unternehmen
Facebook Payments Inc.
Atlas
Instagram LLC
Mobile Technologies Inc.
Onavo
Parse
Moves
Oculus
LiveRail
WhatsApp Inc.

Datenrichtlinie 20723

Grundlagen zum Datenschutz
Research at Facebook
Sicherheitstipps

Was sind Nutzernamen? 1939

Details on Social Reporting 2807

TRUSTe Feedback and Resolution System
U.S.-EU SAFE HARBOR LIST

Was ist der Unterschied zwischen dem Deaktivieren und dem Löschen meines Kontos? 1720

Wie kann ich eine Kopie meiner Facebook-Daten herunterladen? 1450

Mehr über das Aktivitätenprotokoll erfahren 4950

Datennutzung durch Google bei Ihrer Nutzung von Websites oder Apps unserer Partner 3649

Einsatz der Mustererkennung durch Google 3285

Werbung 8117

So verwendet Google Cookies 924

Von Google verwendete Cookie-Arten 6924

Transparenz und Wahlmöglichkeit

Google Apps-Administrator-Hilfe: Wer ist mein Domain-Administrator?

Google Play – Datenschutzerklärung für Books on Google Play
Datenschutzhinweise für Google Payments
Google Fiber Privacy Notice
Leitfaden zum Datenschutz in Google-Produkten
Datenschutzerklärung und zu den Prinzipien
Google Chrome – Datenschutzhinweise

Google's security philosophy 2320

Google-Tools für Sicherheit und Datenschutz 5378

Technologien und Prinzipien 4369

Unsere zehn Grundsätze 10901

Rahmen zur Selbstregulierung
Der Chrome-Browser: Safe Browsing
Google Bestätigung in zwei Schritten: Mehr Sicherheit für Ihr Google-Konto

AdSense-Hilfe: Über Google Anzeigen 2863

http://export.gov/safeharbor/
Safe Harbor-Zertifizierung

Zur Nutzung von Google+ anmelden
Willkommen in der Google+-Hilfe
Google+ Hilfe: Google+ Profil ansehen und bearbeiten
Anzeigeneinstellungen
Zur Nutzung von Google Dashboard anmelden
Mit Ihrem Google-Konto anmelden

Google Konten-Hilfe: Daten herunterladen

Wichtige Begriffe 7065

• Verbundene Unternehmen
• Applikationsdaten-Cache
• Browser-Webspeicher
• Cookies und ähnliche Technologien
• Gerät
• Google-Konto
• IP-Adresse
• Nicht-personenbezogene Daten
• Personenbezogene Daten
• Pixel-Tag
• Sensible Kategorien
• Sensible personenbezogene Daten
• Serverprotokolle
• Eindeutige Gerätekennung

Google Websuche-Hilfe: SSL-Suche 1600

Nicht jugendfreie Inhalte an Bildungseinrichtungen blockieren

95

THE ARCHITECTURE OF THE GRID

Martin Dumont
Metaxia Markaki
Nitin Bathla
Alexander Daxböck

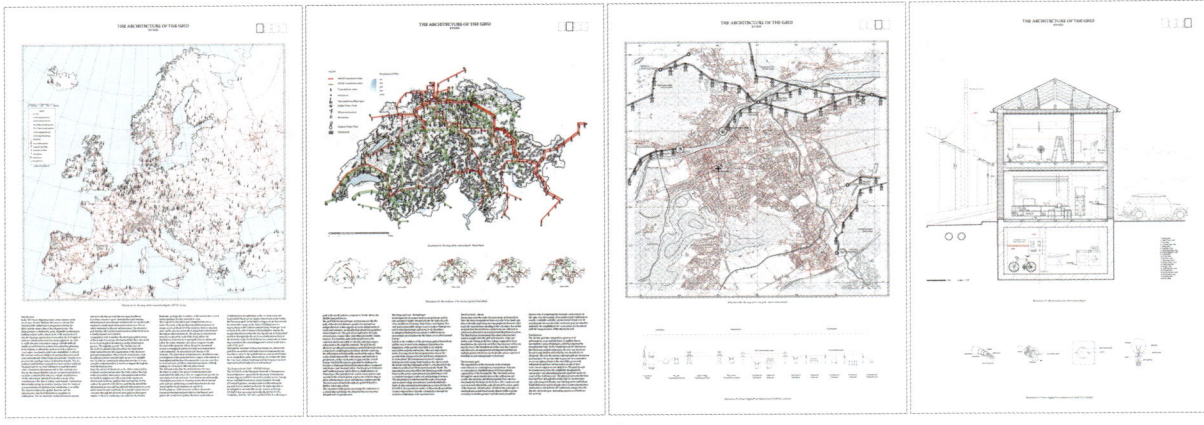

The object at stake is the spatial structure and the infrastructure that lies behind the geographies of urbanisation. Infrastructural systems and networks provide the necessary backbone for urban systems to grow. Traditionally, infrastructural networks like rail tracks and roads are being analysed to understand processes of urbanisation. We are more interested in the "soft" infrastructure of electricity; the electricity grid that has affected the transformation of the territory in a similar manner.

Geographers tend to analyse the electricity grid in terms of flows and of economic development but they often tend to overlook its physical influence on the urbanisation process. The electricity network exists as a physical entity and surrounds us in a very tangible way.

Since the advent of electricity in the 18th century and its later commercial use from the 19th century to the present day, it is hard to imagine one's life without the numerous electric and electronic gadgets surrounding us. The growth of the electric grid has both facilitated urbanisation and allowed a seamless interconnection of cities. This interconnection is a central marker of the Anthropocene, as terrain, landscape and the boundaries of the nation state do not form barriers any longer.

The grid can be described and interpreted at various scales. At the level of the territory, where production and transmission of energy take place, a network of singular production facilities can be identified. At the level of the local the distribution of energy is managed, which can happen within the framework of a city or a region. At the level of the domestic the network is organised around consumption, whereby changes in the domestic co-determine the network structure. The innovation in production, distribution and consumption of electricity – a major achievement of humankind – has determined the way our cities have evolved and holds the possibility of making our cities more efficient and resilient in the future.

Der Gegenstand, um den es geht, ist die Infrastruktur, die hinter den Geografien der Urbanisierung liegt. Infrastrukturelle Systeme und Netzwerke stellen das notwendige Rückgrat für das städtische Wachstum bereit. Traditionellerweise werden, um den Urbanisierungsprozess zu verstehen, infrastrukturelle Netzwerke wie Straßen- und Schienensysteme analysiert. Wir sind eher an der "weichen" Infrastruktur der Elektrizität interessiert; das Stromversorgungsnetz hat die Transformation des Territoriums auf eine ähnliche Weise beeinflusst.

Geografen tendieren dazu, das Stromversorgungsnetz unter dem Aspekt der Energieflüsse und im Hinblick auf die Wirtschaftsentwicklung zu analysieren, doch dabei übersehen sie in der Regel den physischen Einfluss dieses Netzes auf den Prozess der Urbanisierung. Das Elektrizitätsnetz existiert als eine physische Entität, die uns auf eine sehr greifbare Weise umgibt.

Seit dem Aufkommen der Elektrizität im 18. Jahrhundert und ihrer späteren kommerziellen Nutzung vom 19. Jahrhundert bis zum heutigen Tag kann man sich ein Leben ohne die zahllosen elektrischen und elektronischen Geräte, die uns umgeben, schwer vorstellen. Das Wachstum des Strom-

versorgungsnetzes hat sowohl die Verstädterung vorangetrieben als auch die nahtlose Vernetzung der Städte untereinander ermöglicht. Diese Vernetzung ist ein zentrales Kennzeichen des Anthropozäns, da Terrain, Landschaft und die Grenzen des Nationalstaats keine Barrieren mehr bilden.

Das Netz kann auf unterschiedlichen Maßstabsebenen beschrieben und interpretiert werden. Auf der Ebene des Territoriums, wo die Produktion und Transmission von Energie stattfindet, läßt sich ein Netzwerk singulärer Produktionsanlagen ausmachen. Auf der Ebene des Lokalen wird die Verteilung der Elektrizität organisiert, was im Rahmen einer Stadt oder einer Region erfolgen kann. Auf der Ebene des Häuslichen wird das Netz um den Konsum herum organisiert, wobei der Wandel des Häuslichen die Netzstruktur mitbestimmt. Die Innovationen in der Produktion, der Verteilung und im Einsatz von Elektrizität – eine wesentliche Leistung der Menschheit – haben die Art und Weise geprägt, wie sich die Städte entwickelt haben, und sie beinhalten die Chance, dass sie künftig effizienter und flexibler werden.

Die verschiedenen Ebenen, die das Netz abdeckt, fungieren hier als Kameraobjektive, um das Projekt der

The different scales that the grid includes act as lenses to explore the project of urbanisation. Four frames are strategically selected, whereby we zoom into the territorial grid; each of these frames addresses the transformations at each level.

First of all we have chosen the transnational European grid, because it's the largest such grid in the world and signifies the interconnectedness of urbanisation at a planetary scale. Owing to its great potential for renewable energy in the form of hydropower, Switzerland is a major player in the carbon-neutral future of Europe. Then we take a look at the city of Aarau to analyse the energy distribution networks of a typical city in Switzerland and to find out how this taps into the grid. Finally we look at the domestic scale of a Swiss house in the countryside of Aarau; this house constitutes the concluding point, after which we turn to the micro-scale of the grid.

In order to capture the spatial relations and structures that are relevant in the framework of these scalar observations, we reclaim the plan, the very basic architectural drawing, as a medium to represent and critically process information.

The electric grid has emerged as a great tool of urbanisation; its growth has been so sudden that we have failed to acknowledge its unifying impact at the transnational scale. Today we can observe similarities between the electronic gadgets dependent on electricity and the way different national networks are structured and function. We are also able to perceive how we are networked to the city in a physical way and how innovations at any of these scales have an impact on our daily lives. The physical networks depicted in this study call for an alternative way of looking at the urban, one which goes beyond urban-rural dichotomies and propagates a global urbanisation feeding off continuous energy networks.

Urbanisierung zu erkunden. Vier Einzelbilder werden strategisch ausgewählt, mit deren Hilfe wir uns in das territoriale Netz hineinzoomen; jedes dieser Einzelbilder beobachtet die Veränderungen auf der jeweiligen Ebene.

Als erstes haben wir das grenzüberschreitende europäische Netz ausgewählt, da es weltweit das größte Netz dieser Art ist und es die Vernetzung der Urbanisierung in einem globalen Maßstab veranschaulicht. Anschließend zoomen wir auf die Schweiz, die an einem wesentlichen Knotenpunkt innerhalb des europäischen Netzes liegt. Dank ihres enormen Potentials von erneuerbarer Energie in Form von Wasserkraft ist die Schweiz ein wesentlicher Faktor bei der carbonneutralen Zukunft Europas. Dann werfen wir einen Blick auf die Stadt Aarau, um die Energieverteilungsnetzwerke einer typischen Schweizer Stadt zu analysieren und um herauszufinden, wie diese sich in das Netz einklinken. Zu guter Letzt schauen wir auf den häuslichen Maßstab eines Schweizer Wohnhauses in der ländlichen Umgebung Aaraus; dieses Haus bildet den Schlusspunkt, bei dem wir uns dem Mikromaßstab des Netzes zuwenden.

Um die räumlichen Beziehungen und Strukturen zu erfassen, die im Rahmen dieser maßstäblichen Betrachtungen relevant sind, kommen wir auf den Grundriss zurück, auf die klassische architektonische Zeichnung als ein Medium zur Präsentation und kritischen Verarbeitung von Information.

Das Stromversorgungsnetz hat sich als bedeutendes Werkzeug der Urbanisierung erwiesen; sein Wachstum erfolgte dermaßen plötzlich, dass uns seine grenzüberschreitende vereinigende Wirkung entgangen ist. Heute entdecken wir die Ähnlichkeiten zwischen allen Dingen, die auf Elektrizität angewiesen sind, und zwischen der Art und Weise, wie die unterschiedlichen nationalen Netze strukturiert sind und wie sie funktionieren. Wir können auch erkennen, wie wir auf eine physische Weise in der Stadt vernetzt sind und wie eine Innovation auf jeder der genannten Ebenen einen Einfluss auf unser Alltagsleben ausübt. Die physischen Netzwerke, die in dieser Untersuchung gezeigt werden, legen eine alternative Betrachtungsweise der Urbanität nahe, die über die Stadt-Land-Dichotomie hinausgeht und eine globale Urbanisierung propagiert, welche sich aus kontinuierlichen Energienetzwerken speist.

European Network of Transmission System Operators

The ENTSO-E represents 41 electricity transmission system operators from 34 countries across Europe. It was established by the EU's third legislative package for the internal energy market in 2009, aimed at liberalising the gas and electric markets in Europe. It is the largest grid in the world and also connects to North Africa, the Middle East and Russia. Central Europe holds massive potential for hydropower, compared with West Europe where nuclear power dominates and South Europe where there is a high reliance on natural gas. The grid employs interconnected security measures in the event of failing power sources, allowing urbanisation to expand and function uninterruptedly.

Das ENTSO-E besteht aus 41 Stromübertragungsnetzbetreibern aus 34 europäischen Staaten. Es wurde vom dritten Legislativpaket der EU für den Energiebinnenmarkt im Jahr 2009 eingeführt und zielt auf die Liberalisierung des europäischen Gas- und Strommarktes ab. Es ist das größte Netz der Welt und verbindet auch Nordafrika, den Nahen Osten und Russland. Verglichen mit Westeuropa, wo Atomkraft überwiegt, und Südeuropa, wo man sich auf natürliche Gasvorkommen verlässt, verfügt Mitteleuropa über große Wasserkraftreserven. Das Netzwerk arbeitet mit zusammengeschalteten Sicherheitsmaßnahmen im Falle einer Unterbrechung der Stromquellen und erlaubt es Urbanisierungsprozessen so, ununterbrochen voranzuschreiten.

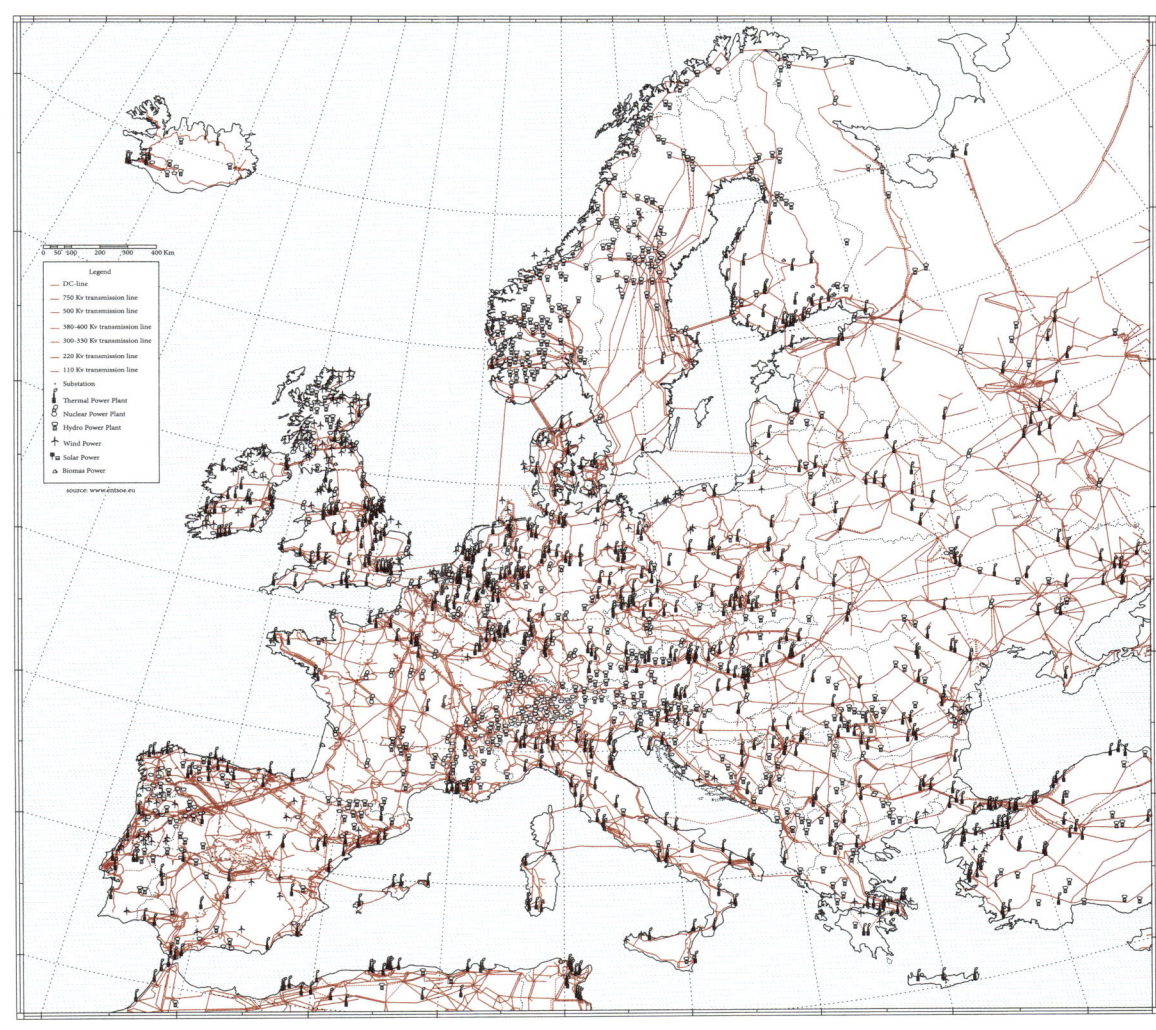

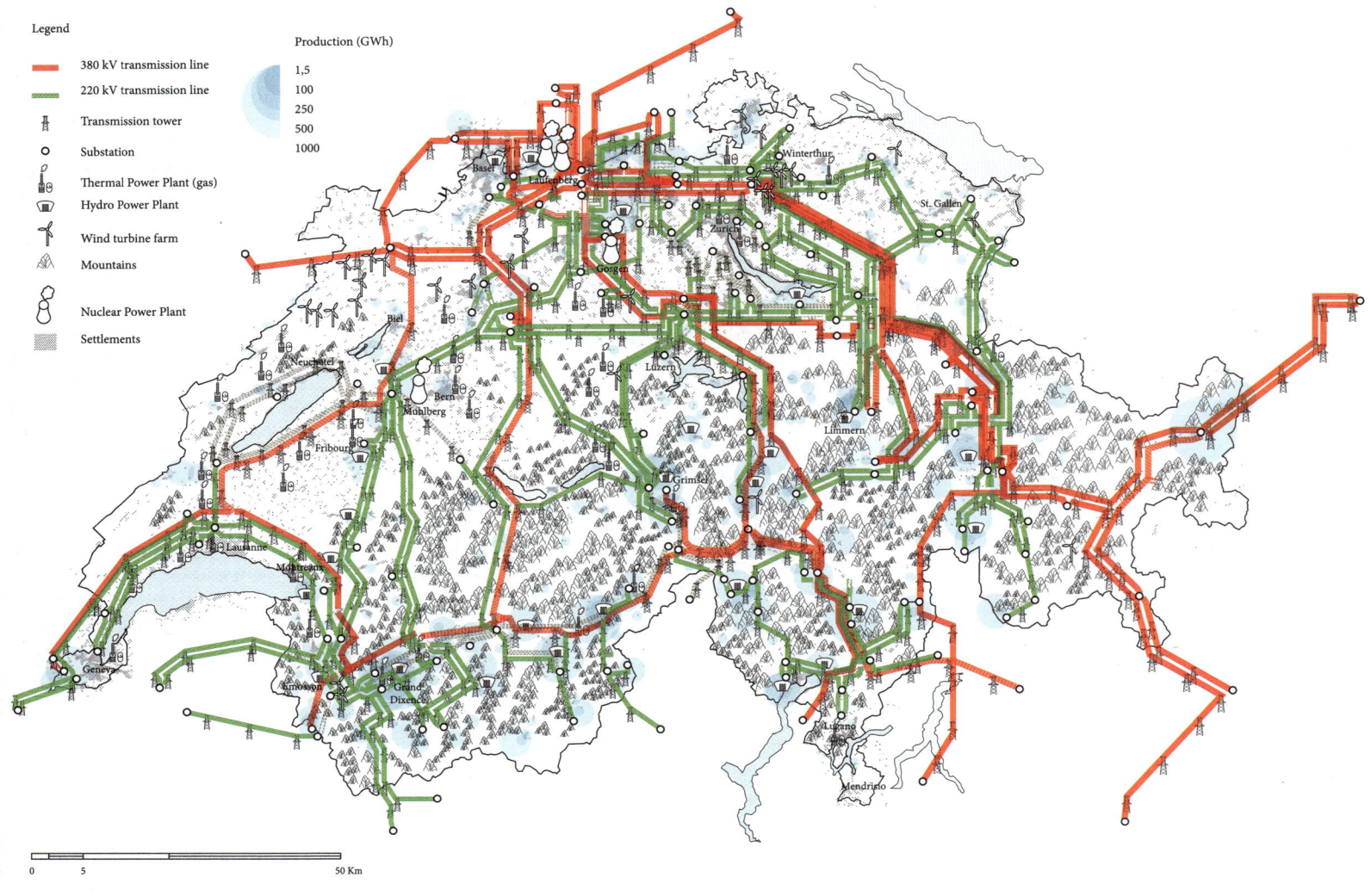

Legend

— 380 kV transmission line
— 220 kV transmission line

⚡ Transmission tower

○ Substation

Thermal Power Plant (gas)

Hydro Power Plant

Wind turbine farm

Mountains

Nuclear Power Plant

Settlements

Production (GWh)

1,5
100
250
500
1000

Illustration 02: The map of the national grid - Switzerland

The National Grid – Switzerland

Switzerland sits at a major nodal point in Europe and its national grid is highly integrated with the national grids of its neighbours. The nation is rich in renewable energy sources such as hydropower and geothermal energy. The transmission network connects the hydropower-rich hinterlands of the Alps with the urbanised areas that are concentrated in the North. Owing to its abundance in untapped hydropower potential, Switzerland will play an important role in the future of a carbon-neutral Europe.

Die Schweiz liegt an einem wichtigen Knotenpunkt in Europa und ihr nationales Netzwerk ist in hohem Maße mit dem ihrer Nachbarstaaten integriert. Der Staat ist reich an erneuerbaren Energiequellen wie Wasserkraft oder geothermische Energie. Überlandleitungen verbinden das wasserkraftreiche Hinterland in den Alpen mit den verstädterten Gebieten im Norden. Dank ihrer Fülle an unerschlossenen Wasserkraftreserven wird die Schweiz eine wichtige Rolle in einer carbon-neutralen Zukunft Europas spielen.

The domestic grid

Electricity arrives through the main transfer lines of the settlement and reaches the domestic distribution panel, from which it is transmitted to house-hold devices. Domestic infrastructure follows the principles of standardisation and functionality that regulate our everyday habits, gestures and discretely mould inhabiting the domestic environment. Similar to an architectural study of a building, usually concluding with the construction details, we intend to underline the connection of a household with the megastructure of the electricity grid by revealing the microscale of the electricity grid.

Strom gelangt durch die Hauptleitungen der Siedlung in den häuslichen Verteilerkasten, aus dem er an Haushaltsgeräte weitergeleitet wird. Die häusliche Infrastruktur folgt Prinzipien der Standardisierung und Funktionalität, die unsere täglichen Gewohnheiten und Gesten regulieren und diskret das Bewohnen der häuslichen Umgebung gestalten. Ähnlich wie bei einer architektonischen Gebäudestudie, die gewöhnlich mit Konstruktionsdetails abschließt, beabsichtigen wir die Verbindung des Haushalts mit der Megastruktur des Stromnetzwerkes aufzuzeigen, indem wir den Mikromaßstab des Stromnetzes darstellen.

The City Grid – Aarau

Aarau represents a typical city in Switzerland. After the main transmission lines cross the Swiss landscape, neglecting almost all topographical obstacles, they reach the transformers at the city's edges. Here, the aerial wire connections are directed to an underground distribution system. The distribution system, much like other infrastructure systems, morphs into the structure of the city. Due to the low voltage required for local distribution, the network is able to follow the street grid.

Aarau steht für eine typische Stadt in der Schweiz. Nachdem die Überlandleitungen die schweizerische Landschaft durchquert und dabei fast alle topographischen Hindernisse außer Acht gelassen haben, erreichen sie die Umspannwerke am Stadtrand. Hier werden die oberirdischen Leitanschlüsse an ein Verteilersystem unter der Erde weitergeleitet. Dieses Verteilersystem, wie auch andere infrastrukturelle Systeme, geht in die Stadtstruktur über. Wegen der niedrigen Spannung, die für örtliche Verteilung benötigt wird, ist es dem Netzwerk möglich, dem Straßennetz zu folgen.

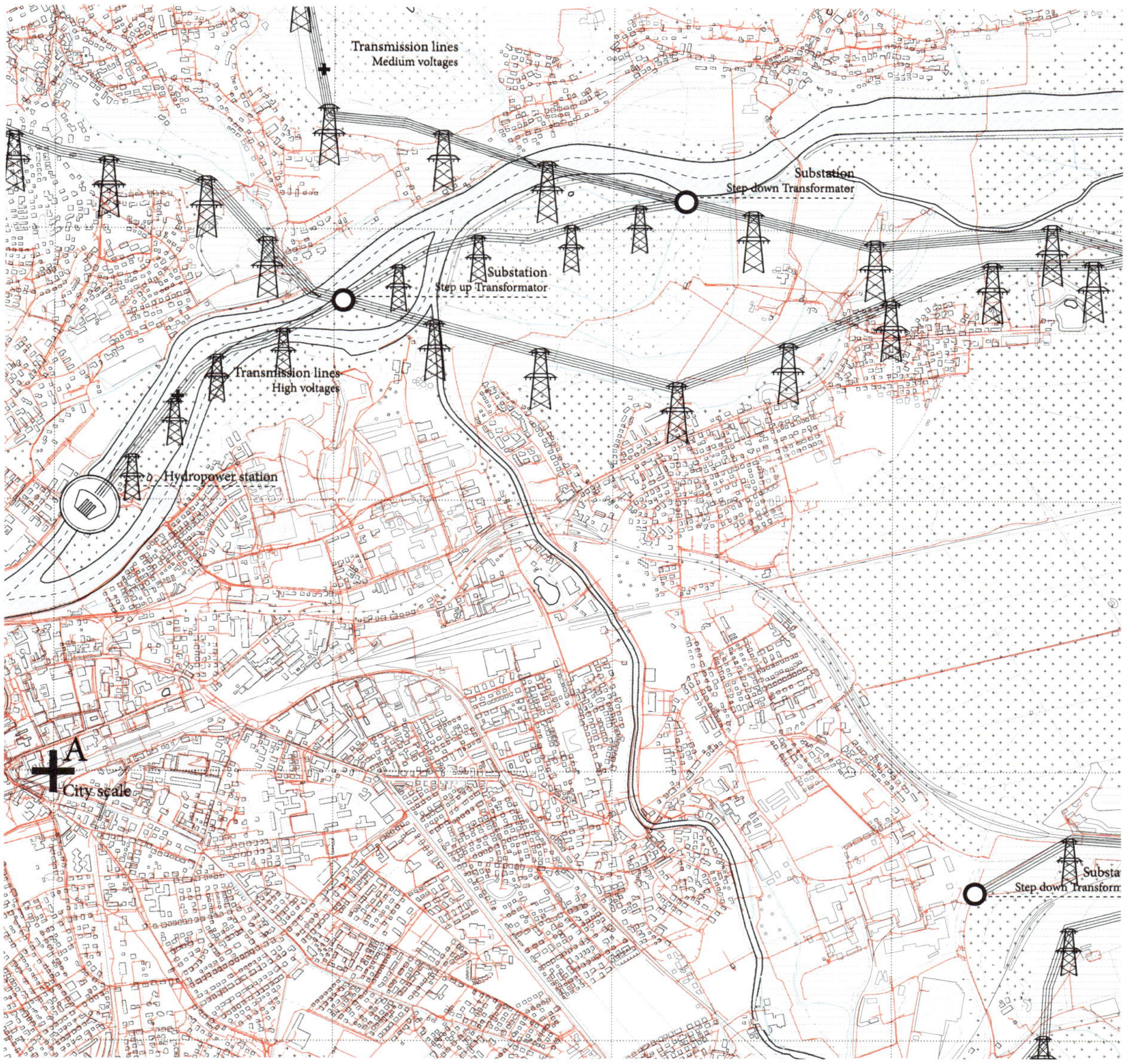

Transmission lines Medium voltages

Substation Step-down Transformator

Substation Step up Transformator

Transmission lines High voltages

Hydropower station

A City scale

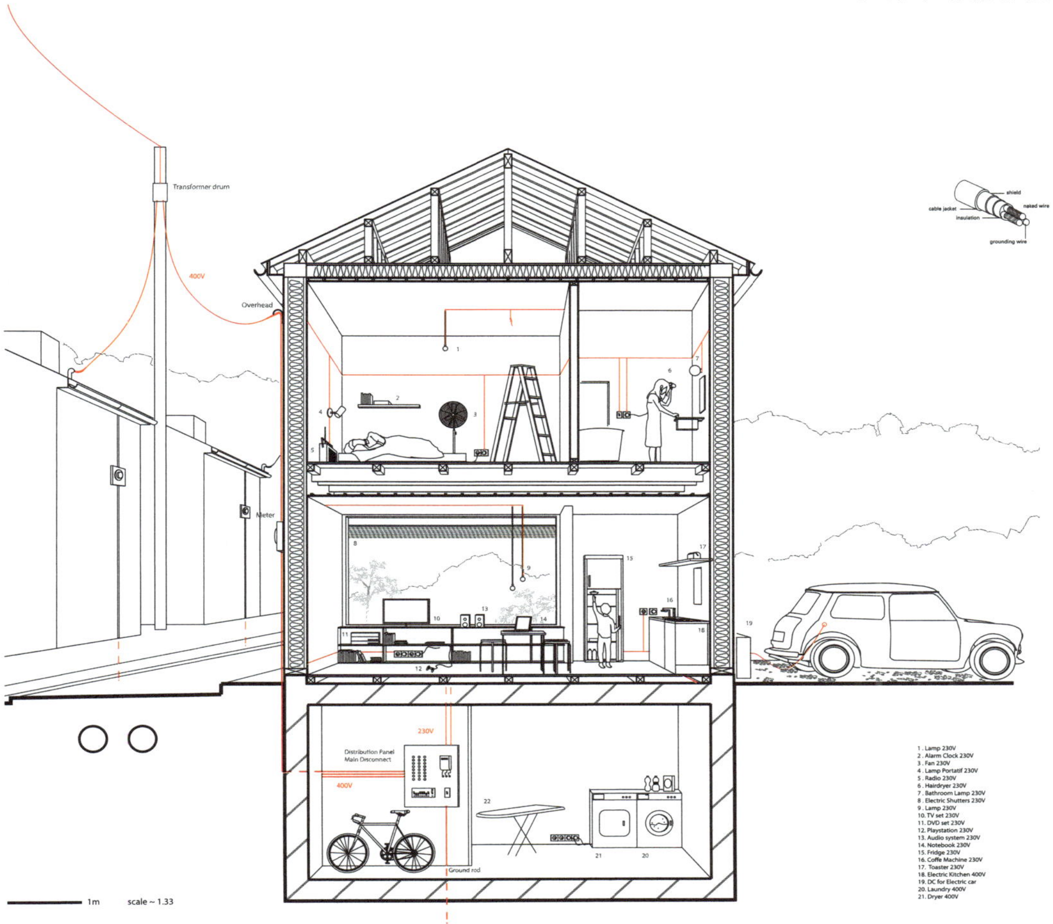

Substation Step down Transformer

Transformer drum

400V

Overhead

Meter

230V

Distribution Panel Main Disconnect

400V

Ground rod

1m   scale ~ 1.33

1. Lamp 230V
2. Alarm Clock 230V
3. Fan 230V
4. Lamp Portabl 230V
5. Radio 230V
6. Hairdryer 230V
7. Bathroom Lamp 230V
8. Electric Shutters 230V
9. Lamp 230V
10. TV set 230V
11. DVD set 230V
12. Playstation 230V
13. Audio system 230V
14. Notebook 230V
15. Fridge 230V
16. Coffe Machine 230V
17. Toaster 230V
18. Electric Kitchen 400V
19. DC for Electric car
20. Laundry 400V
21. Dryer 400V

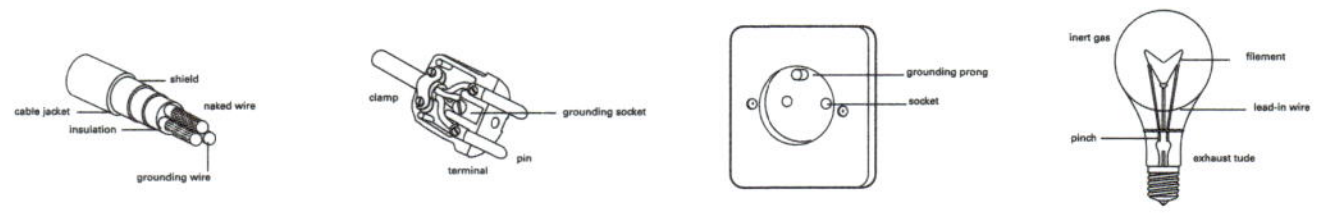

cable jacket / shield / naked wire / insulation / grounding wire

clamp / terminal / pin / grounding socket

grounding prong / socket

inert gas / filament / lead-in wire / pinch / exhaust tube

UNITED REGIONS OF EUROPE

Maximilian Pecher
Philipp Schwarzbauer

The highly interconnected metropolises of the globalised world, involved in increasingly complicated coherences by real and virtual flows of goods and data, supersede the nation state's traditional functions to an ever greater extent. Major economic developments and socio-cultural impulses no longer arise within stately limits, but in and via exchange between cities – and that on a world-spanning scale. Global economic centres attract intellectual inventiveness, innovation and investment: the heterogeneity of possible human activity and ways of life can rightly be described as the most beautiful promise of globalisation and has already made the concept of the nation state, formulated in the 19th century, historically obsolete. Policymakers, however, still cling to rigid national structures, what entails a series of adverse effects: Because the capitals of centralised governments such as France, Great Britain or Japan are in a disproportionally high level responsible for the success of their respective state budget, the surrounding regions desolate – wealth gaps between urban and rural areas become wider. The more competition for work and living space intensifies, the clearer social inequalities emerge. Coexistence in cities, despite its leading role in human development, is turning more and more into a struggle for survival.

An alternative to this dynamic is to be formulated using the example of Europe. In the culturally highly diverse continent exist both small-scale federal structures, functioning well economically and socially, and highly centralised nation states, where metropolitan areas condense more and more, while the periphery "depletes" reciprocally. Through the possibilities of digital technologies to create new relationships of proximity and distance, however, the urban centres can flout the "empty" regional interspace. While the "winners" among cities bestir themselves to adopt characteristics that are valid on a global scale in order not to be eliminated from global competition, the "losers" fall further behind until they align themselves into the global periphery. Paradoxically, instead of heterogeneity, homogeneity is created in the long term: in the centralised European city, regional particularities recede into the background – its inhabitants lose their cultural identity and at best become "urban citizens" empowered to consume constantly.

The project locates Europe's real identity in the smaller federal "metro regions" and proposes a Union of regions, substituting nation states within a European community of values and law. Urbanisation would therefore function increasingly decentralised and would not be determined solely by "capitals". A more even distribution of population growth and prosperity would provide mid-sized cities with more economic and political influence. The respective regions' cultural goods could be maintained and promoted, instead of having to subordinate to the dictum of homogeneity. Especially with regard to the current drifting apart of the European unity, progressive models for future collective living must be found. Will urbanisation create a Europe with swelling, centralised urban clusters and competing states, or a post-national Europe, where a new kind of interconnectedness enables a multipolar urban development, attuned to regional circumstances? The decision is ultimately a political one.

Die hochvernetzten Metropolen der globalisierten Welt, durch reale und virtuelle Waren- und Datenströme in immer komplexere Zusammenhänge verwickelt, lösen die traditionellen Funktionen des Nationalstaats in immer größerem Ausmaß ab. Die wichtigsten wirtschaftlichen Entwicklungen und sozio-kulturellen Impulse entstehen nicht länger innerhalb staatlicher Grenzen, sondern in und im Austausch zwischen den Städten – und das im weltumspannenden Maßstab. Globale Wirtschaftszentren ziehen intellektuelle Schaffenskraft, Innovationen und Investitionen an: Die Heterogenität möglicher menschlicher Aktivität und Lebensweisen kann zurecht als schönste Verheißung der Globalisierung bezeichnet werden und hat das im 19. Jahrhundert formulierte Konzept des Nationalstaats längst historisch obsolet gemacht. Politische Entscheidungsträger klammern sich aber nach wie vor an starre nationalstaatliche Strukturen, was eine Reihe von negativen Auswirkungen nach sich zieht: Weil die Hauptstädte von Zentralstaaten wie Frankreich, Großbritannien oder Japan in einem unverhältnismäßig hohen Maß für den Erfolg ihres jeweiligen Staatshaushalts verantwortlich sind, veröden die umliegenden Regionen – Wohlstandsgefälle zwischen Stadt und Land werden größer. Je mehr sich die Konkurrenz um Arbeit und Lebensraum intensiviert, desto deutlicher treten soziale Ungleichheiten hervor. Das Zusammenleben in den Städten wird, trotz seiner tonangebenden Rolle für die menschliche Entwicklung, zusehends zu einem Kampf ums Überleben.

Eine Alternative zu dieser Dynamik soll am Beispiel Europas formuliert werden. In dem kulturell höchst vielfältigen Kontinent existieren sowohl kleinteilige föderale Strukturen, die wirtschaftlich und gesellschaftlich gut funktionieren als auch stark zentralistische Nationalstaaten, in denen sich die Ballungsräume immer weiter verdichten, während sich die Peripherie reziprok "entleert". Durch die Möglichkeiten digitaler Technologien,

neue Nähe- und Distanzbeziehungen herzustellen, können sich die städtischen Zentren allerdings über den "leeren" Zwischenraum der Regionen hinwegsetzen. Während sich die "Gewinner" unter den Städten bemühen, weltweit gültige Merkmale anzunehmen, um im globalen Wettbewerb nicht auszuscheiden, werden die "Verlierer" weiter abgeschlagen, bis sie sich in die globale Peripherie einordnen. Paradoxerweise wird also langfristig Homogenität statt Heterogenität geschaffen: Regionale Besonderheiten treten in der zentralisierten europäischen Stadt in den Hintergrund, die in ihr lebenden Menschen verlieren ihre kulturelle Identität und werden bestenfalls zu ständigem Konsum befähigten "Stadtbürgern".

Das Projekt verortet in den kleineren föderalen "Metroregionen" die wahre Identität Europas und schlägt eine Union der Regionen vor, die die Nationalstaaten innerhalb einer europäischen Rechts- und Wertegemeinschaft ersetzt. Urbanisierungsprozesse würden somit zunehmend dezentral funktionieren und nicht mehr alleinig durch die "Hauptstädte" bestimmt werden. Eine gleichmäßigere Verteilung von Bevölkerungswachstum und Wohlstand würde mittelgroßen Städten mehr wirtschaftlichen und politischen Einfluss verschaffen. Die jeweiligen kulturellen Güter der Region könnten erhalten und gefördert werden, anstatt sich dem Diktum der Homogenität unterordnen zu müssen. Besonders im Hinblick auf das aktuelle Auseinanderdriften der europäischen Einheit müssen progressive Modelle für zukünftiges kollektives Leben gefunden werden. Wird die Urbanisierung ein Europa mit immer größer anschwellenden, zentralisierten urbanen Clustern und konkurrierenden Staaten schaffen oder ein postnationales Europa, in der eine neue Art der Vernetzung eine multipolare und auf regionale Gegebenheiten abgestimmte städtische Entwicklung möglich macht? Die Entscheidung ist letztendlich eine politische.

Text: Anna Aichinger

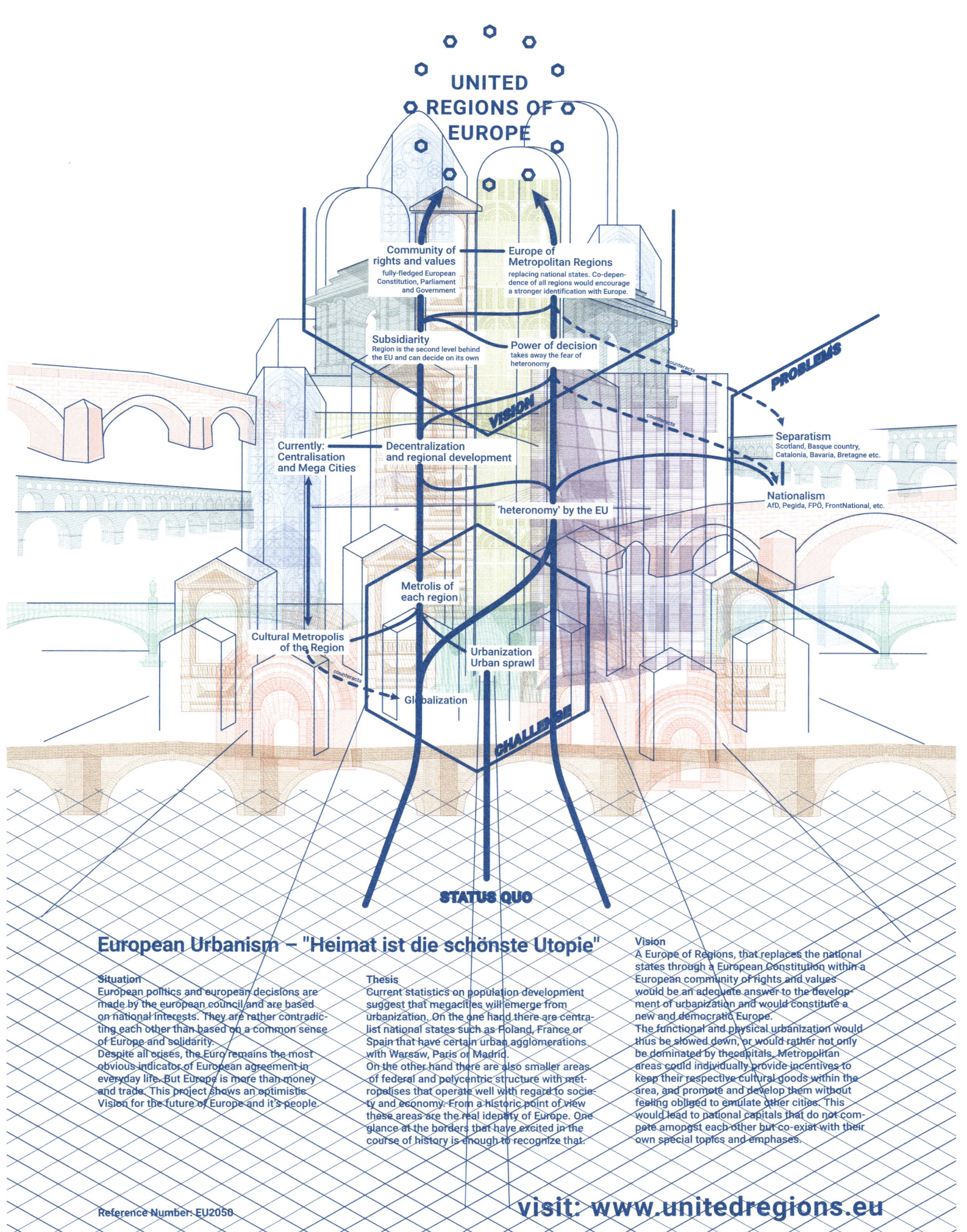

UNITED REGIONS OF EUROPE

Community of rights and values — fully-fledged European Constitution, Parliament and Government

Europe of Metropolitan Regions — replacing national states. Co-dependence of all regions would encourage a stronger identification with Europe.

Subsidiarity — Region is the second level behind the EU and can decide on its own

Power of decision — takes away the fear of heteronomy

PROBLEMS

VISION

Currently: Centralisation and Mega Cities

Decentralization and regional development

Separatism — Scotland, Basque country, Catalonia, Bavaria, Bretagne etc.

counteracts

Nationalism — AfD, Pegida, FPÖ, FrontNational, etc.

'heteronomy' by the EU

Metrolis of each region

Cultural Metropolis of the Region

counteracts

Urbanization Urban sprawl

Globalization

CHALLENGE

STATUS QUO

European Urbanism – "Heimat ist die schönste Utopie"

Situation
European politics and european decisions are made by the european council and are based on national interests. They are rather contradicting each other than based on a common sense of Europe and solidarity.
Despite all crises, the Euro remains the most obvious indicator of European agreement in everyday life. But Europe is more than money and trade. This project shows an optimistic Vision for the future of Europe and it's people.

Thesis
Current statistics on population development suggest that megacities will emerge from urbanization. On the one hand there are centralist national states such as Poland, France or Spain that have certain urban agglomerations with Warsaw, Paris or Madrid.
On the other hand there are also smaller areas of federal and polycentric structure with metropolises that operate well with regard to society and economy. From a historic point of view these areas are the real identity of Europe. One glance at the borders that have existed in the course of history is enough to recognize that.

Vision
A Europe of Regions, that replaces the national states through a European Constitution within a European community of rights and values would be an adequate answer to the development of urbanization and would constitute a new and democratic Europe.
The functional and physical urbanization would thus be slowed down, or would rather not only be dominated by the capitals. Metropolitan areas could individually provide incentives to keep their respective cultural goods within the area, and promote and develop them without feeling obliged to emulate other cities. This would lead to national capitals that do not compete amongst each other but co-exist with their own special topics and emphases.

Reference Number: EU2050

visit: www.unitedregions.eu

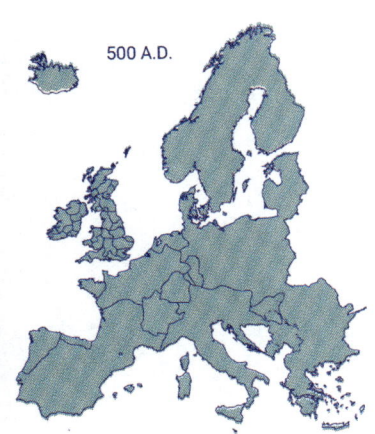

500 A.D.

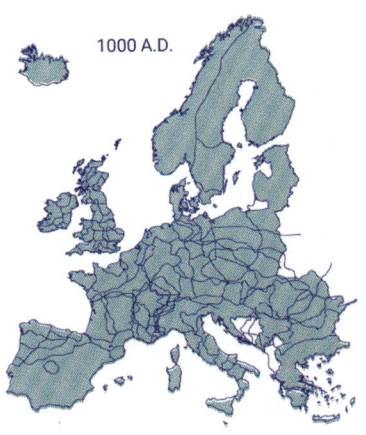

1000 A.D.

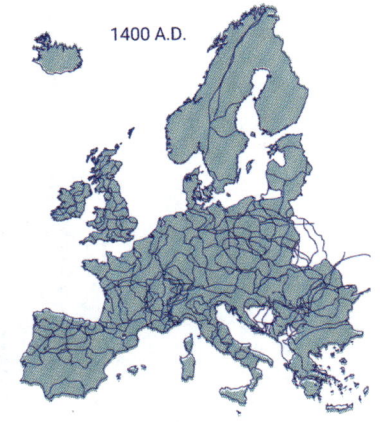

1400 A.D.

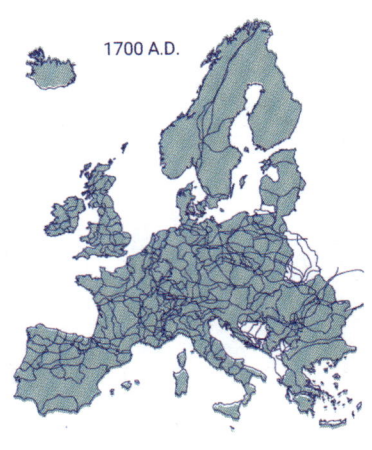

1700 A.D.

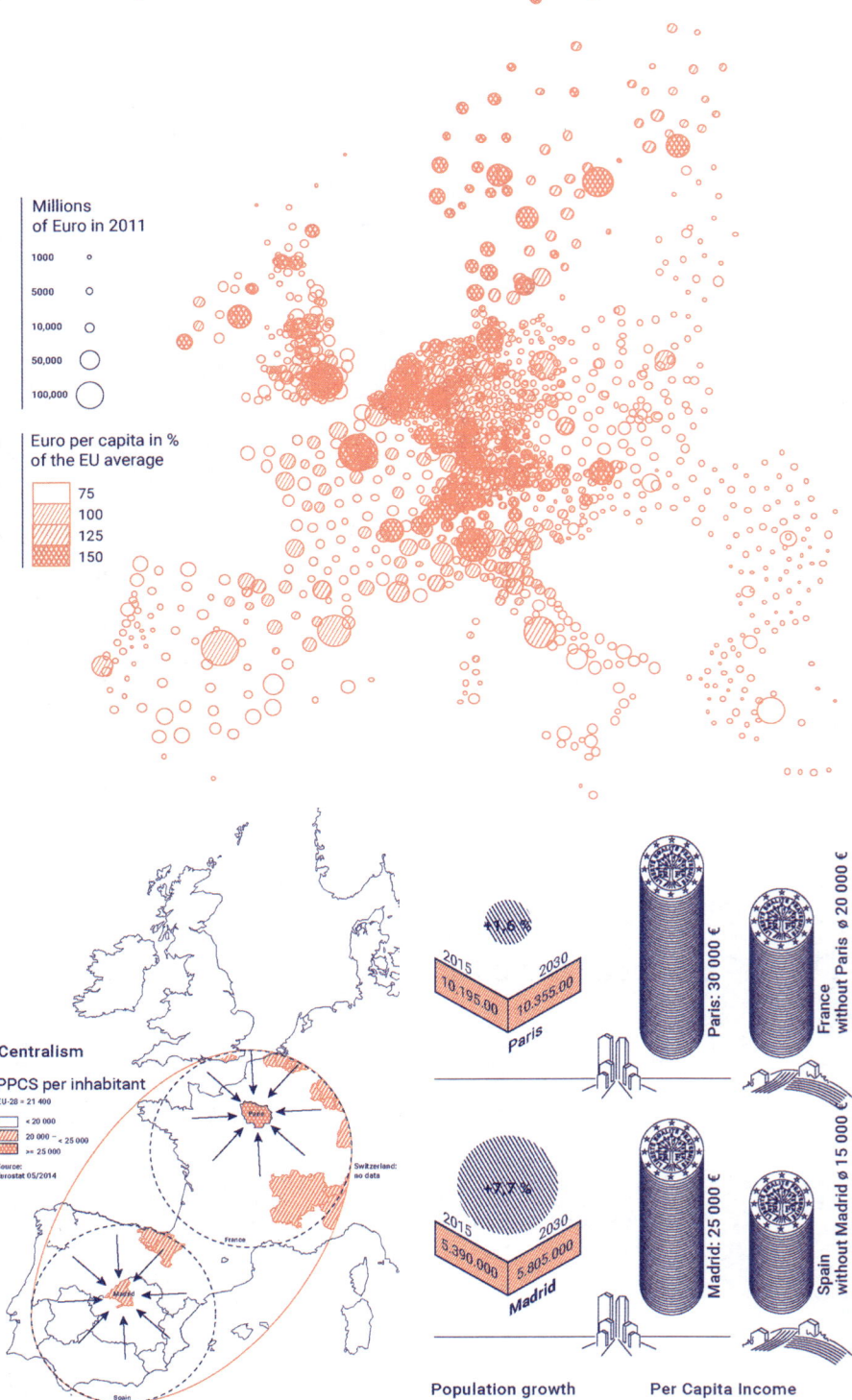

top
"If you took a map of Europe and you drew every political border there ever was in the history of the continent, you would end up with a net of black lines so close-meshed it'd appear as a single, black plain. Which of all these lines on that black plane could strike us a natural border?" Robert Menasse

right
The GDP of national states like Spain, Poland or France is high only in their major cities, whereas it is more evenly distributed in states with federal structures.

bottom right
A large income gap between capital and suburbs is the consequence of centralism. More people are moving to the main cities (urbanisation); the rural area dies out. Madrid especially is bound to grow considerably within the next 15 years. The increasing dependence to Madrid has given rise to separatism movements in e.g. Catalonia.

Millions
of Euro in 2011

1000
5000
10,000
50,000
100,000

Euro per capita in %
of the EU average

75
100
125
150

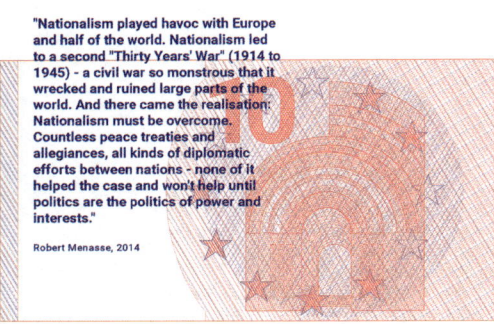

"Nationalism played havoc with Europe and half of the world. Nationalism led to a second "Thirty Years' War" (1914 to 1945) - a civil war so monstrous that it wrecked and ruined large parts of the world. And there came the realisation: Nationalism must be overcome. Countless peace treaties and allegiances, all kinds of diplomatic efforts between nations - none of it helped the case and won't help until politics are the politics of power and interests."

Robert Menasse, 2014

"Free, open-minded, in motion, no more blinkered by nationality and - like the very first European citizens - devoted to a common legal situation: Those are the new Europeans."
Robert Menasse, 2014

Centralism

PPCS per inhabitant
EU-28 = 21 400

< 20 000
20 000 - < 25 000
>= 25 000

Source:
Eurostat 05/2014

Switzerland:
no data

France

Spain

+1.6 %
2015   2030
10.195.00   10.355.00
Paris

Paris: 30 000 €

France
without Paris ⌀ 20 000 €

+7.7 %
2015   2030
5.390.000   5.805.000
Madrid

Madrid: 25 000 €

Spain
without Madrid 15 000 €

Population growth

Per Capita Income

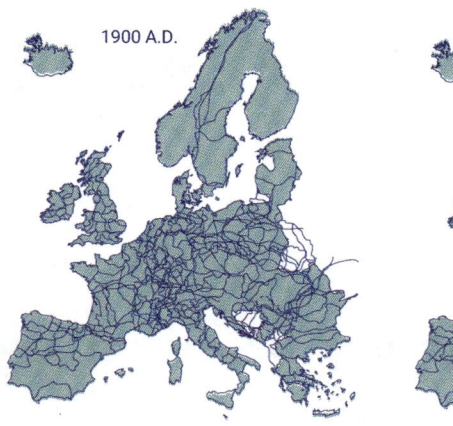

1900 A.D.

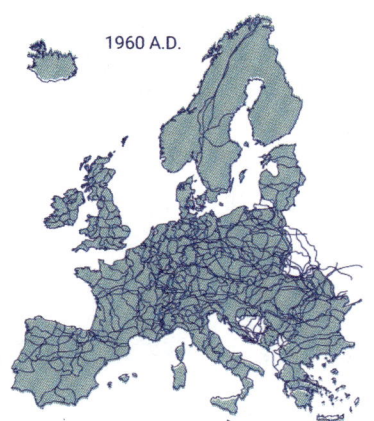

1960 A.D.

STATUS QUO

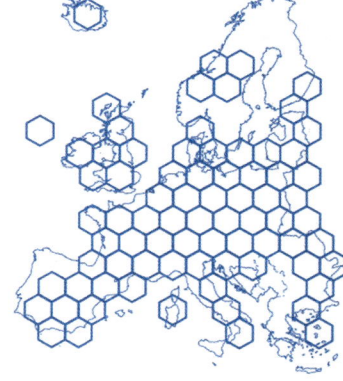

VISION

Europe of Nations

• Contradicting "national interests".
• Centralized urbanization in the national capitals.
• Increasing problems of urbanization.
• Inequality of wealth between the states.

Europe of Regions

• A European constitution and solidarity community
• Decentralized urbanization in regional capitals.
• less problems of urbanization.
• A better spread of wealth.

right
The United Regions of Europe: a possible scenario of Europe's regions.

bottom
The European Constitution provides a community of values based on the human and civil rights. As people's immediate environment, every region has a certain autonomy. The principle of subsidiary is in place: What matters here is decided here, by democratically elected direct representatives in a regional parliament; or by referendum.

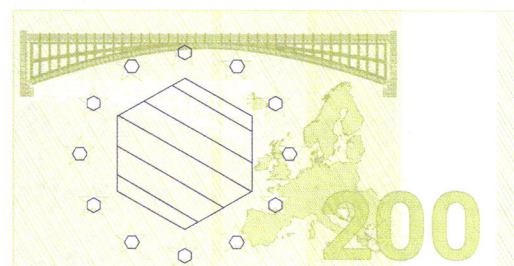

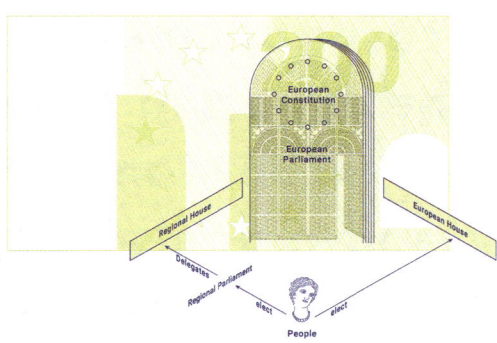

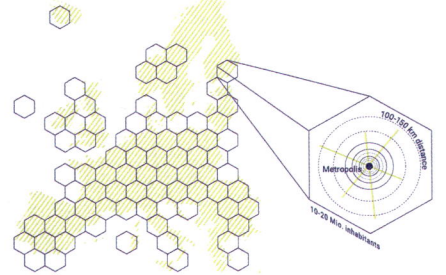

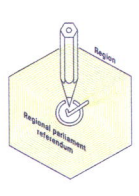

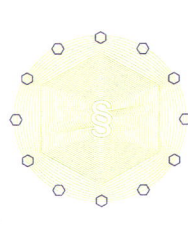

III. INFORMAL

Traditionally, cities function in the clear differentiation between public and private tasks. The security of daily life is based on the fact that the infrastructure for basic supplies is guaranteed by the municipality, or on its behalf, that the forms of urban coexistence are shaped by bureaucratic regulations and structured by administrative routines. But what is life like in the unplanned, unregulated, rapidly growing settlements on the peripheries of megacities, where there is no public responsibility for running water, electricity, sanitation or waste collection, where carrying out everyday tasks is hugely complex and mobility in the city becomes difficult due to a lack of proper roads and means of transportation? When there is no public support system for people in cases of illness or unemployment, and help can only be expected from people in similarly precarious circumstances? In such situations, self-help and self-organisation become the main characteristics of a bottom-up urbanism, the creative potential of which, despite all idealisation, must not obscure the fact that it is born out of the brutal requirement to survive.

VS REGULATED

Städte funktionieren traditionellerweise in der klaren Unterscheidung zwischen öffentlichen und privaten Aufgaben. Die Sicherheit des alltäglichen Lebens beruht darauf, dass die infrastrukturelle Grundversorgung durch die Kommune selbst oder in ihrem Auftrag gewährleistet wird, dass die Formen des städtischen Zusammenlebens von bürokratischen Regelungen geprägt und durch Verwaltungsroutinen strukturiert werden. Wie aber gestaltet sich das Leben in den ungeplanten, unkontrolliert wachsenden Siedlungen an den Rändern der Megacities, wo es keine öffentliche Zuständigkeit für fließendes Wasser, Stromversorgung, Kanalisation oder Müllentsorgung gibt, wenn alltägliche Verrichtungen ungeheuer aufwendig sind und es schwierig wird, sich mangels Straßen, Verkehrsmitteln und -anschlüssen in der Stadt fortzubewegen? Wenn kein öffentliches soziales Netz die Menschen im Falle von Krankheit und Arbeitslosigkeit unterstützt und Hilfe nur von Menschen in ähnlich prekären Verhältnissen zu erwarten ist?

In solchen Situationen wird Selbsthilfe und Selbstorganisation zum zentralen Merkmal eines Bottom-up Urbanismus, dessen schöpferisches Potential jenseits aller Idealisierung nicht darüber hinwegtäuschen darf, dass er aus der brutalen Notwendigkeit des Überlebens hervorgegangen ist.

MANIFESTO OF THE 21st CENTURY'S OWN SETTLEMENT FORM

Barbarism lurks in the very concept of culture – as the concept of a fund of values which is considered independent, not, indeed, of the production process in which these values originated, but of the one in which they survive.
Walter Benjamin, 1937

1. The urban heritage of the 21st century will consist of the world's self-organised settlements.

2. These settlements demonstrate the current conditions of human life on the planet as they result from a historical process: urbanisation under neoliberal regimes. Therefrom – and not from the fact that they might perform as "arrival cities", as stages of "smart informality" or as "urban commons" – derives their value as cultural heritage.

3. We refuse the concept of informality, expression of a functionalist-technocratic top-down perspective on the architectural, philosophical and political question of human settlement. So-called informal practices, mere reaction to the unjust administration of the forces of production worldwide, to successful exclusionary politics and to the protracted denial of the right to housing on the part of deserting states and elitist planners, cannot stop either exploitation or the politics of exclusion.

4. Far from generating cultural value, academics and practitioners that praise and propose to learn from informality – but invariantly fail at that, since its dynamic mechanisms elude fixation – don't but extend the predatory culture of the West: the Global South, be it for economic or scientific interests, is once again instrumentalised.

5. In an age of simultaneity and translocality, the binomial "formal/informal", "A is not B", is obsolete. To term other livelihoods and life forms "informal" means to disqualify them with paternalistic stubbornness.

6. Unauthorised settlements are no aberration: in the 21st century, mirror of the lack of civilisation of capitalist production-consumption that destroyed worldwide ecological and social resources, they will be the habitat of more than 1.5 billion people. It's high time to finally grant them their own place in the history of civilisation, because:

7. the modes of production and forms of organisation that are growing in these settlements beyond or beneath conventional forms of subsistence, articulate – in the present and not in retrospective – own and new values, and

8. vis-à-vis global challenges – from the energy to the food crisis, from the redistribution of resources to climate change – and in contrast to gated communities and privately developed new townships that are spreading as a parallel worldwide trend but fail to generate social value, these settlements define possibilities for human beings' cohesion in the future.

9. All this makes them appear the most hopeful settlement form of the neoliberal age. We hence demand that self-organised settlements be recognised as an own form of civilisation and settlement and, instead of being marginalised, treated as cultural heritage and finally authorised.

10. "Cultural heritage", for us, is nothing to freeze in UNESCO manner. Self-organised, unplanned and unplannable, always contingent: that's how the human settlements of the 21st century have to be!

ON THE MYTH OF INFORMAL URBANISATION: KARAIL BASTI, DHAKA   Elisa T. Bertuzzo

It's still there. Karail Basti lives on, despite everything – despite the major incidents, like the bulldozer operation of 2012 in which 4,000 people were made homeless because a road had to be widened, and the minor ones, such as last week's fire, caused by a faulty gas line, which affected 22 dwellings. In the last eight years, the settlement survived a democratic crisis, a transitional government, two national elections and a reform of the urban administration, not to mention the pressure from the real estate sector, which would be extremely keen to get its hands on the area, located as it is, at the heart of Dhaka's business district. Thus it continues to thrive on Banani Lake with its corrugated tin houses, mosques, trees and palms, whereby the spanking new walls and roofs of its dwellings, gleaming in the sun, seem to want to send a proud message to the surrounding high-rise landscape: we have grown in you and with you, like you we will grow denser and higher. And, we will endure.

They still live there. The seasonal construction workers and migrants from rural areas who built the first temporary dwellings on the peninsula by the lake a good thirty years ago are by now an ever-dwindling minority. Their children have grown up here, their relatives have found refuge here, new neighbours have arrived; today, around 120,000 people work or live in the basti. It is thanks to their efforts, their collective engagement and their spirit of enterprise that meanwhile, Karail functions so well that some describe it as a "luxury slum". Nonetheless, they are classified as squatters and could be evicted at a moment's notice: a reality that denudes the unimaginative cynicism of those who speak of luxury, as well as the blindness of a state apparatus that confuses its own responsibilities with duties of the people or the NGOs. Despite this, they hang on to their settlement – they believe in its future, actively contribute to its development and fight for its recognition. This, more than any topographical or historical characteristics, makes Karail Basti paradigmatic for numerous other success stories of self-organisation and the fight for the right to the city worldwide.

I am there, still. A few days more: then, like every other time, I will have to leave. Leave the friends made over years of discussions, even conflicts; leave the many acquaintances with whom it's always nice to chat over a glass of tea; leave Tanzila, who no longer needs me to explain how far apart Bangladesh and Germany

Noch steht es. Karail Basti bleibt, trotz aller Zwischenfälle – von den großen, wie die Bulldozer-Aktion von 2012, bei der 4.000 Menschen obdachlos wurden, weil eine Straße breiter werden musste, bis zu den kleinen, wie der von einer defekten Gasleitung ausgelöste Brand von letzter Woche, der 22 Wohnräume betraf –, stehen. In den letzten acht Jahren hat die Siedlung einen demokratischen Notstand, eine Übergangsregierung, zwei Nationalwahlen und eine Reform der Stadtverwaltung überstanden, über den Druck der Immobilienwirtschaft ganz zu schweigen, die auf das inmitten von Dhakas Business District liegende Areal besonders scharf wäre. So erhebt sie sich bis heute mit ihren Wellblechhäusern, Moscheen, Bäumen und Palmen auf dem Banani Lake, wobei die nagelneuen Wände und Dächer ihrer Wohnbauten, strahlend unter der Sonne, der umliegenden Hochhäuser-Landschaft eine stolze Botschaft scheinen senden zu wollen: Wir sind in und mit dir zusammen gewachsen, wie du werden wir dichter, sprießen in die Höhe. Und, wir bleiben.

Noch leben sie da. Die saisonalen Bauarbeiter und Migranten aus dem Land, die vor gut 30 Jahren auf der Halbinsel am See die ersten temporären Unterkünfte bauten, stellen inzwischen eine verschwindende Minderheit dar. Ihre Kinder sind hier groß geworden, ihre Verwandten haben hier Zuflucht gefunden, neue Nachbarn kamen dazu; nun arbeiten oder wohnen rund 120.000 Menschen im Basti. Es ist ihren Anstrengungen, ihrem kollektiven Engagement und ihrem Unternehmungsgeist zu verdanken, wenn Karail heute so gut funktioniert, dass es von manchen als "Luxus-Slum" bezeichnet wird. Indessen gelten sie laut Gesetz als Besetzer und könnten jederzeit vertrieben werden: Daran wird der phantasielose Zynismus derer deutlich, die von Luxus reden, ebenso wie die Blindheit eines staatlichen Apparats, der seine eigenen Aufgaben mit Pflichten der Bevölkerung oder allemal der NGOs vertauscht.

left page:
Those imagining unauthorised settlements as idle, unproductive or terribly poor would be surprised entering Karail Basti and discovering its thousands of shops, workshops, eateries and small businesses:

- Improvised food stalls during the upgrading works on the big gathering field Boro Math
- one of many taylor shops
- employee of a recycling workshop carrying waste to a collection area
- ongoing house construction works.

right page:
- In the course of one decade, house production has become a matter for trained builders, carpenters and even masons, involved in the construction of meanwhile common brick-and-corrugated-iron one storey-house forms.

- Varying pavements in the settlement deliver insight into the community's efforts towards upgrading the existing infrastructure, whereby road works can be either steered by the inhabitants or sponsored by NGOs.

- Transportation from and to the settlement is ensured by an efficient, and of course self-organised, boats network.

- Bou bazar, the settlement's well-sorted grocery market, is unaffected by Dhaka's frequent power cuts thanks to the basti's unofficial electricity provision.

Fotos: Günter Nest

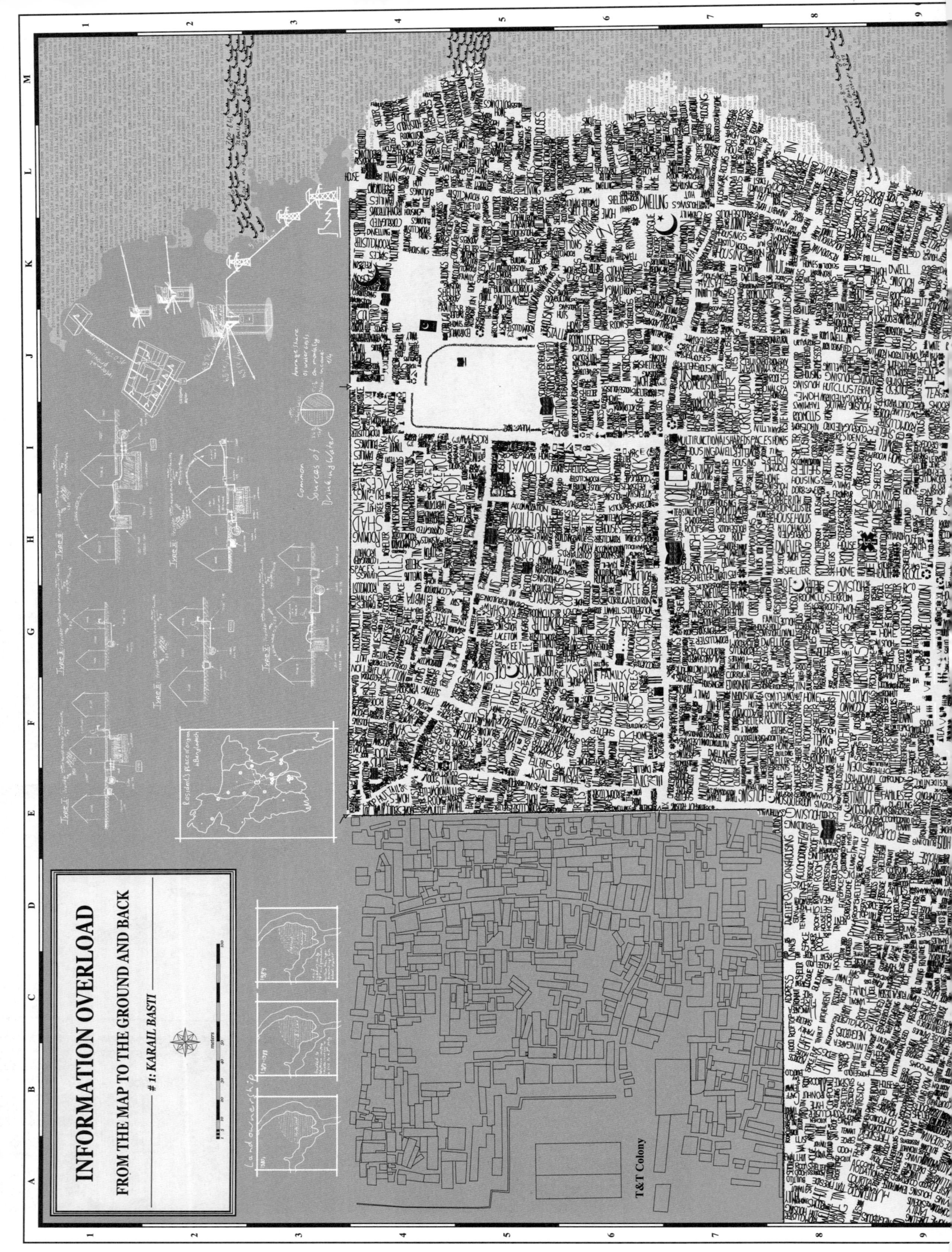

INFORMATION OVERLOAD

FROM THE MAP TO THE GROUND AND BACK

1: KARAIL BASTI

Wettbewerbsteam: Günter Nest, Elisa T. Bertuzzo, Louisa Scherer, Marcus Jeutner, Paul Klever, Anna Sauter
Projektmitarbeiter: Marian Knop, Lisa Lampe, Tamanna Siddiqui, Farhana Kaniz Sharna, Abdul Kader Khan (Komol)

1. Das städtische Kulturerbe des 21. Jahrhunderts wird in den selbstorganisierten Siedlungen aller Welt bestehen.

2. Diese Siedlungsform manifestiert die Lage menschlichen Lebens auf dem Planeten als Produkt eines historischen Prozesses: Urbanisierung unter neoliberalen Bedingungen. Daher – und nicht etwa von der Fähigkeit her, erfolgreiche "arrival city" zu sein, "smart informality" zu lehren oder "urban commoning" zu realisieren – rührt ihr dringender Kulturwert.

3. Wir lehnen das Mantra von der Informalität, Ausdruck einer funktionalistisch-technokratischen Top-Down-Sichtweise auf die architektonische, philosophische und politische Frage ums menschliche Wohnen, ab. Informalität, Folge der ungerechten Handhabung weltweiter Produktivkräfte und bloße Reaktion auf erfolgreiche Politiken der Exklusion und der Verweigerung des Rechts auf Wohnen vonseiten desertierender Staaten und elitärer Planerinnen und Planer, kann an Ausbeutung und Exklusionspolitik nichts ändern.

4. Weit davon entfernt, Kulturwerte zu erzeugen, sichern Akademikerinnen und Akademiker sowie Praktikerinnen und Praktiker, die Informalität loben und reproduzieren möchten – diese aber nie begreifen, weil sie sich stets der Fixierung entzieht – lediglich das Fortbestehen der westlichen Raubkultur: Der globale Süden wird für die eigenen, ob ökonomischen oder wissenschaftlichen Interessen dienlich gemacht.

5. Die westlich geprägte Unterscheidung "Formell/Informell", "A ist nicht B", ist in einer Epoche der Gleichzeitigkeit und Translokalität offensichtlich veraltet. Andere Lebensformen als "informell" zu bezeichnen, bedeutet sie schlicht mit paternalistischer Rechthaberei zu disqualifizieren.

6. Nicht-autorisierte Siedlungen sind keine Abweichung: Im 21. Jahrhundert, Zeugnis der Unzivilisiertheit des kapitalistischen Systems, verantwortlich für die globale Zerstörung ökologischer und sozialer Ressourcen, werden mehr als 1,5 Milliarden Menschen so leben. Es ist an der Zeit, ihnen eine eigene Stelle in der Zivilisationsgeschichte einzuräumen, denn:

7. die für sie charakteristischen Produktionsweisen und Organisationsformen jenseits oder unterhalb herkömmlicher Subsistenzformen bringen – in der Gegenwart und nicht retrospektivisch – eigene und neuartige Werte hervor, und

8. vor dem Hintergrund bevorstehender globaler Herausforderungen, von der Energiekrise bis zur Ernährungskrise, von der Ressourcen-Umverteilung bis zum Klimawandel, definieren nicht-autorisierte Siedlungen, im Gegensatz zu privatisierten Wohnanlagen und "gated commuties", die sich in einem parallelen Trend weltweit vermehren, aber keinen sozialen Wert entwickeln, Möglichkeiten des künftigen menschlichen Zusammenhalts.

9. All dies macht sie zur hoffnungsvollsten Siedlungsform des neoliberalen Zeitalters. Daher fordern wir, dass selbstorganisierte Siedlungen fortan als Zivilisations- und Siedlungsform anerkannt und anstatt marginalisiert, als Kulturerbe behandelt und endlich autorisiert werden.

10. "Kulturerbe" ist für uns nichts, was nach geläufigen UNESCO-Praktiken fixiert und starr wird. Selbstorganisiert, ungeplant und unplanbar, immer kontingent: So sollen die Siedlungen der Menschen im 21. Jahrhundert sein!

Habitat Forum Berlin / Elisa T. Bertuzzo, Günter Nest

The basti's still standing. Impression from the main road.

Self-made architecture, sometimes, means self-expression.
Fotos: Günter Nest

lie: she will smile and with a shy glance, say, "see you soon". The most difficult thing for me is to take leave of Karail as a whole – for although one can make arrangements to see people again, she can't do the same with places.

In Bengali, the official language of Bangladesh, basti (pronounced bosti) means settlement, but self-organised settlements like Karail are increasingly called "slums". The term, if it reflects the academic debate, irritates me, on the one hand because it evokes images of poverty, depraved surroundings and precarious living conditions that overshadow the good or at least open-to-improvement aspects of dwelling and living in such settlements; on the other, because it does not differentiate: it suggests that the poorer or most exploited social groups worldwide have just the one form of housing, the one way of life. However, in Dhaka alone, changing topographical or evolutionary conditions – whether a settlement is compact or scattered, whether it is located in an old or a relatively new neighbourhood, on private or public land – have yielded such diverse social and spatial forms that every basti is essentially an isolated case!

Karail is one such case. Spreading over 190,000 square metres, it is Dhaka's largest and, after other bastis were cleared by force or succumbed to developers, also oldest self-organised settlement. When I first rented a room there in 2009, I was preoccupied with questions revolving around the subject of "informality". How had this parallel universe in the middle of the city come up? How was it possible that, without any urban planning interventions, it did not only avail of water and electricity, but was also maintained by street sweepers and forces of law and order? Where do the potentials, as well as the limitations, of "informal" settlement development lie, and what is the scope of self-sufficiency and self-organisation? Since then, Karail Basti has been widely described and discussed – whether as case study in a research programme sponsored by the German Research Foundation, or as the setting of YouTube videos made by tourists and activists; as "arrival city" in Doug Saunders's eponymous book, or as site for architecture students from all over the world, tasked with solving one of its problems. Despite the variety of these representations, it has retained the label "informal".

"Informality", like "slum", seems to apply to everything. But is it so? On closer examination one rather notices that the overuse of this term meanwhile idealises highly sensitive ways of life in complex (and not to forget, often endangered) systems. Not one of the many studies of Karail Basti, for example, has produced definite figures about the number of people living there, or checked the significant discrepancies between data of varying sources – the Bureau of Statistics lists 30,000 residents, the NGOs in their funding proposals, 200,000. Such a failure is not linked to the high population density of the settlement, for simple demographic methods would enable to perform an on-site survey within an acceptable period of time. Rather, it seems as if Karail's classification as "informal" destroyed the motivation for this undertaking, or even undermined its sense in the eyes of researchers. Why is a settlement defined as informal not deemed worthy of being seriously surveyed, like every other area of the city?

In all this, I must confess that I am no friend of statistical surveys: to study urban processes, I prefer personal approaches to quantitative methods. When maps of the settlement were drawn up in the framework of the documentation project of

Nichtsdestotrotz halten sie an der Siedlung fest – sie glauben an ihre Zukunft, tragen aktiv zu ihrer Entwicklung bei und kämpfen für ihre Anerkennung. Dies, mehr als alle topografischen oder historischen Eigenarten, macht Karail Basti für viele andere Erfolgsgeschichten der Selbstorganisation und des Kampfes um das Recht auf die Stadt in der ganzen Welt paradigmatisch.

Noch bin ich da. Ein paar Tage noch: Dann, wie jedes Mal, werde ich mich verabschieden müssen. Von den in jahrelangen Auseinandersetzungen, gar Reibungen gewonnenen Freunden; von den vielen Bekannten, mit denen man gern ein Glas Tee trinkt und plaudert; von Tanzila, der ich inzwischen nicht mehr erklären brauche, wie weit auseinander Bangladesch und Deutschland liegen: Sie wird lächeln, den flüchtigen Blick nach unten gerichtet, und "bis bald" sagen. Am Schwierigsten finde ich, das Basti als Ganzes zu verabschieden – denn mit Orten, anders als mit Menschen, lässt sich das nächste Wiedersehen nicht verabreden.

In Bengali, der Landessprache Bangladeschs, bedeutet basti (ausgesprochen bosti) Siedlung, aber selbstorganisierte Siedlungen wie Karail werden immer häufiger in Anlehnung an die akademische Debatte lediglich "Slums" genannt. Der Begriff ärgert mich, einerseits weil er überschnell Bilder von Armut, degradierter Umwelt und prekären Lebensbedingungen evoziert, welche die guten oder zumindest ausbaufähigen Aspekte des Wohnens und Lebens in solchen Siedlungen unterdrücken; und andererseits, weil er nicht differenziert: Er suggeriert, dass den ärmeren bzw. ausgebeutetsten Gesellschaftsgruppen weltweit nur noch eine einzige Wohn- bzw. Lebensform zusteht. Dabei haben allein in Dhaka jeweilige topografische oder Entstehungsbedingungen – etwa, ob eine Siedlung kompakt oder gestreut ist, in einem alten oder relativ neuen Stadtteil bzw. auf privatem oder öffentlichem Boden liegt – so unterschiedliche soziale und räumliche Ausformungen zur Folge, dass jedes Basti im Grunde einen Einzelfall darstellt!

Karail, mit einer Fläche von 190.000 Quadratmetern die größte und, nachdem andere Basti Zwangsräumung oder Baudruck zum Opfer gefallen sind, die älteste selbstorganisierte Siedlung von Dhaka, ist einer von diesen Einzelfällen. Als ich mir 2009 zum ersten Mal ein Zimmer dort mietete, trieben mich Fragen rund um das Thema der "Informalität" um. Wie war dieser Parallelkosmos mitten in der Stadt aufgebaut worden? Wie kam es, dass die Siedlung ohne jegliche stadtplanerische Intervention nicht nur mit Wasser und Strom versorgt, sondern auch von eigenen Straßenfegern und Ordnungskräften instand gehalten wurde? Wo liegen die Potenziale, aber auch die Grenzen der "informellen" Siedlungsentwicklung, wie weit reichen Selbstversorgung und -organisation? Seither ist Karail Basti vielfach beschrieben und diskutiert worden – mal als Fallbeispiel eines von der Deutschen Forschungsgemeinschaft geförderten Forschungsprojekts, mal als Kulisse von YouTube-Videos von Touristen und Aktivistinnen, mal als arrival city in Doug Saunders' gleichnamigem Bestseller, mal als Aktionsfeld von Architekturstudierenden aus aller Welt, die irgendeines seiner Probleme lösen sollten. Bei aller Vielfalt der Repräsentationen blieb die Bezeichnung "informell" an ihm haften.

"Informalität" wie "Slum" scheint alles erklären zu können. Stimmt das? Bei näherer Betrachtung lässt sich eher feststellen, dass die Überbeanspruchung dieses

November 2015, the works for the upgrading of the now legalised water delivery are on ...

... while electricity is still provided via a myriad of unofficial contracts.
Fotos: Günter Nest

Begriffs höchst sensible Lebensformen in komplexen (und nicht zu vergessen, oft gefährdeten) Systemen inzwischen verklärt. Keine der vielfältigen Untersuchungen über Karail Basti zum Beispiel hat eindeutige Angaben zur Zahl der dort Wohnenden hervorgebracht oder die äußerst diskrepanten Daten der üblichen Quellen – die Statistikbehörde berichtet von 30.000, die NGOs in ihren Förderanträgen von 200.000 Bewoh-

nern – überprüft. Ein solches Versagen liegt nicht an der hohen Bevölkerungsdichte der Siedlung, denn vermittels einfacher demographischer Methoden könnte eine Erhebung vor Ort ohne übermäßigen Zeitaufwand durchgeführt werden. Es sieht eher danach aus, dass Karails Kennzeichnung als "informell" die Motivation zum Unterfangen vernichtete, oder gar dessen Sinn in den Augen der Forschenden unterminierte. Warum ist es eine als informell bezeichnete Siedlung nicht wert, wie jedes andere Gebiet der Stadt seriös untersucht zu werden?

Dabei muss ich gestehen, dass ich selbst keine Freundin statistischer Erhebungen bin: Zum Erforschen städtischer Prozesse ziehe ich persönliche Zugänge quantitativen Methoden vor. Als im Rahmen des Dokumentationsprojekts, das das Habitat Forum Berlin vor Ort durchführt, Karten der Siedlung entstanden[1], gelang es mir nicht, diese mit dem "gefühlten" Erfahrungsraum in Einklang zu bringen, der sich in meinem Gedächtnis bereits eingeprägt hatte. Weiterhin laufe ich nach Gefühl und den Hinweisen der Bewohner dort durch, wobei ich gern dem Spiel der Bilder nachgebe, die einander überlappend ein Zeit-Raum-Labyrinth schaffen – eines, in dem sich Straßenecken, Teebuden, Wege, Läden und Gesichter der Vergangenheit und der Gegenwart pausenlos abwechseln. Denn alles verändert sich schnell in Karail, bei jeder Rückkehr lässt sich etwas vermissen, etwas Anderes neu kennenlernen.

Der Anblick der neuen Wassertanks führt mich zum Beispiel zu den Wasser-Jungs zurück. April 2009, sechs Uhr morgens: die Plastikkanister sind fast leer, zum scharfen Kartoffel-Gemüse masala, das die meisten zum Frühstück essen, ist kaum was zu trinken da; die Männer bestellen sich an der Bude am Straßenrand ein Glas Tee. Vor allem in den heißen Sommermonaten ist noch nicht mal Wasser fürs Abspülen übrig, weshalb Teller, Töpfe und Besteck an der Türschwelle jeder Hütte gestapelt werden. Die Frage, ob und wann und wie viel Wasser zur Verfügung steht, bestimmt den Alltag der Frauen – vom Abwasch bis zum Gießen der Gemüse- und Gewürzpflanzen, vom Duschen bis zum Waschen der kleineren Kinder. Deswegen ist die Zeit vor der Wasserlieferung, erst recht wenn sie verspätet erfolgt, zugleich von Ungeduld und einer seltenen Untätigkeit geprägt. Nachbarinnen besuchen einander, tauschen sich in den offenen Räumen zwischen den Hütten aus. Sie reden über die Kinder, über Geburten und Tode, über die steigenden Nahrungsmittelpreise und die Verwandten im Dorf. Oft schweigen sie auch. Alle Haushalte im Hüttencluster teilen die gleiche Infrastruktur: abgesehen von Kochstellen und Nasszellen auch die Wasserversorgung, für die jedoch jeder individuell eine Pauschalgebühr bezahlt. Endlich kommen die Jungs. Sie schließen einen herumliegenden Gartenschlauch, die gemeinsame "Wasserleitung", an einen von weiter her kommenden Schlauch an, und das Wasser fließt. Ordentlich, Kanister um Kanister, speichern Frauen und Mädchen ihre Ration für den Tag, wobei das ganze Verfahren nicht länger als 15 Minuten dauert: Auf mehr haben sie keinen Anspruch. Danach beginnen die Haushaltsarbeiten, allen voran das Kochen von Wasser, damit es gefahrlos getrunken werden kann.

Inzwischen gehören die Wasser-Jungs sowie das Warten und Vorräteanlegen der Vergangenheit an, weil Karail und viele andere Siedlungen, die ihres "illegalen" Status wegen nicht ans städtische Wassernetz angeschlossen waren, seit 2013 über eine offizielle Wasserversorgung verfügen[2]. Dass die Wasserbehörde ihr Mandat endlich mit der Wasserlieferung an alle Bewohner Dhakas unabhängig von Einkommen und Adresse identifizierte, kann als großer Erfolg von CBO-Leader[3] wie Mannan angesehen werden, die jahrelang hartnäckig um das Recht auf Wasser für die nicht-autorisierten Siedlungen der Stadt kämpften. Zugleich stellte diese Entwicklung einen ersten Angriff auf jene inoffiziellen Versorger dar, die in Absprache mit den Verwaltern der benachbarten Wohngebäude, oder gleich mit den

---

Habitat Forum Berlin[1], I was unable to reconcile these with the "sensed" space of experience that I had committed to memory living there. Till today, I walk through the area by following my instincts or the advice of residents, and I do like to surrender, now and then, to the game of the images that, overlapping, create a time-space labyrinth – one in which street corners, tea stalls, paths, shops and faces, both past and present, alternate each other without pause. Because everything changes quickly in Karail, and every time I return, something is missing, and there is something new to discover.

Seeing the new water tanks for instance takes me back to the "water boys". April 2009, six in the morning: the plastic canisters are almost empty, there is hardly anything left to drink with the spicy potato and vegetable masala that most eat for breakfast; the men order a glass of tea at the stand on the roadside. Especially in the hot summer months, there is not even any water left to do the dishes, which is why plates, saucepans and cutlery are piled up on the doorstep of every hut. Whether, when and how much water will be available defines the everyday of the women – from washing-up to watering vegetables and spice plants, from showering to washing the youngest children. For this reason, the time that precedes the delivery of water, especially when there are delays, is characterised by a combination of impatience and a seldom idleness. Neighbours visit one another, chat in the open spaces between the huts. They talk about their children, about births and deaths, about the rising food prices and their relatives in the villages. Often, they just keep silent. All the households in one cluster of huts share the same infrastructure: apart from the cooking areas and washrooms, also the water supply, for which each pays an individual flat rate. The boys finally arrive. They connect a garden hose lying around, the shared "water pipeline", to a pipe coming from further afield, and the water flows. In an orderly fashion, one canister after another, women and girls store their ration for the day, whereby the whole process lasts no longer than fifteen minutes: they have no right to more. Then, the domestic chores begin, the priority being to boil water so that it can be drunk without risk.

Meanwhile, the water boys, the waiting as well as the stocking up of supplies have become a thing of the past, because Karail and many other settlements, which were not connected to the municipal water network due to their "illegal" status, obtained an official water supply in 2013[2]. The fact that the water authority finally realised that its mandate is to supply water to all of Dhaka's inhabitants, irrespective of income and address, should be seen as a great achievement of CBO leaders[3] such as Mannan, who for many years fought hard for the right to water of the city's self-organised settlements. At the same time, this evolution represented a first attack on the unofficial suppliers, who in collusion with the managers of the neighbouring residential buildings, or even with the employees of the water

authority – for money, of course – used to tap in to the regular network and offer overpriced water in the basti. Only now that the negotiations have ended on a positive note and the system is operative to the satisfaction of all the inhabitants does Mannan-bhai[4] confide, with a nonchalant grin, how some of these suppliers tried with threats or bribery to force him to give up his endeavour. In the near future, he wants electricity, like water, to be delivered by way of official contracts. Whether this will happen depends on the interaction with the responsible offices and, equally, on the community's ability to emancipate themselves from the current traders. Mannan knows that this will be a lengthy process: unlike the water, the electricity in Dhaka is distributed by a number of public administration bodies and companies that entertain shadowy public-private partnerships and will without a doubt prove more difficult to convince; as far as the unofficial suppliers are concerned – these might now also turn to desperate methods in order to maintain the hitherto system of dependences.

The trade in electricity in unauthorised settlements is highly lucrative. Karail's self-organised electricity network meanwhile serves all the single households: every hut has got at least one light bulb and one fan hanging from the roof; some families own a television. Although every house owner pays according to the actual monthly consumption, which is recorded by an electricity meter, there are additional fees for the connection and for maintenance, which are charged by the electricity traders based on rates that they set themselves, naturally to their own advantage. Their second customer group consists of Karail's small entrepreneurs, who run flourishing food shops, tailoring, recycling and iron workshops, tea stalls, mobile phone and accessory shops, amusement arcades, etc. Those who sell vegetables, fish and meat in the covered part of Bou Bazar (Bride's market) are simultaneously connected to different networks in the nearby neighbourhoods of Mohammadpur, Gulshan and Banani and when one of these fails, they can immediately switch to another. Thus, for the market, the many electricity traders guarantee an almost unbroken supply of electricity, independently of private generators: in a city where power cuts are an everyday occurrence, this is the exclusive privilege of the government buildings, the military zones and the Export Processing Zones (EPZs) filled with foreign textile factories. I can hear it coming now, the usual adage: "Wonders of informality". If I hadn't seen the others, who during power cuts sweat inside their overheated corrugated iron huts, or have to put aside a school book the day before an important test, or fall asleep, exhausted, at their sewing machines, then I, too, would still believe in it.

I'm still here; for a few more days, my focus can remain on everyday life. In conversations and tours, I learn about the status of a wide range of construction projects – from the expansion or fortifying works on private housing blocks to collectively expedited infrastructure interventions, for example on the moorings for the boats with which Karail's inhabitants reach the main road to the south as well as the residential and business district Gulshan to the east of the peninsula. Every year before the monsoon, these moorings have to be reinforced so that they withstand the constant rain and possible flooding. The toilets and wet rooms, if not sponsored by NGOs, likewise depend on joint investments by neighbouring families that maintain them collectively. Currently, in connection with the legalisation of the water supply, the makeshift self-built sewers of entire areas are being expanded.

All the infrastructure projects, including those initiated by NGOs, are coordinated by local shomiti. These committees have different structures, depending on the complexity and nature of their tasks. Alongside those called into being to manage major interventions, there are also shomiti that oversee everyday concerns, be it the appointment of street sweepers, the restoration of a specific alleyway, the

Angestellten der Wasserbehörde – gegen Bezahlung, versteht sich – das reguläre Netz anzapften und im Basti überteuertes Wasser anboten. Nur jetzt, da die Verhandlungen positiv ausgegangen sind und das System zur Freude aller Bewohner funktioniert, vertraut uns Mannan-bhai[4] mit einem gleichgültigen Grinsen an, wie manch einer unter diesen Versorgern mit Drohungen oder Geld versuchte, ihn von seinem Kampf abzubringen. Er möchte, dass Strom, ähnlich wie das Wasser, demnächst über offizielle Verträge in die Siedlung geleitet wird. Ob das gelingt, hängt von der Interaktion mit den verantwortlichen Ämtern ab, ebenso sehr wie von der Fähigkeit der Gemeinschaft, sich von den bisherigen Versorgern zu emanzipieren. Mannan weiß, dass dies ein ungleich langwierigerer Prozess sein wird: Anders als das Wasser wird der Strom in Dhaka über eine wenig transparente öffentlich-private Partnerschaft zwischen vielschichtigen Behörden und Firmen verteilt, die sicherlich schwieriger zu überzeugen sein werden; was die inoffiziellen Versorger anbelangt, dürften diese nun auch auf verzweifelte Methoden zurückgreifen, um das bisherige Abhängigkeitssystem aufrechtzuerhalten.

Der Handel mit Strom in nicht-autorisierten Siedlungen ist besonders rentabel. Das selbstorganisierte Stromnetz Karails bedient inzwischen alle einzelnen Haushalte: In jeder Hütte hängen mindestens eine Glühbirne und ein Ventilator an der Decke; einige Familien besitzen einen Fernseher. Zwar bezahlt jeder Hausbesitzer nach dem tatsächlichen, durch Stromzähler aufgenommenen Monatsverbrauch; aber dazu kommen die Gebühren für die Leitung und Instandhaltung, die von den Stromhändlern nach eigenen Sätzen und natürlich zum eigenen Vorteil festgelegt werden. Ihre zweite Kundengruppe besteht aus den Betreibern von Karails florierenden Lebensmittelgeschäften, Schneidereien, Recycling- und Eisenwerkstätten, Teebuden, Handy- und Zubehörläden, Videogames-Räumen etc. Dabei sind die Geschäftsleute, die im überdachten Teil des Bou Bazar ("Markt der Braut") Gemüse, Fisch und Fleisch verkaufen, gleich mit verschiedenen Netzen der umgebenden Ortschaften Mohammadpur, Gulshan und Banani verbunden, und wann immer eines davon ausfällt, können sie sofort ein anderes einschalten. Die vielen Stromhändler garantieren ihnen also eine beinahe lückenlose und von Privatgeneratoren unabhängige Stromlieferung – in einer Stadt, in der Stromausfälle an der Tagesordnung sind, ist dies das ausschließliche Privileg der Regierungsgebäude, der Militärzonen und der mit ausländischen Textilfabriken gefüllten EPZs ("Export Processing Zones"). Jetzt höre ich ihn kommen, den üblichen Spruch: "Wunder der Informalität". Wenn ich nicht die anderen vor Augen hätte, die während der Stromausfälle in ihren überhitz-

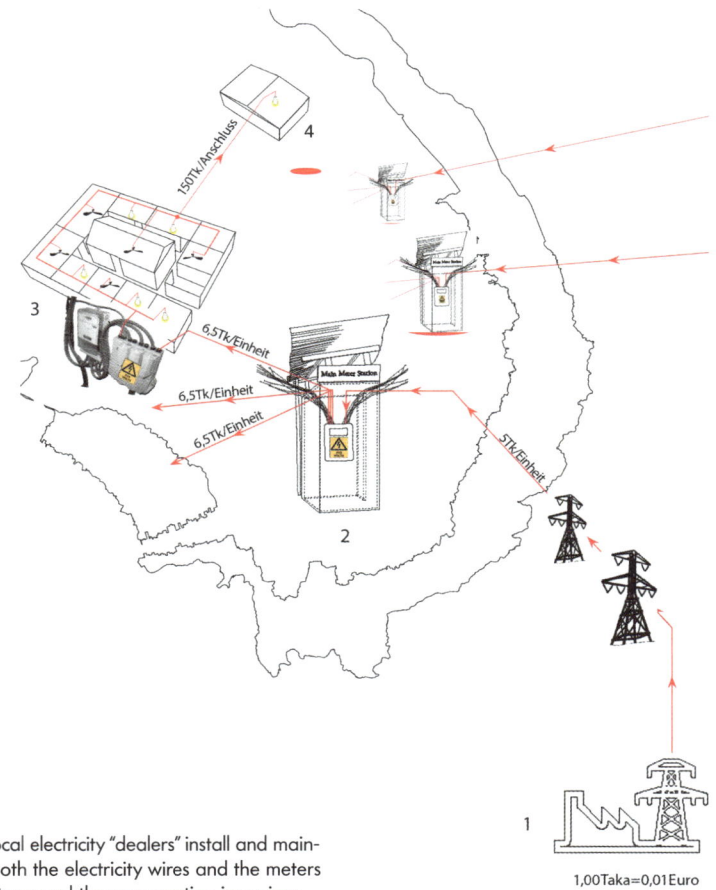

The local electricity "dealers" install and maintain both the electricity wires and the meters used to record the consumption in various residential clusters.
Drawing © Louisa Scherer

1,00 Taka = 0,01 Euro

Shared cooking place in a residential cluster.

development of the bazaars, the organisation of cultural events or the collection of donations for one of the basti's thirteen mosques. Now and again I stumble across the rather private discussions of the members of a third type of shomiti, Karail's numerous savings groups. Savings groups provide access to the banking system for individuals who have too few assets to open a bank account or who had to flee their village and go underground in the city due to excessive debts with creditors or NGOs, or who simply have no official address. The pooled savings go into collective accounts and are registered under the name of a member who can produce proof of a permanent address in the city, for instance with relatives. The fact that all members come from one and the same region ensures that the latter does not disappear with the money: in short, Karail's savings groups rely on the high social control that derives from the lively bonds with the village and strong local networks typical of Bangladesh's society.

Given the government's ongoing neglect, all initiatives that secure basic services in the basti can only be praised. However, these remain only partial and poorly funded emergency solutions: so for example, six to ten housewives have to share a single cooking area; in the mornings, demoralising queues form in front of the washrooms, which likewise have to be shared; makeshift gas lines and electricity networks cause frequent explosions and fires. Many of the sewers are open and run alongside the houses[5], whereby Banani Lake, which absorbs the unfiltered sewage and much of the settlement's refuse, is regularly covered with harmful algae and plants. Outbreaks of waterborne epidemics, among them typhoid and dengue fever, are on the rise here, as in the rest of the city. However, it is when it comes to the conditions and costs of self-organised services compared with functioning public services that the discourse on informality reveals particularly flawed. Why do we so rarely mention that the price of a unit of electricity increases with each further sale, or that far higher prices have to be paid for basic services such as electricity and water in a basti than in officially connected residential areas?[6]

To this circumstance, which brings to light the at least ambivalent implications of "informal" supply, adds the problem that the description of self-organised settlements as "informal" nourishes the myth that they are set up in non-hierarchical ways. Indeed, all of Karail's inhabitants live in hazardous conditions, on an ecologically and hygienically compromised strip of land where flooding and accidents are frequent; they all fled from their native villages due to poverty, land loss or destructive floods and are daunted by the burden of migration and the disappointed hopes of a new beginning in the big city. But they are not all the same. On the contrary, diverse actors protect their own interests by more or less legitimate means: from those who charge extraordinary fees for electricity and gas and those who, claiming the self-appointed right of the first to arrive, demand a kind of land use tax for the construction of houses on "their" land, to those who are proud to have bought land cheaply from neighbours afraid of eviction and then sold it on at a profit.

And what should I say about the powerful mallik[7]? Their clever tactics of "informal investment in residential property" have brought about a radical transformation of Karail's spatial structure over the last eight years. In the early days everyone built their own hut, to which they gradually added shared washrooms and cooking areas in an inner courtyard: in this way, they secured enough room for the rapidly growing extended family or for additional family members arriving from the countryside. But following a devastating fire in 2005, individuals began to seize larger areas and to build on them rows of longish corrugated iron shacks with four to seven rooms, each measuring six to nine square metres, which were then rented out to families of up to seven persons. Such space-saving linearity imposed a geometric discipline on the settlement and created an alienating urban structure that resembles that of barracks in which narrow paths lined with windowless corrugated iron walls are in stark contrast to the vibrant market streets and winding older roads. In the last few years, from around 2012, these mallik have started to build more and more two-storey houses and partly replace the old ones by solid brick houses. The fact that this is causing the population density to increase, even double, too rapidly is a concern for some of the CBO leaders, who are mindful of the greater strain on the shaky infrastructure and its maintenance; few however worry about the quality of the buildings which, even when built by professional carpenters, is still poor.

All this gives me reason to draw three conclusions about "informal" self-sufficiency. Firstly, as the inhabitants of settlements like Karail are able to evolve sophisticated supply systems for water and electricity as well as effective practices

ten vier Wellblechwänden schwitzen oder ihr Schulbuch am Vortag einer wichtigen Prüfung ablegen müssen oder erschöpft über ihrer Nähmaschine einschlafen, würde auch ich immer noch daran glauben.

Noch bin ich hier; ein paar Tage lang steht noch der gelebte Alltag im Vordergrund. Bei Gesprächen und Begehungen erfahre ich vom Stand verschiedenster Bauvorhaben – ob Vergrößerungs- und Befestigungsarbeiten privater Wohnblöcke oder kollektiv vorangetriebene Infrastrukturmaßnahmen wie die Anlegestellen für die Boote, mit denen Karails Bewohner die südlich verlaufende Hauptstraße und das östlich gelegene Wohn- und Businessviertel Gulshan von der Halbinsel aus erreichen. Jedes Jahr vor dem Monsun müssen diese Anlegestellen wieder befestigt werden, damit sie dem Dauerregen und möglichen Überflutungen standhalten. Ebenso gehen Toiletten und Nasszellen, sofern nicht von NGOs gesponsert, auf gemeinsame Investitionen von benachbarten Familien zurück, die sie gemeinsam instand halten. Aktuell, im Zusammenhang mit der Legalisierung der Wasserversorgung im Basti, werden die selbst angelegten behelfsmäßigen Abwasserkanäle in kompletten Nachbarschaften ausgebaut.

Alle Infrastrukturmaßnahmen, auch wenn sie auf die Erstinitiative einer NGO zurückgehen, werden auf lokaler Ebene durch shomiti koordiniert. Diese Komitees sind unterschiedlich aufgestellt, je nachdem, wie aufwendig sie sind und welcher Natur ihre Aufgaben sind. Neben jenen, die für umfangreiche Interventionen ins Leben gerufen wurden, gibt es auch shomiti mit alltagspraktischen Anliegen, von der Anstellung von Straßenfegern bis zur punktuellen Instandsetzung einzelner Gassen, von der Entwicklung der Bazare zur Organisation von Kulturveranstaltungen bis hin zur Sammlung von Spenden für eine der 13 Moscheen des Basti. Ab und zu stoße ich auf die eher privaten Diskussionen der Mitglieder einer dritten shomiti-Kategorie, Karails unzählige Spargruppen. Die Spargruppen sichern für Einzelpersonen, deren Anlagen zur Eröffnung eines Bankkontos nicht ausreichen oder die wegen Überschuldung bei Kreditgebern bzw. NGOs vom Dorf fliehen und in der Stadt untertauchen mussten oder schlicht nicht polizeilich gemeldet sind, einen Zugang zum Bankwesen. Die mit den zusammengelegten Ersparnissen eröffneten gemeinschaftlichen Konten laufen unter dem Namen eines Mitglieds, das eine feste Anschrift in der Stadt, etwa bei Verwandten, vorweisen kann. Um zu vermeiden, dass letzteres mit dem Geld abhaut, setzen Karails Spargruppen auf einen praktischen Vorteil der dorfgebundenen, auf lokalen Netzwerken beruhenden Gesellschaft Bangladeschs, auf soziale Kontrolle: Ihre Mitglieder stammen jeweils aus ein und derselben Region.

Alle Initiativen, die in Karail eine Art Grundversorgung sicherstellen, können angesichts der permanenten staatlichen Vernachlässigung nur positiv bewertet werden. Allerdings handelt es sich dabei lediglich um segmentierte und unterfinanzierte Notlösungen: So teilen sich sechs bis zehn Hausfrauen eine einzige Kochstelle; so formieren sich morgens vor den Nassstellen, die ebenfalls gemeinsam benutzt werden müssen, demütigende Warteschlangen; so verursachen selbstgebastelte Gasleitungen und Stromnetze häufig Explosionen und Brände. Viele der Abwasserkanäle verlaufen unter freiem Himmel, an den Häusern entlang[5]; und im Banani Lake, der die ungefilterten Abwässer und einen Großteil des Mülls der Siedlung aufnimmt, gedeihen schädliche Algen und Pflanzen. Wasserbedingte Seuchen, darunter Typhus und Dengue-Fieber, brechen wie im Rest der Stadt vermehrt aus. Letztlich sind selbstorganisierte gegenüber funktionierenden öffentlichen Dienstleistungen meistens mit höheren Kosten für die Endnutzer verbunden. Vor allem dieses Thema – die Bedingungen und Kosten der Versorgung von nicht-autorisierten Siedlungen – wird im Diskurs über Informalität vernachlässigt. Warum problematisieren wir so selten, dass der Preis einer Stromeinheit bei jedem Weiterverkauf wächst oder dass für Grundgüter wie Strom und Wasser in einem Basti viel mehr bezahlt werden muss, als in offiziell angeschlossenen Wohngebieten?[6]

Zu diesem Sachverhalt, der die "informelle" Versorgung in einem mindestens zwiespältigen Licht erscheinen lässt, kommt das Problem hinzu, dass die Bezeichnung von selbstorganisierten Siedlungen als "informell" die Suggestion nährt, die Verhältnisse vor Ort seien unhierarchisch. Zwar leben alle Bewohner Karails unter prekären Bedingungen, in einem ökologisch und hygienisch beeinträchtigten Landstreifen, in dem es zu häufigen Überschwemmungen und Unfällen kommt; sie alle sind wegen Armut, Landverlusts oder Hochwasserkatastrophen aus ihren Heimatdörfern geflüchtet und bemängeln die Last der Migration, die enttäuschten Hoffnungen auf einen Neuanfang in der Großstadt. Aber sie sind nicht alle gleich. Ganz im Gegenteil, verschiedene Akteure schützen mit mehr oder weniger legitimen Mitteln die eigenen Vorteile: angefangen von denen, die für Strom und Gas außerordentliche Gebühren einziehen; über jene, die unter Berufung auf ein selbstzugeschriebenes Recht des Erstangekommenen eine Art Bodennutzungssteuer für das Errichten von Häusern auf "ihrem" Grund und Boden verlangen; bis zu denen, die stolz darauf sind, das Land von Nachbarn, die eine Vertreibung befürchteten, zu einem niedrigen Preis erworben und später gewinnbringend weiterverkauft zu haben.

Und was sollte ich zu den mächtigen mallik[7] sagen? Auf ihre cleveren Taktiken der "informellen Investition in Wohneigentum" geht die radikale Veränderung von Karails Raumaufteilung in den letzten acht Jahren zurück. In der Anfangszeit baute

sich jeder eine eigene Hütte, die nach und nach um gemeinsame Waschräume und Kochstellen im Innenhof ergänzt wurde: Auf diese Weise wurde genug Platz für die schnell wachsenden Großfamilien oder für weitere vom Land zuwandernde Angehörige sichergestellt. Nach einem verheerenden Brand im Jahr 2005 jedoch begannen Einzelpersonen, größere Gebiete zu beschlagnahmen und darauf meistens längliche Wellblechbaracken mit vier bis sieben Zimmern à 6–9 Quadratmeter zu errichten, die dann an bis zu siebenköpfige Familien vermietet wurden. Die platzsparende Bauform des Riegels hat der Siedlung eine geometrische Disziplinierung aufoktroyiert und ein befremdliches Stadtgefüge geschaffen, das dem

of land speculation and professionalised mass production of living space, the talk of "improvised", "spontaneous" or "unresolved" circumstances proves to be far removed from reality. There are rather tactics, sagacity and power at play when wealthier or stronger residents, also supported by political parties, organise water and electricity networks, monopolize valuable public space, displace neighbours and impose new rental agreements on them or take away their access to the water by building new rows of houses on stilts. Secondly, projects that require large initial investments or ongoing maintenance such as sewers, refuse collection and street lighting or surfacing, cannot be accomplished in a self-organised manner, which is why "informal" infrastructures invariably have serious shortcomings. Thirdly, the unfairly high prices which financially weak households have to pay for unofficial basic services, retarding the improvement of their own living conditions, reveal that the "informal" solutions (like the "informal" economy, which should require no or only intermittent support from the government) are not only counterproductive to real progress, but stand suspiciously close to neoliberal, laissez-faire approaches to development. To be smart, an urban solution, as well as a business, must be equally accessible and affordable for diverse social groups, but above all for the most vulnerable.

This last aspect challenges the myth of informality as an "organising logic" of urbanisation. What is being organised? For whom, for how many? The experiences in Karail Basti, which represents a paradigmatic case of "self-organisation vis-à-vis an urbanisation process based on the unequal distribution of resources", show that although this logic may help organise improvements and services, it leaves unchallenged obsolete norms such as obedience and dependence on protectors (for lack of democratically legitimised structures, it rather supports those) and enduring inequalities concerning the housing and living conditions of the cities' inhabitants. Neither the private sector nor self-organised communities are able and authorised to ensure a just access to the essential resources: this is, still, clearly the task of governments and states – yes, the "formal" sector. After all, to date the latter are the only actors that can provide answers to the question (rarely addressed in academic circles, but increasingly pushed forward by urban dwellers) of the recognition or legalisation of unauthorised settlements in the form of progressive, enabling laws. To remain with the role of research: these days, academics contribute with terms such as "smart informality", "shadow cities" and all kinds of "urbanisms", along with novels, films and comics, to a colourful hagiography of urban life, wherein a positivist, if not mystifying, interpretation of the latter predominates. This inclination to fictionalise stems in part from the pressure to publish and from

einer Kaserne ähnelt – der Kontrast zwischen den vielen schmalen, von fensterlosen Wellblechfronten gesäumten Wegen und den belebten Geschäftsstraßen sowie den weniger geradlinigen älteren Wegen könnte kaum krasser sein. In den letzten Jahren, etwa seit 2012, werden indessen immer mehr zweistöckige Häuser gebaut und teilweise durch stabile Backsteinbauten ersetzt. Dass sich dadurch die Bevölkerungsdichte noch schneller entwickelt, gar verdoppelt, kümmert einige der CBO-Leader, die an die höheren Lasten für die wackelige Infrastruktur und deren Instandhaltung denken; um die Qualität der Bauten, die wenngleich von professionellen Zimmerleuten errichtet, weiterhin mangelhaft bleiben, machen sich jedoch die Wenigsten Sorge.

Das Ganze erlaubt drei Schlussfolgerungen über die "informelle" Selbstversorgung. Erstens: In Siedlungen wie Karail bestehen ausgefeilte Liefersysteme für Wasser und Strom sowie erprobte Praktiken der Bodenspekulation und der professionalisierten Massenproduktion von Wohnraum, sodass sich die Rede von "improvisierten", "spontanen" oder "ungeklärten" Verhältnissen als realitätsfern erweist. Es sind Taktik, Kalkül und Machtspiele am Werk, wenn reichere bzw. stärkere Bewohner, auch von politischen Parteien unterstützt, Wasser- und Stromleitungen organisieren, kostbaren offenen Raum vereinnahmen, Nachbarn vertreiben und zu neuen Mietverhältnissen zwingen oder ihnen durch neue Häuserreihen auf Stelzen die Wassernähe nehmen. Zweitens: Belange, die große Startinvestitionen oder kontinuierliche Pflege erfordern, wie beispielsweise Kanalisation, Müllsammlung, Straßenbeleuchtung und -pflasterung, lassen sich selbstorganisiert nicht bewerkstelligen, weshalb "informelle" Infrastrukturen immer gravierende Unzulänglichkeiten aufweisen. Drittens: Der ungerecht hohe Preis, den finanziell schwache Haushalte für die inoffizielle Grundversorgung bezahlen müssen, hindert sie an der Verbesserung der eigenen, ohnehin schweren Lebensbedingungen und lässt die "informellen" Lösungen (ebenso wie die "informelle" Ökonomie, die keiner oder nur punktueller Unterstützung durch den Staat bedürfen soll) als liberalistisch gefärbte und entwicklungspolitisch kontraproduktive Hülle aufscheinen. Smart ist eine urbane Lösung, ebenso wie ein Business, nur, wenn die verschiedenen Gesellschaftsgruppen, vor allem aber die fragilsten, gleichberechtigt Zugang dazu haben.

Vor allem dieser letzte Aspekt bringt den Mythos der Informalität als "organisierende Logik" der Urbanisierung ins Wanken. Was wird organisiert? Für wen, für wie viele? Die Erfahrungen in Karail Basti, das als paradigmatischer Fall in puncto "Selbstorganisation vor dem Hintergrund einer auf ungleicher Ressourcenverteilung beruhenden Urbanisierung" angesehen werden kann, zeigen, dass anhand dieser vermeintlichen Logik Verbesserungsmaßnahmen und Dienstleistungen zwar organisiert, aber überkommene Normen wie Gehorsam und Abhängigkeit von Protektoren sowie wesentliche Ungleichheiten hinsichtlich der Wohn- und Lebensqualität der Stadtbewohner nicht überholt werden können (mangels demokratisch legitimierter Strukturen werden diese doch noch verstärkt). Weder der Privatsektor noch selbstorganisierte Gemeinschaften sind dazu fähig oder legitimiert, einen gerechten, also universellen Zugang zu lebenswichtigen Ressourcen sicherzustellen: Dies ist, noch, die eindeutige Aufgabe von Regierungen und Staaten – ja, dem "formellen Sektor". Schließlich sind letztere die einzigen Akteure, die der

short research periods, but also from the huge complexity of the social phenomena occurring simultaneously in and around the cities. Because today's technologies make it easier for the increasingly mobile scientist to compare such phenomena on a global scale, it also becomes more tempting to find broader, all-embracing or universal explanations. The suggestive adjectives and metaphors that are mostly deployed to this goal, however, provide little information about the process(es) occurring behind the phenomena. This is what I mean by the "idealisation through overuse" of the term "informality": we are making attempts to bundle disparate phenomena together under one term, which itself belongs more to the phenomenological than the analytical sphere. When something that deviates from the conventional forms of social organisation is described as "informal", our understanding of this object, way of life or phenomenon does not actually increase. Forms, as well as their deviations, are part of the world of perception and phenomena; if we wish to understand and not merely describe these, then we must delve into the world of processes, i.e., of the production of space in capitalist regimes. But since this only leads to focus the responsibilities and irreversible shortcomings of a system which, as we already know, wreaks havoc on the preconditions of human beings' existence on this earth, I will pursue another idea.

Among the many labels circulating in the discourse, from occupancy urbanism or subaltern urbanism to radical urbanism, planetary urbanism could seem to be little more than one additional variant. But the term "urbanism" has always evoked the sense of a challenge to design or plan, and the challenge of training a global view when designing and planning our habitat, which resonates in the term "planetary urbanism", should be taken very seriously – also with regard to the so-called "upgrading of slums", which after all is an important factor of urban planning, development cooperation and of course, economic cooperation (not least for the cement industry!). When the majority today claim that an all-encompassing solution for the problems associated with complex urban phenomena cannot be defined and that specific developments in places as disparate as Dhaka, Lagos, Vienna, Hangzhou, Berlin or Tehran cannot be steered by means of one and the same formula, it seems no less than astonishing that self-organised settlements all over the world are still just called "slums". The living conditions that characterise them as well as the local reasons – whether environmental catastrophes, epidemics, social conflicts or economic dependencies – that led to their formation are viewed in a way that is not only non-specific, but also unhistorical.

Trapped in such a stance, the design and planning disciplines can only regard self-organised settlements such as Karail Basti as inferior physical spaces that must be "upgraded", regulated and better managed. If a planetary perspective were applied, then these settlements would have to be first of all taken seriously in their quality of complex social spaces that are rapidly expanding worldwide. In a further step, the observers might then detect, in their everyday tactics, valid approaches for a self-organised life, and thus for human subsistence in the course of this century. Because every day, their inhabitants – partly without any development programmes and ignored, if not oppressed, by their own governments – refine tactics of social cohesion based on an accepted shortage of resources, which is turned into a motive for collective action (rather than hysterical extractivism). In other words: vis-à-vis questions of social-political deliberation and production, they bank on inventiveness, practical reason as well as process-oriented, locally specific and immanent solutions, whereby they also keep room for enjoyment and conviviality. When frigid talks of rationalistic "austerity" are putting at risk entire populations' lust for life, these emerge as the precise solutions that the current discussion about resilience, that is about appropriate forms of subsistence or resistance for the twenty-first century, calls for.

They are still there. We can still visit them; we can still meet their inhabitants with humility, with our eyes wide open and with the aid of translators, when our language skills prove inadequate. Their everyday struggle for dignified housing and living conditions in the cities and not on their outer fringes can still be supported, too. It still makes sense to work and to research, to hope and to write, to smile and to dream – as long as they are still there.

Elisa T. Bertuzzo has conducted research in Karail Basti as part of the Habitat Forum Berlin team since 2007.

Frage der Anerkennung bzw. Legalisierung von selbstorganisierten Siedlungen – eine Frage, die in der Wissenschaft seltener behandelt, aber von Stadtbewohnern weltweit immer vehementer gestellt wird – Antworten in Form von progressiven, befähigenden Gesetzen geben könnten.

Bleiben wir bei der Rolle der Wissenschaft. Heutzutage tragen Akademiker mit anmutenden Begriffen wie smart informality, shadow cities und allerlei Urbanismen neben Romanen, Filmen und Comics zu einer bunten Hagiographie des Städtischen bei, wobei eine positivistische, wenn nicht mystifizierende Deutung des Städtischen vorherrscht. Dieser Hang zur Fiktionalisierung geht zum Teil auf Publikationsdruck und kurze Recherchezeiten zurück, zum Teil aber auch auf die gewaltige Komplexität der heute gleichzeitig stattfindenden sozialen Phänomene in den Städten und um sie herum. Da es die heutigen Technologien für die selbst zunehmend mobilen Wissenschaftler einfacher machen, solche Phänomene auf globaler Ebene zu vergleichen, wird auch die Versuchung größer, all- bzw. weltumfassende Erklärungen zu erfinden. Dazu werden des Öfteren suggestive Adjektive und Metaphern engagiert, die wenig Auskunft über den sich hinter den Phänomenen abwickelnden Prozess geben. Das ist, was ich unter "Verklärung durch Überbeanspruchung" des Informalität-Begriffs meine: Es wird versucht, disparate Phänomene durch einen Begriff zusammen zu bündeln, der selbst eher zur phänomenologischen denn zur analytischen Sphäre gehört. Indem etwas, das von den üblichen Formen des sozialen Zusammenhalts abweicht, als "informell" bezeichnet wird, wächst dessen Verständnis faktisch nicht. Formen ebenso wie ihre Abweichungen gehören zur Welt der Wahrnehmung und der Phänomene; wollen wir diese begreifen und nicht nur beschreiben, so müssen wir in die Welt der Prozesse, d.h. der Produktion des Raums in kapitalistischen Regimes eintauchen. Aber da dies lediglich dazu führt, die Verantwortungen und nicht wieder gut zu machenden Schäden eines Systems zu fokussieren, das bekanntlich die Bedingungen des Lebens der Menschen auf dieser Erde zerstört, bringe ich einen anderen Gedanken ein.

Unter vielen in der Fachdebatte kursierenden Labels, von occupancy urbanism über subaltern urbanism zu radical urbanism, könnte planetary urbanism nichts Anderes als eine weitere Variante sein. Doch im Begriff "urbanism", also Stadtplanung, schwingt eine gestalterische bzw. planerische Aufforderung mit und die Aufforderung, bei Gestaltung und Planung unseres Habitats einen planetarischen Blick zu trainieren, sollte ernst genommen werden – auch im Bereich des sogenannten "Upgrading von Slums", das ein wichtiger Faktor der Stadtplanung, der Entwicklungszusammenarbeit sowie der wirtschaftlichen Kooperation (die Zementindustrie winkt) ist. Wenn die meisten heute beteuern, dass sich eine allumfassende Lösung für die Probleme, die mit komplexen städtischen Phänomenen einhergehen, nicht definieren lässt und dass spezifische Entwicklungen an so unterschiedlichen Orten wie Dhaka, Lagos, Wien, Hangzhou, Berlin oder Teheran nicht anhand ein und derselben Formel gesteuert werden können, so erscheint es mindestens erstaunlich, dass die weltweit verbreiteten selbstorganisierten Siedlungen in der Fachdiskussion immer noch nur "Slums" genannt werden. Dabei werden die für sie typischen Lebensbedingungen – ebenso wie die lokalen Gründe, ob ökologische Katastrophen, Epidemien, soziale Unruhen oder wirtschaftliche Abhängigkeiten, die zu ihrer Ausbildung führen – nicht nur unspezifisch, sondern unhistorisch betrachtet.

In einer solchen Haltung verkapselt, können die gestaltenden und Planungsdisziplinen nicht-autorisierte Siedlungen wie Karail Basti nur als minderwertige physische Räume auffassen, die es "aufzuwerten", zu reglementieren und besser zu verwalten gilt. Würde ein planetarischer Blick angewandt, so würde zunächst begriffen, dass diese Siedlungen komplexe, weltweit rasant wachsende soziale Räume sind und ernst genommen werden müssen. Im weiteren Schritt könnte es dann gelingen, dass in ihnen valide Ansätze selbstorganisierten Lebens und somit Ansätze für die menschliche Subsistenz im Laufe des begonnenen Jahrhunderts erkannt werden. Denn ihre Bewohner verfeinern täglich – teilweise an Entwicklungsprogrammen vorbei und von den eigenen Regierungen ignoriert, wenn nicht unterdrückt – Taktiken des Zusammenhalts auf der Grundlage einer akzeptierten Knappheit von Ressourcen, welche zum Anlass kollektiven Aushandelns (anstatt hysterischen Extraktivismus) gemacht wird. Mit anderen Worten: Bei Fragen sowohl der Deliberation als auch der Produktion setzen sie auf Erfindungsreichtum, praktischen Sinn sowie auf prozesshafte, lokalspezifische, immanente Lösungen, wobei Freude und Geselligkeit stets ihren Platz haben. In Zeiten, da rationalistische Reden von Austerität die Lebenslust gesamter Bevölkerungsgruppen in Gefahr setzen, sind das die Lösungen, auf die sich die Diskussion rund um die Resilienz, also um geeignete Subsistenz- bzw. Widerstandsformen für das 21. Jahrhundert, berufen sollte.

Noch stehen sie da. Noch können wir sie besuchen; noch können wir mit Demut, offenen Augen und der Hilfe von Übersetzern, wenn unsere Sprachkenntnisse nicht ausreichen, ihren Bewohnern begegnen. Auch ihr alltäglicher Kampf für würdige Wohn- und Lebensbedingungen in den Städten, und nicht an deren äußersten Rändern, kann noch unterstützt werden. Noch hat es Sinn, zu arbeiten und zu forschen, zu hoffen und zu schreiben. Solange sie noch da sind.

Elisa T. Bertuzzo forscht seit 2007 im Habitat Forum Berlin-Team über Karail Basti.

Every 6 months, people of Karail get together to compile a map of their settlement that will be used to facilitate the planning and coordination of infrastructural interventions. These community maps are drawn collectively on sheets of brown paper of approximately A0 size and, along with demographic information gathered by the members, mirror the slightest socio-spatial transformations in the basti.

CIDADE DE DEUS – A BIOGRAPHY

Marc Angélil, Rainer Hehl,
in collaboration with Something Fantastic

"What has been considered as a problem, the favela, offers very specific solutions to the question of housing the masses – what is meant to be the solution, state-sponsored mass housing, represents the real problem for urban developments."
John F.C. Turner, 1968[1]

An evolutionary biography of a social housing misconception

1961: Announcement of the Alliance for Progress program
In March 1961, US president John F. Kennedy announced the Alliance for Progress program as "a vast cooperative effort, unparalleled in magnitude and nobility of purpose"[2] to promote economic growth and political reform in Latin America. In the aftermath of the Cuban Revolution, the program promoted US values with the belief that capitalism can be universally applied to foster economic growth.

1966: Completion of Cidade de Deus, City of God
As part of the Alliance for Progress, Brazilian municipal housing agency CO-HAB received almost $4.5 million in loans to construct several housing complexes on Rio's peripheries.[3] One of these was Cidade de Deus, giving home to more than 3000 families relocated from 23 favelas (illegal squatting in Brazilian cities). Identical tiny houses arranged in neat rows like in American suburbs and identical five-story apartments were cheaply built, providing the bare minimum. As a standardized mass housing solution, its origin traces back to

CIAM's Charta of Athens, as a means of teaching the urban poor to form new habits of hygiene and health. Under the umbrella of the modernist ideal is nevertheless a marriage between government's ambition for economic status and speculators' desire for central land occupied by favelas. Instead of facing urban poverty as a reality, the agenda was to create a new middle class out of low-income groups while modernizing society as a whole.[4]

2003: Worldwide release of film "City of God"
The popular hit film stereotyped Cidade de Deus as a no-go area – a ghetto, where its inhabitants are trapped between violent crime and corrupted police. Set between the end of 1960s and the beginning of 1980s, the film showed how the purified modern settlement grew over the years into a neo-favela; how a capitalist dream faded into criminality and social decay.

2009: Pacification of Cidade de Deus
As part of the community-policing model UPP (the Police Pacification Units), police presence was increased in Rio's various favelas to combat crime and ensure safety, arguably as preparation for the 2016 Summer Olympic Games. In Cidade de Deus, as police officers moved in and drug traffickers were driven out, murder rate was reported to have fallen from 36 in 2008 to 5 in 2012.[5]

2011: Introduction of a local currency in Cidade de Deus
Pacification brought about an immediate increase of property value[6], which

"Was als ein Problem gilt – die Favela –, liefert sehr spezifische Lösungen für die Frage des Massenwohnungsbaus, während das, was man gemeinhin als Lösung betrachtet – der staatlich geförderte Massenwohnungsbau –, das wahre Problem der Stadtentwicklung ist."
John F.C. Turner, 1968[1]

Die Entwicklungsstadien einer falschen Vorstellung von Sozialem Wohnungsbau

1961: Verkündung des Programms der "Allianz für den Fortschritt"
Im März 1961 verkündete US-Präsident John F. Kennedy das Programm der "Allianz für den Fortschritt" und bezeichnete es als "einen gewaltigen, gemeinsamen Versuch, der an Größe und Erhabenheit seiner Zielsetzung nicht seinesgleichen hat"[2]; dabei bezog er sich auf die Förderung des Wirtschaftswachstums und der Demokratisierung in Lateinamerika. Angesichts der Kubanischen Revolution propagierte das Programm US-amerikanische Werte in der Überzeugung, der Kaptalismus sei das ideale Instrument zu einer weltweiten Förderung des Wirtschaftswachstums.

1966: Fertigstellung der Cidade de Deus
Im Rahmen der "Allianz für den Fortschritt" erhielt die städtische Wohnungsbaugesellschaft COHAB Kredite in Höhe von fast 4,5 Millionen Dollar, um eine Reihe von Wohnkomplexen an der Peripherie von Rio de Janeiro zu errichten.[3] Einer dieser Komplexe war die Cidade de Deus, in der mehr als dreitausend, aus dreiundzwanzig Favelas (illegal errichtete Barackensiedlungen in brasilianischen Städten) stammende Familien untergebracht wurden. Identische, wie in amerikanischen Vororten in ordentlichen Reihen angeordnete Häuschen und identische fünfstöckige Wohngebäude wurden in Billigbauweise aus dem Boden gestampft; in Sachen Komfort erfüllten diese nicht mehr als die Mindestanforderungen. Die Ursprünge dieser standardisierten Lösung für das Problem des Massenwohnungsbaus gingen auf die vom CIAM formulierte Charta von Athen zurück, und das Ziel bestand darin, hygienischere und gesündere Wohnbedingungen für die arme Stadtbevölkerung zu schaffen. Unter dem Schirm der Ideale der Moderne kam es indes zu einem Pakt zwischen Regierung und Spekulanten, mit dem Erstere den ökonomischen Status erhöhen und Letztere sich den innerhalb der Stadt gelegenen, von Favelas besetzten Grund und Boden unter den Nagel reißen wollten. Anstatt die städtische Armut als eine Realität zu betrachten, bestand die Agenda darin, aus Bevölkerungsschichten mit niedrigem Einkommen eine neue Mittelschicht zu bilden und gleichzeitig die Gesellschaft insgesamt zu modernisieren.[4]

2003: Weltweiter Kinostart des Films "City of God"
Dieser Erfolgsfilm porträtierte die Cidade de Deus als eine No-go-Area, als ein Ghetto, dessen Bewohner ihr Leben in einem Sumpf aus Gewaltverbrechen und Polizeikorruption fristeten. Der zwischen dem Ende der 1960er und dem Beginn der 1980er Jahre spielende Film zeigte, wie sich die saubere, moderne Wohnsiedlung im Laufe der Zeit in eine neue Favela verwandelte – wie ein kapitalistischer Traum in Kriminalität und sozialem Niedergang endete.

might lead to gentrification or property trade. To build resistance against the incorporation into the market economy, a local currency was introduced to stimulate local informal commerce. The community bank also offers loans for small businesses and invests in community projects.[3]

2013: Publication of the book "Cidade de Deus – City of God"

In collaboration with "Something Fantastic" a research program was initiated as part of the master program "Advanced studies in Urban Design" at the ETH Zürich to study the case of Cidade de Deus. The result is a book documenting the informal practice and asserting its positive aspects. As the original houses become hardly recognizable amidst extensions; informally built kiosks, garages, gardens and workshops form a new streetscape. The harsh divisions are softened; empty spaces are filled; daily social interactions are enabled.

2032:....?

Brazil pledges to cut carbon emissions by 37% by 2025.[7] The building sector accounts for around 44% of its overall energy consumption. Meanwhile three million new homes are to be built in seven years to resolve the housing deficit, according to the 2009 program "Minha Casa, Minha Vida". Instead of giving favelas the due credit and assistance, Brazil is building more low-density, mono-functional and car-reliant settlements, which would further offset an urban problem to a larger urban footprint and create a new generation of suburban ghettos.[8]

On the contrary, by seeing favelas as a starting point for a model of incremental urban growth, authors of the book "Cidade de Deus – City of God" envision "a marvelous city 2032". To achieve that, archipelago structures are designed as top-down stimulators to hold public functions; while bottom-up and do-it-yourself construction is assisted by a catalogue of patterns so that inhabitants could gradually upgrade their own homes.

The future of our planet lies in our vision of urbanity. A compact city is one solution; the compactness, self-organization, and diversity of favelas provide surprising inspirations.[9] One might say that the marvelous city 2032 is optimistic and not aesthetically pleasing to everyone, but what if this is the only way left?

•

All images are from the book
Cidade de Deus – City of God
Marc Angélil & Rainer Hehl (Eds.),
in collaboration with Something Fantastic (Leonard Streich, Elena Schütz und Julian Schubert)
Berlin 2013, Ruby Press.
ISBN: 978-3-944074-02-3

2009: Pazifizierung der Cidade de Deus

Im Rahmen des polizeilichen Gemeindeüberwachungs-Modells UPP (die Abkürzung steht für die polizeilichen Pazifizierungs-Einheiten) wurde die Polizeipräsenz in Rios diversen Favelas erhöht, um die Kriminalität zu bekämpfen und um für mehr Sicherheit zu sorgen, wohl in Vorbereitung auf die Olympischen Sommerspiele von 2016. Nachdem die Polizeibeamten in die Cidade de Deus eingezogen und die Drogenhändler von dort vertrieben worden waren, soll die Zahl der jährlichen Mordfälle von sechsunddreißig im Jahr 2008 auf fünf im Jahr 2012 gesunken sein.[5]

2011: Einführung einer lokalen Währung für die Cidade de Deus

Eine Folge der Pazifizierung war der sofortige Anstieg der Grundstückspreise[6,] eine Entwicklung, die Gentrifizierung und Immobilienspekulation Vorschub leistet. Um sich nicht völlig von der Marktwirtschaft vereinnahmen zu lassen, wurde eine lokalen Währung eingeführt, die den informellen örtlichen Handelsverkehr stimulieren soll. Die Gemeindebank vergibt nicht nur Darlehen an Kleinunternehmer, sondern investiert auch in Gemeindeprojekte.[3]

2013: Veröffentlichung des Buchs "Cidade de Deus – City of God"

Gemeinsam mit "Something Fantastic" fand im Rahmen des Masterstudiengangs "Advanced Studies in Urban Design" an der ETH Zürich ein Forschungsprogramm zur Untersuchung des Falls der Cidade de Deus statt. Daraus resultierte ein Buch, das die informellen Praktiken der Favela-Bewohner dokumentiert und deren positive Aspekte herausgearbeitet. Während die ursprünglichen Häuser wegen ihrer Anbauten kaum noch zu erkennen sind, bilden informell errichtete Kioske, Garagen, Gärten und Werkstätten eine neue Straßenlandschaft. Die strengen Aufteilungen werden gemildert; leere Räume werden gefüllt; tägliche soziale Interaktionen werden ermöglicht.

2032:....?

Brasilien hat sich verpflichtet, seine Kohlendioxidemissionen bis zum Jahr 2025 um 37 % zu verringern.[7] Der Bausektor ist für etwa 44 % des brasilianischen Energieverbrauchs verantwortlich. Laut dem 2009 verabschiedeten Programm "Minha Casa, Minha Vida" sollen in sieben Jahren drei Millionen neue Wohnungen gebaut werden, um den Wohnungsmangel zu beheben. Anstatt den Favelas die ihnen gebührende finanzielle Hilfe und anderweitige Unterstützung zukommen zu lassen, baut Brasilien noch mehr monofunktionale, auf privaten Autoverkehr angewiesene Wohnsiedlungen mit niedriger Bebauungsdichte, eine Entwicklung, die womöglich zu einem zusätzlichen urbanen Problem, einem größeren städtischen Fußabdruck, führt und eine neue Generation von vorstädtischen Ghettos schaffen könnte.[8]

Im Gegensatz dazu stellen sich die Autoren des Buchs "Cidade de Deus – City of Good" eine "herrliche Stadt 2032" vor und betrachten die Favelas als Ausgangspunkt für ein schrittweises städtisches Wachstum. Um das zu erreichen, werden, als "top-down"-Stimulatoren, insulare, einen Archipel bildende Gebäude entworfen, die öffentliche Funktionen beherbergen sollen. Das "bottom-up"- und "Do-it-yourself"-Bauen wird durch einen Musterkatalog unterstützt, sodass die Bewohner ihre eigenen Häuser und Wohnungen nach und nach verbessern können.

Die Zukunft unseres Planeten hängt von unserem Verständnis von Stadt ab. Eine kompakte Stadt wäre eine Lösung; die Kompaktheit, die Selbstorganisation und die bunte Vielfalt der Favelas sorgen für überraschende Inspirationen.[9] Man könnte sagen, die "herrliche Stadt 2032" sei zu optimistisch und nicht nach jedermanns Geschmack, doch womöglich ist sie die einzige uns noch verbliebene Möglichkeit.
Text: Zhen Zhang

1966: Aerial image of Cidade de Deus. Constructed on the periphery of Rio de Janeiro, the housing project was cut off from both public transportation and amenities.

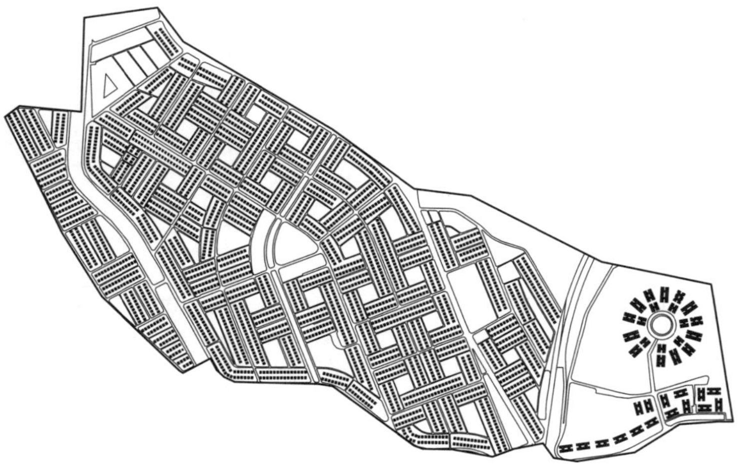

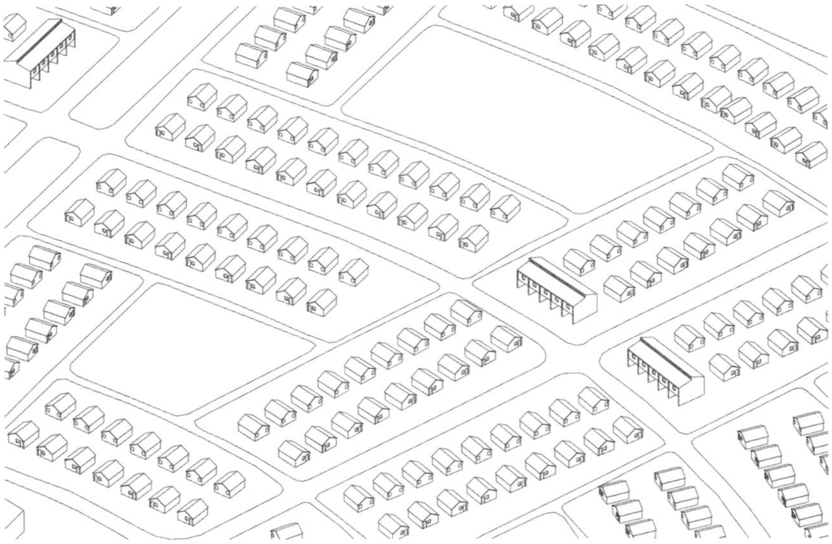

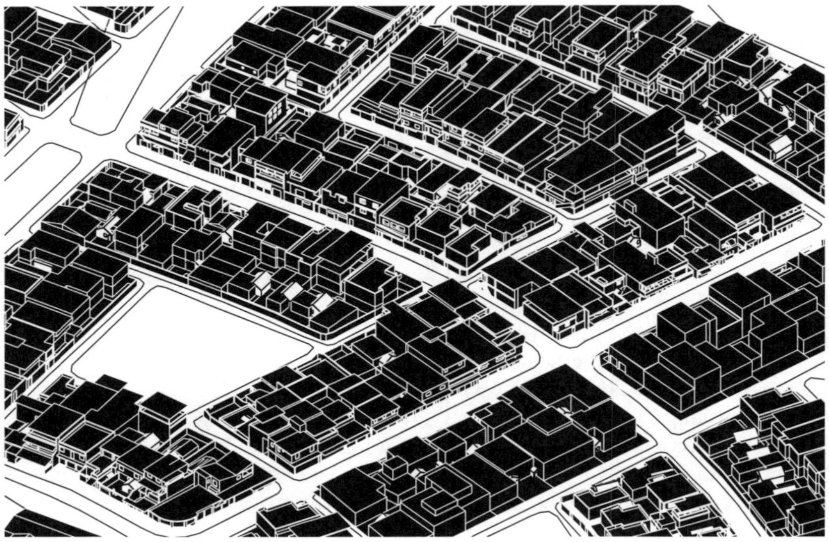

top left
1966: Cidade de Deus' first layout

top right
Like American suburbs, multiple similar
houses were arranged in neat rows and
blocks surrounding an open field.

middle left
2012: Informal growth has inverted the
relationship between figure and ground.

middle right
The original houses are hardly recognizable
amidst the informally built extensions.

bottom
How was the transformation taking place
between 1966 and 2012? The history of four
lots explains how houses in CDD are gradually transformed over time. First, lots were
enclosed by walls and fences and extensions
were added to the ground floor. Further
steps saw the construction of additional
floors. In most cases, the original house
was entirely replaced.

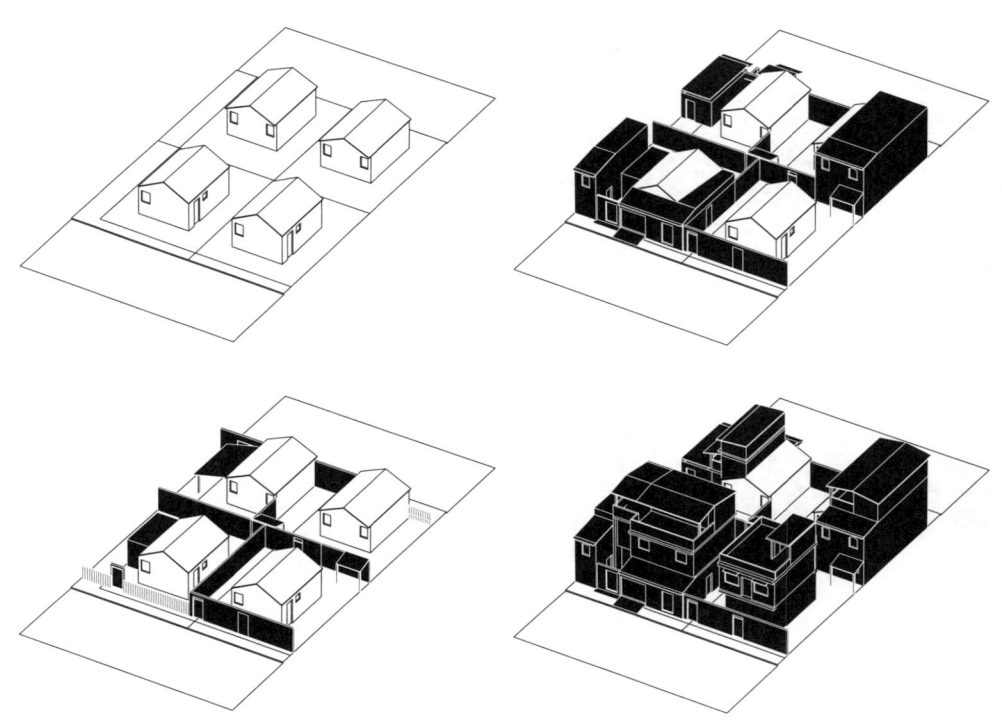

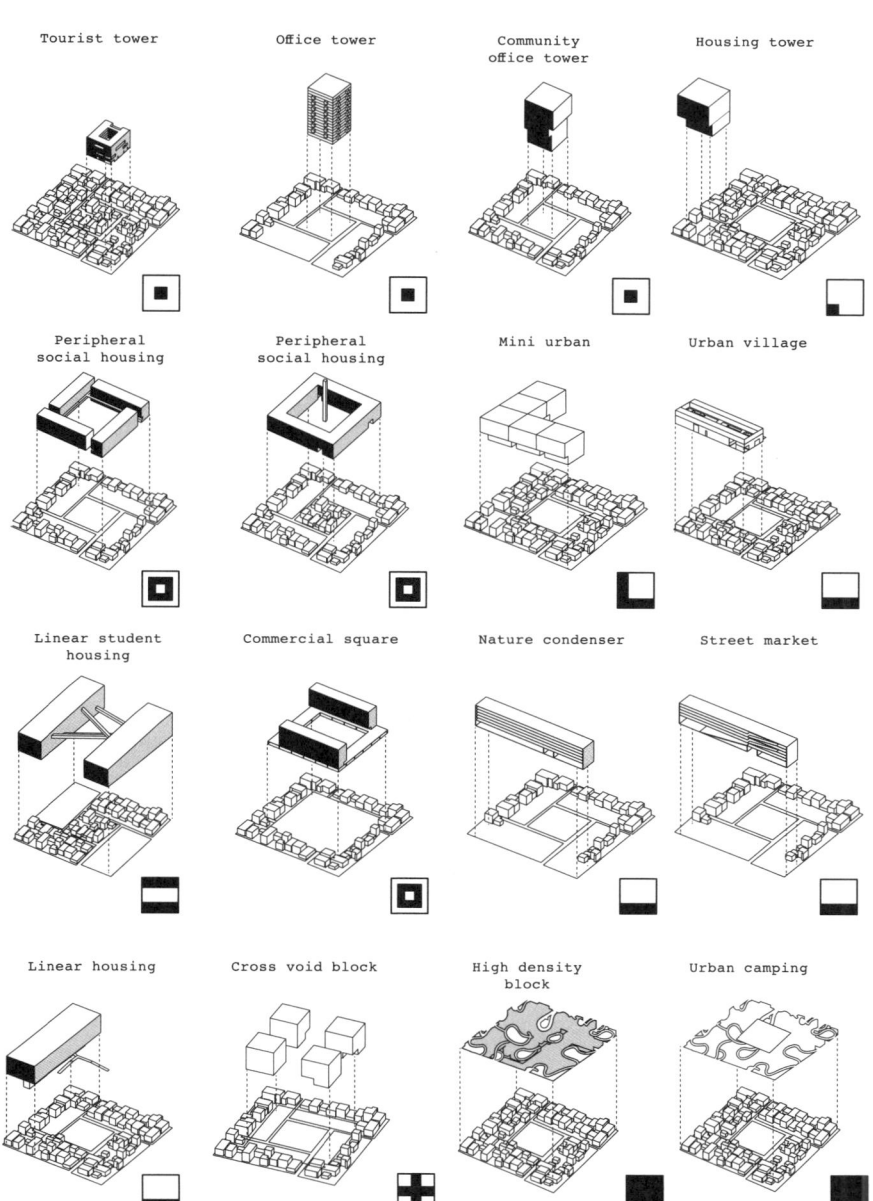

Tourist tower

Office tower

Community office tower

Housing tower

Peripheral social housing

Peripheral social housing

Mini urban

Urban village

Linear student housing

Commercial square

Nature condenser

Street market

Linear housing

Cross void block

High density block

Urban camping

left
Each layer is developed into an architectural design that defines the buildings' volume. The starting point of each prototype is the design of its open spaces.

right
CDD's population density compared to other city centers. Note that CDD's population density is greater than that of Manhattan.

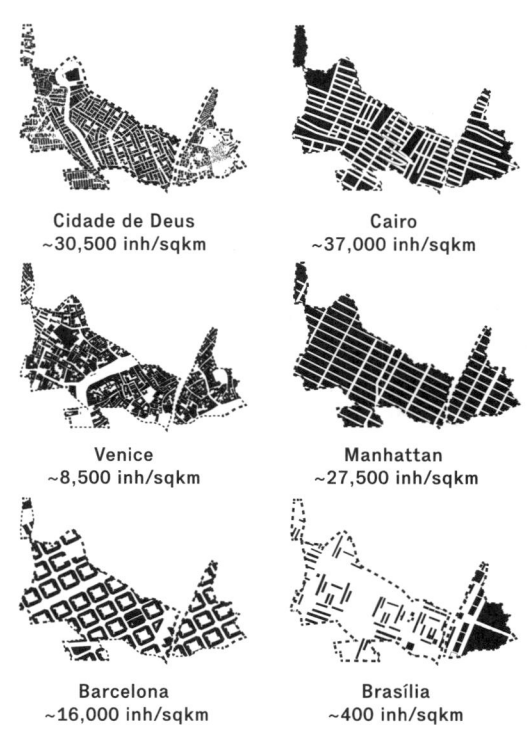

Cidade de Deus
~30,500 inh/sqkm

Cairo
~37,000 inh/sqkm

Venice
~8,500 inh/sqkm

Manhattan
~27,500 inh/sqkm

Barcelona
~16,000 inh/sqkm

Brasília
~400 inh/sqkm

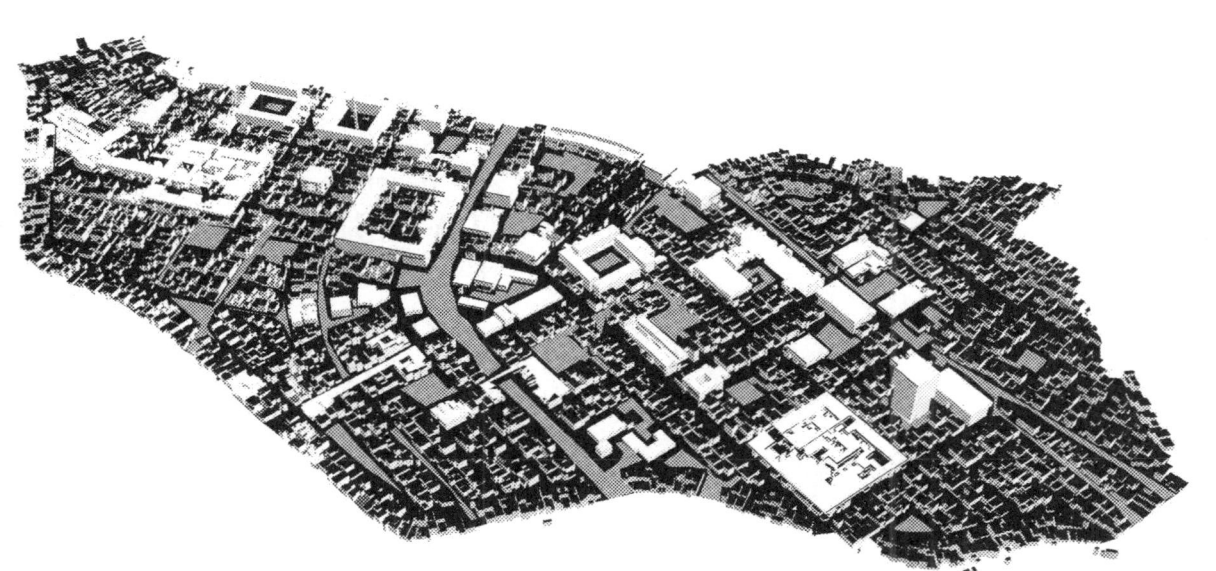

left
Introducing layers into the existing fabric is better suited to the area's informalization processes. Additional layers are not forced upon the area as organizational structure but as catalysts that encourage user-driven development. The sedimented city is formed by constantly updating existing structures with new programs, technologies, and building fragments.

following page
The following page includes a selection of posters that were displayed in Cidade de Deus and in an exhibition at Studio-X, Rio de Janeiro, to communicate to locals MAS's views and ideas on informal urbanization. The posters assemble existing and future inventions to create a pool for sharing and exchanging knowledge. Operating on various scales, these ideas hold the potential of further developing Cidade de Deus into an exemplary model of a marvelous city in 2032, which is inspired by CDD but also points beyond it.

CIDADE DE DEUS!

A marvelous city is a great place—to live, to work, to learn, to love. A marvelous city is safe, children can play outside, shops are never far, and you can rely on your neighbor. It is compact, lively, and welcoming to strangers. It provides facilities, schools, community spaces, and sport fields for everyone, and gratis. A marvelous city is democratic, fair, and inclusive; everybody is free and everybody feels part of the city, because everybody is the city. Collective needs and individual wishes are perfectly balanced. Nature is everywhere and everything is natural in a marvelous city. The architecture of a marvelous city is simple, smart, and beautiful; It adapts to the needs and possibilities of its inhabitants. A marvelous city is one among other marvelous cities, all with their own identities and singularites. Cidade de Deus is the Marvelous City 2032.

The 2032 Marvellous City Award goes to:

CIDADE DE DEUS!

26 Destaques que fazem uma cidade melhor!

Destaque No 13:
A Estrutura-Estante

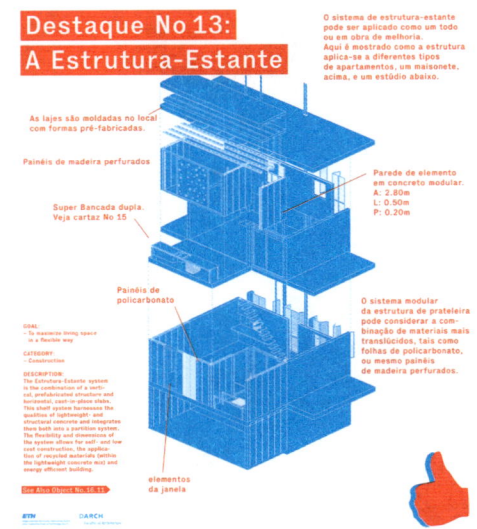

O sistema de estrutura-estante pode ser aplicado como um todo ou em obra de melhoria. Aqui é mostrado como a estrutura aplica-se a diferentes tipos de apartamentos, um maisonete, acima, e um estúdio abaixo.

As lajes são moldadas no local com formas pré-fabricadas.

Painéis de madeira perfurados.

Super Bancada dupla.
Veja cartaz No 15

Parede de elemento em concreto modular.
A: 2.80m
L: 0.50m
P: 0.20m

Painéis de policarbonato.

O sistema modular da estrutura de prateleira pode considerar a combinação de materiais mais translúcidos, tais como folhas de policarbonato, ou mesmo painéis de madeira perfurados.

elementos da janela.

The 2032 Marvellous City Award goes to:

CIDADE DE DEUS!

26 Destaques que fazem uma cidade melhor!

Destaque No 11:
Moeda Local

Da população para a população, a moeda local permite a circulação de bens, dinheiro e realça o espírito de comunidade.

O dinheiro economizado na compra de mantimentos e produtos trazem uma nova visão à comunidade. A riqueza produzida internamente circula entre os moradores, criando uma nova realidade na Cidade de Deus. A moeda local segue a economia informal, o pequeno comércio e torna todos ainda mais fortes.

The 2032 Marvelous City Award goes to:

CIDADE DE DEUS!

26 Destaques que fazem uma cidade melhor!

Destaque No 18:
Telha Reflectora

Durante o Verão, a Telha reflectora chuta os raios do sol de volta para a atmosfera!

Em Inverno el Sol pode entrar profundamente no pátio!

The 2032 Marvelous City Award goes to:

CIDADE DE DEUS!

26 Destaques que fazem uma cidade melhor!

Destaque No 21:
Iluminação Portátil

Com a luz vem de segurança, com pessoal de segurança e com as pessoas vem a alegria.

O refletor de luz pode funcionar tanto como elemento para gerar sombra, quanto coletor de água da chuva.

A base é projetada para permanecer em qualquer superfície também com a ajuda do acréscimo do peso da água.

A luz pode ser gerada adicionando água da chuva assim como água salgada

Produz-se tanto iluminação direta, quanto indireta.

The 2032 Marvelous City Award goes to:

CIDADE DE DEUS!

26 Destaques que fazem uma cidade melhor!

Destaque No 19:
Grade
Noite & Dia

Durante o dia as barras de ferro levantadas funcionam como um perfeito varal.

Durante a noite, ou geralmente quando os moradores estão fora de casa, a grade garante segurança extra contra invasores.

The 2032 Marvelous City Award goes to:

CIDADE DE DEUS!

26 Destaques que fazem uma cidade melhor!

Destaque No 2:
Casa Multifamiliar

As famílias crescem e se multiplicam, a ampliação informal das moradias tornam-se necessárias conforme as diferentes gerações.

entrada de família 3

moradias das famílias 2 e 3

família 3

família 2

entrada compartilhada das famílias 2 e 3

satélite da família 1

entrada de família 1

The 2032 Marvelous City Award goes to:

CIDADE DE DEUS!

26 Destaques que fazem uma cidade melhor!

Destaque No 15:
Super Bancada Dupla

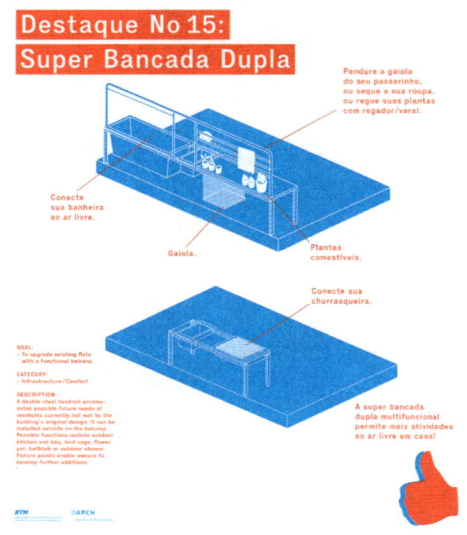

Pendure a gaiola do seu passarinho, ou seque a sua roupa, ou regue suas plantas com regador/varal.

Conecte sua banheira ao ar livre.

Gaiola.

Plantas comestíveis.

Conecte sua churrasqueira.

A super bancada dupla multifuncional permite mais atividades ao ar livre em casa!

The 2032 Marvelous City Award goes to:

CIDADE DE DEUS!

26 Destaques que fazem uma cidade melhor!

Destaque No 26:
Geladeira móvel
para Camelôs

Uma pequena carroça de camelô para refrigerar comida e bebidas

Baseado sobre um chassi de bicicleta a geladeira móvel pode caminhar ruelas estritas e mesmo usar o trem.

A intensidade de refrigeração pode ser regulada pela máquina pneumática de mão.

O mineral poroso funciona como uma pilha que pode ser carregada com o calor do sol.

As pilhas podem ser acampadas e usadas conforme a necessidade dos da refrigeração.

LIMA: CO-PRODUCED CITY

Patricia Caldas Torres, Paula Kapstein Lopez,
Edith Aranda Dioses, Mariel Valdivia Lopez

In the last century, Lima transformed from being a small urban nucleus to a metropolitan area. Compared to the year 1940, its population is now thirteen-fold; its area has multiplied by 45 times. The explosive urbanization began in the mid-1940s with mass migration towards Lima from mostly the impoverished Andean rural areas, resulting in vulnerable urban areas that have absorbed the rural way of living. Informality, being the key characteristic, turns the cityscape into a vast urban sprawl.

"Barriadas" is the Peruvian name for the diffuse settlements commonly referred to as slums. Here people arrive, start a living; then they construct, before installing further services.[1] The temperate marine climate makes such a living possible, while occupation on vacant state-owned lands was tolerated for years. Along the Rimac River are some of Lima's early Barriadas at the city's former northern edge. As the city expanded beyond the river the once peripheral settlements ended up in the centre of a now enlarged city. In spite of the economic development of the city at large, life improvement here has stayed frozen. Separated from the rest of the city by real barriers, a complex and vulnerable urban territory within the city is formed, as an "Inner Peripheries System"[2], with clearly differentiated and interconnected places.

Side by side with these "Barriadas" are "Unidades Vecinales" (UVs), namely "neighbourhood-units". In the 1950s, influenced by European post-war housing developments, self-contained units or satellite cities with green areas and communal equipment were planned, based on an imported urban theory with roots in the Garden City Movement. Aimed to liberate city borders from the proliferating informal settlements, this urban model of social housing failed to solve the mass-housing problem precisely because it ignored the population's real spatial needs.

Ironically the UVs now seem to face its greatest fear, namely being appropriated by their own residents through informal living. A housing unit designed for a nuclear family can sometimes end up tripling its original area to house an "extended family" – a dwelling pattern evident in slums. Five communities of UVs are chosen as case studies to show how various typologies transformed over time. The studies reveal the reality of more than half of Lima's population as being a lower-middle class, whose concrete needs contrast with the "dominated space".

Though vastly different, Barriadas and the modified UVs share deep ties of kinship, respectively manifesting informal living as a "system" and as a "life-process". The systematic existence of Barriadas points to an open and flexible planning, in which the demands of the inhabitants and efforts from various players could be incorporated, to integrate the inner peripheries back into the city at large. The UVs form an urban laboratory staging a process in which everyday life penetrates through formal structures, challenging the traditional perception of social housing as an artefact. A growing collective housing is thus imaginable to be the new typology, in which planning is only the first step. In this way, the formal and informal players might finally team up, together creating a "co-produced city".

Während des vergangenen Jahrhunderts entwickelte sich Lima von einem kleinen, fest umrissenen Stadtkern zu einer regelrechten Metropole: Im Vergleich zum Jahr 1940 hat sich Limas Bevölkerung vervierzehnfacht, und sein Stadtgebiet hat sich seitdem auf das Fünfundvierzigfache ausgedehnt. Die explosionsartige Urbanisierung begann zur Mitte der 1940er Jahre mit einer Massenzuwanderung aus den verarmten ländlichen Regionen der Anden; dadurch entstanden problematische städtische Areale, deren Bewohner ihre ländliche Lebensweise beibehielten. Der informelle Charakter dieser Ansiedlungen ließ die Stadtlandschaft unkontrolliert auswuchern.

"Barriadas" ist der peruanische Begriff für diffuse Ansiedlungen, die man normalerweise als Slums bezeichnet. Dort fangen die frisch eingetroffenen Zuwanderer ein neues Leben an; sie bauen Behausungen, bevor es dort städtische Ver- und Entsorgungseinrichtungen gibt.[1] Das milde Meeresklima gestattet ein solches Leben, und die Besiedlung unbewohnten staatlichen Grund und Bodens wurde jahrelang toleriert. Entlang des Rio Rimac, am einstigen nördlichen Rand Limas, liegen einige der ältesten Barriadas der Stadt. Als Lima über den Fluss hinaus expandierte, fanden sich diese ehemals peripheren Ansiedlungen im Zentrum der nun vergrößerten Stadt wieder. Trotz des wirtschaftlichen Aufschwungs der Stadt insgesamt haben sich die Lebensumstände in den Barriadas nicht verbessert. Vom Rest der Stadt durch reale Barrieren getrennt, hat sich innerhalb der Stadt ein komplexes und problematisches städtisches Areal herausgebildet, ein "System innerer Peripherien"[2] mit klar voneinander geschiedenen und miteinander verbundenen Lokalitäten.

Neben diesen Barriadas gibt es die "Unidades Vecinales" (UVs) bzw. "Nachbarschaftseinheiten". Nach dem Vorbild des europäischen Wohnungsbaus der Nachkriegszeit wurden in den 1950er Jahren autarke Einheiten oder Satellitenstädte mit Grünflächen und kommunalen Einrichtungen geplant, denen eine importierte städtebauliche Theorie mit Wurzeln in der Gartenstadtbewegung zugrunde lag. Dieses städtische Modell des Sozialen Wohnungsbaus sollte die Stadtgrenzen von den auswuchernden informellen Ansiedlungen befreien, war jedoch nicht in der Lage, das Problem der Massenunterbringung zu lösen, weil es die tatsächlichen räumlichen Bedürfnisse der Bevölkerung ignorierte.

Ironischerweise scheint nun genau das einzutreten, was die UVs am meisten befürchten, nämlich eine Beeinträchtigung durch die informelle Lebensweise ihrer Bewohner. Eine für eine Kernfamilie geplante Wohneinheit kann die von ihr beanspruchte Wohnfläche mitunter verdreifachen, um eine "erweiterte Familie" aufzunehmen – ein für Slums typisches Besiedlungsmuster. Fünf Nachbarschaften oder UVs werden als Fallstudien ausgewählt, um zu zeigen, wie sich im Laufe der Zeit unterschiedliche Typologien herausgebildet haben. Diese Studien offenbaren, dass mehr als die Hälfte der Bevölkerung Limas zur unteren Mittelschicht zählt, deren konkrete Bedürfnisse im Gegensatz zum "dominierten Raum" stehen.

Trotz ihrer beträchtlichen Unterschiede sind Barriadas und modifizierte UVs eng miteinander verwandt, denn beide gestalten das informelle Leben als ein "System" bzw. als einen "Lebensprozess". Die systematische Existenz von Barriadas deutet auf eine offene und flexible Planung, bei der die Bedürfnisse der Bewohner und die Bemühungen diverser Akteure berücksichtigt werden können, um die inneren Peripherien wieder in die Stadt als solche zu integrieren. Die UVs bilden ein städtisches Laboratorium, das einen Prozess inszeniert, bei dem das Alltagsleben formale Strukturen durchdringt und bei dem die traditionelle Wahrnehmung des Sozialen Wohnungsbaus als ein Artefakt in Frage gestellt wird. Ein wachsender gemeinschaftlicher Wohnungsbau ist somit als eine neue Typologie denkbar, bei der die Planung lediglich der erste Schritt ist. Auf diese Weise kommen die formellen und die informellen Akteure möglicherweise zusammen, um gemeinsam eine "koproduzierte Stadt" zu erschaffen.

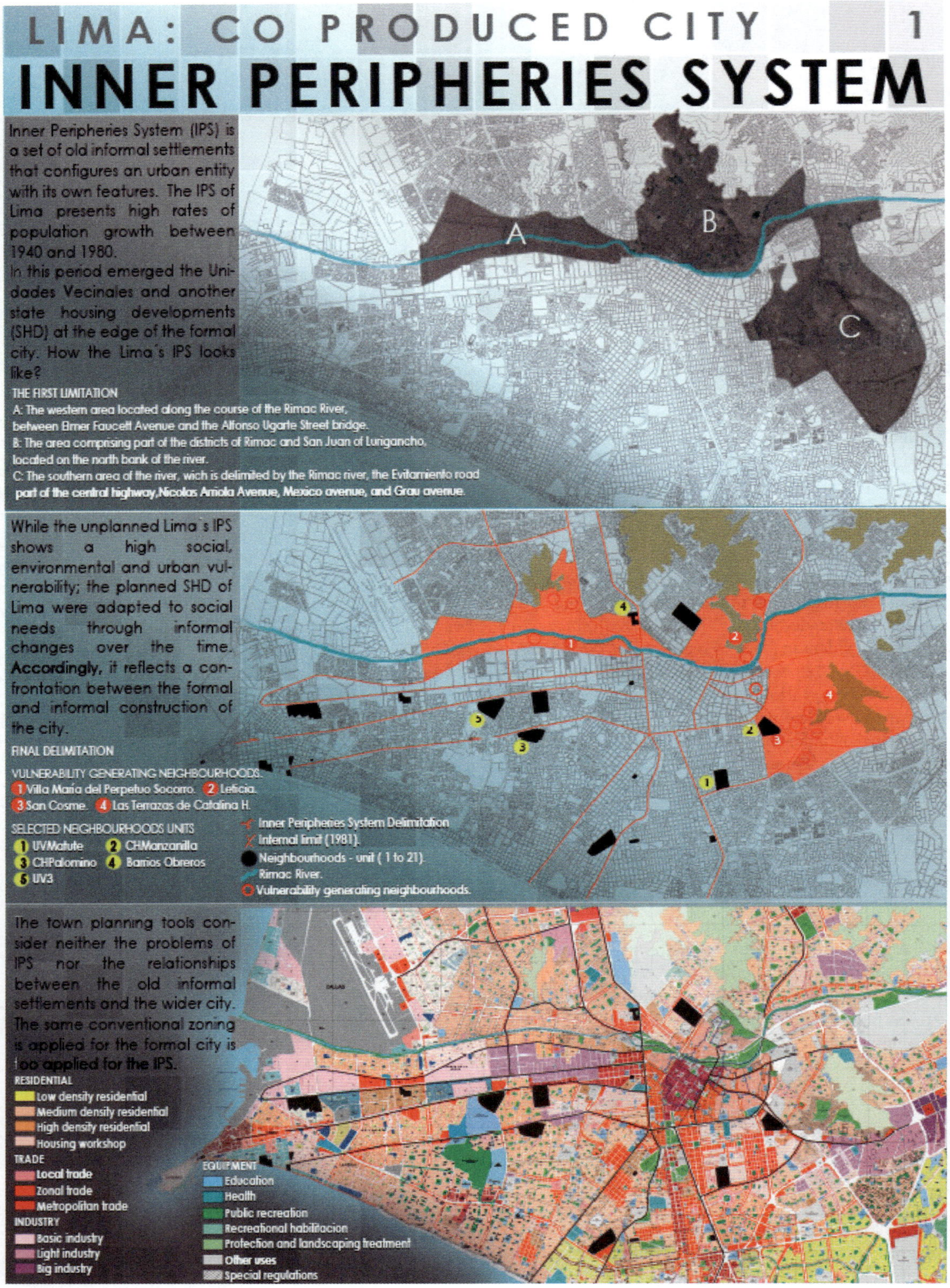

INNER PERIPHERIES SYSTEM

SELECTED NEIGH

represent paradigmati

Inner Peripheries System (IPS) is a set of old informal settlements that configures an urban entity with its own features. The IPS of Lima presents high rates of population growth between 1940 and 1980.
In this period emerged the Unidades Vecinales and another state housing developments (SHD) at the edge of the formal city. How the Lima´s IPS looks like?

THE FIRST LIMITATION
A: The western area located along the course of the Rimac River, between Elmer Faucett Avenue and the Alfonso Ugarte Street bridge.
B: The area comprising part of the districts of Rimac and San Juan of Lurigancho, located on the north bank of the river.
C: The southern area of the river, wich is delimited by the Rimac river, the Evitamiento road part of the central highway,Nicolas Arriola Avenue, Mexico avenue, and Grau avenue.

While the unplanned Lima´s IPS shows a high social, environmental and urban vulnerability; the planned SHD of Lima were adapted to social needs through informal changes over the time. **Accordingly,** it reflects a confrontation between the formal and informal construction of the city.

FINAL DELIMITATION

VULNERABILITY GENERATING NEIGHBOURHOODS:
1 Villa Maria del Perpetuo Socorro. **2** Leticia.
3 San Cosme.   **4** Las Terrazas de Catalina H.

SELECTED NEIGHBOURHOODS UNITS:
1 UVMatute   **2** CHManzanilla
3 CHPalomino   **4** Barrios Obreros
5 UV3

— Inner Peripheries System Delimitation
✓ Internal limit (1981).
● Neighbourhoods - unit (1 to 21).
— Rimac River.
○ Vulnerability generating neighbourhoods.

The town planning tools consider neither the problems of IPS nor the relationships between the old informal settlements and the wider city. The same conventional zoning is applied for the formal city is too applied for the IPS.

RESIDENTIAL
■ Low density residential
■ Medium density residential
■ High density residential
■ Housing workshop

TRADE
■ Local trade
■ Zonal trade
■ Metropolitan trade

INDUSTRY
■ Basic industry
■ Light industry
■ Big industry

EQUIPMENT
■ Education
■ Health
■ Public recreation
■ Recreational habilitacion
■ Protection and landscaping treatment
■ Other uses
■ Special regulations

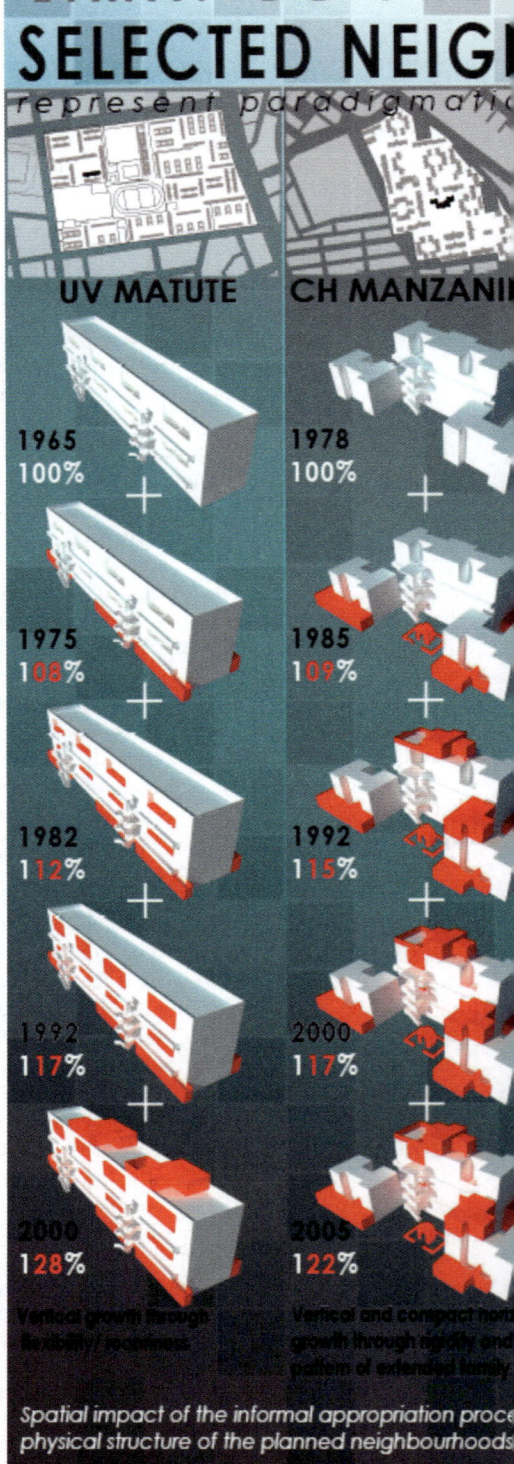

UV MATUTE   CH MANZANI

1965 100%	1978 100%
1975 108%	1985 109%
1982 112%	1992 115%
1992 117%	2000 117%
2000 128%	2005 122%

Vertical growth through flexibility / readiness

Vertical and compact growth through agility and pattern of external growth

Spatial impact of the informal appropriation proce physical structure of the planned neighbourhoods

---

Inner Peripheries System
Along the Rimac River were the early barriadas, which formed the northern periphery of Lima until the 1950s. As the city expanded beyond the Rimac River, which was Lima's natural boundary, the once peripheral slums now become part of the central area of a much larger metropolis.

Unidades Vecinales
Based on the imported theory of the neighborhood unit, Unidades Vecinales (UVs) were planned by the State in the 1950s near to the former periphery of the city. In the context of modernization processes, UVs were considered as an urban model of social

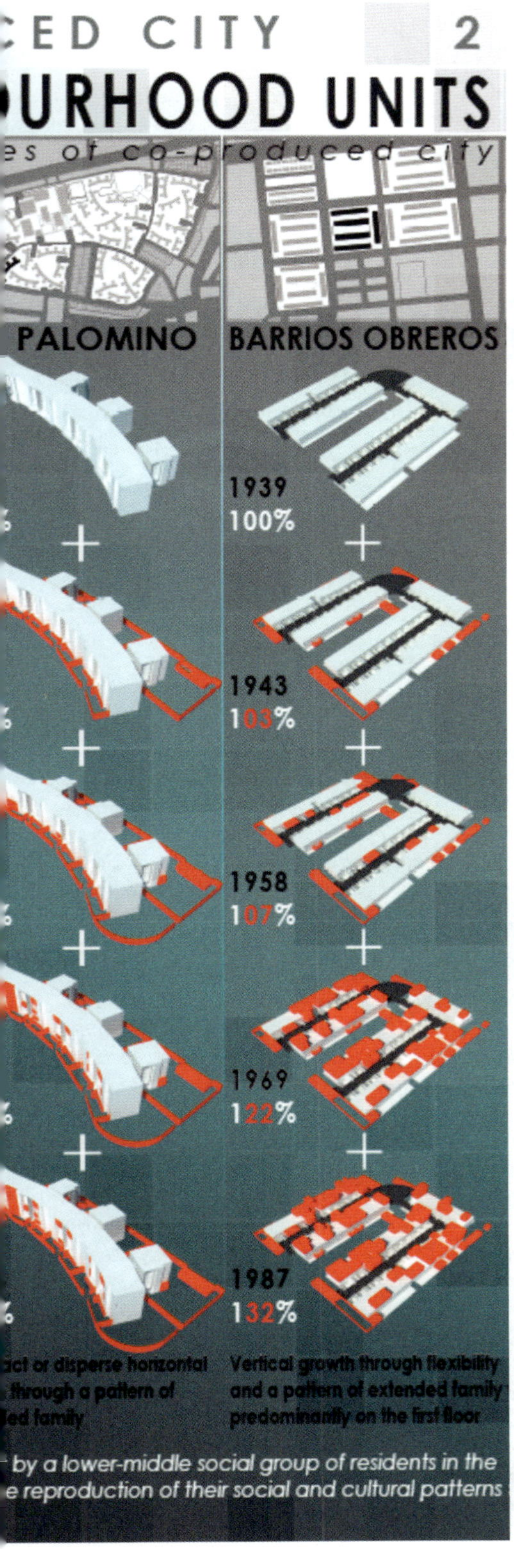

URHOOD UNITS
es of co-produced city

PALOMINO | BARRIOS OBREROS

1939
100%

1943
103%

1958
107%

1969
122%

1987
132%

act or disperse horizontal
through a pattern of
ed family

by a lower-middle social group of residents in the
reproduction of their social and cultural patterns

Vertical growth through flexibility
and a pattern of extended family
predominantly on the first floor

UV3: A CASE STUDY and OPEN PLANNING

Type 1

Type 2

Type 3

1949
2013

DENSITY CHANGE
1950	188 Hab./Ha
1956	188 Hab./Ha
1967	239 Hab./Ha
1978	174 Hab./Ha
2007	133 Hab./Ha

Pedestrian Flow   Vehicular Flow

Housing   Equipment

Equipment
Primary school
Educational center
Technical professional education
Shops
Medical center
Market Kindergarden
Soups kitchen (comedor popular)
Doctor's surgeries
Police station

OPEN PLANNING

The **review** of informal appropriation in the UVs leds **us** to **propose** an open planning for informal urban contexts: Strategic inclusion of civil society´s potentials as well as new collective housing forms. An Strategic Plan of Inner Peripheric System Regeneration in Lima is needed:

1. Participatory government;
2. Urban units with identity;
3. Educational programmes.

Individual garden UV3
Green area maintenance by the residents (individual and collective gardens) in coordination with the municipality

Configurated collective space in the CH Palomino
New public spaces for social interaction through the residents initiative

Collective housing as process for lower-middle social groups typologies

Building additions for collective needs in the neighbourhoods

Phases of growth of a housing type in UV MATUTE

A small building for kindergarten was added in a housing block UV3

Type 3

1949
100%

1963
114%

1983
123%

1995
131%

Through a pattern of extended family

New spatial pattern: square and semi public space between two parallel housing blocks

Shop in green area

Workshop in green area

Co-Produced City
The informal changes in the UVs can be regarded as a social-spatial appropriation that contrasts with the "dominated space", suggesting a deeper connection to the informal barriadas. The analysis leads to the concept of a co-produced city that combines the formal structure with the informal process.

housing in a period of explosive population growth. Over the years, the planned and formal UVs have been modified through extensions carried out by their residents.

ARTIFICIAL REEF Olivia Grandi

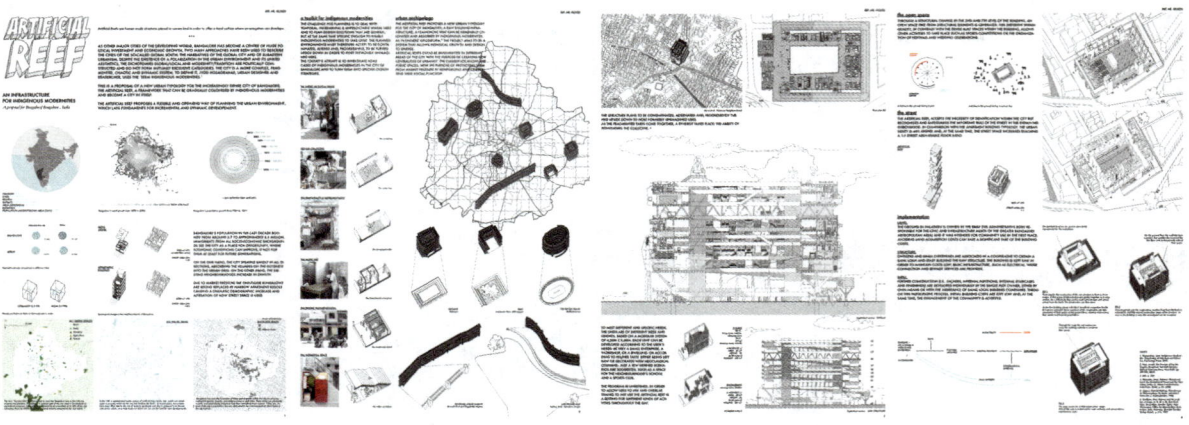

"Die Großform schafft den Rahmen, die Ordnung und den geplanten Raum für einen unvorhersehbaren, nicht planbaren, lebendigen Prozess, für eine parasitäre Architektur. Ohne diese Komponente bleibt jede Planung starr und leblos…Erst wenn zu der Summe von Einzelteilen eine neue Qualität hinzukommt und eine höhere Entwicklungsstufe erreicht wird, entsteht eine Großform. Kennzeichnend ist nicht die numerische Größe. Ein im Volumen kleines Haus kann ebensogut eine Großform sein wie ein Häuserblock, eine Stadtteil oder eine ganze Stadt."[1]

O.M. Ungers: Großformen im Wohnungsbau, 1966

Since the nineties, a completely new and unprecedented urban landscape has come into being as a product of the new booming economy in the Indian city of Bangalore, partly due to its fast growing IT branch.[2] New morphologies have emerged from scratch forming landscapes of luxury townships, corporate parks and special economic zones. Mega governmental development plans exist alongside incremental growth initiated by the inhabitants.

Global City vs. Subaltern Urbanism

The experience strolling through the city reveals two contrasting aesthetical images. On the one hand, the so-called Silicon Valley is a deliberately constructed model of technological development with fully glazed high-end office buildings, clean roads, and exclusive residential communities, where success is assured.[3] On the other hand, beyond the gated areas, a territory generating fear and uncertainty is kept apart from the IT elites; residents of a poorer group are creators of "architecture without architects", leading a more chaotic yet more democratic process and silently opposing and modifying the rigidly planned city.[4]

The two contrasting formal languages of order and of chaos correspond to the two main tendencies in urban studies describing cities of the so-called Global South: the narratives of the "Global City" and of "Subaltern Urbanism". Bangalore's Silicon Valley presents an image of a constructed "Global City", where the city is a functional node in an integrated planetary capitalism[5], connected with other global cities around the world but detached from its local context of the physical, social and symbolic dimension[6]. "Subaltern Urbanism" summarizes the vast chaotic territory of the city, where the dominant political power is resisted, the elitism of historiography is questioned, and a history from below is proposed.[7]

Of other spaces:
Indigenous modernities

Despite the existence of a polarization in the urban environment and its linked aesthetics, the dichotomies global vs. local and modernity vs. tradition are politically constructed and do not form mutually exclusive categories. The city is a more complex, fragmented, chaotic and dynamic system. The term "indigenous modernities" questions direct adoption of the western "modern" model in the developing world and thus recognizes other forms of modernity through contamination of the local context. By seeing the polarization of "tra-

Seit den 1990er Jahren bildet sich in der indischen Stadt Bangalore eine völlig neue und beispiellose urbane Landschaft heraus – als Resultat eines Wirtschaftsbooms, der zum Teil auf die rasant wachsende IT-Branche zurückzuführen ist.[2] Neue Morphologien entstehen gleichsam aus dem Nichts und bilden Landschaften aus luxuriösen Wohnanlagen, Firmenparks und wirtschaftlichen Sonderzonen. Von staatlichen Behörden vorgelegte Mega-Entwicklungspläne existieren parallel zu einem inkrementalen, von den Bewohnern initiierten Wachstum.

"Globale Stadt" vs. "Subalterner Urbanismus"

Ein Spaziergang durch die Stadt offenbart zwei gegensätzliche ästhetische Bilder. Auf der einen Seite befindet sich das sogenannte Silicon Valley, ein bewusst errichtetes Modell der technischen Entwicklung mit vollverglasten Hightech-Bürogebäuden, gepflegten Straßen und exklusiven Wohnanlagen, wo man den Erfolg förmlich riechen kann.[3] Auf der anderen Seite, jenseits der umzäunten Areale, liegt ein Angst und Unsicherheit hervorrufendes, von den IT-Eliten abgesondertes Territorium; die einer ärmeren Bevölkerungsschicht angehörigen Bewohner erschaffen eine "Architektur ohne Architekten", die zu einem chaotischeren, aber demokratischeren Prozess führt und die stumm gegen die rigide geplante Stadt aufbegehrt und die Planung modifiziert.[4]

Von anderen Räumen:
"Indigene Modernitäten"

Trotz der bestehenden Polarisierung in der urbanen Umgebung und der damit verbundenen Ästhetik sind die Dichotomien "global vs. lokal" und "modern vs. traditionell" politisch erzeugt und stellen keine einander ausschließenden Kategorien dar. Die Stadt ist ein komplexeres, fragmentierteres, chaotischeres und dynamischeres System. Der Begriff "indigene Modernitäten" stellt

Die beiden entgegengesetzten formalen Sprachen der Ordnung und des Chaos entsprechen den beiden Haupttendenzen in den gegenwärtigen Untersuchungen zum Städtebau, die die Städte des sogenannten Globalen Südens beschreiben: die Narrative der Globalen Stadt und des Subalternen Urbanismus. Bangalores Silicon Valley präsentiert das Bild einer bewusst errichteten Globalen Stadt, wo die Stadt ein funktionaler Knoten innerhalb eines vernetzten, weltweit operierenden Kapitalismus ist[5], verbunden mit anderen globalen Städten überall auf der Welt, aber herausgelöst aus den physischen, sozialen und symbolischen Dimensionen ihres örtlichen Kontexts.[6] Der Subalterne Urbanismus fasst das ausgedehnte chaotische Territorium der Stadt zusammen, all jene Areale, wo man sich der dominanten politischen Macht widersetzt, das elitäre Denken der Historiografie in Frage stellt und eine "Geschichte von unten" propagiert.[7]

ditional" and "modern" as politically derived and socially constructed, this perspective seeks to break the juxtaposition and celebrate simultaneity and engagement.[8]

As in the context of Indian cities, squatter settlements proliferate along gated zones of residence and industries, being separated by a visible, artificial, constructed, and not-always-functioning wall. In reality, actors can't be neatly mapped in belonging either to the power side or to the resistance side[9], but are part of an interlinked, tangled structure. The urban environment must be seen as formed by multiscale theatres of action, in which the global and local actors and economies are interlinked and interdependent.

One certainly cannot deny the current presence of the two polarizing images of being top-down vs. bottom up, planned vs. self-organized, state controlled vs. entrepreneurial, big vs. small, uniform vs. fragmented, homogeneous vs. heterogeneous, western vs. non-western. The aim is not to question its presence but to question the narratives that claim its justification and try to keep the two worlds further apart. Therefore, the challenge for planners is to deal with what is unplannable, temporal, unpredictable and flexible and to plan design solutions that are generic but at the same time specific enough to enable "indigenous modernities". The planned environments must accept to be contaminated, alternated and, progressively turned upside down to host formerly unimagined uses, eventually forming a heterogeneous terrain whose aesthetics is presented as territories of multiple hues.[10]

Artificial Reef

"An artificial reef is a human-made underwater structure, typically built to promote marine life in areas with a generally featureless bottom, to control erosion, to block ship passage, or to improve surfing. Many reefs are built using objects that were intended for other purposes, for example by sinking oil rigs, scuttling ships, or by deploying rubble or construction debris. Other artificial reefs are built from PVC or concrete. Shipwrecks may become artificial reefs when preserved on the sea floor. Regardless of construction methods, artificial reefs provide hard surfaces where algae and invertebrates such as barnacles, corals, and oysters attach themselves; the accumulation of attached marine life, in turn, provides intricate structure and food for assemblages of fish."[11]

This is a proposal for a new urban typology for the city of Bangalore that could be implemented in different areas of the city: the Artificial Reef, raw building-infrastructure and framework that can be gradually colonized and absorbed by "indigenous modernities".

Designed as a "Großform" as defined by Ungers[1], it is aimed to allow maximal freedom for individual elements to be uniquely defined within a larger scheme that holds the fragmented parts together[12]. Each fragment of the Artificial Reef can be developed according to the user's necessities – be it a small enterprise, a workshop, or a dwelling – or taste – by either being left raw or decorated with neoclassical columns.

Kinship ties with several other theoretical works are visible throughout the conception and design. The analogy with individual reef islands and the graphic presentation reminds one of the green archipelago project in Berlin, "the city in the city" project of Ungers. In an ocean of chaos, an archipelago of giant reefs forms systems that hopefully allow individual growth and design to emerge. The giant structure echoes Koolhaas' concept of Bigness, in which a sort of programmatic alchemy takes place, enabling programmatic elements to react with each other and create new events.[13] Fundamentally being a "Großform", the elements from different contexts come together; the structure as a whole achieves a new locality[14]. The occupation of the structure also bears a resemblance of the famous "Torre David"; but in this case, appropriation is invited rather than being an accidental outcome.

Through the use of two different scales, the whole and its fragmented parts, the structure aims to dialog with both concepts of cities in the global south – the Global City and the City of the Subaltern. It is an attempt to bring the top-down and the bottom-up face to face, to bridge the gap between the two polarizations, and to turn a parallel juxtaposition into a multiscale coexistence.

•

die pauschale Übernahme des westlichen "modernen" Modells in den Entwicklungsländern in Frage und erkennt somit andere Formen der Modernität an, das heißt, Formen, die durch eine Kontamination des lokalen Kontexts entstehen. Indem sie die Polarisierung "traditionell vs. modern" als politisch hergeleitet und sozial konstruiert betrachtet, möchte diese Sichtweise die starre Gegenüberstellung aufbrechen und stattdessen Simultanität und Engagement zelebrieren.[8]

Wie im Kontext der indischen Städte zu beobachten ist, breiten sich entlang der umzäunten Wohn- und Industriezonen illegal errichtete Wohnsiedlungen aus, die durch eine sichtbare, künstliche, gebaute und nicht immer funktionierende Mauer abgetrennt sind. In Wirklichkeit lassen sich die Akteure nicht fein säuberlich der Seite der Macht oder der Seite des Widerstands

zuordnen[9], denn alle sind Teil einer vernetzten, komplexen Struktur. Die urbane Umgebung muss als etwas betrachtet werden, was von vielfältigen, unterschiedliche Maßstäbe annehmenden Handlungsschauplätzen geformt wird, in denen globale und lokale Akteure und Ökonomien miteinander verbunden und voneinander abhängig sind.

Die aktuelle Präsenz der zwei polarisierenden Bilder "top-down" vs. "bottom-up" organisiert, geplant vs. selbst organisiert, staatlich kontrolliert vs. privatwirtschaftlich kontrolliert, groß vs. klein, einheitlich vs. fragmentiert, homogen vs. heterogen, westlich vs. nicht westlich – das lässt sich sicher nicht leugnen. Das Ziel besteht indes nicht darin, diese Präsenz in Frage zu stellen, sondern darin, die Narrative zu hinterfragen, die zu ihrer Rechtfertigung herangezogen werden und die diese beiden Welten noch stärker voneinander zu trennen versuchen. Deshalb besteht die Herausforderung für Planer darin, sich mit etwas zu befassen, was unplanbar, temporär, nicht voraussagbar und flexibel ist, und Entwurfslösungen zu ersinnen, die generisch und gleichzeitig spezifisch genug sind, um indigene Modernitäten zu ermöglichen. Die geplanten Umgebungen müssen akzeptieren, dass sie kontaminiert, verändert und in zunehmendem Maße auf den Kopf gestellt werden, um einstmals unvorstellbare Nutzungen zu beherbergen, wobei sie schließlich ein heterogenes Terrain bilden werden, dessen Ästhetik sich als eine Ansammlung von Territorien mit mannigfaltigen Farbtönen präsentiert.[10]

Künstliches Riff

"Ein künstliches Riff ist ein von Menschenhand geschaffenes Unterwasserbauwerk, das normalerweise errichtet wird, um die Meeresflora und -fauna in Gegenden zu unterstützen, wo der Meeresboden kahl und öde ist, oder um der Erosion entgegenzuwirken, die Durchfahrt von Schiffen zu blockieren oder die Bedingungen für das Surfen zu verbessern. Viele Riffe werden gebaut, indem man Objekte verwendet, die ursprünglich anderen Zwecken dienten, etwa indem man Bohrinseln versenkt, die Bodenventile von Schiffen öffnet oder Trümmer und Bauschutt im Meer abslädt. Andere künstliche Riffe werden aus PVC oder Beton gebaut. Schiffswracks können sich zu künstlichen Riffen entwickeln, wenn man sie dem Meeresboden überlässt. Unabhängig von der jeweiligen Baumethode sorgen künstliche Riffe für stabile Oberflächen, an denen sich Algen und wirbellose Tiere wie Entenmuscheln, Korallen und Austern festsetzen; diese Anballung von festgewachsener Meeresflora und -fauna wiederum lässt ein verschlungenes,

komplexes Gefüge entstehen und liefert Nahrung für Schwärme von Fischen."[11]

Was wir hier vorschlagen, ist eine neue urbane Typologie für die Stadt Bangalore, etwas, was sich in unterschiedlichen Gegenden der Stadt implementieren ließe: das Künstliche Riff, eine Rohbau-Infrastruktur oder ein Rahmen, der schrittweise von indigenen Modernitäten kolonisiert und absorbiert werden kann. Als eine Ungers'sche Großform konzipiert[1], möchte das Künstliche Riff den individuellen Elementen die größtmögliche Freiheit gewähren und es diesen ermöglichen, sich innerhalb eines größeren, die fragmentierten Einzelteile zusammenhaltenden Schemas auf eine einmalige Weise zu definieren.[12] Jedes Fragment des Künstlichen Riffs kann entsprechend den Bedürfnissen des Nutzers entwickelt werden – sei es ein Kleinunternehmen, eine Werkstatt, eine Wohnunterkunft – und entsprechend dem Geschmack des Nutzers – schlicht und unverziert oder mit klassizistischen Säulen dekoriert.

Verwandtschaftliche Beziehungen zu einigen anderen theoretischen Werken sind bei der Konzeption und beim Entwurf nicht zu übersehen. Die Analogie mit den individuellen Riffinseln und die grafische Präsentation erinnern an Ungers' Planungskonzept "Berlin, das grüne Stadtarchipel", sein Projekt "Die Stadt in der Stadt". In einem Ozean aus Chaos produziert ein Archipel aus riesigen Riffen Systeme, die, wie wir hoffen, ein individuelles Wachstum und einen individuellen Entwurf ermöglichen. Das riesige Bauwerk weckt auch Erinnerungen an Koolhaas' Konzept von Bigness, bei dem so etwas wie eine programmatische Alchimie stattfindet, die dafür sorgt, dass programmatische Elemente aufeinander reagieren und neue Ereignisse hervorbringen.[13] Die im Grunde eine Großform darstellenden Elemente aus unterschiedlichen Kontexten verbinden sich miteinander; das Bauwerk als Ganzes bringt eine neue Lokalität hervor.[14] Die geplante Besetzung des Bauwerks erinnert auch an den berühmten Torre David; doch in diesem Fall ist die Aneignung kein Zufallsergebnis, sondern bewusst gewollt.

Durch die Verwendung von zwei unterschiedlichen Maßstäben, den des Ganzen und den von dessen fragmentierten Einzelteilen, möchte das Bauwerk einen Dialog mit beiden Konzepten der Stadt des globalen Südens – die Globale Stadt und die Stadt des Subalternen Urbanismus – führen. Es ist ein Versuch, den top-down-Ansatz mit dem bottom-up-Ansatz zu vereinbaren, ein Versuch, die Kluft zwischen den beiden Polarisierungen zu überbrücken und eine parallele Gegenüberstellung in eine multiple Maßstäbe berücksichtigende Koexistenz zu verwandeln.

a toolkit for indigenous modernities

THE CHALLENGE FOR PLANNERS IS TO DEAL WITH
TEMPORAL, INCREMENTAL & UNPREDICTABLE SPATIAL USES
AND TO PLAN DESIGN SOLUTIONS THAT ARE GENERIC,
BUT AT THE SAME TIME SPECIFIC ENOUGH TO ENABLE
INDIGENOUS MODERNITIES TO TAKE OVER. THE PLANNED
ENVIRONMENTS MUST THEREFORE ACCEPT TO BE CONTA-
MINATED, ALTERED AND, PROGRESSIVELY, TO BE TURNED
UPSIDE DOWN IN ORDER TO HOST PREVIOUSLY UNIMAGI-
NED USES.
THE TOOLKIT'S ATTEMPT IS TO INVESTIGATE SOME
CASES OF INDIGENOUS MODERNITIES IN THE CITY OF
BANGALORE AND TO TURN THEM INTO SPECIFIC DESIGN
STRATEGIES.

urban archipelago

THE ARTIFICIAL REEF PROPOSES A NEW URBAN TYPOLOGY
FOR THE CITY OF BANGALORE; A RAW BUILDING-INFRA-
STRUCTURE, A FRAMEWORK THAT CAN BE GRADUALLY CO-
LONIZED AND ABSORBED BY INDIGENOUS MODERNITES.
AS IN UNGERS' GROSSFORM,[5] THE PROJECT AIMS TO BE A
SYSTEM THAT ALLOWS INDIVIDUAL GROWTH AND DESIGN
TO EMERGE.
ARTIFICIAL REEFS COULD BE IMPLEMENTED IN DIFFERENT
AREAS OF THE CITY WITH THE PURPOSE OF CREATING NEW
CENTRALITIES OF URBANITY. THE CHOSEN LOCATIONS ARE
PUBLIC SPACES, WITH THE PURPOSE OF PROTECTING THEM
FROM MARKET PRESSURE BY REINFORCING AND CELEBRA-
TING THEIR SOCIAL FUNCTION.

T01 STREET AS SOCIAL SPACE

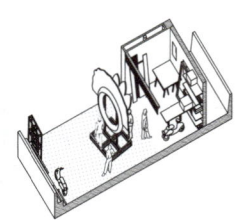

the workshop

T02 THE COLLECTIVE

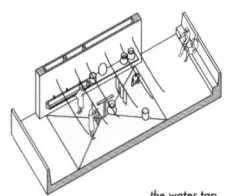

the water tap

T03 TEMPORALITY & INCREMENTALITY

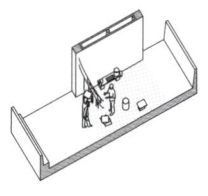

the newspaperseller

T04 MIXED USE

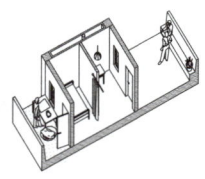

the home-based enterprise

T05 TENURE FRAGMENTATION

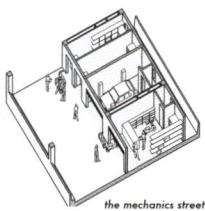

the mechanics street

T06 INTERSTITAL SPACE

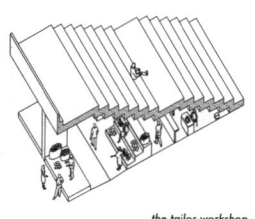

the tailor workshop

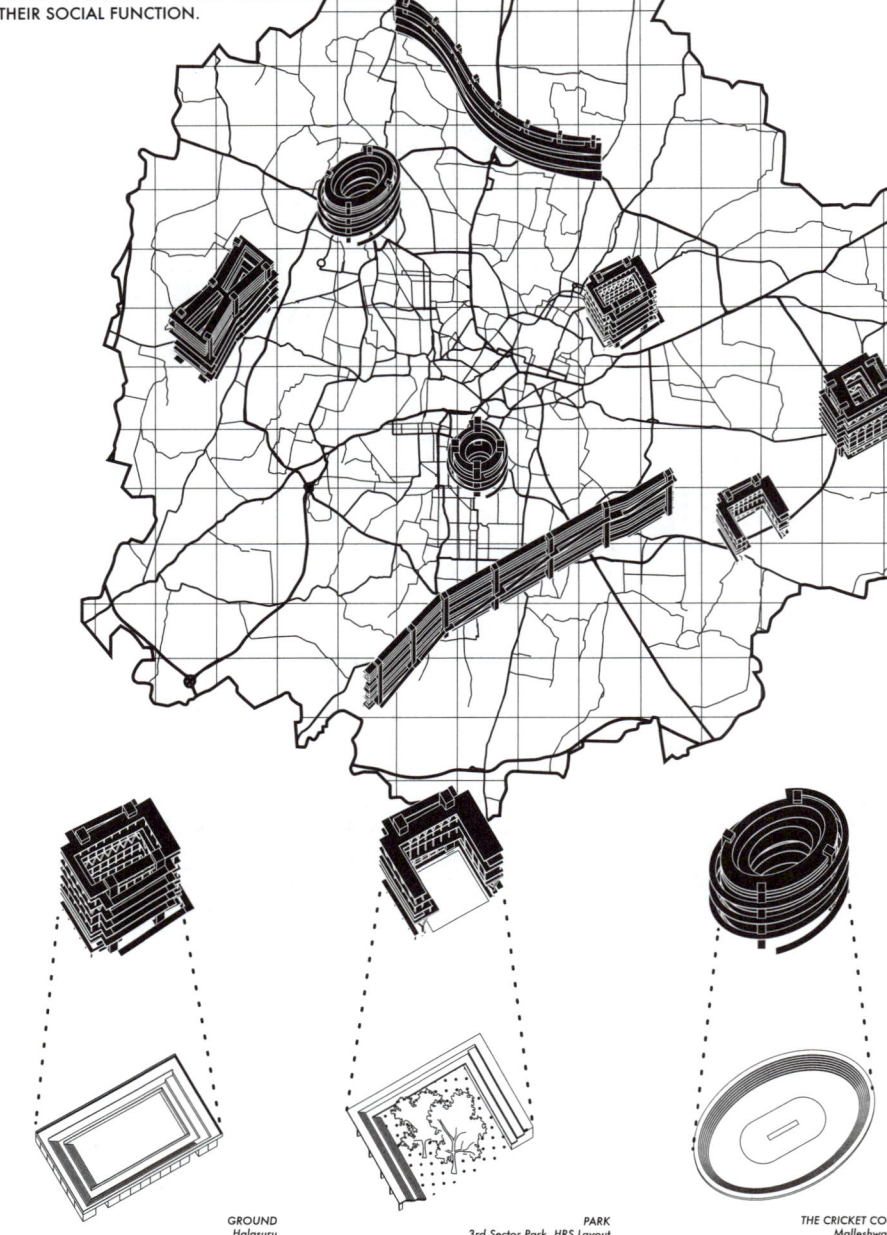

GROUND
Halasuru

PARK
3rd Sector Park, HRS Layout

THE CRICKET COURT
Malleshwaram

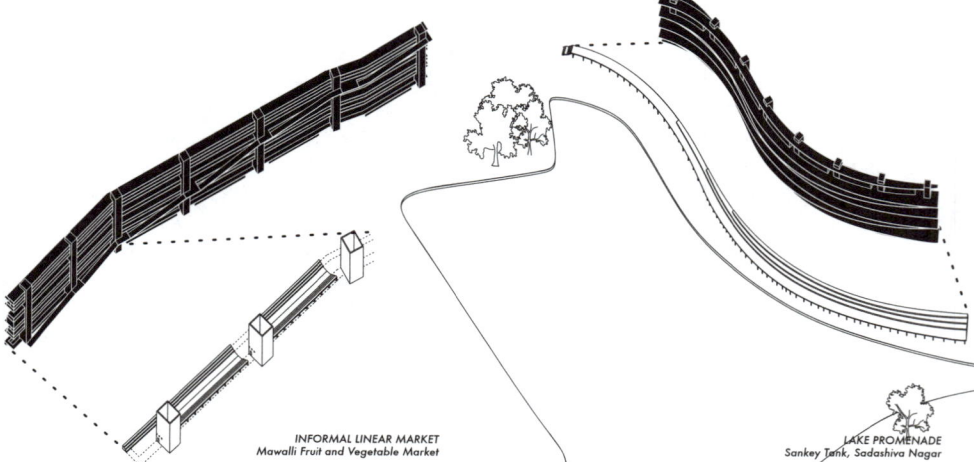

INFORMAL LINEAR MARKET
Mawalli Fruit and Vegetable Market

LAKE PROMENADE
Sankey Tank, Sadashiva Nagar

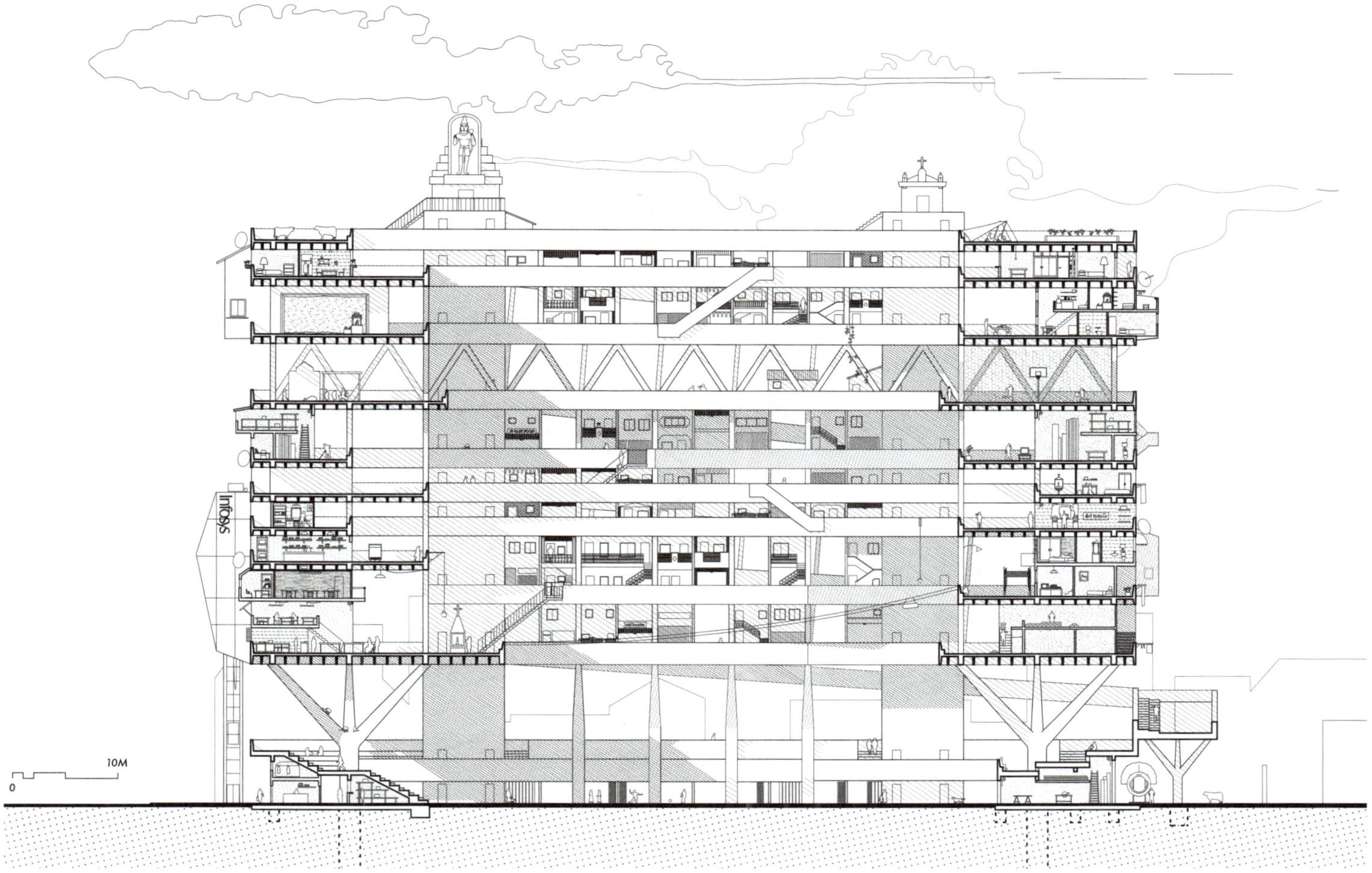

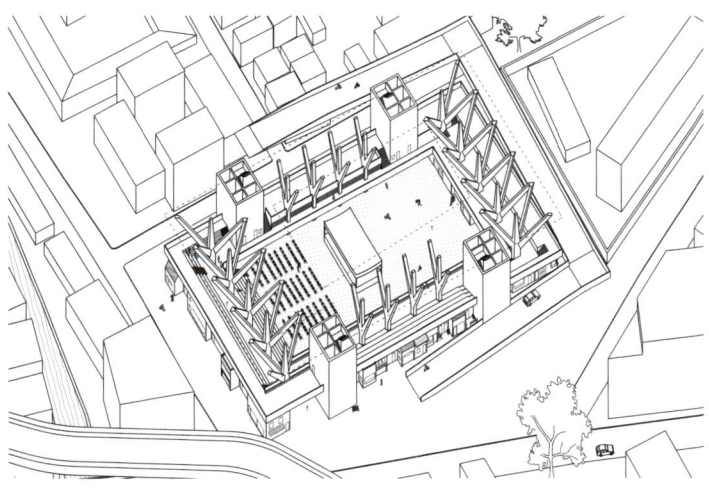

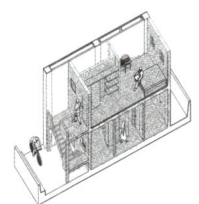

2 FLATS
flat A .
living room, toilette,
sleeping room
flat B .
living/
sleeping room, toilette

4 MODULES //
AREA . 65 m²
HEIGHT . 2h
(6,20 meters)
VOLUME . 301 m³

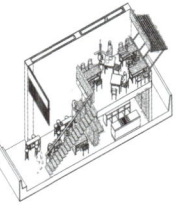

RESTAURANT
dinning room, kitchen

4 MODULES //
AREA . 49 m²
HEIGHT . 2h
(6,20 meters)
VOLUME . 301 m³

POSSIBLE INFILLS

TO MEET DIFFERENT AND SPECIFIC NEEDS, THE UNITS ARE OF DIFFERENT SIZES AND HEIGHTS, BASED ON A MODULAR SYSTEM OF 4,50M X 3,60M. EACH UNIT CAN BE DEVELOPED ACCORDING TO THE USER'S NEEDS -BE THEY A SMALL ENTERPRISE, A WORKSHOP, OR A DWELLING- OR ACCORDING TO HIS/HER TASTE -EITHER BEING LEFT RAW OR DECORATED WITH NEOCLASSICAL COLUMNS-. JUST A FEW DEFINED SCENARIOS ARE SUGGESTED, SUCH AS A SPACE FOR THE NEIGHBOURHOOD'S SCHOOL AND A SPORTS CLUB.

THE PROGRAM IS UNDEFINED, IN ORDER TO ALLOW USES TO MIX AND OVERLAP. THANKS TO MIX USE THE ARTIFICIAL REEF IS A SETTING FOR DIFFERENT KINDS OF ACTIVITIES THROUGHOUT THE DAY.

the open space

THROUGH A STRUCTURAL CHANGE IN THE 2ND AND 7TH LEVEL OF THE BUILDING, AN OPEN SPACE FREE FROM STRUCTURAL ELEMENTS IS GENERATED. THIS DIFFERENT SPATIAL QUALITY, IN CONTRAST WITH THE DENSE BUILT SPACES WITHIN THE BUILDING, ALLOWS OTHER ACTIVITIES TO TAKE PLACE SUCH AS SPORTS COMPETITIONS OR THE ORGANIZATION OF FESTIVALS AND WEDDING CELEBRATIONS.

the street

THE ARTIFICIAL REEF, ACCEPTS THE NECESSITY OF DENSIFICATION WITHIN THE CITY BUT RECOGNIZES AND SAFEGUARDS THE IMPORTANT ROLE OF THE STREET IN THE INDIAN NEIGHBOUHOOD. IN COMPARISON WITH THE APARTMENT BUILDING TYPOLOGY, THE URBAN DESITY IS 60% HIGHER AND, AT THE SAME TIME, THE STREET SPACE INCREASES REACHING A 1:1 STREET AREA:USABLE FLOOR RATIO.

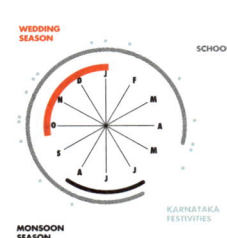

Activities in the ground during a year.

Activities in the ground during a normal day.

ARTIFICIAL REEF

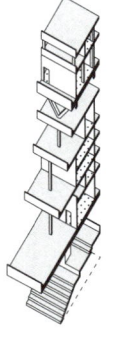

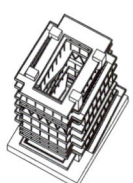

1600 m² UFA

STREET AREA:UFA
1:1

IV. NEOLIBERAL

In the context of a neoliberal urban policy, many hitherto public infrastructure services in cities have been privatised in recent years. This policy, urged by the World Bank, has also been pursued in developing and emerging nations, and has worsened living conditions for large sections of the population, especially with respect to housing for the urban poor. The deregulation of the housing and property market has hastened the process of social segregation in cities. With the sale of municipal properties and social housing to private investors, the municipalities lose an important management tool to offset social disparities.

URBAN POLICY

Im Kontext einer neoliberalen Stadtpolitik sind in den letzten Jahrzehnten viele ehemals öffentliche Aufgaben der infrastrukturellen Versorgung der Städte privatisiert worden. Diese Politik, die auch in den Entwicklungs- und Schwellenländern auf Druck der Weltbank betrieben wurde, hat die Lebensverhältnisse größerer Teile der Bevölkerung nachhaltig verschlechtert, vor allem die Wohnungsversorgung der städtisch Armen. Durch die Deregulierung des Wohnungs- und Immobilienmarktes beschleunigt sich in den Städten der Prozess der sozialen Segregation. Durch den Verkauf kommunaler Liegenschaften und Bestände aus dem sozialen Wohnungsbau an private Investoren verlieren die Kommunen ein wichtiges Steuerungsinstrument im Ausgleich sozialer Disparitäten.

MEDELLÍN – HUMAN RIGHT ON WATER

Marcela López, Miodrag Kuc, Juan Esteban Naranjo

Shifts towards neoliberal policies since the 1980s in Latin America have facilitated the configuration of urban waterscapes in ways that inequalities are (re)produced. This economic model holds the promise that market-oriented practices and private ownership are necessary solutions to deliver water services to the growing urban population. Despite the widespread implementation of market oriented reforms, the continent continues facing the ethical dilemma of how to improve adequate water supply services to low-income households in urban areas. This study investigates how the emergence of new forms of neoliberal governance constructs and reconstructs uneven urban waterscapes. This will be assessed by exploring recent patterns of water access in Medellín.

The city hosts one of the most successful public multi-utility companies in Latin America – Empresas Públicas de Medellín (EPM) – in terms of efficiency, profitability and provision of high quality services. The company enjoys a "natural" monopoly condition, not just by providing water, but also sanitation, energy, gas and telecommunication services to over 4 million people in Medellín's metropolitan area. In the last decades, the company has increasingly been required to behave in ways comparable to privately owned operators by adopting a competitive and profit-driven logic, despite remaining publicly owned by the city of Medellín, to which it pays 30% of its utilities. Because of this, the company has positioned itself as an active player in cultural and planning issues in the city

by financing cultural institutions, educational programs as well as providing facilities such as parks and libraries.[1]

The transformation of the water supply sector from a public service to a business organization is largely the result of two key changes in the economic and spatial organization of EPM: First, the company initiated in 1997 a process of commercialization through the implementation of market logics in public services provision.[2] The second key spatial and economical change of the company took place in the late 2010 and early 2011 with the trans-nationalization of operations into other geographical areas. While EPM successfully integrates into the global market, the city reports rising levels of non-payment of bills as a consequence of the steady increment in water tariffs. In response, the company embarked on aggressive measures of disconnecting those households from the formal water supply network. By 2011, company reports estimate that 46,166 households were disconnected for non-payment (near 6.5% of the total).

Additionally, the city reports estimate that around 35,000 households (near 5% of the total) do not have access to the formal network due to their illegal land tenure status. Although prepaid water technologies and a free basic allowance program (2.5 m³/person/month) have been deployed as solutions to ameliorate the current water crisis, many social groups question the efficiency of these strategies as they tend to benefit the water company by recovering unpaid bills. Existing research has primarily shown that neo-

Die seit den 1980er Jahren in Lateinamerika zu beobachtende Wende zu einer neoliberalen Politik hat die sozialen Ungleichheiten in der Gestaltung der städtischen Wasserlandschaft (re)produziert. Dieses wirtschaftspolitische Modell behauptet, marktorientierte Praktiken und Privateigentum seien unabdingbare Voraussetzungen für eine adäquate Wasserversorgung der ständig wachsenden Stadtbevölkerung. Trotz der weitverbreiteten marktorientierten Reformen steht der Kontinent weiterhin vor dem ethischen Dilemma, wie man in den städtischen Ballungsgebieten die Wasserversorgung für Haushalte mit geringem Einkommen verbessern kann. Unsere Untersuchung beschäftigt sich mit der Frage, wie neue Formen einer neoliberalen Politik ungleiche städtische Wasserlandschaften entstehen lassen. Dazu werfen wir einen näheren Blick auf die Wasserversorgung in Medellín.

Die Stadt ist Sitz eines der erfolgreichsten öffentlichen Versorgungsunternehmen Lateinamerikas, der Empresas Públicas de Medellín (EPM) – erfolgreich, was Effizienz, Rentabilität und die Versorgung mit hochwertigen Dienstleistungen betrifft. Das Unternehmen genießt eine "natürliche" Monopolstellung; es ist nicht nur für die Wasserversorgung von mehr als vier Millionen Einwohner des Großraums Medellín zuständig, sondern auch für die Abwasserbeseitigung, Gas- und Stromversorgung und die Telekommunikation. In den vergangenen Jahrzehnten hat sich die EPM zunehmend wie ein Privatunternehmen verhalten und sich eine wettbewerbs- und profitorientierte Logik zu eigen gemacht, obwohl die EPM nach wie vor ein öffentlicher Versorgungsbetrieb der Stadt Medellín ist, an die sie 30 % ihrer Leistungen abführt. Von daher ist das Unternehmen auch maßgeblich in kulturelle und planerische Fragen der Stadt involviert und finanziert nicht nur kulturelle Institutionen und Erziehungsprogramme, sondern auch öffentliche Einrichtungen wie Parks und Bibliotheken.[1]

Die Transformation der Wasserversorgung von einer öffentlichen Dienstleistung in eine unternehmerisch orientierte Organisation ist größtenteils das Ergebnis zweier zentraler Veränderungen: Zum einen begann die EPM 1997 einen Prozess der Kommerzialisierung ihrer Dienstleistungen nach Marktkriterien.[2] Zum anderen fand Ende 2010 und Anfang 2011 mit der multinationalen Ausweitung der Geschäftstätigkeit auf andere geografische Gebiete die zweite räumliche und ökonomische Veränderung des Unternehmens statt. Während sich die EPM erfolgreich auf dem Weltmarkt engagiert, berichtet die Stadt von einer Zunahme nichtbezahlter Rechnungen infolge der ständigen Erhöhung der Wassertarife. Das Unternehmen reagierte darauf mit drastischen Maßnahmen und sperrte den betroffenen Haushalten den Zugang zum öffentlichen Wassernetz. Im Jahresbericht 2011 wird die Anzahl der Haushalte, denen wegen nichtbezahlter Rechnungen das Wasser abgesperrt wurde, auf 46.166 beziffert (das sind etwa 6,5 % aller Haushalte). Außerdem berichtet die Stadt, dass schätzungsweise 35.000 Haushalte (d.h. rund 5 % aller Haushalte) wegen der illegalen Landaneignung keinen Zugang zum öffentlichen Wassernetz haben. Obwohl technische Einrichtungen zu einer Vorausbezahlung des Wassers und ein städtisches Programm einer unentgeltlichen Grundversorgung (monatlich 2,5 Kubikmeter pro Person) als Maßnahmen zur Linderung der gegenwärtigen Wasserkrise eingesetzt werden, ist die Effizienz solcher Strategien zweifelhaft, da in erster Linie das Wasserversorgungsunternehmen davon profitiert und nicht mehr auf unbezahlten Rechnungen sitzen bleibt.

Jüngere Untersuchungen[3,4] haben vor allem gezeigt, dass neoliberale Reformen im Wasserversorgungssektor eng mit einer Verbesserung der Wasserqualität, der Steigerung der wirtschaftlichen Leistung und der Effizienz der Versorgung verbunden sind, doch

liberal reforms in the water sector are closely associated to improvement of water quality, increment of economic performance and efficiency in service provision[3,4] however, it has paid insufficient attention to the socio-economic impacts, especially in urban areas characterized by high levels of inequalities. This project intends to address this gap by exploring how the recent transformation of Medellín's multi-utility company has significantly contributed to reinforcing and deepening the already protracted conditions of inequality by taking the case of water disconnection as the main empirical reference. Dominant narratives deployed by the municipality and the water company tend to interpret disconnection as a problem rooted in a "culture of non-payment" while inability to extend infrastructure network to unserved areas is justified by the technical difficulties arising from the topographic conditions of the city's periphery. In contrast, the first argument to be investigated in this project is that disconnection for non-payment represents a particular spatial-temporal moment in the process of insertion of EPM into transnational networks of capital accumulation.

The exclusion from access to the infrastructure networks is based on the grounds that formal water provision implies legalization of land. The latter argument holds significant importance for the case of Colombia as hundreds of campesinos (farmers) have been forced to migrate to the cities as consequence of decades of civil war and their struggle to be recognized as citizens has been translated in a struggle for securing access to land. To capture uneven power relations inherent in processes of capital accumulation, this project follows the circulation of water through the hydro-social cycle.[5,6] This interpretation provides new avenues for understanding how water access and control depends not only on its physical availability (hydrological cycle) but also on political and economic processes operating at different scales of time and space. The recent transformation of EPM is a well-suited case study to document how water circulation in low-income households has shifted from a continuous flow to a prepaid drop. Here is where our story begins.

Panel 1: Transnational connections and local disconnections
A historical and multi-scale analysis explains how the transformation of EPM is strongly embedded in international, national and municipal discourses, defending and legitimizing particular forms of circulating water through the waterscape. The outcomes are detrimental for low-income households.

Panel 2: Governing the hydro-social cycle
The EPM monopoly alleviates particular forms of controlling the hydro-social cycle. The circulation of water as a commodity, combined with the existing conditions of inequality reflected in the socio-economic stratification of the city (Strata 1: poorest and Strata 6: richest), provide a suitable ground for (re)constructing uneven waterscapes.

Panel 3: (Un)commodifying the waterscape
The third page analyses different informal strategies and struggles faced by disconnected households to secure access to water. To capture this complexity, the project classifies desconectados in three groups according to the nature and length of disconnection: suspended (non-payment of 2 to 7 bills), cut off (non-payment of more than 7 bills) and unserved (excluded from the formal water network).

Panel 4: From disconnection to self-disconnection
Water disconnection needs to be understood beyond economic and technical factors. The story of Don Mario and his family depicts the struggles of a low-income family to secure access to water and explains why prepaid systems are presented as the "only viable solution" to reduce water inequalities, while the company uses them as a tool to re-educate low-income households into a "culture of payment".

diese Untersuchungen haben den sozioökonomischen Folgen zu wenig Aufmerksamkeit geschenkt, insbesondere in städtischen Gebieten, die durch ein hohes Ausmaß an Ungleichheit gekennzeichnet sind. Unser Projekt soll diese Lücke füllen, indem es auf der empirischen Grundlage der Wasserabsperrung untersucht, wie die Transformation von Medellíns öffentlichem Versorgungsunternehmen signifikant dazu beigetragen hat, die bereits stark ausgeprägte soziale Ungleichheit noch zu verstärken und zu vertiefen. Die vorherrschenden Erklärungen der Kommunalverwaltung und des Wasserversorgungsunternehmens tendieren dazu, die Absperrung als ein Problem darzustellen, das aus einer "Kultur des Nichtbezahlens" resultiert, während die Unfähigkeit, das infrastrukturelle Versorgungsnetz auf bislang unversorgte Gebiete auszudehnen, mit den technischen Schwierigkeiten gerechtfertigt wird, die sich aus den topografischen Bedingungen am Stadtrand ergeben. Im Unterschied dazu argumentieren wir, dass die Absperrung wegen Nichtbezahlung einen besonderen Moment im Prozess der Eingliederung der EPM in das multinationale Netzwerk der Kapitalakkumulation darstellt.

Der Ausschluss von den infrastrukturellen Netzen ist darauf zurückzuführen, dass eine formale Versorgung mit Wasser eine Legalisierung der Landnahme voraussetzt. Das letztgenannte Argument ist im Falle Kolumbiens von besonderer Bedeutung, denn Hunderte von campesinos (Bauern) sind, als Folge des jahrzehntelangen Bürgerkriegs, dazu gezwungen worden, in die Städte überzusiedeln, und ihr Kampf um eine Anerkennung als Einwohner ist identisch mit dem Kampf um die Sicherung des Zugangs zu Grund und Boden. Um die ungleichen Machtverhältnisse aufzudecken, die den Prozess der Kapitalakkumulation begleiten, folgt unser Projekt der Zirkulation des Wassers durch den hydrosozialen Zyklus.[5,6] Diese Interpretation ermöglicht neue Einsichten darüber, wie Zugänglichkeit und Kontrolle des Wassers nicht nur von dessen physikalischer Verfügbarkeit (hydrologischer Zyklus) abhängen, sondern auch von den politischen und wirtschaftlichen Prozessen, die sich auf unterschiedlichen Maßstabsebenen vollziehen. Die Transformation der EPM bietet eine exemplarische Fallstudie darüber, wie sich die Wasserzirkulation in Haushalten mit niedrigem Einkommen von einem stetigen Fließen in ein vorausbezahltes Tropfen verwandelt hat. Und hier beginnt unsere Geschichte.

Tafel 1: Transnationale Verbindungen und lokale Absperrungen
Eine historische und unterschiedliche Maßstäbe berücksichtigende Analyse erklärt, wie die Transformation der EPM in internationale, nationale und kommunale Diskurse eingebettet ist, die spezifische Formen der Zirkulation des Wassers durch die Wasserlandschaft verteidigen und legitimieren. Die Auswirkungen sind nachteilig für Haushalte mit niedrigem Einkommen.

Tafel 2: Kontrolle des hydro-sozialen Zyklus
Die Monopolstellung der EPM erleichtert bestimmte Formen der Kontrolle des hydro-sozialen Zyklus. Die Zirkulation des Wassers als ein kommerzielles Produkt, in Kombination mit der herrschenden sozialen Ungleichheit, wie sie sich in der sozioökonomischen Schichtung der Stadt widerspiegelt (Schicht 1: die Ärmsten; Schicht 6: die Reichsten), – schafft eine geeignete Grundlage für die (Re)Konstruktion ungleicher Wasserlandschaften.

Tafel 3: (Ent)Kommerzialisierung der Wasserlandschaft
Die dritte Tafel analysiert unterschiedliche informelle Strategien, mittels derer sich abgesperrte Haushalte einen Zugang zu Wasser verschaffen, sowie die Schwierigkeiten, mit denen sie dabei zu rechnen haben. Unser Projekt unterteilt die desconectados in drei Gruppen, entsprechend Art und Dauer der Absperrung: zeitweilig unterbrochen (Nichtbezahlung von 2–7 Rechnungen), abgestellt (Nichtbezahlung von mehr als sieben Rechnungen) und unversorgt (vom öffentlichen Wasserversorgungsnetz komplett ausgeschlossene Haushalte).

Tafel 4: Von der Absperrung zur Selbstabsperrung
Bei Wasserabsperrung spielen nicht nur ökonomische und technische Faktoren eine Rolle. Die Geschichte von Don Mario und seiner Familie veranschaulicht die Anstrengungen, die eine Familie mit geringem Einkommen unternehmen muss, um einen Zugang zu Wasser zu bekommen, und erklärt, warum Vorauszahlungssysteme als die "einzige realisierbare Lösung" zur Reduzierung der Ungleichheiten der Wasserversorgung postuliert werden, während das Versorgungsunternehmen solche Systeme als Erziehungsmittel benutzt, um Haushalte mit geringem Einkommen an eine "Kultur des Bezahlens" zu gewöhnen.

Transnational connection and local disconnections:
The contradictory representation of water through scales of time and space

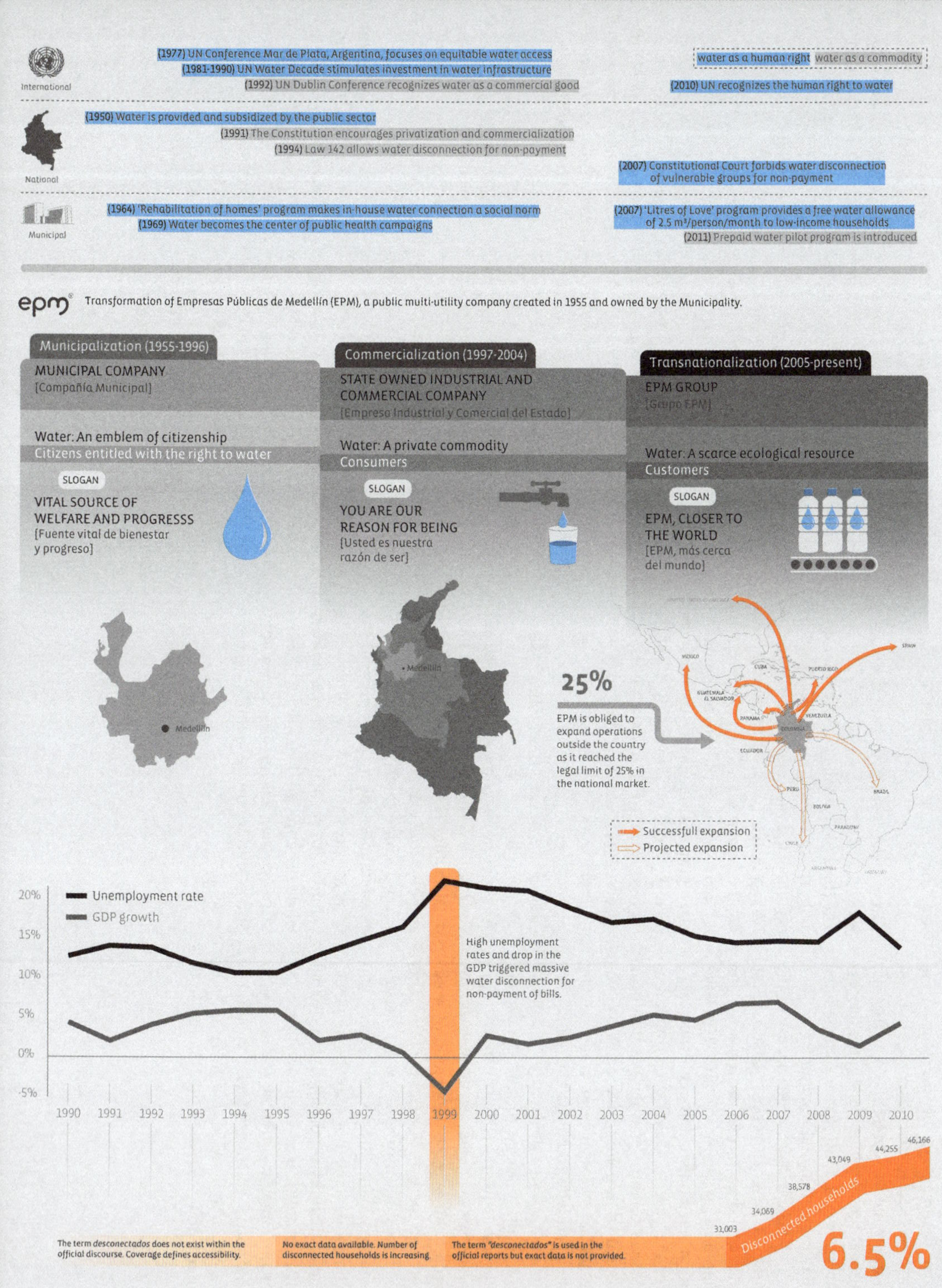

Governing the hydro-social cycle:
Deepening inequalities by creating socio-spatial differentiation

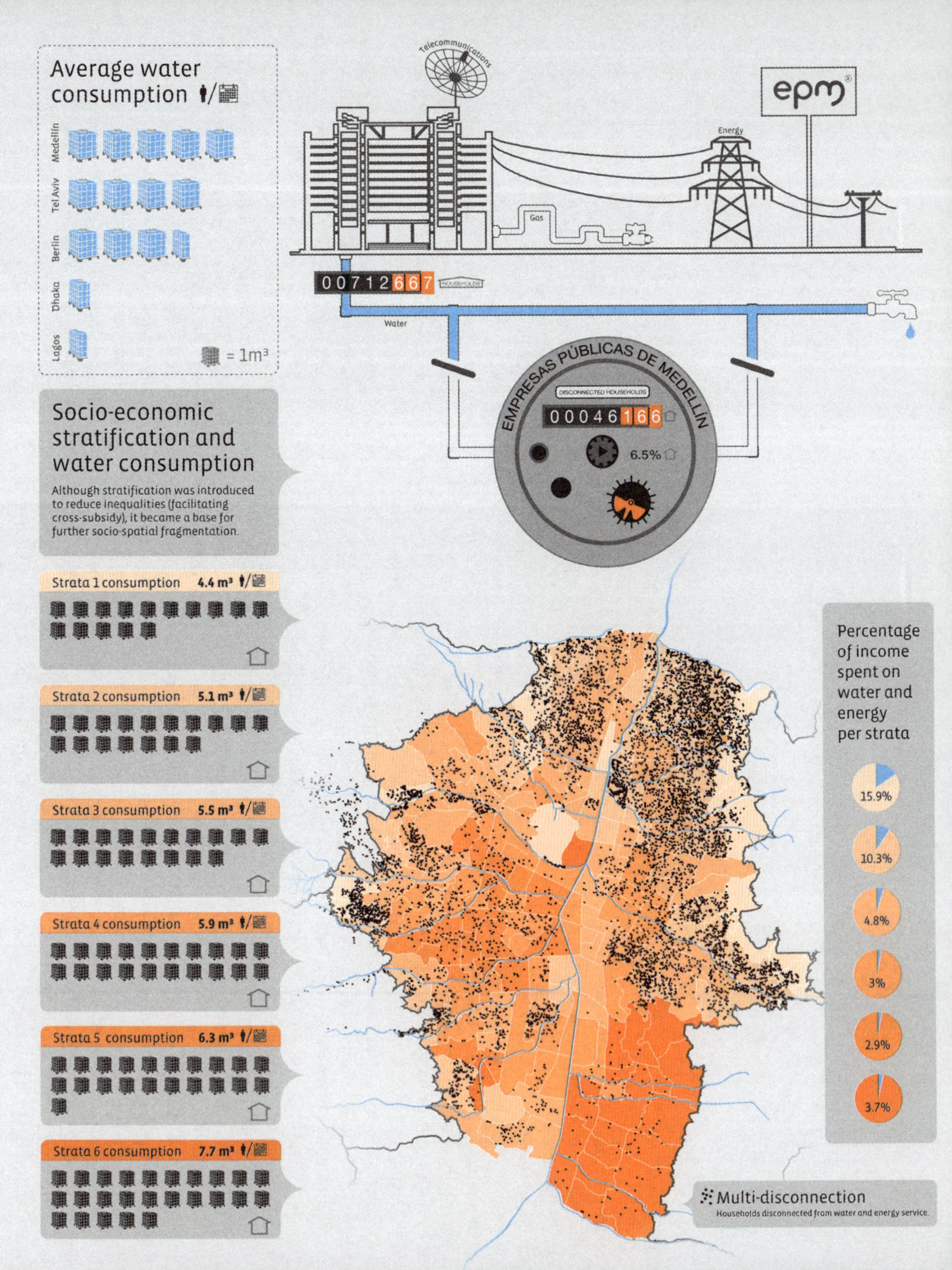

From continuous flow to prepaid drops: Medellín's uneven waterscape

COS741

EMPRESAS PÚBLICAS DE MEDELLÍN

6.5%

Energy
Gas
Telecommunications
Water

Percentage of income spent on water and energy per strata

15.9% 10.3% 4.8% 3% 2.9% 3.7%

Multi-disconnection
Households disconnected from water and energy service.

Average water consumption 👤/🏠

Medellín
Tel Aviv
Berlin
Dhaka
Lagos

🏠 = 1m³

Socio-economic stratification and water consumption

Although stratification was introduced to reduce inequalities (facilitating cross-subsidy), it became a base for further socio-spatial fragmentation.

Strata 1 consumption   4.4 m³
Strata 2 consumption   5.1 m³
Strata 3 consumption   5.5 m³
Strata 4 consumption   5.9 m³
Strata 5 consumption   6.3 m³
Strata 6 consumption   7.7 m³

International
[1977] UN Conference Mar del Plata, Argentina, focuses on equitable water access
[1981-1990] UN Water Decade stimulates investment in water infrastructure
[1992] UN Dublin Conference recognizes water as a commercial good

water as a human right
water as a commodity

[2010] UN recognizes the human right to water

National
[1950] Water is provided and subsidized by the public sector
[1991] The Constitution encourages privatization and commercialization
[1994] Law 142 allows water disconnection for non-payment

[2007] Constitutional Court forbids water disconnection of vulnerable groups for non-payment

Municipal
[1964] 'Rehabilitation of homes' program makes in-house water connection a social norm
[1989] Water becomes the center of public health campaigns

[2007] 'Liters of Love' program provides a free water allowance of 2.5 m³/person/month to low-income households
[2011] Prepaid water pilot program is introduced

Transformation of Empresas Públicas de Medellín (EPM), a public multi-utility company created in 1955 and owned by the Municipality.

Municipalization (1955-1996)
MUNICIPAL COMPANY
[Compañía Municipal]

Water: An emblem of citizenship
Citizens entitled with the right to water

SLOGAN
VITAL SOURCE OF WELFARE AND PROGRESS
[Fuente vital de bienestar y progreso]

Commercialization (1997-2004)
STATE OWNED INDUSTRIAL AND COMMERCIAL COMPANY
[Empresa Industrial y Comercial del Estado]

Water: A private commodity
Consumers

SLOGAN
YOU ARE OUR REASON FOR BEING
[Usted es nuestra razón de ser]

Transnationalization (2005-present)
EPM GROUP
[Grupo EPM]

Water: A scarce ecological resource
Customers

SLOGAN
EPM, CLOSER TO THE WORLD
[EPM, más cerca del mundo]

25%

EPM is obliged to expand operations outside the country as it reached the legal limit of 25% in the national market.

Successful expansion
Projected expansion

High unemployment rates and drop in the GDP triggered massive water disconnection for non-payment of bills.

6.5%
Disconnection projection households

31.003 34.089 38.578 42.049 44.255 46.266

— Unemployment rate
— GDP growth

20% 15% 10% 5% 0% -5%

1990 1991 1992 1993 1994 1995 1996 1997 1998 1999 2000 2001 2002 2003 2004 2005 2006 2007 2008 2009 2010

The term "desconectados" does not exist within the official discourse.

No exact data available. Number of disconnected households is increasing.

The term "desconectados" is used in the official reports but exact data is not provided.

Coverage defines accessibility.

(Un)commodifying the urban waterscape:
Building particular spatial knowledge through informal practices

From disconnection to self-disconnection:
Educating customers in a 'culture of pre-payment'

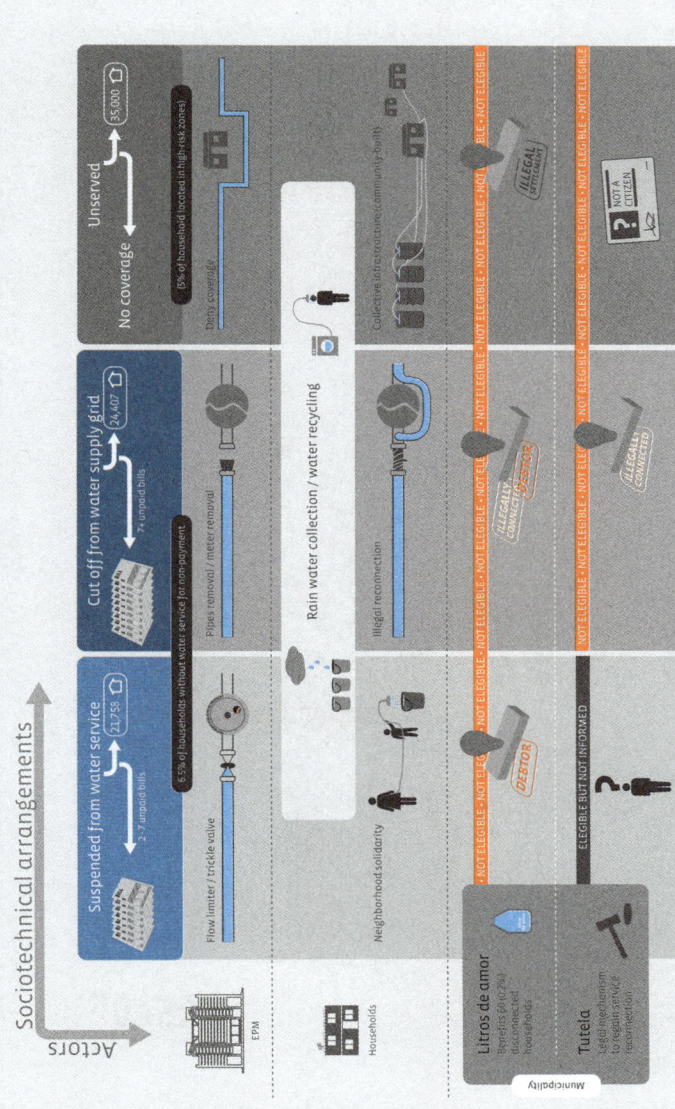

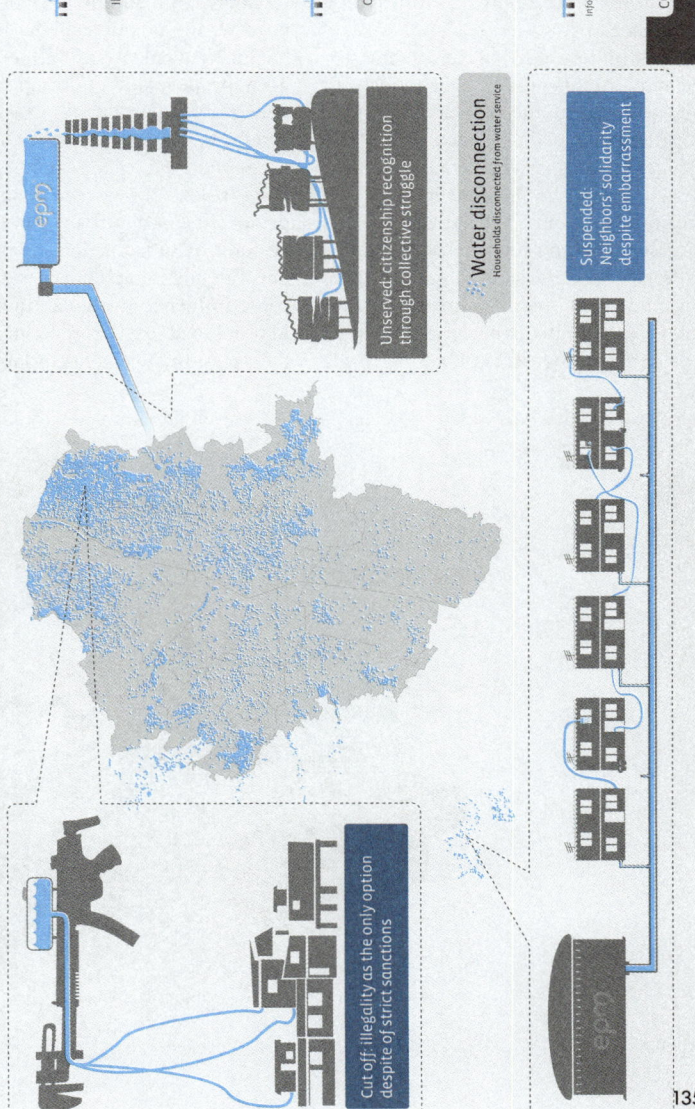

The story of Don Mario and his family

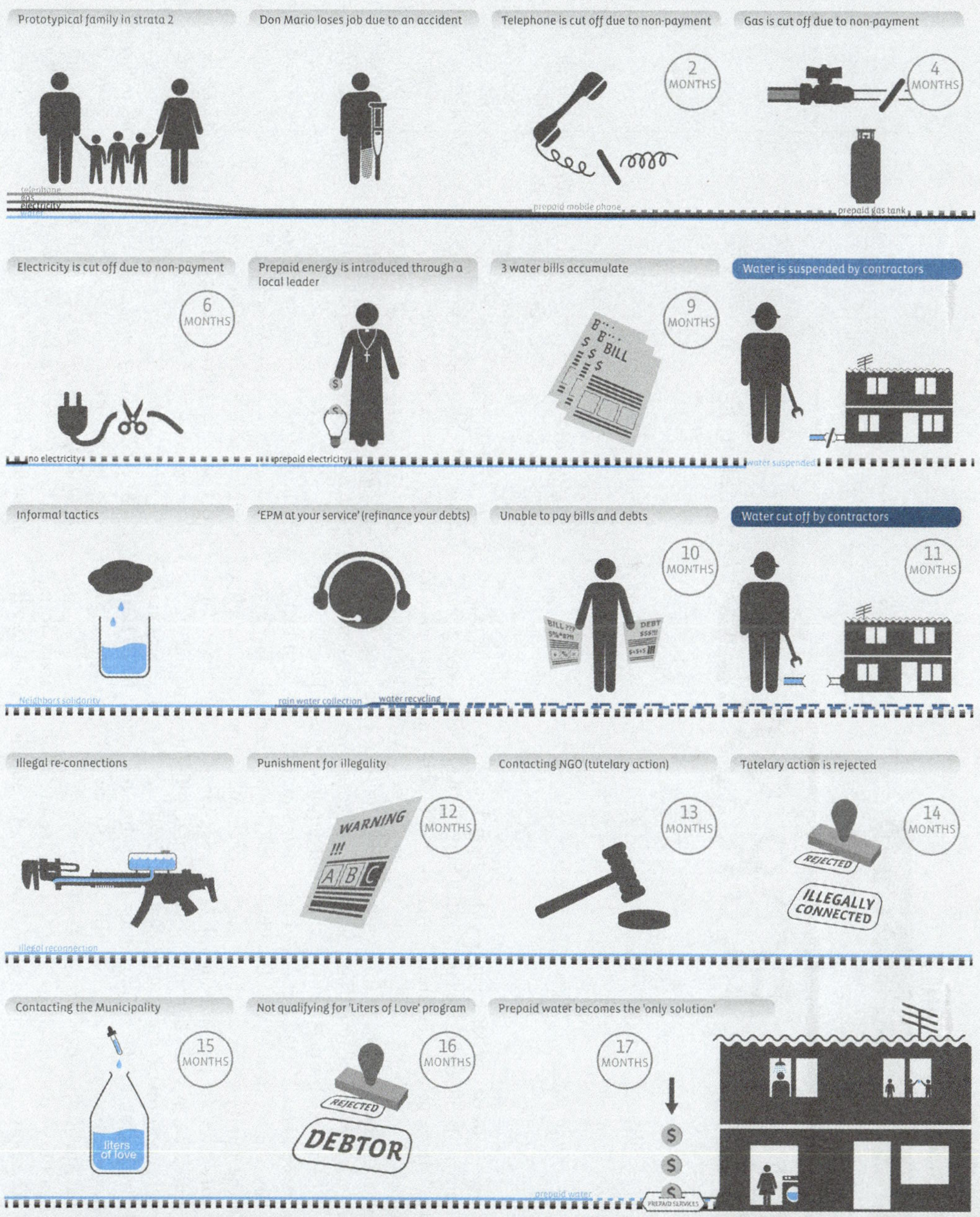

Sociotechnical arrangements

Actors

EPM · Households · Litros de amor · Tutela · Municipality

Suspended from water service · Cut off from water supply grid · No coverage · Unserved

Rain water collection / water recycling

Neighbourhood solidarity · Illegal reconnection

Water disconnection — Households disconnected from water service

Suspended: Neighbors solidarity despite embarrassment

Cut off: illegality as the only option despite of strict sanctions

Unserved: citizenship recognition through collective struggle

COS741

From continuous flow to prepaid drops: Medellín's uneven waterscape

BERLIN FOR SALE Maximilian Pecher

Since 2001, the city of Berlin has been selling off some of its publicly owned real estate. 47% of the total urban area is public property, of which 87% is used for public services and 6% is for sale. The sales are being justified on the grounds of balancing the deeply indebted municipal budget. Yet this debt-reduction policy, the lifespan of which is limited by the number of available plots, will hardly alleviate the colossal municipal debt. This privatisation of public real estate conforms to the usual shortsighted neoliberal urban policy, which eschews steering mechanisms to offset social inequality and limits the scope of political participation if urban areas are removed from public influence.

With the aid of an interactive animation, this project aims to identify the players in the procurement process and to explain how it works. It is a process that otherwise remains hidden. It will show the unequal influence of politics, economy and citizens on the decision-making to this effect. Various official channels, small cogs in a large machine that interlock to set in motion the sellout of the city, determine the selling process. At a selling price

of less than 3 million euros, the caucus of the Senate, the federal state government of Berlin, can make the sale with a simple majority. With sales valued at more than 3 million euros the federal state parliament serves as a second cog that co-determines the selling process. The population itself has no direct influence on the proceedings. The quantitative basis for the project is supplied by the research of the initiative "Open Berlin" and official statistics of the state of Berlin and the "Liegenschaftsfonds" (public real estate fund) Berlin, Berlin's city-owned real estate company.

The animated infographic format illustrates, in addition to the selling process, the position of the initiatives "Stadt Neudenken" and "Open Berlin". They propose a "bottom-up planning" that enables participation in decisions and the exertion of influence in relation to public real estate and, moreover, aims to lead the way to a sustainable perspective on urban development. A body of citizens and experts could develop planning concepts that have some influence on the selling process in order to at least exert an influence on the use of the lost areas of land.

Seit 2001 verkauft die Stadt Berlin einen Teil ihrer öffentlichen Stadtflächen. 47 % der gesamten Stadtfläche sind öffentliches Eigentum, davon dienen 87 % der Daseinsvorsorge, 6 % stehen zum Verkauf. Die Verkäufe werden mit der Sanierung des schwer verschuldeten städtischen Haushalts gerechtfertigt. Tatsächlich lässt sich der städtische Schuldenberg durch diese 'Entschuldungspolitik', die zeitlich durch die Anzahl der zur Verfügung stehenden Grundstücke begrenzt ist, kaum merklich vermindern. Diese Privatisierung öffentlichen Eigentums entspricht der üblichen kurzsichtigen neoliberalen Stadtpolitik, die auf Steuerungsmöglichkeiten im Ausgleich sozialer Ungleichheit verzichtet und das Feld politischer Partizipation begrenzt, wenn Stadträume dem Einfluss der Öffentlichkeit entzogen werden.

Dieses Projekt soll mit Hilfe einer interaktiven Animation transparent machen, wer die Akteure im Vergabeprozess sind und wie dieser abläuft. Es ist ein Prozess, der sonst im Verborgenen bleibt. Gezeigt wird der ungleiche Einfluss von Politik, Wirtschaft und Bevölkerung auf die Entscheidung. Der Verkaufsablauf wird von unterschiedlichen

Instanzen bestimmt, die zahnradartig ineinandergreifen und den Ausverkauf der Stadt in Gang setzen. Bei einem Verkaufswert von unter 3 Millionen Euro kann der Ausschuss der Senatsverwaltung den Verkauf mit einfacher Mehrheit durchführen. Bei Verkäufen von über 3 Millionen Euro bestimmt das Abgeordnetenhaus als zweites Zahnrad den Verkaufsprozess mit. Die Bevölkerung selbst hat keinen direkten Einfluss auf den Ablauf. Quantitative Grundlage der Arbeit sind die Recherchen der Initiative "Open Berlin" und offizielle Statistiken des Landes und des Liegenschaftsfonds.

Die animierte Form der Infografik zeigt neben dem Verkaufsablauf auch die Position der Initiativen "Stadt Neudenken" und "Open Berlin". Sie schlagen eine "Planung von unten" vor, die eine Teilhabe an Entscheidungen und die Einflussnahme auf öffentliches Eigentum ermöglichen und darüber hinaus auch einen nachhaltigen Blick auf die Stadtentwicklung lenken soll. Eine Gemeinschaft aus Bürgern und Experten könnte Planungskonzepte entwickeln, die in den Verkaufsprozess einfließen, um wenigstens einen Einfluss auf die Nutzung der verlorenen Flächen nehmen zu können.

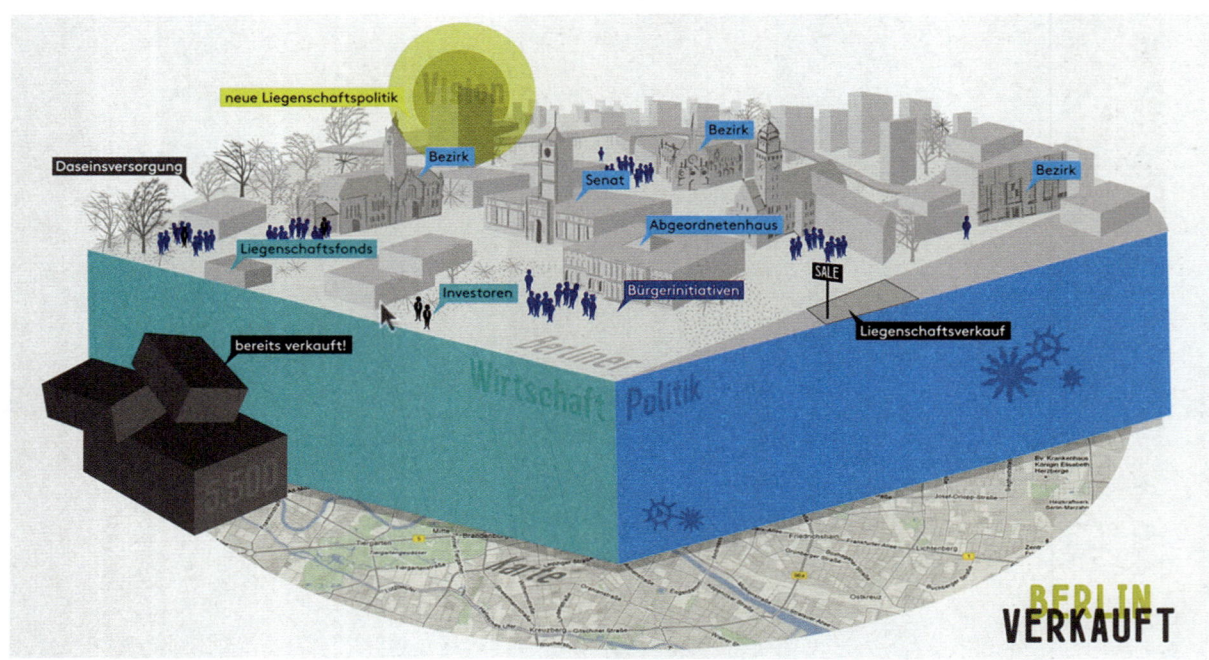

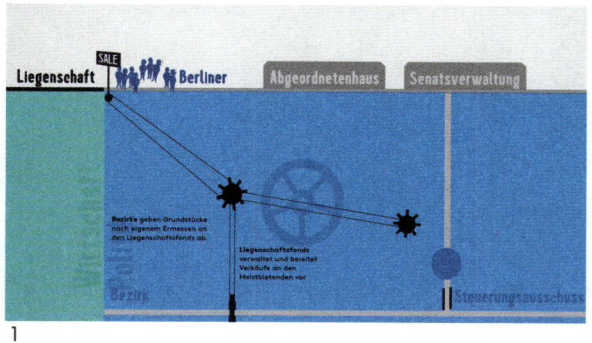

1

2

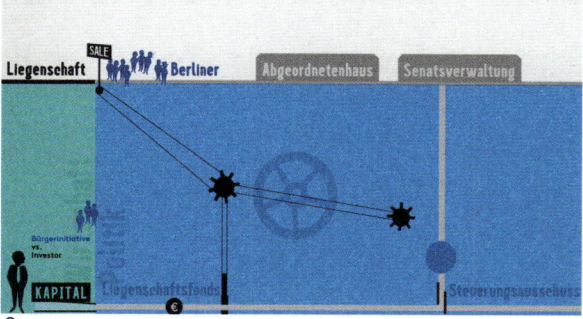

3

4

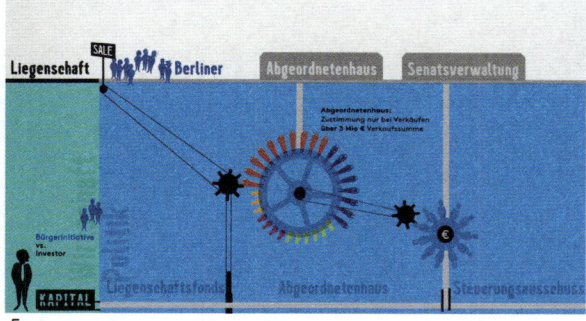

5

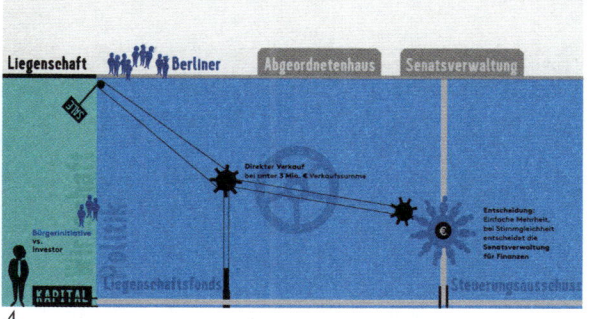

6

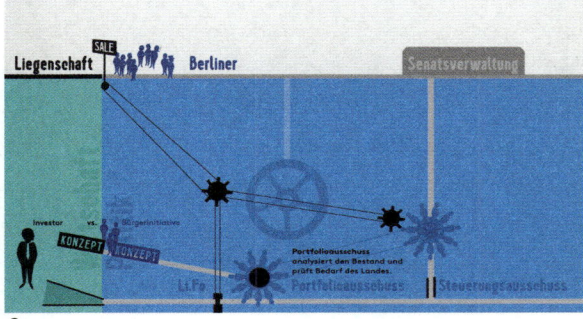

7

8

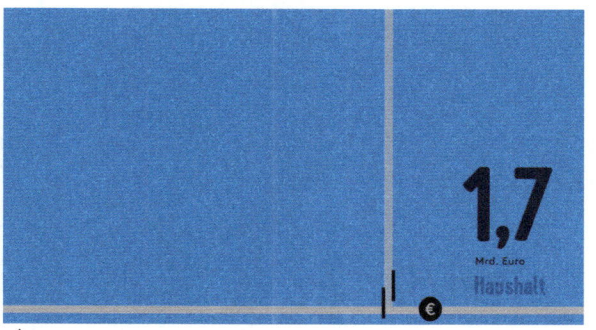

9

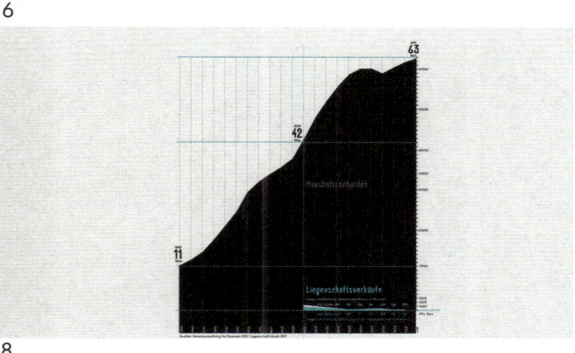

10

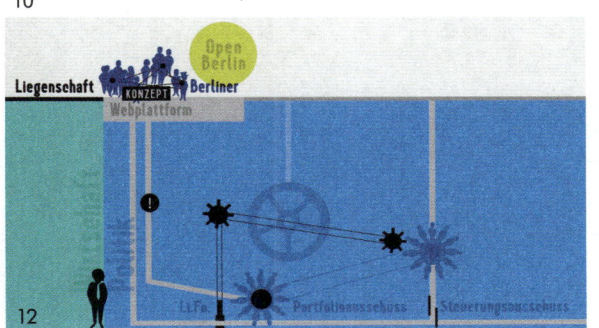

11

12

1. The districts of Berlin hand plots of land to the "Liegenschaftsfonds" (public real estate fund), which prepares the sale without the citizens having any influence on the matter.
2. In effect, anyone can buy the property. In practice, however, capital holds sway. Usage concepts for the plot remain unheeded.
3. With financially strong investors, the sale process begins. The steering committee decides on the sale with a simple majority; where there is no majority, the decision is made by the Senate Department for Finance.
4. Accordingly, plots with a selling price of less than 3 million euros can be sold directly.
5. With regards to higher-priced real estate only, the federal state parliament, which represents the citizens, has a say in the decision and becomes an important cog in the process.
6. Since 2001, 1.7 billion euros have been raised for Berlin's budget by these means.
7+8. A small sum when compared with the budget deficit of 63 billion euros.
9. In 2012 the Senate Department for Finance put forward a proposal for more transparency in the real estate policy with the introduction of a portfolio committee.
10+11. For the citizens this committee is unsatisfactory due to shortcomings in the selection criteria; the initiatives "Stadt Neudenken" and "Open Berlin" envisage creating a body of citizens and experts.
12. Here, alternative concepts are being developed so that sales of publicly owned real estate are not based solely on capital gains but also include reasonable proposals for usage.

1. Die Berliner Bezirke geben Grundstücke an den Liegenschaftsfonds ab, der den Verkauf vorbereitet, ohne dass die Bürger darauf Einfluss nehmen können.
2. Faktisch hat jeder die Chance, die Liegenschaft zu erwerben. In der Praxis entscheidet jedoch nur das Kapital. Nutzungskonzepte für das Grundstück bleiben unbeachtet.
3. Durch zahlungskräftige Investoren kommt der Verkauf in Gang. Der Steuerungsausschuss entscheidet über den Verkauf mit einfacher Mehrheit, bei Stimmengleichheit entscheidet die Senatsverwaltung für Finanzen.
4. Grundstücke mit einem Verkaufswert von unter 3 Millionen Euro können so direkt verkauft werden.
5. Nur bei Liegenschaften mit höherem Wert entscheidet das Abgeordnetenhaus als Repräsentanten der Bevölkerung mit und wird ein wichtiger Teil des Zahnradprozesses.
6. Seit 2001 konnten so 1,7 Mrd. Euro für den Berliner Haushalt eingenommen werden.
7+8. Im Vergleich zu den Haushaltsschulden von 63 Mrd. Euro eine geringe Summe.
9. 2012 hat die Senatsverwaltung für Finanzen mit der Einführung eines Portfolioausschusses einen Vorschlag für mehr Transparenz in der Liegenschaftspolitik gemacht.
10+11. Für die Bürger ist dieser Ausschuss aufgrund fehlender Auswahlkriterien ungenügend; die Initiative "Stadt Neudenken" und "Open Berlin" hat die Vision einer Gemeinschaft aus Bürgern und Experten.
12. Hier werden alternative Konzepte entwickelt, um die öffentlichen Flächen nicht allein aufgrund des Kapitaleintrags zu verkaufen, sondern sinnvolle Nutzungsvorschläge miteinzubeziehen.

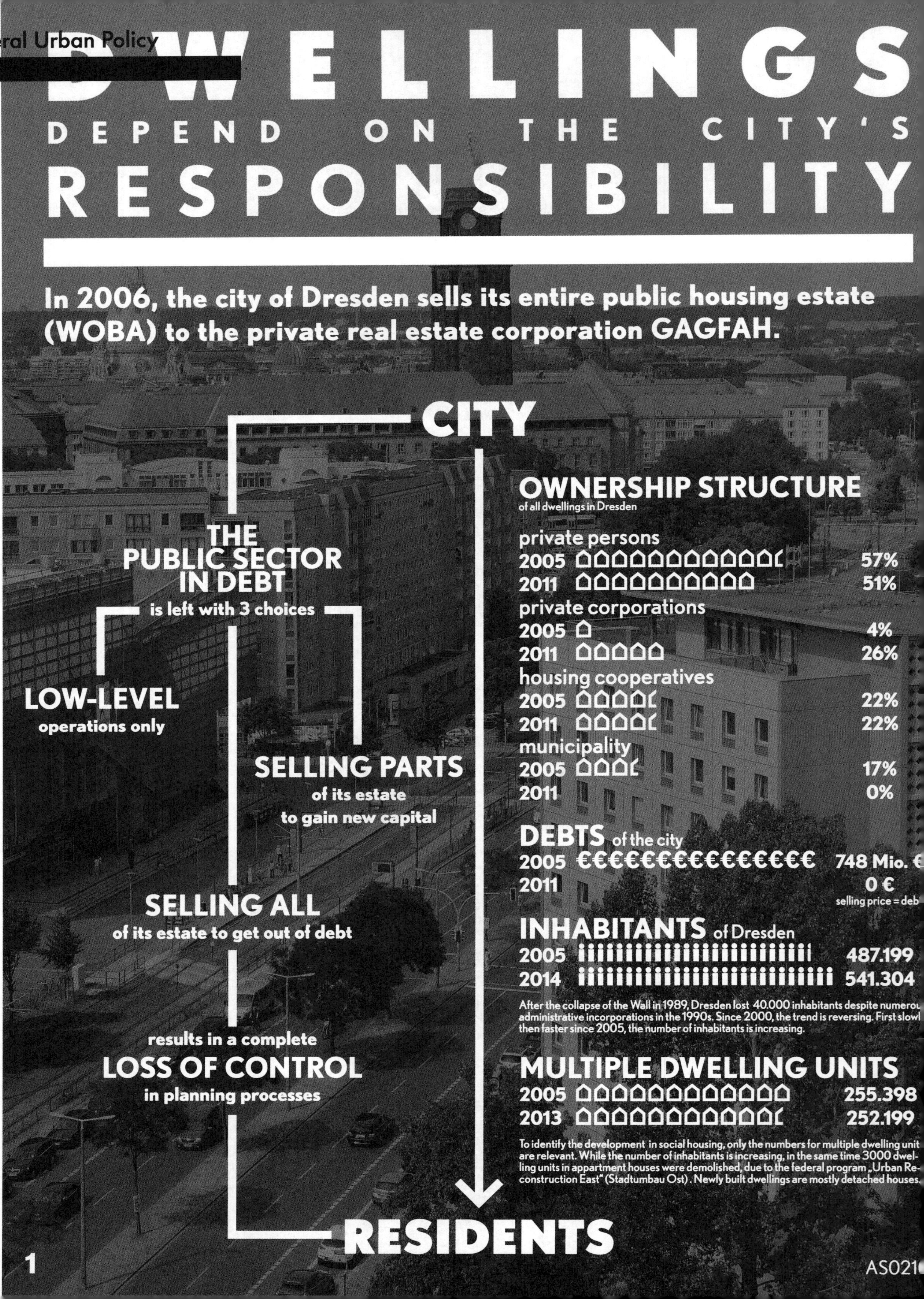

DWELLINGS
DEPEND ON THE CITY'S
RESPONSIBILITY

In 2006, the city of Dresden sells its entire public housing estate (WOBA) to the private real estate corporation GAGFAH.

CITY

THE PUBLIC SECTOR IN DEBT
is left with 3 choices

LOW-LEVEL
operations only

SELLING PARTS
of its estate
to gain new capital

SELLING ALL
of its estate to get out of debt

results in a complete
LOSS OF CONTROL
in planning processes

OWNERSHIP STRUCTURE
of all dwellings in Dresden

private persons
2005   57%
2011   51%

private corporations
2005   4%
2011   26%

housing cooperatives
2005   22%
2011   22%

municipality
2005   17%
2011   0%

DEBTS of the city
2005   748 Mio. €
2011   0 €
selling price = deb‍

INHABITANTS of Dresden
2005   487.199
2014   541.304

After the collapse of the Wall in 1989, Dresden lost 40.000 inhabitants despite numerou‍ administrative incorporations in the 1990s. Since 2000, the trend is reversing. First slowl‍ then faster since 2005, the number of inhabitants is increasing.

MULTIPLE DWELLING UNITS
2005   255.398
2013   252.199

To identify the development in social housing, only the numbers for multiple dwelling unit‍ are relevant. While the number of inhabitants is increasing, in the same time 3000 dwel‍ ling units in appartment houses were demolished, due to the federal program „Urban Re‍ construction East" (Stadtumbau Ost) . Newly built dwellings are mostly detached houses.

RESIDENTS

Diana Felber, Michael Wicke, Arne Schmitt

DWELLINGS
ARE INSTRUMENTS OF
CITY DEVELOPMENT

A real estate corporation such as GAGFAH has no interest in the social structure of a city, but in maximizing profit.

REAL ESTATE CORPORATION

MAXIMIZING PROFIT
by
distinguishing locations:

DOWNGRADING
large parts of
substandard real estate

UPGRADING
a small part of
promising real estate

leads to

URBAN SEGREGATION

SOCIAL CHARTA (for 10 years only)
As a part of the sale contract, the city implemented certain regulations, including:

- a limitation in rent increases
- life-long right of residence for renters 60+ and severely handicapped
- preference for renters in case of sale, price must be 15% under market value
- luxury refurbishment is prohibited
- limitation for resale (at least 35.000 units must be kept)
- involvement of GAGFAH in urban planning processes (INSEK)

In 2011, there was a legal battle around the social charta: the city sued GAGFAH for violating the agreement by not preferring renters in case of sale. The parties settled in an out-of-court agreement in 2012.

NUMBER of all (former) WOBA dwellings
2005 ⌂⌂⌂⌂⌂⌂⌂⌂⌂⌂⌂⌂   ~48.000
2011 ⌂⌂⌂⌂⌂⌂⌂⌂⌂   ~37.000

This decline is referrable to the sale of most lucrative items and demolition of peripheral buildings. On a segregation index of German cities, Dresden was ranked 5th, right behind Frankfurt a.M., Leipzig, Berlin and Hamburg. Only there, high and low earners lived further apart from each other.

AVERAGE SALE PRICE per dwelling
2005 €€€€€€€€€   ~35.000 €
2015 €€€€€€€€€€€€€€€€€   ~64.000 €

Meaning: a profit margin of 91% in 9 years, 10% per year, supplemented by profits from selling the most lucrative items cited above. The latter occur in upscale locations mainly, leading to an increase in rent and a decline in social housing in these inner-city or popular neighborhoods.

CITY

DWELLINGS
ARE USED AS OBJECTS OF
SPECULATION

In 2015, GAGFAH merges with Deutsche Annington to form Germany's largest real estate corporation VONOVIA.

REAL ESTATE CORPORATION

MORE AND MORE MERGERS

between large corporations lead to further

ACCUMULATION OF CAPITAL

which leads to a

DECLINE IN:
- **DIVERSITY**
- **TRANSPARENCY**
- **COMPETITION**

all resulting in

LESS AND LESS HOUSING QUALITY

SHAREHOLDERS of GAGFAH S.A.
stock corporation, place of business: Luxembourg, numbers from 17/04/15

Lansdowne Partners hedge fund, place of business: London (UK), Vienna (AUT), Cayman Islands	8,5%
Sun Life Financial stock corporation, place of business: Toronto (CAN)	7,2%
2004 - 2013:	
Fortress Investment Group hedge fund, place of business: N.Y.C. (USA), shares since 2013 in free float	60%

SHAREHOLDERS of Deutsche Annington
stock corporation, place of business: Düsseldorf (GER); numbers from 17/04/15

Abu Dhabi Investment Authority sovereign wealth fund of United Arab Emirates, place of business: Luxembourg	11,9%
Norges Bank central bank of Norway, place of business: Oslo (NOR)	7,8%
The Wellcome Trust biomedical research charity, place of business: London (UK)	11,9%
BlackRock world's largest asset manager, place of business: N.Y.C. (USA)	6%
Sun Life Financial stock corporation, place of business: Toronto (CAN)	3,1%

THE RENTER'S VOICE
from newspaper articles on the practice of Deutsche Annington and GAGFAH

ℹ „They told me on the phone that a little water would be reason to move out immediatly." «Water damage dislodges renters» Ruhr Nachrichten, 29/5/15

ℹ „The call-center employees told me they have orders t serve no applicants on welfare." «Apartment search with pitfall» General-Anzeiger Bonn, 3/2/15

ℹ „Rent had just been raised by 20%, and there wasn't ev a phone number on the letter." «Renters angry: Complaints about GAGFAH pile up» DNN-online, 2/

RESIDENTS

DWELLING
IS THE BASIS FOR SOCIAL
COEXISTENCE

When a city has lost direct control, it has to find alternative ways to engage in housing policy.

CITY

The broader the range of participants in the development process, **the more resilient the structure of a city can get.** This is why we think that besides political actors, **grassroot movements have to be promoted.** If political structures are supposed to **provide the basic elements** that make a city work, people have to be granted the right to adapt the city to their needs. We think further concentration on neoliberal phantasies in which **few powerful players pull the strings** will do harm to the cities of the future. For that reason, the city should become involved in various ways: **buy back and build new MUNICIPAL HOUSING ASSOCIATIONS** to fit the basic needs of city residents and to counteract segregation. In addition, private **BUILDERS COMMUNITIES have to be promoted, ranging from multi-generational living to grant-aided small houses. Platforms for interaction of all actors** have to be provided and moderated, enabling people to **shape their habitat by themselves**, to adapt it to new needs and to securly **invest in their own neighborhoods. COOPERATIVES** in the field of **real estate** (Leipzig Ostblock), **energy** (Bürger Energie Berlin)**, etc.** with **fresh social concepts and participation rights** ranging from domestic rules to the further development of the cooperative, are a much more responsive alternative than investments driven by the rate of return. Transparent, community-based processes promote **participation, accountability and trust:** therefore, cooperatives should be granted finacial aid and be favored in leasing land which is still in possession of the city. **APPROPRIATION OF SPACE** (Berlin Tempelhof)**, Open Space** (urban gardening, makerspace, etc.) and **room laboratories** are temporary urban development tools which enable the inhabitants to **adapt the city to their needs. DYNAMIC AND STRICT RULES** which are able to **react to segregation and gentrification** (Hamburg 3×⅓) and keep governmental structures transparent, are an important means of regulation.

RESIDENTS

BUY BUY B€RLIN Dominik Rau

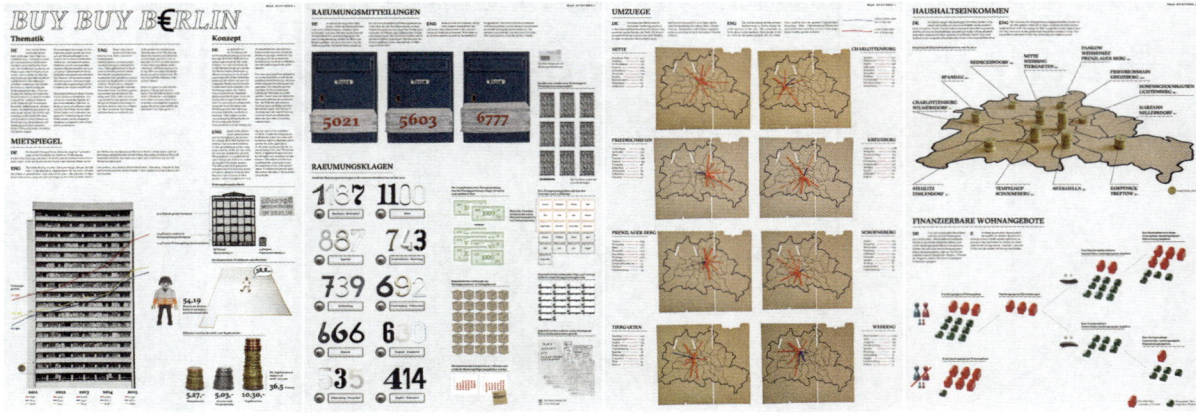

Those who can no longer afford the rent have to move – a result of gentrification: Neighborhoods are modernised, rebuilt and revalued, the resident population is displaced by a richer social stratum. Since a few years this process of gentrifcation can be found in Berlin. The capital pressure on inner-city areas is higher in Berlin than in any other German city.

The process often follows the same pattern. First students, artists and subcultural groups move into a certain quarter because of cheap rents. They raise the interest in the quarter and bring about a first upvaluation. The housing demand rises and investors wind chances for increased profit. First houses and apartments are restored, new clubs, restaurants and bars develop. The rents rise. The resident population, the students and artists, cannot afford the increased rents, and are being displaced. They move to different quarters. A new richer clientele sets different standards for living. Real Estate Companies discover the demand, further luxury renovations occur until the character of the quarter has fundamentally changed and the original socio-economical structure is disposed of.

Wer sich die Miete nicht mehr leisten kann, zieht weg – eine Folge von Gentrifizierung: Stadtviertel werden durch Sanierungen oder Umbauten aufgewertet, die dort ansässige Bevölkerung durch wohlhabendere Bevölkerungsschichten verdrängt, das Wohnungspreisniveau steigt. Seit einigen Jahren ist dieser Prozess auch in Berlin zu beobachten. Zurzeit ist der Druck des Kapitals auf die innenstadtnahen Flächen in Berlin so groß wie in keiner anderen deutschen Stadt.

Es ist ein Prozess, der häufig nach einem typischen Muster abläuft: Aufgrund der niedrigen Mieten wird ein Stadtteil für Studierende, Künstler, Subkulturen etc. attraktiv; sie machen das Viertel interessant und sorgen für eine erste Aufwertung. Die Wohnungsnachfrage steigt und Investoren sehen Chancen zur Wertsteigerung. Erste Häuser und Wohnungen werden restauriert, Szene-Clubs und Kneipen entstehen. Die Mieten steigen. Die ansässigen Bewohner, die Studierenden und Künstler, können sich die Mieterhöhungen nicht leisten und werden verdrängt. Sie siedeln in andere Stadtteile um. Eine neue wohlhabendere Klientel setzt andere Lebensstandards durch. Immobilienunternehmen entdecken das Interesse, es folgen weitere Luxussanierungen, bis der Charakter des Viertels sich grundlegend gewandelt hat und die ursprüngliche sozialökonomische Struktur beseitigt wurde.

RENT INDEX

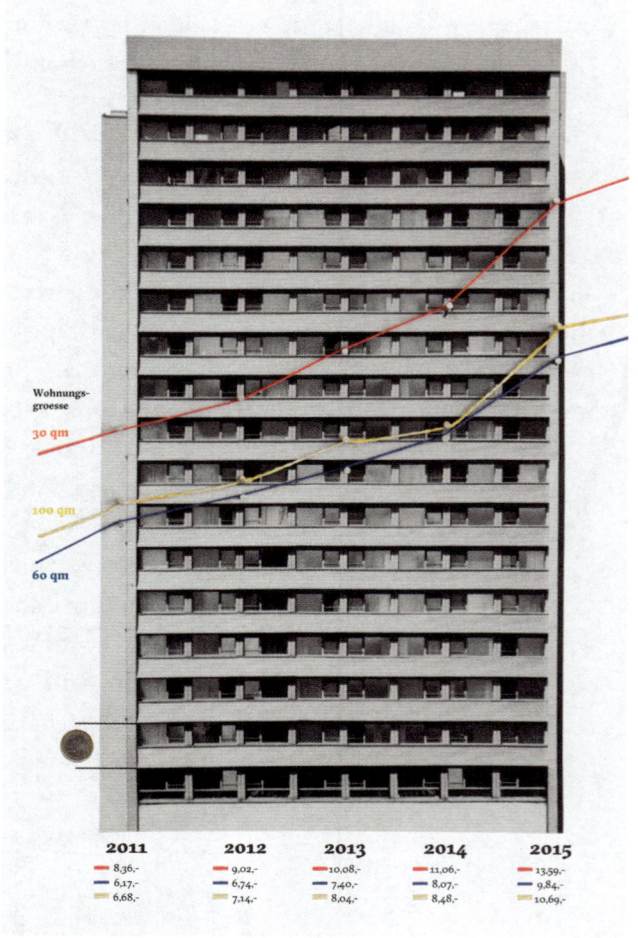

Wohnungs-groesse
30 qm
100 qm
60 qm

2011	2012	2013	2014	2015
8,36,-	9,02,-	10,08,-	11,06,-	13,59,-
6,17,-	6,74,-	7,40,-	8,07,-	9,84,-
6,68,-	7,14,-	8,04,-	8,48,-	10,69,-

ACTIONS OF EVICTION

In Germany, rent arrears are among the most common reasons for dismissal. In the case of eviction, tenants are sued by their landlord to leave the apartment. The amount of eviction notices has increased in recent years. The most evictions took place within the S-Bahn ring of Berlin.

Mietrückstände sind einer der häufigsten Kündigungsgründe in Deutschland. Bei einer Zwangsräumung werden die Mieter per Räumungsklage von ihrem Vermieter aus der Wohnung geklagt. In den letzten Jahren sind die Mitteilungen über anberaumte Zwangsräumungen angestiegen. Ein Großteil der Räumungsklagen findet innerhalb des S-Bahnrings von Berlin statt.

MITTE

Prenzlauer Berg	411
Wedding	250
Friedrichshain	191
Pankow	135
Lichtenberg	104
Neukoelln	102
Steglitz	72
Reinickendorf	62
Weissensee	62
Hellersdorf	58

CHARLOTTENBURG

Spandau	521
Wilmersdorf	203
Steglitz	146
Zehlendorf	134
Tiergarten	93
Tempelhof	78
Wedding	76
Reinickendorf	73
Prenzlauer Berg	59
Schoeneberg	37

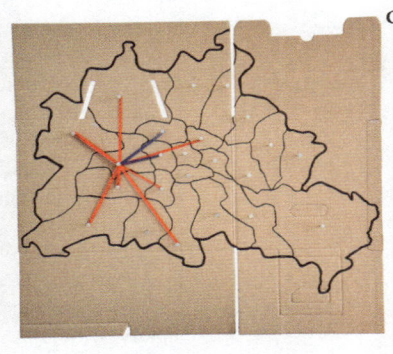

FRIEDRICHSHAIN

Lichtenberg	793
Neukoelln	531
Mitte	191
Treptow	158
Pankow	129
Tiergarten	98
Koepenick	97
Weissensee	84
Hellersdorf	83
Marzahn	57

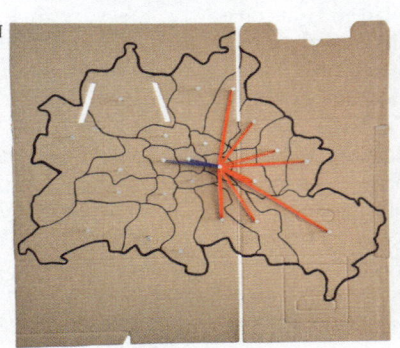

KREUZBERG

Neukoelln	1188
Tempelhof	409
Prenzlauer Berg	219
Treptow	183
Schoeneberg	176
Reinickendorf	146
Wedding	114
Steglitz	100
Zehlendorf	62
Pankow	54

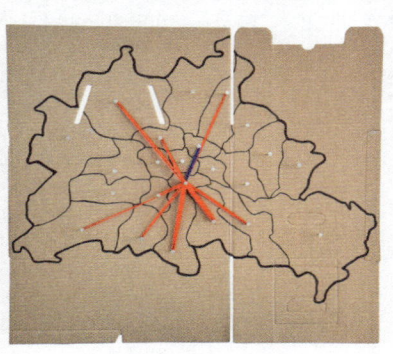

RELOCATIONS

The increasing rents and the growing displacement pressure in Berlin change the social structure of the city. The movements in Berlin show a clear tendency to suburbanisation: The more centralised the quarter, the greater the migration.

Die steigenden Mieten und der wachsende Verdrängungsdruck in den Innenstadtbezirken haben Einfluss auf die sozialräumliche Struktur der Stadt. Die Umzüge innerhalb Berlins weisen eine klare Tendenz zu einer verstärkten Randwanderung auf: Je zentraler das Viertel, desto größer die Abwanderung.

HOUSEHOLD INCOME

Life in the inner-city of Berlin only can be afforded by a wealthy social stratum. 39 percent of the existing appartments are suitable for families, but only 29 percent of the apartments are financially affordable for average income households, only 7 percent for low-income families.

Das Leben in den Innenstadtbezirken kann sich nur noch eine einkommensstarke Bevölkerungsschicht leisten. Von den existierenden Berliner Wohnungen sind 39 % für Familien geeignet, jedoch nur 29 % für den Durchschnittsverdiener und nur 7 % für Familien mit geringem Einkommen bezahlbar.

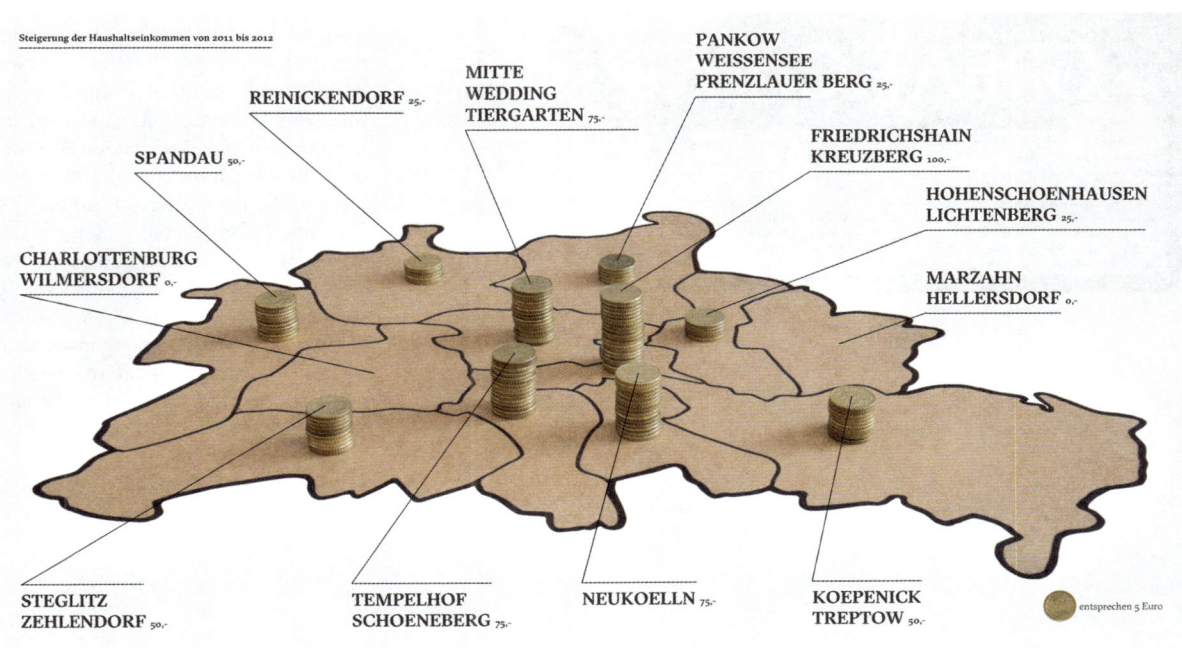

Steigerung der Haushaltseinkommen von 2011 bis 2012

REINICKENDORF 25,-
SPANDAU 50,-
CHARLOTTENBURG WILMERSDORF 0,-
MITTE WEDDING TIERGARTEN 75,-
PANKOW WEISSENSEE PRENZLAUER BERG 25,-
FRIEDRICHSHAIN KREUZBERG 100,-
HOHENSCHOENHAUSEN LICHTENBERG 25,-
MARZAHN HELLERSDORF 0,-
STEGLITZ ZEHLENDORF 50,-
TEMPELHOF SCHOENEBERG 75,-
NEUKOELLN 75,-
KOEPENICK TREPTOW 50,-

entsprechen 5 Euro

ISTANBUL – GREAT CITY LIFE

Andreas Lang, Simon Delbeck,
Evgeniya Panova, Marina Petrova

Tarlabaşi, a historical low-income neighbourhood in the heart of Istanbul, is less than a five-minute walk away from the illustrious Istiklal Caddesi shopping street.[1] Its inhabitants have to cope with high crime rates, illegal trade and prostitution and a highly dilapidated building mass. Yet, Tarlabaşi has been a haven for mainly Kurdish migrants from rural Turkey, refugees from neighbouring states and Africa, as well as marginalised groups such as transsexuals.[1] Informal or illegal labourers are settling in the neighbourhood because it is central, thus offering more employment opportunities in adjacent upmarket areas like Istiklal.

Its central location also led to the stately Housing Development Administration (TOKI) targeting the area in 2006 as a possible zone for large-scale – and highly profitable – urban renewal. TOKI, a public agency on the surface, is essentially a "state led real estate business" that administers the sale of public assets to private enterprises, thus privatising public land and real estate on a grand scale. The colossal profits from real estate and construction industry are supposed to make Turkey one of the world's leading economic powers.[2]

In addition, a newly introduced law extended local municipalities' expropriation power by making it possible to implement renewal for various blocks without the assent of property owners or tenants.[1] After years of court battles over property rights, renewal projects took off in 2012. Re-development includes shopping malls, upmarket apartments and recreation facilities on a 20,000 sqm area of Tarlabaşi, as well as the demolition of around 200 authentic Ottoman-era buildings.[3] Also at risk is the neighbourhood's diverse community. TOKI announced on its website that redevelopment would encompass the relocation of inhabitants to new housing estates and the eviction of squatter households, so that the area would be "cleansed" for future regeneration.

Text: Anna Aichinger

Tarlabaşi, ein historisches, sozial benachteiligtes Stadtviertel im Herzen Istanbuls, ist zu Fuß weniger als fünf Minuten entfernt von der bedeutenden Einkaufsstraße Istiklal Caddesi.[1] Seine Einwohner haben mit hoher Kriminalität, illegalem Handel und Prostitution sowie einer stark verfallenen Bausubstanz zu kämpfen. Dennoch bietet Tarlabaşi einen Zufluchtsort für hauptsächlich kurdische Migranten aus dem türkischen Umland, Flüchtlinge aus Nachbarstaaten und Afrika und marginalisierte Gruppen wie z.B. Transsexuelle.[1] Informelle oder illegale Arbeiter lassen sich im Viertel nieder, weil es zentral gelegen ist und somit mehr Arbeitsmöglichkeiten in den benachbarten gehobenen Gegenden wie Istiklal bietet.

Seine zentrale Lage führte außerdem dazu, dass das Viertel von der staatlichen Wohnungsbaubehörde (TOKI) im Jahr 2006 als eine mögliche Zone für großmaßstäbliche – und höchst profitable –Stadterneuerungsprojekte ins Visier genommen wurde. TOKI, oberflächlich betrachtet ein öffentlicher Bedarfsträger, ist im Grunde ein "staatliches Immobilienunternehmen", das den Verkauf von öffentlichen Liegenschaften an Private verwaltet und so öffentliches Land und Immobilien im großen Stil privatisiert. Die horrenden Profite aus der Immobilien- und Bauindustrie sollen die Türkei zu einer der weltweit führenden Wirtschaftsnationen machen.[2]

Ein neu verfasstes Gesetz erweiterte zudem das Enteignungsrecht von lokalen Stadtverwaltungen, indem es ihnen ermöglicht, die Erneuerung vieler Wohnblöcke ohne die Zustimmung der Hausbesitzer oder Mieter in Gang zu setzen.[1] Nach jahrelangen Gerichtsverhandlungen über Eigentumsrechte wurden die Stadterneuerungsprojekte im Jahr 2012 eingeleitet. Die baulichen Entwicklungen schließen Einkaufszentren, Luxusappartements und Freizeiteinrichtungen auf einer 20.000 qm großen Fläche von Tarlabaşi mit ein sowie den Abriss von etwa 200 authentischen ottomanischen Gebäuden.[3] Auf dem Spiel steht auch die vielfältige Gemeinschaft des Viertels. TOKI gab auf seiner Website bekannt, dass die Stadterneuerungsprojekte die Umsiedelung von Einwohnern in neue Wohnsiedlungen und die Zwangsräumung von Hausbesetzern umfassen würden, um das Viertel für die zukünftige Regenierung zu "säubern".

so easy to play ...

find... grab...

throw!

but be aware of the residents!

If they stay in the neighborhood or return and reoccupy the houses – GAME OVER!

locals
- mainly large families
- easy to deal with as many of them are not aware of their rights
- prevent them from gathering in groups
- they become stronger to break through the fence!

craftsmen
- strong and skilled - they can break fences easily
- they use hammers, automobile tools, scissors and other inventive instruments from their workshops
- keep an eye on them and try to neutralize them faster than locals

shop owners
- they can spread information and gossips about your renewal plans and unite them in the district
- gain them over by using angry shop owner button and they will help you with eviction process

activists
- they inform inhabitants about your renewal plans and unite everyone
- once everyone is against you, it's going to be even harder to win

bazaar of ITEMS

From the MAIN MENU you can enter the BAZAAR. Here you can discover a wide range of ITEMS, which will help you improve your high score! ITEMS are tools you can use to keep the locals in a new outskirt housing settlement or prevent them from moving back to the neighborhood. Once you purchase an item it will immediately appear in the game.

explore a huge set of ITEMS!

storehouses

Mass housing is an efficient investment - cheap and fast way to accommodate the unwanted people in the outskirts. The higher building you purchase - the more people you can get rid of. Mass Housing Blocks are usually located far away from the city center - you can be sure that the resettled people will never come back.

provisional shack extension shack prefabricated house concrete block building high-rise building

streets

To expand the traffic area is a very easy, but effective way to set obstacles to the renewal area. As it was already proved by a successful extension of Tarlabasi Boulevard inhabitants will hardly find the way to cross the traffic area. To narrow the traffic area you can buy to isolate the unwanted from the renewal area.

path one lane street two lane street four lane street six lane street

fences

Fences are a powerful tool to increase security of the area you are renovating. It serves as an effective barrier and holds back your opponent. One of the favorite fences of the urban developers in Istanbul is a high metal fence that prevents locals to enter the neighborhood or even see what happens to their houses. Don't forget to upgrade your fences and prevent the invasion of your renewal project!

barricades bushes wooden fence mesh wire fences metal fence concrete wall

---

bazaar of BUTTONS

BUTTONS are time limited actions you can purchase to evict inhabitants easier and faster or to prevent them from trying to go back to the renewal area. Very useful, as they can make you even more efficient and powerful. Buy BUTTONS by spending the credits you have already earned and use it to raise your score.

choose from a wide range of BUTTONS!

gated communities
- discover a fascinating method to gate out the house from renovation
- build a fence around a house to isolate it from locals breaking through the flat fence
- by out a unique quality fence that withstood the projects against renewal project in the Sulukule neighborhood

angry shop owners
- sell the shop owners that their business can be threatened by locals
- follow the advice of your partners from Tarlabasi 360 project and offer them a shop unit after renovation
- gain support of angry shop owners to get rid of the people inside the house

parking lot
- destroy one of the houses and use it as a parking space to earn extra money!
- just move the habitants to the outskirts they have no way to come back home
- be sure this tool perfectly works in in the whole historic peninsula in Istanbul

media campaign
- be inspired by Tarlabasi media representation - show how dangerous today the district is: beggars, pickpockets, drug dealers, and even tenants
- mention that your only concern is people's safety and locals will leave the renewal area immediately

law 6306
- use the law to easily declare the district as an earthquake risk zone and drive all the inhabitants from the houses
- don't worry, this legal instrument worked pretty well in the Osreydlar and Ayazma residential districts

power cut-off
- turn off the electricity in the neighborhood
- locals will go outside very angry as they are very tired of this infrastructural problem happening in more than 50% of the houses
- don't miss the chance to relocate them to the outskirts!

law 5366
- announce that historical and cultural assets of the district are in danger
- get the property rights for 3 houses and empty them at once
- try the legal power of expropriation already proven in Sulukule
- be prepared, it makes activists unusually angry!

law 2985
- construct cheap houses with the support of the city administration
- build up more low quality housing blocks to accommodate more people for a certain time
- use as an example Kayabasi or Tasoluk and try to locate the houses at least 2 hours from the city center

and plenty more...

set fire raise the rent hard traffic TV show police operation fancy french street

begging children slimit seller tricky shoe cleaner

145

CITIZEN RIGHTS IN PLANNING

Quynh Doan Truc, Tan Nguyen Minh, Tri Hua Tran Minh, Hien Dang The, Phuc Nguyen Vinh, Tay Ho Son, Duong Nguyen Dinh Que

"The Generic City presents the final death of planning. Why? Not because it is not planned – in fact, huge complementary universes of bureaucrats and developers funnel unimaginable flows of energy and money into its completion; for the same money, its plains can be fertilized by diamonds, its mud fields paved in gold bricks…

But its most dangerous and most exhilarating discovery is that planning makes no difference whatsoever."

Rem Koolhaas & Bruce Mau
S, M, L, XL

Metropolises like Tokyo, Hong Kong, Shanghai, and Bangkok form the heart of East and Southeast Asia's new economic life. Other potential areas strive to become the next international economic center. Clusters of skyscrapers are being erected throughout the region. The wish is clear: if an area is planned and built to be prosperous, it will also turn out to be.

The next big plan of Ho Chi Minh City's "Thanh Da – Binh Quoi" is one example of such ambition. Located 8 km away from city center, Thanh Da is a wetland peninsular where tourist villages, established from the 1970s to the 1990s, represent a romantic image of rural Vietnam. Green coverage and informal settlements dominate the rest of the peninsular. In May 2014, Bitexco, a multi-industry corporation and high-profile developer is chosen to zone the area to be home to 41,000 – 50,000 citizens at the cost of 1.34 billion USD. Exciting renderings depict a densely built area with high-rise, waterfront villas and ecological parks.

So far it sounds like a story almost cliché in Asia: a generic urban area replacing ecological wetlands, "trigger[ing] the boom that put the city on the map"[1] – the global map of potential investment. In the case of Binh Quoi, however, the plan has been "hanging" for two decades without implementation. Ever since 1992, the approved plan was expired and modified repeatedly; the land use right was handed to Saigon Construction Holding in 2004 and taken away in 2010 after years of little progress. As the new developer is now taking over, a new 1:2000 zoning plan is being prepared; meanwhile two bridges are to be built to connect the area to the rest of the city.

Behind the phenomenon is Vietnam's "fiscal socialism", in which "local officials can require that private developers build the infrastructure the city has planned in exchange for approval of the developer's investment project and the administration of land titles."[3] Private capital accounted for 60% of the city's total investment capital between 2001 and 2010. Behind the figure is a negotiation between the government's wish lists and investors' interests, using planning as a facilitator for a private-public partnership, in which the private sector helps the city to achieve high economic growth and fiscal political autonomy.[2] As in a "generic city", "the surface of the city explodes, the economy accelerates, slows down, bursts, collapses".[1]

In other cases, it is a wish that never came true: Binh Quoi project remains merely a "hanging plan". Vietnam Law does not recognize private land ownership; therefore residents have little power against land appropriation. During the "hanging" decades, they are not allowed to transact land use right, to renovate or build new houses. Technical infrastructure has not been further developed. Residents suffer under unofficial power supply, lack of municipal water supply, and missing wastewater and solid waste disposal systems.

How a new round of the story unfolds is hard to predict. We have heard the story of the generic and iconic Dubai Waterfront project being suspended with 2008 global financial crisis. A parallel uncertainty could be vaguely traced. Those whose fates are most uncertain, however, are those who live on an undetermined land.

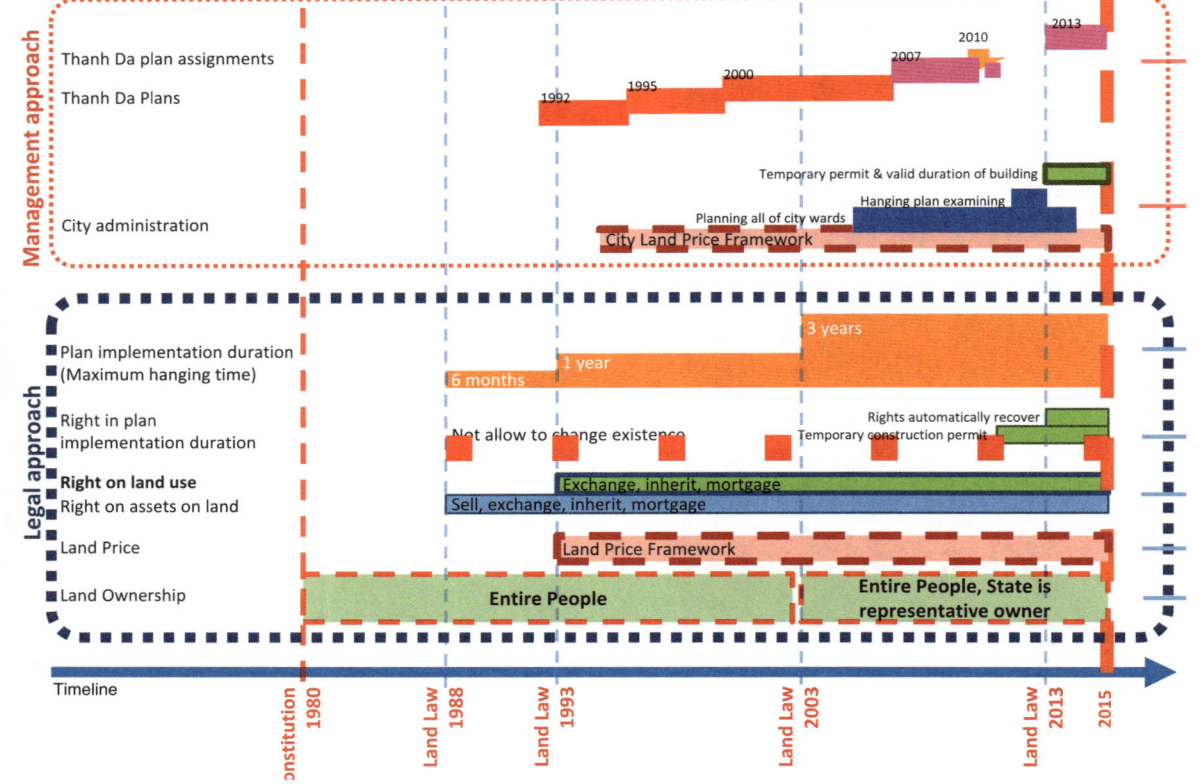

Project development timeline: managerial and legal processes between 1992 and 2015

1992: Introduction of a plan to develop the area
1995: Plan approved
2000: Plan expired
2004 - 2010: Saigon Construction Holding owns land use rights
2014: Land use rights go to Bitexco Holdings – a new plan is being prepared.

2014: Introduction of a time-limited permission (3-5 years) for construction. The owner of land use rights can apply to upgrade a house or build a new one.

2003: According to Land Law, a plan should be executed within 3 years.

2013: Unimplemented plans have to be modified or dismissed.

2009: Beginning of public participation in urban planning processes.
Official price used for land acquisition; received compensation payment far below market price.
"Land belongs to all people": Vietnam Law does not recognize private land ownership. Residents only own land use rights thus the asset value of the land.

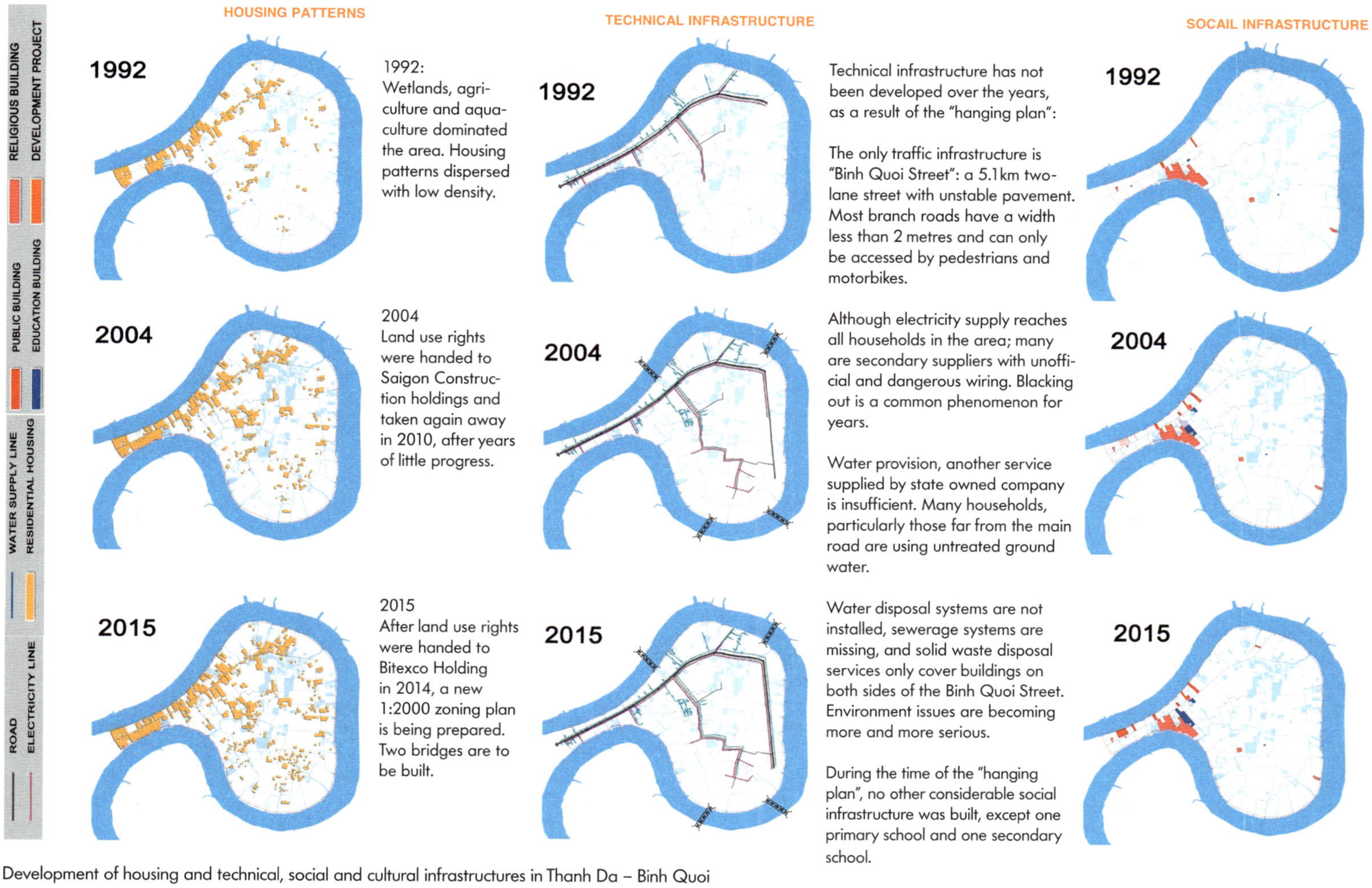

Legend (left column):
RELIGIOUS BUILDING · DEVELOPMENT PROJECT
PUBLIC BUILDING · EDUCATION BUILDING
WATER SUPPLY LINE · RESIDENTIAL HOUSING
ROAD · ELECTRICITY LINE

1992

1992:
Wetlands, agri-culture and aqua-culture dominated the area. Housing patterns dispersed with low density.

2004

2004
Land use rights were handed to Saigon Construc-tion holdings and taken again away in 2010, after years of little progress.

2015

2015
After land use rights were handed to Bitexco Holding in 2014, a new 1:2000 zoning plan is being prepared. Two bridges are to be built.

1992

Technical infrastructure has not been developed over the years, as a result of the "hanging plan":

The only traffic infrastructure is "Binh Quoi Street": a 5.1km two-lane street with unstable pavement. Most branch roads have a width less than 2 metres and can only be accessed by pedestrians and motorbikes.

2004

Although electricity supply reaches all households in the area; many are secondary suppliers with unoffi-cial and dangerous wiring. Blacking out is a common phenomenon for years.

Water provision, another service supplied by state owned company is insufficient. Many households, particularly those far from the main road are using untreated ground water.

2015

Water disposal systems are not installed, sewerage systems are missing, and solid waste disposal services only cover buildings on both sides of the Binh Quoi Street. Environment issues are becoming more and more serious.

During the time of the "hanging plan", no other considerable social infrastructure was built, except one primary school and one secondary school.

1992

2004

2015

Development of housing and technical, social and cultural infrastructures in Thanh Da – Binh Quoi

---

"Die eigenschaftslose Stadt markiert den endgültigen Tod jeder Planung. Wieso? Nicht, weil sie nicht geplant wäre – in Wirklichkeit lassen unge-heure, einander ergänzende Univer-sen von Bürokraten und Bauträgern unvorstellbare Ströme von Energie und Finanzmitteln in ihre Fertigstellung fließen; für dasselbe Geld könnte man ihre Ebenen mit Diamanten düngen und ihre Schlammfelder mit goldenen Ziegelsteinen pflastern. Doch ihre gefährlichste und zugleich erheiternds-te Entdeckung ist die, dass Planung völlig irrelevant ist."
Rem Koolhaas & Bruce Mau
S, M, L, XL

Metropolen wie Tokio, HongKong, Shanghai und Bangkok bilden das Herz des neuen Wirtschaftslebens in Ost- und Südostasien. Andere potenzielle Metropolen sind bestrebt, zum näch-sten internationalen Wirtschaftszentrum zu avancieren. Wolkenkratzer werden überall in der Region gleich gruppen-weise aus dem Boden gestampft. Wird ein Areal geplant und gebaut, um wirt-schaftlich zu prosperieren, so will man, dass sich dieser Wunsch auch erfüllt.

Der nächste große Plan von Ho-Chi-Minh-Stadt, "Thanh Da – Binh Quoi", ist ein Beispiel für diesen Ehr-geiz. Das acht Kilometer vom Stadtzen-trum entfernte Thanh Da ist eine aus Marschland bestehende Halbinsel, auf der zwischen den 1970er und 1990er Jahren Touristendörfer errichtet wur-den, die das Bild eines ländlichen ro-mantischen Vietnams heraufbeschwö-ren. Die übrige Halbinsel wird von Vegetation und informellen Siedlungen beherrscht. Im Mai 2014 wurde der in-dustrielle Mischkonzern und profilierte Bauträger Bitexco dazu ausersehen, das Areal in Zonen einzuteilen, um dort für 41.000 bis 50.000 Personen Wohnraum zu schaffen – für insgesamt 1,34 Milliarden US-Dollar. Atembe-raubende Zeichnungen zeigen ein dicht bebautes Areal mit Hochhäusern, am Wasser gelegenen Villen und naturna-hen Parks.

Bis hierher klingt das wie eine Geschichte, die in Asien fast schon ein Klischee ist: Ein eigenschaftsloses städtische Areal soll an die Stelle von naturbelassenem Marschland treten und "[löst] dadurch den Boom aus, der die ... Stadt auf der Landkarte er-scheinen [lässt]"[1], der globalen Land-karte potenzieller Investitionen. Im Fall von Binh Quoi ist der Plan jedoch zwei Jahrzehnte lang nicht umgesetzt worden. Seit 1992 wurde der offiziell abgesegnete Plan mehrmals überar-beitet und die festgelegten Fristen sind verstrichen und wieder verlängert wor-den. Das Landnutzungsrecht ging 2004 an die Saigon Construction Holding und wurde dieser 2010, nach Jahren ohne nennenswerte Fortschritte, wieder entzogen. Als der neue Bauträger über-nahm, wurde ein neuer Zonierungsplan im Maßstab von 1:2000 erstellt; mittler-weile werden zwei Brücken gebaut, die das Areal mit der Stadt verbinden sollen.

Hinter diesem Phänomen verbirgt sich der vietnamesische "Fiskalsozia-lismus", bei dem "örtliche Amtsträger verlangen können, dass private Bau-träger die Infrastruktur errichten, die die Stadt geplant hat – als Gegenleis-tung für die Baugenehmigung und das Landnutzungsrecht."[3] Der Anteil des privaten Kapitals am gesamten Investi-tionskapital der Stadt lag zwischen 2001 und 2010 bei 60 %. Hinter dieser Zahl verbirgt sich ein Kompromiss zwischen den Wunschlisten der Behörden und den Interessen der Investoren; die Stadtpla-nung fungiert in diesem Zusammenhang als Förderer einer privat-öffentlichen Partnerschaft, bei der der private Sektor der Stadt hilft, ein hohes Wirt-schaftswachstum und fiskalpolitische Autonomie zu erlangen.[2] Ganz so, wie es sich für eine "Stadt ohne Eigenschaf-ten" gehört: "Die Oberfläche der Stadt explodiert, die Wirtschaft startet voll durch, bremst ab, bricht auseinander, kollabiert."[1]

Das Binh Quoi-Projekt bleibt je-doch ein unerfüllter Wunsch: Es hängt in der Schwebe. Das vietnamesische Recht kennt kein privates Grundeigen-tum; deshalb können die Bewohner kaum etwas gegen die geplante Verwen-dung tun. Während der Wartezeit dürfen sie ihr Landnutzungsrecht nicht aus-üben; es ist ihnen untersagt, ihre Häuser zu renovieren oder neue zu bauen. Die technische Infrastruktur ist nicht weiter-entwickelt worden. Die Bewohner leiden unter der inoffiziellen Stromversorgung, dem Fehlen städtischer Wasserversor-gung und Abwasser- bzw. Abfallentsor-gung.

Wie das nächste Kapitel dieser Geschichte aussehen wird, ist schwer zu sagen. Wir kennen die Geschichte vom Aussetzen des generischen und ikonischen Dubai-Waterfront-Projekts in Folge der globalen Finanzkrise des Jahres 2008. Eine ähnlich ungewisse Geschichte deutet sich auch hier an. Diejenigen, deren Schicksal jedoch am ungewissesten ist, sind die Bewohner, die nach wie vor auf einem Stück Land leben, über dessen Zukunft noch nicht entschieden worden ist.
Text: Zhen Zhang

GATED COMMUNITIES

Nina Schengber, Madeline Rasche,
Sven Hendrik Olde, Monika Paul

USA: Celebration City by Walt Disney in the state of Florida, built on 27,7 sq km and for 7,427 inhabitants, is an utopia of a small-town, harmonic and uniform world. The idyll is based on a seventy page rulebook, determining hedge heights and curtain colours, and calling on children to hang their fishing rods in picturesque blue lakes like little Huckleberry Finns.

South Africa: The sparkling multi-storey buildings of Century City still attest to the history of apartheid in South Africa. One enters the hermetically sealed housing complex through gates under video surveillance. The security system is regarded as one of the most innovative worldwide and, with their especially trained security guards, has won several awards.

The first gated community goes back to 1857. It was established in New Jersey, USA. Ever since, their number has been increasing continuously. The size varies from single monitored blocks of flats up to extensive estates with over 100,000 residents and private infrastructure. Since the 1970s the trend of gated communities is unabated. While in the 20th century gated communities were to be found primarily in the agglomerations of North and South America, this kind of housing estate now has also taken hold in Asia and Europe. Whereas gated communities in North America established themselves at first as second homes for prosperous pensioners in the autumn of their lives, they served the isolation of the wealthy from the rest of the urban population in South America. However, by now the less wealthy social strata can also afford a life in private estates. This has led to a new movement of distinction including even more exclusive forms of gated communities. Today, in the USA there are just over 20,000 gated communities with more than nine million residents. In the case of accounting for housing complexes under video surveillance, more than 20 million Americans live in estates with special security measures.

Gated communities can be differentiated into the three types of security, prestige, and lifestyle estates, although these types often merge. Characteristic of a security estate is, that the security obsession with electronic surveillance systems, fences, walls and cameras eventually turns against its inhabitants. Demarcation of the outside corresponds with a high degree of order, control and disciplining on the inside. Lifestyle communities are based on a similar way of life, and similar leisure activities like e.g. belonging to a sports club. Prestige estates are exclusive luxury communities, characterised by their prominent and influential residents in particular. Finally, the wish for co-determination in one's own quarter or dissatisfaction with municipal administration play a role in the decision to live in a gated community.

The consequences of the proliferation of gated communities are widely known. They intensify the tendencies for social segregation already in place in urban agglomerations and increase social disparities within a population. Real estates are finance projects with high return, for which less profitable uses have to make way. Balancing social inequalities thus becomes more and more unlikely. Moreover, communities diminish their scope of action for creating public space with the instalment of extensive gated areas, and hand it over to the finance and real estate industry. This is a clear contradiction to what public space in a city should be like: an interplay and exchange of cultural ways of life. Urbanisation processes on a global scale offer the chance for great diversity of urban life, if stimuli through migration of people, their ways of life and spatial concepts, are incorporated and mediated with the status quo. The poster series "Gated communities" is a visual plea for planning and building urban agglomerations in such a way that these relations can unfold freely.

USA: Celebration City von Walt Disney im Bundesstaat Florida, eine auf 27,7 qkm für 7.427 Einwohner erbaute Utopie einer kleinstädtischen, harmonischen und uniformierten Welt. Als Basis für diese Idylle fungiert ein siebzigseitiger Regelkatalog, der Heckenhöhe und Gardinenfarbe bestimmt und Kinder dazu auffordert, ihre Angelrute wie kleine Huckleberry Finns in malerische blaue Seen zu hängen.

Südafrika: Die glitzernden Hochhäuser von Century City in Kapstadt bezeugen die Geschichte der Apartheid in Südafrika. Durch videoüberwachte Tore betritt man die hermetisch geschlossene Wohnanlage. Das Sicherheitssystem gilt als eines der innovativsten weltweit und hat mit seinem besonders geschulten Sicherheitspersonal schon mehrere Preise errungen.

Die erste Gated Community wurde 1857 in New Jersey gegründet. Seitdem hat ihre Zahl stetig zugenommen. Die Größe variiert von einzelnen bewachten Appartementblöcken bis hin zu großflächigen Siedlungen mit über 100.000 Bewohnern und eigener Infrastruktur. Seit den 1970er Jahren ist der Trend zur Gated Community ungebrochen. Waren sie im 20. Jahrhundert vor allem in den Ballungszentren Nord- und Südamerikas zu finden, setzt sich diese Wohn- und Siedlungsform nun auch in Asien und Europa durch. Während sich in Nordamerika das Modell Gated Community in erster Linie als Zweitwohnsitz für den Lebensabend wohlhabender Rentner etablierte, ging es in Südamerika vor allem um die Abschottung der wohlhabenden Schicht gegenüber dem Rest der städtischen Bevölkerung. Aber inzwischen können sich auch weniger vermögenden Mittelschichten ein Leben in privaten Wohnsiedlungen leisten, was eine neue Abgrenzungsbewegung mit noch exklusiveren Formen der Gated Communities nach sich gezogen hat. In den USA gibt es mittlerweile knapp über 20.000 Gated Communities mit mehr als neun Millionen Einwohnern. Zählt man die überwachten Wohnanlagen dazu, so leben mehr als 20 Millionen Amerikaner in Siedlungen mit besonderen Sicherheitsmaßnahmen.

Die Gated Communities lassen sich nach den Typen "Security", "Lifestyle" und "Prestige Communities" unterscheiden, wobei sich diese Aspekte vielfach überlagern. Kennzeichen der Security Estates ist, dass der Sicherheitswahn mit elektronischen Überwachungssystemen, Zäunen, Mauern und Kameras sich letztlich gegen die Bewohner wendet. Die Abschottung nach Außen korrespondiert mit einem hohen Maß an Ordnung, Kontrolle und Disziplinierung im Inneren. Grundlage der Lifestyle Estates ist ein ähnlicher Lebensstil oder ähnlich verbrachte Freizeit der Bewohner, z.B. durch die Zugehörigkeit zu einem Sportclub. Die Prestige Estates sind exklusive Luxus Communities, die sich vor allem durch ihre prominenten Bewohner auszeichnen. Schließlich spielen auch der Wille nach Mitbestimmung im eigenen Quartier oder Unzufriedenheit mit der kommunalen Verwaltung eine Rolle bei der Entscheidung für ein Leben in einer Gated Community.

Die Folgen der Verbreitung von Gated Communities sind bekannt. Sie verstärken die vorhandenen Segregationstendenzen in den urbanen Ballungsräumen und vergrößern die sozialen Disparitäten in einer Gesellschaft. Die Immobilien sind Anlageobjekte mit hoher Rendite, denen weniger profitable Nutzungen weichen müssen. Das Ausbalancieren sozialer Ungerechtigkeiten wird so immer unwahrscheinlicher. Darüber hinaus geben die Kommunen mit der flächendeckenden Einrichtung von Gated Communities Handlungsoptionen zur Gestaltung des öffentlichen Raumes an die Finanz- und Bauindustrie ab – ein deutlicher Widerspruch zu dem, was den öffentlichen Raum einer Stadt ausmachen sollte: das Zusammenspiel und den Austausch kultureller Lebensweisen. Der globale Verstädterungsprozess bietet die Chance einer großen Vielfalt des urbanen Lebens, wenn es gelingt, die Anreize durch die Migration von Menschen, durch ihre Lebensweisen und Raumkonzepte aufzunehmen und mit dem Bestehenden zu vermitteln. Die Plakatserie "Gated Communities" versteht sich als ein visuelles Plädoyer, die urbanen Ballungsräume so zu planen und zu bauen, dass sich diese Vielfalt entfalten kann.

An overview of GATED COMMUNITIES

The global map shows position, size and type of Gated Communities worldwide.

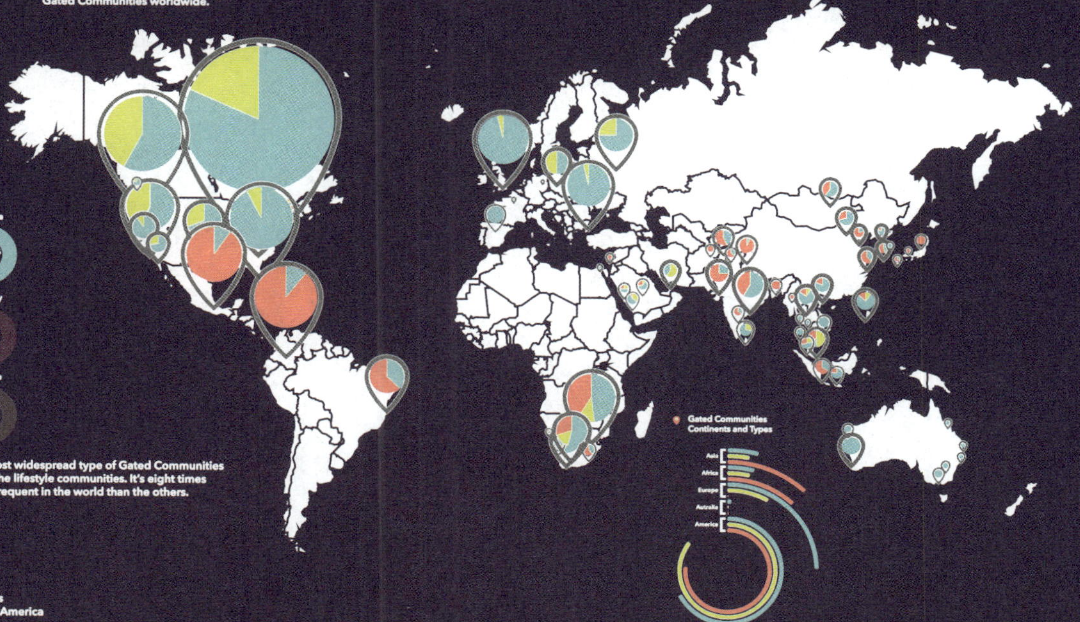

The ice chunk illustrates the official number of Gated Communities in comparison to the unknown amount.

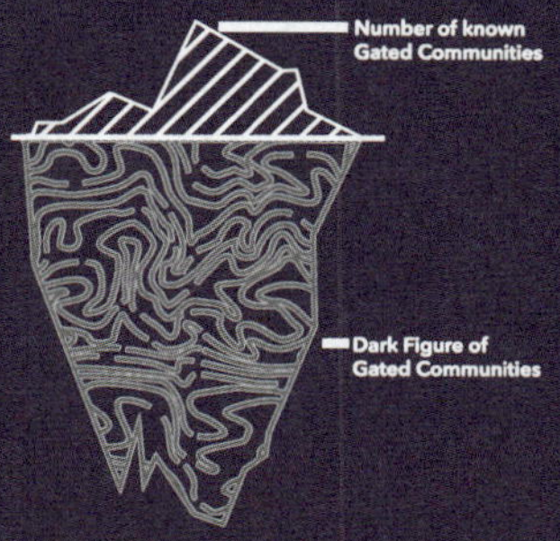

— Number of known Gated Communities

— Dark Figure of Gated Communities

Lifestyle
79%

Security
13%

Prestige
8%

The most widespread type of Gated Communities is the lifestyle communities. It's eight times more frequent in the world than the others.

Gated Communities Continents and Types

Asia
Africa
Europe
Australia
America

Timeline of Gated Communties

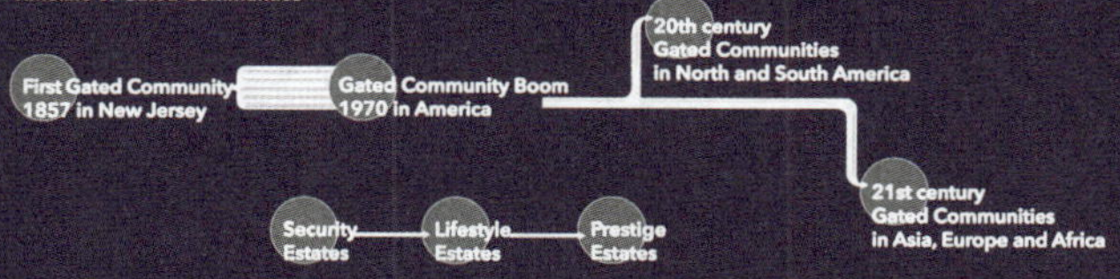

First Gated Community 1857 in New Jersey

Gated Community Boom 1970 in America

20th century Gated Communities in North and South America

21st century Gated Communities in Asia, Europe and Africa

Security Estates — Lifestyle Estates — Prestige Estates

The direction that the ongoing process of global urbanisation is taking, is essentially determined by the way in which human beings define their relationships. Wherever massive urbanisation is in progress around the globe and people with various socio-cultural backgrounds meet, a rise of population density is the result, a process which often leads to growing tensions.

For one thing these developments have increased the need for demarcation in the population, to the perception that a barrier between yourself and the world would lead to an increase in safety. Thus, tensions come into existence in places where walls and fences are a living testimony to inequality, no matter whether they are made of steel, wood, concrete or created by laws or emotions. Residents

seeking a safe haven in a Gated Community will sacrifice a good deal of their personal freedom, exposing themselves to a surveillance system and other security measures. Fear is one of the major factors in the decision to move into a secluded space, as well as a dissatisfaction with public administration which brings about the wish for self governance, but the desire to gain a certain social prestige by owing a plot in such a community is equally important as a driving force. The following map of the world shows present day socio-spacial disparities on a global scale. Each of these Gated Communities causes a fragmentation of the modern city, undermining the basic principle of each city, that of a shared space and cooperation, leading in essence to a gated NON-community.

Blakely and Snyder's (1997) general typology of Gated Communities

Types	A : Lifestyle Estate			B : Prestige Estate			C : Security Estate		
Features	These projects emphasize common amenities and cater to a leisure class with shared interests; may reflect small-town nostalgia; may be urban villages, luxury villages, or resort villages.			These projects reflect desire for image, privacy, and control; they focus on exclusivity over community; few shared facilities and amenities.			These projects reflect fear; involve retrofitting fences and gates on public streets; controlling access		
Subtypes	Retirement	Golf and Leisure	Suburban new town	Enclaves of rich and famous	Top-fifth developments	Executive middle class	City perch	Suburban perch	Barricade perch
Characteristics	age-related complexes with suite of amenities and activities	shared access to amenities for an active lifestyle	shared access to amenities for an active lifestyle	mas-ter-planned project with suite of amenities and facilities; often in the Sunbelt	secured and guarded privacy to restrict access for celebrities and very wealthy; attractive locations	secured access for the nouveau riche; often have guards	restricted access; usually without guards	restricted public access in inner city area to limit crime or traffic	closed access or some streets to limit through traffic

GATED NON-COMMUNITY
Gated Communties as a result of planetary urbanism

WOULD YOU LIKE TO LIVE IN A GATED COMMUNITY?

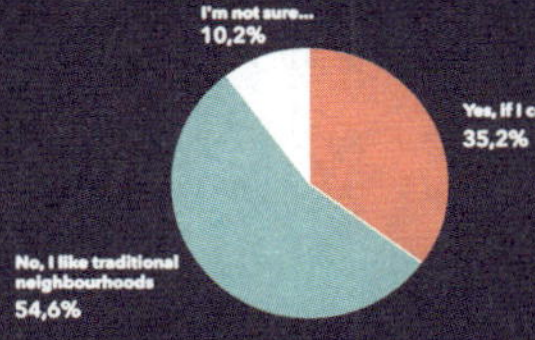

I'm not sure... 10,2%

Yes, if I could afford it 35,2%

No, I like traditional neighbourhoods 54,6%

The spread of Gated Communities, which is predominantly encouraged by real estate agents, illustrates the gap between rich and poor in populaces. Nevertheless, the building of Gated Community is a process in society which seems to make the balancing out of social inequalities become even more unlikely. The actual number of gated communities existing in the world is hard to come by, because data is not made public and there exist various terms for the concept on the market, another safety measure against those who harbor resentments against this brave new world of estates, communities, resorts und enclosed neighborhoods. An increasing number of communities built however, makes it even more difficult to get this problematic development under control, let alone solve it.

Thus, next to the empirical data, it is the emotional friction between parties within and outside the Gated Community as well as the promises made by real estate agents, which should be taken seriously.

MOTIVATION TO RESIDE IN A GATED COMMUNITY

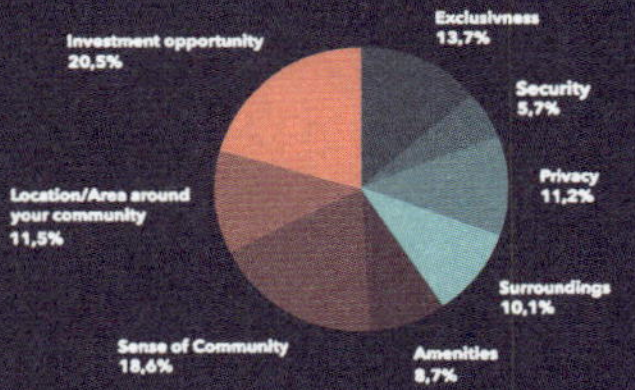

Investment opportunity 20,5%

Exclusiveness 13,7%

Security 5,7%

Privacy 11,2%

Location/Area around your community 11,5%

Surroundings 10,1%

Amenities 8,7%

Sense of Community 18,6%

All materials used in the model for Century City in South Africa, were chosen to match the type and character for this sort of gated community. They are cold, hard and metallic, and appear fortified like e.g. concrete blocks signifying sky scrapers, threateningly lined up nails as fences and walls, electronic components as surveillance systems, and stones and sand for street scenes. It is a composition that above all symbolises seclusion. The crime rate within the community, particularly regarding murders and sex crimes, is not significantly lower than in the rest of Cape Town.

Für das Modell von Century City in Südafrika wurden Materialien verwendet, die dem Typ und Charakter dieser abgeschotteten Gated Community entsprechen. Sie sind kühl, hart, metallisch und erscheinen wehrhaft wie z.B. Betonklötze als Wolkenkratzer, bedrohlich aufgereihte Nägel als Mauern und Zäune, Computerteile als Überwachungssysteme, aber auch Steine und Sand für das Straßenbild. Eine Anordnung, die vor allem Abwehr symbolisiert. Die Kriminalitätsrate innerhalb der Community, insbesondere was Morde und Sexualstraftaten betrifft, ist nicht geringer als in Kapstadt.

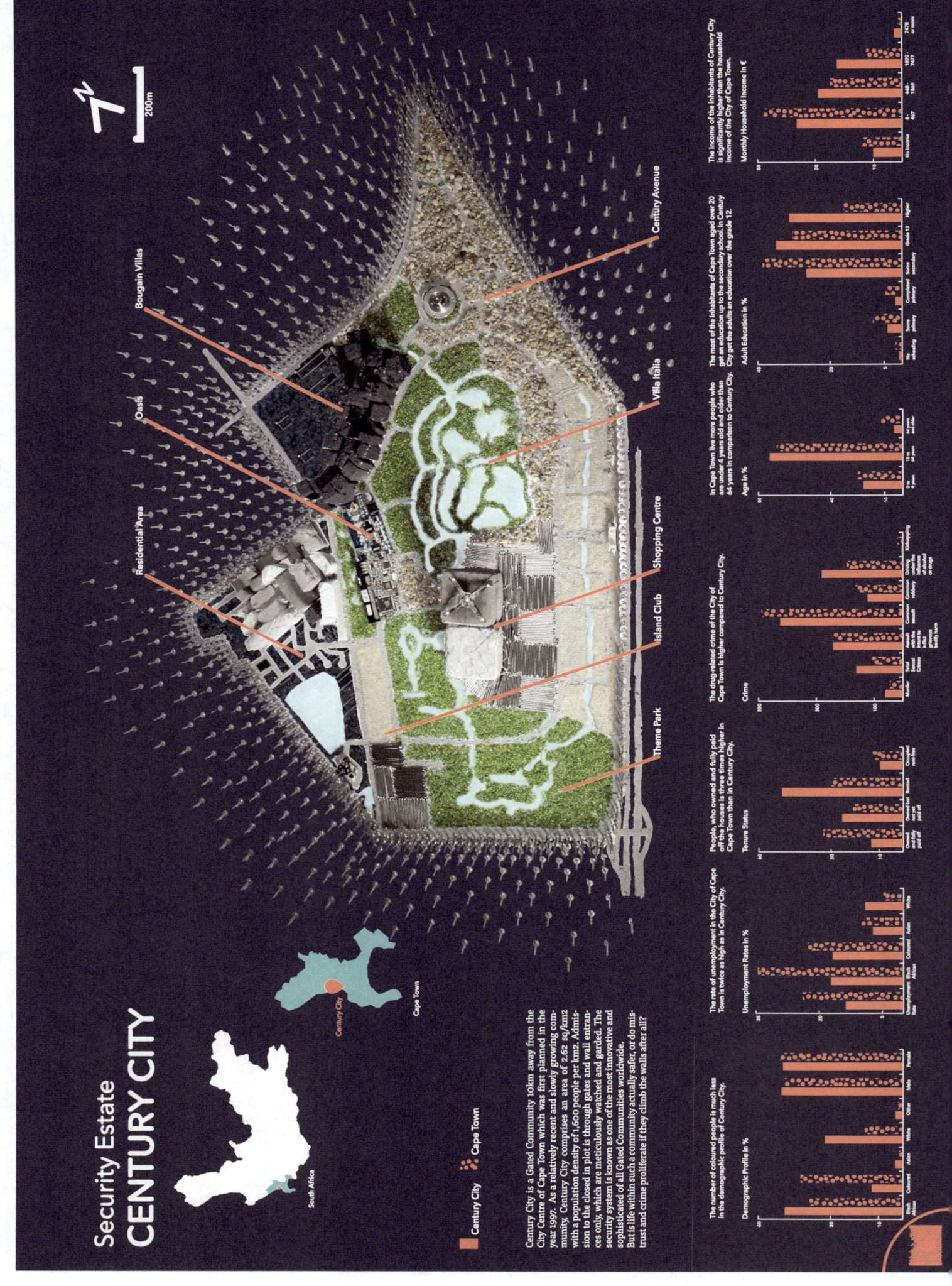

Security Estate
CENTURY CITY

Century City is a Gated Community 10km away from the City Centre of Cape Town which was first planned in the year 1997. As a relatively recent and slowly growing community, Century City comprises an area of 2.62 sq/km2 with a population density of 1,500 people per km2. Admission to the closed in plot is through gates and wall entrances only which are meticulously watched and guarded. The security system is known as one of the most innovative and sophisticated of all Gated Communities worldwide. But is life within such a community actually safer, or do mistrust and crime proliferate if they climb the walls after all?

Lifestyle Estate
CELEBRATION

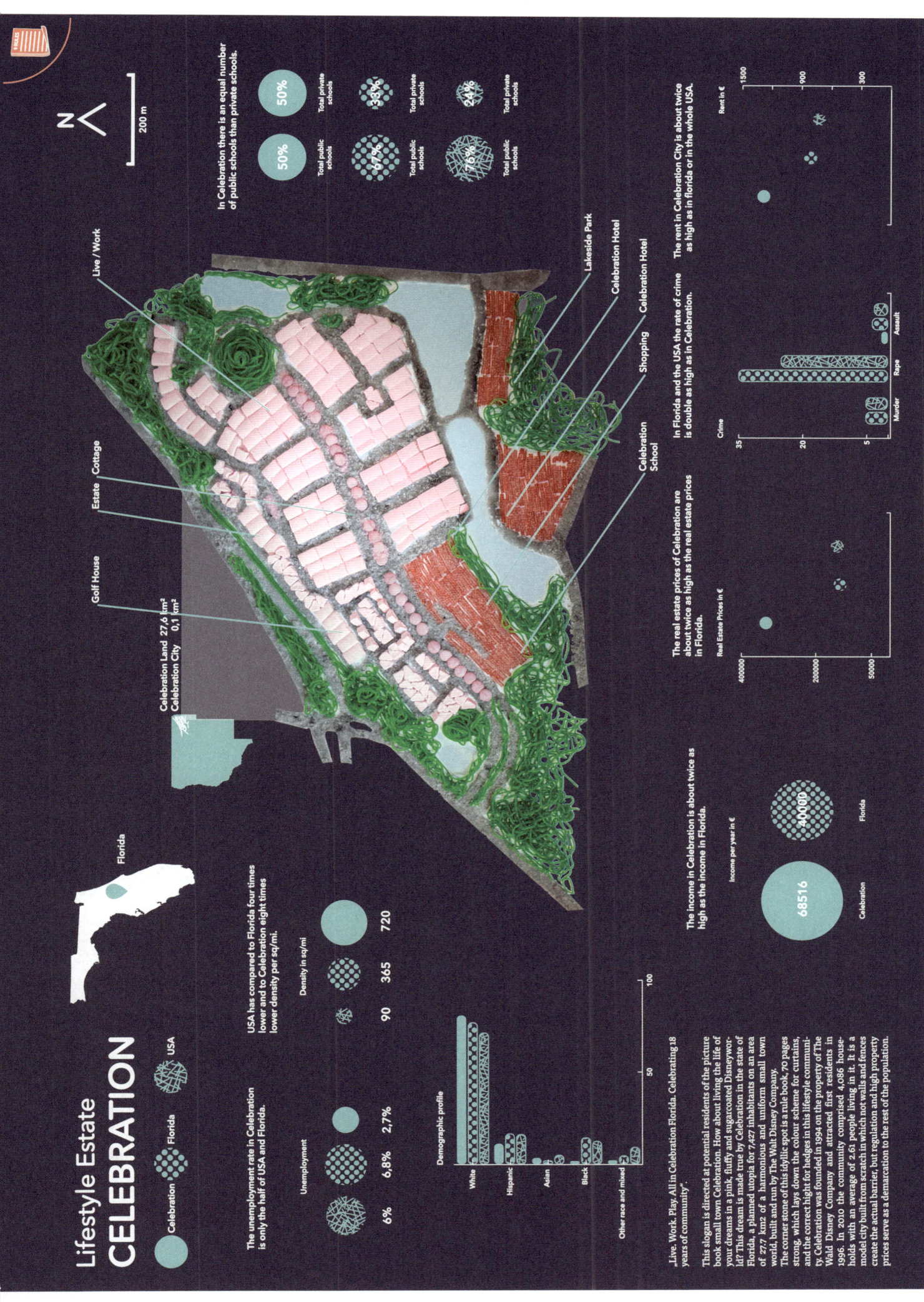

● Celebration ● Florida ◉ USA

Florida

The unemployment rate in Celebration is only the half of USA and Florida.

Unemployment

6% 6,8% 2,7%

USA has compared to Florida four times lower and to Celebration eight times lower density per sq/mi.

Density in sq/mi

90 365 720

Demographic profile

100

White
Hispanic
Asian
Black
Other race and mixed

50

„Live. Work. Play. All in Celebration Florida. Celebrating 18 years of community".

This slogan is directed at potential residents of the picture book small town Celebration. How about living the life of your dreams in a pink, fluffy and sugarcoated Disneyworld? This dream is made true by Celebration in the state of Florida, a planned utopia for 7,427 inhabitants on an area of 27.7 km2 of a harmonious and uniform small town world, built and run by The Walt Disney Company.
The corner stone of this idyllic spot is a rule book, 70 pages strong, which lays down the colour scheme for curtains, and the correct hight for hedges in this lifestyle community. Celebration was founded in 1994 on the property of The Walt Disney Company and attracted first residents in 1996. In 2010 the community comprised 4,086 households with an average of 2.61 people living in it. It is a model city built from scratch in which not walls and fences create the actual barrier, but regulation and high property prices serve as a demarcation to the rest of the population.

In Celebration there is an equal number of public schools than private schools.

50% Total private schools
50% Total public schools

38% Total private schools
67% Total public schools

24% Total private schools
76% Total public schools

The rent in Celebration City is about twice as high as in florida or in the whole USA.

Rent in €

1500
900
300

Golf House Estate Cottage Live / Work

Celebration Land 27,6 km²
Celebration City   0,1 km²

Lakeside Park
Celebration Hotel
Shopping Celebration Hotel
Celebration School

N
200 m

In Florida and the USA the rate of crime is double as high as in Celebration.

Crime

35
20
5

Murder Rape Assault

The real estate prices of Celebration are about twice as high as the real estate prices in Florida.

Real Estate Prices in €

400000
200000
50000

The income in Celebration is about as high as the income in Florida.

Income per year in €

68516 Celebration
40000 Florida

The model of Celebration City, Florida, is made out of candy, representative of the town's artificial character: pink marshmallows and chocolate beans depict dwellings, while the city centre consists of over-sugared wine gum. This centre is framed by picturesque lakes created from turquoise gelatine and woods made out of green sugar cords. Paths of dyed sugar stand for the traffic-calmed street network. Celebration City's inhabitants are mostly white US-Americans with above-average wages. Rents are high.

Das Modell von Celebration City besteht aus Süßigkeiten, stellvertretend für den artifiziellen Charakter der Stadt: Rosarofer Mäusespeck und Schokolinsen stellen Wohnhäuser dar, während der Stadtkern von überzuckerten Wein-gummis gebildet wird. Dieser Kern wird eingerahmt von malerisch türkisfarbenen Seen aus Gelatine und Wäldern aus grünen Gummischlangen. Wege aus gefärbtem Zucker stehen für die tempobeschränkten Straßen im überschaubaren Verkehrsnetz. In Celebration City leben überwiegend weiße Amerikaner mit überdurchschnittlichen Einkommen. Die Mieten sind hoch.

URBAN EXILE

David Stephens
Alessia De Simone
Ke Xie

By means of the cities of Atlanta, USA, Naples, Italy, and Hong Kong, China, the displacement of low-income population strata from preferred urban locations is described in global comparison. Individual daily routines and personal narratives regarding livelihoods in the less privileged, often peripheral urban quarters are paramount.

"The displacement of the poor from cities is exacerbating. Everywhere in the world the urban underclass is suffering most from the consequences of the crisis."[1]

"Since capitalist cities exist, there has been displacement of the poor. But the political attitude and the governmental

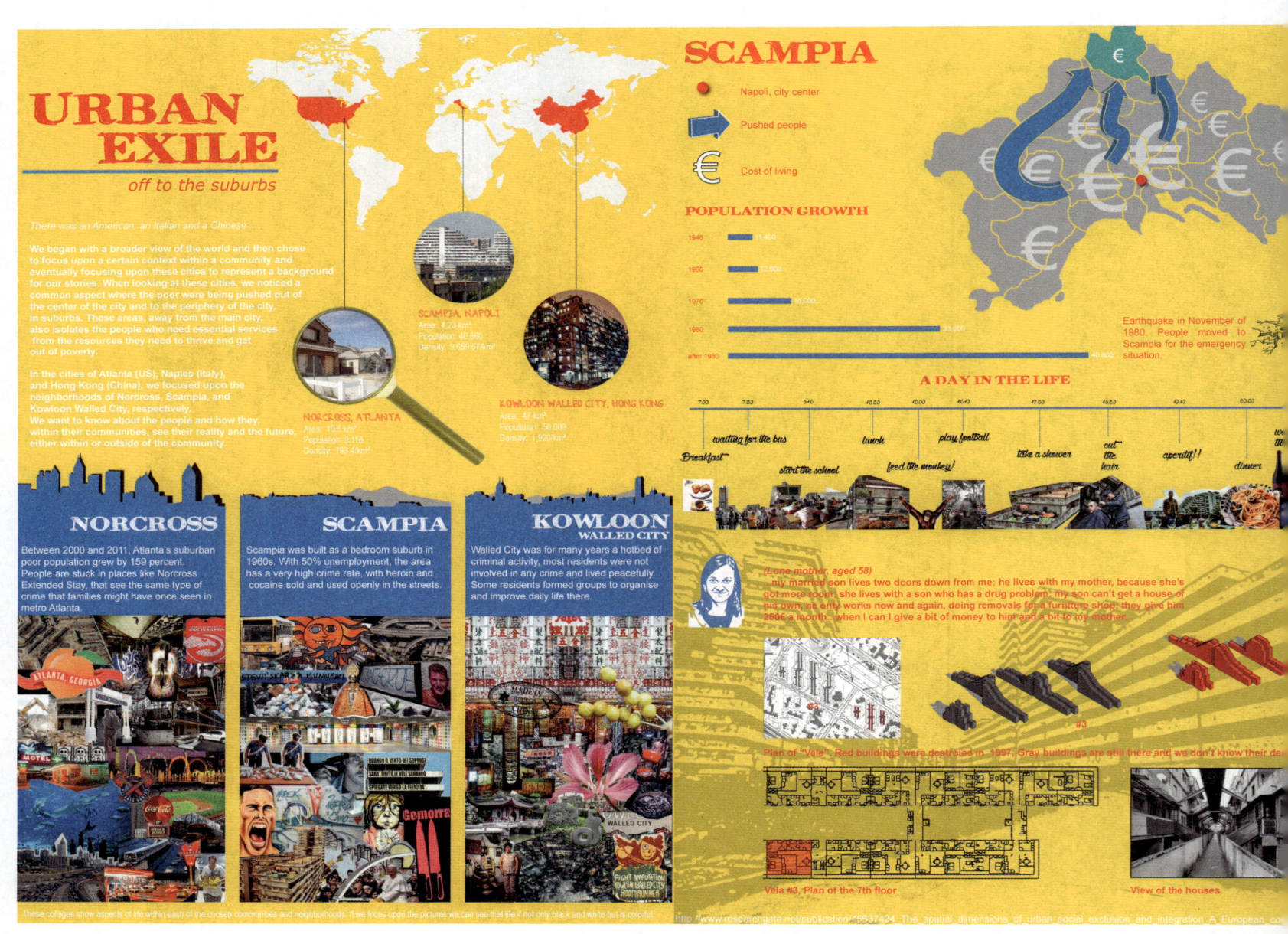

regulation to such displacement tendencies have changed. By now many municipalities very deliberately rely on gentrification as a strategy of urban renewal."[1]

"When will the people start to wage class war back? One of the places to start would be to focus on the rapidly degrading qualities of urban life, through foreclosures, the persistence of predatory practices in urban housing markets, reductions in services, and above all the lack of viable employment opportunities in urban labour markets almost everywhere, with some cities […] utterly bereft of employment prospects. The crisis now is as much an urban crisis as it ever was." p. 105 [2]

"Capitalist urbanization perpetually tends to destroy the city as a social, political and liveable commons." p.80 [2]

•

Anhand der Städte Atlanta, USA, Neapel, Italien, und HongKong, China wird die Vertreibung einkommensschwacher Bevölkerungsschichten aus bevorzugten städtischen Lagen im weltweiten Vergleich beschrieben. Im Vordergrund stehen individuelle Tagesabläufe und persönliche Narrative über den Lebensunterhalt in den weniger bevorzugten, oft peripheren Stadtvierteln.

"Die Verdrängung von Armen aus den Städten verschärft sich. Überall auf der Welt sind es die städtischen Unterschichten, die am meisten unter den Krisenfolgen leiden."[1]

"Seit es kapitalistische Städte gibt, werden Arme vertrieben. Aber die politische Einstellung und die staatliche Regulierung zu solchen Verdrängungstendenzen haben sich verändert. Mittlerweile setzen viele städtische Verwaltungen ganz bewusst auf Gentrifizierung als Strategie der Stadterneuerung."[1]

"Wann wird das Volk zurückschlagen? Was als Ausgangspunkt dienen könnte,

ist die rapide Abnahme der Lebensqualität in den Städten durch Zwangsvollstreckungen, räuberische Methoden auf den Immobilienmärkten der urbanen Zentren und durch den Abbau von Dienstleistungen. Vor allem fehlen aber in beinahe allen Städten vernünftige Arbeitsplätze, wobei es mancherorts […] schlicht und ergreifend überhaupt keine Beschäftigungsmöglichkeiten mehr gibt. Wie alle anderen Krisen ist auch die heutige eine urbane Krise." S. 105 [2]

"Die kapitalistische Urbanisierung neigt fortwährend dazu, die Stadt als soziales, politisches und lebenswertes Gemeingut zu zerstören." S. 148 [2]

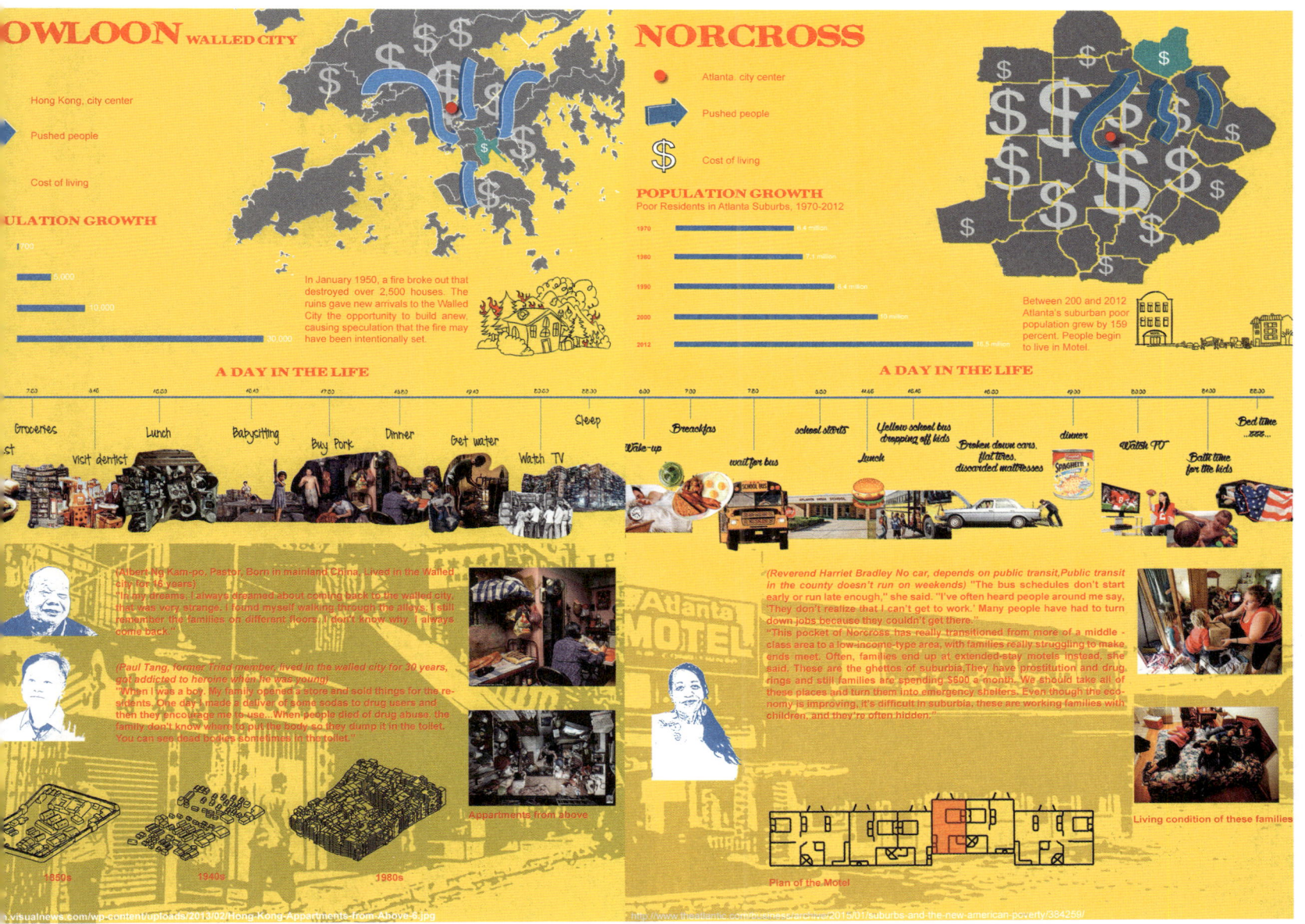

MOTION POSTER: **ANGRY99**

Gerrit Hoffschulte

The work is devoted to the advancing unequal monetary distribution in the societies of the economic powers as a result of deregulated financial markets. Neo-liberal economic activity in recent decades has resulted in a few individuals more and more drastically enriching themselves at public expense, and without sustainably. The project title "Angry99" hints at the slogan of the Occupy Wall Street movement – "We are the 99%" – and discusses society's anger towards the greed of a few, culminating in the Occupy-movement's world-wide demonstrations and camps. This work aims at shedding light on the substantial data concerning the economic situation, and making it intelligible in public space. The "Motion Poster" – as a combination of the classic demonstration poster and moving footage of demonstrators – is to be placed in public space in the form of beamer projections or video-capable "City-Lights" and are directed towards the affected majority (the 99% in question) of the population. They are intended to convey the triggers for the Occupy movement's legitimate anger via well-established facts and to provoke the confrontation with and questioning of the global financial policy. The "Motion Poster's" beamer projections at unusual places for posters ought to keep a whiff of the Occupy movement's activism, now vanished from the cityscapes, alive.

•

Die Arbeit widmet sich der fortschreitenden ungleichen monetären Verteilung in den Gesellschaften der Wirtschaftsmächte als Folge der dere-gulierten Finanzmärkte. Das neoliberale Wirtschaften der letzten Jahrzehnte hat zur Folge, dass einige wenige Individuen sich immer drastischer auf Kosten der Allgemeinheit bereichern, ohne dabei nachhaltig zu wirtschaften. Der Projekt-Titel "Angry99" spielt auf den Slogan der Occupy-Wallstreet-Bewegung – "We are the 99%" – an und thematisiert den gegen diese Gier einiger Weniger gerichteten Zorn der Gesellschaft, der in den weltweiten Demonstrationen und Camps der Occupy-Bewegung gipfelte. Ziel dieser Arbeit ist es, die durchaus vorhandenen Daten zur wirtschaftlichen Lage allgemein verständlich und an öffentlich zugänglichen Orten zu beleuchten. Die "Motion Poster" – als eine Kombination des klassischen Demonstrationsplakats und bewegten Aufnahmen von Demonstranten – sollen in Form von Beamer-Projektionen oder videofähigen "City-Lights" im öffentlichen Raum platziert werden und richten sich an den betroffenen Großteil (besagte 99 %) der Gesellschaft. Sie sollen den Betrachtern durch fundierte Fakten die Auslöser des berechtigten Zorns der Occupy-Bewegung vermitteln und die Auseinandersetzung mit und das Hinterfragen der globalen Finanzpolitik provozieren. Beamer-Projektionen der "Motion Poster" an für Plakate unübliche Orte sollen einen Hauch des Aktionismus der inzwischen aus den Stadtbildern verschwundenen Occupy-Bewegung am Leben erhalten.

WORLD METROPOLS: ABOUT WAGES AND PRICES

Indre Grumbinaite, Darjan Hil, Safak Korkut,
Nicole Lachenmeier, YAAY.ch

Cities are focal points for social developments and control systems for social order – also regarding the wages paid to the workforces. The unabated allure of the cities is due not least to the fact that compared with rural areas, they offer their inhabitants a wealth of financial opportunities. Often, it is important to settle in a city in order to try to hook up with the labour market or to earn a higher wage. But even when these things are possible, the situation for entrants to the labour market differs from city to city worldwide. The aim of the project is to shed light on these differences.

Not only are the income gaps within one city striking, they become even more questionable when they are compared from city to city on a global scale. One basic premise of the neoliberal social system is that it rewards each individual according to his or her performance. The individual's performance should have a direct impact on their personal income. In other words, those who contribute a lot to society deserve a significant monetary return. In reality however, it is debatable whether the distribution of income according to performance is fairly balanced and, even more so, whether there are indeed objective criteria that allow one to assess the value of one particular service in comparison with another in monetary units. This uncertainty inherent to the postulate of performance and hence the remuneration system's failure to explain itself becomes greater the more extreme the differences between the different professions.

The actual breach of norms of the neoliberal social system, which sees itself as globally operative and universally valid, however becomes all the more obvious when the remuneration systems are compared with one another, and one is compelled to question why a teacher in Johannesburg earns so much less than a teacher in London. Although there are economic explanations for the differences, such as the

varying productive strengths of specific countries, the international comparison shows just how unsatisfactory the performance-based explanatory model is. Even if one accepts the concept of fairness that underpins this model as a social norm, reality does not follow this norm – neither within the individual countries, nor in the relationship between rich and poor countries.

poster 1 shows the income gap as a geometric representation of social disparities. Five selected professions – labourer, car mechanic, teacher, engineer and financial analyst – are presented. The positions of the professions within the range of the gap indicate their social status by means of the different wages. Lines representing mean values provide an overview and allow comparison. In addition, the chart shows the GDP of the given country, whereby the shown wage level for the professions may be placed in the overall social context.

The diagram on poster 2 again offers a comparison of wage levels. The single dot now more closely approximates the iconography of money. "Piled up", it becomes a potential opportunity to distribute the wage across products and services. The price level of five selected goods and services adds the domestic purchasing power to the wage comparison and places it in relation to typical European consumer behaviour. On a second tier, the prices of goods and services may be compared.

The focus in poster 3 is on the city line with its dot-shaped units, which represent the purchasing power of the local worker in food and, below, its inverted mirror image which shows in comparison the purchasing power of a visitor from Zurich, who, it must be noted, has the same profession. Here, the theme of purchasing power addressed in the second poster is assigned by way of example to three goods, illustrated by the dots. In addition to basic foodstuffs of rice and bread, the branded food product Big Mac is listed as an unit.

Städte sind Brennpunkte gesellschaftlicher Entwicklungen und Leitsysteme gesellschaftlicher Ordnung – auch was die Entlohnung der Arbeitskräfte betrifft. Nicht zuletzt ist die ungebrochene Sogkraft der Städte darauf zurückzuführen, dass sie ihren Bewohnern im Vergleich zu ruralen Gebieten ein Vielfaches an finanziellen Möglichkeiten eröffnen. Ein wichtiger Grund sich in einer Stadt niederzulassen, wird oftmals der Versuch sein, Anschluss an den Arbeitsmarkt zu finden oder einen höheren Lohn zu erzielen. Doch selbst wenn dies gelingt, ist global gesehen die Situation für die Arbeitsmarktteilnehmer in den einzelnen Städten ganz unterschiedlich. Diese Unterscheidungen offensichtlich zu machen, ist das Ziel des Projekts.

Die Einkommensunterschiede sind nicht nur innerhalb einer Stadt frappierend, sondern werden durch den globalen Vergleich Stadt versus Stadt nochmals fragwürdiger. Ein Grundpostulat des neoliberalen Gesellschaftssystems ist, dass jeder angemessen und entsprechend seiner Anstrengungen vom System entlohnt wird. Die eigene Leistung soll direkten Einfluss auf das persönliche Einkommen haben. Sprich, wer viel für die Gesellschaft leistet, hat viel monetäre Gegenleistung verdient. In der Realität ist allerdings fraglich, ob die Einkommensverteilung nach Leistung ausbalanciert ist, und mehr noch, ob es tatsächlich objektive Kriterien gibt, die den Nutzen einer bestimmten Leistung im Vergleich mit einer anderen in monetären Einheiten bewerten können. Diese interne Unsicherheit des Leistungspostulats und damit die Erklärungsnot des Entlohnungssystems wird umso größer, je extremer die Unterschiede bei den verschiedenen Berufen ausfallen.

Der eigentliche Normbruch des neoliberalen Gesellschaftssystems, das sich selber als global agierend und universal gültig versteht, wird jedoch dann um so offenbarer, wenn die Entlohnungssysteme untereinander verglichen werden, und man sich unweigerlich die Frage stellen muss, warum ein Lehrer in Johannesburg so viel weniger verdient wie ein Lehrer in London. Obwohl es ökonomische Erklärungen der Unter-

schiede gibt, wie die verschiedene Produktivkraft einzelner Länder, zeigt doch gerade der internationale Vergleich, wie unzulänglich das leistungsbasierte Erklärungsmodell ist. Selbst wenn man die Gerechtigkeitsvorstellung dieses Modells als gesellschaftliche Norm akzeptiert, folgt die Realität nicht dieser Norm – nicht länderintern und nicht im Verhältnis zwischen reichen und armen Ländern.

Plakat 1 zeigt die Einkommensschere als geometrischen Ausdruck sozialen Gefälles. Fünf ausgewählte Berufe: Arbeiter, Automechaniker, Lehrer, Ingenieur und Finanzanalyst werden vorgestellt. Die Position der Berufe auf der Schere gibt über die unterschiedliche Entlohnung Hinweise auf ihre soziale Einordnung. Mittelwertlinien unterstützen die Übersicht und Vergleichbarkeit. Die Grafik wird durch das BIP des betreffenden Landes ergänzt, wodurch das abgebildete Lohnniveau der Berufe in den gesamtgesellschaftlichen Zusammenhang gestellt werden kann.

Die Grafik auf Plakat 2 bietet nochmals die Lohnvergleichsperspektive. Der einzelne Punkt rückt nun der Ikonographie des Geldes näher. Er wird in der "Anhäufung" zur potentiellen Möglichkeit, den Lohn auf Produkte und Dienstleistungen aufzuteilen. Das Preisniveau von fünf ausgewählten Waren und Dienstleistungen ergänzt den Lohnvergleich mit der Binnenkaufkraft und stellt sie in Relation zu typisch europäischem Konsumverhalten. Auf einer zweiten Ebene lassen sich die Waren- und Dienstleistungspreise vergleichen.

Im Zentrum von Plakat 3 steht die Städtelinie mit ihren Punkteeinheiten, welche die Kaufkraft des lokalen Arbeiters in Lebensmitteln darstellen, und ihrem massiven inversen Spiegelbild darunter, welches im Vergleich die Kaufkraft eines Zürcher Besuchers darstellt, der wohlgemerkt den gleichen Beruf hat. Die im zweiten Plakat aufgeworfene Thematik der Kaufkraft wird hier exemplarisch für drei Güter in die Punktedarstellung übertragen. Zu den Grundnahrungsmitteln Reis und Brot wird das Markenlebensmittel Big Mac als Einheit aufgeführt.

Income Index

The income gap diagram represents the disparities
between the monthly wages in various cities of the world
for five selected professions. The two extreme values,
usually worker and financial analyst, define the extent of
the gap.

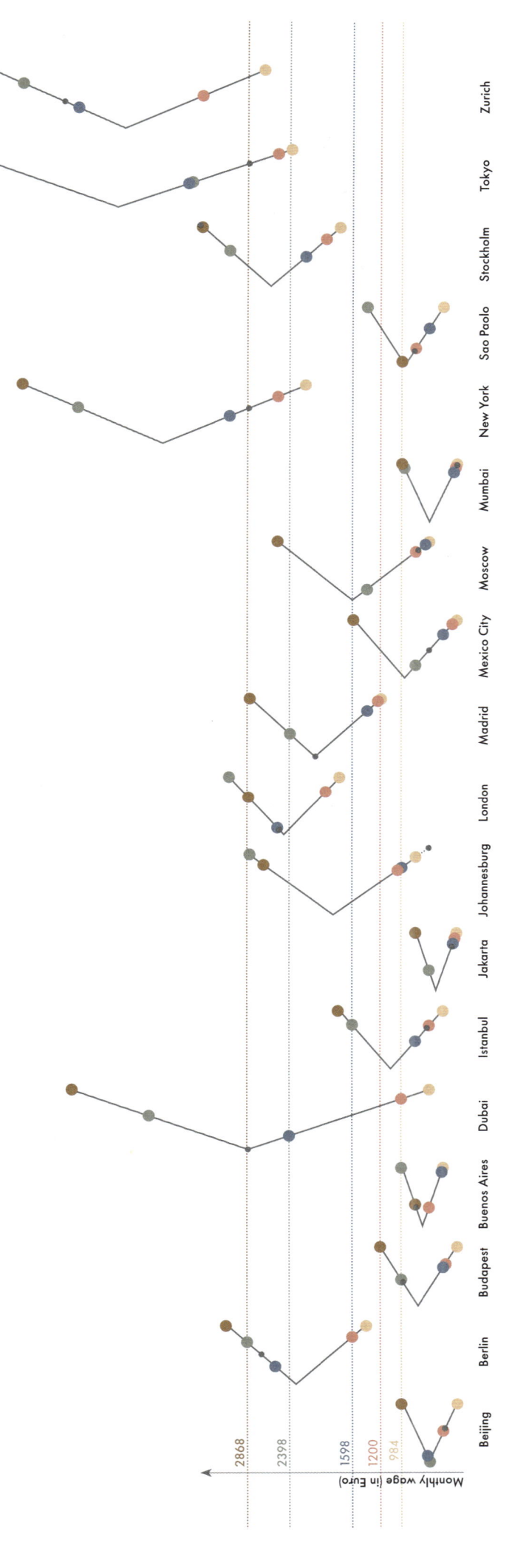

Monthly wage (in Euro)

2868
2398
1598
1200
984

Beijing · Berlin · Budapest · Buenos Aires · Dubai · Istanbul · Jakarta · Johannesburg · London · Madrid · Mexico City · Moscow · Mumbai · New York · Sao Paolo · Stockholm · Tokyo · Zurich

Legend

● Financial analyst
● Engineer
● Teacher
● Car mechanic
● Worker
⋮ Average wage in 18 cities
● GDP

● **Financial analyst**
30–35 years old, single, no children, working in a major bank,
graduate (university, technical university, some technical college)
and at least 5 years of experience.

● **Engineer**
35 years old, married, two children, working in an industrial company
in the electronics industry, graduate (university, technical university,
some technical college) and at least 5 years of experience.

● **Teacher**
35 years old, married, two children, already working in the state
education system (not in private schools) for around 10 years.

● **Car mechanic**
25 years old, no children, has an apprenticeship certificate and around
5 years of professional experience.

● **Worker**
25 years old, no children, working in a medium-sized business
(primarily in the textile industry) as a semi-skilled or unskilled labourer.

● **GDP** (Gross domestic product per citizen per month)
Gives the total monetary value of all finished goods and services
produced within the boundaries of a national economy in one year,
which are intended for consumption.

Concept and Graphics: YAAY.ch, Basel, Out of Balance Competition 13
Sources: UBS AG, CIO WM Research (Publisher): Preise und Löhne, pp. 26 ff., Zurich, 2012, Primary source: YA747_20130131_Data.pdf, CIO Wealth Management Research, UBS AG, recieved on
23.10.2012, Calculation basis: Monthly wage = Net yearly wage / 12. Worldbank Database /GDP 2011, accessed on 11.01.2013: http://data.worldbank.org/indicator/NY.GDP.PCAP.CD

Prices Index

The dots represent the monthly wage for the 5 selected professions. To the side of the larger view, the comparison of the wage levels is supplemented by the local prices for exemplary products, i.e. data pertaining to domestic purchasing power.

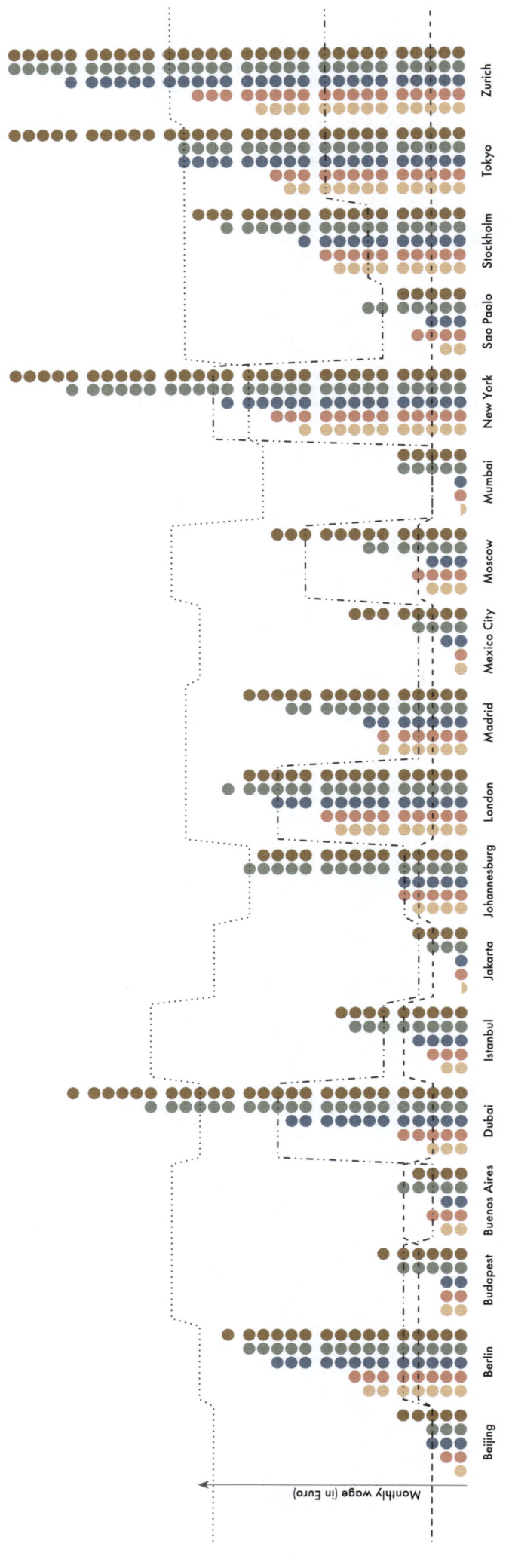

Monthly wage (in Euro)

Beijing · Berlin · Budapest · Buenos Aires · Dubai · Istanbul · Jakarta · Johannesburg · London · Madrid · Mexico City · Moscow · Mumbai · New York · Sao Paolo · Stockholm · Tokyo · Zurich

Legend

○ 200 Euro
◡ under 200 Euro
● Financial analyst
● Engineer
● Teacher
● Car mechanic
● Worker

··· Shopping cart of electronic and household goods
This shopping cart price is made up of electronic products with market prices that tend to be homogeneous worldwide (TV, PC, Notebook, Smartphone, digital camera) as well as predominantly locally produced household products (refrigerator, vacuum cleaner, skillet and hair dryer).

– · – Unfurnished 3-room flat
The rental charge should be regarded as a point of reference for the average local rent level (gross rent per month) and refers to flats built after 1980 (3 rooms, kitchen, bathroom, no garage) incl. all utilities, with average comfort and size for the locality, near the city centre.

– – iPhone
The iPhone represents a desirable luxury product that is relatively unaffected by economic fluctuations and costs more or less the same worldwide.

Concept and Graphics: YAAY.ch, Basel. Out of Balance Competition 13
Sources: UBS AG, CIO WM Research (Publisher): Prices and Earnings, pp. 6 ff., 10–14, 23 - 24, Zurich, 2012; Primary source: YA7447_20130131_Data.pdf, CIO Wealth Management Research, UBS AG, received on 23.10.2012. Calculation basis: Monthly wage=Net yearly wage/12. Data are rounded up 200 Euro units.

Food Index

The dots represent the monthly purchasing power of a worker in food, i. e. Big Mac, rice and bread. The dots above the city names show the purchasing power of a local worker in his hometown. By comparison, the dots below the city names show the purchasing power of a worker in Zurich who, with his wage from Zurich, shops in the various cities of the world.

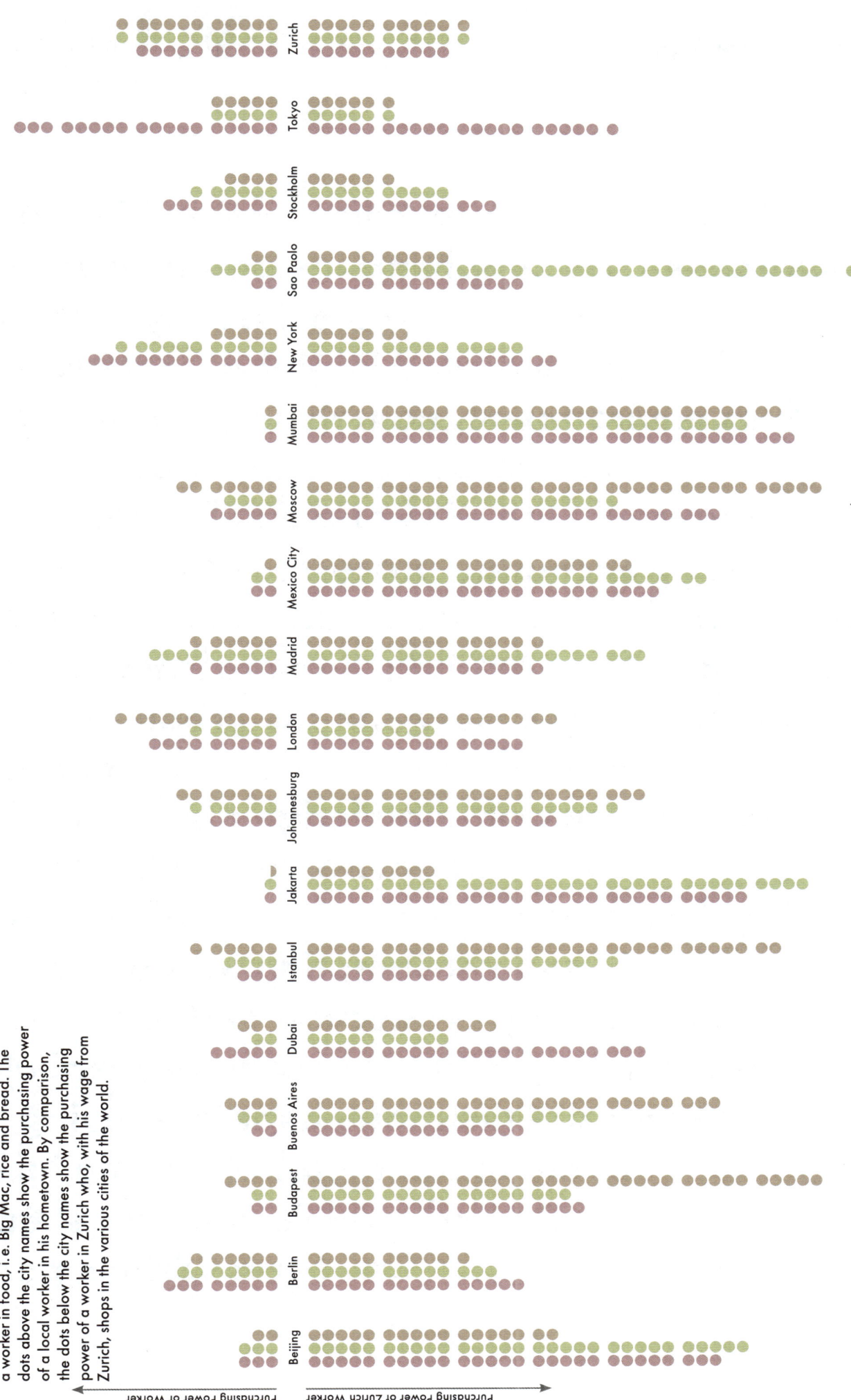

Purchasing Power of Worker

Purchasing Power of Zurich Worker

Legend

- 50kg Big Macs
- 100kg Rice
- 100kg Bread
- under 100kg Bread

Big Mac
E. g. In Mexico City, one Big Mac costs 2.34 euros. A worker with a monthly wage of 183.33 Euro can afford 78 Big Macs. In Zurich, a Big Mac costs 5.42 euros. A worker with a monthly wage of 2800 euros can afford 517 Big Macs. A worker from Zurich who travels to Mexico City can afford 1197 Big Macs with the same wage.

Rice
E. g. In Mexico City, 1 kg rice costs 1.04 euros. A worker with a monthly wage of 183.33 euros can afford 176 kg rice. In Zurich, 1 kg rice costs 2.48 euros. A worker with a monthly wage of 2800 can afford 1129 kg rice. A worker from Zurich who travels to Mexico City can afford 2692 kg rice with the same wage.

Bread
E. g. In Mexico City, 1 kg bread costs 1.25 euros. A worker with a monthly wage of 183.33 euros can afford 147 kg bread. In Zurich, 1 kg bread costs 2.47 euros. A worker with a monthly wage of 2800 can afford 1134 kg bread. A worker from Zurich who travels to Mexico City can afford 2240 kg bread with the same wage.

Concept and Graphics: YAAY.ch. Basel. Out of Balance Competition 13

Cities have a parasitic relationship with their environment. By supplying the people gathered in them, they generate a distinct eco system, which, although integrated in global material cycles, feeds off its environment, namely land, water, air and local resources, and offloads its waste products in the environment. The material and energy exchange processes of cities transform traditional agricultural structures, intervene deeply in natural reproduction processes and drive climate change. How can the urban metabolism be made environmentally compatible? There is no lack of knowledge about sustainable production and environmentally compatible material cycles, about models of self-sufficient growth and consumption, about alternative forms of energy production and energy-saving construction. What is lacking are real utopias that integrate the many aspects playing a role in the urban metabolism into inclusive concepts and models and that shed light on what is possible.

METABOLISM

Städte verhalten sich parasitär gegenüber ihrer Umwelt. Sie erzeugen in der Versorgung der in ihnen versammelten Menschen ein eigenes Ökosystem, das zwar in globale Stoffkreisläufe eingebunden ist, sich aber von seiner Umgebung, sprich Land, Wasser, Luft und lokalen Ressourcen ernährt und seine Ausscheidungsprodukte in der Umwelt ablädt. Die materiell-energetischen Austauschprozesse von Städten wälzen überkommene, agrarische Strukturen um, greifen tief in natürliche Reproduktionsprozesse ein und treiben den Klimawandel an. Wie kann der städtische Stoffwechsel umweltverträglich gestaltet werden? Es fehlt nicht an Wissen über nachhaltige Produktion und umweltverträgliche Stoffkreisläufe, über Modelle selbstgenügsamen Wachstums und Konsums, über alternative Formen der Energiegewinnung und energiesparenden Bauens, woran es fehlt, sind Realutopien, welche die Vielzahl von Aspekten, die in den städtischen Stoffwechsel hereinspielen, zu ganzheitlichen Konzepten und Modellen integrieren und den Spielraum des Machbaren aufzeigen.

WHERE THERE IS LIGHT – THERE IS SHADOW

Vanessa Lang, Daniel Grasmeier, Sascha Hermanns

There is light ever since there was man. In former times it came as fire, a place where people came together, warmed themselves and felt good. The invention of the first light bulb in 1879, the rapid industrialisation and with it urbanisation abruptly turned the tide around.

Nowadays light gathers around us instead of the other way around – and it does day and night. Quietly and unnoticed a new kind of environmental pollution developed, which is still unnoticed by the majority of the population.

Light pollution is one of the biggest problems of the present and it has a deeper impact than one might think. Nowadays, a city counting over 500,000 inhabitants is exposed to a continuous light pollution of at least 60%. No matter if it's street lighting to improve safety or decadent city-marketing like skybeamers or illuminated buildings. Extensive and wrong lighting is not only dangerous for the fauna, but for the whole planet and especially for us. Everyone of us is already affected.

The following infographics show facts and deep impacts, which are connected to light pollution, a problem increasing about 6% per year. Since our basis refers to the area of a city, we use the abstract shape of a square for visualisation.

Like bees round a honeypot

Insects have a huge influence on our food. They pollinate our crop plants and, although their status in the food chain seems low, they play a decisive role therein.

In the night normally the moon is the brightest source of light and the insects' point of reference. With the invention of light bulbs the grade of illumination grew more and more and finally outshone the moon. For comparison:

The full moon has a lighting intensity of less than 0.25 lux. Usual street lighting counts up to 100 lux.

Furthermore the illumination interferes with the insects' inner compass. Flying through lightened streets and passing a street lamp every few meters, they don't find a fixed point of reference. The steadily changing light misleads them and makes them fly non-directional. While normally flying an angle of 90° to the moon they now fly in an 80° angle to the light source and thus draw nearer and nearer, circle the light bulb and die of exhaustion or burning.

Especially the white light, for example of high-pressure mercury lamps, strongly attracts insects. Yellow light has a much lower effect on them.

Sleepless

Sleeping less than five to six hours daily causes a permanent lack of sleep and serious health problems. After already two weeks of insomnia the doctor should be consulted.

Insomnia may be based on a variety of factors. Physical and psychological problems, as well as external influences like noise or light, often keep us awake. An emerging problem in large cities is light pollution. Street light and skybeamers light up the night and stop the human production of melatonin – the hormone rocking us to sleep. Thereby the choice of light is an important aspect, not only regarding the energy balance. The more white and blue the light contains, the bigger is the impact on humans, animals and plants.

Which consequences sleep deprivation can have is also reflected by the fact that there is an increase of 25% of heart problems directly after the clock change in spring. The number of accidents is also 30% higher than year average.

Seit Anbeginn der Menschheit war Licht, damals noch in Form von Feuer, ein Ort, an dem sich Menschen versammelten, wärmten und wohlfühlten. Mit der Erfindung der ersten Glühbirne 1879, der rasch folgenden Industrialisierung und damit verbundenen Urbanisierung hat sich dieses Blatt stark gewendet. Das Licht schart sich jetzt um uns, statt andersherum und das rund um die Uhr. Still und heimlich entstand eine neue Art der Umweltverschmutzung, von der selbst heute der Großteil der Menschen keinen blassen Schimmer hat.

Lichtverschmutzung ist eines der größten Probleme der Gegenwart und zieht mehr Folgen nach sich, als man zunächst glauben mag. Heutzutage ist jede Stadt mit einer Einwohnerzahl ab zirka 500.000 Menschen einer konstanten Lichtverschmutzung von mindestens 60 % ausgesetzt. Ob Straßenbeleuchtung zur angeblichen Steigerung der Sicherheit oder dekadentes City-Marketing in Form von Skybeamern und Gebäudeanstrahlung. Durch großflächige und falsche Beleuchtung schaden wir nicht nur der Tierwelt, sondern auch dem ganzen Planeten und letztendlich uns selbst. Jeder von uns ist bereits betroffen.

Die folgenden Informationsgrafiken vermitteln Fakten und weitreichende Folgen, die mit der jährlich um 6 % steigenden Lichtverschmutzung einhergehen. Da sich die Basis unserer Arbeit auf die jeweilige Fläche einer Stadt bezieht, nutzen wir dafür die abstrakte Form des Quadrates zur Visualisierung.

Wie die Motten zum Licht

Insekten haben einen wichtigen Einfluss auf unsere Nahrung, sie bestäuben unsere Nutzpflanzen und sind so trotz ihres niederen Ranges in der Nahrungskette ein wichtiger Bestandteil derselben.

Normalerweise orientieren sich Insekten nachts am Mond, der hellsten Lichtquelle. Mit der Erfindung der Glühbirne kam immer mehr und immer hellere Beleuchtung dazu, die den Mond überstrahlt. Zum Vergleich: Der Vollmond strahlt mit einer Intensität von weniger als 0,25 Lux, während herkömmliche Straßenbeleuchtung bei bis zu 100 Lux liegen kann.

Durch die schnellen Wechsel der Lichtorientierungspunkte beim Vorbeifliegen an Beleuchtung wird ihr innerer Kompass gestört und die Falter fliegen ungerichtet durch die Gegend. Statt des üblichen 90°-Winkels zum Mond, fliegen sie im 80°-Winkel zur Lichtquelle und nähern sich dieser so immer mehr, umkreisen sie und sterben durch Erschöpfung oder Verglühen. Vor allem weißes Licht, wie das der Quecksilberdampflampe, übt eine starke Anziehungskraft auf Insekten aus, gelbes Licht hingegen weitaus weniger.

Schlafloser Alltag

Weniger als fünf bis sechs Stunden Schlaf täglich rufen auf Dauer Schlafmangel und gravierende gesundheitliche Probleme hervor. Schon nach zwei Wochen anhaltender Schlafstörungen sollte deshalb ein Arzt aufgesucht werden.

Schlafprobleme können vielerlei Ursachen haben. Körperliche und psychische Probleme, aber auch äußere Einflüsse wie Lärm oder Licht verhindern oft das Ein- oder Durchschlafen. Gerade die Lichtverschmutzung in Großstädten wird zunehmend zum Problem. Straßenbeleuchtung und Skybeamer erhellen die Nacht und hemmen durch ihr grelles Licht die Melatoninproduktion des Menschen – das Hormon, das uns schlafen lässt. Je weißer und blauer das Licht, desto größer ist der Einfluss auf Menschen, Tiere und Pflanzen, weshalb die Wahl des richtigen Leuchtmittels von großer Bedeutung ist und nicht nur die Energiebilanz betrifft.

Welche Folgen Schlafmangel haben kann, zeigt sich auch durch die Tatsache, dass es einen Anstieg um 25 % an Herzbeschwerden direkt nach der Zeitumstellung im Frühjahr gibt. Auch die Unfallzahlen liegen im Durchschnitt eines Jahres um 30 % höher als sonst.

WIE DIE MOTTEN ZUM LICHT

Insekten haben einen wichtigen Einfluss auf unsere Nahrung, sie bestäuben unsere Nutzpflanzen und sind so trotz ihres niederen Ranges in der Nahrungskette ein wichtiger Bestandteil derer.

Normalerweise orientieren sich Insekten nachts am Mond, der hellsten Lichtquelle. Mit der Erfindung der Glühbirne kam immer mehr und immer hellere Beleuchtung dazu, die den Mond überstrahlt. Zum Vergleich: Der Vollmond strahlt mit einer Intensität von weniger als 0,25 Lux, während herkömmliche Straßenbeleuchtung bei bis zu 100 Lux liegen kann.

Durch die schnellen Wechsel der Lichtorientierungspunkte beim Vorbeifliegen an Beleuchtung wird ihr innerer Kompass gestört und die Falter fliegen ungerichtet durch die Gegend. Statt des üblichen 90°-Winkels zum Mond fliegen sie im 80°-Winkel zur Lichtquelle und nähern sich dieser so immer mehr, umkreisen sie und sterben durch Erschöpfung oder Verglühen. Vor allem weißes Licht, wie das der Quecksilberdampflampe, übt eine starke Anziehungskraft auf Insekten aus, gelbes Licht hingegen weitaus weniger.

ÜBERFLÜSSIGE LICHTABSTRAHLUNG

Überflüssige Strahlung von Straßenlaternen mit unterschiedlichen Ausrichtungen.
Wasted radiance of streetlights due to different angles.

82 %
überflüssige Abstrahlung

3 %
überflüssige Abstrahlung

keine
überflüssige Abstrahlung

100 %
Lichtstreuung

24 %
Lichtstreuung

18 %
Lichtstreuung

● Leuchtmedium ● Lichtstreuung in die Umgebung ● Überflüssige Abstrahlung

LED vs. QSDL

Effektivitätsduell eines modernen und eines veralteten Leuchtmittels.
Efficiency of a modern versus an outdated source of light.

20 W LED

50 W Quecksilberdampflampe

● Energieverbrauch, gemessen in Watt
⁄⁄ Lichtausbeute

VERALTETES LEUCHTMITTEL

Eine einzige Quecksilberdampflampe verbraucht 2.347,68 kWh im Jahr.
Die Grafik zeigt, wie diese Energie alternativ genutzt werden kann.
One mercury vapour lamp uses up to 2.347.68 kWh per year.
The graphic below shows how this energy could be used alternatively.

- **114,52 Tage** MacBook Pro-Betrieb
- **489,1 Tage** Radio-Betrieb
- **554,2 Tage** Fernseher-Betrieb - LCD - 32"
- **813,29 Tage** Waschmaschinen-Betrieb - 5,5 kg
- **732,56 Tage** Gefriertruhen-Betrieb - 200 l
- **11.269 Tassen** Kaffee kochen
- **669,41 Tage** Kühlschrank-Betrieb - 154 l
- **13.042,65 Ladungen** eines Smartphones

365 Tage
Quecksilberdampflampe

■ Eine Einheit entspricht 23,48 kWh

BELEUCHTUNGSDAUER

Entwicklung der Laternenbrennzeiten von 1849 bis heute.
Average burning time of streetlights from 1849 until now.

3,6 h pro Tag bis 1849

6,6 h pro Tag ab 1849

12 h pro Tag heute

HELLER ALS DER MOND

Vergleich der Lichtausbeute vom Mond und einer herkömmlichen Straßenlaterne.
Light efficiency of the moon compared to a conventional streetlight.

● Beleuchtungsstärke gemessen in LUX
● Leuchtmittel/-medium
● Anziehungskraft auf Insekten

0,25 Lux Mond

100 Lux Straßenlaterne

1:133.296

33 %
der nächtlich anfliegenden Insekten werden an den Lampen bzw. im Umfeld der Lampen geschädigt oder kommen zu Tode.

LICHTAUSBEUTE BEI LEUCHTMITTELN

Prozentualer Vergleich der vier Hauptleuchtmittel in Straßenlaternen in Bezug auf ihre Lichtausbeute (gemessen in Lumen pro Watt).
Comparison of the four main illuminants in streetlights related to their efficiency (measured in lumen per watt).

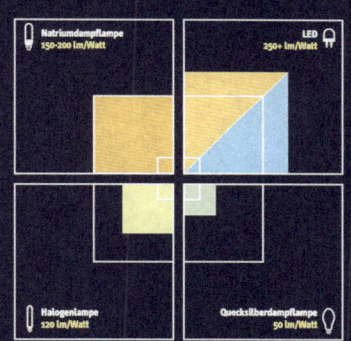

Natriumdampflampe 150-200 lm/Watt

LED 250+ lm/Watt

Halogenlampe 120 lm/Watt

Quecksilberdampflampe 50 lm/Watt

■ 1900-3000K warmes Licht Kerzenlicht

■ 4000-6000K direktes Sonnenlicht / Tageslicht

■ 5000-10000K kaltweiß blauer Himmel

INSEKTENSTERBEN DURCH STRASSENBELEUCHTUNG

Anzahl der stündlich sterbenden Insekten durch falsche Beleuchtung.
Number of insects dying per hour due to wrong lighting.

150 Ins/Std
je Straßenlaterne

13.425.000 Ins/Std
in Paris

9.300.000 Ins/Std
in Köln

3.150.000 Ins/Std
in Reykjavik

SICHERHEIT IM DUNKLEN

Eine Studie aus Bristol belegt, dass die Kriminalitätsrate nach dem regelmäßigen Abschalten der Straßenbeleuchtung zwischen 0.00 und 5.00 Uhr in einem Jahr um die Hälfte gesunken ist.
A study from Bristol proves a decrease of crime of 50 % within one year just by turning off streetlights between 0.00 and 5.00 am.

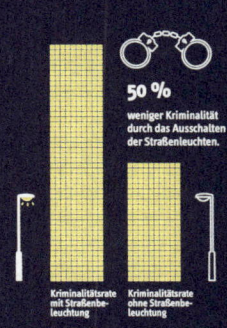

50 %
weniger Kriminalität durch das Ausschalten der Straßenleuchten.

Kriminalitätsrate mit Straßenbeleuchtung

Kriminalitätsrate ohne Straßenbeleuchtung

URSACHEN DES INSEKTENSTERBENS

Neben der enormen Lichtverschmutzung tragen selbstverständlich noch weitere Faktoren zum steigenden Insektensterben bei, wodurch unter anderem die Ernte bestäubungsabhängiger Lebensmittel leidet.
Besides the vast amount of light pollution there are other factors affecting mass extinction of insects, resulting also in decreasing harvests of foods dependent on pollination.

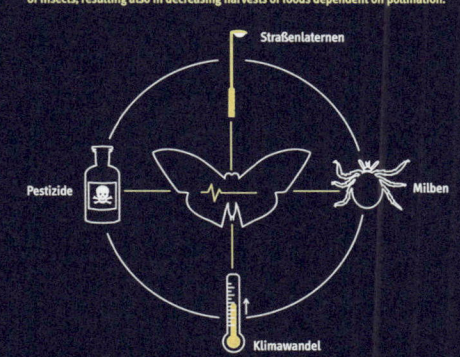

Straßenlaternen

Pestizide

Milben

Klimawandel

AUSWIRKUNGEN

Das steigende Insektensterben bringt eine weitreichende Folgenvielfalt mit sich.
The increasing mortality of insects has resulted in far-reaching consequences.

Zunahme von Schädlingen

Gebremste Textilproduktion

Störungen der Nahrungspyramide

STEIGENDE LEBENSMITTELPREISE

Die jährliche Preiszunahme von unterschiedlichen Lebensmitteln aufgrund der fehlenden Bestäubung durch die nötige Insekten.
The annual increase of different foods resulting from the lack of pollination by insects. (1993 to 2009)

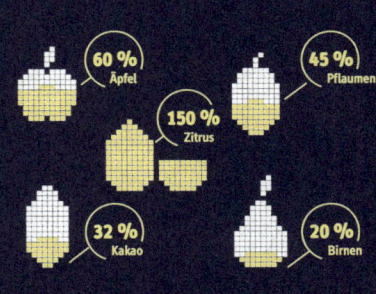

60 % Äpfel

45 % Pflaumen

150 % Zitrus

32 % Kakao

20 % Birnen

■ Eine Einheit entspricht 1 %

164

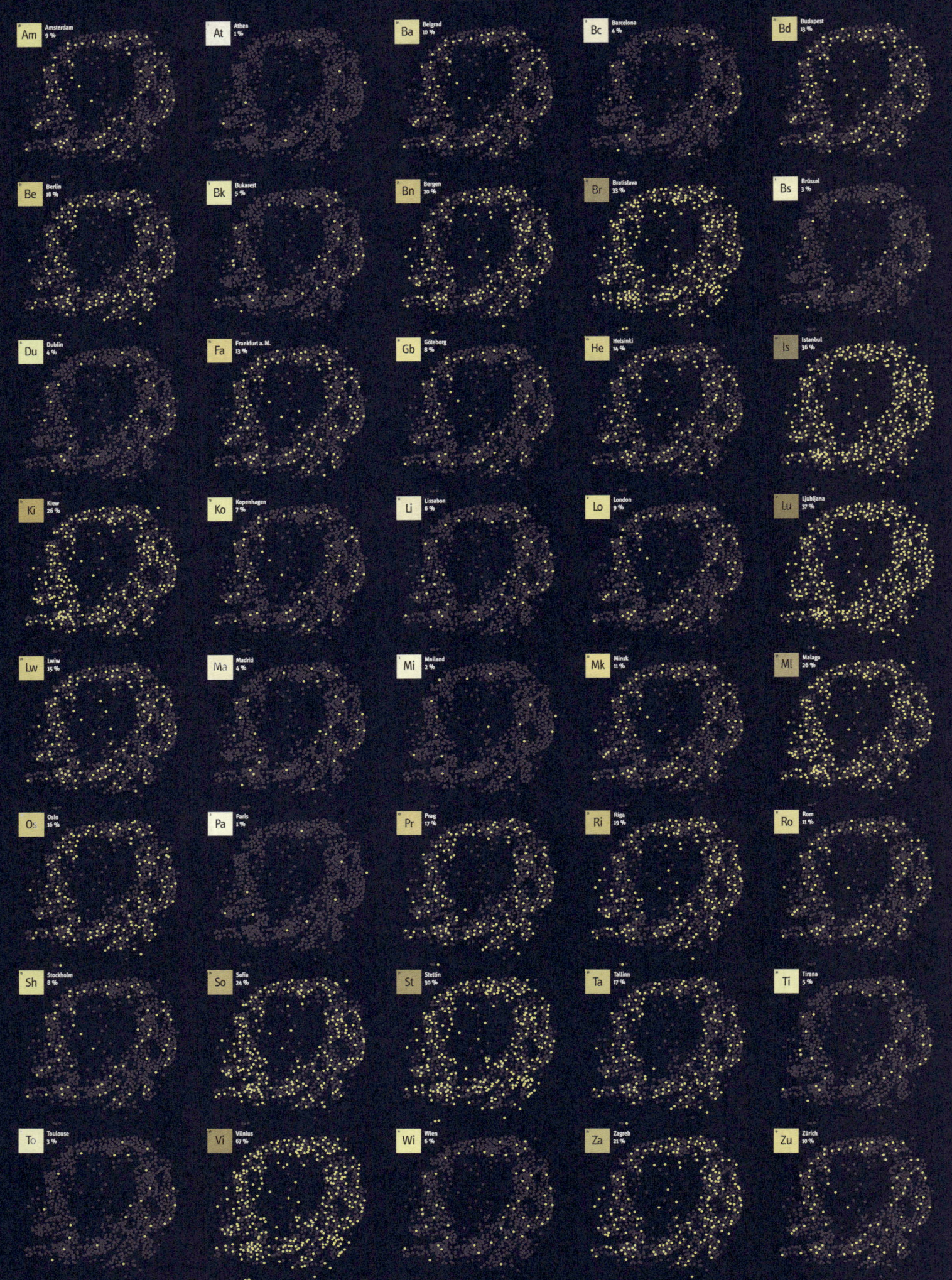

163

WHERE THERE IS LIGHT, THERE IS SHADOW

Seit Anbeginn der Menschheit war Licht, damals noch in Form von Feuer, ein Ort, an dem sich Menschen versammelten, wärmten und wohlfühlten. Mit der Erfindung der ersten Glühbirne 1879, der rasch folgenden Industrialisierung und damit verbundenen Urbanisierung hat sich dieses Blatt stark gewendet. Das Licht schart sich jetzt um uns, statt andersherum und das rund um die Uhr. Still und heimlich entstand eine neue Art der Umweltverschmutzung, von der selbst heute der Großteil der Menschen keinen blassen Schimmer hat.

Lichtverschmutzung ist eines der größten Probleme der Gegenwart und zieht mehr Folgen mit sich, als man zunächst glauben mag. Heutzutage ist jede Stadt mit einer Einwohnerzahl ab zirka 500.000 Menschen einer konstanten Lichtverschmutzung von mindestens 60 % ausgesetzt. Ob Straßenbeleuchtung zur angeblichen Steigerung der Sicherheit oder dekadentes City-Marketing in Form von Skybeamern und Gebäudeanstrahlung. Durch großflächige und falsche Beleuchtung schaden wir nicht nur der Tierwelt, sondern auch dem ganzen Planeten und letztendlich uns selbst. Jeder von uns ist bereits betroffen.

Die folgenden Informationsgrafiken vermitteln Fakten und weitreichende Folgen, die mit der jährlich um 6 % steigenden Lichtverschmutzung einhergehen. Da sich die Basis unserer Arbeit auf die jeweilige Fläche einer Stadt bezieht, nutzen wir dafür die abstrakte Form des Quadrates zur Visualisierung.

There has been light ever since the very beginning of civilization. In former times it came as campfires, a place where people came together, warmed themselves and felt good. The invention of the first light bulb in 1879, the rapid industrialisation and with it urbanisation abruptly turned the tide around. Nowadays light surrounds us rather than the other way around – and it does so constantly, day and night. Quietly a new kind of environmental pollution has developed, which is still unnoticed by the majority of the population.

Light pollution is one of the biggest problems of the present and it has a stronger impact than one might think. Nowadays a city with approximately more than 500.000 inhabitants is exposed to a continuous light pollution of at least 60 %. No matter what kind: streetlights to improve safety, decadent city-marketing tools such as skybeamers or illuminated buildings. Extensive and wrong lighting endangers not only our fauna, but our whole planet and thus, mankind. Every one of us is already affected.

The following infographics show facts and far-reaching implications connected to light pollution, a problem increasing steadily at a rate of approximately 6 % per annum. Since our point of reference relates to the individual surface area of a city, we use the abstract shape of a square for visualisation.

PERIODENSYSTEM DER LUMINANZDICHTE

Auf Basis der BLACK MARBLE-Daten der NASA wurde eine einzigartige Methode entwickelt, die sowohl den visuellen, als auch den prozentualen Grad der Lichtverschmutzungsdichte für jede beliebige Stadt der Welt errechnen kann.

Diese Tabelle zeigt die Lichtverschmutzungsdichte europäischer Städte, die nach ihrer Intensität geordnet wurden. (Stand: 2012)

Based on the BLACK MARBLE data by NASA we developed a method for calculating the level of light pollution for every city. In this table the denseness of light pollution of European cities is shown, ordered by intensity. (Status: 2012)

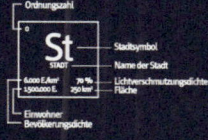

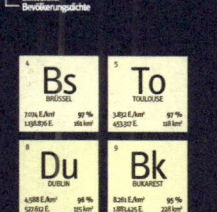

STERNENLOSE NACHT

In großen Städten (z.B. Warschau) sind nur noch 8 % der um 1900 erkennbaren Sterne sichtbar.
In big cities (e.g. Warsaw) only 8 % of the stars that could be seen in 1900 are still visible.

Ländliche Gebiete (●) 2500 Sterne

INEFFIZIENTE BELEUCHTUNG

Der Hauptteil der Lichtverschmutzung wird durch ineffiziente oder falsch ausgerichtete Leuchtmittel in Straßenlaternen verursacht.
The main part of light pollution is caused by inefficient or wrongly angled bulbs in streetlights.

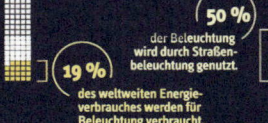

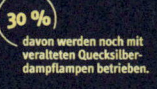

50 % der Beleuchtung wird durch Straßenbeleuchtung genutzt.

19 % des weltweiten Energieverbrauches werden für Beleuchtung verbraucht.

30 % davon werden noch mit veralteten Quecksilberdampflampen betrieben.

WACHSENDE LICHTGLOCKEN

Die weltweit betroffensten Gebiete der Lichtverschmutzung sind Großstädte in Europa, Ostasien und der Ostküste Nordamerikas. Die Grafik zeigt den jährlichen, prozentualen Anstieg der Lichtverschmutzung in diesen Gebieten.
The world's most affected areas of light pollution are major cities in Europe, East Asia and the east coast of North America. The graphic shows the annual increase of light pollution in these areas.

WELTWEIT	DEUTSCHLAND	ITALIEN	SÜDONTARIO	JAPAN	TUCSON
6 %	6 %	10 %	10 %	12 %	15 %

jährlicher Zuwachs der Lichtverschmutzung

SCHLAFLOSER ALLTAG

Weniger als fünf bis sechs Stunden Schlaf täglich rufen auf Dauer Schlafmangel und gravierende gesundheitliche Probleme hervor. Schon nach zwei Wochen anhaltender Schlafstörungen sollte deshalb ein Arzt aufgesucht werden.

Schlafprobleme können vielerlei Ursachen haben. Körperliche und psychische Probleme, aber auch äußere Einflüsse wie Lärm oder Licht verhindern oft das Ein- oder Durchschlafen. Gerade die Lichtverschmutzung in Großstädten wird zunehmend zum Problem. Straßenbeleuchtung und Skybeamer erhellen die Nacht und hemmen durch ihr grelles Licht die Melatoninproduktion des Menschen – das Hormon, das uns schlafen lässt. Je weißer und blauer das Licht, desto größer ist der Einfluss auf Menschen, Tiere und Pflanzen, weshalb die Wahl des richtigen Leuchtmittels von großer Bedeutung ist und nicht nur die Energiebilanz betrifft.

Welche Folgen Schlafmangel haben kann, zeigt sich auch durch die Tatsache, dass es einen Anstieg um 25% an Herzbeschwerden direkt nach der Zeitumstellung im Frühjahr gibt. Auch die Unfallzahlen liegen um 30% höher als sonst im Durchschnitt eines Jahres.

DIE INNERE UHR

Die nächtliche Melatoninbildung steuert unseren Tag-Nacht-Rhythmus. Diese sinkt stetig mit dem Alter und wird durch Nachtarbeit oder der Aussetzung künstlicher Lichtquellen, z.B. einem Monitor, gehemmt.
Our circadian rhythm is controlled by the nocturnal generation of melatonin which decreases with increasing age and is stunted by night work or the permanent exposure of artificial light, e.g. a monitor.

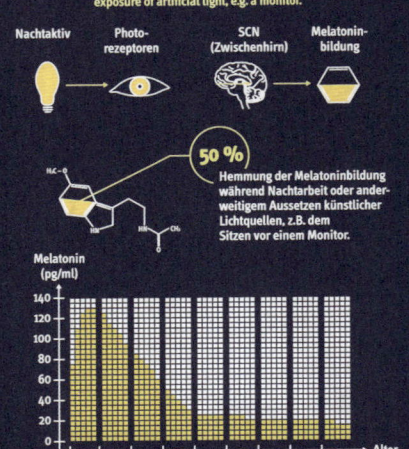

Nachtaktiv — Photorezeptoren — SCN (Zwischenhirn) — Melatoninbildung

50 % Hemmung der Melatoninbildung während Nachtarbeit oder anderweitiger Aussetzen künstlicher Lichtquellen, z.B. dem Sitzen vor einem Monitor.

Melatonin (pg/ml)
140 120 100 80 60 40 20
0 10 20 30 40 50 60 70 80 → Alter

FOLGEN VON SCHLAFMANGEL

Schlafmangel birgt unabsehbare Risiken.
Lack of sleep bears unpredictable risks.

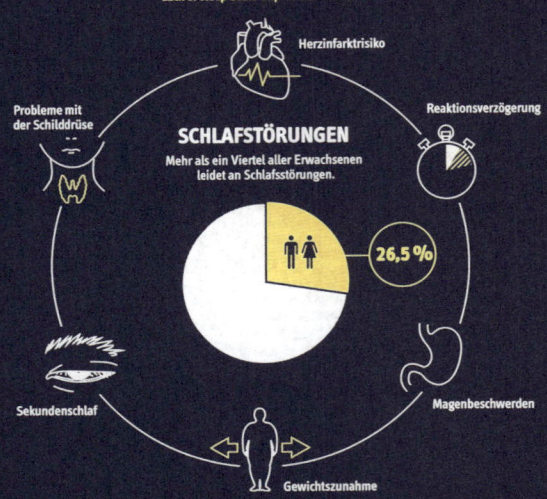

Herzinfarktrisiko
Reaktionsverzögerung
Probleme mit der Schilddrüse
Magenbeschwerden
Sekundenschlaf
Gewichtszunahme

SCHLAFSTÖRUNGEN
Mehr als ein Viertel aller Erwachsenen leidet an Schlafstörungen.
26,5 %

SCHLAFTRUNKENHEIT

Wie betrunken wird man durch Schlafmangel?
How intoxicating is lack of sleep?

17 Std. = **0,5 ‰**

Ein Glas entspricht 100 ml Wein mit einem Alkoholgehalt von 11 %.
Die Umrechnung der Promilleangabe basiert auf einer Person mit ca. 60 kg Körpergewicht.

FOLGEN VON SCHLAFENTZUG

Auswirkungen nach mehreren wachen Nächten.
Effects of several sleepless nights in a row.

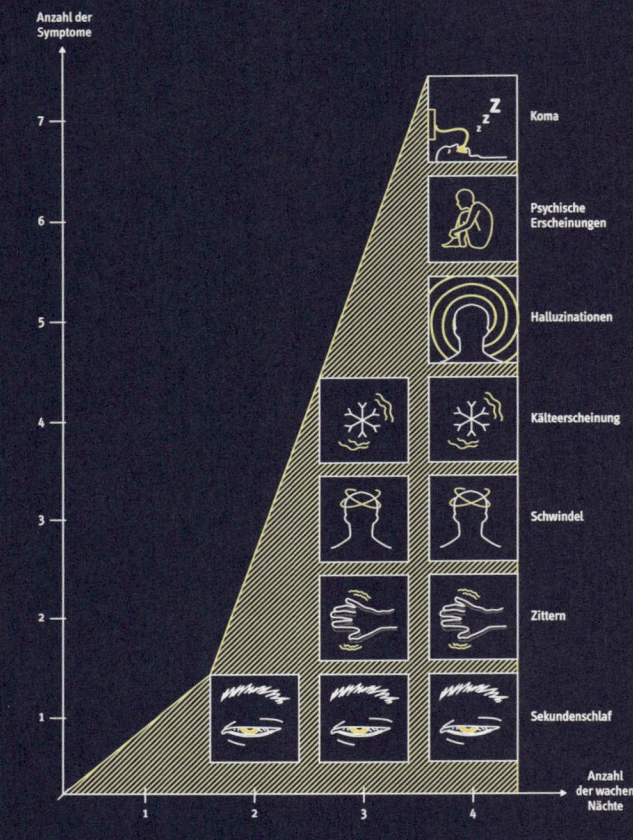

Anzahl der Symptome
7 6 5 4 3 2 1

Koma
Psychische Erscheinungen
Halluzinationen
Kälteerscheinung
Schwindel
Zittern
Sekundenschlaf

Anzahl der wachen Nächte
1 2 3 4

NACHTARBEIT IN DEUTSCHLAND

Anzahl der Nachtarbeiter in der Bundesrepublik.
Number of night workers in Germany.

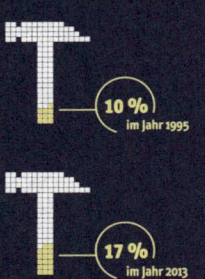

10 % im Jahr 1995
17 % im Jahr 2013

▪ Eine Einheit entspricht 1 %

NACHTAKTIVE STERBEN FRÜHER

Krankheitsrisiken durch Nachtarbeit (gehemmte Melatoninbildung) im Vergleich zu regelmäßigen Rauchern.
Health risks resulting from night work versus regular smoking.

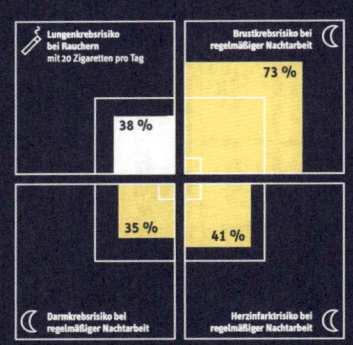

Lungenkrebsrisiko bei Rauchern mit 20 Zigaretten pro Tag **38 %**
Brustkrebsrisiko bei regelmäßiger Nachtarbeit **73 %**
Darmkrebsrisiko bei regelmäßiger Nachtarbeit **35 %**
Herzinfarktrisiko bei regelmäßiger Nachtarbeit **41 %**

NACHTARBEIT ALS RISIKOFAKTOR

Steigendes Unfallrisiko durch Übermüdung.
Increasing accident risk due to fatigue.

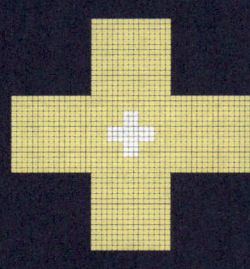

500 % höheres Unfallrisiko während der Nachtarbeit

▪ Eine Einheit entspricht 1 %

AUTOUNFÄLLE DURCH ÜBERMÜDUNG

10 bis 20 Prozent der Verkehrsunfälle in Deutschland entstehen durch Müdigkeit am Steuer. Das wären bei 300.000 registrierten Unfällen mit Personenschaden im Jahr 2014 bis zu 60.000.
10 to 20 percent of traffic accidents in Germany are caused by tiredness of the driver, that is up to 60.000 accidents of 300.000 registered with personal injury in 2004.

SEKUNDENSCHLAF

Die unterschätzte Gefahr des Sekundenschlafes beim Autofahren.
Microsleep – an underestimated risk.

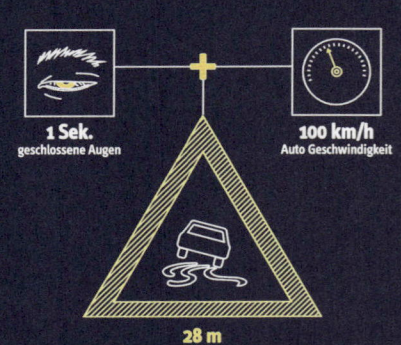

1 Sek. geschlossene Augen
100 km/h Auto Geschwindigkeit
28 m unkontrollierte Fahrt

DIAGNOSIS CITY Olga Schweigert

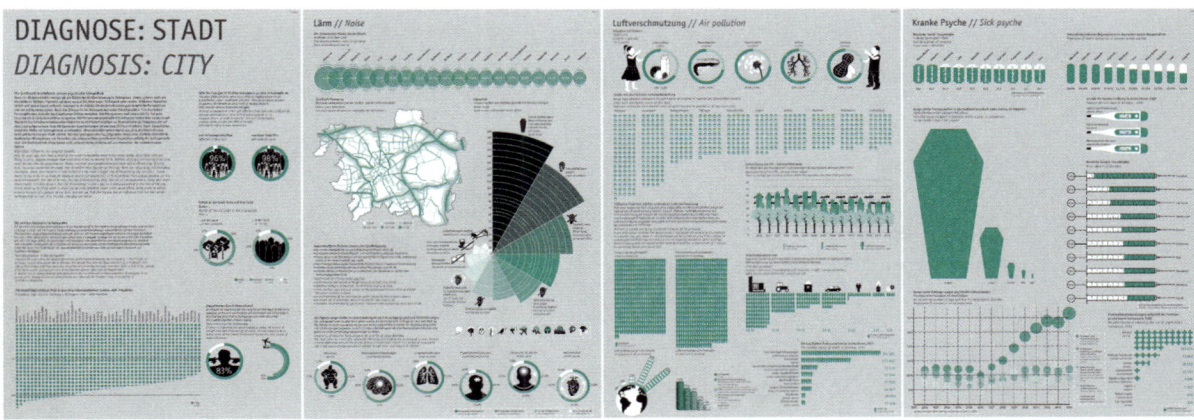

Millions of people are moving from rural areas to the cities – for good reasons. It is in the city that one finds good professional prospects and a vibrant way of living. Still, the urban home has its shady side.

Between 2009 and 2011, up to 96% of urban residents in the European Union are, at least temporarily, exposed to fine dust concentrations, which are classified as harmful by the WHO. 98% had to endure too high ozone levels.[1] Every year, 7 million people are dying worldwide because of air pollution. About 3.7 million death cases can be ascribed to smog in the ambient air; 4.3 million are caused by polluted air within buildings.[2]

Noise is another health risk factor for city dwellers. In Germany, 83% people feel harassed by street noise, 45% by aircraft noise and 40% by rail noise.[3] Chronic noise exposure results in disruption of communication or concentration, increasing risk of heart and circulatory diseases, etc.[4] Sleeping disorder, another possible effect of noise, correlates further with other health problems. Around 13.1% of respondents with a high degree of sleeping disturbance are reported to suffer from lung diseases in addition.[5]

Sick leaves of employees because of mental illnesses are on the rise. 24.9 days of sick leave in Germany are caused by mental illness, while the average number of sick leave days caused by all diseases is 11.8.[6] Psychological problems partly account for the high suicide rate. In Germany, deaths caused by suicide are three times as many as deaths caused by traffic accidents, 9 times as many as by drugs and 35 times as many as by murders. Scientists have figured out that big cities are influencing and changing our brains. Those who are rooted in a city have a bigger risk of becoming city neurotics. Inhabitants of big cities in Germany for example are 40% more liable to get depressions than people growing up in a rural environment; the rate of anxiety disorder is increased by 20%.[7] The risk of schizophrenia is rising even more dramatically. Those grown up in cities seem to show similar brain activities under stress as those being prone to schizophrenia because of a genetic disposition. Scholars assume that the threat to one's psyche rises with the size of the city. One can say that the big city has an influence that has been underestimated up to now: it is actually changing our brains.[8]

60 years ago, less than a third of the world's population lived in big cities. Today, more than 50% are living in cities. Experts estimate that until 2050 it will be around 70%. The looming diagnosis of "city" being the root of our health decline pushes us to seriously seek for a cure for our urban future.

Aus gutem Grund ziehen Millionen Menschen weltweit vom Land in die Städte. Die Großstadt bietet gute berufliche Perspektiven und ein pulsierendes Leben. Doch das Zuhause in der Metropole hat auch seine Schattenseiten.

Zwischen 2009 und 2011 waren bis zu 96 Prozent der Stadtbewohner in der Europäischen Union, zumindest zeitweise, Feinstaubkonzentrationen ausgesetzt, die die WHO als gesundheitsschädlich einstuft. 98 Prozent mussten zu hohe Ozonwerte ertragen.[1] Jährlich sterben etwa sieben Millionen Menschen infolge der weltweiten Luftverschmutzung. Etwa 3,7 Millionen Todesfälle lassen sich auf Smog in der Umgebungsluft zurückführen; 4,3 Millionen haben verschmutzte Luft in Gebäuden als Ursache.[2]

Für die Stadtbewohner ist Lärm ein weiterer Gesundheitsrisikofaktor. In Deutschland fühlen sich 83 Prozent der Bevölkerung durch Straßenlärm belästigt, 45 Prozent von Fluglärm und 40 Prozent von Schienenlärm.[3] Chronische Lärmbelastung führt zu Störungen der Kommunikation oder Konzentration, Erhöhung des Risikos von Herzkrankheiten und Kreislauferkrankungen usw.[4] Schlafstörungen, eine weitere mögliche Auswirkung von Lärm, korrelieren weiterhin mit anderen gesundheitlichen Problemen. Rund 13,1 Prozent der Befragten mit einer hochgradigen Schlafstörung gaben an, zudem unter Lungenerkrankungen zu leiden.[5]

Der durch psychische Erkrankungen verursachte Krankenstand der Arbeitnehmer steigt weiter an. Die dadurch verursachten Ausfalltage sind mit 24,9 Tagen mehr als doppelt so hoch wie der Durchschnitt aller Erkrankungen mit 11,8 Tagen je Fall.[6] Psychische

Probleme schlagen sich teilweise in einer hohen Selbstmordrate nieder. Es gibt in Deutschland 3-mal so viel durch Selbstmord verursachte Todesfälle wie durch Verkehrsunfälle, 9-mal so viel wie durch Drogen und 35-mal so viel wie durch Mord.

Forscher haben herausgefunden, dass die Großstadt unser Gehirn verändert. Wer hier geboren und verwurzelt ist, hat gute Chancen, ein Großstadtneurotiker zu werden. Etliche schwere psychische Erkrankungen treten hier verstärkt auf. Deutsche Großstädter beispielsweise leiden bis zu 40 Prozent häufiger an Depressionen als Menschen, die auf dem Land aufgewachsen sind, die Quote der Angststörungen ist bei Stadtbewohnern um rund 20 Prozent erhöht.[7] Noch dramatischer erhöht sich das Risiko, an Schizophrenie zu erkranken. Wer in der Stadt aufgewachsen ist, zeigt unter Stress in bestimmten Hirnregionen eine ähnliche Aktivität wie Menschen, die aufgrund einer genetischen Disposition anfällig für Schizophrenie sind. Wissenschaftler gehen davon aus, dass die Gefahr für den Geist mit der Größe der Stadt zunimmt. Die Großstadt hat einen bisher wohl unterschätzten Einfluss auf uns Menschen: Sie verändert unser Gehirn.[8]

Noch vor 60 Jahren lebte weniger als ein Drittel der Weltbevölkerung in Metropolen. Heute wohnen mehr als die Hälfte aller Menschen in Städten. Experten schätzen, dass es bis 2050 sogar 70 Prozent sein werden. Die sich abzeichnende Diagnose von "der Stadt" als die Wurzel unserer schwindenden Gesundheit fordert uns dringlich auf, ernsthaft nach einem Heilmittel für unsere urbane Zukunft zu suchen.

Lärm // *Noise*

Die 20 lautesten Städte deutschlands
Anteil des Lärms über 55dB
The twenty noisiest cities in Germany
Share of decibel noise over 50

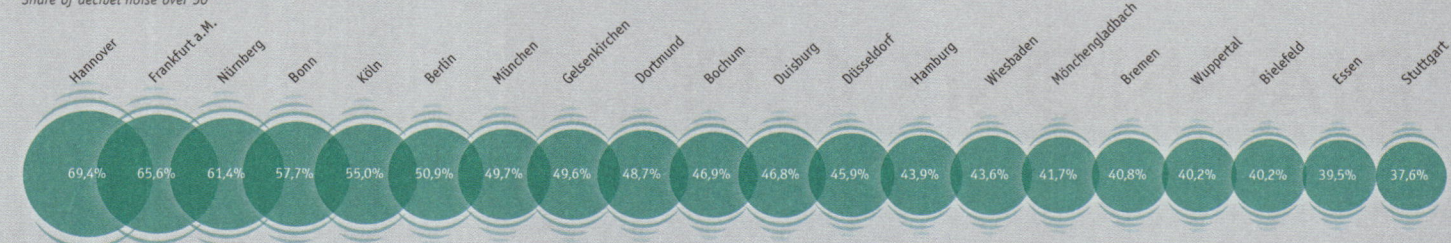

Hannover	Frankfurt a.M.	Nürnberg	Bonn	Köln	Berlin	München	Gelsenkirchen	Dortmund	Bochum	Duisburg	Düsseldorf	Hamburg	Wiesbaden	Mönchengladbach	Bremen	Wuppertal	Bielefeld	Essen	Stuttgart
69,4%	65,6%	61,4%	57,7%	55,0%	50,9%	49,7%	49,6%	48,7%	46,9%	46,8%	45,9%	43,9%	43,6%	41,7%	40,8%	40,2%	40,2%	39,5%	37,6%

Lärmkarte Hannover
Die Haupt-Lärmquellen sind der Straßen- und der Schienenverkehr.
Noise chart Hannover
The main sources of noise are road traffic and rail transport.

< 55 dB > 55-60 dB > 60-65 dB
> 65-70 dB > 70-75 dB > 75 dB

Lärmskala
Geräuschquellen und mögliche gesundheitliche Auswirkungen
Noise scale
Noise sources and possible health effects

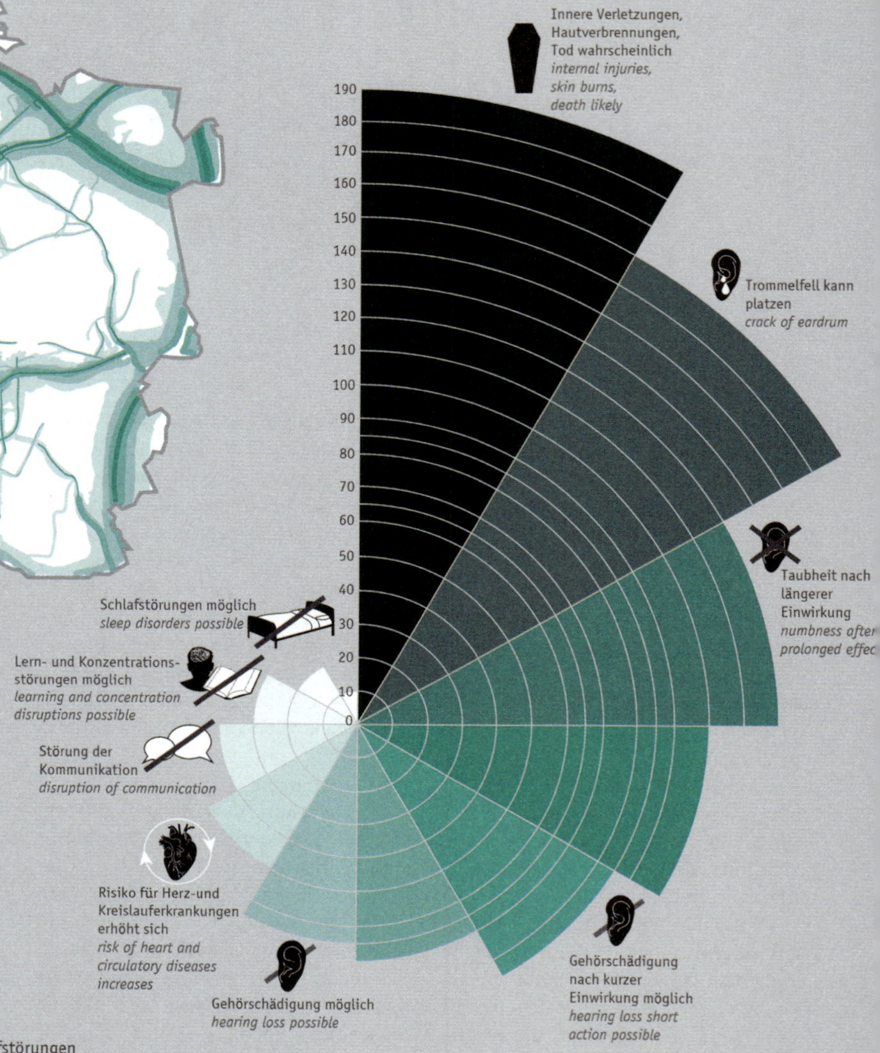

Innere Verletzungen, Hautverbrennungen, Tod wahrscheinlich
internal injuries, skin burns, death likely

Trommelfell kann platzen
crack of eardrum

Taubheit nach längerer Einwirkung
numbness after prolonged effect

Schlafstörungen möglich
sleep disorders possible

Lern- und Konzentrationsstörungen möglich
learning and concentration disruptions possible

Störung der Kommunikation
disruption of communication

Risiko für Herz-und Kreislauferkrankungen erhöht sich
risk of heart and circulatory diseases increases

Gehörschädigung nach kurzer Einwirkung möglich
hearing loss short action possible

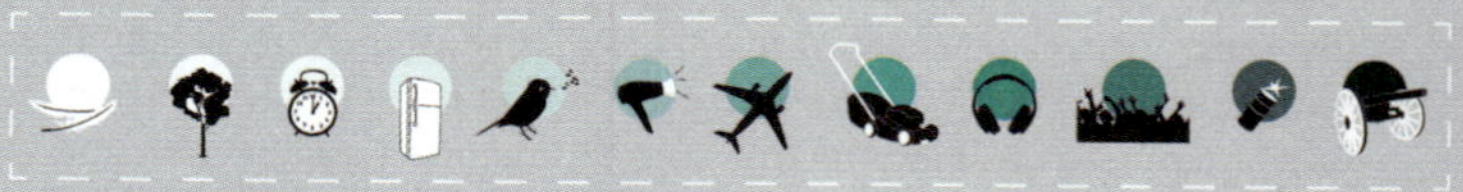

Gehörschädigung möglich
hearing loss possible

Gesundheitliche Risiken chronischer Lärmbelastung
- Lärmschwerhörigkeit bei längerer Belastung mit Pegeln ab 85 dB,
- verringerte Konzentrationsfähigkeit und verminderte Qualität der Nachtruhe,
- Stress, da Lärm als Stressfaktor auf den menschlichen Organismus wirkt, unabhängig davon, ob der Mensch schläft oder wacht,
- beschleunigte Alterung des Herz-Kreislaufsystems durch chronische Lärmbelastung,
- erhöhtes Herzinfarktrisiko bei chronischen Belastungen über 65 dB,
- erhöhtes Risiko, an Bluthochdruck zu erkranken, bei dauerhaftem nächtlichen Geräuschpegel über 55 dB

Health risks of chronic noise exposure
- *noise-induced hearing with prolonged exposure at levels from 85 dB,*
- *decreased ability to concentrate, and diminished quality of sleep,*
- *stress because noise acts as a stressor on the human organism, regardless of whether the person is asleep or awake,*
- *accelerated aging of the cardiovascular system caused by chronic noise exposure,*
- *increased risk of myocardial infarction in chronic stress than 65 dB,*
- *increased risk of developing hypertension, nocturnal when permanently noise level 55 dB*

Häufigkeit ausgewählter Grunderkrankungen nach Ausprägungsgrad von Schlafstörungen
Die vorliegende Statistik zeigt die Ergebnisse einer bundesweiten DAK-Umfrage aus dem Jahr 2009 zur Häufigkeit von sechs Grunderkrankungen, bei denen Unterschiede zwischen den Ausprägungsgeraden von Schlafstörungen bestehen. Rund 13,1 Prozent der Befragten mit einer hochgradigen Schlafstörung gaben an, zudem unter Lungenerkrankungen zu leiden.
Frequency of selected basic diseases by severity of sleep disorders
This table shows the results of a nationwide DAK survey from 2009 on the incidence of six basic diseases in which differences between the severity of sleep disorders exist. Around 13,1 percent of respondents with a high degree of sleep disturbance reported to suffer from lung diseases in addition.

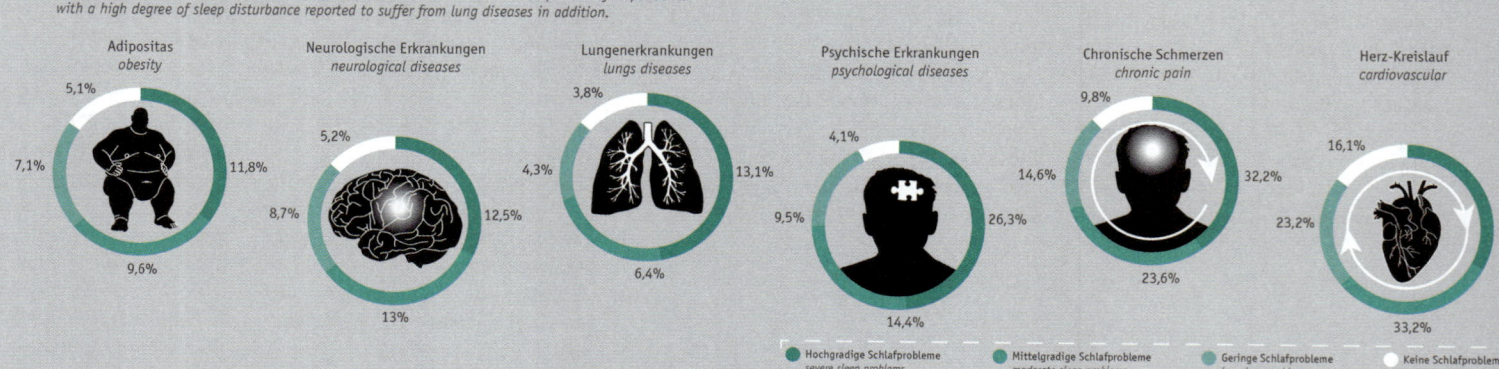

Adipositas *obesity*
5,1% 7,1% 11,8% 9,6%

Neurologische Erkrankungen *neurological diseases*
5,2% 8,7% 12,5% 13%

Lungenerkrankungen *lungs diseases*
3,8% 4,3% 13,1% 6,4%

Psychische Erkrankungen *psychological diseases*
4,1% 9,5% 26,3% 14,4%

Chronische Schmerzen *chronic pain*
9,8% 14,6% 32,2% 23,6%

Herz-Kreislauf *cardiovascular*
16,1% 23,2% 33,2%

Hochgradige Schlafprobleme *severe sleep problems*   Mittelgradige Schlafprobleme *moderate sleep problems*   Geringe Schlafprobleme *low sleep problems*   Keine Schlafprobleme *no sleep problems*

Luftverschmutzung // *Air pollution*

Allergien bei Kindern
Stadt | Land
Children´s allergies
city | country

Lebensmittel *edibles*	Meeresfrüchte *seafood*	Heuschnupfen *hay fever*	Asthma *asthma*	Erdnüsse *peanuts*

  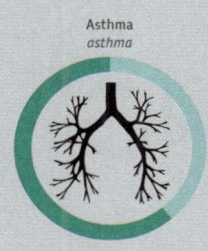 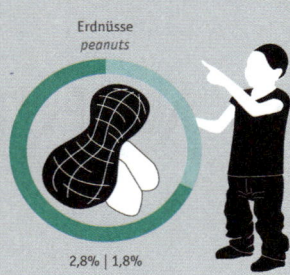

9,8% | 6,2%   2,4% | 0,8%   10,5% | 4,1%   5,9% | 3,1%   2,8% | 1,8%

Städte mit der höchsten Feinstaubbelastung
Bezug Tagesmittelwert (Grenzwert: 50 µg/m³ dürfen an maximal 35 Tagen im Jahr überschritten werden):
Cities with the highest strain of fine dust
Reference: daylie mean value (treshold value: 50 µg/m³ may only be exceeded on 35 days max a year)

Stuttgart Reutlingen Markgröningen Tübingen Gelsenkirchen Hagen Leipzig München Mühlhausen Ludwigsburg

Millionen Menschen sterben weltweit an Luftverschmutzung
Eine neue Analyse der WHO zeigt, dass etwa sieben Millionen Menschen jährlich infolge der weltweiten Luftverschmutzung sterben. Etwa 3,7 Millionen Todesfälle lassen sich laut WHO-Hochrechnung auf Smog in der Umgebungsluft zurückführen, 4,3 Millionen haben verschmutzte Luft in Gebäuden als Ursache. Weil zahlreiche Menschen beiden Arten von Luftverschmutzung ausgesetzt sind, ergibt sich eine statistisch hochgerechnete (nicht absolute) Gesamtzahl von 7 Millionen.

Millions of people are dying worldwide because of air pollution
A new WHO analysis indicates that approximately 7 mio peoples die because of the worldwide air pollution every year. about 3,7 mio deathcases can be ascribed to smog in the ambient air according the the WHO projection. and 4,3 mio are caused by polluted air within buildings. Because many peoples are exposed to both kinds of air pollution, a total number of 7 mio can be statistically forcast (non absolutely).

Entwicklung der PM₁₀-Jahresmittelwerte
Im Mittel über alle Messstationen in der jeweiligen Belastungszone, Zeitraum 2000–2014.
Development of the PM₁₀ annual mean value
Taken in average over all survey stations within the according zone from 2000 until 2014.

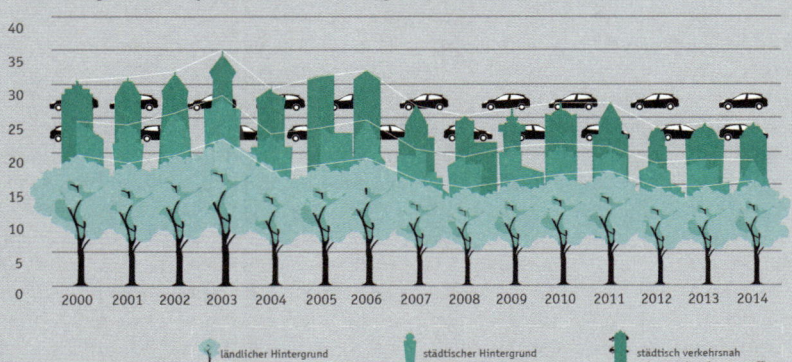

40 35 30 25 20 15 10 5 0

2000 2001 2002 2003 2004 2005 2006 2007 2008 2009 2010 2011 2012 2013 2014

ländlicher Hintergrund *rural setting* — städtischer Hintergrund *urban setting* — städtisch verkehrsnah *urban setting close to traffic*

Smog in der Umgebungsluft
smog in ambient air

Verschmutzte Luft in Gebäuden
polluted air in buildings

◆ 10 000 Tote *10 000 dead people*

Luftverschmutzung in der Umwelt
air pollution in the enviroment

Luftverschmutzung in Gebäuden
air pollution in buildings

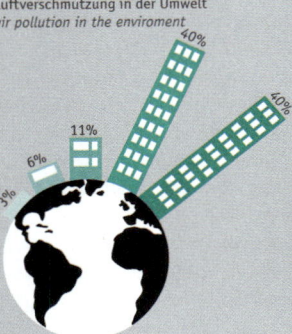

3% 6% 11% 40% 40%

Feinstaubproduzenten
Industrie | Landwirtschaft | Haushalte & Kleinverbraucher | Verkehr | Energiewirtschaft | Diffuse Emissionen aus Brennstoffen | Verarbeitendes Gewerbe
Fine dust producers
industry | agriculture | housekeeping/small consumers | traffic | energy economics | diffus emission from combustible | processing craft

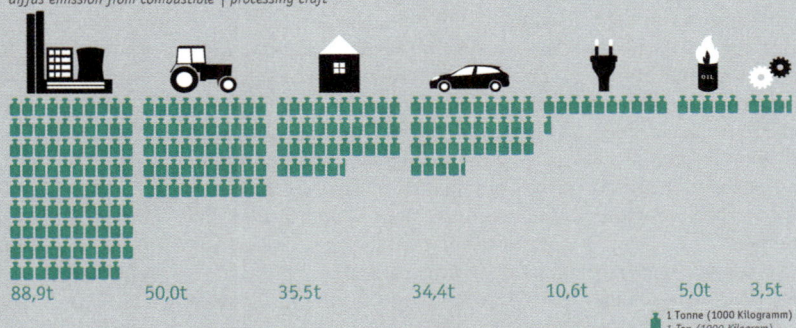

88,9t   50,0t   35,5t   34,4t   10,6t   5,0t   3,5t

🭬 1 Tonne (1000 Kilogramm)
1 Ton (1000 Kilogram)

34% 26% 22% 12% 6%

● Schlaganfall *stroke*
● Ischämische Herzerkrankungen (Durchblutungsstörung des Herzmuskels) *ischemic heart disease (circulatory disorder of the heart muscle)*
● COPD (Chronisch obstruktive Lungenerkrankung) *COPD (Chronic Obstructive Pulmonary Disease)*
● Akute Atemwegserkrankungen bei Kindern *acute respiratory diseases in children*
● Lungenkrebs *lung cancer*

Die häufigsten Todesursachen in Deutschland, 2013
The leading causes of death in Germany, 2013

Herz-Kreislauf-Erkrankungen *cardiovascula diseases*	354 493
Krebsleiden *cancer*	223 842
Chronische ischämische Herzkrankheit *chronic ischemicheart disease*	73 176
Akuter Myokardinfarkt *acute myocardial infarction*	52 044
Herzinsuffizienz *heart failure*	45 815
Lungen-/Bronchialkrebs *lung and bronchial cancer*	44 813
Brustkrebs *breast cancer*	18 009
Dickdarmkrebs *colon cancer*	17 108

🭬 10 000 Tote
10 000 dead people

URBAN MINING

Tobias Hahn

Raw material consumption is on the rise globally, causing a series of implications for the global economy that will be hard to overcome. In the 20th century, politicians' and industrialists' standard policy was to downplay the continual rise in demand for resources; raw materials were relatively cheap and hence not a big factor in economic calculations. Since the 2000s however, emerging countries, particularly China, began hording sought-after raw materials for their own need: around 95% of global deposits in rare earth elements, necessary for the production of smart phones, laser devices and plasma display panels exist in China. The resulting significant price rise for many metals and minerals and, above all, the looming restraint on replenishments put European and US-American firms under pressure.

By today, advocates of the so-called "circular economy" are being heard again even by institutions such as the World Economic Forum, promoting a mode of economic production whereby the life cycle of a product does not stop at its disposal. Taking natural metabolic cycles as role models, waste materials are to be taken up again and transformed into new commodities, sparing the planets ecosystems. A mounting number of firms is incorporating the notion of a circular economy in their production processes, albeit never entirely and never with the help of an extensive network between businesses to exchange waste and commodity materials.

Instead, the main purpose seems to be to optimise production processes internally in order to circumvent the problem of replenishment restraint on a short term basis. An advantageous side effect is the creation of a "green" corporate identity, spurring sales to the increasingly environmentally friendly European and US-American average consumer. However, highly networked zerowaste production processes, verging on something that could be deemed a "natural cycle", are still far from reality.

New areas of intervention and the search for new materials not yet deemed as recycle-worthy could provide much-needed impulses on the way to a circular economy. The project defines the recovery of raw material in an urban area as "urban mining"; hinting at the various opportunities for material, energy and commodity extraction that exist in building construction and demolition. In Germany for example, 80% of all waste is construction site waste: concrete, metal, glass and sand are only a few of the materials that could be generating a hugely profitable recycling market in the future.

The handling of electronic waste is another field that needs considerable optimisation: the United Nations Environment Programme (UNEP) assumes that in the case of over 30 metals, 99% are wasted after only one application. Globally, there are just a few machines capable of separating rare metals from complex electronic articles like mobile phones or computers, which makes routinized recycling virtually impossible.

Even with regards to vital elements like phosphor, indispensable for large-scale crop production in the form of phosphatic fertilizer, some scientists predict that natural reserves will be consumed in 50–100 years. The project proposes the extraction of phosphor from dry matter in sewage canals as one possible solution, and further discusses the use of sewage for heat extraction in urban areas.

Despite major efforts to innovate recycling technologies, the question remains whether a circular economy and industrial production are compatible at all. Circular economies generate certain restrictions (modular assembly, easy disassembly, exclusive use of recycleable materials and enormous expenditures for the recycling of complex products) that do not agree with the current dictate of economic efficiency and profit maximisation.

Weltweit steigt der Verbrauch von Rohstoffen an, was eine Reihe schwer überwindbarer Konsequenzen für die Weltwirtschaft haben wird. Noch im 20. Jahrhundert war es gängige Praxis vieler Politiker und Unternehmer, den problematischen Anstieg der Rohstoffnachfrage herunterzuspielen; Rohstoffe waren relativ günstig und daher kein großer Faktor in wirtschaftlichen Berechnungen. Seit den 2000ern begannen jedoch viele Schwellenländer, insbesondere China, begehrte Rohstoffe zu horten, um ihren Eigenbedarf zu decken: rund 95 % der weltweiten Vorkommen seltener Erden, die für die Herstellung von Smartphones, Lasern und Plasma-Displays benötigt werden, gibt es in China. Der daraus resultierende deutliche Preisanstieg vieler Metalle und Mineralien und vor allem der sich abzeichnende Nachschubstau brachten viele europäische und US-amerikanische Firmen in Bedrängnis.

Heute wird den Befürwortern der so genannten "Kreislaufwirtschaft" sogar von Institutionen wie dem Weltwirtschaftsforum wieder Gehör geschenkt. Sie propagieren eine Wirtschaftsweise, in der der Lebenszyklus eines Produkts nicht mit seiner Entsorgung endet. Natürliche Stoffkreisläufe dienen als Vorbilder dafür, Abfallmaterialien wiederzuverwenden, sie in neue Rohstoffe umzuwandeln und so die Ökosysteme des Planeten zu schonen. Eine wachsende Anzahl von Unternehmen beginnt, Aspekte der Kreislaufwirtschaft in ihre Produktionsprozesse mit einzubeziehen, allerdings nicht vollständig und oft ohne die Unterstützung eines umfangreichen Austauschnetzwerks von Abfall- und Rohstoffmaterialien zwischen einzelnen Unternehmen.

Das eigentliche Ziel scheint hier zu sein, interne Produktionsprozesse zu optimieren, um das Problem des Nachschubstaus kurzfristig zu umgehen. Ein vorteilhafter Nebeneffekt ist die Schaffung einer "grünen" Unternehmensidentität, was Verkäufe an den zunehmend umweltfreundlichen europäischen und US-amerikanischen Durchschnittsverbraucher ankurbelt. Stark vernetzte Produktionsprozesse ohne Abfall, die an so etwas wie "natürliche Kreisläufe" grenzen, sind nach wie vor von der Realität weit entfernt.

Neue Interventionsbereiche und die Suche nach neuen Materialien, die

noch nicht als recycle-würdig gelten, könnten dringend benötigte Impulse auf dem Weg zu einer Kreislaufwirtschaft darstellen. Das Projekt bezeichnet die Rückgewinnung von Rohstoffen im städtischen Gebiet als "Urban Mining" und spielt so auf die verschiedenen Möglichkeiten für Material-, Energie- und Rohstoffgewinnung an, die in der Bau- und Abbruchindustrie existieren. In Deutschland sind beispielsweise 80 % aller Abfälle Baustoffe: Beton, Metall, Glas und Sand sind nur einige der Materialien, durch die in Zukunft ein äußerst profitabler Recyclingmarkt entstehen könnte.

Auch bei der Handhabung von Elektronikschrott besteht erheblicher Optimierungsbedarf: das Umweltprogramm der Vereinten Nationen (UNEP) geht davon aus, dass bei mehr als 30 Metallen 99 % nach nur einer Anwendung verschrottet werden. Weltweit gibt es nur einige wenige Maschinen, die seltene Metalle aus komplexen elektronischen Artikeln wie Mobiltelefonen oder Computern trennen können, was routiniertes, großmaßstäbliches Recycling praktisch unmöglich macht.

Auch in Bezug auf lebenswichtige Elemente wie Phosphor, das in Form von Phosphatdünger für den großmaßstäblichen Anbau von Nutzpflanzen unerlässlich ist, prognostizieren einige Wissenschaftler, dass die natürlichen Reserven in 50 bis 100 Jahren verbraucht sein werden. Das Projekt schlägt als eine mögliche Lösung die Extraktion von Phosphor aus der Trockenmasse in Abwasserkanälen vor und bespricht auch die Verwendung von Abwasser für Wärmegewinnung in städtischen Gebieten.

Trotz massiver Anstrengungen um Innovationen im Bereich der Recyclingtechnologien bleibt die Frage offen, ob sich industrielle Produktion und Kreislaufwirtschaft nicht eigentlich ausschließen. Die Kreislaufwirtschaft erzeugt einige Restriktionen (modularer Aufbau, leichte Demontage, Verwendung von ausschließlich recyclebaren Materialien und enorme Ausgaben für das Recycling von komplexen Produkten), die mit dem gegenwärtigen Diktat von wirtschaftlicher Effizienz und Profitmaximierung nur sehr schwer vereinbar sind.

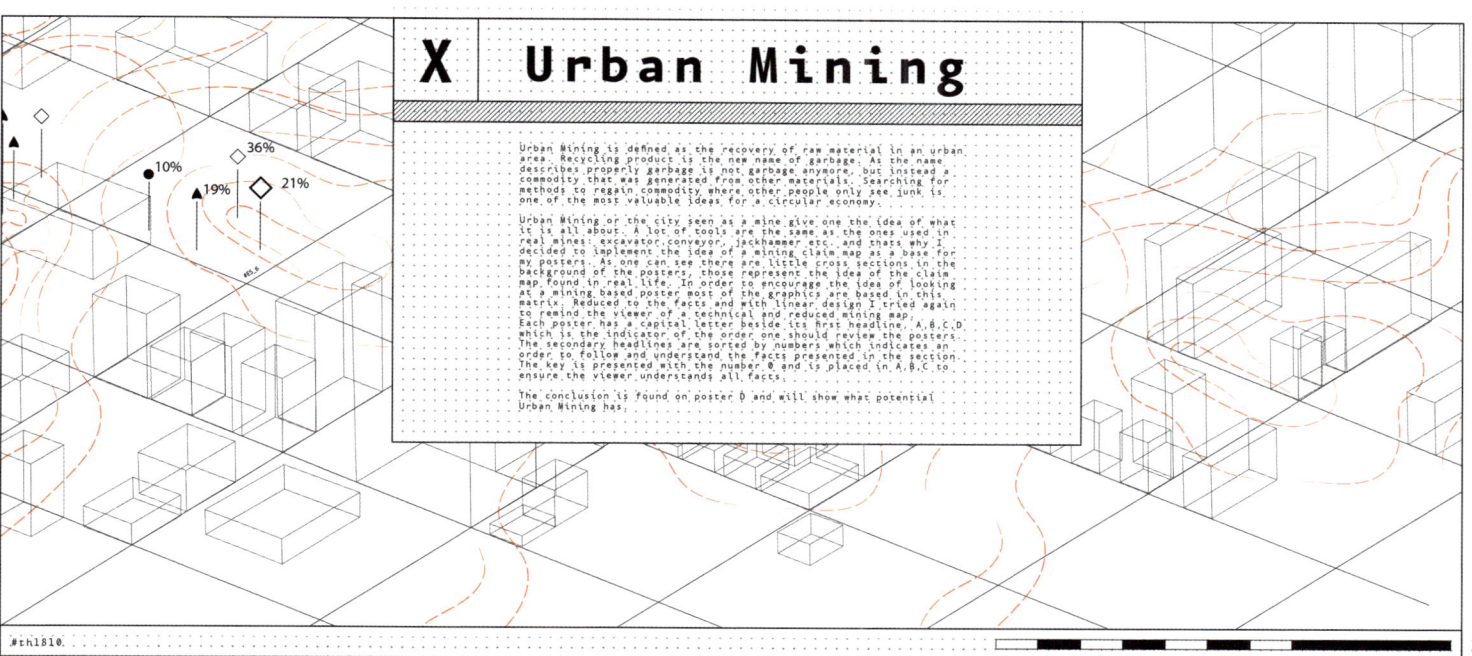

X Urban Mining

Urban Mining is defined as the recovery of raw material in an urban area. Recycling product is the new name of garbage. As the name describes properly garbage is not garbage anymore, but instead a commodity that was generated from other materials. Searching for methods to regain commodity where other people only see junk is one of the most valuable ideas for a circular economy.

Urban Mining or the city seen as a mine give one the idea of what it is all about. A lot of tools are the same as the ones used in real mines: excavator,conveyor, jackhammer etc. and that's why I decided to implement the idea of a mining claim map as a base for my posters. As one can see there are little cross sections in the background of the posters, those represent the idea of the claim map found in real life. In order to encourage the idea of looking at a mining based poster most of the graphics are based in this matrix. Reduced to the facts and with linear design I tried again to remind the viewer of a technical and reduced mining map. Each poster has a capital letter beside its first headline, A,B,C,D which is the indicator of the order one should review the posters. The secondary headlines are sorted by numbers which indicates an order to follow and understand the facts presented in the section. The key is presented with the number 0 and is placed in A,B,C to ensure the viewer understands all facts.

The conclusion is found on poster D and will show what potential Urban Mining has.

#th1810.

A House Dismantling

In Germany 80% of all waste is construction site waste. Concrete, metal, glass, wood are only a few of the materials that are used. A lot of these materials are recyclable. Especially metal is already well recycled but still there is potential - our future: circular economy.

0 Key

□ 1000t.
◺ less than 1000t.

Utilization

■ Thermal processing
■ Recycling
■ Not processed / fuel value under 11.000 kJ/kg
■ not correctly disposed of/. lost for recycling

Commodity key

◺ Glass/Ceramics.
Plastic.
◇ Metal.
  ◆ Iron
  ◆ Aluminum
  ◆ Copper
  ◆ Silver
  ◆ Gold
◤ Rare earth metal
  ◤ Palladium
  ◤ Samarium
  ◤ Holmium
■ Stone/sand.
  ■ Concrete
  ■ Gravel
  ■ Bricks
  ■ Asphalt.
● Chemical compound.
○ Phosphor.
▨ Dry matter.

INFORMATION

As the deconstruction of buildings produces a lot of material and is one of the most promising recycling methods of the future. As raw material prices are rising and a shortage of construction materials is not far away the idea of putting valuable materials back in the ground as filler should not be called recycling. Because the amount which is filled in the ground to reduce the environmental damage the mining companies created.

1 Dismantling material
average from 3 types of buildings

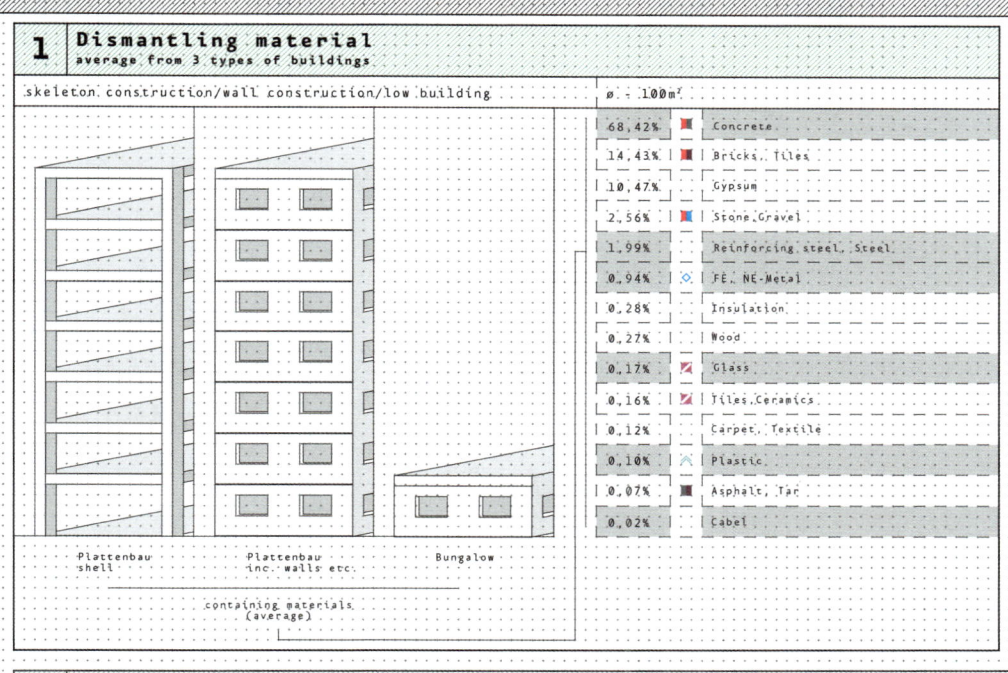

skeleton construction/wall construction/low building

ø. - 100m²

68,42%	■	Concrete
14,43%	■	Bricks, Tiles
10,47%		Gypsum
2,56%	■	Stone,Gravel
1,99%		Reinforcing steel, Steel
0,94%	◇	FE, NE-Metal
0,28%		Insulation
0,27%		Wood
0,17%	◺	Glass
0,16%		Tiles,Ceramics
0,12%		Carpet, Textile
0,10%		Plastic
0,07%	■	Asphalt, Tar
0,02%		Cabel

Plattenbau shell — Plattenbau inc. walls etc. — Bungalow

containing materials (average)

2 Germany-wide waste average
calculation of materials that could be recycled every year

skeleton construction/wall construction/low building

202.735.000t

		Material prices are based on third party purchase prices July/2015	Conclusion
Concrete ■	138.711.287t — Material can be recycled and be used as filling for mining holes.	527.089.441,05€	**1.015.470.489,35€**
Reinforcing steel ◇	4.034.426,5t — Material can be recycled 100%	215.695.756,81€	worth of raw material is produced with these 6 waste materials from deconstruction sites every year.
FE, NE-Metal ◇	1.905.709t — Material can be recycled 100%	248.997.279,46€	As raw materials are becoming more and more scarce the future will change the idea of handling raw materials from filling holes in the ground to creating secondary raw materials from waste.
Glass ◺	138.711.287t — Material can be recycled 100%	3.363.866,35€	
Plastic	344.649,5t — Material can be recycled or used for thermal treatment	4.098.295,30€	Especially concrete and sand are to be dealt with carefully
Cabel	40.547t — Material can be recycled or used for thermal treatment	16.225.850,38€	

169

B Electronic Waste

Every year Germany produces 1.777.500t. electronic waste. Mobiles, refrigerator or remote controller and other electronic devices are found in the garbage. All electronic devices have a high share of metals which are specially valuable for recycling.

#th1810

0 Key

- ☐ 1000t.
- ◿ less than 1000t.

Utilization
- ◼ Thermal processing
- ◼ Recycling
- ◼ Not processed / fuel value under 11.000 kJ/kg
- ◼ not correctly disposed of / lost for recycling

Commodity key
- Glas/Ceramics
- Plastic
- Metal:
  - Iron
  - Aluminum
  - Copper
  - Silver
  - Gold
- Rar.earth metal
  - Palladium
  - Samarium
  - Holmium
- Stone/sand
  - Concrete
  - Gravel
  - Bricks
  - Asphalt
- ● Chemical compound
- ○ Phosphor
- Dry matter

1 Only 40% electronic waste reaches the recycling depot

In total 711.000t/1.777.500t.

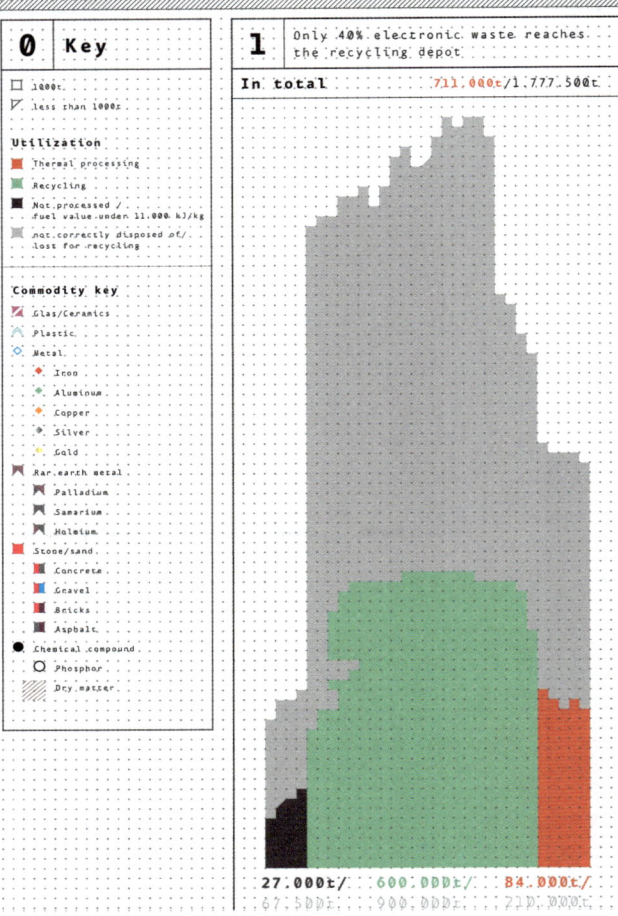

27.000t/ 600.000t/ 84.000t/ 67.500t. 900.000t. 710.000t.

2 Recycling
Waste reduction

Recycling electronic waste contains around 34,3% metal. The metal is a mix of the following materials

Recycling 600.000t/1.500.000t.

Metal	composition	% - rounded
Palladium	18/131t.	0,01%
Gold	36/79Dt.	0,02%
Silver	444/111Dt.	0,21%
Aluminum	14.000/211.000t.	6,67%
Iron	17.000/431.000t.	8,41%
Others	67.772/159.410t.	32,51%
Copper	108.000/270.000t.	52%

207.000/517.000t.

Plastic

2.05% of the imported plastic is currently recycled from electronic waste.

5.11% could be recycled

172.000t./422.000t.

Other Materials

Boards
Glass
Ceramics
Textiles

221.000/353.000t.

D Wasted Waste

Urban Mining - Idea for the future ?
On this poster everything comes together, comparing demand and supply, material pricing and what Germany is wasting every year. This section presents the importance of handling your waste correctly in order to present Germany another huge money generating market. As one of the countries with the highest recycling rates we could become an importer of waste material instead of selling it to 3rd world countries.

#th1810

1 Consumption, Use and Waste
Germany's raw material demand and its prices

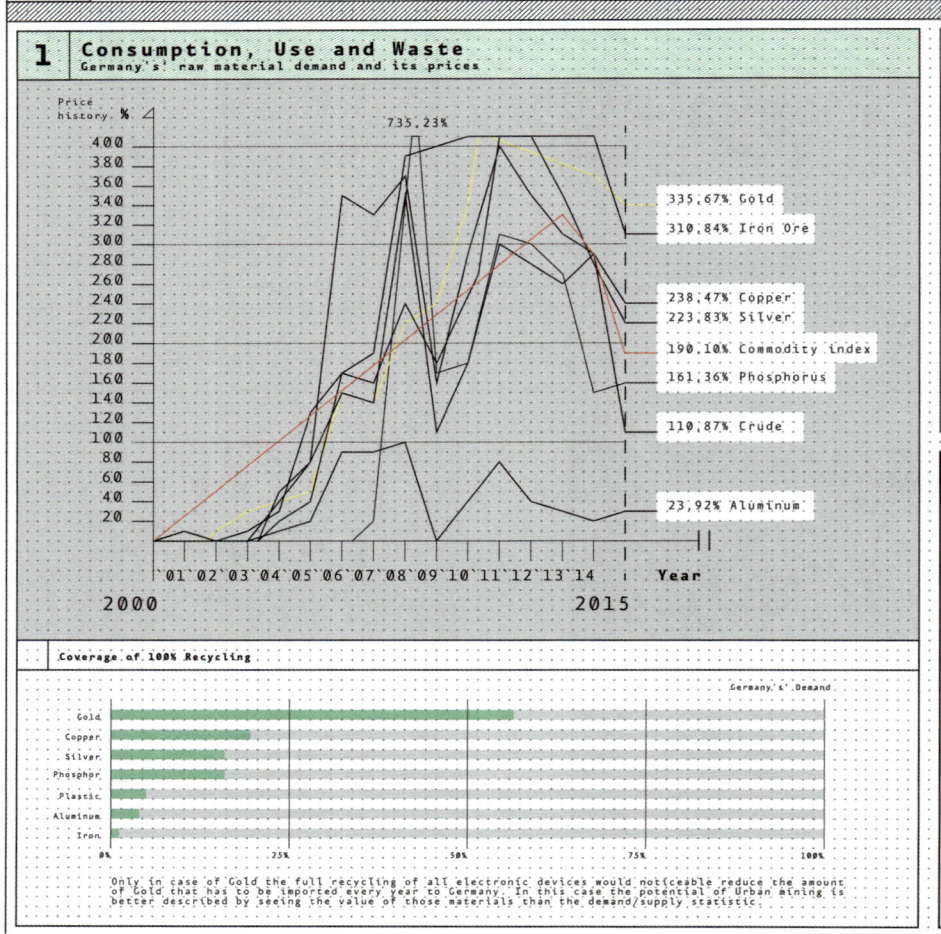

Price history. %

735,23%

- 335,67% Gold
- 310,84% Iron Ore
- 238,47% Copper
- 223,83% Silver
- 190,10% Commodity index
- 161,36% Phosphorus
- 110,87% Crude
- 23,92% Aluminum

'01 '02 '03 '04 '05 '06 '07 '08 '09 '10 '11 '12 '13 '14   Year
2000   2015

Coverage of 100% Recycling

Germany's Demand

- Gold
- Copper
- Silver
- Phosphor
- Plastic
- Aluminum
- Iron

0%   25%   50%   75%   100%

Only in case of Gold the full recycling of all electronic devices would noticeable reduce the amount of Gold that has to be imported every year to Germany. In this case the potential of urban mining is better described by seeing the value of those materials than the demand/supply statistic.

2 Energy Recovery
Germany's prospect of recovering Energy

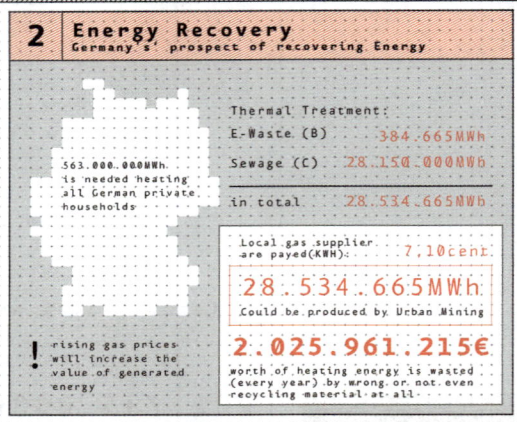

563.000.000MWh is needed heating all German private households

Thermal Treatment:	
E-Waste (B)	384.665MWh
Sewage (C)	28.150.000MWh
in total	28.534.665MWh

Local gas supplier are payed(KWH): 7,10cent.

28.534.665MWh Could be produced by Urban Mining

2.025.961.215€ worth of heating energy is wasted (every year) by wrong or not even recycling material at all.

! rising gas prices will increase the value of generated energy

INFORMATION

1 If one wants to analyze the potential of urban mining, one has to keep in mind the rising prices of every raw material. The value of every raw material rises or falls in different rates but the commodity index of the shown example is 190% in 15 years. If this rate would be steady by 2030, the raw material price would double again.

'Coverage of 100% Recycling' shows the potential cover rate of the electronic waste recycling if the recycling rate is 100%.

2 The result of the energy recovery section only concentrates on the wasted energy. Thermal recycling methods are already in use but could be enhanced. The Sewage (C) value is shorten by not implementing the industrially, governmentally and not privately owned houses. As described in Sewage (C) Urban Mining could cover 5% of Germany's heating energy.

3 One can see what one is able to pay for with the material wasted in Germany every year by not recycling correctly or not using the full potential of current technology.

In this section you can only see what is not used for recycling and the potential for Germany every year. As shown on the Graphic 1, the value of Urban Mining is steadily rising. Besides the raw material a lot of the energy to mine, transport and further processing is reduced.

In order to become a circular economy, Germany has to appreciate the value of urban mining. It is not just about normal recycling, but also about finding new ways to gain and improve the collection of secondary raw materials in fields no one is currently thinking about.

Germany is one of the countries depending highly on imported commodity. On the other hand Germany has one of the highest export rates world wide. Advancement of science can give Germany another way to generate commodity from waste and reduce the import of that commodity. Phosphor is one of those commodities which is found in the sewage. Scientists have found a way to regain the Phosphor and use it as raw material.

#th1810

0   Key

☐ 1000t
◹ less than 1000t

Utilization
■ Thermal processing
■ Recycling
■ Not processed /
  fuel value under 11.000 kJ/kg
■ not correctly disposed of /
  lost for recycling

Commodity key
◩ Glass/Ceramics
◈ Plastic
◇ Metal
  • Iron
  • Aluminum
  • Copper
  • Silver
  • Gold
◣ Rar earth metal
  ◤ Palladium
  ◥ Samarium
  ◤ Holmium
■ Stone/sand
  ■ Concrete
  ■ Gravel
  ■ Bricks
  ■ Asphalt
● Chemical compound
○ Phosphor
▨ Dry matter

1   Phosphor Demand
in Germany and its import origin

Demand   300.000t

1 hr
70kg-
100kg
a year

Phosphor usage
per hectare per year,
for heavy harvesting

100m

300.000t
Germany's
Phosphor import

Jordan 7%
China 8%
USA 8%
South Africa 12%
others 18%
Morocco 47%

Phosphor
reserves
worldwide

INFORMATION

A shortage of Phosphor will be a problem in the future, because we need a lot of Phosphor to harvest our crops. Germany is importing 300.000t every year and prices are rising. One solution could be in our sewage as scientist can extract Phosphor from the dry matter.

Even heat can be extracted from the sewers, this method is still in pilot phase but promises to cover 5% of Germany's heating energy.

The result of the sewage recycling will be shown on poster D

D

2   Human Mine
excretion of Phosphor

Excretion   48.000t

Every human being and even every animal on the planet earth produces Phosphor. When the body has enough Phosphor it secretes the rest. A human produces around

**2gr/day
730gr/year**

Because of our sewage system we can recycle this material and extract the Phosphor. Along with other materials the Phosphor is found in the 2.400.000t sewage dry matter, but one can only find around 2% Phosphor in it.

59.000t
human production

11.000t
Phosphor are
lost on the way

48.000t
are to be found in
the dry matter

2.400.000t
Sewage dry matter

2% Phosphor

4   Sewerage heat recycling
Heat out of the sink

Sewerage heat recycling is not used much in real life application, its potential is proven but also highly depended on the place it is used. Especially for steady heat consuming buildings like indoor swimming pools or administrative bodies it could generate a lot of cheap heating solutions.

This section shows a pilot project regarding the usage of sewage heat and its application in an indoor swimming pool. As the sewage pipe has an average temperature of 14° Celsius one can see the potential application of a recuperator. It uses the heat from the sewage pipe in order to heat up water for the building. Some machines even generate electricity in the process, lessening the energy consumption.

Jan Feb Mr Apr Mai Jun Jul Aug Sep Oct Nov Dec

20
14
9

Sewage water temperature

3.000 households at least are needed

Calculated costs before using sewerage heat recycling

■ 1440kW heater
◹ 3.000MWh/year

7.10 cent/kWh **213.000€**
month of gas

583€ daily month of gas

Calculated costs using sewerage heat recycling

■ recuperator
■ cogeneration unit

both produce ..... 280kW power
.... 3,6 working factor

resulting in ...... 195kW power
.... 75kW power

maximum capacity usage over time ... 4.500h

resulting in 1.800MWh/year

Result

covers electric energy demand

60%

of the 3000MWh could be substituted for with sewerage heat recycling

127.800€
month of gas per year

According to scientist

5%

of Germany's heating energy can be produced by sewage heat recycling

28.534.665MWh

February 2011 till March 2012

CO₂ reduction **160t**

163.000.000km traveled by car

SECURING WATER FOR FOOD

Angela Million
Grit Bürgow
Tim Nebert
Anja Steglich
Jürgen Höfler
Andreas Brück

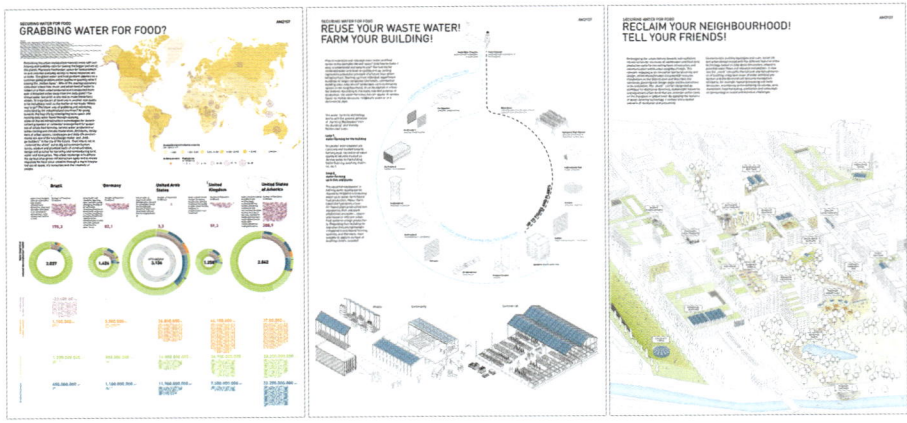

Rethinking the urban metabolism towards more self-sufficiency and livability calls for seeing the bigger, global picture. Freshwater, space for food production and common everyday access to these resources are at stake globally, particularly in big cities. Which way to go? The linear way of grabbing and colonizing yet more land by the industrial countries? Or aiming at rethinking local space use, water cycles and food production practices? The challenge of reorganising the supply and disposal of urban water and food is taken up by a growing number of research initiatives and pilot projects, exploring the transformation of linear, centralized infrastructures towards local, circular approaches. Daily water flows can be reused through applying state of the art infrastructure technologies, e.g. greywater and rainwater management for the purpose of urban food farming, service water production or urban cooling and climate moderation.

Architects and urban designers are among the "bridge-builders" in the city of the future. Their role is not to reinvent the wheel, but to dig out common human sense for reintroducing local water and food cycles. The urban challenge is to create impulses for local value creation through a multipurpose use of space and its resources, and to introduce various blue-green infrastructure types. The result would be a multifunctional infrastructure that links urban water management and food production. For example, waste water could be collected and treated towards bathing water quality to then use it as basis for hydroponic vegetable or fish farming. Water-farm systems are of high productivity and lightweight compared to soil-based farming, what makes them suitable for application on roofs and facades of high-rise buildings. What sounds like a major innovation and an abundance of technology has been practiced in combined wastewater and food production in the Global South, e.g. as early as the millenary traditions of integrated aquaculture farming in Asia and South America.

The question is whether this water-farm technology approach can be successfully adapted to western metropolises meeting 21st century needs, their urban development and design, and their urban ways of life.

Das Überdenken des urbanen Stoffwechsels hin zu mehr Selbstversorgung und Bewohnbarkeit erfordert es, globale Zusammenhänge im Auge zu behalten. Süßwasser, Raum für die Nahrungsmittelproduktion und der gemeinschaftliche tägliche Zugang zu diesen Ressourcen stehen weltweit auf dem Spiel, vor allem in den großen Städten. Welcher Weg ist einzuschlagen? Der lineare Weg hin zu noch mehr Landnahme und Kolonisierung durch die Industrieländer? Oder das Abzielen auf eine Umgestaltung von lokalen Raumpraktiken, Wasserkreisläufen und Lebensmittelproduktion? Eine wachsende Zahl von Forschungsinitiativen und Pilotprojekten nimmt die Herausforderung der Neuorganisation der Ver- und Entsorgung von städtischem Wasser und städtischer Nahrung an und erkundet die Überführung linearer, transregionaler Infrastrukturen hin zu kreisförmigen, lokalen Ansätzen. Tägliche Wasserströme können durch die Anwendung modernster Technologien wiederverwendet werden, beispielsweise durch Grauwasser und Regenwasser-Management für städtische Nahrungsmittelproduktion, Brauchwassererzeugung oder städtische Kühlung und Klimaregelung.

Architekten und Stadtplaner sind die "Brückenbauer" der Stadt der Zukunft. Ihre Rolle sollte nicht sein, das Rad neu zu erfinden, sondern den gesunden Menschenverstand für die Wiedereinführung lokaler Wasser- und Nahrungszyklen zu fördern. Die Herausforderung besteht darin, Impulse für lokale Wertschöpfung durch eine Mehrzwecknutzung von urbanem Raum und seinen Ressourcen zu schaffen, und verschiedene "blau-grüne" Infrastrukturen einzuführen. Das Ergebnis wäre eine multifunktionale Infrastruktur, die städtische Wasserwirtschaft und Nahrungsmittelproduktion verbindet. Abwasser kann beispielsweise gesammelt und hin zu Badewasserqualität behandelt werden, um es anschließend als Grundlage für Gemüse- und Fischzucht in Hydrokulturen zu verwenden. Hydrokulturen sind in hohem Maße produktiv und haben im Vergleich zu einer bodengebundenen Landwirtschaft wenig Gewicht, was sie für den Einsatz auf Dächern und Fassaden von Hochhäusern geeignet macht. Was nach großer Innovation und einer Fülle von Technologie klingt, wurde in kombinierter Mischwasser- und Lebensmittelproduktion im globalen Süden praktiziert, z.B. schon im Rahmen der tausendjährigen Tradition integrierter Aquakultur und Landwirtschaft in Asien und Südamerika.

Die Frage ist, ob diese Technologie der wasserbasierten Landwirtschaft erfolgreich an die westlichen Städte, deren Stadtentwicklung und Design, und an die Bedürfnisse und städtischen Lebensweisen des 21. Jahrhunderts angepasst werden kann.

left
Global freshwater capacity: internal freshwater resources and the securing of additional freshwater resources in foreign countries.

rechts
Weltweite Süßwasservermögen: Inländische Süßwasservorkommen und die Sicherung von zusätzlichen Süßwasservorkommen im Ausland.

bottom
The "water farming loop" treats a building's wastewater in order to reuse it for fish and vegetable aquacultures.

unten
Der "Wasserwirtschaftskreislauf" klärt das Abwasser eines Gebäudes, um es für Fisch- und Gemüseaquakulturen wiederzuverwenden.

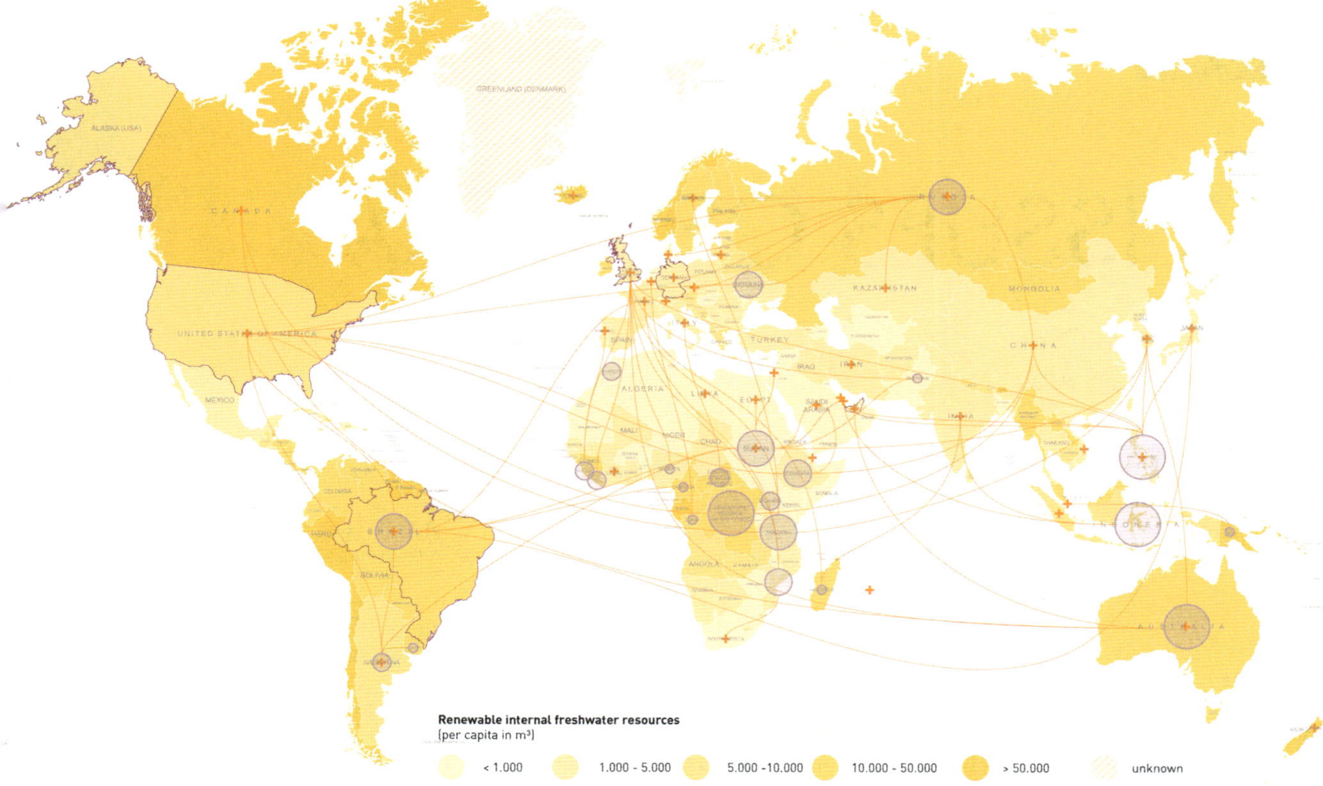

CANADA
UNITED STATES OF AMERICA
KAZAKHSTAN
MONGOLIA
CHINA
ALGERIA
AUSTRALIA
Renewable internal freshwater resources
(per capita in m³)
< 1.000
1.000 - 5.000
5.000 -10.000
10.000 - 50.000
> 50.000
unknown

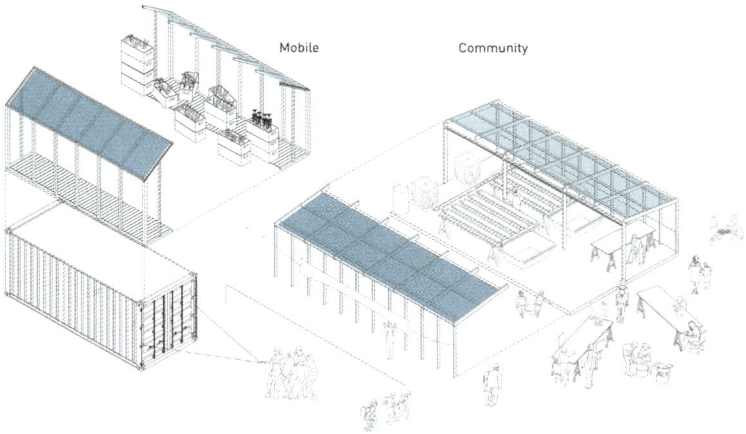

Mobile
Community

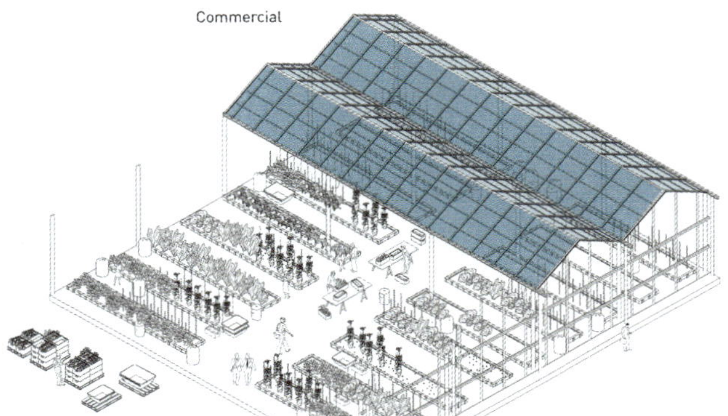

Commercial

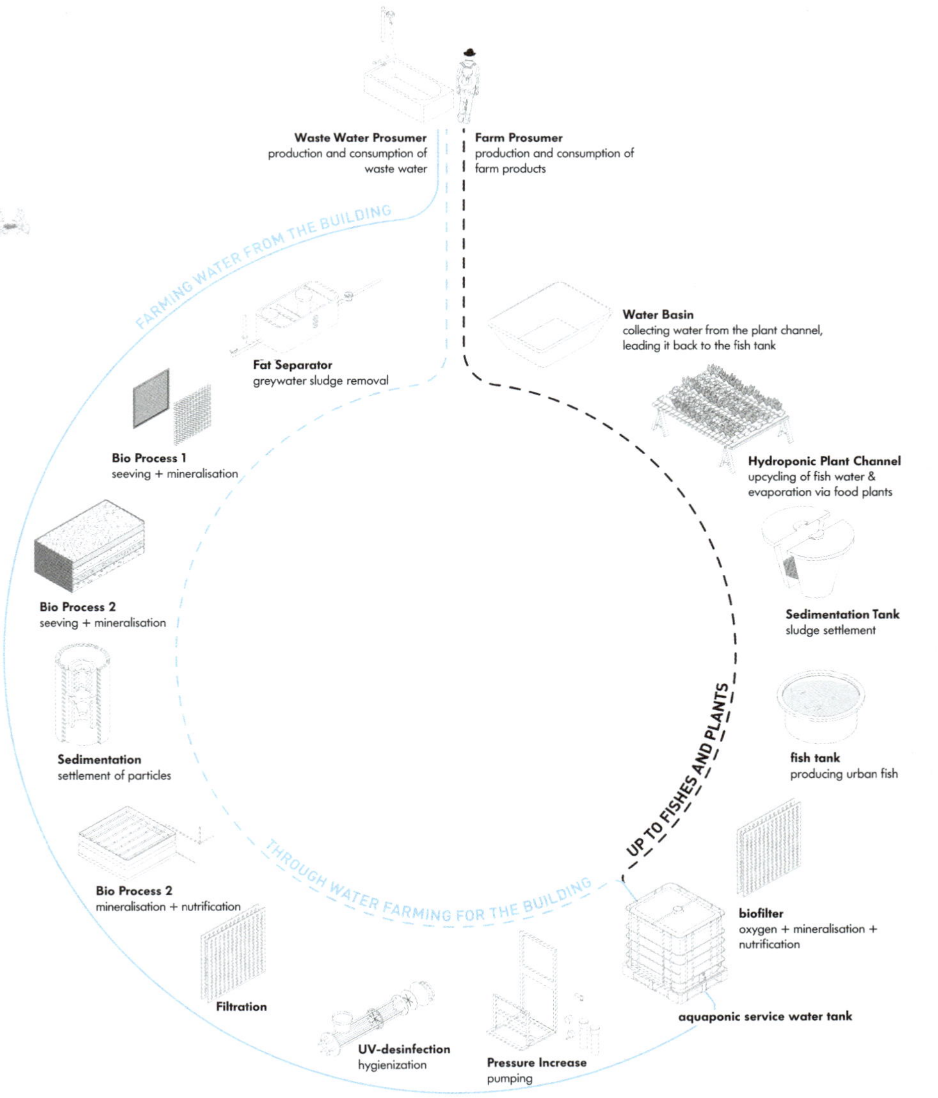

Waste Water Prosumer
production and consumption of waste water
Farm Prosumer
production and consumption of farm products
FARMING WATER FROM THE BUILDING
Water Basin
collecting water from the plant channel, leading it back to the fish tank
Fat Separator
greywater sludge removal
Bio Process 1
seeving + mineralisation
Hydroponic Plant Channel
upcycling of fish water & evaporation via food plants
Bio Process 2
seeving + mineralisation
Sedimentation Tank
sludge settlement
Sedimentation
settlement of particles
UP TO FISHES AND PLANTS
fish tank
producing urban fish
THROUGH WATER FARMING FOR THE BUILDING
Bio Process 2
mineralisation + nutrification
biofilter
oxygen + mineralisation + nutrification
Filtration
aquaponic service water tank
UV-desinfection
hygienization
Pressure Increase
pumping

THE WATER ISSUES OF ACCRA

WaterPower: Antje Bruns, Richard Appiah Otoo,
Felipe Coelho Costa, Lara Bartels, Rossella Alba,
Fanny Frick, Emily Raab
BTK: Lilian Stathogiannoopoulou, Sarah Costa,
Daniel von Pazatka Lipinski, Sophia Wulf,
Cyrus Khazaeli

"Water is indispensable 'stuff' for maintaining the metabolism, not only of our human bodies, but also of the wider social fabric. The very sustainability of cities and the practices of everyday life that constitute 'the urban' are predicated upon and conditioned by the supply, circulation, and elimination of water."[1]

Ensuring the sustainability of the urban water metabolism represents a fundamental challenge for the 21st century and the whole Anthropocene period. Rapidly increasing land, food, energy and freshwater demand drives regional land cover and land use change with global consequences that are distributed unevenly across the planet.[2] African cities are hotspots where these environmental and socio-political megatrends – that operate on global, regional and local levels – culminate. This becomes especially apparent in Western Africa, where urbanization increases more rapidly than governance capacities, causing detrimental effects on human and environmental health.[3] Even in the absence of climate change – it is uncertain how rainfall patterns will affect future water availability – water stresses are likely to increase, since the provision of water services and infrastructure does not keep pace with urban population growth and increasing demand.[4]

In Accra, Ghana, water is physically abundant; yet at the same time drinking water is scarce.[5] Here, as in many other cities of the Global South, it is "the social actors [...] that ultimately decide who will have access to or control over, and who will be excluded from access to or control over [water] resources."[6] The water utilities provide water only to a limited part of the city, and nowadays only about half of the population has direct access to tap water.[7] Where infrastructure is not present or supply is erratic, urban dwellers chase for water, becoming themselves the "water infrastructure".[8]

The animated infographic explores the interlinked dynamics of urbanisation and water security in the light of urban population increase and changing lifestyles, and the consequent increase in consumption and demand of water. It highlights the physical, socio-economic and political challenges related with the availability of and access to freshwater resources and questions the strategies put in place by governments and citizens to provide for the flow of water to and within the city.

•

"Wasser ist unverzichtbares 'Material' um den Stoffwechsel aufrechzuerhalten, nicht nur für unsere menschlichen Körper, sondern auch für das breitere soziale Gefüge. Die Nachhaltigkeit der Städte und die Praktiken des alltäglichen Lebens, die 'das Urbane' konstituieren, basieren auf und sind bedingt durch die Zufuhr, den Kreislauf und den Entzug von Wasser."[1]

Die Nachhaltigkeit des städtischen Wasserstoffwechsels zu gewährleisten, stellt eine grundlegende Herausforderung für das 21. Jahrhundert und das gesamte Zeitalter des Anthropozäns dar. Der rapide steigende Land-, Nahrungsmittel-, Energie- und Frischwasserbedarf feuert Landfraß und Veränderungen in der regionalen Landnutzung an und verursacht globale Konsequenzen, die weltweit unregelmäßig verteilt sind.[2] Afrikanische Städte sind Hot-Spots, in denen diese ökologischen und gesellschaftspolitischen Megatrends – die auf globaler, regionaler und lokaler Ebene operieren – zusammenlaufen. Dies wird besonders in Westafrika deutlich, wo die Urbanisierung schneller voranschreitet, als staatliche Kapazitäten ausge-

baut werden können, was sich schädlich auf die Gesundheit von Mensch und Umwelt auswirkt.[3] Selbst wenn der Klimawandel nicht berücksichtigt wird – es ist unsicher, wie Niederschlagsmuster sich auf die zukünftige Verfügbarkeit von Wasser auswirken werden – wird sich die Wasserknappheit verschlimmern, da die Bereitstellung von Wasserdienstleistungen und deren Infrastruktur nicht mit der Zunahme der Stadtbevölkerung und der erhöhten Nachfrage Schritt hält.[4]

In Accra, Ghana, ist Wasser physikalisch reichlich vorhanden; gleichzeitig ist Trinkwasser knapp.[5] Hier, wie auch in vielen anderen Städten des globalen Südens, sind es "die gesellschaftlichen Akteure [...] die letztlich darüber entscheiden, wer Zugang oder Kontrolle über Wasservorkommen hat und wer davon ausgeschlossen wird."[6] Die Wasserversorgungsunternehmen stellen Wasser nur für einen begrenzten Teil der Stadt zur Verfügung, und heute hat nur noch die Hälfte der Bevölkerung direkten Zugang zu Leitungswasser.[7] Wo Infrastruktur nicht vorhanden ist oder die Versorgung unregelmäßig bleibt, müssen die Stadtbewohner dem Wasser "nachjagen", indem sie selbst zur "Wasserinfrastruktur" werden.[8]

Die animierte Infografik untersucht die verflochtenen Dynamiken der Urbanisierung und der Wassersicherheit im Lichte des städtischen Bevölkerungswachstums und der sich verändernden Lebensgewohnheiten sowie den daraus resultierenden Anstieg des Verbrauchs und der Nachfrage von Wasser. Sie zeigt die materiellen, sozioökonomischen und politischen Herausforderungen im Zusammenhang mit der Verfügbarkeit von und dem Zugang zu Süßwasserressourcen und hinterfragt die staatlichen und zivilgesellschaftlichen Strategien, die das Fließen des Wassers hin zur und innerhalb der Stadt gewährleisten sollen.

The people in the capital of Ghana don't get enough fresh water.

Accra lies between two water reservoirs, which could provide water in abundance.

Every person should have 131 liters of water per day to spend on drinking, washing, cleaning, gardening and other purposes.

In fact, with only 68 liters being available, the deficit of water demand and supply in Accra is 40%.

The poorest have to manage on only 47 liters per day…

…in comparison, an average American spends as much as 300 liters.

In Accra, the taps just won't give any water sometimes. For example, when the unstable electricity network fails only for one minute, the pumping stations might need six hours to get the water system back to work.

About 400,000,000 liters of water are flowing through Accra everyday. Unfortunately, the 2000 km of pipes are partly leaking or cloaked, so they loose about 23% of water on the way.

Every fifth person in Accra doesn't even have access to piped water at all.

In the 1970s the water infrastructure was sufficient for the people living in Accra. But then the city got hit by an enormous population growth and the water supplies and system could not keep up.

There are simply not enough pipes and pumps.

But the budget of the country has to cover health care, energy, infrastructure and education.

Still, water is vital. Shouldn't it be priority number one for the government to think of solutions?

The population of Accra is still growing and the water demand rises constantly. If politicians don't put up much more effort into this issue, there will be a severe crisis.

But the people in Accra are not yet losing their spirit. They have gone to old habits and carry out water on tanks and gallons.

With no investments in water infrastructure, the people in Accra have no choice but being the infrastructure itself.

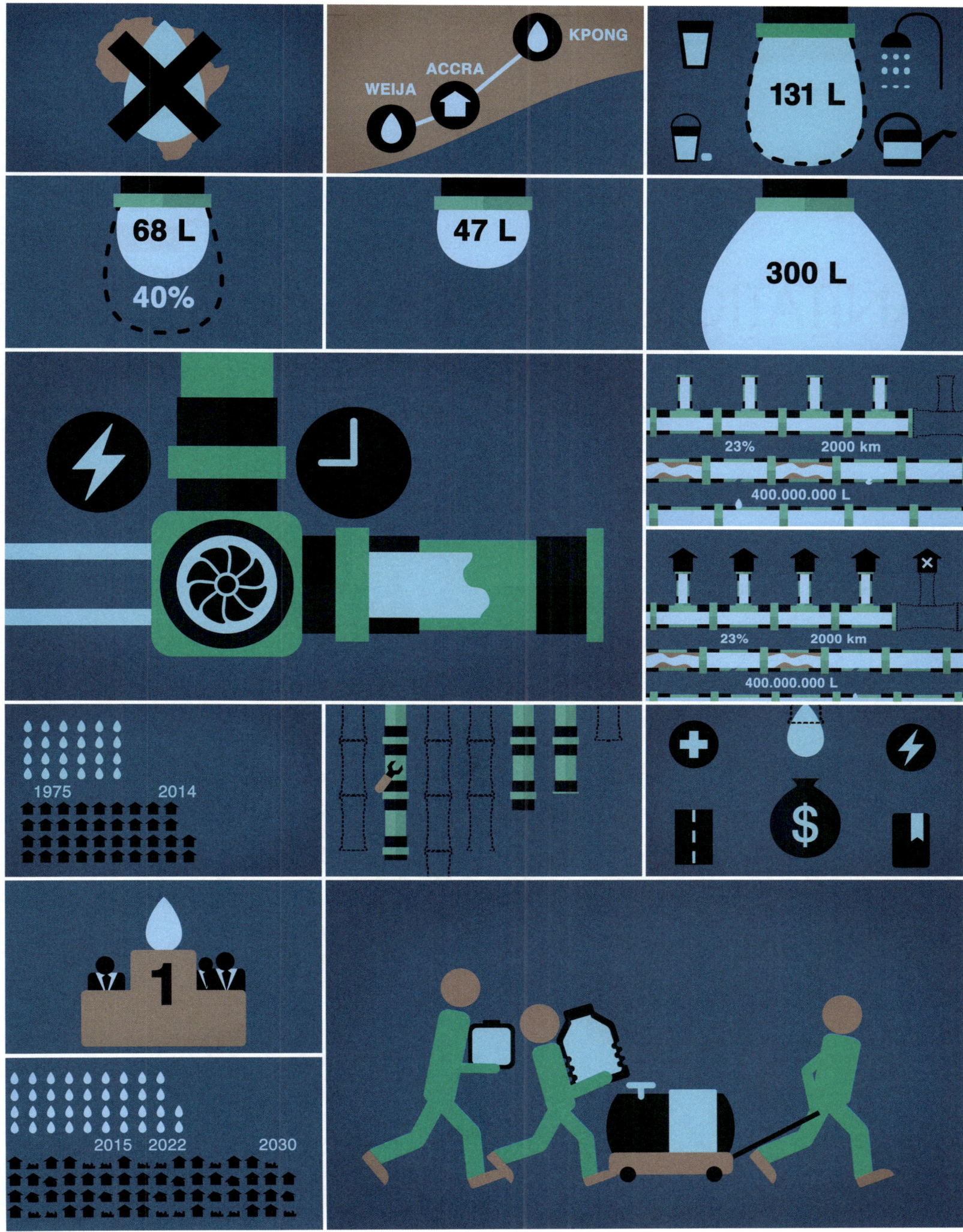

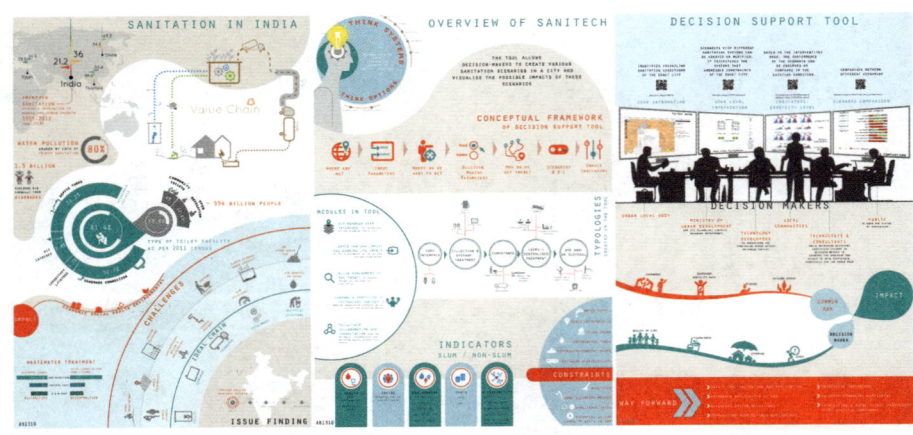

SANITATION IN INDIA
Bhawna Welturkar

One of the most urgent health and environmental challenges in contemporary India is the upgrading of insufficient sanitation systems. About 80% of water pollution in India stems from poor sanitation, causing a perpetual spread of diseases and millions of causalities. No Indian city has a thorough wastewater processing strategy, and nearly a fifth of the population has no access to household toilets. It is estimated that at least 620 million Indians defecate outdoors.

Despite decades of lasting efforts by governmental and administrative bodies to improve sanitation networks, and increased levels of investment in sanitation since 2000, implementation poses significant challenges. In India's highly centralised civil service, local urban administrative bodies (ULBs), responsible for maintenance and operation, often do not hold enough financial agency or technical know-how to effectively upgrade existing sanitary arrangements.

In response, the "Centre for Study of Science, Technology and Policy" (CSTEP) in Bangalore has developed the decision-making tool "San-Tool", targeted at ULBs in particular. While existing available tools are mainly aimed at planners and engineering specialists, "San-Tool" provides local decision-makers with information about available technologies and investment sources. Various indicators are used to help determine urban settlements' characteristics in order to reach a context-based solution.

Resulting sanitary systems ideally encompass entire wastewater processing cycles: from the provision of toilets, storage and transfer, to ecological treatment and recycling. Such self-sustaining systems call for a context-sensitive, decentralised mode of planning, with each measure developed in respect to local specificities.

Eines der größten Gesundheits- und Umweltprobleme in Indien wird durch ausbleibende Modernisierung sanitärer Einrichtungen verursacht. Rund 80 % der Wasserverschmutzung sind katastrophalen sanitären Bedingungen geschuldet, durch die sich fortwährend Krankheiten ausbreiten und Millionen Todesfälle zu beklagen sind. Keine indische Stadt verfügt über eine umfassende Abwasserentsorgung, und fast ein Fünftel der Bevölkerung hat keinen Zugang zu internen Toiletten. Es wird geschätzt, dass sich mindestens 620 Millionen Inder im Freien entleeren.

Die Verbesserung sanitärer Netzwerke wirft, trotz jahrzehntelanger staatlicher Bemühungen und erhöhter

Investitionen in die Abwasserentsorgung seit 2000, erhebliche Probleme auf. Innerhalb Indiens stark zentralisiertem Staatsdienst verfügen die für Wartung und Betrieb zuständigen lokalen Behörden (ULB) oft nicht über genug finanziellen Spielraum oder technisches Wissen, um sanitäre Einrichtungen neu zu schaffen bzw. nachhaltig zu modernisieren.

Das "Zentrum für das Studium der Wissenschaft, Technologie und Politik" (CSTEP) in Bangalore entwickelte die Planungshilfe "San-Tool" insbesondere für lokale Behörden. Während bislang zugängliche Tools vor allem auf Planer und Ingenieure zugeschnitten waren, versorgt "San-Tool" lokale Beamte mit Informationen über verfügbare

Technologien und Investitionsquellen. Eine Reihe von Indikatoren hilft bei der Analyse städtischer Siedlungsräume, um eine möglichst kontextbezogene Lösung zu erzielen.

Im Idealfall umfasst das resultierende sanitäre System einen vollständigen Abwasserverarbeitungskreislauf: von der Bereitstellung von Toiletten über Sickergruben und deren Entleerung zu ökologischer Verarbeitung und Recycling. Nachhaltige Abwassersysteme erfordern dezentrale Planungsmodi, die jede Maßnahme im Kontext lokaler Besonderheiten entwickeln.

Text: Anna Aichinger

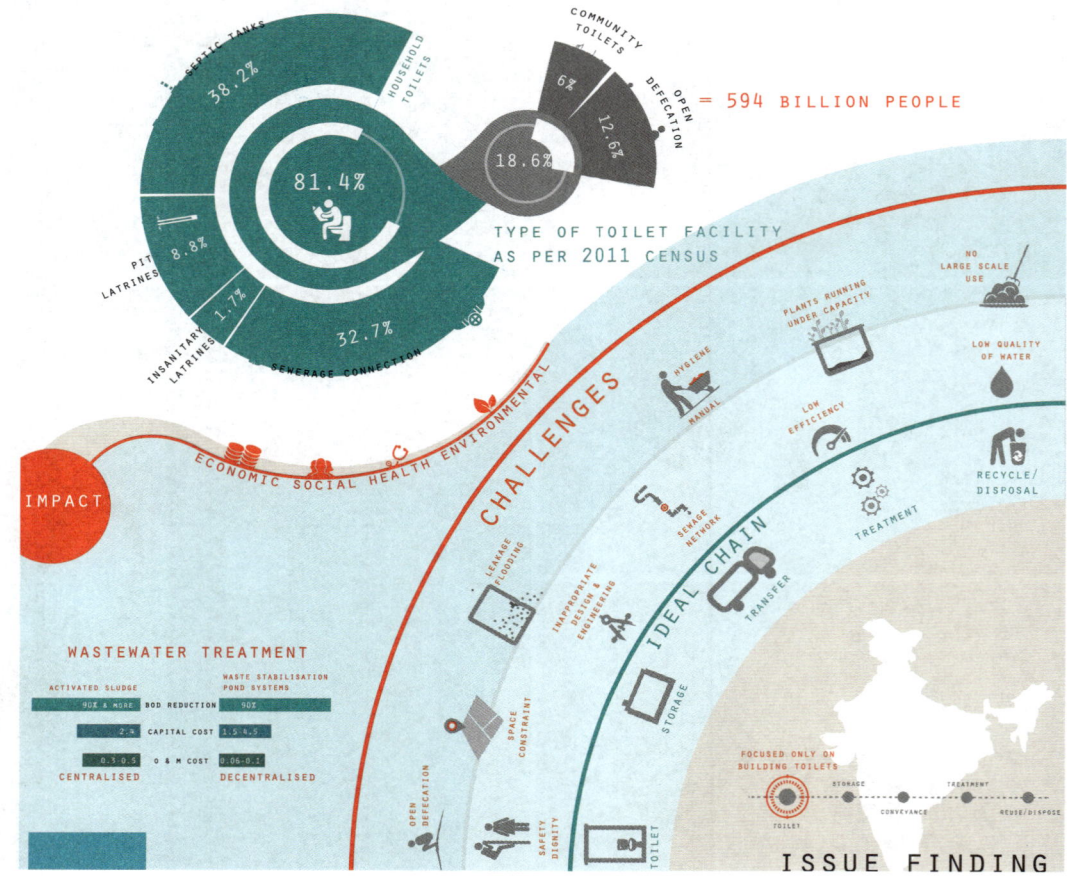

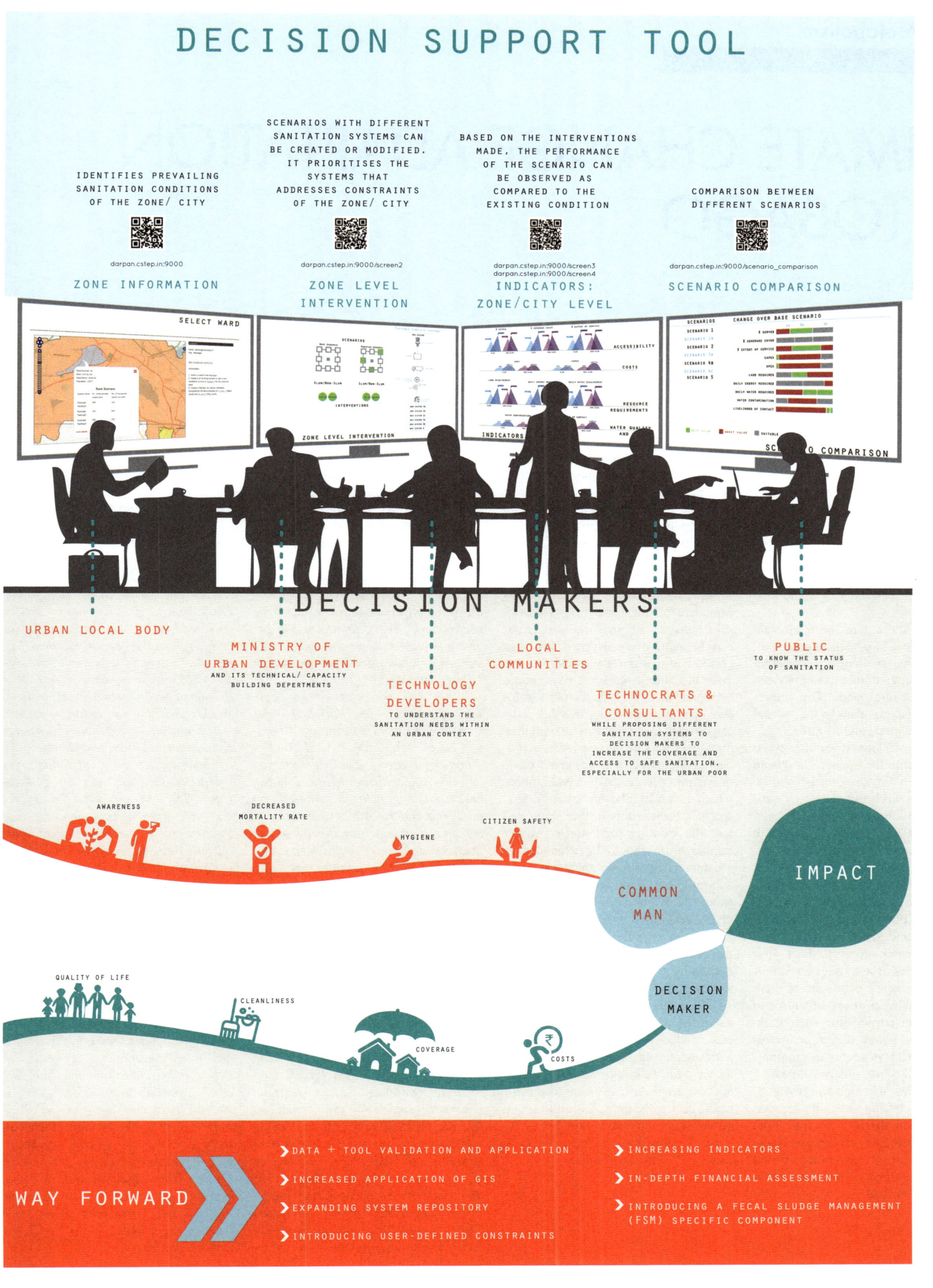

DECISION SUPPORT TOOL

IDENTIFIES PREVAILING SANITATION CONDITIONS OF THE ZONE/ CITY

darpan.cstep.in:9000

ZONE INFORMATION

SCENARIOS WITH DIFFERENT SANITATION SYSTEMS CAN BE CREATED OR MODIFIED. IT PRIORITISES THE SYSTEMS THAT ADDRESSES CONSTRAINTS OF THE ZONE/ CITY

darpan.cstep.in:9000/screen2

ZONE LEVEL INTERVENTION

BASED ON THE INTERVENTIONS MADE, THE PERFORMANCE OF THE SCENARIO CAN BE OBSERVED AS COMPARED TO THE EXISTING CONDITION

darpan.cstep.in:9000/screen3
darpan.cstep.in:9000/screen4

INDICATORS: ZONE/CITY LEVEL

COMPARISON BETWEEN DIFFERENT SCENARIOS

darpan.cstep.in:9000/scenario_comparison

SCENARIO COMPARISON

DECISION MAKERS

URBAN LOCAL BODY

MINISTRY OF URBAN DEVELOPMENT
AND ITS TECHNICAL/ CAPACITY BUILDING DEPERTMENTS

TECHNOLOGY DEVELOPERS
TO UNDERSTAND THE SANITATION NEEDS WITHIN AN URBAN CONTEXT

LOCAL COMMUNITIES

TECHNOCRATS & CONSULTANTS
WHILE PROPOSING DIFFERENT SANITATION SYSTEMS TO DECISION MAKERS TO INCREASE THE COVERAGE AND ACCESS TO SAFE SANITATION, ESPECIALLY FOR THE URBAN POOR

PUBLIC
TO KNOW THE STATUS OF SANITATION

AWARENESS

DECREASED MORTALITY RATE

HYGIENE

CITIZEN SAFETY

IMPACT

COMMON MAN

DECISION MAKER

QUALITY OF LIFE

CLEANLINESS

COVERAGE

COSTS

WAY FORWARD

> DATA + TOOL VALIDATION AND APPLICATION

> INCREASED APPLICATION OF GIS

> EXPANDING SYSTEM REPOSITORY

> INTRODUCING USER-DEFINED CONSTRAINTS

> INCREASING INDICATORS

> IN-DEPTH FINANCIAL ASSESSMENT

> INTRODUCING A FECAL SLUDGE MANAGEMENT (FSM) SPECIFIC COMPONENT

CLIMATE CHANGE ADAPTATION IN TOBAGO

Luna Khirfan, Mandy Zhang

Human settlements are increasingly threatened by global climate change. Sea-level rise, in particular, is putting coastal wetlands of islands in the Indian Ocean, the Caribbean, and the Pacific Ocean at risk.[1] It is predicted that an estimated 0.5 metre rise in sea level by 2100 would lead to a loss of over 38% of the total current beach area in the Caribbean region.[2]

Tobago, located in the Caribbean Sea, is one such small island state, facing increasing challenge since 2006 with a dropping number of tourists and loss of agricultural land.[3] The vulnerable area needs to adapt to the "actual or expected climate and its effects"[4].

As part of a large research project, the "Partnership for Canada-Caribbean Community Climate Change Adaption"[5], a research-based design proposal for the southwest area of Tobago is developed. Responding to the dearth of in-depth empirical research, the proposal seeks for adaptation strategies through urban planning and urban design[6], and tries to generate the strategies through bottom-up participation of local communities.[7]

The research comprised of four distinct phases. First, relevant literature and secondary data sources were reviewed, giving a priori structures to facilitate later participatory fieldwork. In the second phase, design charrettes were held with various subcommunities. 77 local stakeholders formed 15 charrette teams; three student researchers joined each team to facilitate activities, document discussions and assist visual expression of participants. In the third phase, all the textual and visual data collected through the design charrettes were overlaid into one summary map, enabling comparison and classification of the themes identified by various charrette teams. Through review of literature, exploration of fieldwork data and through comparison and combination of these approaches, design options were proposed by each team as the outcome of the fourth phase.

One major design proposal was to capitalize on the contiguous relationship between the reef, the sea grass, and the mangrove ecosystem. It is suggested that mangrove wetlands, a vital asset in battling sea level rise, should be replenished. To help the propagules (seed pods) of red mangrove fall vertically into the sand and stay so until they propagate into mangrove trees, a biodegradable carpet was designed, made of woven coconut leaves and bamboo, which is said to be an invasive species in Tobago. It is further suggested that the existing road and rainwater infrastructure should be expanded in a manner that would capitalize on the natural gentle slope whereby the rainwater runoff could be channelled to the drying mangrove wetlands and replenish it, which would in turn benefit the mangrove forests, whose healthiness eventually would benefit the sea grass and the reefs.[8]

Recognizing the interconnected nature of the ecosystem, the research tries to identify key factors to promote a virtuous cycle; while the design tries to put these factors in action. Oscillating between the micro, the meso, and the macro scales, the pragmatic attitude and participatory approach will hopefully inspire further practical engagement in coping with climate change.

Menschliche Ansiedlungen werden zunehmend durch den weltweiten Klimawandel bedroht. Es ist vor allem der Anstieg des Meeresspiegels, der die Küstenregionen von Inseln im Indischen Ozean, in der Karibik und im Pazifik gefährdet.[1] Treffen die heutigen Prognosen zu, so wird der im Jahr 2100 um etwa 0,5 Meter gestiegene Meeresspiegel zu einem Verlust von mehr als 38 % der gegenwärtigen Strandgebiete der Karibik führen.[2]

Die in der Karibik gelegene Insel Tobago, ein Teil des Staates Trinidad und Tobago, sieht sich seit 2006 mit einem ständigen Rückgang der Touristenzahlen und einem kontinuierlichen Verlust von landwirtschaftlicher Nutzfläche konfrontiert.[3] Die gefährdeten Küstenareale müssen sich an das "gegenwärtige und das künftige Klima und dessen Folgen" anpassen.[4]

Als Teil des umfassenden Forschungsprojekts "The Partnership for Canada-Carribean Community Climate Change Adaptation"[5] wird ein forschungsgestützter Entwurfsvorschlag für die südwestliche Küste Tobagos entwickelt. Angesichts des Mangels an fundierter empirischer Forschung sucht der Vorschlag mittels Stadtplanung und Stadtentwurf nach Anpassungsstrategien[6] und möchte Letztere mit einer "bottom-up"-Beteiligung der örtlichen Gemeinden entwickeln.[7]

Das Forschungsprojekt umfasste vier Phasen. Zunächst wurden die relevante Literatur und die sekundären Datenquellen ausgewertet, wodurch sich a priori Strukturen ergaben, die die später vor Ort erfolgende praktische Arbeit erleichtern sollten. In der zweiten Phase wurden Charrette-Verfahren mit diversen Unterkomitees in Gang gebracht. Siebenundsiebzig an dem Projekt interessierte Anwohner bildeten fünfzehn Charrette-Teams; um die Aktivitäten und die Diskussion der Dokumente zu erleichtern und um den Beteiligten beim visuellen Ausdruck unter die Arme zu greifen, wurden jedem dieser Teams drei studentische Berater zugewiesen. In der dritten Phase wurden die in den Charrette-Verfahren gesammelten textlichen und visuellen Daten zu einer zusammenfassenden Overlay-Landkarte kombiniert, die einen Vergleich und eine Klassifizierung der von den diversen Charrette-Teams entwickelten Themen ermöglichte. Als Resultat der vierten Phase wurden Designvorschläge erstellt, die auf den Themen basierten, die sich aus der deduktiven Auswertung der Literatur und der induktiven Untersuchung der in der praktischen Arbeit gewonnenen Daten ergeben hatten.

Ein wesentlicher Entwurfsvorschlag lief darauf hinaus, sich die enge Beziehung zwischen dem Riff, dem Seegras und dem Mangroven-Ökosystem zunutze zu machen: Das Mangroven-Feuchtbiotop, ein elementarer Faktor im Kampf gegen den Anstieg des Meeresspiegels, soll regeneriert werden. Damit die Propagula (Samenschoten) der Roten Mangrove vertikal in den Sand fallen und auch dort bleiben können, um zu Mangrovenbäumen heranzuwachsen, wurde ein biologisch abbaubarer, aus Kokospalmenblättern und Bambus (der ein ursprünglich nicht auf Tobago einheimisches Gewächs sein soll) geflochtener "Teppich" entworfen. Des Weiteren wird vorgeschlagen, die bestehende Straßen- und Regenwasserinfrastruktur auf eine Weise zu erweitern, die sich das natürliche, leichte Gefälle des Geländes zunutze machen würde, indem sie das abfließende Regenwasser in die vertrocknenden Mangroven-Feuchtbiotope leiten und Letztere regenerieren, was wiederum den Mangrovenwäldern zugute käme, von deren Gesundheit schließlich auch das Seegras und die Riffe profitieren würden.[8]

Unter Berücksichtigung der vernetzten Natur des Ökosystems versucht das Forschungsprojekt, die maßgeblichen Faktoren zu identifizieren, die einen vorbildhaften Zyklus fördern könnten, während der Entwurf diese Faktoren in die Praxis umzusetzen versucht. Zwischen den Mikro-, den Meso- und den Makromaßstäben oszillierend, könnten die pragmatische Einstellung und der partizipatorische Ansatz dieses Projekts zu weiteren praktischen Maßnahmen gegen die Folgen des Klimawandels anregen.

CONTEXT

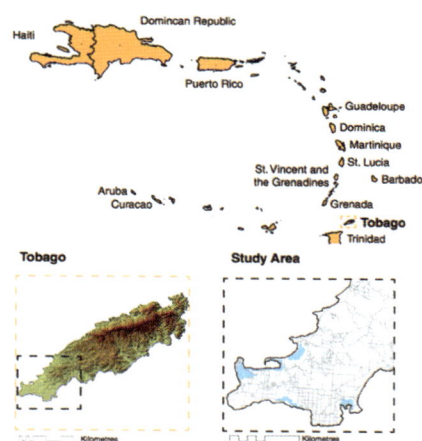

Tobago

Study Area

1) INDUCTIVE: LITERATURE REVIEW

2) DEDUCTIVE: DESIGN CHARRETTES

Four Communities

Four Design Charrettes

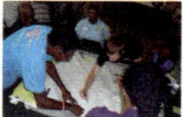

SUMMARY MAP THAT EMERGED FROM THE FOUR DESIGN CHARRETTES

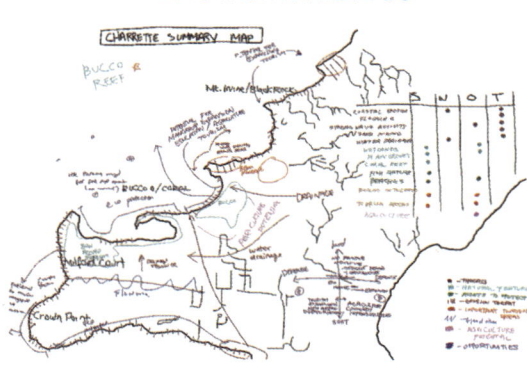

DATA ANALYSIS AND FINDINGS

Stressors — Sea Level Rise, Coral Bleaching, Ocean Acidification, Extreme Weather, Pollution

Impacts — Wild Life Habitat Loss, Landslides, Coastal Erosion, Water Security, Food Security, Flooding

Adaptation Priorities — Home & Settlements, Food Security, Transportation, Waste & Water, Coastal Infrastructure

ASSETS

1) EXISTING ROAD, WATER, AND SEWAGE INFRASTRUCTURE

2) MANGROVES & WETLANDS

Buttonwood Mangrove   White Mangrove   Black Mangrove   Red Mangrove   Sea Grass   Coral Reef

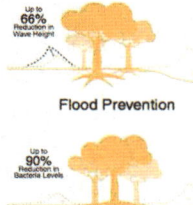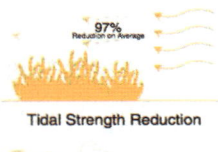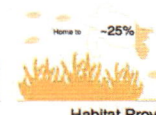

Flood Prevention   Flood Prevention   Flood Prevention   Flood Prevention   Tidal Strength Reduction   Tidal Strength Reduction

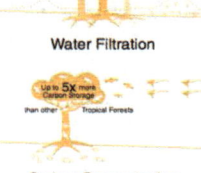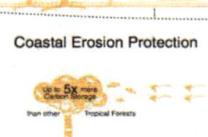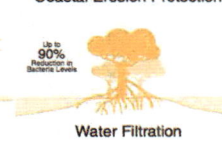

Water Filtration   Water Filtration   Coastal Erosion Protection   Coastal Erosion Protection   Oxygen Production   Habitat Provision

Carbon Sequestration   Carbon Sequestration   Carbon Sequestration   Water Filtration   Suspended Solid Filtration   Tourism

REGENERATE THE MANGROVE FOREST

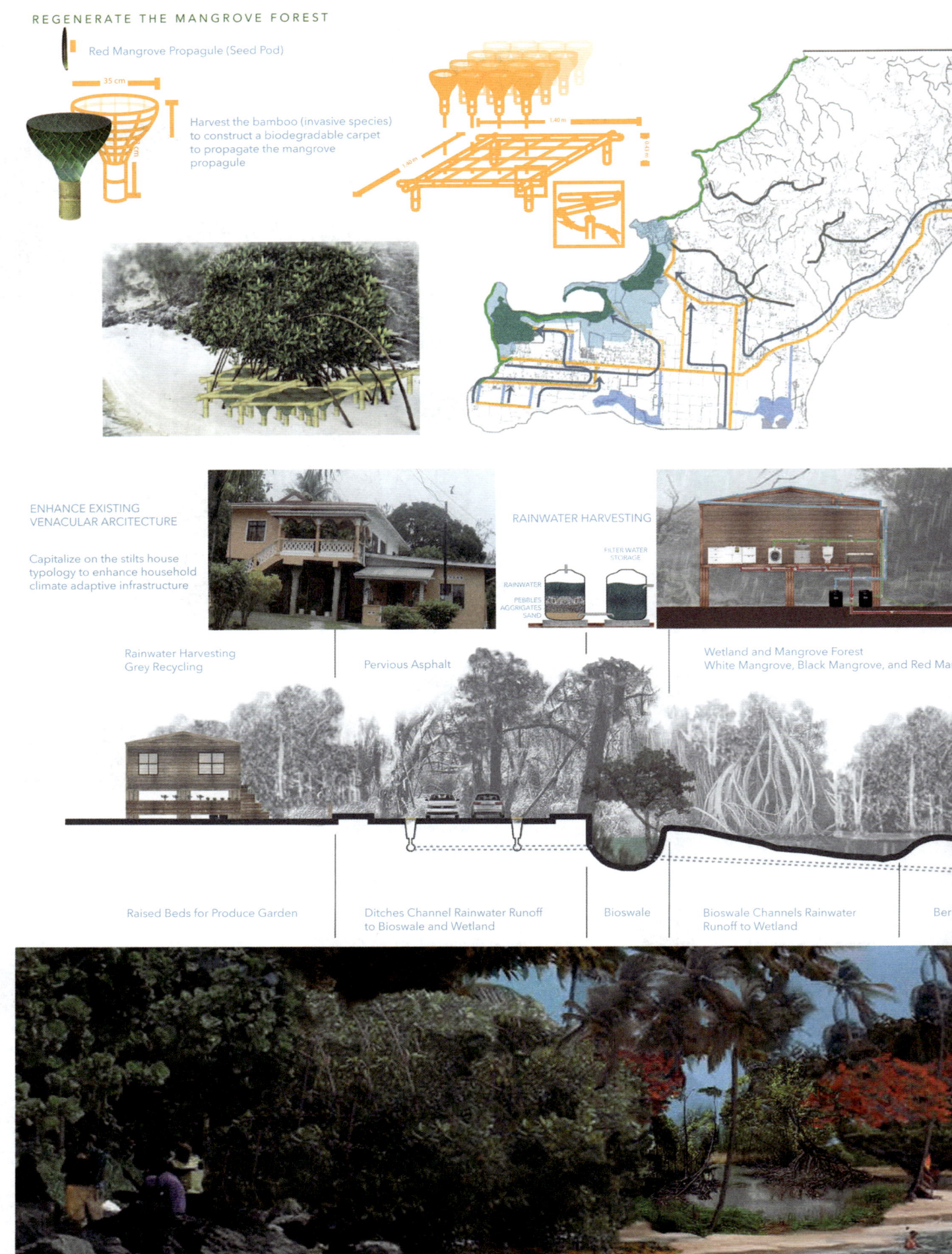

Red Mangrove Propagule (Seed Pod)

35 cm

Harvest the bamboo (invasive species) to construct a biodegradable carpet to propagate the mangrove propagule

1.40 m

ENHANCE EXISTING VENACULAR ARCITECTURE

Capitalize on the stilts house typology to enhance household climate adaptive infrastructure

RAINWATER HARVESTING

FILTER WATER STORAGE

RAINWATER

PEBBLES AGGREGATES SAND

Rainwater Harvesting
Grey Recycling

Pervious Asphalt

Wetland and Mangrove Forest
White Mangrove, Black Mangrove, and Red Man

Raised Beds for Produce Garden

Ditches Channel Rainwater Runoff to Bioswale and Wetland

Bioswale

Bioswale Channels Rainwater Runoff to Wetland

Ber

N ISLAND ROAD

BEFORE

AFTER

Harvest the bamboo to enhance the public realm

AND ROAD

BEFORE

AFTER

Deepen and cover the open ditches with bamboo and channel the rainwater runoff to replenish the wetland

GABION BASKET   EROSIONAL CARPET

ASTAL ROAD

BEFORE

AFTER

Shirvan Road

Use harvested bamboo to construct biodegradable and flexible gryones

YWATER RECYCLING

FILTER WATER STORAGE

Raised bed gardens to support food security and beautify stilt construction by concealing infrastructure

Biodegradable Mangrove Carpet

Berm

Biodegradable And Reversible Gryones

RE-GENERATOR

Gabriel Munoz Moreno

What if we design building systems that not only support our society, but also support the natural environments that we inhabit?

The constant change and growth of the human population that we are experiencing today produce a collateral damage in the natural ecosystems where cities stand all around the world. This damage is produced by today's building systems and by urban designs that do not take into account the natural environment where they are built. The expected and rapid population growth in the first half of the 21st century, propelled especially by the developing countries (from 7.2 billion to 9.6 billion people estimated in UN's "World Population Prospects" report), results in a need to search alternatives to contemporary building methods in order to provide construction tools and guides that makes urban growth compatible with the preservation of our environment. Moreover, I believe in the power of architecture to change the future of our cities and the lives of its inhabitants.

The intention of the research is to provide a construction system that solves the problems caused by the massive population growth and the provision of shelter to these people. Up to now, cities have largely prioritized quickness and simplicity in their building methods at the expense of the natural ecosystems; they impose physical obstacles to the earth's cycles. The first step that we do in construction is to erase all the natural characteristics of a certain piece of land to impose our necessities. By doing this, we seal the ground and thus interrupt the water, air and sun cycles, impacting negatively on the different natural phases of the ecosystems. The project does not intend to restrain the human instinct to inhabit nature, rather it intends to guide it with a series of architectural concepts in order to achieve a sustainable development between human beings and their environment.

I propose an alternative construction system for the city of Hangzhou, selected for its rapid population growth, its natural ecosystem, the wetlands, and its coastal location. The construction system is organized and distributed like cells throughout the city. Such cells are elevated above the ground, to make way for the recovery of the wetlands. The cells should be translucent and permeable, without disrupting the natural cycles of the sun, air and water. Moreover, not only this elevated structure, but also the wetlands make it resilient to sea level rise. The net of cells and its connections will be the new constantly changing living space for the inhabitants of the city.

Hangzhou is built on a bay that allows the formation of large wetlands, standing as one of the most important natural ecosystems on earth because they contain a wide variety of species that help cleaning the water, balance the temperature and control water excesses and water scarcities. The direct consequence of the population growth observed was the partial destruction of the ecosystem on which the city stands: the wetlands. The construction systems used so far do not support them because they seal and waterproof the wetlands, destroying all their properties.

First of all, in order not to alter the preexisting natural ecosystem, the methodology must avoid as much as possible construction at ground level. By moving the city to an elevated plane above ground, the relationship between the city and the wetlands is improved because we can have two things at the same time, inhabitants and the preexisting natural ecosystem. Here, it is important to design vertical supports and restraints adapted to this environment.

Secondly, the construction system must be as transparent and permeable as possible in order not to interrupt the natural water, sun and air cycles. It is necessary to explore the structural and material limits of this system in

Was wäre, wenn wir Bausysteme entwickeln, die nicht nur unserer Gesellschaft dienen, sondern auch der natürlichen Umgebung, die wir bewohnen?

Das beständige Bevölkerungswachstum, das wir derzeit erfahren, erzeugt einen Kollateralschaden in den natürlichen Ökosystemen an den Standorten der Städte rund um die Welt. Dieser Schaden wird durch die heutigen Bausysteme und Stadtentwürfe erzeugt, die keine Rücksicht auf ihre natürliche Umgebung nehmen. Die erwartete rasante Bevölkerungszunahme für die erste Hälfte des 21. Jahrhunderts (von 7,2 Millionen zu 9,6 Millionen Menschen laut UN-Bericht World Population Prospects), die vor allem von den Entwicklungsländern vorangetrieben wird, erfordert verstärkt Forschung über Alternativen zu den heutigen Baumethoden, um Werkzeuge und Richtlinien für das Bauen zu entwickeln, die ein für unsere Umwelt erträgliches Stadtwachstum erlauben. Ich glaube an die Macht der Architektur, die Zukunft unserer Städte und das Leben ihrer Bewohner zu verändern.

Der Forschung liegt die Absicht zugrunde, ein Bausystem zu entwickeln, das die Probleme des massiven Bevölkerungswachstums und der Bereitstellung von Unterkunft für diese Menschen löst. Bisher haben Städte in ihren Baumethoden Schnelligkeit und Einfachheit auf Kosten natürlicher Ökosysteme bevorzugt; sie haben natürliche Kreisläufe mit physischen Hindernissen verstellt. Der erste Schritt beim Bauen ist, dass wir alle natürlichen Charakteristika des Stück Landes beseitigen, um unsere Erfordernisse durchzusetzen. Damit versiegeln wir den Boden und unterbrechen die Zyklen von Wasser, Luft und Sonne und beeinflussen die verschiedenen natürlichen Phasen des Ökosystems negativ. Das Projekt will nicht den menschlichen Instinkt, sich die Natur zunutze zu machen, unterdrücken, vielmehr geht es darum mit einer Reihe architektonischer Konzepte eine nachhaltige Entwicklung zwischen den Menschen und ihrer Umgebung zu fördern.

Es wird ein alternatives Bausystem für die chinesische Stadt Hangzhou vorgeschlagen, sie wurde ausgewählt wegen ihres rasanten Bevölkerungswachstums, ihres natürlichen Ökosystems, dem Marschland und ihrer Küstenlage. Das Bausystem ist in Form von Zellen organisiert, die sich über das gesamte

Areal der Stadt verteilen. Diese Zellen sollen aufgeständert sein, damit sich das darunter liegende Marschland erholen kann. Sie sollen lichtdurchlässig und permeabel sein, ohne die natürlichen Zyklen von Sonne, Luft und Wasser zu beeinträchtigen. Außerdem widersteht diese aufgeständerte Konstruktion dem für dieses Jahrhundert vorhergesagten, das Marschland bedrohenden Anstieg des Meeresspiegels. Das Netzwerk von Zellen und deren Verbindungen wird den neuen, sich ständig verändernden Lebensraum für die Bewohner der Stadt bilden.

Hangzhou liegt an einer Bucht, die das Entstehen weitläufiger Marschen begünstigt – die Region gilt als eines der weltweit bedeutendsten Ökosysteme, denn sie beherbergt ein weites Spektrum von Spezies, die nicht nur zur Reinigung des Wassers und zum Temperaturausgleich beitragen, sondern auch Wasserüberfluss und Wassermangel kontrollieren. Die unmittelbare Folge des Bevölkerungswachstums ist die partielle Zerstörung des Ökosystems der Marschen, das gleichsam das Fundament Hangzhous bildet. Die bisherigen Baumethoden sind dem Marschland abträglich, da sie dieses versiegeln und wasserundurchlässig machen und somit dessen nützliche Eigenschaften zerstören.

1. Um das bestehende Ökosystem nicht zu beeinträchtigen, muss nach Möglichkeit vermieden werden, ebenerdig zu bauen. Wenn man die Stadt aufständert, wird die Beziehung zwischen Stadt und Marschland verbessert, weil man auf diese Weise zwei Dinge gleichzeitig beherbergt: Bewohner und das bestehende natürliche Ökosystem. Hier wird der Entwurf von in die Umgebung eingepassten vertikalen Stützen und Verspannungen bedeutsam.

2. Das Bausystem muss, damit die natürlichen Zyklen von Sonne, Luft und Wasser nicht unterbrochen werden, möglichst lichtdurchlässig und permeabel sein. Die Erforschung seiner strukturellen und materiellen Grenzen hilft, den Materialaufwand zu reduzieren und physische Auswirkungen auf das natürliche Ökosystem zu vermeiden. Dies führte mich zu einer Untersuchung von Leichtbaustrukturen, bei der die modifizierte Tensegrity-Konstruktion, die Diller & Scofidio bei "The Blur Building" verwendet haben, ein herausragendes

BUH
Basic Unit of Habitability

CONCEPTS:
- Lightness
- Habitability

★ Prefabricated ALUMINIUM enclosure
1mm alum./3mm plastic / 1mm alum.
reinforced with fiberglass

- laser cut
- lamination
- on site bending

★ Sandwich panel of POLYESTER

- construct
- laser cut
- heat bending

BUA
Basic Unity of Accessibility

CONCEPTS:
- Lightness
- Permeability
- Transparency

★ TRAMEX with mesh =
1mm alum./3mm;
carrier = 50 x 3mm;

- recycling of
- buildings
- construct
- simplicity
- laser cut

★ RETENTION NET against falling objects
15x15mm high resistance

- recycling of
- buildings
- construct
- simplicity
- yarn with
- machine

WATER FILTER

BUR
Basic Unity of Regeneration

CONCEPTS:
- Self sufficiency
- Lightness
- Greenhouse

★ Sandwich panel of translucent POLYESTER
with layer silica x AEROGEL

- laser cut
- heat bending
- aerogel acrylic.

water pump
Trapac

RE GENERATOR

K X 2 8 4 6

Plan to regenerate & recover the Wetlands of Hangzhou
Hangzhou, People's Republic of China

The project stems from an analysis of the World's population growth. Is expected a rapid growth for the first half of the 21st century, propelled specially by the developing countries (from 7.2 billion to 9.6 billion people estimated in UN's World Population Prospects' report). The direct consequence observed is the partial destruction of the natural ecosystems where the cities. Part of this damage is produced by today's building systems and by urban designs that do not take into account the natural environment where they are built. This growth will result into the need to provide shelter to the inhabitants of the different cities. The continued use of the current construction system will end up destroying part of the ecosystems of the word.

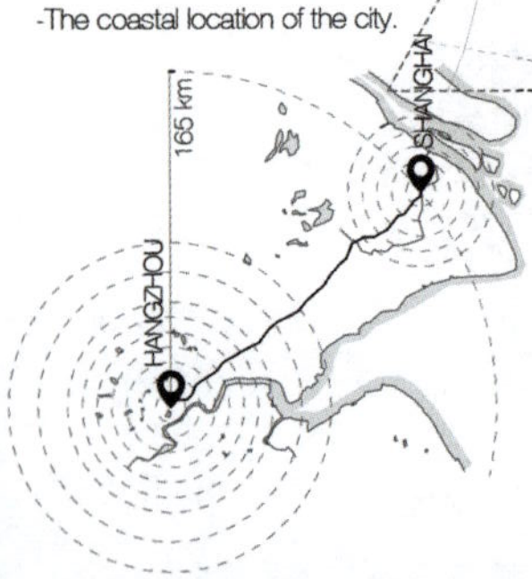

RWM
Cities & Ecosystems
Resilient World Map

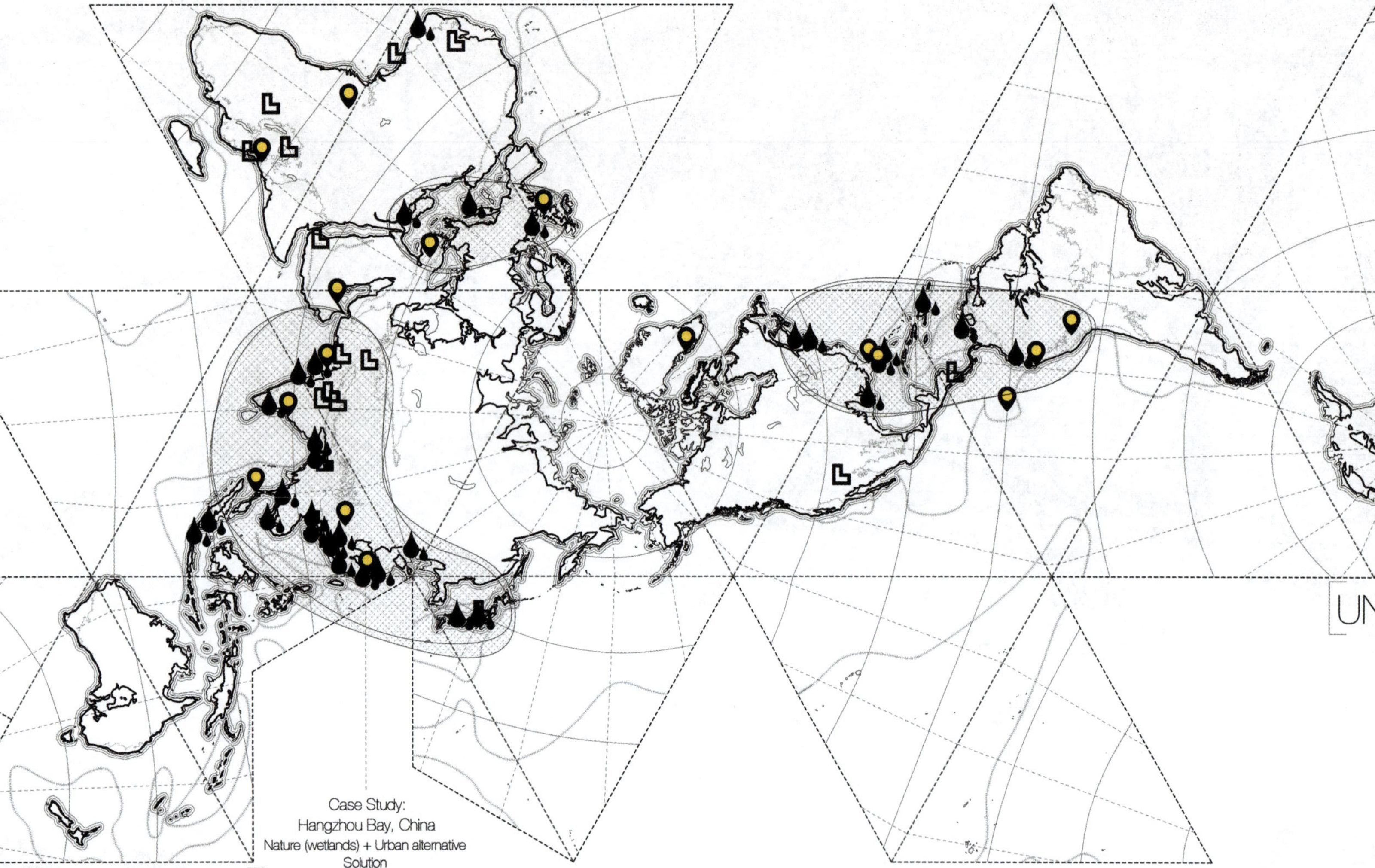

- Ecosystems in Danger
- Boundary of ecosystems
- Ecosystems most affected hotspots
- Sea Level Rise Risk
- Flooded boundary with over 65m sea level rise
- Urban Growth
- Areas with cities & ecosystems most affected

RUD
A Resilient Urban Design

The design of an elevated structure and the construction of the wetlands will make of a city resilient to the sea level rise that it is forecasted to happen in this century by the Intergovernmental Panel on Climate Change. The net of cels and its connections will be the new living plane for the inhabitants of the city, which is intended to be a progressive change.

T5C
TOP 5 Countries at Risk (Sea Rise Level)

	Country	Exposed (thousands)
①	China	50465
②	Vietnam	23407
③	Japan	12751
④	India	12643
⑤	Bangladesh	10230
⑥	Indonesia	10157
⑦	Thailand	8176
⑧	Netherlands	7793
⑨	Philippines	6205
⑩	Myanmar	4742

Case Study:
Hangzhou Bay, China
Nature (Wetlands) + Urban alternative Solution

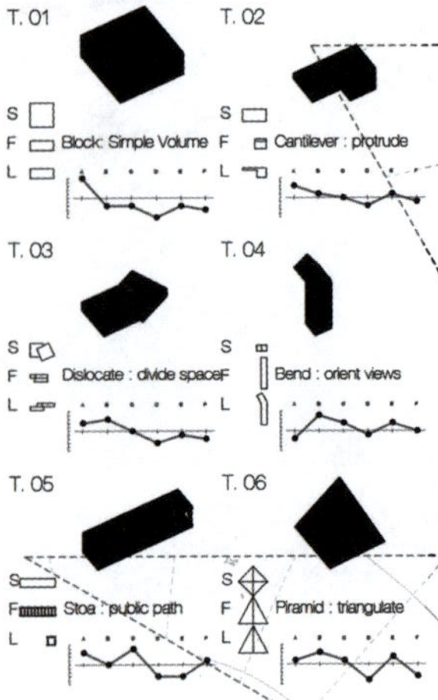

For this case, it is selected the city of Hangzhou, in China, for the following reasons:
-Its rapid population increase.
-The natural ecosystems that are being erased by the construction system used.
-The coastal location of the city.

UN
United Nations Population Growth Forecast

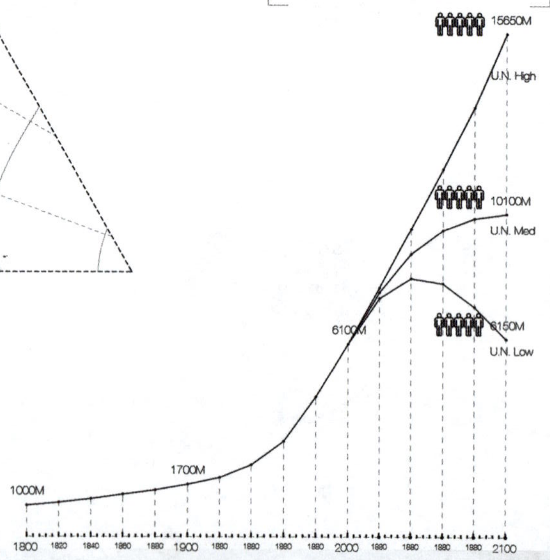

UN High
UN Med
UN Low

T.01
T.02
T.03
T.04
T.05
T.06

S — Shoe : public path
F — Book : Simple Volume
L — Cantilever : porticus
S — Decade : divide space
F — Band : orient views
S — Frame : triangles

HANGZHOU
SHANGHAI
165 km

183

CCL

Problem: The construction method used is not sustainable with the ecosystems of the place. It destroys them by building on top of the wetlands.

CITY VS WETLANDS

1978
1984
1991
2000
2010

560M
1340M
1400M

RELATIONSHIP POPULATION / WETLANDS

Population / China
Wetlands / Hangzhou

IMO

Incompatible Models

ECOSYSTEM // WETLANDS

URBAN GROWTH

CSH

Construction Solution
Hangzhou Case

As a solution to this, it is proposed an alternative construction system that is organized and distributed like cells throughout the city. Such cells are elevated above the ground, to make way for the recovery of the wetlands. The cells should be transluscent and permeable, without disrupting the natural cycles of the regeneration of any ecosystem.

The proposed network of structural cells visualize a temporal limit on the 2060 date, from which it is impossible to forecast.

PROBLEM / 01
INTERVENTION

8. REGENERATION OF WETLANDS

CLL

Regenerative Cell

REGENERATIVE CELL
The cell is supplied with different 'inputs' to enable the habitability and the clearing of the wetlands, using its waste to encourage self-sufficiency. Such inputs mimic different functions of natural cells and enable our construction cell to be a living element, a system in constant change and growth.

REPRODUCTION / EXPANSION
FEEDING / ACCESS, ENERGY
CONNECTIONS

membrane
nucleus
cytoplasm

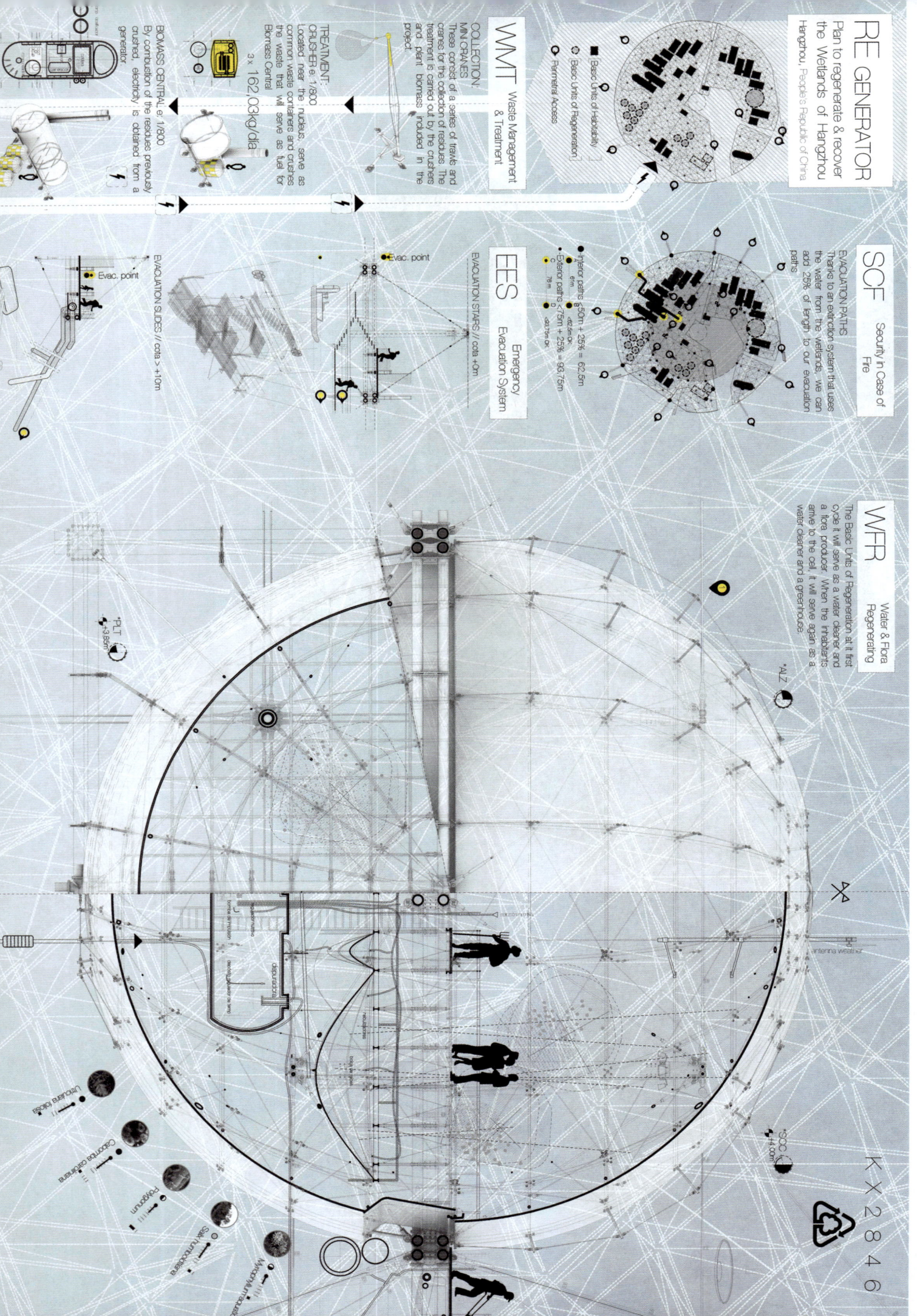

RE GENERATOR

Plan to regenerate & recover the Wetlands of Hangzhou
Hangzhou, People's Republic of China

■ Basic Units of Habitabilty
◇ Basic Units of Regeneration
● Perimetral Access

SCF
Security in Case of Fire

EVACUATION PATHS
Thanks to an extinction system that uses the water from the wetlands, we can add 25% of length to our evacuation paths

Interior paths ≥50m + 25% = 62,5m
Exterior paths ≥75m + 25% = 93,75m
6m — —
75m — —
78m — —
93,75m ---

EES
Emergency Evacuation System

EVALUATION SYSTEM
EVACUATION STAIRS // cota +0m
EVACUATION SLIDES // cota > +10m
● Evac. point

WFR
Water & Flora Regenerating

The Basic Units of Regeneration at it first cycle it will serve as a water cleaner and a flora producer. When the inhabitants arrive to the cell it will serve again as a water cleaner and a greenhouse.

WMT
Waste Management & Treatment

COLLECTION:
MINI CRANES
These consist of a series of trawls and cranes for the collection of residues. The treatment is carried out by the crushers and plant biomass included in the project.

3 x 162,03kg/dia

TREATMENT
CRUSHER e: 1/800
Located near the nucleus, serve as common waste containers and crushes the waste that will serve as fuel for Biomass Central.

BIOMASS CENTRAL e: 1/800
By combustion of the residues previously crushed, electricity is obtained from a generator.

KX 28 46

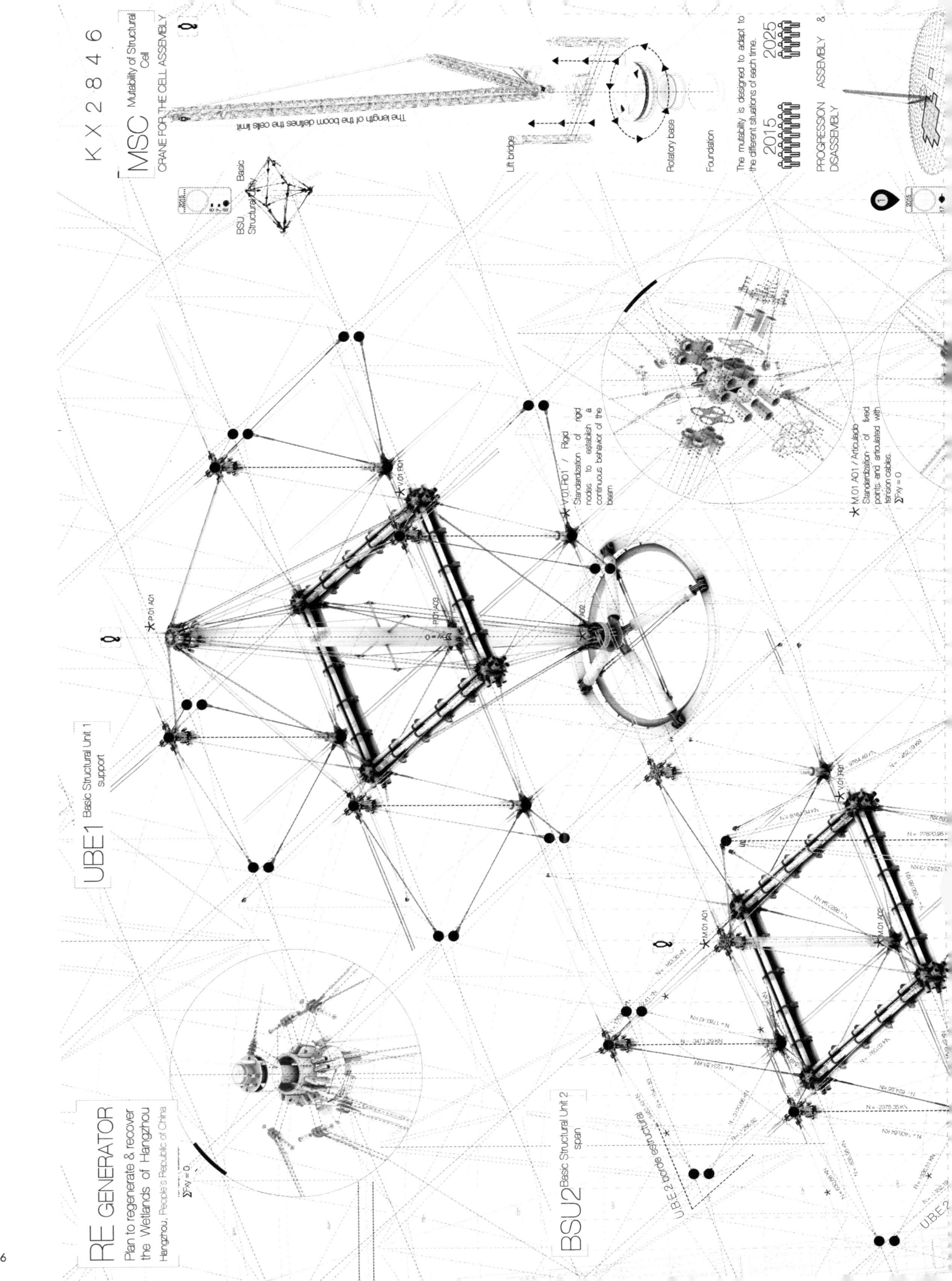

K X 2 8 4 6

MSC Mutability of Structural Cell
CRANE FOR THE CELL ASSEMBLY

The length of the boom defines the cells limit

Lift bridge

Rotatory base

Foundation

The mutability is designed to adapt to the different situations of each time.

2015   2025

PROGRESSION ASSEMBLY &
DISASSEMBLY

Basic
BSU
Structural Unit

★ V01 R01 / Rigid
Standardization of rigid nodes to establish a continuous behavior of the beam

★ M01 A01 / Articulado
Standardization of fixed points and articulated with tension cables.
$\Sigma Fv = 0$

RE GENERATOR
Plan to regenerate & recover
the Wetlands of Hangzhou
Hangzhou, People's Republic of China

UBE1 Basic Structural Unit 1
support

$\Sigma Fv = 0$

★ P01 A01

P01 A03

A02

$\Sigma Fv = 0$

BSU2 Basic Structural Unit 2
span

U.B.E.2 borde estructural

★ M01 A01

★ V01 R01

A02

186

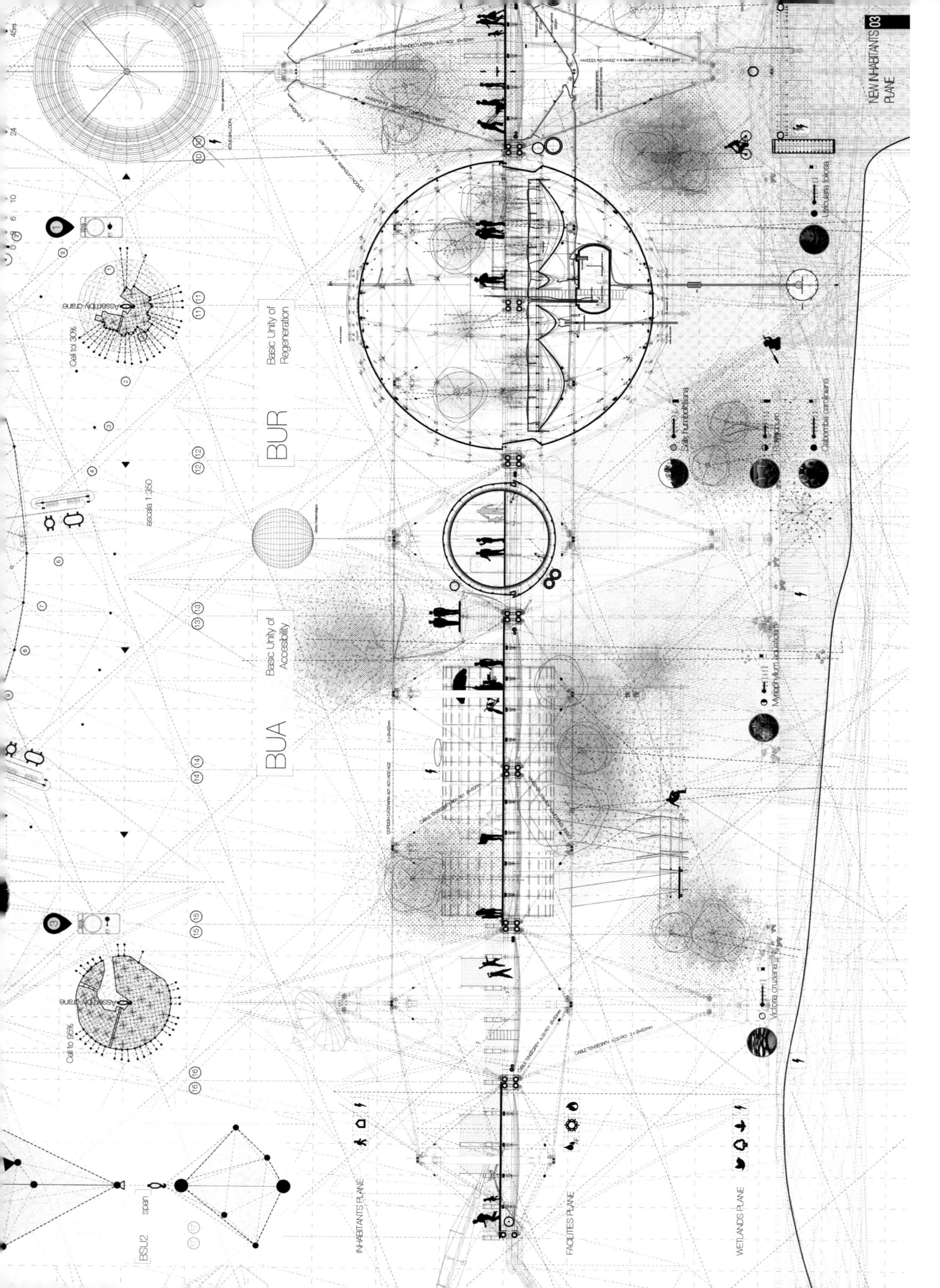

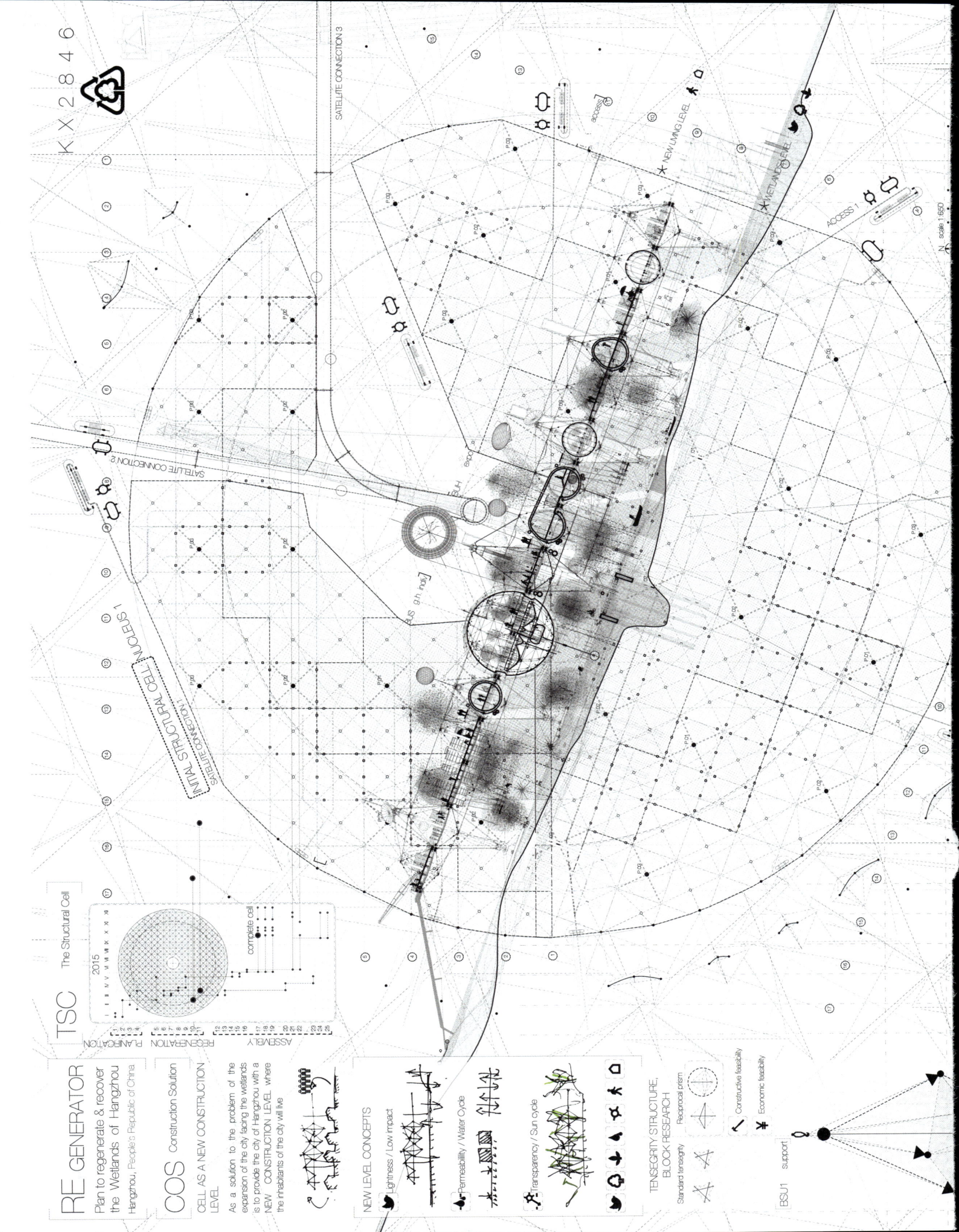

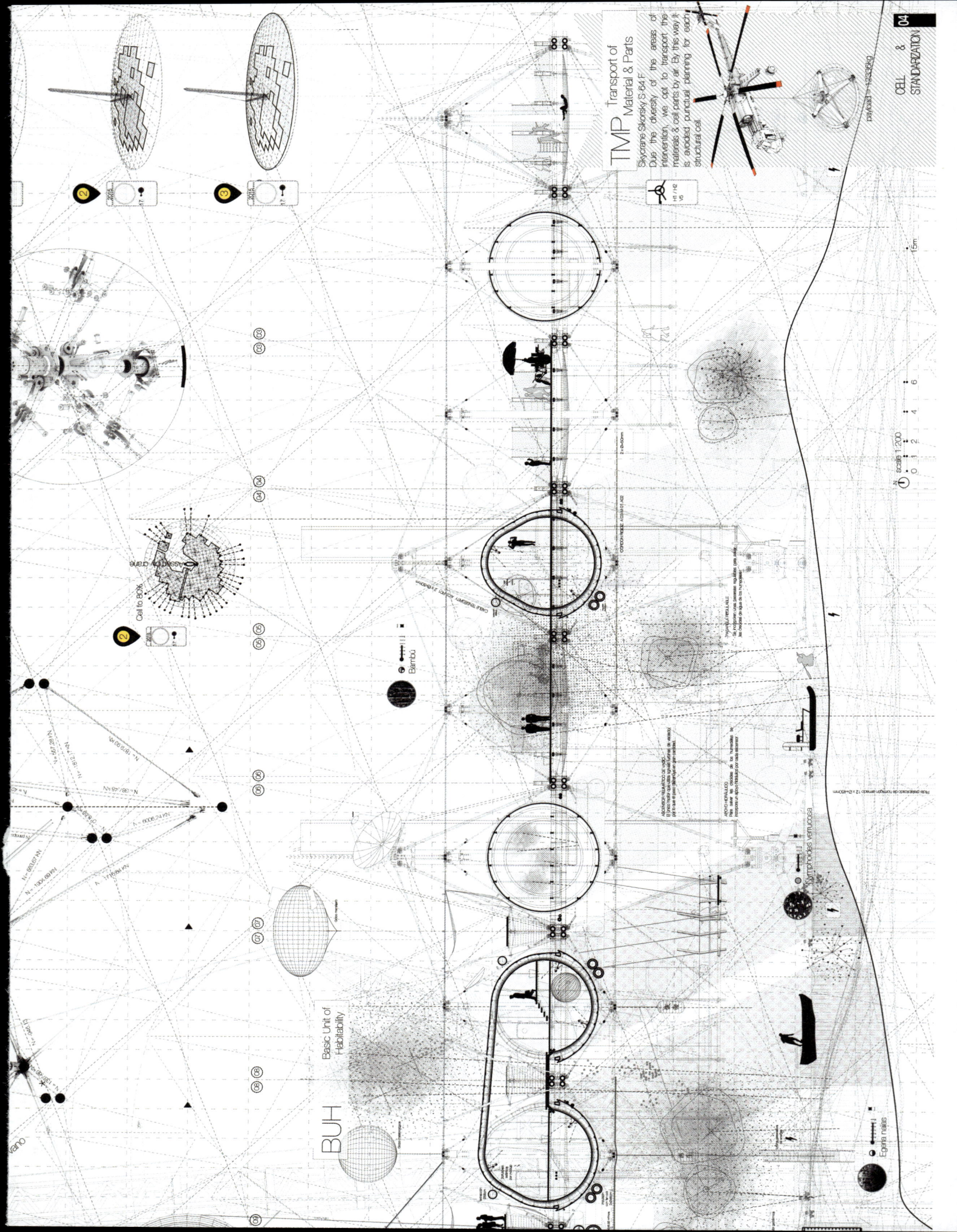

TMP Transport of Material & Parts

Skycrane Sikorsky S-64 F

Due the diversity of the areas of intervention, we opt to transport the materials & cell parts by air. By this way it is avoided punctual planning for each structural cell

payload = 14333kg

BUH

Basic Unit of Habitability

scale 1:200

order to reduce the amount of material and to produce no physical impact on the natural ecosystem where it will be raised. This brings me to a study of light structures, finding a great example in the semi-tensegrity structure used in "The Blur Building" by Diller & Scofidio. By implementing it with a catenary system I am able to increase its transparency and permeability. The structural system works as a slab hanging from the main pillars. This structure is provided with a dynamic tensegrity system that makes it more rigid by reducing the deflection caused by the big spans and cantilevers.

Third, the system's adaption capabilities to the necessities of each situation are very important in order to save energy and resources. Here, the system will be characterized by being assigned two structural modules allowing the mutability of the project according to the use required in each moment. Of course, the utilities system is linked to the mutability of the project. For this purpose, I decided to associate the different networks to the structural units.

Regarding the extension of the proposal throughout the city, the structure will reproduce alongside Hangzhou with these parameters: Connectivity will be achieved along the water canals, and HUBs (centers of activities) will be located where the canals intersect. Construction will star where free spaces are available. There is a limit on the height, because the concepts of permeability and transparency do not allow the same population density as towers do.

Fourth, in order to achieve both a maximum industrial and assemblage energy efficiency, standardization of the pieces and assemblies that form the system is a key part in this extended design. In all these components, the production and income of energy must be a priority, proposing different units integrated in the whole design that will help produce this energy since its first deployment.

When the inhabitants' connectivity comes into play, we must think about an organism that changes through time and is able to adapt to the different locations of the city. Therefore the structure will be distributed and expands like cells throughout the city. The HUBs will be connected by water along Hangzhou's canals, by air through a funicular system resulting from the new requirements of an elevated construction, and by ground through walk and bicycle paths.

The construction period plays a very important role in the intervention. So, the land movement will serve to partially recover the wetlands, and the location of the supports are to be chosen as not to damage the structure of the Wetlands. The next step will be the assemblage of the structural modules. The final step will be the localization of the basic units of habitability, service and accessibility on the structural modules and the positioning of the basic units for housing, service and accessibility.

– Basic Unit of Housing. These are inspired by the light construction systems in the aircraft industry. These units will adopt different forms to take advantage of every space to give the user more versatility.

– Basic Unit of Service. There will be two types: private and common greenhouses. They will provide support for the users. To avoid the use of flora's soil, which would dramatically increase the load on the structure, the greenhouse system used will be aeroponic. This also takes advantage of the water of the wetlands, which are used as the water tanks of the greenhouses.

– Basic Units of Accessibility. These will be composed by the paths and outer slabs that will be used as the entry points by the people. Some of them will use the residual spaces of the structure. Furthermore, the cell is supplied with different inputs to make possible the cleaning of the wetlands, using its waste to encourage self-sufficiency. These mimic different parts of a natural cell and enable our structural cell to be a living element, a system in constant change and growth, regenerating the ecosystems, in this case the wetlands of Hangzhou.

The materiality is linked to the main concepts of transparency and permeability. The materials will be aluminum for the basic units of habitability because of its reflectivity, "Tramex" in the units of accessibility due to its permeability, glass to provide transparency and polyester due to its capacity to adapt to the project proposed.

In the end, the system results in an architecture capable of changing and finding the equilibrium between our living ways and the different ecosystems that we inhabit, an architecture that is formed by the natural ecosystem where it is deployed instead of imposing its necessities on it. By treating architecture as a natural element carved by the multiple elements that affect it, we achieve a balance between our construction methods and the natural environments that we inhabit.

Beispiel lieferte. Wenn ich diese Konstruktion mit einem Seilaufhängungssystem versehe, kann ich ihre Transparenz und Permeabilität steigern. Die Tragstruktur besteht aus einer von der Hauptstütze abgehängten Platte. Diese Struktur wird mit einem dynamischen Tensegrity-System ausgestattet, welches sie steifer macht, indem es die Durchbiegung reduziert, die durch die großen Spannweiten und Auskragungen erzeugt wird.

3. Die Fähigkeiten dieses Systems, sich an verschiedene Situationen anpassen zu können, sind sehr wichtig, um Energie und Ressourcen zu sparen. In unserem Fall sind es zwei strukturelle Module, die die Veränderbarkeit des Projekts hinsichtlich der jeweils erforderten Verwendung ermöglichen. Selbstverständlich ist das Versorgungssystem in die Veränderbarkeit des Projekts einbezogen. Daher sind die verschiedenen Netzwerke mit den strukturellen Einheiten verbunden.

Bezüglich der Ausweitung dieses Vorschlags auf die gesamte Stadt wird sich die Struktur längsseits Hangzhous mit den folgenden Parametern fortpflanzen: Konnektivität entsteht über die Wasserkanäle, und wo sich Kanäle kreuzen, werden HUBs (Zentren von Aktivität) eingerichtet. Der Bauprozess wird dort beginnen, wo freie Areale verfügbar sind. Es wird eine Höhenbegrenzung geben, da die Konzepte der Permeabilität und Lichtdurchlässigkeit nicht die gleiche Bevölkerungsdichte erlauben wie Hochhäuser.

4. Um ein Maximum an industrieller und montagetechnischer Energieeffizienz zu erzielen, ist die Standardisierung der Komponenten und Verbindungsstücke des Systems ein wesentlicher Gesichtspunkt dieses erweiterten Entwurfs. Bei allen Komponenten muss die Erzeugung und der Ertrag von Energie Vorrang haben; der Vorschlag ist, verschiedene Einheiten in den gesamten Entwurf zu integrieren, mittels derer diese Energie gleich von der Umsetzung des Entwurfs an erzeugt werden kann.

Wenn es um die Konnektivität der Bewohner geht, müssen wir uns einen Organismus vorstellen, der sich im Laufe der Zeit verändert und an die unterschiedlichen Standorte der Stadt anzupassen vermag. Deshalb wird die Struktur über die gesamte Stadt verteilt und sich dort in Form von Zellen ausbreiten. Die HUBs werden auf dreifache Weise miteinander verbunden: über das Wasser entlang der Kanäle Hangzhous; durch die Luft über ein Seilsystem, das den Anforderungen einer aufgeständerten Konstruktion entspricht; auf dem Erdboden über Fußgänger- und Fahrradwege.

Die Bauperiode spielt eine bedeutsame Rolle bei dem Eingriff. So wird die Erdbewegung zu einer partiellen Regeneration des Marschlands

beitragen und die Standorte für die Stützen und Fundamente sind so festzulegen, dass sie die Struktur des Marschlands nicht beeinträchtigen. Der nächste Schritt wird in der Montage der strukturellen Module bestehen und der Festlegung der Basiseinheiten für Wohnen, Versorgung und Erschließung der strukturellen Module.

– Die Wohneinheiten orientieren sich an den Leichtbaukonstruktionen der Flugzeugindustrie; sie werden unterschiedliche Formen annehmen, um jeden Raum so nutzen zu können, dass er den Bewohnern ein Optimum an Flexibilität gewährt.

– Als Versorgungseinheiten wird es private und öffentliche Gewächshäuser geben. Sie werden die Bewohner unterstützen. Da Erde für die Pflanzen die Belastung der Struktur dramatisch erhöhen würde, wird das Gewächshaussystem aeroponisch sein. Es nutzt das Wasser der Marschen, das in den Reservoirs der Gewächshäuser zur Verfügung steht.

– Die Erschließungseinheiten werden aus den Wegen und den äußeren Platten bestehen, die den Leuten als Eingang dienen. Dafür werden auch die Restflächen der Struktur genutzt.

Darüber hinaus wird die Zelle mit verschiedenen "Inputs" versehen, die es möglich machen, das Marschland zu säubern, und die den Abfall in einer Weise nutzen, die Autarkie fördert. Diese Inputs ahmen die verschiedenen Funktionen natürlicher Zellen nach und machen unsere Bauzelle zu einem lebenden Element, zu einem System, das wächst und sich unablässig verändert und dabei die Ökosysteme regeneriert, in diesem Fall die Marschen von Hangzhou.

Das Material folgt den grundlegenden Konzepten der Lichtdurchlässigkeit und Permeabilität. Bei den Wohneinheiten wird das Material Aluminium sein (wegen seines Reflexionsvermögens). Bei den Erschließungseinheiten kommen "Tramex" (wegen seiner Permeabilität), Glas (wegen seiner Lichtdurchlässigkeit) und Polyester (wegen seiner Anpassbarkeit an das vorgeschlagene Projekt) zur Verwendung.

Am Ende resultiert das System in einer Architektur, die sich verändern und ein Gleichgewicht zwischen unseren Lebensweisen und den unterschiedlichen, von uns bewohnten Ökosystemen finden kann, eine Architektur, die dort, wo man sie realisiert, vom natürlichen Ökosystem geformt wird, statt es ihren Bedürfnissen unterzuordnen. Indem wir die Architektur wie ein natürliches Element behandeln, das von den mannigfaltigen auf sie einwirkenden Kräften geprägt wird, vermag sie eine Balance zwischen unseren Baumethoden und den natürlichen, von uns bewohnten Umgebungen herzustellen.

HYBRID PRACTICES IN THE VENICE LAGOON

Klaus K. Loenhart, Daniel Baumgartner, Patrick Fresner, Bianca Nedwetzky,
Regina Nemecz, Theresa-Alena Platzer, Roberto Viforcos Giron,
Sandra Weinrauch, Katharina Wernig, Maria Theres Baumgartner, Jörg Dittus,
Walter Frühwirth, Michael Keser, Philip Marzona, Magdalena Schepe,
Anne Schlebbe, Sebastian Wattenberg, Maki Stolberg

This project focuses on the cultural dimension of the impending ecological and resource shift. As a consequence, our society is confronted in with fundamental interventions in the traditional understanding of landscape and technology. How can a cultural practice, an integral design of this future living-environment look like? What links between large-scale infrastructures, technologies and social practices are desirable?

Starting from architecture and landscape as a field of activity, it shall be shown that these future challenges and scenarios carry the unique potential to unlock the corresponding social sphere of action, and to develop a new and integrative "cultural ecology". The architectures presented here arise from partly unexpected relationships between energy production, social and cultural activities and nature.

The lagoon of Venice existed for centuries as an "urban archipelago". With its rich ecosystem it provides an ideal location for us to develop new systemic scenarios and their cultural formations. For this purpose, the project uncovers stories that are deeply rooted in the region. These stories tell us of care and harvesting, preservation

of the landscape system, which has established a unique infrastructure, a network of channels, growing areas, dams and temporary structures that coexist in an exceptionally diverse wetland. In the last century, however, the progress of modernity led to the near disappearance of the lagoon and its small and contemplative stories. In economics, it was designated as empty, and its ecosystem neglected. The primarily agricultural area witnessed the ruthless, efficient landscaping of contemporary management methods.

Now that the myth of limitless growth shows visible cracks, a new understanding of the lagoon archipelago can be created by developing sustainable economic scenarios, tailored to local circumstances. Through a new productive landscape, supporting a regional community of small settlements, a holistic and environmentally stable system is to be created that builds on local knowledge, existing infrastructure and existing biodiversity. Our thesis is that the future architectures of the energy and resource shift will write the future from local knowledge, history and everyday practices – or rather, a variety of "futures" as living culture.

Das vorliegende Projekt thematisiert die kulturelle Dimension der bevorstehenden Ökologie- und Rohstoffwende. Unsere Gesellschaft wird in der Folge mit grundlegenden Eingriffen in das tradierte Verständnis von Landschaft und Technologie konfrontiert. Wie kann eine kulturelle Praxis, eine integrale Gestaltung dieser zukünftigen Lebenswelt aussehen? Welche Bezüge zwischen großräumigen Infrastrukturen, Technologien und sozialen Praktiken sind erstrebenswert?

Ausgehend vom Tätigkeitsfeld Architektur und Landschaft soll dargestellt werden, dass diese zukünftigen Herausforderungen und Szenarien auch das einmalige Potenzial beinhalten, den zugehörigen gesellschaftlichen Handlungsraum zu erschließen, um eine neue und integrative "kulturelle Ökologie" zu entwickeln. Die hier präsentierten Architekturen entstehen dann aus einem, teilweise unerwarteten, Beziehungsgeflecht zwischen Energiegewinnung, sozialen und kulturellen Handlungen und Natur.

Die Lagune von Venedig existiert seit Jahrhunderten als "urbaner Archipel". Sie stellt mit ihrem reichen Ökosystem für uns einen anschaulichen Ort dar, um neue systemische Szenarien und deren kulturelle Überformungen zu entwickeln. Dazu deckt das Projekt Geschichten auf, die tief in der Region verwurzelt sind. Diese Geschichten erzählen von Pflege und Ernten, Fürsorge

und Erhaltung des Landschaftssystems, das eine einmalige Infrastruktur etabliert hat, ein Netzwerk aus Kanälen, Anbaugebieten, Dämmen und temporären Strukturen, die in einem außergewöhnlich vielfältigen Feuchtbiotop koexistieren. Im letzten Jahrhundert hat aber der Fortschritt der Moderne die Lagune mit ihren kleinen und beschaulichen Erzählungen fast verschwinden lassen. In der Ökonomie wurde sie als leer bezeichnet und ihr Ökosystem vernachlässigt. Die primär landwirtschaftlich genutzte Fläche bezeugt die rücksichtslose, effiziente Flächengestaltung zeitgenössischer wirtschaftlicher Methoden.

Zum jetzigen Zeitpunkt, wo der Mythos des grenzenlosen Wachstums sichtbare Risse zeigt, können nachhaltige und auf lokale Gegebenheiten abgestimmte wirtschaftliche Szenarien ein neues Verständnis des Archipels der Lagune erzeugen. Durch eine neue produktive Landschaft, die eine regionale Gemeinschaft kleiner Siedlungen tragen kann, soll ein ganzheitliches und ökologisch stabiles System entstehen, das auf lokalem Wissen, bestehender Infrastruktur und vorhandener Biodiversität aufbaut. Die künftigen Architekturen der Energie- und Rohstoffwende, so unsere These, werden aus lokalem Wissen, Geschichte und Alltag Zukunft schreiben – oder besser, eine Vielzahl von "Zukünften" als gelebte Kultur.

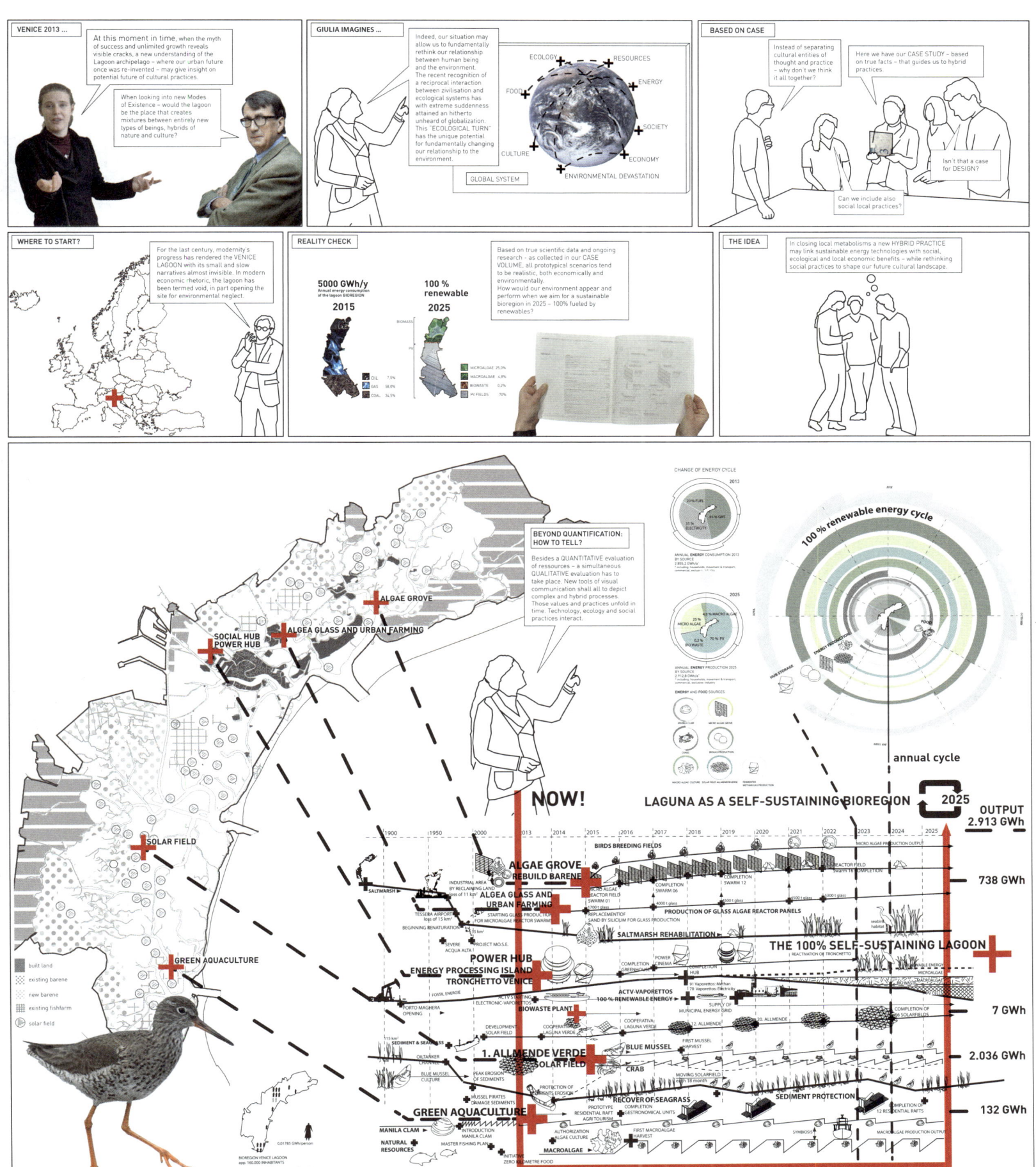

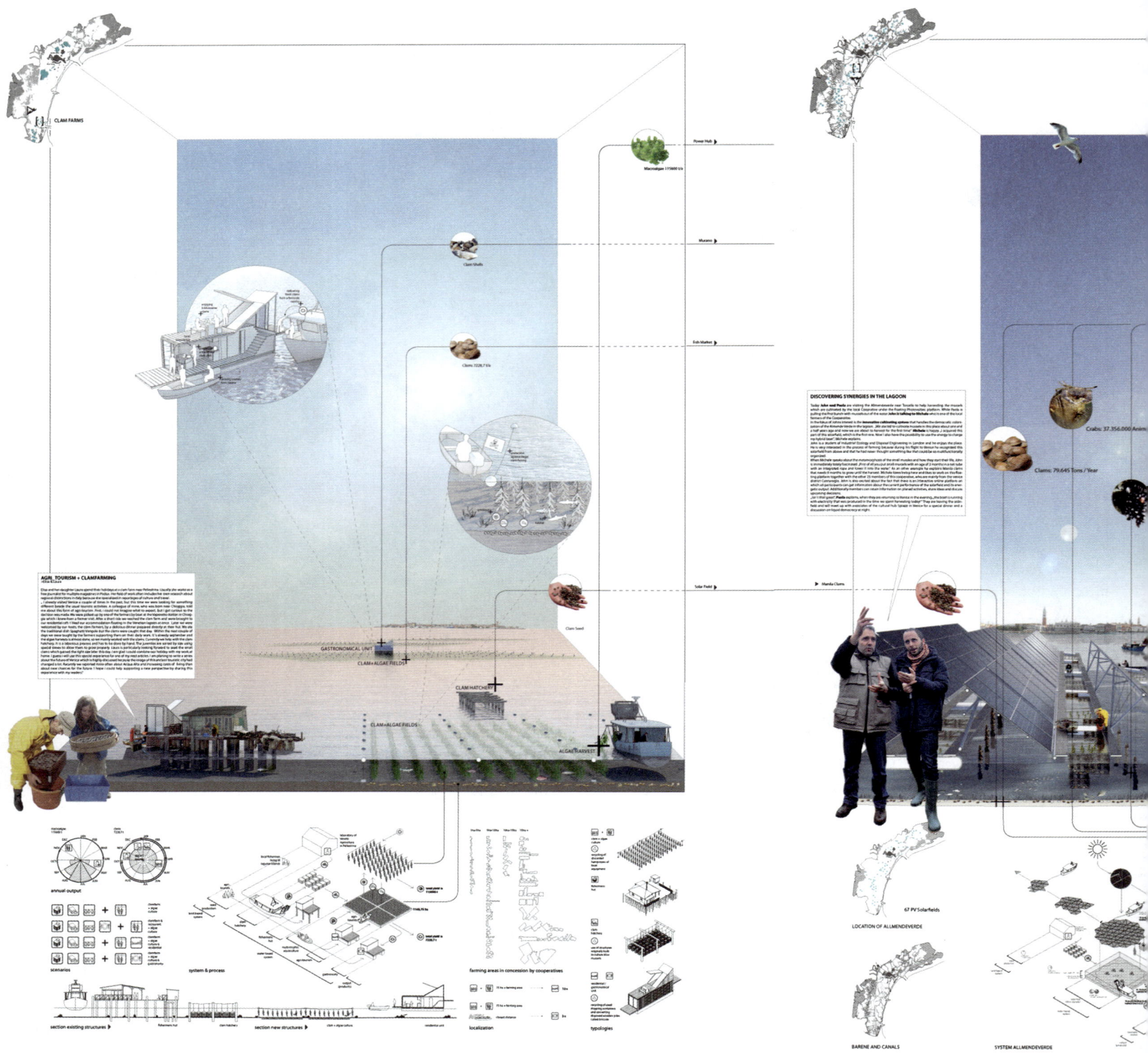

Green Aquaculture

The project contains the extension of the currently existing Manila clam farms in different ways to provide higher income and enhanced sustainability. The monoculture of clams is to be combined with the culture of macro algae. This multi-trophic aquaculture stimulates the growth of both species and decreases seawater pollution through deposited substances of dense clam cultures. The biomass of macro algae is used to produce sustainable fuel for local boat traffic or biological fertilizer for agriculture. In addition, the algae cultures protect the degradation of sediments and seagrass populations on the lagoon bottom because the water movement caused by boat traffic is calmed. Moreover, the algae above the clam fields build a mechanical barrier as a protection from illegal harvesting activities. Particular units are constructed providing clam farm tourism and gastronomical services.

Solar Field or Allmendeverde

"Allmendeverde" are floating structures for energy production and traditional aquaculture in the Venetian lagoon, organised collaboratively and as common goods. 67 moveable fields with a diameter of 600 metres protect areas that before were exploited by illegal clam fishery, which caused bad impacts on the lagoon fauna and sediment. The photovoltaic panels, which are designed and constructed near Murano, produce 70% of the energy demand of the

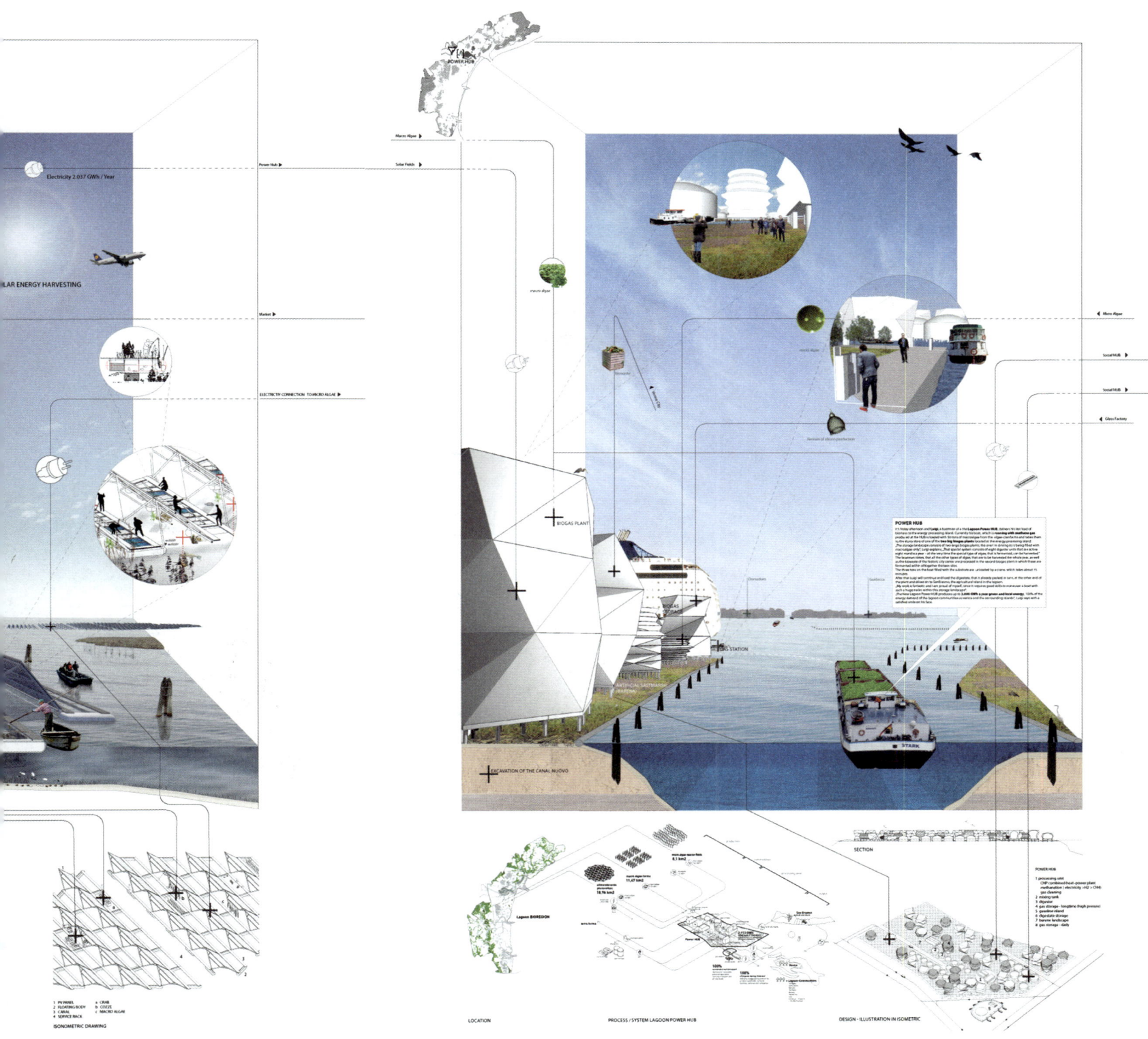

LOCATION   PROCESS / SYSTEM LAGOON POWER HUB   DESIGN - ILLUSTRATION IN ISOMETRIC

1 PV PANEL   4 CRAB
2 FLOATING BODY 5 COZZE
3 CANAL   6 MACRO ALGAE
4 SERVICE RACK
ISONOMETRIC DRAWING

nice lagoon BIOREGION's 160,000 inhabitants.
nctioning as a photovoltaic-field above surface,
low surface the entire farm is fitted for mussel and
ab cultures, which do especially well in the slightly
aded environment. Subscribers of solar power can
nt space on the same structure for cultivating mus-
s for a very low fee. Positioned in the currents of
al change, the harvest shows a great bunch of fine
goon-food.

Lagoon Power Hub

The 20 hectare large storage landscape consists
of two large biogas plants, and 32 gas storages
for the daily biogas output. Appendix 1 is active for
eight months (from March to November) and digests
macro algae within eight silos. The second biogas
plant is composed out of 13 fermenters, in which
microalgae and organic waste from the historic city
centre are processed. Every biogas process takes about
40 days. Part of the produced biogas is converted
into electricity and heat in one of two block heating
stations, while the other part is purified to methane
and transported to the gas station, as well as being
applied to the existing natural gas network of Venice
and the lagoon. Gas storage units are structured by
membranes and change their shapes during the day,
dependant on the amount of gas within, swelling and
folding.

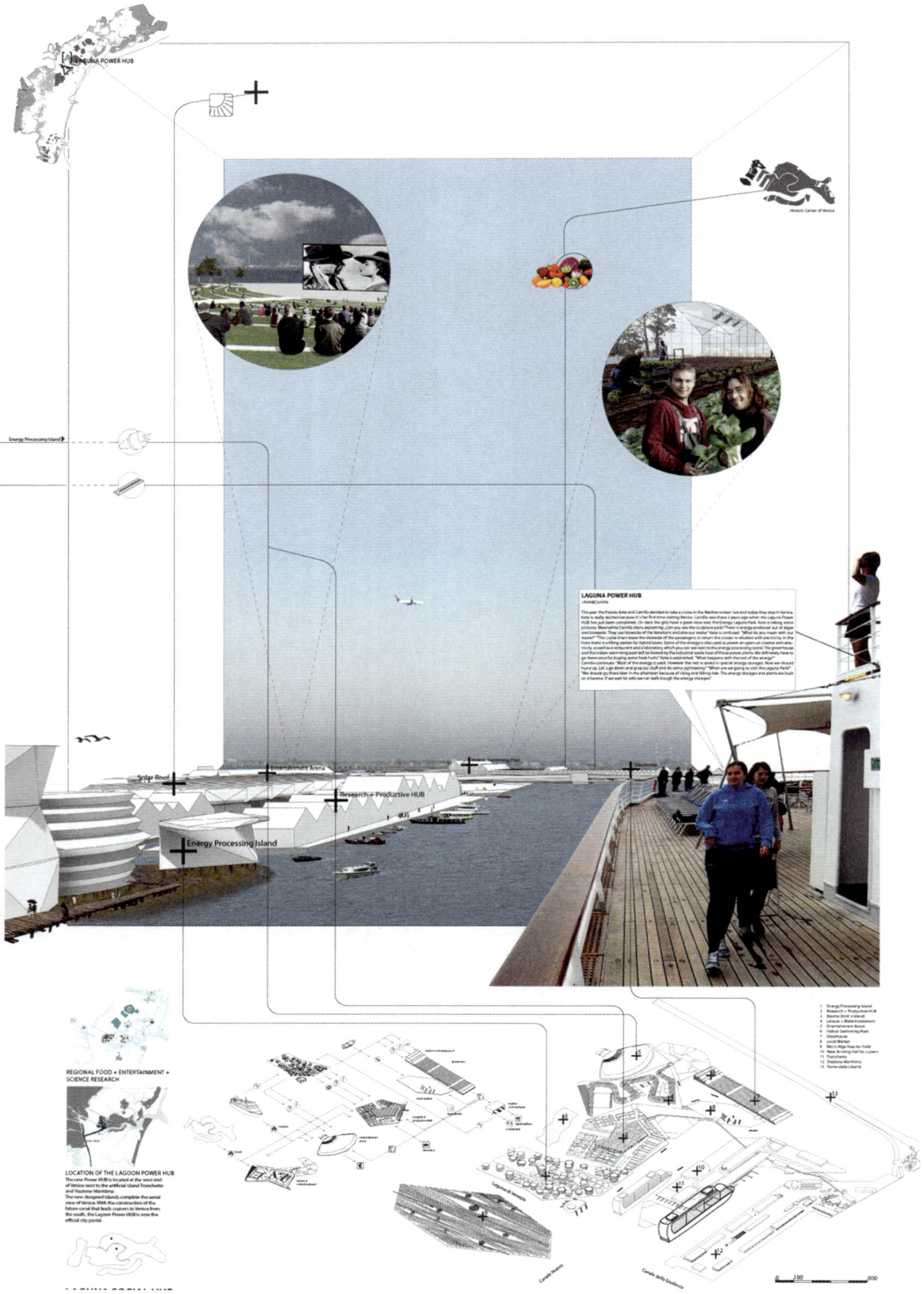

Lagoon Social Hub

The Lagoon Power Hub is a hybrid lagoon park located next to Tronchetto, an artificial island in the west of Venice's historic city centre. The differently shaped islands, linked by bridges and reachable by boat or the People Mover, offer various features: a sports island, that also works as a natural purification plant, a market island for fresh vegetables and seafood, a laboratory island for research and development, an arena for cultural events, different restaurants and bars, and a greenhouse with an indoor pool.

In the greenhouse tomatoes, cucumbers, eggplants, artichokes and herbs are cultivated, which are sold on the local market island and in a wholesale market in Tronchetto. Visitors have the possibility to visit every part of the Power Hub, even the production plants, situated on an artificial saltmarsh island. The new Laguna Park is a highly productive place exchanging energy, information and culture, and combining industry, research and entertainment with ecological benefit.

Algae Glass & Urban Farming

Murano is one of the most famous areas for producing glass. Still, the sector was struggling in the past years, with the influx of cheap glass from China as the main problem. However, energy-intensive production and unwillingness to use local raw materials are also responsible. Diatoms, a specific kind of micro algae, can be an alternative source for the required silicon. The algae is grown on the roof of the production building, and, along with other algae types, on fields in the lagoon. The production site is located in

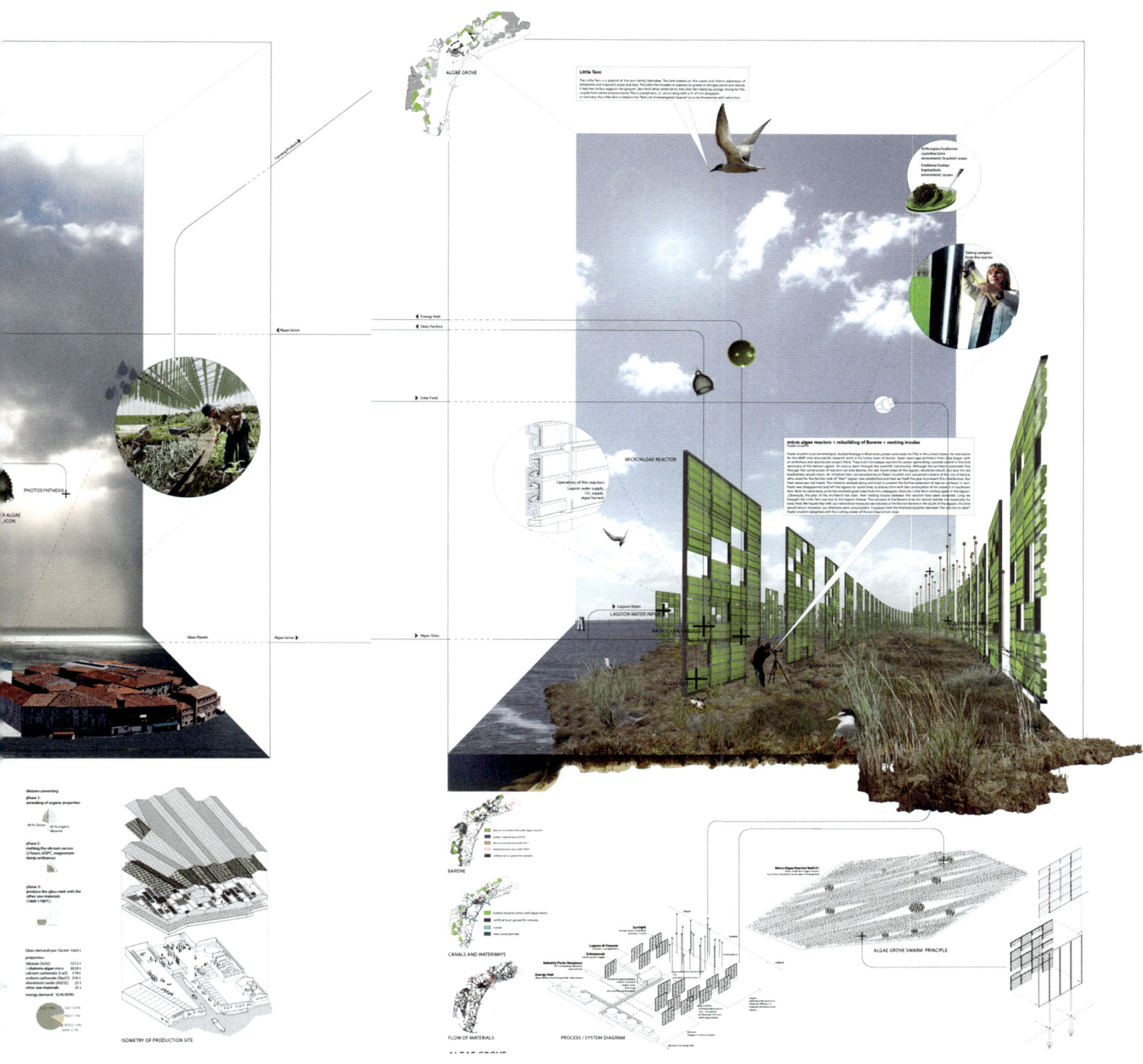

Algae Grove

...rmerly vacant halls in East Murano, also hosting
...semi-public greenhouse that provides green space
...d the possibility to plant fruits and vegetables in
...e densely built Murano. Another glass component
...at can be partially replaced by local substances is
...e. Therefore, a collecting point for conches, which
...nsist of nearly 100% lime, is set up. The required
...mount is covered by restaurants, factories and tour-
...s who visit the production site. The resulting glass
...ay be a bit dimmer, but that could become a new
...ature of Murano glass.

The backbone of the project are algae reactors
cultivating micro algae that can serve as starting materials for various processes, e.g. biomass and silicon
production. The micro algae species can be varied
in the future to also serve the production of biofuel
or hydrogen. The reactors use lagoon water and are
arranged on artificial islands in a flock pattern, with
a minimum distance to prevent obscuring, and a
maximum distance to ensure efficient land use. Before

long, these islands will have the same ecosystem as
the Barene salt marshes, which not only have a great
biodiversity, but also serve as retention areas. CO_2
is injected to increase algae growth, which is compressed in the industrial plants of Mestre and then
transported to the supply unit. The electric current for
the operation of the supply unit is generated by the
solar panels. The algae can be harvested daily and is
transported to the Power Hub regularly, where the
bio mass is processed to produce biogas or glass.

TEHRAN: GREEN MEETING BLUE

Shadi Azizi

Hamid Reza Mousavi

Alireza Delpazir

Mohammad M. Zanjanian

Shadnaz Azizi

Nima Vahedi

Arezoo Khamesi

Hesam Tavasoli

Siavash Ghorbani Jazi

Milad Heidari

Seyed Ali Chavoshian

Alireza Ghazizadeh

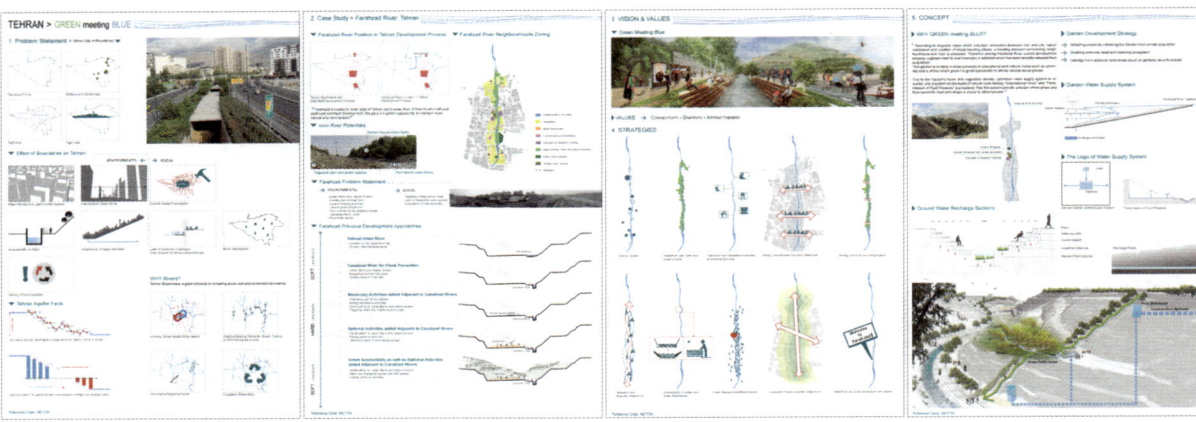

Despite being described as one of the major economic and cultural hubs in the Middle East, over the last 30 years urban policies and construction processes in Tehran have converted social and environmental fringes into boundaries. Highways directly pass through residential towns and divide the city into different socio-economical areas. Besides particular municipalities following mostly economic interests by increasing prescribed building densities, military land ownership and unregulated construction also affect the permeability of urban space. Streets, small sidewalks and high-rise residential blocks are largely without in-between open spaces.

Tehran's divided spatial organization causes social segregation of different ethnic and language groups. Lack of interactive open spaces in the public realm has increased conflict and decreased the strength of social connection: Unequally distributed park and forest areas only make up 6.5% of the urban fabric, while immethodical construction on hills serves the destruction of open green spaces. The canalization of rivers, carried out mostly for flood control purposes, not only gave rise to the omission of rivers from the ecological space of city, but has also created an impenetrable line between the communities on each side. Thus, Tehran's

seven rivers are inaccessible and play no role in the daily lives of the cities inhabitants. The last decade's urban management policies have also dramatically reduced underground water resources, so that Tehran faces severe dryness and lack of water: the underground storage water level declined by around 7% per year.

However, Tehran's rivers have a great potential for breaking sociospatial boundaries, connecting neighborhoods, restoring the ecosystem and creating meeting places for cultural and social events. The project proposes raising connectivity between, and attractiveness of, river banks on various scales ranging from local urban design to the city's overall spatial development. Design principles, understood as a combination of formal and participatory planning methods, should establish a close relation of urban fabric and water, as well as facilitate social integration of people of different age, sex, nationality and religious belief. A private green area next to Farahzad River, for example, is to be converted into a public Persian garden with extensive greening and recharge ponds to supply river water to ground water levels, and the river canal to be substituted with open terracing and flood plains for flood protection.

Obwohl Teheran als eines der wichtigsten wirtschaftlichen und kulturellen Zentren im Nahen Osten bezeichnet werden kann, haben Stadtpolitik und Bauwesen in den letzten 30 Jahren soziale und ökologische Randzonen zu Grenzen verhärtet. Autobahnen wurden direkt durch Wohngebiete gezogen und teilen die Stadt in verschiedene sozioökonomische Bereiche. Neben den einzelnen Stadtverwaltungen, die mit der Erhöhung der vorgeschriebenen Baudichte meist wirtschaftliche Interessen verfolgen, haben auch militärischer Grundbesitz und unkontrolliertes Bauen Auswirkungen auf die Durchlässigkeit des Stadtraums. Straßen, kleinere Gehwege und vielgeschossige Wohnblöcke müssen weitgehend ohne Zwischenräume und Freiflächen auskommen.

Teherans zersplitterte räumliche Organisation verursacht die soziale Segregation verschiedener ethnischer und sprachlicher Gruppen. Der Mangel an interaktivem öffentlichem Raum hat Konflikte gesteigert und sozialen Zusammenhalt verringert: Die unregelmäßig verteilten Park- und Waldflächen machen nur 6,5 % des städtischen Gefüges aus, während die unsystematische Bebauung auf den Hügeln der Stadt Grünflächen zerstört. Die Kanalisierung von Flüssen, die größtenteils zum Zwecke des Hochwasserschutzes durchgeführt wurde, führte nicht nur dazu, dass die Flüsse vom ökologischen Gefüge der Stadt abgeschnitten wurden, sondern hat auch eine unüberbrückbare Grenze zwischen den Bezirken an jeder Seite geschaffen. Die sie-

ben kanalisierten Flüsse Teherans sind für die Stadtbewohner unzugänglich und spielen keine Rolle im alltäglichen Leben. Im letzten Jahrzehnt hat diese Stadtplanungspolitik auch die unterirdischen Wasserressourcen dramatisch verringert, sodass Teheran heute mit Trockenheit und ständigem Wassermangel konfrontiert ist: Der Grundwasserspiegel ist jährlich um ca. 7 % abgesunken.

Teherans Flüsse haben aber ein großes Potenzial, sozialräumliche Grenzen aufzubrechen, Stadtteile zu verbinden, Ökosysteme wiederherzustellen und Treffpunkte für kulturelle und gesellschaftliche Veranstaltungen bereitzustellen. Das Projekt schlägt vor, die Konnektivität zwischen und die Attraktivität von Flussufern auf mehreren Maßstabsebenen auszubauen, ausgehend von lokaler Stadtgestaltung bis hin zu der gesamten städtischen Entwicklung. Entwurfsprinzipien, verstanden als eine Kombination von formalen und partizipativen Planungsmethoden, sollten eine enge Beziehung zwischen städtischen Gefügen und Wasser herstellen und die soziale Integration von Menschen unterschiedlichen Alters, Geschlechts und unterschiedlicher Nationalität und Religion erleichtern. Eine private Grünfläche neben dem Fluss Farahzad wird beispielsweise in einen öffentlichen persischen Garten mit umfangreicher Begrünung und Teichen zur Grundwasseranreicherung umgestaltet und der Flusskanal mit offener Terrassierung und Überflutungsflächen zum Hochwasserschutz ersetzt.

Effect of Boundaries on Tehran

ENVIRONMENTAL ← → SOCIAL

Mass Intensity and Lack of Green Spaces

Impermeable Urban Fronts

Divided Spatial Organization

BOOM_I

Inaccessibility to Water

Unbalanced Underground Water

Lack of Interactive in-between Open Spaces for Various Social Groups

Tehran Aquiifer Facts

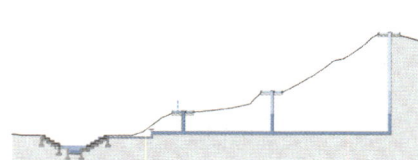

"Six meter drop of water table is observed from 1994 to 2014 in Tehran"

1850 MCM
1710 MCM
1570 MCM
1430 MCM

Extracted Unrenewable Water

Extracted Renewable Water

-810 MCM
-950 MCM

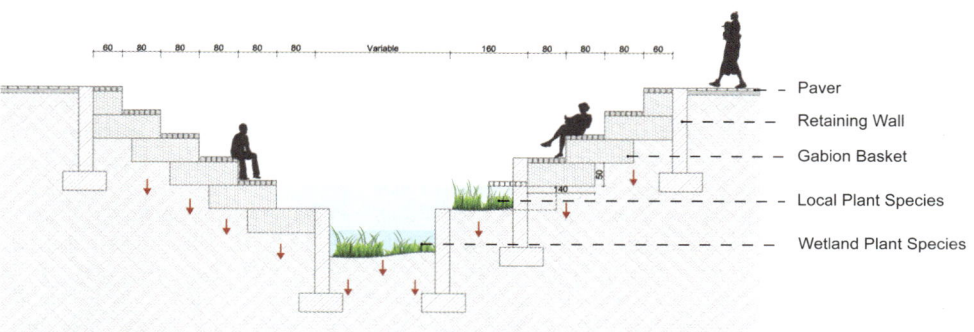

| Paver |
| Retaining Wall |
| Gabion Basket |
| Local Plant Species |
| Wetland Plant Species |

Persian Garden Terracing

Transmission of Fluid Pressure

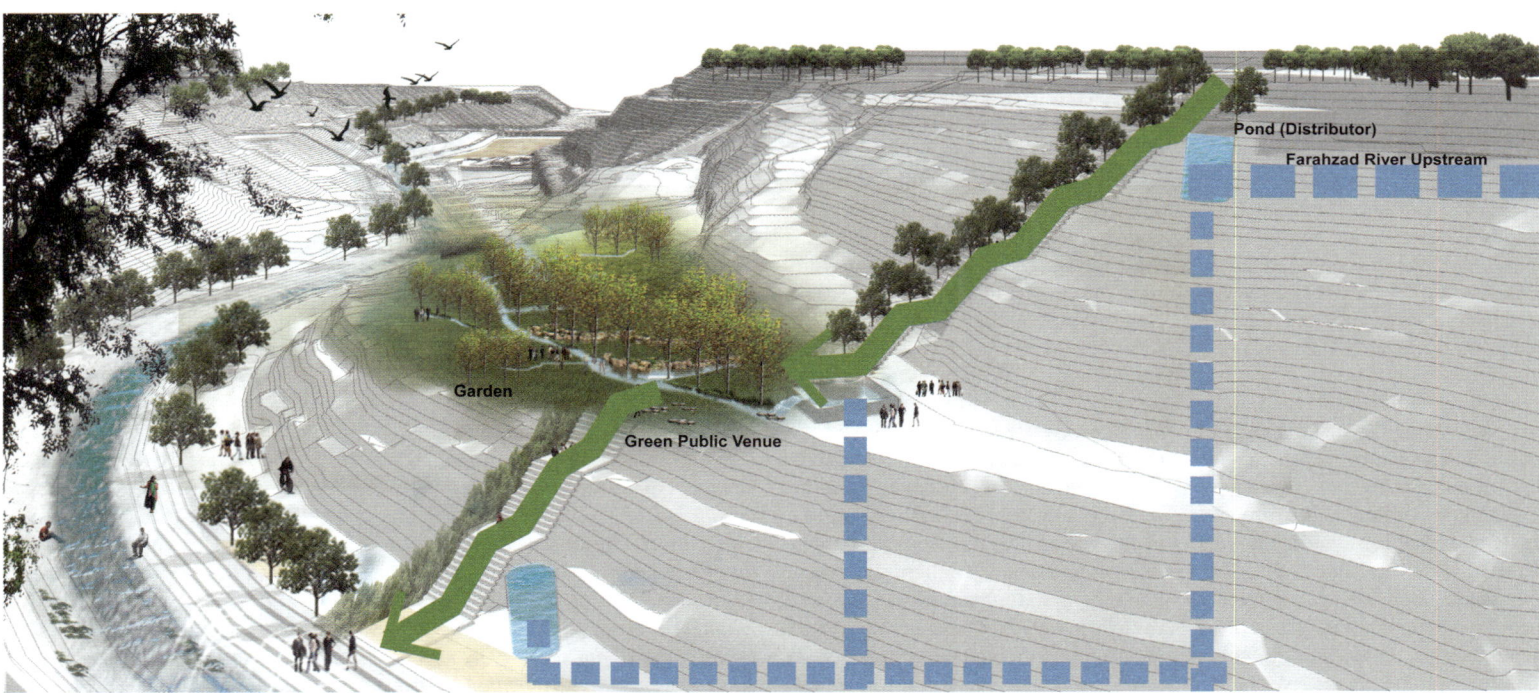

Pond (Distributor)

Farahzad River Upstream

Garden

Green Public Venue

Ground Water Recharge System showing recharge points and underground distribution

Green meeting Blue

195

ECOLOGY WITHOUT NATURE

Ariadna Weisshaar, Simranjit Kaur

Floodplains and Rivers in Europe

European landscapes are often the product of technocratic regulations and strong human engineering intervention. Control over rivers is essential for human habitation and economy. Human settlements along the rivers either manipulate existing natural high points in the terrain or, by means of dykes and dams, protect the lower land. Dykes and dams are also essential for both the use and diversion of river water for the purpose of irrigation. The need for inland navigation in Europe has been the main motive to manipulate the river form and to straighten it. This reduces the river length and volume to contain water during extreme flooding. Consolidation of extensive farming in the floodplains of Europe have led to the disappearance of physical elements that gave the land its legibility and dynamic system of movement, change and regulation.

Recent flooding events in Europe are an outcome of the insufficiency of structural flood control measures such as increased channel cross-sections, the construction of flood embankments, straightening channels, and removing vegetation to create flood diversion channels and flood storage reservoirs. Pioneering within new methods of flood prevention is the Dutch policy "room for the river" or "letting the river be".

The understanding of a landscape should begin with the understanding of its geomorphological aspects and the natural processes of land formation that are constantly changing its natural shape over different times and scales. The point is not to imitate forms found in nature, but to understand how to work with the natural processes and forces that are constantly shaping the landscape. If nature shapes the land, then human intervention should take into account those natural forces by viewing them not as a threat, but as a tool to achieve a new urban and landscape design approach.

Shrinkage in Saxony-Anhalt, Germany

The project focuses on the river Saale, a tributary of the river Elbe, and the city of Halle in the region of Saxony-Anhalt, Germany. This region was famous as a chemical triangle, including the cities of Halle, Bitterfeld and Leipzig. Until the 1990s, it was a landscape of open lignite mines and polluted rivers. The area faced massive deindustrialization after the German reunification, with most of the industries unable to withstand the competition of an open market. Hence it suffered manifold: deindustrialization, suburbanization, demographic ageing and unfavorable economic reforms.

Recently, various incentives of regeneration have been targeted with the prime aim of providing specific "service industries" to each of the city in the region ranging from education, tourism and health to alternate energy. Ecology and tourism landscapes are being advocated, open mines converted to lakes and floodplains restored. All towns around the region are independently trying to consolidate and extend their economies. Internally, having faced urban shrinkage, the city of Halle has specific areas that face major vacancy; mainly prefab housing sectors and industrial plots. Housing formerly inhabited by chemical factory workers and professionals lies majorly vacant as detached housing is preferred.

Überflutungsflächen und Flüsse in Europa

Europäische Landschaften sind häufig das Ergebnis technokratischer Regulierungen und massiver technischer Eingriffe von Menschenhand. Die Kontrolle über die Flüsse ist eine unabdingbare Voraussetzung für die Habitation und die Wirtschaft der Menschen. Ansiedlungen entlang der Flüsse nutzen entweder natürliche Hochpunkte des Terrains oder schützen das tiefer gelegene Land mittels Deichen und Dämmen. Letztere sind ebenfalls unabdingbar für die Nutzung und die Umleitung des Flusswassers zum Zwecke der Bewässerung. Die Erfordernisse der europäischen Binnenschifffahrt sind der Hauptgrund für die bauliche Umgestaltung und Begradigung von Flüssen. Das reduziert die Länge der Flüsse und deren Kapazität, Wassermengen bei extremen Überschwemmungen aufzunehmen. Der Ausbau der extensiven landwirtschaftlichen Nutzung der europäischen Überflutungsflächen hat zum Verschwinden jener physischen Elemente geführt, die dem Land nicht nur seine Erkennbarkeit verliehen haben, sondern auch sein System der Bewegung, der Veränderung und der Regulierung.

Die jüngsten Überschwemmungsereignisse in Europa sind ein Resultat der Unzulänglichkeit der baulichen Hochwasserschutzmaßnahmen (Vergrößerung des Flussbettquerschnitts, Bau von Hochwasserdeichen, Begradigung des Flussbetts, Entfernung der Vegetation, Bau von Hochwasserumleitungskanälen und Rückhaltebecken). Pionierarbeit auf dem Gebiet der Überschwemmungsprävention leisten derzeit die Niederlande mit ihrer Politik des "dem Fluss Raum geben" oder "den Fluss in Ruhe lassen".

Das Verstehen einer Landschaft sollte beginnen mit dem Verstehen ihrer geomorphologischen Aspekte und der natürlichen Prozesse der Landformung, die die natürliche Gestalt der Landschaft unaufhörlich verändern, zu unterschiedlichen Zeiten und in unterschiedlichen Größenordnungen. Es geht nicht darum, die in der Natur vorgefundenen Formen zu imitieren, sondern darum zu verstehen, wie man mit den natürlichen Prozessen und Kräften arbeiten kann, die die Landschaft ununterbrochen formen. Wenn die Natur das Land formt, dann sollten die Eingriffe des Menschen diesen natürlichen Kräften Rechnung tragen und sie nicht als eine Bedrohung sehen, sondern als ein Werkzeug, mit dessen Hilfe man einen neuartigen Ansatz für städtische und landschaftliche Entwürfe entwickeln kann.

Schrumpfung in Sachsen-Anhalt

Das Projekt konzentriert sich auf den Fluss Saale, einen Nebenfluss der Elbe, und auf die Stadt Halle in der Region Sachsen-Anhalt. Diese Region, einschließlich der Städte Halle, Bitterfeld und Leipzig, war als "chemisches Dreieck" berühmt. Bis in die 1990er Jahre war das eine Landschaft aus Braunkohletagen und verunreinigten Flüssen. Die Region erlebte nach der Wiedervereinigung eine massive Deindustrialisierung, da die Mehrzahl der dort ansässigen Industrien auf dem freien Markt nicht konkurrenzfähig war. Und so litt diese Region gleich in mehrfacher Hinsicht: Deindustrialisierung, Zersiedelung, demografische Überalterung sowie unvorteilhafte Wirtschaftsreformen.

In jüngster Zeit sind diverse Anreize zu einer wirtschaftlichen Wiederbelebung geschaffen worden, die in erster Linie darauf abzielen, jede Stadt in der Region mit besonderen "Service-Industrien" zu versehen, die von Bildung und Tourismus bis zu Gesundheitsvorsorge und alternativen Energien reichen. Man befürwortet eine weitläufige Landschaft aus Ökologie und Tourismus; die Tagebaue werden in Seen verwandelt, und die Überflutungsflächen werden wiederhergestellt. Alle Städte in der Region versuchen im Alleingang, ihre Wirtschaft zu konsolidieren und auszubauen. Da Halle mit Schrumpfung konfrontiert wurde, gibt es im Innern der Stadt bestimmte Areale, die mehr oder weniger unbewohnt sind, vor allem Plattenbausiedlungen und Industriestätten. Wohnkomplexe, die früher von Arbeitern aus den Chemiefabriken und von Angehörigen freier Berufe bewohnt wurden, stehen überwiegend leer, da heute Einfamilienhäuser bevorzugt werden.

Design Proposal for Halle

The project investigates how two parallel processes, economic and ecological, stand to reinform each other. Within the framework of "ecology without nature", the river form and process is used as a tool to redefine urbanity. In Saxony-Anhalt, shrinkage and the state policy of urban restructuring – demolition – is speculated to create a fragmented city, an archipelago of settlements. This fragmented city could be mediated through the use of the river to create new territories, with their uses changing over time. It is investigated whether the vacant land of shrinking cities in floodplain areas can be put to a new use; helping the local economy and mitigating the problem of flooding. The redundant prefab housing is mostly situated to the left bank of the River Saale: an often flooded, low lying area. Hence the left bank becomes the project site for flooding and the creation of a land form that can be put to use of inundation, water storage and agriculture. One option is the use of these vacant containments as agricultural fields, willing to bear the risk of flooding in the time of extreme flooding. The creation of inundation zones and stable non-floodable islands for the construction of infrastructure is based on the degrowth pattern of the city and the surrounding region. Hence, the design of such land pockets is closely tied to the manipulation of the river form.

In the design process, river dynamics in the floodplain areas and the spatial structures formed by both natural forces and man-made interventions are examined. In the specific case of River Elbe and its tributary Saale, two kinds of river channel systems are observed: meandering and anastomosing. The former creates oxbow lakes while the latter creates islands. The design intervention seeks to create floodable zones in vacant floodplains areas of the shrinking cities by utilizing natural forms in the search for new economic uses.

Entwurfsvorschlag für Halle

Wir untersuchen, wie zwei parallele Prozesse ökonomisch und ökologisch zu einander stehen, um sich gegenseitig zu beeinflussen. Innerhalb eines Rahmens aus einer Ökologie ohne Natur werden Form und Verlauf des Flusses als ein Werkzeug benutzt, mit dem sich Urbanität bestimmen und neu definieren lässt. Schrumpfung und die staatliche Politik der städtischen Umstrukturierung (Abriss) soll angeblich eine fragmentierte Stadt erschaffen, einen Archipel von Ansiedlungen. Diese fragmentierte Form wird durch eine Nutzung des Flusses vermittelt, die darauf hinausläuft, dass neue Territorien erschaffen werden, deren Nutzung sich im Laufe der Zeit verändert. Unsere Untersuchung will herausfinden, ob das unbewohnte Land auf den Überflutungsflächen der schrumpfenden Städte einer neuen Nutzung zugeführt werden kann, die der örtlichen Wirtschaft hilft und gleichzeitig das Überschwemmungsproblem mildert. Die leerstehenden Plattenbauareale befinden sich hauptsächlich am linken Ufer der Saale, das ein häufig überschwemmtes, tief gelegenes Stück Land ist. Daher wird das unbewohnte Areal am linken Flussufer im Projekt als Gebiet für Überschwemmungen ausgewiesen und für die Erschaffung von Landformen, welche für Überflu-tung, Wasserspeicherung und landwirtschaftliche Zwecke genutzt werden können. Eine der Optionen besteht in der Nutzung dieser Eindämmungen als landwirtschaftliche Flächen, bei denen man es in Kauf nimmt, dass sie zu Zeiten extremen Hochwassers überschwemmt werden. Die Einrichtung von Überflutungszonen und stabiler nicht überschwemmbarer Inseln für die Schaffung einer "umstrukturierten und reduzierten" Infrastruktur basiert auf dem degressiven Wachstumsmuster der Stadt und der umliegenden Region. Von daher ist der Entwurf von solchen Landeinschlüssen eng mit der Umgestaltung des Flussverlaufs verbunden.

Im Entwurfsprozess werden die Dynamik des Flusses in den Überflutungsflächen und die räumlichen Strukturen, die durch die natürlichen Prozesse und durch Eingriffe des Menschen geformt werden, untersucht. Im spezifischen Fall der Elbe und ihres Nebenflusses Saale lassen sich zwei Arten von Flussbettsystemen beobachten: mäandernde und anastomosisierende. Erstere erzeugen Gewässer mit U-förmigen Schleifen, während letztere Inseln entstehen lassen. Der geplante Entwurf versucht in den unbewohnten Arealen der schrumpfenden Stadt Überflutungsflächen zu schaffen und dafür natürliche Formen für neue/zusätzliche wirtschaftliche Nutzungen heranzuziehen.

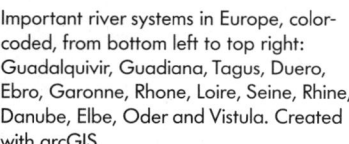

Important river systems in Europe, color-coded, from bottom left to top right: Guadalquivir, Guadiana, Tagus, Duero, Ebro, Garonne, Rhone, Loire, Seine, Rhine, Danube, Elbe, Oder and Vistula. Created with arcGIS.

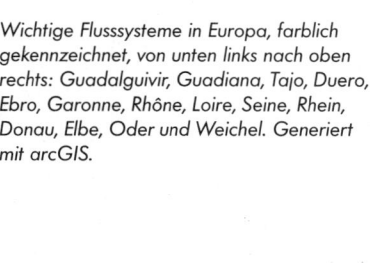

Wichtige Flusssysteme in Europa, farblich gekennzeichnet, von unten links nach oben rechts: Guadalguivir, Guadiana, Tajo, Duero, Ebro, Garonne, Rhône, Loire, Seine, Rhein, Donau, Elbe, Oder und Weichel. Generiert mit arcGIS.

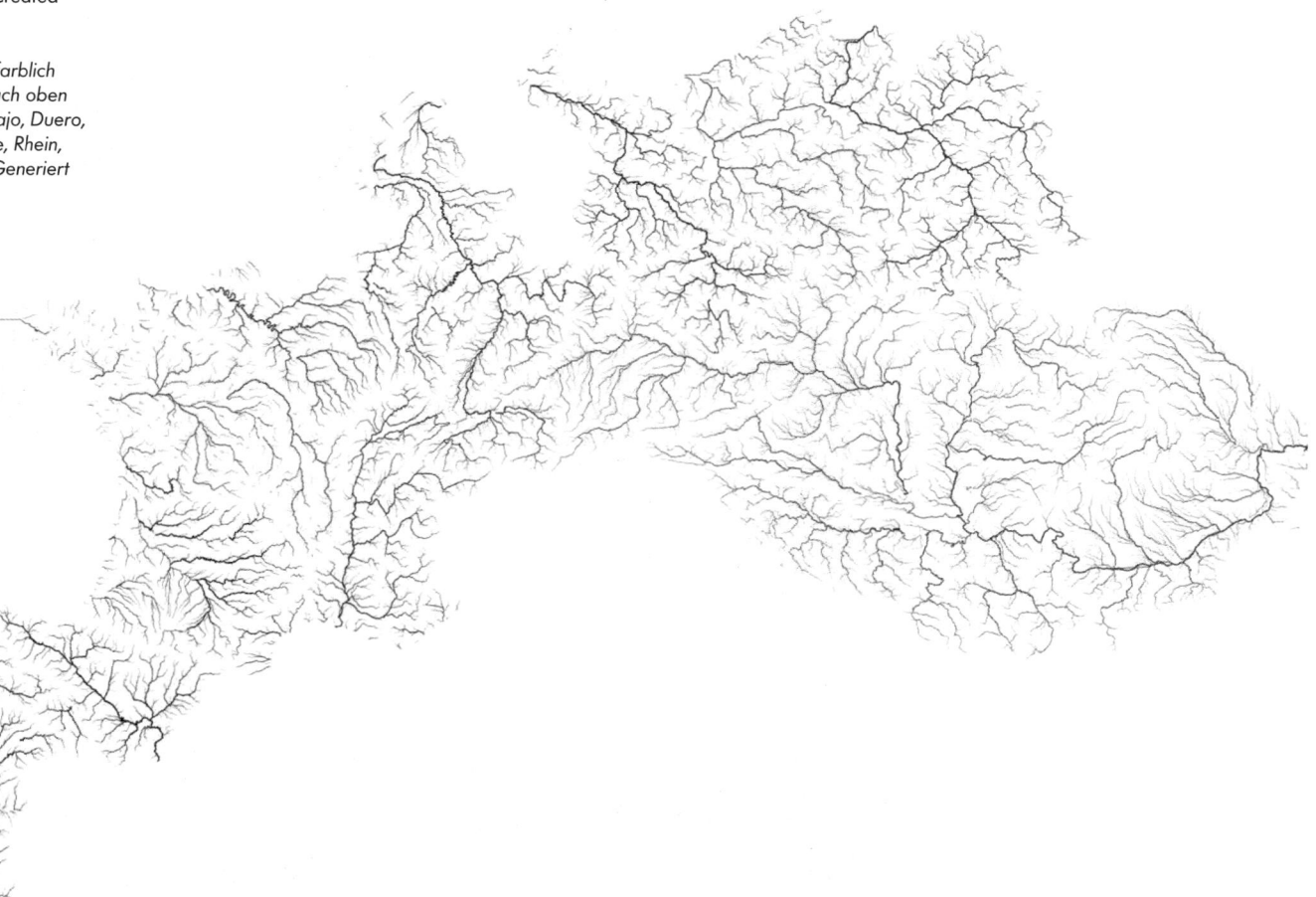

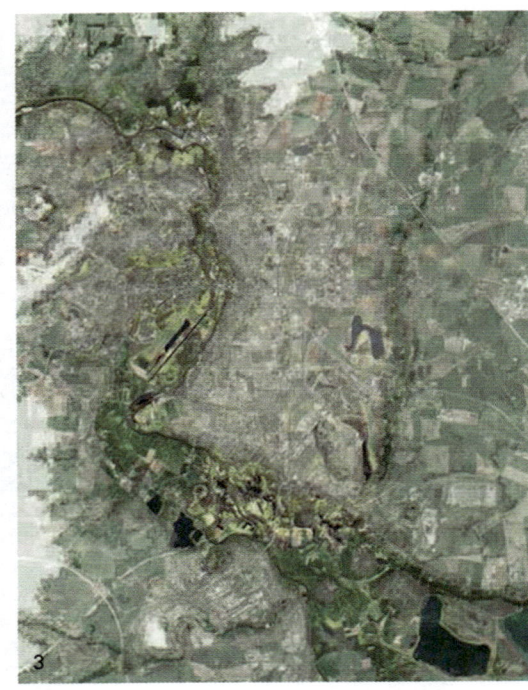

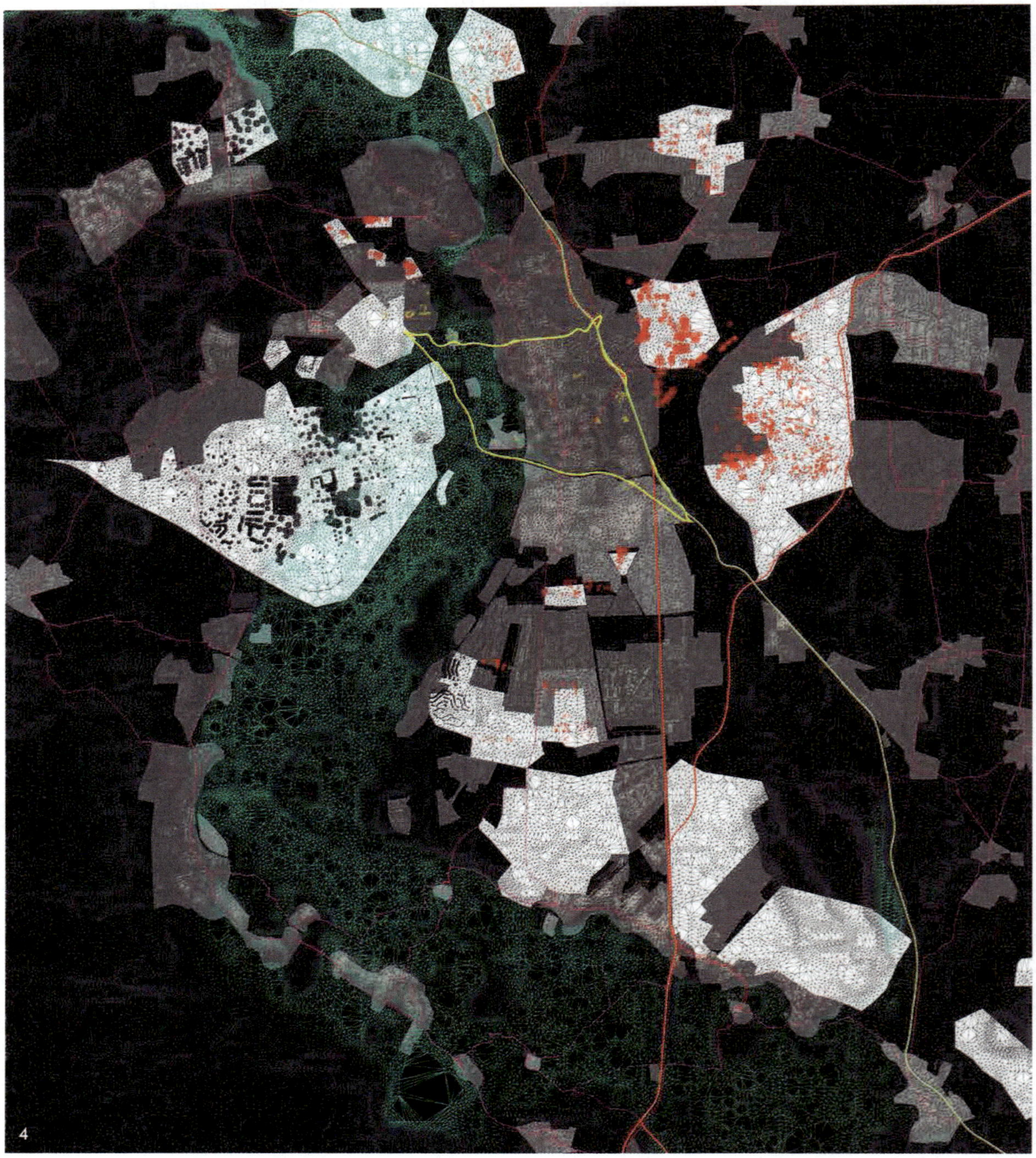

1. Network analysis of Halle including street network (red), building structure (grey) and potential inner city green spaces (green). Institutional (yellow), commercial (orange) and tourism routes (green) are marked as main infrastructural axes and are to be taken into consideration during the planning process. The inner city core, ca. 5 km wide, is marked as a dashed line.

2. Inner city vacancy (white) is resulting from shrinkage processes in the city of Halle. Three vacant areas within the floodplain area are marked with green dots.

3. Overlay of topographic floodplain data (green) with historical data of a 200-year-flooding (blue).

4. Overlay of 1 – 3. Regarding the three earlier defined vacant areas within the floodplain, there is the possibility of renaturation into potential flooding areas.

5. Floodplain and contours overlay (using arcGIS)

1. Netzwerkanalyse von Halle mit Straßennetz (rot), Bebauungsstruktur (grau) und potenziellen innerstädtischen Grünflächen (grün). Institutions- (gelb), Kommerz- (orange) und Tourismusrouten (grün) sind als Hauptverkehrsachsen gekennzeichnet und sollen im Planungsprozess berücksichtigt werden. Der ca. 5 km breite innerstädtische Kernbereich ist mit gestrichelter Linie gekennzeichnet.

2. Innerstädtischer Leerstand (weiß) ist das Resultat von Schrumpfungsprozessen in Halle. Drei Leerstandsflächen, welche sich innerhalb des Überflutungsgebietes befinden, sind mit einem grünen Punkt gekennzeichnet.

3. Überlagerung von topografischen Daten des Flussbettes (grün) mit historischen Daten einer 200-Jahres-Flut (blau).

4. Überlagerung von 1 – 3. Bei den drei zuvor identifizieren Lehrstandsflächen innerhalb des Überflutungsgebietes besteht die Möglichkeit des Rückbaus, um sie als potenzielle Flutungszonen zu renaturieren.

5. Überlagerung von Überflutungsflächen und Flusskonturen (nach arcGIS)

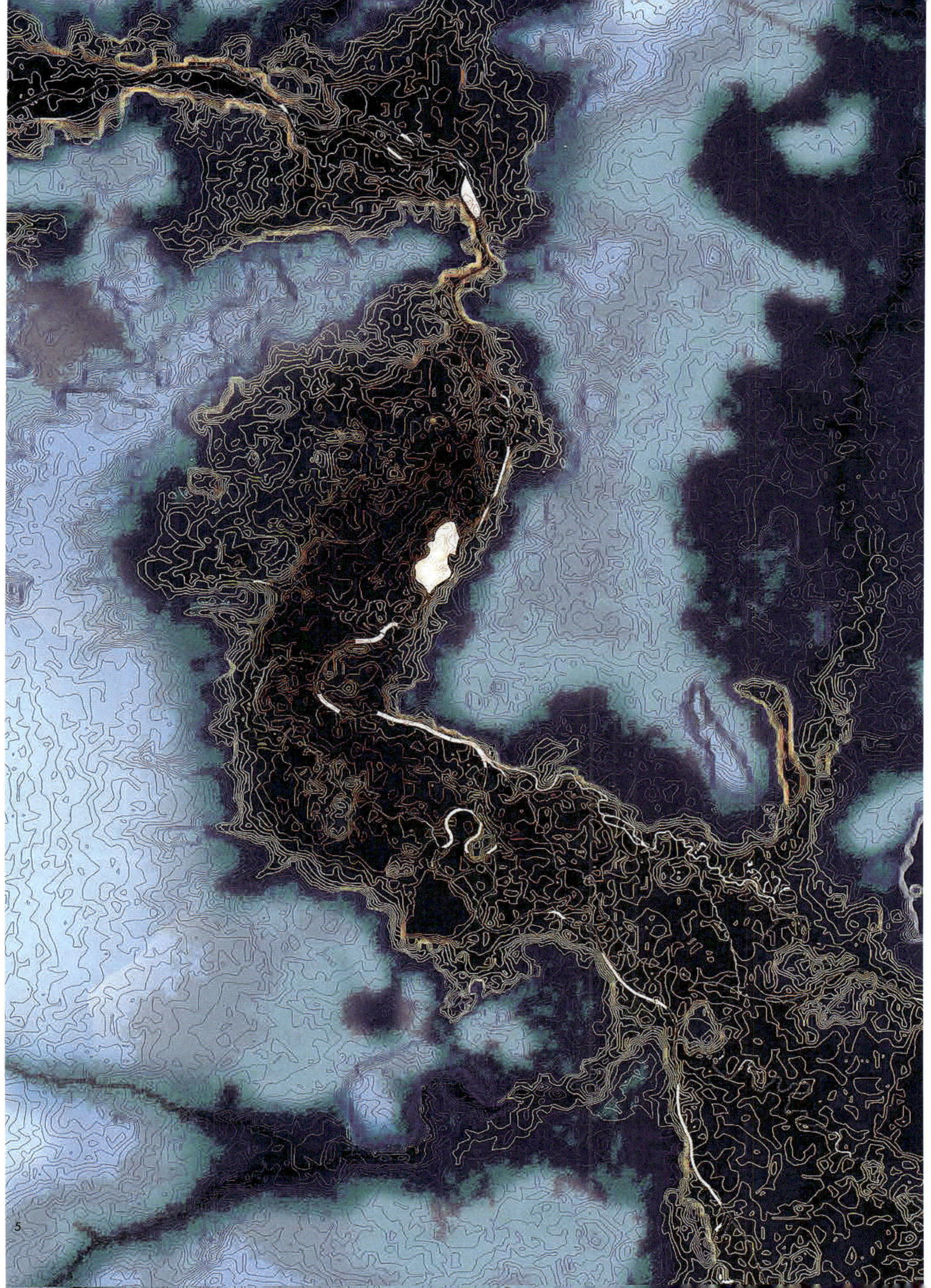

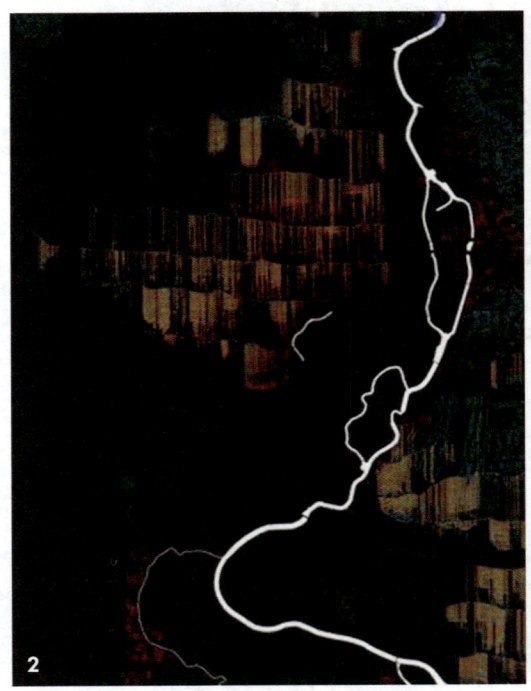

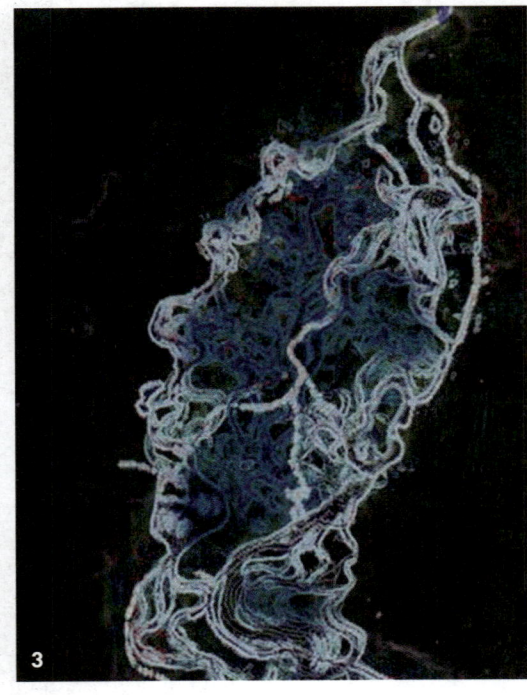

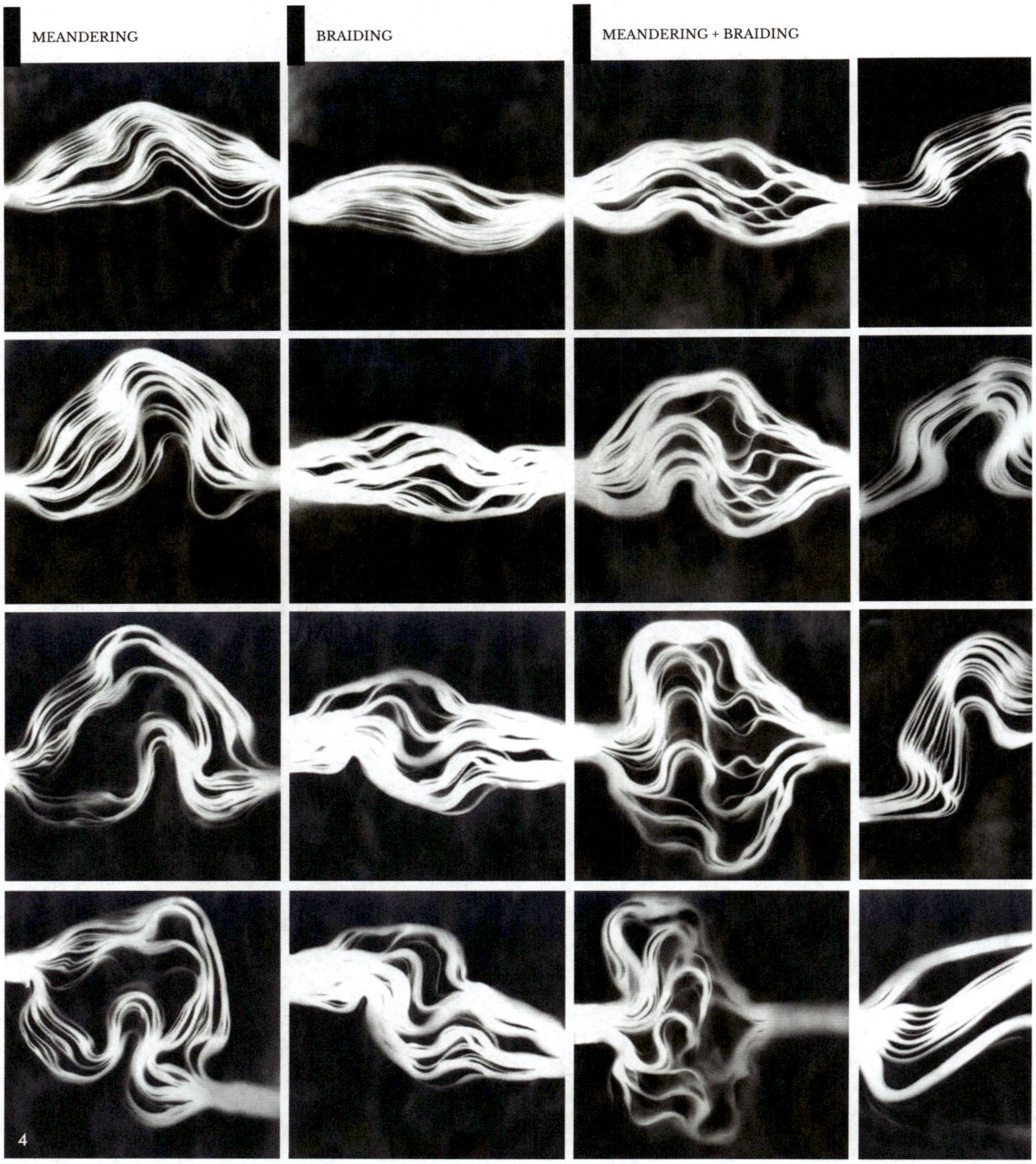

1. Depiction of the building structure (red) and areas of water (blue-green) in the city of Halle. The flooding area of the river Saale is analysed through terrain sections.

2. Depiction of the inner city vacancy's density (yellow) in close proximity to the river Saale (white).

3. Prognosis of the flood plain area in case of a 200-year-flood, incorporating a conscious modelling of surfaces. Non-sloping cavities within the flood plain area are forming collection points for water and sediment. Such cavities can be used to manipulate the river course with little effort.

4. Three models forms, chosen to affect change in the floodplain:
– more capability of storing water
– keep certain infrastructure zones free of flooding
– convert vacant areas into agriculture and inundation zones.

5. Overlay of 1 and 2. A potential flooding scenario in case of the conscious modelling of surfaces (white), taking account of the earlier identified vacancy areas (red).

1. Darstellung der Gebäudestruktur (rot) und Wasserflächen (blaugrün) in der Stadt Halle. Das Überflutungsgebiet der Saale wird anhand von Geländeschnitten analysiert (braun).

2. Darstellung der Dichte von innerstädtischem Leerstand (gelb) nahe der Saale (weiß).

3. Prognose des Überflutungsgebietes bei einer 200-Jahres-Flut im Falle einer bewussten Flächenmodellierung. Steigungsfreie Hohlräume innerhalb des Überflutungsgebietes bilden Sammelstellen für Wasser und Sediment. Mit nur geringem Aufwand können solche Hohlräume genutzt werden, um den Flusslauf zu manipulieren.

4. Drei Modellstudien der Steuerung von Überflutung:
– mehr Wasseraufnahmekapazität
– überflutungsfreie Infrastrukturzonen
– freie Zonen für Landwirtschaft und Überflutung.

5. Überlagerung von 1 und 2. Mögliches Überflutungsszenario im Falle einer bewussten Flächenmodellierung (weiß) unter Berücksichtigung der zuvor identifizierten Leerstandsflächen (rot).

MEANDERING   BRAIDING   MEANDERING + BRAIDING

5   HALLE: CARTOGENESIS-CHANNEL MULTIPLICATION

ABOUT MIGRATING SPECIES AND HUMAN HAPPINESS

Jasmin Honold, Myriel Milicevic, Leonie Fischer

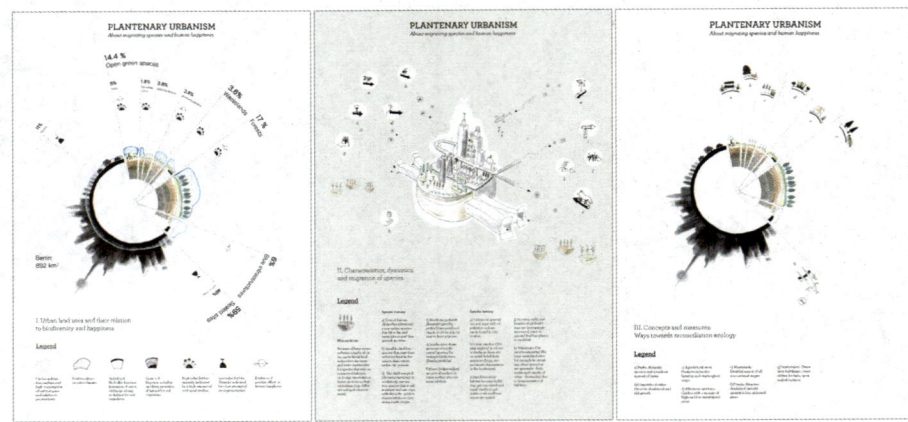

Together with the human population, urban areas are growing worldwide – in dimensions barely conceivable: China alone has used more cement between 2011 and 2013 than the US in the entire 20th century.[1] In Germany, each day about 73 hectares of unsealed surface are transformed into mostly impervious, built-up areas, which is a lot more than the 2020 aim of 30 hectares of daily land consumption.[2] This surface sealing destroys or fragments habitats of diverse animal and plant species, and even entire ecosystems. Thus, urbanisation causes a general decline in biodiversity, for example, of rare and endemic species. Besides climate change, the loss of biodiversity is understood to be the biggest ecological catastrophe of the present: Even though quantitative estimations must be treated with care, 20 species may become extinct each day.[3]

The urban densification poses risks to the physical and mental health of us humans, particularly by causing stress-related illnesses. However, staying in, or views of vegetated urban areas can reduce stress and thus, improve city residents' health. Here, a high diversity in vegetation may be especially beneficial for human well-being.[4] Although many native moisture-loving species migrate or become extinct within cities, other native species, e.g. dry grassland species on former demolition sites, as well as Mediterranean species that rely

on higher temperatures may profit.[5] Thus, the urban habitat provides potentials for biodiversity that should not be underestimated:

a) Traffic areas or their edges such as road verges may offer habitat for specialised species (e.g. thrift seapink, Armeria maritima). Vegetated facades and roofs can function similarly and can also provide habitat for insects and birds.

b) Traditional parks offer high restoration potential and high urban biodiversity: For example, the potential of very old trees as a habitat for rare species such as the Great Capricorn beetle (Cerambyx cerdo) was determined. Some meadows that are mown only once or twice a year can even possess a legal conservation status due to their special species composition. Patches with old-growth and dying trees as well as dead wood should be left in wooded areas of parks.

c) Allotment gardens are estimated richer in species if a mosaic of high- and low-maintenance areas exists. Moreover, views of or gardening in allotment gardens can be beneficial to health and foster social networks.

d) In some typical urban land uses (e.g. residential developments), a lot can be achieved by simple measures, e.g. the conservation of habitat for bats by keeping open small cracks in roof beams.

Weltweit wachsen mit der Bevölkerung die städtischen Gebiete – in fast unvorstellbaren Ausmaßen: China hat allein zwischen 2011 und 2013 mehr Zement verbraucht als die USA im gesamten 20. Jahrhundert.[1] In Deutschland werden täglich noch immer ca. 73 Hektar unversiegelter Boden in eine meist bebaute Fläche umgewandelt, also weit mehr als der für das Jahr 2020 anvisierte Flächenverbrauch von 30 Hektar täglich.[2] Dabei werden die Lebensräume zahlreicher Tier- und Pflanzenarten zerstört oder fragmentiert, sodass sie nicht mehr als intakte Ökosysteme funktionieren können. Die Urbanisierung führt daher zu einem generellen Rückgang der Biodiversität seltener oder einheimischer Arten. Biodiversitätsverlust gilt neben dem Klimawandel als größte ökologische Katastrophe der Gegenwart: Wenngleich quantitative Schätzungen schwierig sind, muss global mit einem Verlust von 20 Arten täglich gerechnet werden.[3]

Diese Umweltbedingungen gefährden auch die körperliche und psychische Gesundheit von uns Menschen, insbesondere durch stressbezogene Erkrankungen. Der Aufenthalt in oder der Blick auf begrünte Umgebungen kann aber innerhalb urbaner Gebiete Stress reduzieren und so die Gesundheit von Stadtbewohnern fördern. Dabei scheint insbesondere eine hohe Artenvielfalt vorteilhaft zu sein.[4] Auch wenn viele feuchtigkeitsliebende einheimische Arten aus Städten abwandern oder dort aussterben, profitieren sowohl andere

einheimische Arten, z.B. Trockenrasenarten auf ehemaligen Abrissflächen, als auch mediterrane Arten, die auf höhere Temperaturen angewiesen sind.[5] Somit bieten städtische Lebensräume ein nicht zu unterschätzendes Potenzial für Biodiversität:

a) Verkehrswege und ihre Ränder können Lebensraum für spezialisierte Arten bieten (z.B. Strand-Grasnelke, Armeria maritima). Diese Funktion kann auch die Begrünung von Fassaden und Dächern erfüllen, die zudem etwa Insekten und Vögeln Lebensraum gibt.

b) Traditionelle Parkanlagen bieten starkes Erholungspotential und eine hohe urbane Biodiversität: Das Potenzial sehr alter Baumbestände als Lebensraum für seltene Arten wie den Heldbock (Cerambyx cerdo) wurde bestätigt. Selten im Jahr gemähte Wiesen genießen teilweise sogar gesetzlichen Schutzstatus aufgrund ihrer besonderen Artenzusammensetzung. Alte und absterbende Gehölze sowie Biotopholz sollten im Bestand belassen werden.

c) Kleingärten werden als artenreicher eingeschätzt, wenn ein kleinflächiges Mosaik von gepflegten und wilderen Bereichen besteht. Zudem kann die gärtnerische Aktivität in Gartenanlagen Gesundheit und Sozialleben fördern.

d) In typisch städtischen Flächennutzungen (z.B. Wohnbebauung) kann durch einfache Maßnahmen viel erreicht werden, beispielsweise mit dem Erhalt von Lebensräumen für Fledermäuse durch Offenhalten kleiner Ritzen und Spalten im Dachgebälk.

PLANTENARY URBANISM
About migrating species and human happiness

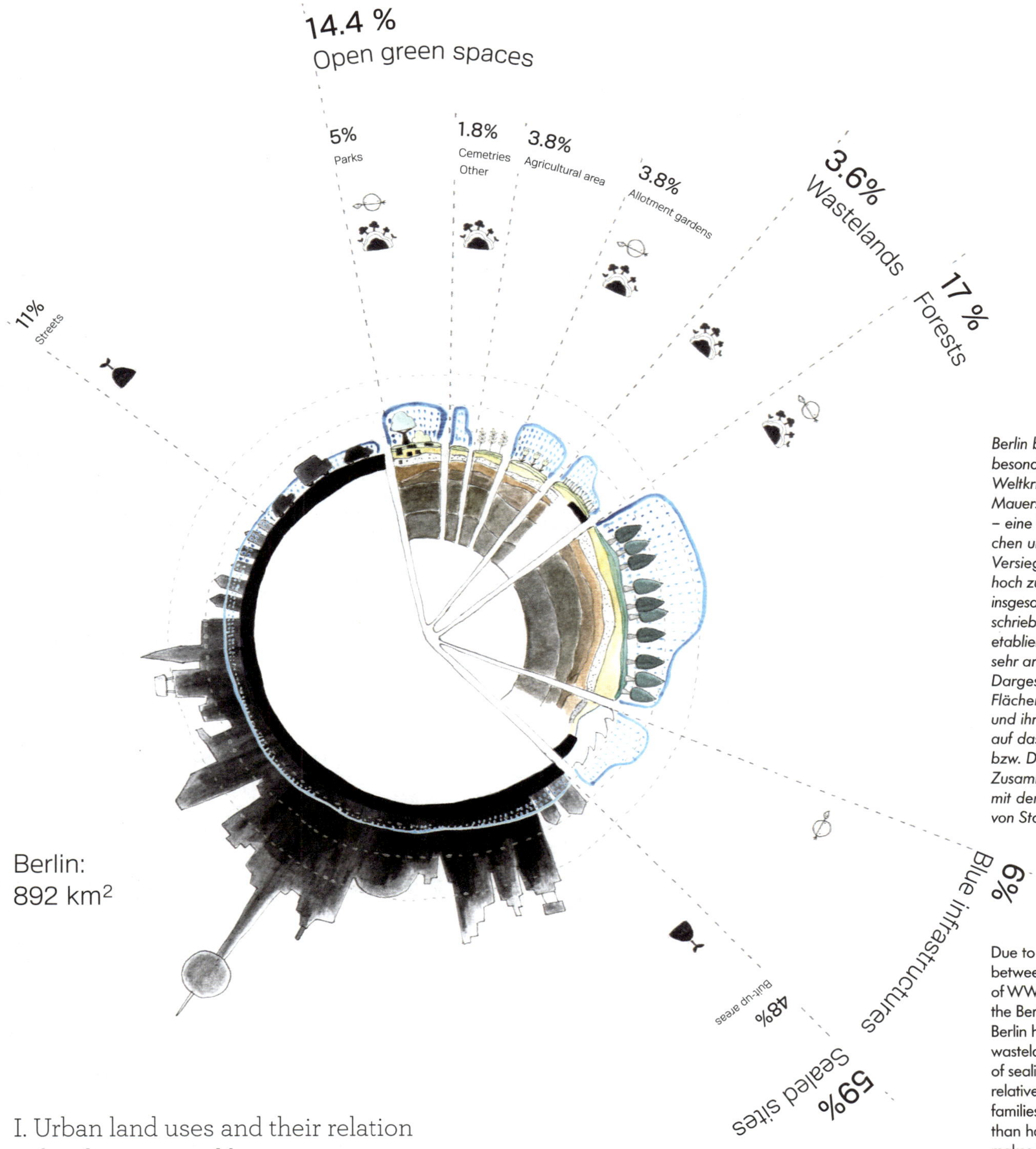

14.4 %
Open green spaces

5%
Parks

1.8%
Cemetries
Other

3.8%
Agricultural area

3.8%
Allotment gardens

3.6%
Wastelands

17 %
Forests

11%
Streets

3.6%

Berlin:
892 km²

Berlin besitzt durch seine Geschichte – insbesondere durch Baulücken aus dem Zweiten Weltkrieg und den lange Zeit unbebauten Mauerstreifen nach der deutschen Trennung – eine Vielzahl unterschiedlicher Grünflächen und Brachen. Dennoch ist der aktuelle Versiegelungsgrad um 35 % als relativ hoch zu bewerten.[6] Im Jahr 2014 werden insgesamt 2445 Pflanzensippen für Berlin beschrieben, von denen mehr als die Hälfte als etabliert gilt – demnach kann Berlin als eine sehr artenreiche Stadt eingestuft werden.[7] Dargestellt werden die unterschiedlichen Flächennutzungen im Berliner Stadtgebiet und ihre ökologischen Funktionen: Effekte auf das Mikroklima, Versiegelungsgrad bzw. Durchlässigkeit und Tiefe des Bodens, Zusammenhänge mit der Artenvielfalt und mit dem "Glück" bzw. dem Wohlbefinden von Stadtbewohnern.

6%
Blue infrastructures

48%
Built-up areas

59%
Sealed sites

Due to its specific history – resulting in gaps between buildings caused by the destructions of WW II and the undeveloped areas around the Berlin wall after German reunification – Berlin has multiple different green spaces and wastelands. Nevertheless, the present degree of sealing of about 35% is determined to be relatively high.[6] In 2014, a total of 2445 plant families were described for Berlin, and more than half of these are established – which makes Berlin a very species-rich city.[7] Depicted are the different land uses in the urban area of Berlin and their ecological functions: effects on microclimate, sealing degree/impervious layers and soil depth, relations with biodiversity and with the "happiness", or well-being, of city dwellers.

I. Urban land uses and their relation to biodiversity and happiness

Legend

Circles indicate low, medium and high consumption of vertical space and relation to microclimate

Positive effects on microclimate

Sealed soil
No buffer function (retention of water, exchange of air), no habitat for soil organisms

Open soil
Function as buffer and filter, provision of habitat for soil organisms

High value for biodiversity indicated by a high amount of ecological studies

Low value for biodiversity indicated by a low amount of ecological studies

Evidence of positive effect or human happines

Although cities have harboured the promise of a better life since time immemorial, migration is rarely voluntary. Global migration has two main causes: Flight from crisis- and war-torn regions, and migration because the basis for self-sustenance is no longer in place. In the developing and emerging nations, urbanisation results above all because the traditional agrarian way of life is no longer able to sustain families. Besides environmental hazards due not least to climate change, the reasons for this are found in the local effects of a global economy at the expense of the developing and emerging nations. One unique type of migration is temporary migration, whereby individual family members engage in migratory labour. Migrant workers make a significant contribution to economic growth, but in many cases their living conditions may be described as little more than a modern form of slavery.

MIGRATION

Städte bergen seit jeher das Versprechen eines besseren Lebens, aber Migration erfolgt selten freiwillig. Die weltweite Migrationsbewegung hat vor allem zwei Gründe: Flucht aus Krisen- und Kriegsgebieten und Abwanderung, weil die Grundlage der Subsistenz nicht mehr gegeben ist. Vor allem die Urbanisierung in den Entwicklungs- und Schwellenländern resultiert daraus, dass die traditionelle agrarische Lebensweise die Familien nicht mehr ernährt. Neben Umweltrisiken, die nicht zuletzt dem Klimawandel geschuldet sind, liegen die Ursachen bei den lokalen Effekten globaler Ökonomie auf Kosten der Entwicklungs- und Schwellenländer.

Ein besonderer Fall der Migration ist die Migration auf Zeit, wie sie durch Wanderarbeit einzelner Familienmitglieder gegeben ist. Wanderarbeiter leisten einen großen Beitrag zum wirtschaftlichen Wachstum, ihre Lebensverhältnisse lassen sich vielfach nur als moderne Form der Sklavenhaltung bezeichnen.

OUT OF PROPORTIONS Mariya Nesheva, Christos Antoniou

Worldwide around 60 million people are fleeing from wars, persecution and environmental disasters; the highest number recorded since World War II. Since 2010, refugee numbers have quadrupled globally; the highest rise since the beginning of records. According to the UN High Commissioner of Refugees António Guterres, we are "[…] witnessing a paradigm change, an unchecked slide into an era in which the scale of global forced displacement […] is now clearly dwarfing anything seen before."[1] In all regions of the world new conflicts are breaking out, continuing or flaring up again, which is why it is increasingly impossible for refugees to return to their home countries. As displaced people with little or no future prospects they live on the fringes of society for an indefinite period. After around 1.6 million people from, among other places, Syria, Afghanistan, Iraq and Eritrea reached Europe via the Mediterranean and the so-called Balkan route in 2015, the refugee movement will proceed with unchanged intensity in the year to follow – for an end of the war in Syria, the origin of the biggest refugee movement of our time, is not in sight.

The Syrian Civil War and the strengthening of the terrorist militia IS (so-called Islamic State) are viewed by the West as a global threat, particularly since the Paris attacks on November 13th, 2015. While the majority of the western world ascribes the war in the Middle East to a diffuse, unpredictable enemy with a "medieval" worldview, the political reality is much more complex: By now, even the former British prime minister Tony Blair admitted that the 2003 western invasion in Iraq, conducted without any genuine strategy or financing model for a democratic reconstruction of the country, gener-

ated the chaos in which terrorist militias could gain a foothold in the first place.[2] This decade-long European and US-American foreign policy allowed that no functioning constitutional states could be built up in the "liberated" areas, and that, by today, a whole generation of youths is confronted with virtually insolvable militant conflicts, an inscrutable thicket of religious fundamentalist militias and a hopeless economic outlook. The IS uses this lack of perspective for its goals by mobilising young Muslims under the pretext of "oppressed Sunnism", and justifies unscrupulous war crimes as a preliminary stage of a triumphant, world-spanning IS-Caliphate. However, the majority of the Syrian population is faced with the decision for a dangerous escape to Syria's neighbouring countries or Europe, or else for more years in constant mortal danger in the midst of civil war and Islamist extremism.

Meanwhile, the EU member states' reaction to the refugee movement is characterised by discord and reciprocal denunciation. Several nations are practicing isolationist policies, while in Germany, the declared dream destination of most refugees, a capacity crisis has arisen as of 2015. The expansion of asylum structures does not keep step with the new arrivals; in part, because politics and administration react too late to the looming mass immigration. The protection of EU external borders and the registration of refugees barely functions, while a fair intake of expelled people has failed for lack of cooperation between the 28 EU member states. Meanwhile, in the (crumbling) welfare bastions of Central Europe and Scandinavia, asylum procedures are exacerbated and legal barriers for immigration restrictions removed. However, the main burden of the Syrian crisis is born

Weltweit sind ca. 60 Millionen Menschen auf der Flucht vor Kriegen, Verfolgung und Umweltkatastrophen; das ist die höchste Zahl, die seit dem Zweiten Weltkrieg verzeichnet wurde. Seit 2010 haben sich die Flüchtlingszahlen zudem weltweit vervierfacht; der höchste Anstieg seit Beginn der Aufzeichnungen. Nach dem UN-Flüchtlingskommissar António Guterres, werden wir "[…] aktuell Zeugen eines Paradigmenwechsels. Wir geraten in eine Epoche, in der das Ausmaß der globalen Flucht und Vertreibung […] alles davor Gewesene in den Schatten stell[t]."[1] In allen Regionen der Welt brechen neue Konflikte aus, dauern an oder flammen wieder auf, weswegen es geflüchteten Menschen immer weniger möglich ist, in ihre Heimat zurückzukehren. Als Vertriebene mit geringer oder keiner Zukunftsperspektive leben sie auf ungewisse Zeit an den Rändern der Gesellschaft. Nachdem im Jahr 2015 ca. 1,6 Millionen Menschen aus u.a. Syrien, Afghanistan, dem Irak und Eritrea über das Mittelmeer und die sog. Balkanroute Europa erreicht haben, wird die Fluchtbewegung im nächsten Jahr mit unveränderter Heftigkeit voranschreiten – denn ein Ende des Krieges in Syrien, Ursprung einer der größten Fluchtbewegungen unserer Zeit, ist nicht in Sicht.

Der syrische Bürgerkrieg und die Erstarkung der terroristischen Miliz IS (sog. Islamischer Staat) werden im Westen vor allem seit den Pariser Attentaten vom 13.11.2015 als globale Bedrohung wahrgenommen. Während der Großteil der westlichen Welt den Krieg im Nahen Osten den Machenschaften eines diffusen, unberechenbaren Feinds mit "mittelalterlicher" Weltsicht zuschreibt, ist die politische Wirklichkeit um einiges differenzierter: Inzwischen hat sogar der ehemalige britische Premierminister Tony Blair eingeräumt, dass die westliche Invasion im Irak 2003, die ohne ernsthafte Strategien oder Finanzierungsmodelle für einen demokratischen Wiederaufbau des Landes durchgeführt wurde, das Chaos verursacht hat, in dem terroristische Milizen überhaupt erst in der Region Fuß fassen konnten.[2] Diese über Jahrzehnte

andauernde außenpolitische Haltung der USA und Europas hat es zugelassen, dass sich in den "befreiten" Gebieten keine funktionierenden Rechtsstaaten aufbauen konnten, und eine ganze Generation Jugendlicher heute mit schier unlösbaren bewaffneten Konflikten, einem undurchschaubaren Dickicht religiös-fundamentalistischer Milizen und einer aussichtslosen wirtschaftlichen Lage konfrontiert ist. Der IS nutzt diese Perspektivlosigkeit für seine Ziele, indem er junge Muslime unter dem Vorwand des "unterdrückten Sunnismus" mobilisiert und skrupellose Kriegsverbrechen als Vorstufe eines siegreichen, weltumspannenden IS-Kalifats rechtfertigt. Der Großteil der syrischen Bevölkerung steht allerdings vor der Entscheidung für die gefährliche Flucht in die Nachbarländer Syriens und nach Europa oder für weitere Jahre in ständiger Lebensgefahr inmitten von Bürgerkrieg und islamistischem Extremismus.

Die Reaktion der EU-Mitgliedsstaaten auf die Flüchtlingsbewegung ist derweilen von Uneinigkeit und gegenseitiger Denunzierung geprägt. Einzelne Nationen betreiben eine Abschottungspolitik, während es in Deutschland, erklärtes Wunschziel eines Großteils der Flüchtlinge, ab 2015 zu einer Kapazitätskrise kommt. Der Ausbau der Asylstrukturen hält nicht mit der Anzahl der Neuankommenden Schritt; auch, weil Politik und Verwaltung zu spät auf die sich abzeichnende massenhafte Einwanderung reagieren. Die Sicherung der EU-Außengrenzen und die Registrierung flüchtender Menschen funktioniert kaum, während eine faire Aufnahme der Vertriebenen mangels Zusammenarbeit der 28 EU-Mitgliedsstaaten gescheitert ist. Inzwischen werden in den (bröckelnden) wohlfahrtsstaatlichen Bastionen Skandinaviens und Mitteleuropas Asylverfahren verschärft und die rechtlichen Hürden zur Einwanderungsbeschränkung abgebaut. Dabei wird die Hauptlast der Syrienkrise nicht von Europa getragen, sondern von den Nachbarländern in der Levante: allein in der Türkei leben zurzeit ca. 2,5 Millionen vertriebene Syrer. Die bis zuletzt fehlgeschlagene europäische Flücht-

not by Europe, but by the neighbouring countries in the Levant: around 2.5 Million displaced Syrians are currently living in Turkey alone. The European refugee policy, so far failing, threatens the stability of the European Union and blames the refugees for its own malfunction, who, without any political voice or lobby, are an easy target.

However, the true problems are social and economic. In the aftermath of the 1st World War, the Middle East was divided into arbitrarily fixed "spheres of influence" by the victorious Entente Cordiale, shortly thereafter ratified by the League of Nations. Today, the resulting unstable political formations are proxies of competing power interests, and particularly location of the global run for fossil fuels, be it from the side of the West, authoritarian regimes or the IS. What is more, the economic agenda of leading Western states, favoured for decades, has been accompanied by extensive deregulation of global financial markets and the delegation of stately responsibility to the "invisible hand of the market". In the process of globalisation, this policy has also been imposed on less developed countries, which have been incorporated into late capitalism without a transition phase by, for instance, the International Monetary Fund's (IMF) neoliberally slanted Structural Adjustment Programs (SAPs) since the 1980s. The pretence of "free" competition on the global market often conceals a brutal exploitation mechanism: young states in the Global South are urged to deregulate their stately structures – seemingly to attract foreign "sponsors" – while profitable access to resources and land is made available for international businesses. So, in all parts of the world social safety nets are thinning and social disparity is growing, while individual commercial agents are enriching themselves beyond all measure. But, as social resources are getting scarcer, so the flames of rivalry and conflict are fanned: Europe is more and more surrounded by states threatening to slide into instable or authoritarian political conditions. The spreading phenomenon of "failed states" and the subsequent refugee movements constitute the flipside of exploitative global economic activity. Within Europe, the advance of right-wing populist parties is fed to a large part from fear of social descent. Targets of right-wing smear campaigns are often people of different faith: every day discrimination leads to frustration and alienation of a considerable minority of young Muslims, which in turn drives them into the hands of radical Islamists.

It is time for EU states to formulate a long-term policy for the curtailment of social differences. Through generously funded, supranational asylum and integration programs, through the protection of precarious livelihoods by progressive welfare state measures, through a housing policy that focuses on social desegregation, and, indispensably, through a renunciation of highly destructive neo-colonial and neo-liberal practices, the ongoing radicalisation of society could be prevented. On the global political stage, Europe needs to demonstrate determination and to pursue politics in the name of the EUs' core values – democracy, state of law, human dignity. That requires a clear dissociation from discrimination and fundamentalism, be it with regards to right-wing European groups or with regards to radical Islamists – putting an end to the hypocritical value pluralism of European politics. A clear diplomatic European position in the Syrian crisis, propagating a long-term ceasefire and military de-escalation instead of western air strikes as the primary objective, could lessen the distress of refugees and the intensity of the refugee movement and, simultaneously, create a meaningful identity for the disbanding European community.

lingspolitik bedroht die Stabilität der Europäischen Union und lastet das Problem der eigenen Überforderung den Flüchtenden an, die ohne jegliche politische Stimme oder Lobby ein leichtes Ziel abgeben.

Die wahren Probleme sind allerdings sozialer und ökonomischer Art. Schon nach dem 1. Weltkrieg wurde der Nahe Osten durch die siegreiche Entente in willkürlich festgelegte "Einflussgebiete" unterteilt, die kurz darauf durch den Völkerbund ratifiziert wurden. Die daraus hervorgegangenen labilen politischen Gefüge sind heute Stellvertreter konkurrierender Machtinteressen und insbesondere Schauplatz des globalen Runs auf fossile Rohstoffe, sei es von Seiten des Westens, autoritärer Regime oder des IS. Darüber hinaus geht die seit Jahrzehnten favorisierte wirtschaftliche Agenda führender westlicher Staaten einher mit der weitgehenden Deregulierung der globalen Finanzmärkte und der Delegation sozialstaatlicher Verantwortung an die "unsichtbare Hand des Marktes". Im Prozess der Globalisierung wurde diese Politik auch weniger entwickelten Staaten aufgezwungen, die beispielsweise ab den 1980ern durch neoliberal gefärbte Strukturanpassungsprogramme des Internationalen Währungsfonds (IWF) und der Weltbank ohne Überleitung in spätkapitalistische Verhältnisse eingegliedert wurden. Hinter dem Vorwand des "freien" Mitwettbewerbs am globalen Markt verbirgt sich oft eine brutale Ausbeutungsmethode: Von jungen Staaten wird gefordert, ihre staatlichen Gefüge weitgehend zu deregulieren – scheinbar um ausländische "Geldgeber" anzulocken – während internationalen Unternehmen profitabler Zugang zu Rohstoffen und Land verschafft wird. In allen Teilen der Welt kommt es also zu einer Ausdünnung gesellschaftlicher Auffangnetze und wachsender sozialer Disparität, während sich einzelne privatwirtschaftliche Akteure über die Maßen bereichern. Werden gesellschaftliche Ressourcen aber immer knapper, befeuert das Konkurrenz und Konflikte: Europa ist heute mehr und mehr von Staaten umgeben, die in instabile oder autoritäre politische Verhältnisse abzugleiten drohen. Das sich ausbreitende Phänomen der "gescheiterten Staaten" und die damit verbundenen Fluchtbewegungen bilden die Kehrseite des ausbeuterischen globalen Wirtschaftens. Innerhalb Europas speist sich der Vormarsch rechtspopulistischer Parteien zu einem großen Teil aus Angst vor gesellschaftlichem Abstieg. Zielscheibe rechter Hetze sind oft Andersgläubige: Die alltägliche Diskriminierung führt zu Frustration und Entfremdung einer nennenswerten Minderheit junger Muslime, was sie wiederum radikal-islamistischen Gruppen in die Hände treibt.

Es ist an der Zeit, dass die EU-Staaten eine langfristige Politik zur Schmälerung gesellschaftlicher Differenzen formulieren. Durch großzügig durchfinanzierte, überstaatlich geregelte Asyl- und Integrationsprogramme, durch progressive wohlfahrtsstaatliche Modelle zur Sicherung prekärer Existenzen, durch eine Wohnungspolitik, die soziale Durchmischung forciert, und – unumgänglich, weil im hohem Maße zerstörerisch – durch eine Abkehr von neo-kolonialen und neoliberalen Praktiken könnte die fortschreitende gesellschaftliche Radikalisierung verhindert werden. Auf der weltpolitischen Bühne ist Europa angehalten, entschlossen aufzutreten und Politik im Namen der Grundwerte der Europäischen Union zu betreiben – Demokratie, Rechtsstaat, Menschenwürde. Dazu gehört, sich klar von Diskriminierung und Fundamentalismus abzugrenzen, sei es in Bezug auf rechtsradikale europäische Gruppierungen oder auf radikale Islamisten – und somit dem scheinheiligen Wertepluralismus europäischer Politik ein Ende zu bereiten. Durch einen klaren diplomatischen Standpunkt Europas in der Syrienkrise, der anstatt westlicher Luftangriffe einen langfristigen Waffenstillstand und militärische Deeskalation als übergeordnetes Ziel propagiert, können die Not der Flüchtenden und die Intensität der Fluchtbewegung gemindert und gleichzeitig eine sinnstiftende Identität für die sich in Auflösung begriffene europäische Gemeinschaft geschaffen werden.
Text: Anna Aichinger

OUT OF PROPORTIONS

WORLDWIDE ARE BEING DISPLACED:

51 MILL. PEOPLE

16,7 MILLION REFUGEES According to the United Nations Convention (1967 Protocol), a Refugee is a person who is outside his or her country and is a well-founded fear of persecution due to his/her race, religion, nationality, membership of a particular social group or political opinion, and is unable or unwilling to return.

33,3 MILLION IDP's An Internally Displaced Person is someone who is living inside the borders of the country, but is unable to safely live in their own home or region.

1,2 MILLION ASYLUM-SEEKERS An Asylum Seeker is a person who has fled from his or her own country due to fear of persecution and has applied for (legal and physical) protection in another country but has not yet had their claim for protection assessed. A person remains an asylum seeker until his protection "status" has been determined.

The amount of forcibly displaced individuals worldwide increases tremendously every year. The number of the emigrants is so big by now, that all of them put together in one place would make the 26th largest nation in the world. There are three main groups of forcibly displaced people: refugees, asylum-seekers and stateless persons. Round 80 percent of them come to Europe using some of the well-known emigration routes. Once they reach their destination, the immigrants don't have many options.

Entering Europe the immigrants often imagine a brighter future for them and normal living conditions in one peaceful country. The Asylum policy in between the Shengen borders is the same, but the implementation in each country appears to be different. Because of that the image of the united Europe, functioning as one, remains an utopia for the foreigners. Those extreme situations show that Europe is not as united as it should be. It is divided and overbalanced and this is a problem that is often overlooked and ignored, but it affects all of us.

REFUGEE AND ASYLUM SEEKER POPULATIONS BY COUNTRY OF DESTINATION, 2013

TOTAL EUROPE 29%

USA & CANADA 16%

JAPAN & SOUTH KOREA 1%

AUSTRALIA & NEW ZEALAND 4%

TOP 20 REFUGEE-HOSTING COUNTRIES IN THE WORLD, 2013

DEVELOPING COUNTRIES HOSTED 86% OF THE WORLD'S REFUGEES, COMPARED TO 70% 10 YEARS AGO.

MAJOR SOURCE COUNTRIES OF REFUGEES, 2013 (IN MILLIONS)

REASONS:

The main migrating reasons listed below belong to the push factors from the origin countries. Important should be to consider also the pull factors in the hosted countries attracting the immigrating population.

POVERTY

ARMED CONFLICT

SOCIAL STRIFE

POLITICAL TURMOIL

ECONOMIC HARDSHIPS

CLIMATE CHANGE

A WAY TO GO

THE DIFFERENT FACES OF EUROPE: COMPARISON BETWEEN GERMANY AND GREECE

128 902 were stopped on their way to Europe

1.786.500 refugees manage to go through the Shengen boarders (end of 2013)

UNDOCUMENTED POPULATION **391 000** is the approximate number of the undocumented people in Greece at the end of 2012.

In 2004 **44** countries reported to have undocumented citizens. Nowadays those countries are **94**

INFORMAL LIVING CONDITIONS
Asylum seeker living area:
European dog living area:
Average european living area:

PASS

STOP

DEATH

ARREST

The number of deaths increased from **1500** to **3077** during the period 2013-14.

PRISON
The number of arrested immigrants on the Greece borders is decreasing. In the last 2 years, **41.930** were arrested in 2014.

ASYLUM SEEKERS
The total number of initial and subsequent asylum applications for 2014 in Europe is **435 000**

ASYLUM FACILITIES
The average size of the living area in the asylum facilities per person in Germany is **4,5** square meters. In comparison, the average living area of the normal german is **42,8** square meters.

DETENTION FACILITIES
There are 31 camps and detention centers in Germany where ca **50 000** people are being hold.

108 315 people are being hold in camps and detention borders in Greece right now.

SENT TO PREVIOUS EU COUNTRY
In 2013 **4.741** applicants that didn't become an asylum were sent from Germany to the previous european land they entered.

SENT BACK

EXPECTATIONS

REALITY

VS.

ACCESS TO EDUCATIONAL SYSTEM AND LABOUR MARKET

In Germany the asylum seekers under 18 have the rights to go to primary school. Yet the older ones may face many barriers accessing higher education, including a lack of information, advice and individual guidance sensitive to their specific needs. Inadequate provision of intensive language courses for academic purposes, and restricted access to government student finance schemes. The access to the labour market remains also very difficult. The asylum seekers were not allowed to work during the first nine months spent in the country. After some reforms in juny 2014 the time they had to walt was reduced to 3 months.

In Greece over **33%** of the immigrants were unemployed in 2014. Access to the education system. Access to the education system in 2014. Access to the education system, however shall not be postponed for more than three months from the date of reception of the asylum application by the child or the child's parents. This period may be extended to one year where specific language education is provided in order to facilitate access to the education system.

EUROPE:

MAP ON IRREGULAR AND MIXED MIGRATION ROUTES INTO THE EU, 2014:

30.000
50.000
200.000

▲ Main Airplane Destinations
⬦ Sea Routes
— Land Routes
● Main Transit Cities

DIED WHILE TRYING TO GET TO EUROPE:

First years of Shengen Borders
(1 July 1994 to 30 June 1998)

From the introduction of the integrated electronic system for outdoor surveillance (SIVE)
(1 July 1998 - 30 June 2002)

From the Sevilla peak till the peak of Rabat
(1 July 2002 - 30 June 2006)

Since the shift of control to the outside (Frontex)
(1 July 2006 - 30 June 2009)

WHERE ARE EUROPE'S BORDERS?

Europe's migration policy, which has developed to strengthen external border controls and to organize solidarity between transit and destination countries doesn't seem to work properly.
Comparing the Shengen border with the detention centers of each country, someone can easily conclude that there is no operational cooperation and every country acts autonomously violating the rights of immigrants and sometimes the other EU member states.

Shengen Borders
● Camps for foreigners awaiting Deportation
● Camps for foreigners pending examination before-extraditing both functions
● Civil Law prison used for detention

EASTERN BORDERS
768

WESTERN BALKAN ROUTE
7 000

CIRCULAR ROUTE FROM ALBANIA TO GREECE
5 750

CENTRAL-MEDIT. ROUTE
32 000

WESTERN-MEDIT. ROUTE
6 200

EASTERN-MEDIT. ROUTE
43 200

APULIA & CALABRIA ROUTE
7 761

FOR A BETTER FUTURE

DEFINING SOME MEASURES THAT COULD IMPROVE THE CURRENT SITUATION:

REDUCE:

"OVER THE LAST FEW YEARS, EU COUNTRIES HAVE BEEN BUSY BUILDING FENCES, REAL AND INVISIBLE, TO KEEP PEOPLE OUT."

Keeping people out is an expensive business. A legitimate way to avoid it, is the intervention of international organizations and states of developed countries, in the origin countries, to create better living conditions, by advancing the infrastructure, spreading technology, knowledge and declining the possible conflicts.

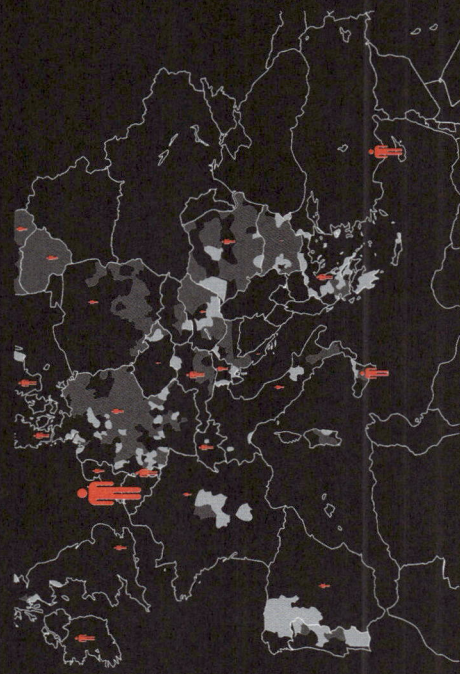

3.8 b.
border control 1.9 b.
asylum procedures 0.7 b.
0.2 b. help for the origin countries

★★★★
3.8
BILLION
★★★★

140 million € will spent EU for projects assisting refugees and IDPs in 33 origin countries.

3800 million € has been set up for the period 2014-20 for the Internal Security Strategy, law enforcement cooperation and the management of the Union's external borders

REDISTRIBUTE:

The problem of the accumulation of irregular populations in some eu countries can be solved with an integrated program for the reception of immigrants from all countries, depending on the absorption capacity, the local population and the circumstances.

To achieve this, a European or international organization should be set up to objectively assess the potential of each country and take care of the distribution and their integration in the local communities.

Furthermore the immigrant inflow in the EU can be seen as a potential solution to the EU demographic problem.

■ POPULATION DECREASE, MIGRATORY BALANCE+
■ POPULATION DECREASE, MIGRATORY BALANCE-
■ MIGRATORS, 2012 (I) (PER 1.000 INHABITANTS)

RECREATE:

IN ORDER TO BE EQUAL TO THE VALUES THAT IT PROMOTES, THE EU CANNOT SIMPLY STRENGTHEN ITS BORDER CONTROLS AND OUTSOURCE ITS MIGRATION POLICY.

The EU could benefit a lot through a common immigration policy. Neglected areas can be upgraded by absorbing immigrant population. Common plans for the immigrants should be implemented to improve the living conditions and promote the integration in the local communities. The main focus to achieve this should be in education and employment programs, such as social inclusion and active citizenship.

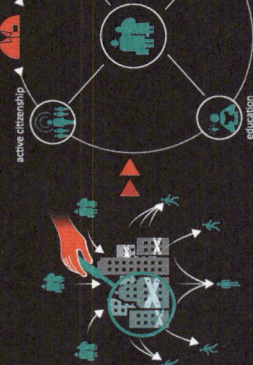
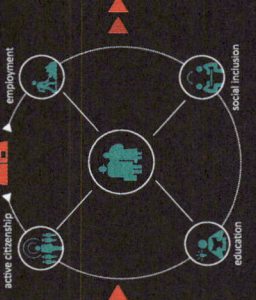

employment

social inclusion

active citizenship

education

STATES OF REFUGE

Nina Valerie Kolowratnik, Johannes Pointl
with Martina Soi Gunelas, Birgit Miksch, Lea Soltau,
Anton Wagner, Mario Weisböck

Asylum and Architecture

Built spaces and spatial coherencies are an integral part of the state of refuge and waiting and on various levels and to different degrees one of the realities of the asylum system. The project "Fluchtraum Österreich" calls attention to the effects of spatial action and planning – or the lack of it – and argues for a proactive inclusion of architecture in the asylum discourse.

Aside from the refugee route itself, which is characterised by diverse spatial manifestations of borders and border areas, on arriving in Austria asylum seekers are again confronted by built spaces of inclusion and exclusion. In the course of the asylum process the physical barriers and limits to movement in initial reception centres, allocated accommodation facilities and federal states are added to by social and institutional barriers that have an influence on the built environment and spatial decisions, or are caused by these.

On the spatial planning and policy level, regional building regulations and spatial development policies mean that local building authorities become important players in the asylum context. They can prevent or delay the flexible and location-specific accommodation of asylum seekers through insistence on official or building inspectorate requirements. The repurposing of vacant buildings for asylum seekers for instance is made impossible in many places because the change of use must be reclassified according to building law. Detailed specifications for repurposed buildings such as the obligatory provision of elevators for those over four storeys high are likewise proscribed by building law, but often involve high investment costs. The like also applies to the required approval of residential containers that can be set up quickly for temporary accommodation, which in many cases is precluded by bureaucratic hurdles concerning the repurposing of the land in question. Where tents are concerned, in some federal states permission for these

first becomes necessary after six months of use, which is one of the reasons for the current rise in the accommodation of asylum seekers in tent camps.

The spatial decision about the choice of location and the accessibility of accommodation facilities for asylum seekers has a direct influence on their inhabitants' social environment. In many cases their geographical isolation inhibits social inclusion and undermines the asylum seekers' political capacity to act due to a lack of presence in the public sphere. Because the shortage of opportunities to take control of their own lives is a major reason why asylum seekers flee from their states of origin in the first place, it is all the more necessary to allow asylum seekers to organise themselves, so that they are not once again pushed into a state of social and political paralysis. The current employment restrictions for asylum seekers however contribute to their lack of social and economic agency. They are denied access to regular working environments and conditions and this leads to diffuse and insecure grey areas in employment.

The smallest spatial scale that asylum seekers experience is created by the housing in accommodation facilities for asylum seekers and the relationship between guest and host: a regimented hospitality that prescribes the use of space and freedom of movement and establishes clear rules and hierarchies. Whether the rooms provided there offer not only physical but also psychological refuge and offer an environment with which their inhabitants can identify and which preserve their identity is often entrusted to those who run the accommodation centres, who in most cases are not trained to deal with people in need of protection and their housing needs. One of the few requirements that the accommodation providers must meet is the minimum standard established by the federal states for living space per asylum seeker, allowing for example former hotel rooms designed for two tourists to be occupied by up to six asy-

Asyl und Architektur

Gebaute Räume und räumliche Zusammenhänge sind ein maßgebender Bestandteil des Zustands der Flucht und des Wartens, und auf unterschiedlichen Ebenen und Maßstäben Teil der Asylrealität. Fluchtraum Österreich ist ein Projekt, welches die Auswirkungen räumlichen Handelns und Planens – oder dessen Abwesenheit – aufzeigt und für ein proaktives Eintreten der Architektur in den Asyldiskurs argumentiert.

Neben dem Fluchtweg an sich, der von unterschiedlichen räumlichen Manifestationen von Grenzen und Grenzräumen geprägt ist, sind Asylsuchende an ihrem Ankunftsort in Österreich erneut mit gebauten Räumen der Ein- und Ausgrenzung konfrontiert. Zu den physischen Barrieren und Bewegungseinschränkungen in Erstaufnahmezentren, zugewiesenen Unterkünften und Bundesländern kommen im Laufe des Asylverfahrens soziale und institutionelle Hürden, die Einfluss auf die gebaute Umwelt und räumliche Entscheidungen nehmen oder durch eben diese hervorgerufen werden.

Auf raumplanerischer und raumpolitischer Ebene werden die Baubehörden der Gemeinden durch die regionalen Baugesetze und Raumordnungen zu wichtigen Akteuren im Asylkontext. Sie können flexible und ortspezifische Unterbringung von Asylwerbern durch das Bestehen auf behördliche und baupolizeiliche Auflagen verhindern oder verzögern. Die Umnutzung von leerstehenden Gebäuden für Asylwerber wird zum Beispiel vielerorts unmöglich gemacht, da für die geänderte Nutzung laut Baurecht eine Umwidmung notwendig ist. Darüber hinaus gibt es Detailvorschriften, wie etwa ein verpflichtender Aufzug für Häuser mit mehr als vier Stockwerken, welche durch die neue Nutzung baurechtlich notwendig werden, aber oftmals zu hohe Investitionskosten darstellen. Ähnliches gilt für die nötige Bewilligung von Wohncontainern, die als temporäre Unterkunftsmöglichkeiten rasch aufgestellt werden könnten, dem jedoch in vielen Fällen bürokratische Hürden bei der Umwidmung der betreffenden Grundstücke entgegenstehen. Bei Zelten wird in einigen Bundesländern eine Genehmigung erst ab einer sechsmonatigen Nutzung

notwendig, was mit ein Grund für die derzeit vermehrte Unterbringung von Asylwerbern in Zeltlagern ist.

Die räumliche Entscheidung über die Standortwahl von Asylwerberunterkünften und deren Erreichbarkeit hat direkten Einfluss auf den sozialen Raum ihrer Bewohner. In vielen Fällen wird durch geographische Abgelegenheit sozialer Anschluss verhindert und die politische Handlungsfähigkeit der Asylsuchenden durch fehlende Präsenz im öffentlichen Raum untergraben. Da gerade die fehlenden Möglichkeiten, ihr Leben selbst zu bestimmen, ein wichtiger Grund sind, warum Asylbewerber aus ihren Herkunftsländern flüchten, ist es umso notwendiger, Selbst-Organisation von Asylwerbern zuzulassen, um sie nicht erneut in einen Zustand der sozialen und politischen Handlungsunfähigkeit abzudrängen. Geltende Arbeitsmarktbeschränkungen für Asylwerber tragen aber zur sozialen und ökonomischen Handlungsunfähigkeit bei. Der Zutritt zu regulären Arbeitsräumen und -verhältnissen bleibt ihnen verwehrt und führt dadurch zu diffusen und unsicheren Grauzonen der Beschäftigung.

Der kleinste räumliche Maßstab, den Asylsuchende erfahren, entsteht durch die Beherbergung und Beziehung zwischen Gast und Gastgeber in Asylwerberunterkünften: eine reglementierte Gastfreundschaft, die Möglichkeiten der Raumnutzung und Bewegungsfreiheit vorschreibt und klare Regeln und Hierarchien festlegt. Ob die in Asylunterkünften zur Verfügung gestellten Räume nicht nur der physischen, sondern auch psychischen Zuflucht dienen, eine Umgebung anbieten, mit der Geflüchtete sich identifizieren können und die ihre Identität bewahrt, ist zu oft dem Willen von Betreibern der Unterkünfte überlassen, die meist über keine Ausbildung im Umgang mit schutzbedürftigen Personen und deren Wohnbedürfnissen verfügen. Eine der wenigen Bestimmungen, welche die Unterkunftgeber erfüllen müssen, sind die von den Bundesländern festgelegten Mindeststandards der Wohnfläche pro Asylwerber. Diese machen es möglich, dass beispielsweise ehemalige Hotelzimmer, die für zwei Touristen ausgelegt waren, in ihrer neuen Nutzung mit bis zu maximal sechs Asylwerber belegt werden

lum seekers. The minimum standards do not take into account the need for privacy and the freedom to make lifestyle choices, such as when to do something, which are baseline requirements for living in a positive sense.

Unlike the tourism infrastructure or the public health system, the asylum system in Austria lacks long-term planning for crucial infrastructure for asylum seekers and legally recognised refugees. The seemingly temporary nature of migration which is perpetuated by the recurring institutional state of emergency does not permit a strategic approach, and as a result this has to date been kept out of the architectural discourse. Migration movements however have a permanent presence in the current geopolitical climate. Host countries must therefore begin to work with long-term spatial solutions, rather than implement ad hoc spatial solutions behind the smokescreen of impermanence.

Panel 1: Institution of Asylum
The set of rules of the Austrian asylum system is spatialised in an architectural design – the building "Institution of Asylum Austria". Structures and processes within the system are illustrated with architectural subjects, making them graspable. The assignment of different meanings to the various architectural elements shows subjective emotions, degrees of pressure and forces asylum seekers experience at certain stations. First, activists and interested people may use the design for making the system itself understandable – most importantly for asylum seekers themselves. Then, "Institution of Asylum Austria" should be used as a basis for constructive criticism and discussion about the redesign of existing asylum policies.[1-4]

Panel II: Borders and Movements
Escape routes are commonly represented in numbers and figures, which are supposed to reflect general movements across the globe and serve as factual findings. Yet, every one of these abstract arrows is made up of real people, who have their own histories, experiences and sufferings and therefore deserve to be looked at individually. This mapping utilizes data used in strategic maps by official actors in the European border protection[5] and recent data of displaced persons by the UNHCR[6] and couples these with narratives by two refugees currently applying for asylum in Austria. Since Djadi and Kalil escaped from Syria in 2012 and 2014 respectively[7], changing border crossing situations become visible; developing towards hardened frontiers within this two year span.

What remains steady is numbing subjection to the power structures facilitating or preventing movement across borders.

Panel III: Living Biography
The illustration was formed during long conversations with Mrs. H. (50 years) in May 2015 about her and her daughter N.'s (18 years) direct residential environment after escaping from Ramallah to Vienna. In the interviews she was drawing basic room structures which were transferred into architectural plans and refined from meeting to meeting. The level of detail grew up to the description of tapestries, the daily routine and their favourite places. "Home is not a room or a house", explains H. "I feel like living standby." No living, more a being-located, a forced feeling of comfort. "I have to feel home to complete myself." Self-determination, retreat, space requirement and the possibility of creating a personal atmosphere are basic needs of living and are rarely implemented in refugee hostels. "I sit in my bed. I don't have a choice."[8]

Panel IV: Knowledge Landscapes and Structural Access Barriers
Asylum seekers are structurally deprived of their chances to leverage their previous life experiences and knowledge or to utilize them as an initial position for their private life. The Austrian province Tyrol collects data on spoken languages, professions or interests of persons who are taken into basic welfare support in Tyrol. By means of these entries, this mapping aims to visualise and locate a basic evaluation of the range and variety of knowledge in refugee homes. The data produces an interesting knowledge landscape in the context of migration and asylum policies in Austria.[9-16]

•

The cartographies and essays are the result of a long-term research project on migration spaces and spaces of waiting in Austria, initiated by Nina Valerie Kolowratnik and Johannes Pointl in 2014. They were developed in the framework of a seminar at the guest institution TU Wien (Vienna) and in collaboration with Asylkoordination Österreich, and published under the title "Fluchtraum Österreich". The project is part of the Echoing Borders Initiative at the Columbia University in New York. Team: Nina Valerie Kolowratnik and Johannes Pointl with Martina Soi Gunelas, Birgit Miksch, Lea Soltau, Anton Wagner, Mario Weisböck
www.fluchtraum.at

können. Privater Rückzugsraum und das Bedürfnis nach individueller Freiheit der Lebensführung, wie etwa die Wahl des Zeitpunktes einer Handlung, welche die Mindestanforderungen für ein Gefühl des Wohnens darstellen, sind in den Mindeststandards nicht berücksichtigt.

Anders als der Tourismusinfrastruktur oder dem öffentlichen Gesundheitssystem in Österreich fehlt dem Asylsystem in Österreich die langfristige Planung von unbedingt notwendiger Infrastruktur für Asylwerber und rechtlich anerkannte Flüchtlinge. Die scheinbare Temporalität der Flucht, die durch den wiederkehrenden institutionellen Ausnahmezustand aufrechterhalten wird, lässt keine strategische Herangehensweise zu und diese wird dadurch bis dato vom Architekturdiskurs ferngehalten. Migrationsbewegungen stellen jedoch einen permanenten Zustand im gegenwärtigen geopolitischen Geschehen dar. Aufnahmeländer müssen deshalb beginnen mit langfristigen räumlichen Lösungen zu arbeiten, anstatt sich unter dem Deckmantel der Temporalität räumlicher ad hoc Lösungen zu bedienen.

Tafel I: Institution des Asyls
Das Regelwerk des österreichischen Asylsystems wird in einem architektonischen Entwurf verräumlicht, dem Gebäude "Institution des Asyls Österreich". Strukturen und Prozesse innerhalb dieses Systems werden mittels architektonischer Subjekte veranschaulicht, wodurch Erstere greifbar werden. Die den diversen architektonischen Elementen zugewiesenen unterschiedlichen Bedeutungen offenbaren subjektive Emotionen, Abstufungen der Zwänge und der Gewalt, denen sich Asylsuchende in bestimmten Stadien ausgesetzt sehen. Als Erstes könnten Aktivisten und interessierte Bürger den Entwurf verwenden, um das System als solches verständlich zu machen. Anschließend sollte "Institution des Asyls Österreich" für eine konstruktive Kritik und eine Diskussion über die Reform der gegenwärtigen Asylpolitik herangezogen werden.[1-4]

Tafel II: Grenzen und Bewegungen
Fluchtrouten werden für gewöhnlich mit Zahlen und Symbolen veranschaulicht, die allgemeine Wanderbewegungen über den Erdball widerspiegeln sollen und die als faktische Erkenntnisse dienen. Doch jeder dieser abstrakten Pfeile steht für Menschen aus Fleisch und Blut, für Menschen mit ihrer eigenen Geschichte und ihren eigenen, meist schlimmen Erfahrungen, und deshalb verdienen sie es, als Individuen betrachtet zu werden. Diese Kartierung verwendet Daten, die aus strategischen Karten von offiziellen Akteuren des europäischen Grenzschutzes[5] stammen, sowie jüngst veröffentlichte UNHCR-

Daten zur Flüchtlingssituation[6] und verknüpft diese Daten mit den Erfahrungsberichten zweier Flüchtlinge, die sich derzeit in Österreich um Asyl bewerben. Seitdem Djadi und Kalil 2012 beziehungsweise 2014 aus Syrien geflüchtet sind[7], haben sich die Grenzüberquerungssituationen deutlich verändert; innerhalb dieser Spanne von zwei Jahren sind die Grenzen weniger durchlässig geworden. Was sich nicht verändert hat, ist die frustrierende Unterwerfung unter die Machtstrukturen, die die Überquerung von Grenzen entweder erleichtern oder verhindern.

Tafel III: Lebende Biografie
Die Illustration entstand während der ausgedehnten Gespräche, die wir im Mai 2015 mit der fünfzigjährigen, von Ramallah nach Wien geflüchteten Frau H. geführt haben und in denen es um die Wohnsituation von Frau H. und ihrer achtzehnjährigen Tochter N. ging. Bei den Interviews zeichnete sie rudimentäre Raumanordnungen, die anschließend in architektonische Grundrisse überführt und im Laufe der Zeit zunehmend verfeinert wurden. Die berücksichtigten Details umfassten schließlich die Beschreibung der Gobelins, die alltäglichen Verrichtungen und die Lieblingsorte der beiden Frauen. "Ein Zuhause ist mehr als ein Zimmer oder ein Haus", erklärt Frau H. "Ich führe so etwas wie ein Standby-Leben." Kein Leben, sondern eher ein Untergebrachtsein, ein erzwungenes Gefühl von Behaglichkeit. "Ich muss mich zu Hause fühlen, um ein vollständiger Mensch zu sein." Selbstbestimmung, Rückzugsmöglichkeiten, genügend Raum und die Möglichkeit, sich eine persönliche Atmosphäre zu erschaffen, sind Grunderfordernisse des Lebens, die in den Flüchtlingshostels selten berücksichtigt werden. "Ich sitze auf meinem Bett. Mir bleibt keine andere Wahl."[8]

Tafel IV: Wissenslandschaften und strukturelle Zugangsbarrieren
Asylsuchende werden strukturell daran gehindert, ihre früheren Lebenserfahrungen und ihr Wissen sinnvoll einzubringen oder diese Dinge als einen Ausgangspunkt für ihr Privatleben zu nutzen. Das österreichische Bundesland Tirol sammelt Daten über die gesprochenen Sprachen, die Berufe und die Interessen von Personen, die in Tirol eine die Grundversorgung gewährleistende Sozialhilfe beziehen. Anhand dieser Daten möchte diese Karte eine grundlegende Evaluation des Ausmaßes und der Vielfalt des in Flüchtlingsheimen vorhandenen Wissens veranschaulichen und räumlich verorten. Diese Daten ergeben eine interessante Wissenslandschaft "Wissenslandschaften" im Zusammenhang mit der Migration und der österreichischen Asylpolitik.[9-16]

STATES OF REFUGE / FLUCHTRAUM ÖSTERREICH –
Institution of Asylum Austria by Birgit Miksch

POINTS OF ENTRY INTO THE SYSTEM

A   Entry Initial Reception Center Traiskirchen
B   Entry Airport Vienna
C   Entry Police
D   Entry Initial Reception Center Thalham

SEQUENCE OF STATIONS

01   Application for International Protection
02   Data acquisition
03   Photographs
04   Impressions of the papillary ridges on the fingers
05   Baggage screening
06   Initial Reception Center Traiskirchen
07   Initial Reception Center Thalham
08   Medical examination
09   First interrogation
10   Legal advice from NGOs
11   Second interrogation
12   Exit area for green identity card
13   Administrative decision on application for International Protection
14   Complaint with Federal Administrative Court
15   Administrative decision on complaint concerning admission procedure
16   „Voluntary return"
17   Custody to secure deportation
18   Deportation
19   Distribution to federal states
20   Exit area for white identity card
21   Interview with the Federal Office for Immigration and Asylum
22   Administrative decision on asylum procedure
23   Exit for people with asylum status
24   Exit area for persons holding Subsidiary Protection or Residence Entitlement
25   Complaint with Federal Administrative Court and retrial
26   Administrative decision by Federal Administrative Court
27   Renewed asylum procedure
28   Level of NGOs

BASIC WELFARE SUPPORT IN THE FEDERAL STATES

a   Vienna
b   Vorarlberg
c   Tirol
d   Styria
e   Salzburg
f   Upper Austria
g   Lower Austria
h   Carinthia
i   Burgenland

POLICE DETENTION CENTERS IN AUSTRIA

I   Pre-Deportation Detention Center Vordernberg
II   Bludenz
III   Eisenstadt 1
IV   Eisenstadt 2
V   Graz
VI   Innsbruck
VII   Klagenfurt
VIII   Leoben
IX   Linz
X   Salzburg
XI   Schwechat
XII   St. Pölten
XIII   Steyr
XIV   Villach
XV   Wels
XVI   Vienna Hernalser Gürtel
XVII   Vienna Rossauerlände
XVIII   Wiener Neustadt

People
frequentation of stations, points of congestion and waiting rooms

Room size
duration of stay in the station

Wall
limitation and barrier to the environment

Exterior wall
barrier to the environment

Section wall
barrier between sections

Partition wall
connected stations

Glass wall
barrier with visual connection to the environment

Door
showing directions through the system

Door
guiding through the system

Swinging door
one-time entry and exit point

Revolving door
repeated entry and exit point

Sliding door
points out an important stage

Rolling grilles
compulsory departure

Window
contact to the environment

Fixed glazing
visual relationship - contact only to a limited extent

Tilt and turn window
physical contact with the environment to a limited extent

Check point
important station - can only be crossed with an administrative decree

Court yard
limited freedom within the system

With the green identity card leaving the IRC is allowed, but the movement is restricted to the district level.

Initial Reception Center

With the white identity card full mobility within Austria is granted, but leaving the country is prohibited. Depending on the accommodation of the asylum seeker he can not be absent longer than 1-3 nights.

Basic Welfare Support

Full mobility within Austria is granted and also leaving the country is allowed, but people holding Subsidiary Protection can not travel to their home country. People with a residence permit card need to apply for extension regularly.

Subsidiary Protection and Residence Entitlement

Spiral staircase
points of supportive interventions of NGOs within the system

This visualisation is based on Austrian asylum laws which were in effect in June of 2015.

STATES OF REFUGE / FLUCHTRAUM ÖSTERREICH –
Living Biography by Lea Soltau

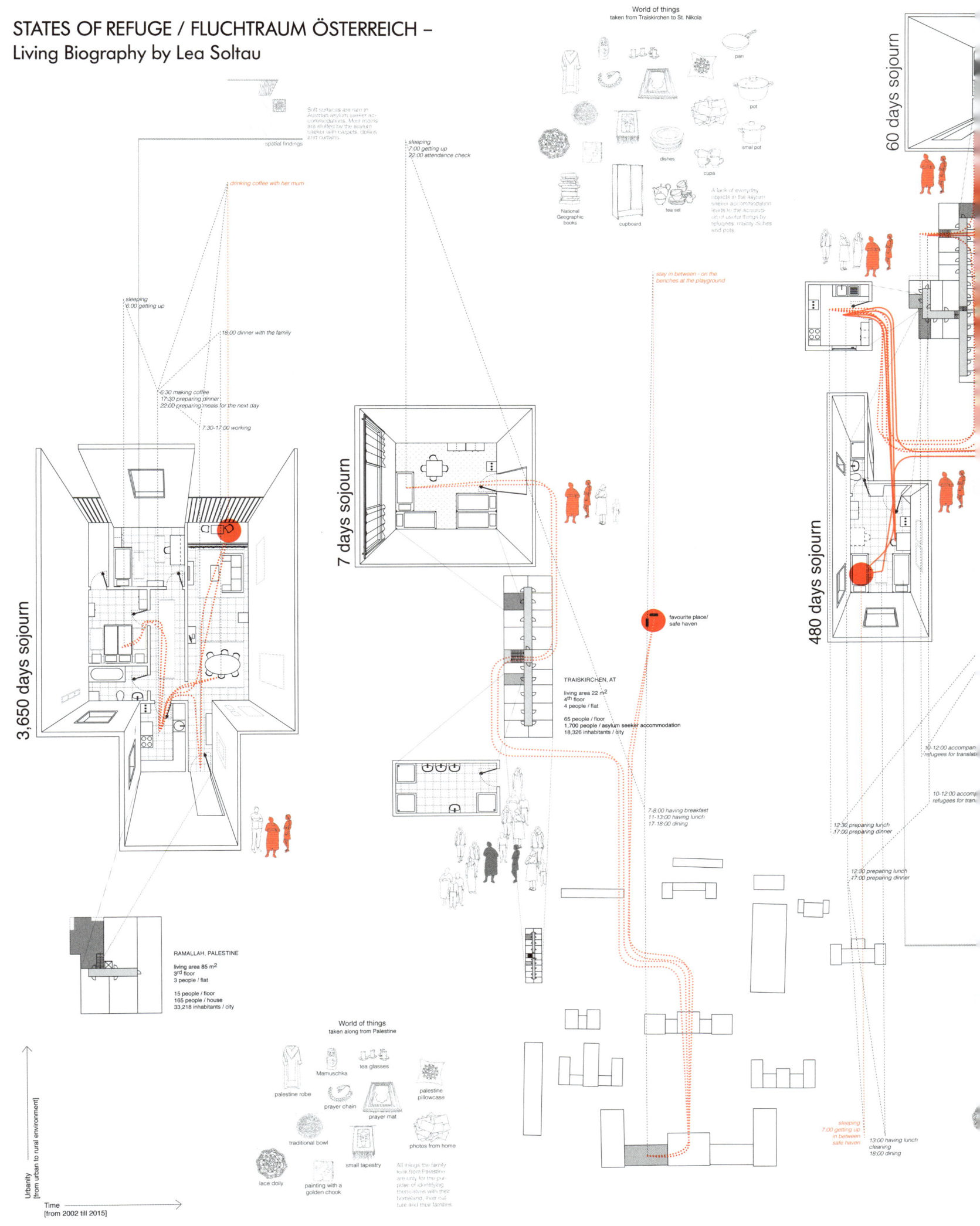

60 days sojourn

World of things
taken from Traiskirchen to St. Nikola

pan

pot

smal pot

dishes

cupa

National
Geographic
books

tea set

cupboard

A lack of everyday
objects in the asylum
seeker accommodation
leads to the accumula-
tion of useful things by
refugees: mainly dishes
and pots

sleeping
7:00 getting up
22:00 attendance check

spatial findings

Sptt surfaces are rare in
Austrian asylum seeker ac-
commodations. Most rooms
are stuffed by the asylum
seeker with carpets, doilies
and curtains.

drinking coffee with her mum

sleeping
6:00 getting up

18:00 dinner with the family

6:30 making coffee
17:30 preparing dinner
22:00 preparing meals for the next day

7:30-17:00 working

7 days sojourn

480 days sojourn

*stay in between - on the
benches at the playground*

favourite place/
safe haven

3,650 days sojourn

TRAISKIRCHEN, AT

living area 22 m²
4th floor
4 people / flat

65 people / floor
1,700 people / asylum seeker accommodation
18,326 inhabitants / city

10-12:00 accompan
refugees for translati

10-12:00 accomp
refugees for tran

12:30 preparing lunch
17:00 preparing dinner

12:30 preparing lunch
17:00 preparing dinner

7-8:00 having breakfast
11-13:00 having lunch
17-18:00 dining

RAMALLAH, PALESTINE

living area 85 m²
3rd floor
3 people / flat

15 people / floor
165 people / house
33,218 inhabitants / city

World of things
taken along from Palestine

Mamuschka

tea glasses

palestine robe

prayer chain

prayer mat

palestine
pillowcase

traditional bowl

photos from home

lace doily

small tapestry

painting with a
golden chook

All things the family
took from Palestine
are only for the pur-
pose of identifying
themselves with their
homeland, their cul-
ture and their families.

*sleeping
7:00 getting up
in between
safe haven*

13:00 having lunch
cleaning
18:00 dining

Urbanity
[from urban to rural environment]

Time
[from 2002 till 2015]

214

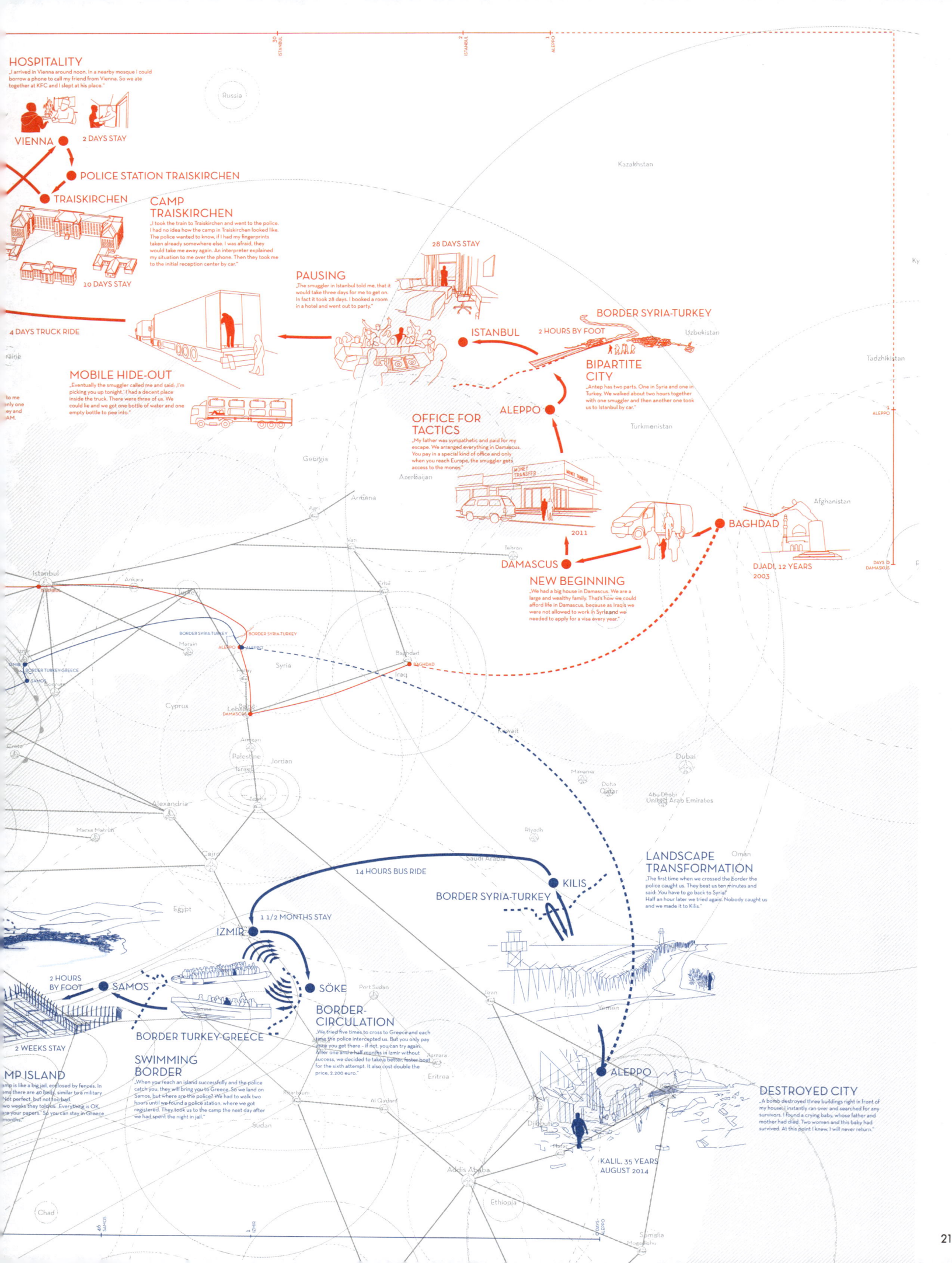

HOSPITALITY

„I arrived in Vienna around noon. In a nearby mosque I could borrow a phone to call my friend from Vienna. So we ate together at KFC and I slept at his place."

VIENNA

2 DAYS STAY

POLICE STATION TRAISKIRCHEN

TRAISKIRCHEN

CAMP TRAISKIRCHEN

„I took the train to Traiskirchen and went to the police. I had no idea how the camp in Traiskirchen looked like. The police wanted to know, if I had my fingerprints taken already somewhere else. I was afraid, they would take me away again. An interpreter explained my situation to me over the phone. Then they took me to the initial reception center by car."

10 DAYS STAY

28 DAYS STAY

PAUSING

„The smuggler in Istanbul told me, that it would take three days for me to get on. In fact it took 28 days. I booked a room in a hotel and went out to party."

4 DAYS TRUCK RIDE

ISTANBUL

BORDER SYRIA-TURKEY

2 HOURS BY FOOT

MOBILE HIDE-OUT

„Eventually the smuggler called me and said: „I'm picking you up tonight. I had a decent place inside the truck. There were three of us. We could lie and we got one bottle of water and one empty bottle to pee into."

BIPARTITE CITY

„Antep has two parts. One in Syria and one in Turkey. We walked about two hours together with one smuggler and then another one took us to Istanbul by car."

ALEPPO

OFFICE FOR TACTICS

„My father was sympathetic and paid for my escape. We arranged everything in Damascus. You pay in a special kind of office and only when you reach Europe, the smuggler gets access to the money."

2011

BAGHDAD

DAMASCUS

NEW BEGINNING

„We had a big house in Damascus. We are a large and wealthy family. That's how we could afford life in Damascus, because as Iraqis we were not allowed to work in Syria and we needed to apply for a visa every year."

DJADI, 12 YEARS 2003

LANDSCAPE TRANSFORMATION

„The first time when we crossed the Border the police caught us. They beat us ten minutes and said: You have to go back to Syria!
Half an hour later we tried again. Nobody caught us and we made it to Kilis."

KILIS

BORDER SYRIA-TURKEY

14 HOURS BUS RIDE

1 1/2 MONTHS STAY

IZMIR

2 HOURS BY FOOT

SAMOS

SÖKE

BORDER-CIRCULATION

„We tried five times to cross to Greece and each time the police intercepted us. But you only pay once you get there - if not, you can try again. After one and a half months in Izmir without success, we decided to take a better, faster boat for the sixth attempt. It also cost double the price, 2.200 euro."

2 WEEKS STAY

BORDER TURKEY-GREECE

SWIMMING BORDER

„When you reach an island successfully and the police catch you, they will bring you to Greece. So we land on Samos, but where are the police? We had to walk two hours until we found a police station, where we got registered. They took us to the camp the next day after we had spent the night in jail."

CAMP ISLAND

Camp is like a big jail, enclosed by fences. In rooms there are 40 beds, similar to a military base. Not perfect, but not too bad.
After two weeks they told us: „Everything is OK, here are your papers." So you can stay in Greece three months."

ALEPPO

DESTROYED CITY

„A bomb destroyed three buildings right in front of my house. I instantly ran over and searched for any survivors. I found a crying baby, whose father and mother had died. Two women and this baby had survived. At this point I knew, I will never return."

KALIL, 35 YEARS AUGUST 2014

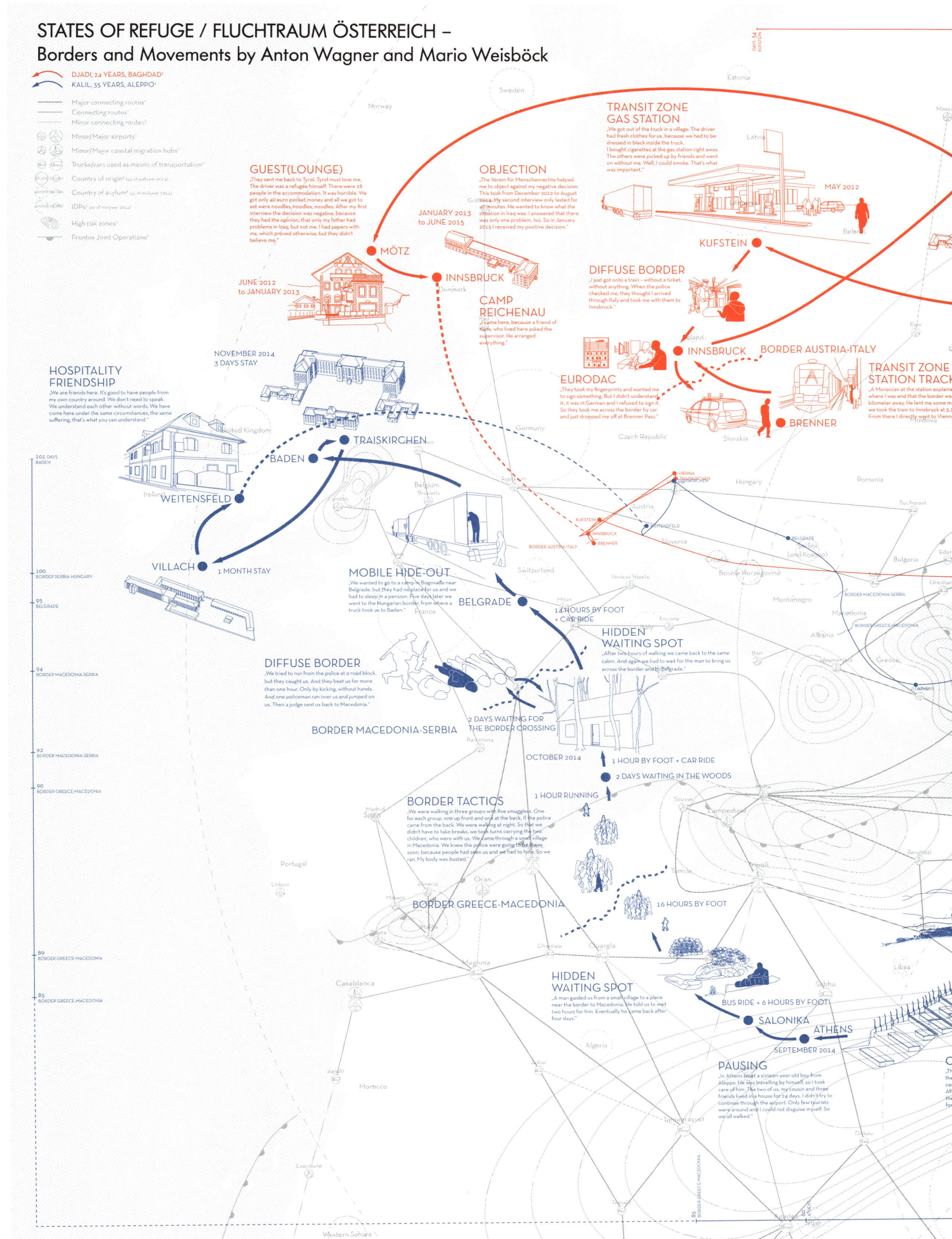

STATES OF REFUGE / FLUCHTRAUM ÖSTERREICH –
Borders and Movements by Anton Wagner and Mario Weisböck

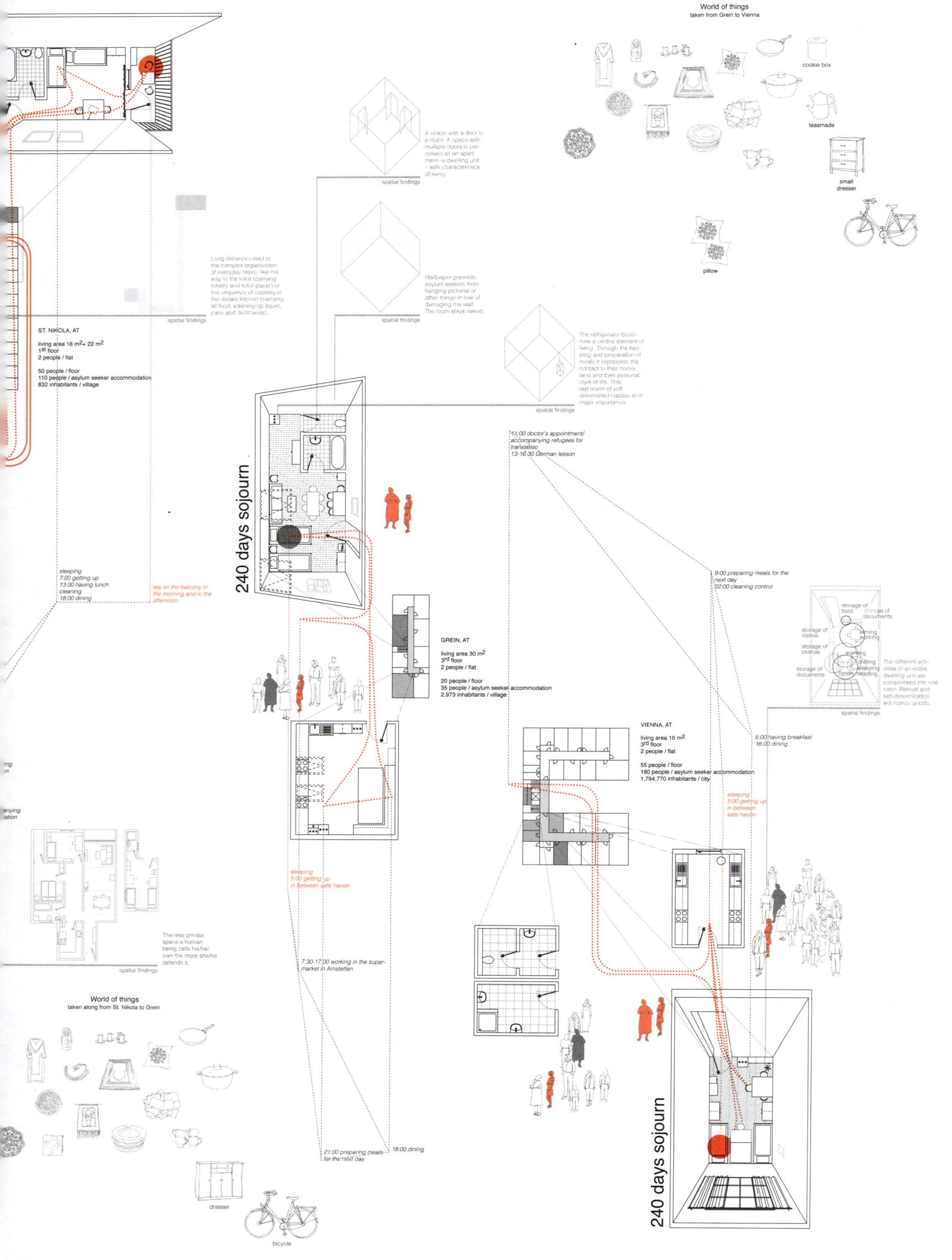

World of things
taken from Grein to Vienna

cookie box
teasmade
small dresser
pillow

A space with a door is a room. A space with multiple doors is perceived as an apartment - a dwelling unit - with characteristics of living.
spatial findings

Wallpaper prevents asylum seekers from hanging pictures or other things in fear of damaging the wall. The room stays naked.
spatial findings

The refrigerator becomes a central element of living. Through the keeping and preparation of meals it represents the contact to their homeland and their personal style of life. This last resort of self-determined habitus is of major importance.
spatial findings

Long distances lead to the complex organisation of everyday tasks, like the way to the toilet (carrying toiletry and toilet paper) or the sequence of cooking in the distant kitchen (carrying all food, washing-up liquid, pans and dishtowels).
spatial findings

ST. NIKOLA, AT

living area 18 m² + 22 m²
1st floor
2 people / flat

50 people / floor
110 people / asylum seeker accommodation
832 inhabitants / village

sleeping
7:00 getting up
13:00 having lunch
cleaning
18:00 dining

tea on the balcony in the morning and in the afternoon

240 days sojourn

11:00 doctor's appointment/ accompanying refugees for translation
13-16:30 German lesson

9:00 preparing meals for the next day
22:00 cleaning control

storage of food
storage of documents
storage of dishes
learning
working
storage of clothes
working
chatting
sleeping
storage of documents
sewing reading

The different activities of an entire dwelling unit are compressed into one room. Retreat and self-determination are scarce goods.
spatial findings

GREIN, AT

living area 30 m²
3rd floor
2 people / flat

20 people / floor
35 people / asylum seeker accommodation
2,973 inhabitants / village

VIENNA, AT

living area 16 m²
3rd floor
2 people / flat

55 people / floor
180 people / asylum seeker accommodation
1,794,770 inhabitants / city

8:00 having breakfast
18:00 dining

sleeping
5:00 getting up
in between safe haven

sleeping
5:00 getting up
in between safe haven

7:30-17:00 working in the supermarket in Amstetten

The less private space a human being calls his/her own the more she/he defends it.
spatial findings

World of things
taken along from St. Nikola to Grein

dresser
bicycle

21:00 preparing meals for the next day
18:00 dining

240 days sojourn

STATES OF REFUGE / FLUCHTRAUM ÖSTERREICH –
Knowledge Landscapes by Martina Soi Gunelas

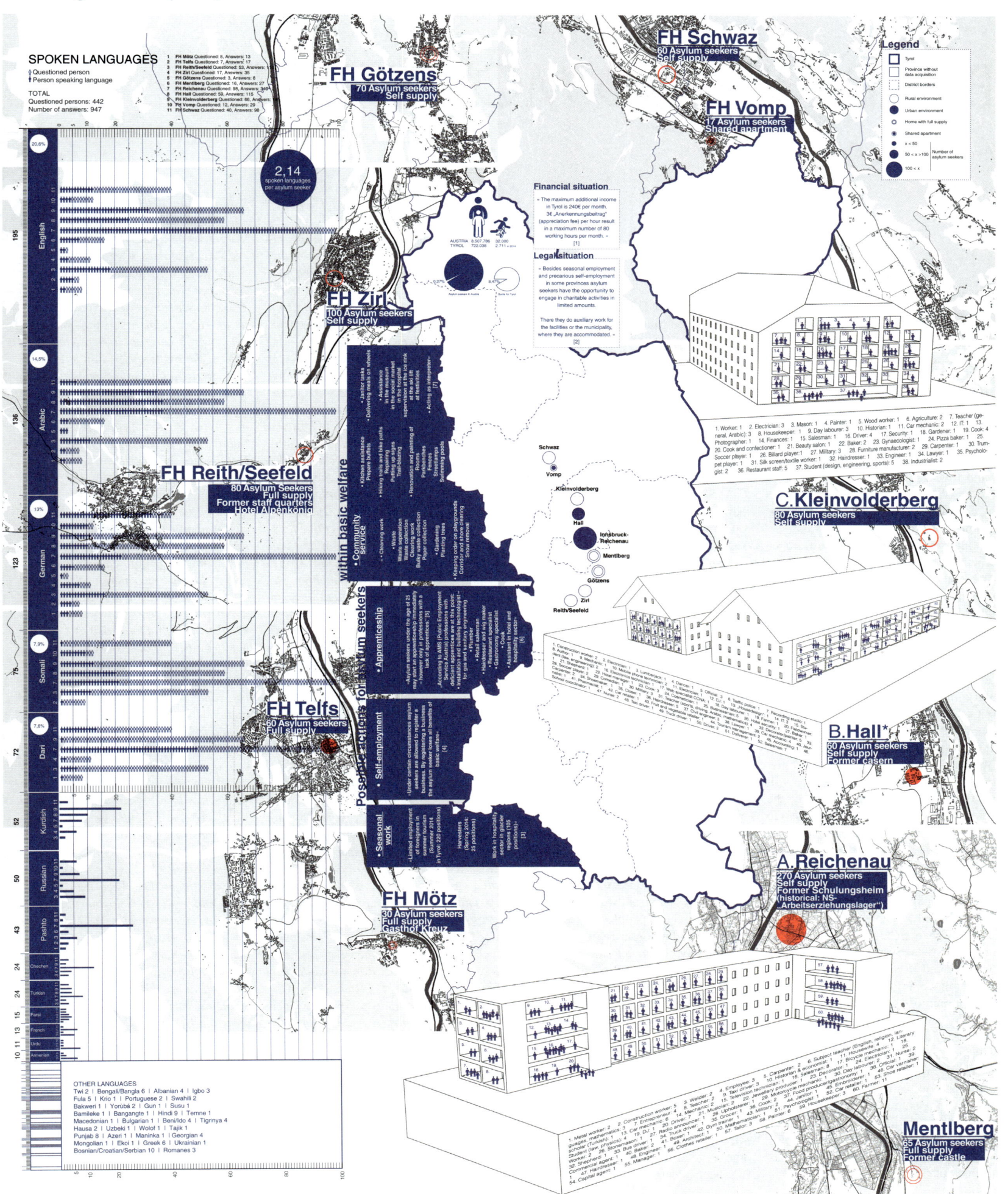

BORDERS AND MOVEMENTS

Anton Wagner, Mario Weisböck

Two refugee stories and their stages

Looking at the individual experiences of Djadi[1] and Kalil[2] should paint a picture that allows one to see behind the public facts and figures of the "flood of refugees". The analysis of the conversations that took place shows that migration must be understood as a complex construct of spatial, political, legal and human interactions that on the one hand reveal patterns and systems, but on the other frequently appear to arise by coincidence from the dynamic of the moment.

It therefore makes a difference whether Djadi fled in 2012 or in 2014 like Kalil, because some borders open up while others close, although the latter – that borders are tightened and become impassable – is observed more frequently, with nations or communities attempting to shut down their own territory to others so that they can see and control precisely who travels in and out[3]. Thus, the government of Bulgaria has been working to strengthen the EU external border since 2012. At the start of construction the Bulgarian Minister of Defence stated, "This fence will stop illegal immigration".[4] In 2015 the Prime Minister of Hungary contrived to construct a 150-metre-long and 4-metre-high fence along the border crossing with Serbia, and Austria was at the same time reconsidering border controls and operational assistance.[5] Borders believed to be open – also within the European Schengen Area – have proven to be subject to the vagaries of the time and have become fluid spaces undergoing many changes. This creates "a community that no longer defines itself by its commonalities, but by the strict guarding of its boundaries"[6] so that the own territory within can exist "without strange looking foreigners that creep out of dark corners and the streets of the slums".[7]

This is precisely what is happening, both at simple border fences where soldiers equipped with weapons sit in watchtowers, able to monitor the cleared strip of land along the border area, and at automated multi-fenced borders equipped with tear gas and monitored by cameras.[8] At topographical features that can act as boundaries, constructional changes become obsolete: seas, rivers, deserts and mountains present barriers that are insurmountable or can only be passed with huge difficulty and that not only entail the risk of attack, but also endanger life.

Should the outsiders overcome the barriers and come through with their otherness intact, they can always be segregated and locked away, interned in camps or be sent "back". But this begs the question of where this "back" should be, because the refugees do not have, or no longer have, a place of their own. In transit, they are always the others, the foreigners, who are neither inside nor outside and move in a grey area between the two.

For the refugee, this is also invariably about whether they can be seen and discovered or whether they must hide or disguise themselves. While Syrian refugees for example are able move freely in Turkey, are permitted to work there, even if only as cheap labour,[9] and are therefore free to choose and determine their own paths, this self-determination ends when it comes to crossing a border. This requires helpers who are familiar with the local situation, the geographical context and the surveillance system: in short, people who know the strategy of the border regime and how to tactically circumvent it.

The border fence – Transformation of the landscape

When Kalil fled from Aleppo in August 2014, the first border at which he and two friends arrived, was the border strip between Syria and Turkey, some distance away from a typical border crossing. The wire mesh fence there is ca. 3.5 metres high and has barbed wire at the top to prevent climbing. The vegetation in front of the fence has been cleared, making it impossi-

Zwei Fluchtgeschichten und deren Stationen

Durch die Betrachtung der individuell erlebten Geschichten von Djadi[1] und Kalil[2] soll ein Bild gezeichnet werden, das einen persönlichen Blick hinter allgemeine Zahlen und Fakten von "Flüchtlingsströmen" ermöglicht. Die Analyse der Gespräche zeigt, dass Flucht als ein komplexes Konstrukt von räumlichen, politischen, juristischen und zwischenmenschlichen Verflechtungen verstanden werden muss, an denen sich einerseits Muster und Systeme erkennen lassen, diese aber andererseits oft zufällig aus der Dynamik des Augenblickes zu entstehen scheinen.

So macht es einen Unterschied, ob man wie Djadi im Jahr 2012 oder wie Kalil im Jahr 2014 geflohen ist, weil sich manche Grenzen öffnen und andere wiederum schließen. Wobei Letzteres häufiger zu beobachten ist: Dass sich Grenzen verdichten und undurchlässig werden. Also Staaten oder Gemeinschaften den Ort des Eigenen gegenüber dem Fremden abzuschließen versuchen,[3] um genau beobachten und kontrollieren zu können, wer ein- und wer ausreist. So baut die bulgarische Regierung seit 2012 an der Verhärtung der EU-Außengrenze. Zum Baubeginn wünschte sich der bulgarische Verteidigungsminister: "Dieser Zaun wird die illegale Einwanderung stoppen."[4] 2015 plant der ungarische Premierminister, einen 150 Meter langen und vier Meter hohen Grenzzaun an der serbisch-ungarischen Grenze zu errichten, und Österreich zieht parallel dazu erneute Grenzkontrollen und Assistenzeinsätze in Betracht.[5] Offen geglaubte Grenzen – auch innerhalb des EU-Schengenraumes – erweisen sich als Gegenstand der Zeit und unterliegen als fluide Räume vielfacher Veränderung. Somit entsteht "eine Gemeinschaft, die sich nicht mehr über ihre Gemeinsamkeit, sondern über die scharfe Bewachung ihrer Grenzen definiert,"[6] damit im Inneren der eigene Bereich "ohne komisch dreinschauende Fremde, die aus dunklen Ecken und den Straßen der Elendsviertel hervorkriechen"[7] existieren kann.

Und genau das passiert sowohl an einfachen Grenzzäunen – an denen Soldaten in Wachtürmen sitzen und mit einem Gewehr ausgestattet den leergeräumten Landstreifen entlang des Grenzgebietes überblicken können – als auch an automatisierten mehrschaligen Grenzzäunen, die mit einer Tränengassprühvorrichtung ausgestattet und über Kameras genau einsehbar sind.[8] An topographischen Gegebenheiten, die als Grenzen fungieren können, werden bauliche Veränderungen obsolet: Meere, Flüsse, Wüsten und Gebirge stellen unüberwindbare oder nur unter großer Anstrengung bewältigbare Barrieren dar, die nicht nur die Gefahr des Aufgegriffenwerdens, sondern eine Gefährdung des Lebens mit sich bringen.

Sollten die Fremden nun die Barrieren überwinden und ihre Andersartigkeit mit hineinnehmen, kann man sie immer noch segregieren und wegsperren, in Lagern internieren oder wieder "zurück" schicken. Die Frage, die sich dabei stellt ist jedoch, wo dieses "Zurück" sein soll, denn einen Ort des Eigenen gibt es für die Flüchtenden nicht, beziehungsweise nicht mehr. Auf ihrer Flucht sind sie immer die Anderen, die Fremden, die sich weder innen noch außen befinden und sich in einer Grauzone dazwischen bewegen.

Das heißt also auch, dass es immer darum geht, ob man gesehen und entdeckt werden kann oder ob man sich verstecken bzw. tarnen muss. Während sich syrische Flüchtlinge z.B. innerhalb der Türkei frei bewegen und dort – wenn auch als billige Arbeitskräfte – arbeiten dürfen,[9] sie sich also frei und selbstbestimmt ihre Wege wählen können, endet diese Selbstbestimmtheit, wenn es darum geht, eine Grenze zu überqueren. Dazu braucht es HelferInnen, welche die Situation vor Ort, die geographischen Gegebenheiten, das Überwachungssystem oder kurz: die Strategie des Grenzregimes kennen und diese taktisch zu umgehen wissen.

Der Grenzzaun – Transformation der Landschaft

Als Kalil im August 2014 aus Aleppo floh, war die erste Grenze, an die er mit zwei Freunden traf, der Grenzstreifen zwischen Syrien und der Türkei, fern von einem regulären Grenzübergang. Der

ble to hide anywhere near the border fence. Watchtowers and patrols ensure that the strip is visible and monitored. Therefore, in order to cross the border unseen, it was done at night. On their first attempt to reach Turkey Kalil's group were discovered by the police, beaten for ten whole minutes and then sent back to Syria.

For Djadi two years earlier, crossing the border near Antep was much easier.[10] He travelled in a car to a border town, where he formed a group with six others. Transformed like the natural landscape by the construction of fences, in an urban context there are no buildings inside the border zone. Instead, police and military checkpoints are set up on roads and transit routes. An individual who helped refugees, familiar with the local circumstances and networks, led the group on foot from the Syrian to the Turkish part of the city inside two hours, then drove them in a bus from there to Istanbul. The border between the two countries was relatively open to movement in both directions. It was possible to cross guarded border crossings in cities with just a Syrian ID; no passport was required. The Orontes boundary river and the poorly monitored, penetrable fence permitted people and goods such as weapons and diesel to be smuggled from Turkey to Syria and vice versa.[11]

Under pressure from the USA and the EU[12] to cap the supply route to IS-occupied territory, the Turkish government increased checks along the border zone in order to stop supplies to the IS and potential IS fighters from entering Syria – but this likewise affects people leaving Syria seeking protection.

For a few hours in June 2015 Turkey closed the border near the town of Akçakale, a major border crossing, and using water cannons and warning shots prevented thousands of people from entering – people fleeing from skirmishes between IS and Kurdish fighters around the Syrian border town Tal Abjad. At the same time, presumed IS fighters attempted to stop the refugees from leaving.[13] In this desperate situation, some of the refugees broke through the border fence or attempted to climb over it.[14]

The topographical boundary

While landscape is transformed for the construction of fences and in order to be able to erect buildings and optimise surveillance, certain topographical features form border systems that create barriers without the need for transformation. These however make progress significantly harder for refugees and endanger the lives of those who can no longer enter by the overland route. On the sea route over the Mediterranean since 2000, more than 23,000 people have died.[15]

Crossing the Aegean, in 2014 more than 26,000 people reached the Greek islands of Lesbos, Samos and Chios, which lie just a short distance away from the Turkish mainland. One of these was Kalil, who had tried to reach Greece from Izmir in an over-loaded rubber dinghy five times, but was caught by the Turkish police each time and returned to Turkey.[16] The sixth attempt with a faster, but twice as expensive, boat successfully brought the group to Samos.[17]

For Kalil, it was important to be registered in Greece and on the EU-RODAC fingerprint database so that he could subsequently apply for asylum in another EU country. The Dublin III Regulation applicable in the EU states that asylum seekers can be returned to the Member State through which they first entered the EU. In 2012 the European Court of Human Rights ruled that to return asylum seekers to Greece was unjustifiable in view of serious short-comings in the accommodation available to them.[18]

So that Kalil could legally stay in Greece and subsequently leave the country without being sent back there, he deliberately sought out the police. Usually, the Greek coastguard service as well as Frontex monitor movements in the Mediterranean and asylum seekers are taken into custody as soon as they arrive on an island.[19] But Kalil's group had to search Samos on foot for two hours before they found a police station, in which they were registered. Two days later, they were brought to a camp.

Diffuse borders

Border systems are not only connected to their geographical location and should not be understood only in the linear sense. For refugees travelling through a country, checks in trains, roadblocks and police identity checks in the public sphere constitute mobile borders that seem diffuse and remain invisible for travellers with the right passport. Without the right documents however, a lack of information about the given border situation causes major anxieties.

Following a walk across the border from Macedonia to Serbia, the car that was to bring Kalil to Belgrade was stopped at a roadblock. In an attempt to run away from the police the group were caught and held at the side of the road for over an hour, in which they were kicked, ill-treated and questioned at gunpoint: "Are you a Christian, or are you a Muslim?" Kalil's answer shows the strength of his will to find a new home and how little he had to lose: "I am a Muslim! I have survived the civil war in Syria, I have come this far. You are a policeman, you will not shoot me!" After a few hours, they were eventually brought to a police station, where a magistrate had them returned to Macedonia again.

When Djadi got on a train to Innsbruck shortly after having arrived in

Maschendrahtzaun dort ist ungefähr 3,5 Meter hoch, Stacheldraht als oberer Abschluss soll das Überklettern verhindern. In dem Bereich vor dem Zaun wurde die Vegetation entfernt, wodurch in unmittelbarer Nähe zum Grenzzaun ein Verstecken unmöglich gemacht wird. Die Einsichtigkeit und Überwachbarkeit des Streifens wird durch Wachtürme und Patrouillen sichergestellt. Um also ungesehen die Grenze zu passieren, geschahen die Bewegungen in der Nacht. Beim ersten Versuch, die Türkei zu erreichen, wurde Kalils Gruppe von der Polizei entdeckt, zehn Minuten lang geschlagen und danach wieder zurück nach Syrien geschickt.

Für Djadi – zwei Jahre früher – war der Grenzübertritt in der Nähe von Antep noch wesentlich einfacher.[10] Mit einem Auto fuhr er zu einer Grenzstadt, in der er sich mit sechs weiteren Personen zu einer Gruppe zusammenschloss. In einer ähnlichen Transformation, wie sie die natürliche Landschaft durch das Errichten von Zäunen erfährt, existieren im urbanen Kontext keine Gebäude innerhalb der Grenzzone. Stattdessen entstehen von Polizei und Militär bewachte Checkpoints an Straßen und Transitrouten.

Ein Fluchthelfer, der die örtlichen Gegebenheiten und Personennetzwerke kannte, führte die Gruppe zu Fuß innerhalb von zwei Stunden vom syrischen in den türkischen Teil der Stadt, von der aus sie ein Kleinbus nach Istanbul brachte. Die Grenze zwischen den beiden Ländern war relativ offen für Bewegungen in beide Richtungen. Bewachte Grenzübergänge in Städten konnten mit syrischem Ausweis überquert werden, ohne einen Reisepass zu benötigen. Der Grenzfluss Orontes sowie der wenig bewachte, poröse Zaun ermöglichten das Schmuggeln von Personen und Waren, wie Waffen und Diesel sowohl von der Türkei nach Syrien als auch in umgekehrter Richtung.[11]

Unter dem Druck von USA und EU,[12] die Versorgungsroute in IS-besetztes Gebiet zu kappen, verstärkte die türkische Regierung die Kontrollen entlang der Grenzzone, um Lieferungen an den IS und dem Einreisen von potentiellen IS-Kämpfern nach Syrien Einhalt zu gebieten, was Schutzsuchende, die versuchen, aus Syrien zu fliehen gleichermaßen trifft.

Im Juni 2015 schloss die Türkei für wenige Stunden die Grenze bei der Stadt Akçakale – die einen wichtigen Grenzübergang darstellte – und hinderte mit Wasserwerfern und Warnschüssen tausende Menschen an der Einreise, die vor Gefechten zwischen

dem IS und kurdischen Kämpfern um die syrische Grenzstadt Tal Abjad flohen. Gleichzeitig versuchten mutmaßliche IS-Kämpfer die Flüchtenden an der Ausreise zu hindern.[13] In dieser verzweifelten Situation durchbrachen einige Flüchtende den Grenzzaun oder versuchten ihn zu überklettern.[14]

Die topographische Grenze

Während für das Errichten von Zäunen die Landschaft verändert wird, um bauliche Strukturen schaffen zu können und ein Maximum an Überwachbarkeit zu sichern, stellen gewisse topographische Gegebenheiten Grenzsysteme dar, die ohne Transformation Barrieren bilden. Diese erschweren wiederum maßgeblich das Weiterkommen während der Flucht und bringen die Schutzsuchenden, die nicht mehr über den Landweg einreisen können, in Lebensgefahr. So endete der Seeweg über das Mittelmeer seit dem Jahr 2000 für mehr als 23.000 Menschen tödlich.[15]

Über die Ägäis haben im Jahr 2014 mehr als 26.000 Menschen die griechischen Inseln Lesbos, Samos und Chios erreicht, die in nur kurzer Entfernung zum türkischen Festland liegen. Einer von ihnen war Kalil, der fünf Mal versucht hatte, in einem überfüllten Gummiboot von Izmir aus nach Griechenland zu gelangen, aber jedes Mal von der türkischen Polizei abgefangen und zurück in die Türkei gebracht worden war.[16] Der sechste Versuch mit einem schnelleren, auch doppelt so teuren Boot brachte die Gruppe erfolgreich nach Samos.[17]

Für Kalil war es wichtig, sich in Griechenland registrieren und in der Fingerabdruckdatenbank EURODAC speichern zu lassen, um später in einem anderen EU-Land Asyl beantragen zu können. Die Dublin III-Verordnung regelt innerhalb der EU, dass Flüchtlinge in jenes EU-Land abgeschoben werden können, in dem sie das erste Mal europäischen Boden betreten haben. Der Europäische Gerichtshof für Menschenrechte stufte in einem Urteil im Jahr 2012 Rückführungen nach Griechenland – aufgrund schwerer Mängel in der Unterbringung von Flüchtlingen – als unverantwortbar ein.[18]

Damit Kalil sich legal in Griechenland aufhalten und später das Land verlassen konnte, ohne wieder dahin zurück geschickt zu werden, suchte er bewusst die Polizei auf. Üblicherweise beobachten sowohl die griechische Küstenwache als auch Frontex Bewegungen im Mittelmeer, und Flüchtlinge werden sofort nach ihrer Ankunft auf einer Insel in Gewahrsam genommen.[19]

Kufstein, he was checked during the journey by police officers. Because he could produce neither proof of his identity nor a ticket, he was taken to a police station. There, his fingerprints were taken and compared with the EU-RODAC database in order to determine whether Austria was responsible for his asylum proceedings. After questioning, he refused to sign a document written in German because he did not understand it. Although there was no evidence whatsoever that Djadi had entered Austria from Italy, the police deported him to the Italian town of Brenner.

A trilateral agreement between the Austrian, Italian and German authorities facilitates the handing over and deportation of asylum seekers across their national borders when it can be assumed that the flight route has crossed one of them. This occurs outside the jurisdiction of the Dublin III Regulation and does not have to be verified by a judicial body. Thus for the police, a receipt from Italy is always enough evidence to enforce the deportation of refugees to that country. This means that for refugees, crossing a border does not end with crossing a line. The border as a line exists de facto only on a map and regulates only the responsibilities of the executive. Refugees only gain the right to be in a territory when their application for asylum is being processed and only this ensures that they cannot be deported at will.

The borders themselves are thus reduced to the smallest possible dimension, the human body. Through the recording of fingerprints and other biometric characteristics, registered refugees carry their border areas with them like shackles, irrespective of location. The human body and the border merge and become indistinguishable from one another. This spatial reduction results in the expansion of the scope of the border regime and reduces people with political and legal status to their mere physical existence, to nothing but their lives.

The camp – Legal limitations

Alongside these delocalised borders that adhere to the human body, camps represent tangible materialised structures in which refugees are interned and lack autonomy, because they are dependent on the camp organisation. "Because its inhabitants are divested of all political status and reduced to mere existence, the camp is also the most biopolitical environment ever created, where power is good for nothing but pure biological life with no agency whatsoever." [20]

Camps may be described on the one hand as governmental structures that assume functions of internment and control: The function of the camp on Samos in Greece in which Kalil spent two weeks is to intern newly arrived refugees for a few days while their documents are checked. But the few days often turn into weeks, which means that the camp originally designed for 280 persons is consistently overcrowded. [21] On the other hand, studies show that the interdependencies formed between asylum seekers and those who help them also reflect the spirit of the camp. The people in these camps find themselves in exceptional circumstances; they have been taken out of society and from their political lives extending beyond the purely existential.

Limits of hospitality

If the flood of refugees is seen as a state of emergency that overwhelms the individual, then it stands that asylum seekers en route are excluded from being part of a society. They are the "others" who belong to another society which is no longer theirs. Europe has committed to protect these people, because "everyone has the right to life, liberty and security of person" [22] and "[...] to leave any country, including his own [...]" [23]. It is precisely this obligation that the progressive hardening of Europe's external borders is working against, which is shown by the comparison of the refugee stories of Djadi (2012) and Kalil (2014) and by contemporary reports about the routes taken by refugees. [24]

●

Kalils Gruppe musste aber erst zwei Stunden auf Samos zu Fuß suchen, bis sie eine Polizeistation fand, in der sie registriert und zwei Tage später in ein Lager gebracht wurde.

Diffuse Grenzen

Grenzsysteme sind nicht nur an ihren geographischen Ort gebunden und nicht nur als eine einzige Linie zu sehen. Für Flüchtende auf der Durchreise durch ein Land stellen Kontrollen im Zug, Straßensperren und polizeiliche Identitätsfeststellungen im öffentlichen Raum mobile Grenzen dar, die diffus erscheinen und für Reisende mit dem passenden Ausweis unsichtbar bleiben. Ohne die richtigen Papiere bringt eine Unwissenheit über die konkrete Grenzsituation jedoch große Unsicherheiten mit sich.

Nach einem Fußmarsch über die Grenze von Mazedonien nach Serbien wurde das Auto, das Kalil bis Belgrad bringen sollte, bei einer Sperre auf einer Landstraße aufgehalten. Beim Versuch vor der Polizei davonzulaufen, wurde die Gruppe erwischt und von einem Polizisten mehr als eine Stunde lang am Straßenrand mit Füßen getreten, misshandelt und mit vorgehaltener Pistole gefragt: "Bist du Christ oder bist du Moslem?" Kalils Antwort lässt erkennen, wie viel Wille eine neue Heimat zu finden und wie wenig zu verlieren er hatte: "Ich bin Moslem! Ich habe den Bürgerkrieg in Syrien überlebt, ich bin bis hierher gekommen. Du bist Polizist, du erschießt mich nicht!" Erst einige Stunden später wurden sie zu einer Polizeistation gebracht, von der aus sie ein Richter wieder nach Mazedonien bringen ließ.

Als Djadi kurz nach seiner Ankunft in Kufstein in einen Zug nach Innsbruck eingestiegen war, wurde er während der Fahrt von Polizeibeamten kontrolliert. Da er sich weder ausweisen noch ein Ticket vorzeigen konnte, wurde er auf eine Polizeistation mitgenommen. Dort wurden ihm die Fingerabdrücke abgenommen und mit dem EURODAC System abgeglichen, um festzustellen, ob Österreich für Djadis Asylverfahren zuständig war. Er weigerte sich nach der Einvernahme ein deutschsprachiges Dokument zu unterschreiben, weil er es nicht verstand. Obwohl es keinerlei Anhaltspunkte und Beweise dafür gab, dass Djadi über Italien nach Österreich eingereist war, wurde er von der Polizei in die italienische Ortschaft Brenner abgeschoben.

Ein trilaterales Abkommen zwischen den österreichischen, italienischen und deutschen Behörden erlaubt es, Schutzsuchende über unterschiedliche Staatsgebiete durchzureichen und abzuschieben, wenn davon auszugehen ist, dass die Fluchtroute über eines der Länder verlaufen ist. Dies geschieht nicht im Rahmen eines Dublin-Verfahrens und muss nicht von einer juristischen Instanz geprüft werden. So genügt der Polizei ein Rechnungsbeleg aus Italien jederzeit als Beweis, um Flüchtlinge dorthin abzuschieben. Das bedeutet, dass für Flüchtlinge der Grenzübertritt nicht durch das Überqueren einer Linie abgeschlossen ist. Die Grenze als Linie existiert de facto nur auf einer Landkarte und regelt ausschließlich die Zuständigkeiten der Exekutive. Flüchtlinge erhalten erst durch eine Aufnahme in das Asylverfahren die Berechtigung, sich auf diesem Territorium zu befinden, und erst damit die Sicherheit, nicht willkürlich abgeschoben werden zu können.

Die Grenzen selbst werden dabei auf den kleinstmöglichen Maßstab reduziert, den menschlichen Körper. Durch die Speicherung der Fingerabdrücke und anderer biometrischer Eigenschaften tragen registrierte Flücht-

linge ihren Grenzraum wie Fußfesseln ortsunabhängig mit sich. Der menschliche Körper und die Grenze gehen ineinander über und werden ununterscheidbar. Diese räumliche Reduktion bewirkt die Vergrößerung der Tragweite des Grenzregimes und reduziert den Menschen mit politischem und juristischem Status auf seine bloße physische Existenz, auf sein nacktes Leben.

Das Lager – Juristische Grenzen

Neben diesen dem menschlichen Körper anhaftenden, ortsunabhängigen Grenzen, stellen Lager konkrete materialisierte Strukturen dar, in denen Flüchtende interniert werden und in Abhängigkeit der Lagerführung über keine Selbstbestimmtheit verfügen. "Weil seine Insassen jedes politischen Status beraubt und gänzlich auf bloßes Leben reduziert wurden, ist das Lager auch der absoluteste biopolitische Raum, der je realisiert wurde, wo die Macht nichts als das reine biologische Leben ohne jegliche Vermittlung vor sich hat." [20]

Von Lagern kann einerseits in Zusammenhang mit staatlichen Strukturen, die eine Internierungs- und Überprüfungsfunktion übernehmen, gesprochen werden: Das Camp auf Samos in Griechenland, in dem Kalil zwei Wochen verbrachte, hat die Funktion, neu angekommene Flüchtlinge während der Zeit der Überprüfung ihrer Papiere wenige Tage zu internieren. Jedoch werden häufig aus den wenigen Tagen Wochen, wodurch das eigentlich für 280 Personen ausgelegte Lager ständig mehr als überfüllt ist. [21] Andererseits trifft auch in Untersuchungen der Abhängigkeitsverhältnisse zwischen Schutzsuchenden und Fluchthelfern in Verstecken vor einem Grenzübertritt der Begriff des Lagers zu. Die Menschen in diesen Lagern befinden sich in einem Ausnahmezustand; sie wurden heraus genommen aus der Gesellschaft und ihrem politischen Leben, das über das reine Am-Leben-Sein hinausgeht.

Grenzen der Gastfreundschaft

Betrachtet man die gesamte Flucht als einen Ausnahmezustand, der über einen Menschen hereinbricht, bedeutet das, dass Schutzsuchende auf ihrem Weg davon ausgenommen sind, Teil einer Gesellschaft zu sein. Sie sind die Fremden, die einer anderen Gesellschaft angehören, die nicht mehr ihre eigene ist. Für den Schutz dieser Fremden hat sich Europa verpflichtet, denn "jeder hat das Recht auf Leben, Freiheit und Sicherheit der Person" [22] und "[...]jedes Land, einschließlich seines eigenen, zu verlassen[...]." [23] Genau dieser Verpflichtung wirkt die voranschreitende Verhärtung der europäischen Außengrenzen entgegen, welche im Vergleich der Fluchtgeschichten von Djadi (2012) und Kalil (2014) sowie an aktuellen Berichten über Fluchtrouten sichtbar werden. [24]

A STRANGER AT HOME
Kristina Mostovaia
Jamila Bräunlich
Doreen Ahmed

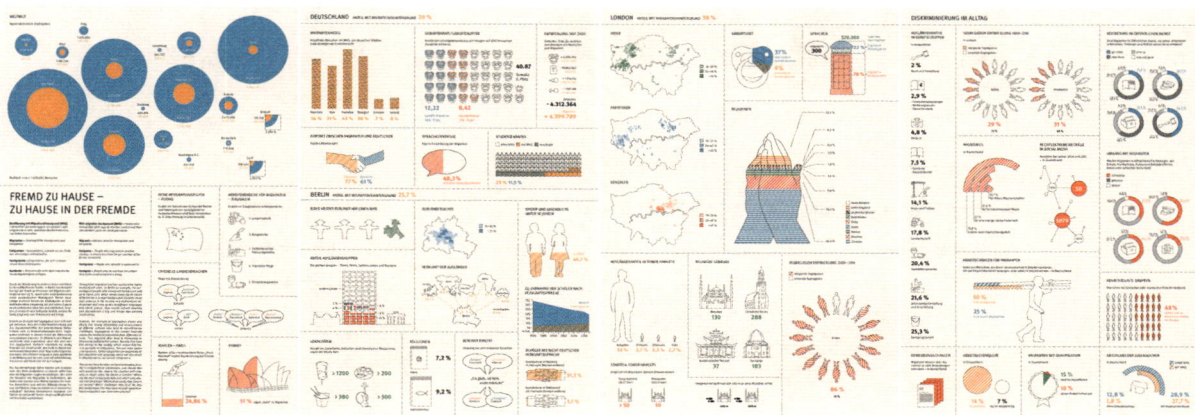

With migration background – People who immigrated after 1949 to another country and their descendants up to the third generation.

Emigrants – People who migrated to another country, in most cases seen from the perspective of the former homeland.

Immigrants – People who relocate in a new country.

Foreigner – A person who does not have the citizenship of the country he or she is living in.

Through transnational migration, increasingly multicultural cities are developing. In Berlin, for example, the percentage of people with a migration background adds up to about 30%, which means every third Berlin citizen has a foreign background. 38% of Londoners have a migration background: in Greater London more than 300 languages exist, as well as a multitude of religious communities. Today, children are growing up in a multicultural environment as early as in the nursery, and have access to different languages and ethnic groups. The result is cultural diversity that shapes a city in new ways and brings along many positive implications.

When considering social segregation processes, one can easily see that strong intermixing and co-occurrence of different cultures also lead to miscellaneous challenges. In this context, segregation basically means the separation of different cultures, spatially and with regards to their living worlds. In European migrant quarters, many immigrants keep to themselves or are excluded by natives. Right-wing populist parties are expanding in all European countries; here, the scapegoats for the stagnating economic development since 2007 are people with a migration background. Discrimination, racism and intolerance lead to little contacts with society as a whole; integration is not happening in many cases. Failed integration can negatively affect education and language, and thus lead to a vicious circle of disadvantage, also for the generations to follow: In Germany, only 3% of foreigners are employed in the finance service sector or in tax consultancy, while 25% are employed in cleaning. Out of 15% highly qualified migrants, every tenth person cannot find a job.

In order to analyse these complex connections, one should ask the following questions: What is the situation of migrants in major cities like Berlin or London? Where do most immigrants come from and which educational level do they have? What chances do they have in our society? Which challenges do they face? Do they feel comfortable? Do they have opportunities to enjoy their own cultures?

Bevölkerung mit Migrationshintergrund – Menschen, die nach 1949 in ein anderes Land eingewandert sind, sowie deren Nachkommen bis zur dritten Generation.

Emigranten – Auswanderer, zumeist aus der Sicht des ehemaligen Heimatlandes

Immigranten – Einwanderer, die sich in einem neuen Staat niederlassen.

Ausländer – Personen, die nicht über inländische Staatsangehörigkeit verfügen.

Durch die transnationalen Wanderbewegungen entstehen zunehmend multikulturelle Städte. In Berlin beträgt der Anteil an Personen mit Migrationshintergrund beispielsweise rund 30 %, sprich rund jeder dritte Berliner hat einen ausländischen Hintergrund. 38 % der Londoner haben einen Migrationshintergrund: im Großraum London werden über 300 verschiedene Sprachen gesprochen, und es existiert eine Vielfalt an religiösen Glaubensgemeinschaften. Heutzutage wachsen Kinder bereits im Kindergarten in einer multikulturellen Umgebung auf und haben Zugang zu verschiedenen Sprachen und Kontakt zu verschiedenen ethnischen Gruppen. Es entsteht eine kulturelle Vielfalt, welche die Stadt in neuer Weise prägt und viele Vorteile mit sich bringt.

Betrachtet man aber gesellschaftliche Segregationsprozesse, lässt sich sehr gut erkennen, dass die starke Durchmischung und das Zusammentreffen der verschiedenen Kulturkreise auch zu Herausforderungen führen.

Segregation bedeutet in diesem Sinne die Trennung verschiedener Kulturen, räumlich und in Bezug auf ihre alltäglichen Lebenswelten. So bleiben in den europäischen Migrantenvierteln viele Zuwanderer unter sich oder werden ausgegrenzt. Rechtspopulistische Parteien finden in allen europäischen Ländern immer stärkeren Zulauf; die Sündenböcke für die stagnierende wirtschaftliche Entwicklung seit 2007 sind oft Menschen mit Migrationshintergrund. So führen Diskriminierung, Rassismus und Intoleranz dazu, dass nur wenige Kontakte zur Gesellschaft entstehen; es findet teilweise keine Integration statt. Gescheiterte Integration kann Nachteile in der Bildung und Sprache mit sich bringen und so einen Teufelskreis der Benachteiligung, auch für nachfolgende Generationen, auslösen: In Deutschland sind beispielsweise nur knapp 3 % der Ausländer im Finanzwesen und in der Steuerberatung tätig, während 25 % Reinigungsberufe ausüben. Von den 15 % hochqualifizierten Migranten findet jede zehnte Person keinen Job.

Um diese meist sehr komplexen Zusammenhänge analysieren zu können, sollte man sich folgende Fragen stellen: Wie sieht die Situation von Migranten in Großstädten wie Berlin oder London aus? Woher kommen die meisten Zuwanderer und welches Bildungsniveau haben sie? Welche Chancen haben sie in unserer Gesellschaft? Welchen Hindernissen begegnen sie? Fühlen sie sich wohl? Haben sie die Möglichkeit, ihre Kultur auszuleben?

DEUTSCHLAND ANTEIL MIT MIGRATIONSHINTERGRUND 20 %

MIGRANTENANTEIL

Anzahl der Menschen mit MHG, von deutschen Städten, nach absteigender Einwohnerzahl

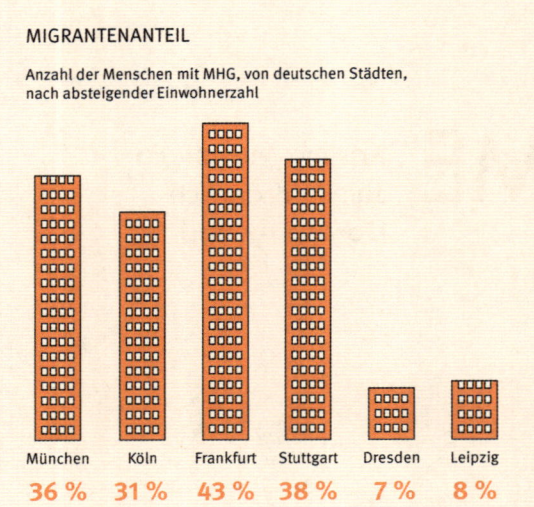

München	Köln	Frankfurt	Stuttgart	Dresden	Leipzig
36 %	31 %	43 %	38 %	7 %	8 %

GEBURTENRATE/GEBURTENZIFFER

Anzahl der Lebendgeborenen pro Jahr bezogen auf 1000 Einwohner (Rangliste weltweit)

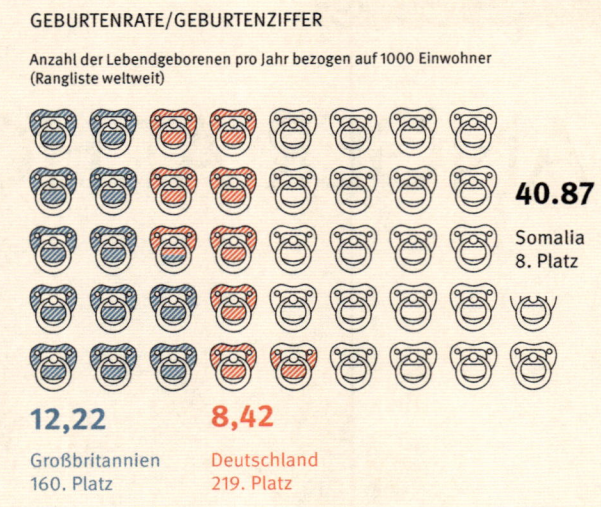

40.87
Somalia
8. Platz

12,22
Großbritannien
160. Platz

8,42
Deutschland
219. Platz

ENTWICKLUNG SEIT 2000

Geburten, Tode, Zu- und Auswanderungen von Deutschen und Migranten

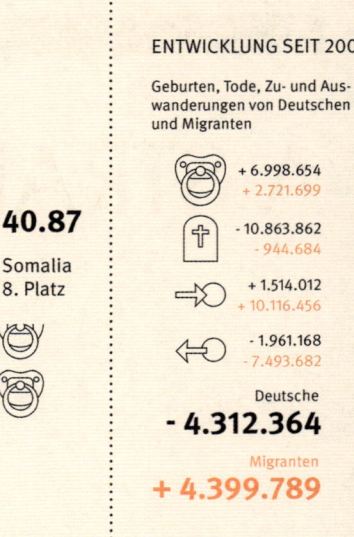

+ 6.998.654
+ 2.721.699

- 10.863.862
- 944.684

+ 1.514.012
+ 10.116.456

- 1.961.168
- 7.493.682

Deutsche
- 4.312.364

Migranten
+ 4.399.789

KONTAKT ZWISCHEN MIGRANTEN UND DEUTSCHEN

Positive Bewertungen

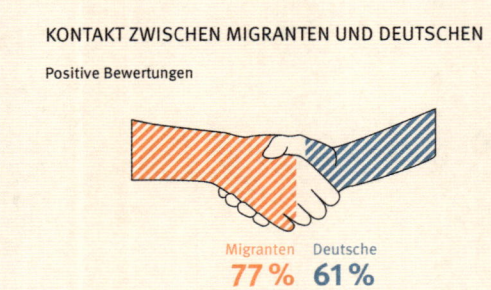

Migranten **77 %** Deutsche **61 %**

SPRACHKENNTNISSE

Eigene Einschätzung der Migranten

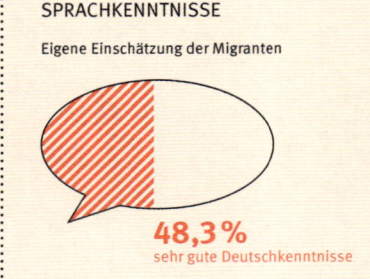

48,3 %
sehr gute Deutschkenntnisse

STUDENTENANTEIL

☐ ohne MHG ☐ mit MHG ☐ Ausländer

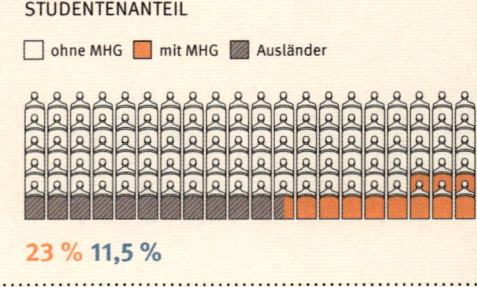

23 % 11,5 %

BERLIN ANTEIL MIT MIGRATIONSHINTERGRUND 25,7 %

JEDER VIERTER BERLINER HAT EINEN MHG

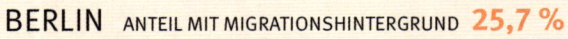

AUSLÄNDERDICHTE

☐ 15–25 %
☐ ‹ 25 %

KINDER UND JUGENDLICHE UNTER 18 JAHREN

mit MHG
44,7 %

ANTEIL AUSLÄNDERGRUPPEN

Die größten Gruppen – Türkei, Polen, Serbien, Italien und Russland

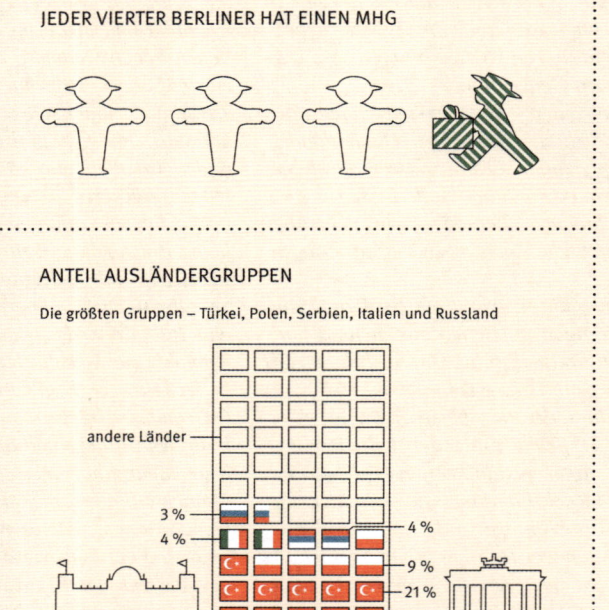

andere Länder

3 %
4 %   4 %
9 %
21 %

HERKUNFT DER AUSLÄNDER

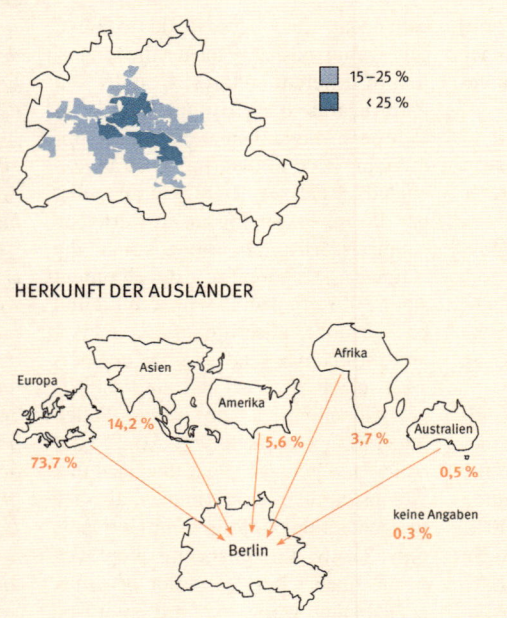

Europa 73,7 %
Asien 14,2 %
Amerika 5,6 %
Afrika 3,7 %
Australien 0,5 %
keine Angaben 0.3 %
Berlin

ZU-/ABNAHME DER SCHÜLER NACH HERKUNFTSSPRACHE

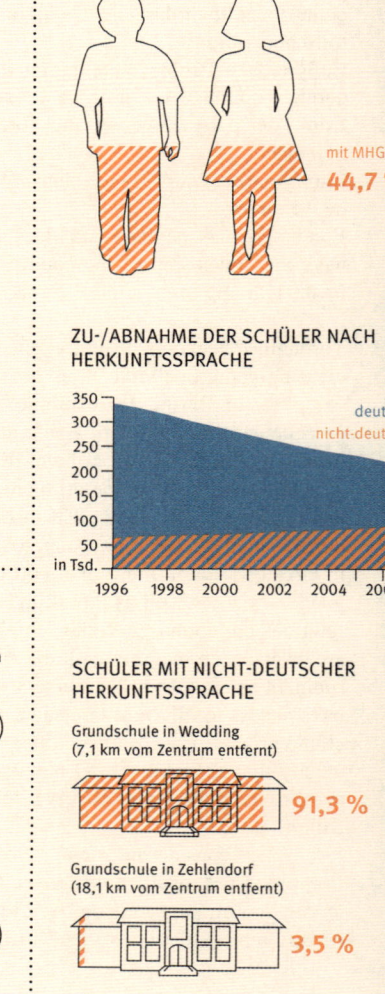

deutsch
nicht-deutsch

in Tsd.
1996 1998 2000 2002 2004 2006

LOKALITÄTEN

Anzahl der Dönerläden, indischen- und chinesischen Restaurants, sowie der Shisha Bars

›1200   ›200
›380   ›500

RELIGIONEN

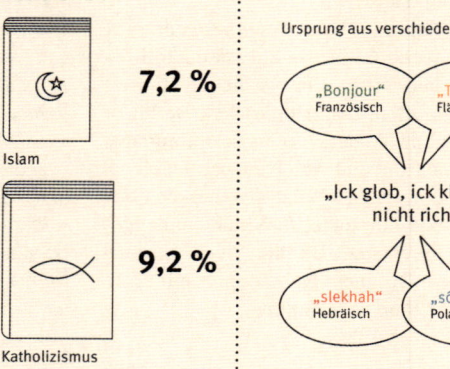

7,2 %
Islam

9,2 %
Katholizismus

BERLINER DIALEKT

Ursprung aus verschiedenen Sprachen

„Bonjour" Französisch   „Tot ziens" Flämisch

„Ick glob, ick kiek nicht richtich!"

„slekhah" Hebräisch   „sõbügöm!" Polabisch

SCHÜLER MIT NICHT-DEUTSCHER HERKUNFTSSPRACHE

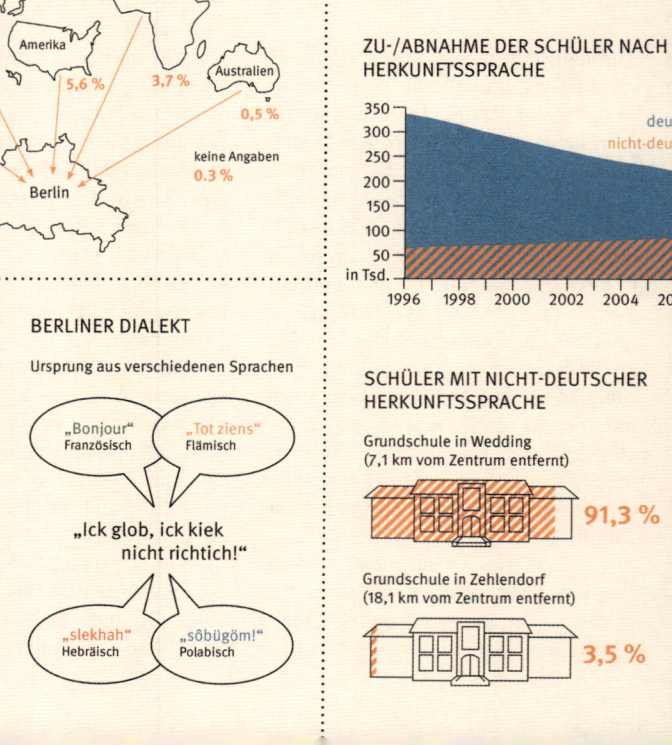

Grundschule in Wedding (7,1 km vom Zentrum entfernt)
91,3 %

Grundschule in Zehlendorf (18,1 km vom Zentrum entfernt)
3,5 %

NDER

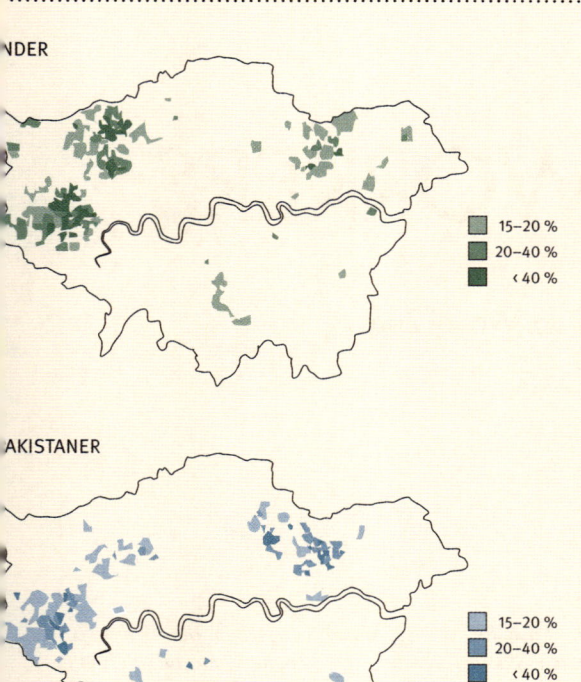

15–20 %
20–40 %
‹ 40 %

AKISTANER

15–20 %
20–40 %
‹ 40 %

ENGALEN

10–25 %
25–45 %
‹ 45 %

GEBURTSORT

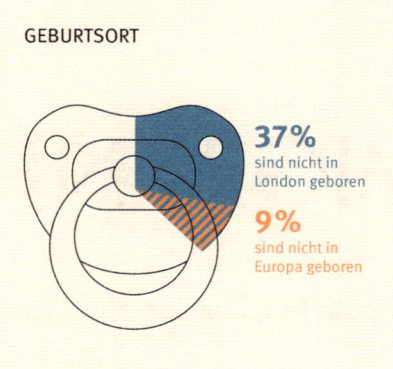

37 %
sind nicht in
London geboren

9 %
sind nicht in
Europa geboren

SPRACHEN

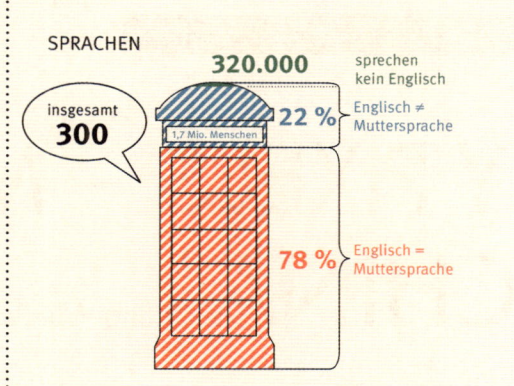

insgesamt
300

320.000

sprechen
kein Englisch

1,7 Mio. Menschen

22 % Englisch ≠
Muttersprache

78 % Englisch =
Muttersprache

RELIGIONEN

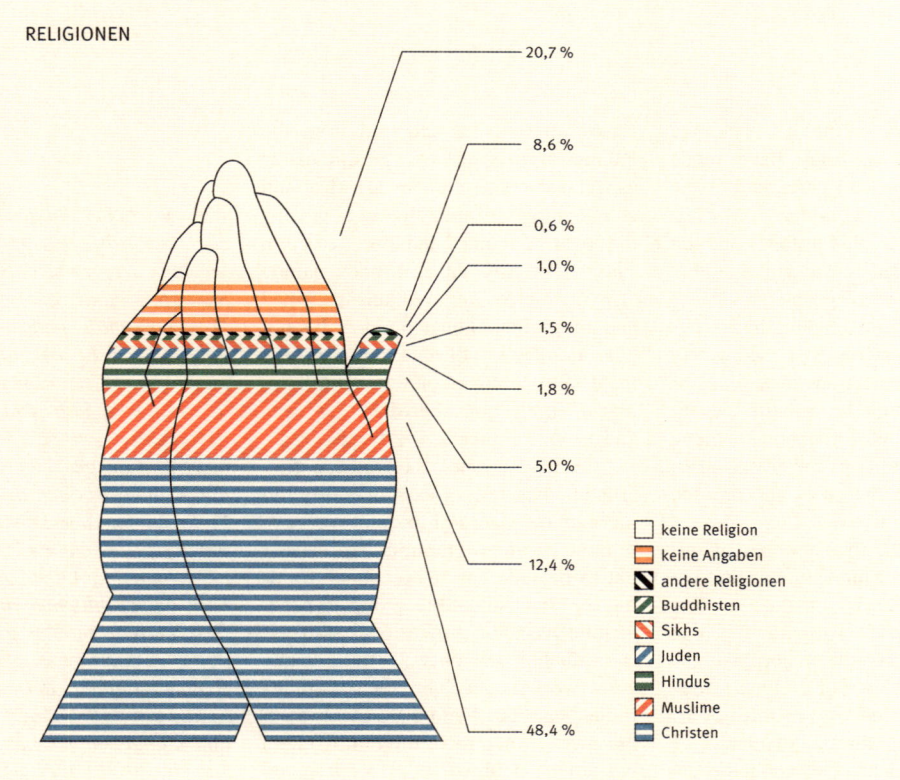

20,7 %

8,6 %

0,6 %

1,0 %

1,5 %

1,8 %

5,0 %

12,4 %

48,4 %

☐ keine Religion
▨ keine Angaben
◩ andere Religionen
▨ Buddhisten
◪ Sikhs
◩ Juden
▤ Hindus
◪ Muslime
▤ Christen

USLÄNDERANTEIL IN TOWER HAMLETS

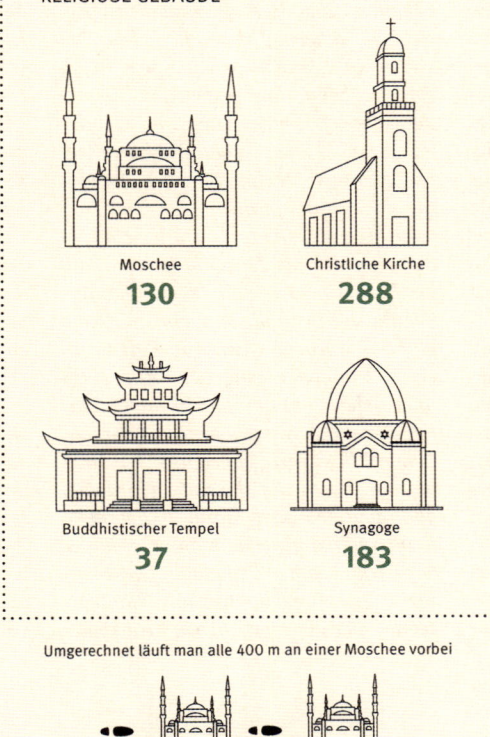

Bengalen Afrikaner Chinesen Inder
32 % **3,7 %** **3,2 %** **2,7 %**

TADTTEIL TOWER HAMLETS

ergleich mit Wiesbaden (gleiche Einwohnerzahl)

Tower Hamlets
(19,77 km²)

Wiesbaden
(203,9 km²)

› 50 **10**

RELIGIÖSE GEBÄUDE

Moschee
130

Christliche Kirche
288

Buddhistischer Tempel
37

Synagoge
183

Umgerechnet läuft man alle 400 m an einer Moschee vorbei

400 m **800 m**

SEGREGATION ENTWICKLUNG 2001–2011

◩ steigende Segregation
☐ sinkende Segregation

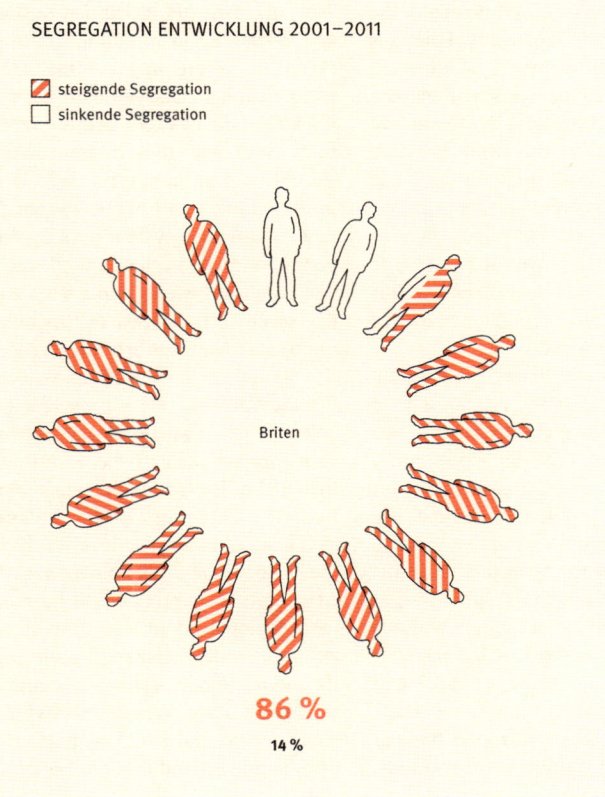

Briten

86 %

14 %

CITY PIXELS – MIGRANT WORKERS IN CHINA
Yiting Wu, Pengbin Ma, Ruimiao Huo, Yang Gao, Wenqi Zhu

Migrant workers are the real backbone of Chinese cities. They have made great contributions to cities and to the whole national economy, however, they have been treated unfairly and are commonly considered as a vulnerable group with various problems. Being discriminated and excluded, they struggle at the lowest rung of the society without basic protections over rights of living and working. Worse still, the city residents seem indifferent and apathetic about the inequality of the city contributors who build the cities and provide convenience for lives.

In 2015, the total number of migrant workers in China amounts to over 270 millions.[1] There are such a great number of migrant workers in China that they comprise the majority of the working population. For designers, they are like pixels. Under given rules of urban development, through the gathering power of individuals, they spontaneously and orderly scrabble up what we can now see as a real city. In this regard, the city is a result, just like the vivid pictures orderly formed by pixels of different colours when we enter instructions and programs into computers. However, we have to admit that sometimes we only care about the result, judging the value from our own different perspectives. We seldomly care about the minor but also strong individual power that supports the whole real world behind reality. This distorted value proposition is the root of the problem discussed.

Living as machines, the migrant workers have to work relentlessly to make ends meet. By listening to their expectation and dreams about cities, the authors aim to express their support concerning the problem of the marginalization of migrant workers, and to arouse social concern for this anomaly. In order to see through the superficial to the depth of problem of migrant workers and to seek for reasons of the inequality and its due influence, research and investigation about migrant workers are carried out in an all-round manner through various channels and methods.

Based on statistics acquired from the internet and the library, questionnaires as well as on-site interviews, a clear and enlightening information design unveils the covered, avoided and forgotten truth. The work turns out as a book named "City Pixels, Migrant Workers in China" and an original animated video. It's not only a collection of data, but also uses the data to comment on the social facts, reveal connections between the facts and provide a direction of discussion.

In recent years, the Chinese government has been focusing more and more on the issues of migrant workers. A number of programmes are carried out to provide various technical trainings to this vulnerable group in order to improve their professional skills. It is estimated that over 20 million migrant workers received such trainings in the years 2014 and 2015. Moreover, the average income of migrant workers has almost doubled in 2015 compared to 2010.[1] At the beginning of the year 2016, the Ministry of Human Resources and Social Security announced a new policy, requiring that contracts in the construction industry should be signed with migrant workers before construction starts and that migrant workers should be registered with their identity information as part of the system. This new "real-name system" policy would hopefully integrate the payroll into formal banking systems and put an end to the current informal cash distribution that often results in wage arrears or debts.[2]

It is nevertheless questionable whether or how the city pixels could enjoy a fairer share of the economic gain, proportional to the contributions they make. The scale of China's internal rural-urban migration in such a short period reaches an unseen level throughout the history.[3] The phenomenon of China's migrant workers could be seen as part of global population flow of arrivals in the cities, challenging the capacity and resilience of urban systems on a worldwide scale. Whether the words on paper would and could be put into actions on the ground is yet to be seen.

Wanderarbeiter bilden das tatsächliche Rückgrat der chinesischen Städte. Sie haben unschätzbare Beiträge zum Städtebau und auch zur gesamten Volkswirtschaft geleistet, werden jedoch ungerecht behandelt, so dass sie unter einer Vielzahl von Problemen zu leiden haben und gemeinhin als eine "schutzlose Gruppe" gelten. Diskriminiert und ausgeschlossen, plagen sich die Wanderarbeiter auf der untersten Stufe der sozialen Leiter ab, ohne dass ihnen irgendwelche Grundrechte, etwa auf Leben und Arbeit, gewährt werden. Und, noch schlimmer, die ortsansässige Bevölkerung scheint gleichgültig und desinteressiert gegenüber der sozialen Benachteiligung derjenigen, die die Städte bauen und deren Einwohnern zu einem angenehmen Leben verhelfen.

In 2015 belief sich die Zahl der Wanderarbeiter in China auf über 270 Millionen.[1] Es gibt so viele Wanderarbeiter, dass sie den Großteil der Erwerbsbevölkerung darstellen. Für Designer sind Wanderarbeiter wie Pixel. Entsprechend den gegebenen Regeln der urbanen Entwicklung und mit der geballten Macht unzähliger Einzelwesen stampfen sie spontan und planmäßig das aus dem Boden, was über kurz oder lang als eine reale Stadt zu erkennen ist. In dieser Hinsicht ist die Stadt ein Resultat, so wie die lebendigen Bilder, die von verschiedenfarbigen Pixeln geformt werden, wenn wir Befehle in einen Computer eingeben. Allerdings interessiert uns mitunter allein das Ergebnis, das wir aus unserem persönlichen Blickwinkel beurteilen. Wir achten nur selten auf die untergeordnete, aber zugleich auch starke individuelle Kraft, die die gesamte reale Welt hinter der Wirklichkeit in Gang hält. Diese verzerrte, einseitige Sichtweise ist die Wurzel des hier angesprochenen Problems.

Wie Maschinen leben die Wanderarbeiter. Sie arbeiten unermüdlich, um über die Runden zu kommen. Indem die Autoren sich die Hoffnungen und Träume anhören, die die Wanderarbeiter mit den Städten verknüpfen, möchten die Autoren ausdrücken, dass sie das Problem der Marginalisierung von Wanderarbeitern ernst nehmen und die Öffentlichkeit für diesen Missstand sensibilisieren wollen. Um diese oberflächliche Wahrnehmung zu überwinden und zum Kern des Problems der Wanderarbeiter vorzustoßen, um die Ursachen für die beschriebene Ungleichheit und deren zwangsläufige Folgen ergründen zu können, wird das Phänomen der Wanderarbeiter allumfassend, über alle möglichen Kanäle und Methoden untersucht. Aufgrund von Statistiken aus dem Internet oder Bibliotheken, von Fragebögen sowie von vor Ort geführten Interviews bringt ein eindeutiges und aufklärendes Information Design die unterdrückte, ignorierte und vergessene Wahrheit ans Tageslicht. Das Projekt hat ein Buch mit dem Titel "City Pixels, Migrant Workers in China" und ein animiertes Video ergeben. Es handelt sich nicht nur um eine Erhebung von Daten, sondern diese Daten werden auch herangezogen, um soziale Sachverhalte zu kommentieren, Verbindungen zwischen solchen Sachverhalten zu offenbaren und der Diskussion eine bestimmte Richtung zu geben.

In der Hoffnung, die soziale Gerechtigkeit zu verbessern, hat sich die chinesische Regierung in den letzten Jahren mehr und mehr auf die Probleme der Wanderarbeiter fokussiert. Eine Reihe von Programmen zur technischen Ausbildung wurde durchgeführt, um die beruflichen Kenntnisse dieser schwachen Gruppe zu verbessern. Es wird geschätzt, dass mehr als 20 Millionen

Overall Size of Migrant Workers

Migrant Workers of Different Regions and the Growth Rate in 2008

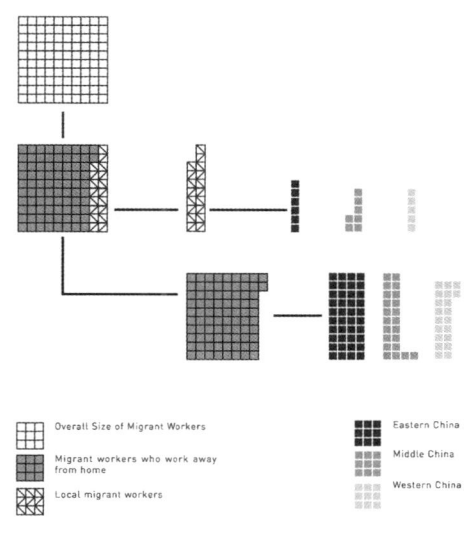

Overall Size of Migrant Workers

Migrant workers who work away from home

Local migrant workers

Eastern China

Middle China

Western China

Overall Size of Migrant Workers

Migrant workers who work away from home

Local migrant workers

Migrant workers that go out for work individually

Migrant workers that go out for work with his/her whole family

Sex Ratio of Migrant Workers

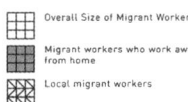

Total number of migrant workers

Number of males

Number of females

Education Level of Migrant Workers

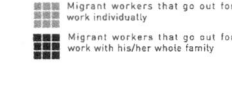

Total number of migrant workers

Illiterate or semi-illiterate

Primary school education

Junior high school education

High school/technical secondary school

Age Ratio of Migrant Workers

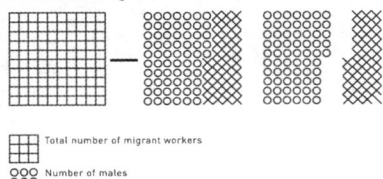

Total number of migrant workers

16 – 25 years old

26 – 30 years old

31 – 40 years old

40 – 50 years old

Above 50 years old

Working Industries of Migrant Workers

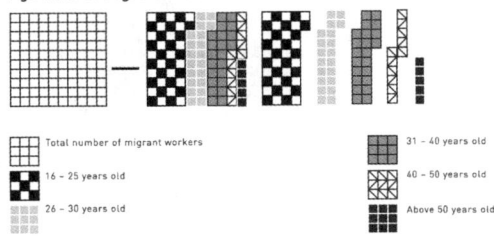

Total number of migrant workers

Manufacturing

Construction

Service industry

Wholesale

Mining

Catering

Other industries

The Percentage of Migrant Workers Signing Labor Contracts (%)

The percentage of migrant workers signing labor contracts is relatively low. 57.2% of migrant workers have not signed any labor contract.

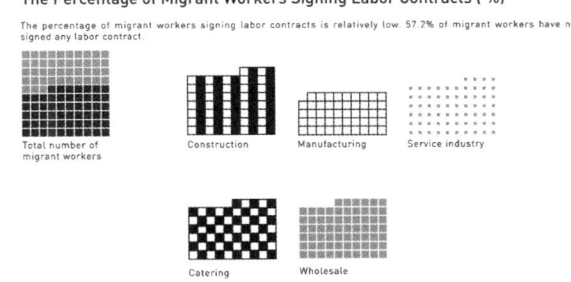

Total number of migrant workers

Construction

Manufacturing

Service industry

Catering

Wholesale

The Percentage of Migrant Workers Protected by Social Security in Different Regions (%)

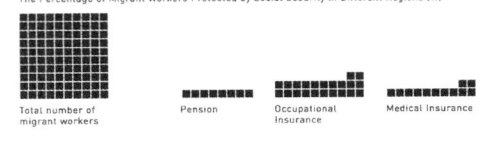

Total number of migrant workers

Pension

Occupational Insurance

Medical Insurance

Unemployment Insurance

Maternity Insurance

Marriage Status of Migrant Workers

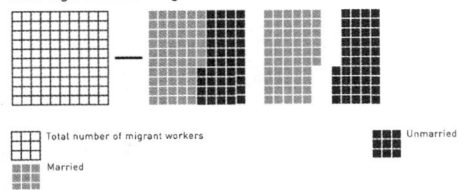

Total number of migrant workers

Married

Unmarried

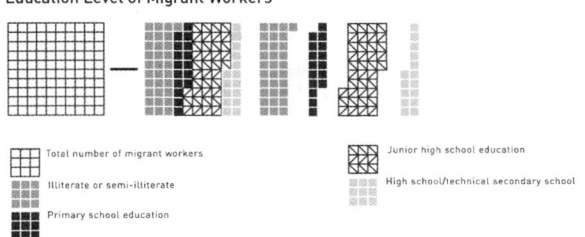
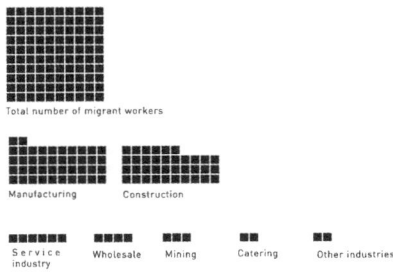

Wanderarbeiter solche Schulungen in den Jahren 2014 und 2015 durchlaufen haben. Im Vergleich zu 2010 hat das sich durchschnittliche Einkommen von Wanderarbeitern im Jahr 2015 fast verdoppelt.[1] Zu Beginn des Jahres 2016 hat das Ministerium für Humanressourcen und soziale Sicherheit eine neue Politik angekündigt, in der verlangt wird, dass Verträge mit Wanderarbeitern vor dem Baubeginn unterzeichnet und dass Wanderarbeiter mit ihren Identitätsinformationen als Teil des Systems registriert werden müssen. Diese neue "Real-Name-System"-Politik wird hoffentlich die Lohnabrechnung in das formelle Bankensystem integrieren und die derzeitige informelle Barzahlung beenden, die oft zu Lohnrückständen oder Schulden führt.[2]

Es ist jedoch fraglich, ob und wie die City Pixels einen fairen Anteil am wirtschaftlichen Gewinn genießen könnten, der proportional dem von ihnen gemachten Beitrag entspricht. Solch ein Ausmaß der chinesischen internen Migration vom Land in die Stadt in einer so kurzen Zeit hat es im Laufe der Geschichte noch nie gegeben.[3] Das Phänomen der Wanderarbeiter in China könnte als Teil der globalen Völkerwanderung in die Städte gesehen werden, die die Kapazität und Belastbarkeit von urbanen Systemen im weltweiten Maßstab herausfordern. Ob die Worte auf dem Papier in Handlungen auf dem Boden umgewandelt werden können, wird noch zu sehen sein.

right
Animated video about the difficult living conditions of migrant workers in Chinese cities

rechts
Animiertes Video zu den schwierigen Lebensbedingungen der Wanderarbeiter in chinesischen Städten

Chinas main production sector has always been agriculture.

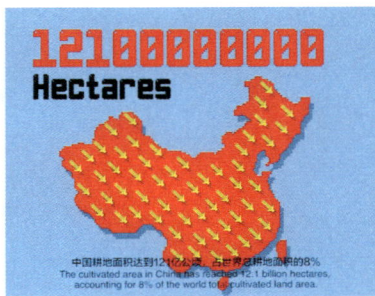
The livelihoods of the majority of the population was dependent on it for a long time.

… and virtually flooded the cities.

Nevertheless, most guest workers enter a new employment without such a course.

Because there is a shortage of people in the labour force in cities …

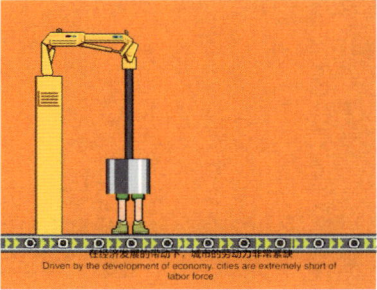
… the guest workers, eager to work, …

Compared to white-collar workers in Peking, the salary of a guest worker is low.

With city rents rising, a worker works for 10 years, …

… to be able to afford a 6 sqm WC, without money for food or drink.

Moreover they suffer from emotional problems …

… and long for physical closeness.

80% of guest workers go hungry to be able to afford a prostitute.

… and the cities would no longer be overcrowded.

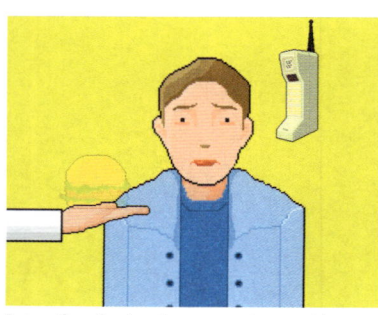
But on the other hand, many services would disappear …

… and the construction industry would have to face major cutbacks, …

8% of agricultural surfaces worldwide are located in China.

Half of the population are farmers.

In the course of industrialisation, China developed into an industrial nation.

Because of modernisation, farmers left the country …

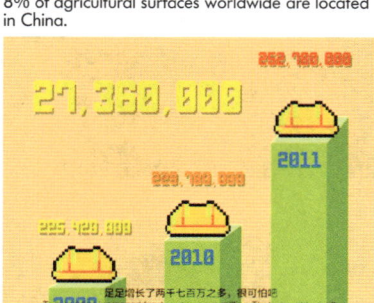

Since 2009, the number of migrant workers is on a record-breaking rise.

But why do so many workers exchange the country for the city?

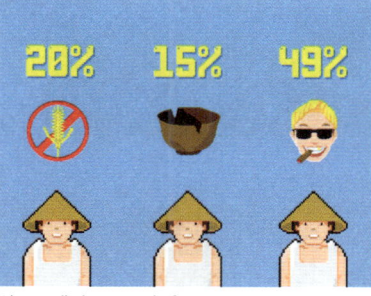

Above all, the appeal of major cities drives many guest workers.

Factories and schools offer preparation and re-education courses.

… almost like in extrusion processing, …

… are wedged into different roles and professions.

The majority eventually finds a job in the factory industry.

Migrant workers live and work under strikingly different circumstances.

Children of migrant workers also suffer from the difficult life circumstances …

… and, for example, do not receive school education.

The guest workers neither receive long-term work contracts, …

… nor sufficient medical care.

What if there were no guest workers in China?

For a start, above all there would be more space …

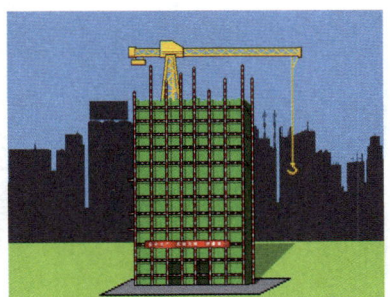

… because the construction of cities only functions through the employment of guest workers.

Chinas economic ascent occurred, above all, thanks to the numerous guest workers. In the future, injustice and marginalisation towards guest workers need to be rectified, because they are the pixels without which the overall image of the city would not be possible.

Their so-called dreams about city

Most of the time they are... they are dumb, telling our listen to what they think, they have no beliefs, sustainable dreams, seldom have in depth thinking about life. Living as machines, they have to work relentlessly to make end meet.

Li Cheng
24
Hubei
Safeguard in campus

I wish I will go to art school next year.
I hope all dreams of my classmates come true.

Luan Gongzheng
21
Henan
Deliverer

Free as wind

Yu Jingxian
21
Henan
Waiter

I hope my family live healthy and happy.

Liu Xiaojun
41
Gansu
Builder

I have no other wish in my age other than that my child can go to university.

Tan Dongwei
24
Hubei
Waiter

I hope I have a chain restaurant of my own in two to three years.

Xv Hongxia
36
Hebei
Bookstore assistant

I wish my child can go to college entrance examination in Beijing. I also hope my business could flourish.

Yang Pengbo
24
Hunan
Milkman

There's only excuse for failure but no reason for success. Think what I think and do what I do.

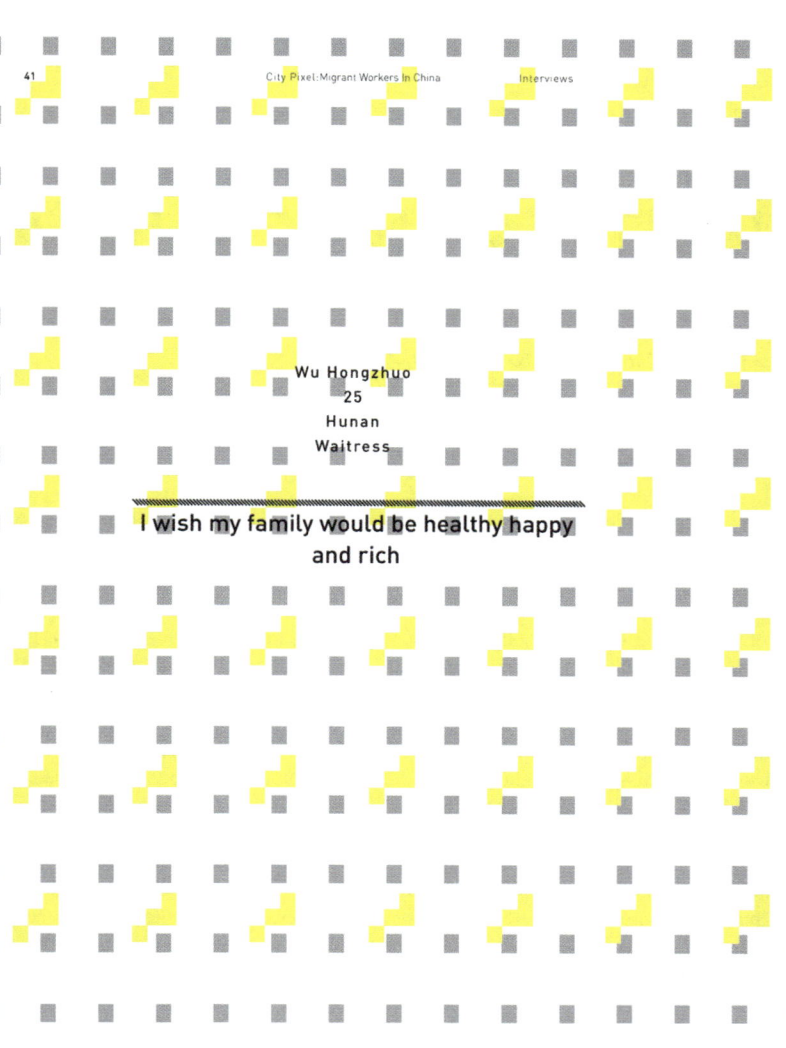

Wu Hongzhuo
25
Hunan
Waitress

I wish my family would be healthy happy and rich

Ma QiRi
28
Sichuan
Flower store assistant

I wish I could establish myself in Beijing.

Zhong Na
24
Henan
Flower store assistant

My flower store will become as flourishing as the flowers.

Xiao Chengshi
43
Henan
Butcher

I hope my income can increase so that I can buy a house in hometown.

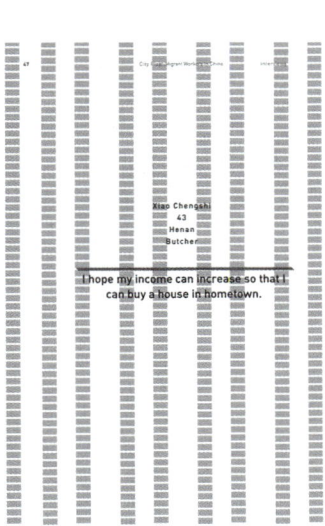

Liu Jv
43
Hebei
Vendor

I wish I can earn more money and have a grandchild earlier.

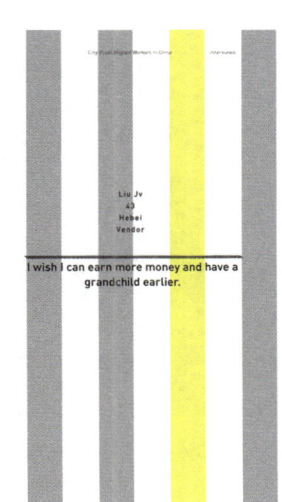
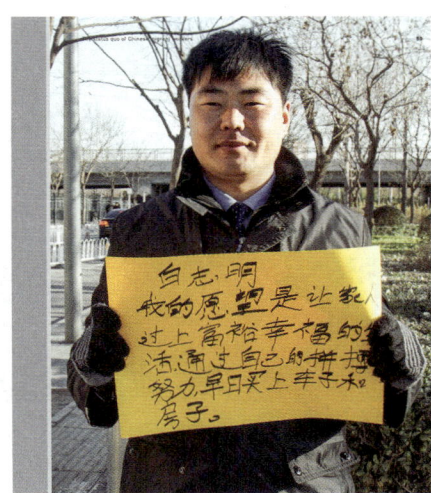

MIGRANT COMMUNITIES IN CHINA

Li Tian, Xinyi Niu, Boyi Wang, Pu Chen, Jihuan Li, Xuecong Yang, Yixiang Ma, Yuan Zhao, Jingwei Li, Liang Ding, Yiqin Wu, Jiayi Hu

"(Social) space is a (social) product… the space thus produced also serves as a tool of thought and of action…in addition to being a means of production it is also a means of control, and hence of domination, of power."
Henri Lefebvre, "The Production of Space"

Leaving hometown, moving to a bigger city in search of better opportunities is, historically speaking, not a new phenomenon. Britain's industrialization attracting rural surplus labor into big cities marked its significance in modern times. China's migrant problem, however, has its special institutional precondition, namely the "Hukou" system – a household registration system originally adopted in 1958. While the system was used to ensure resource allocation in the previous planned economy, to regulate national migration and to enhance social security, today it is rather a barrier for a vast number of migrants. Away from registration location and living in a different city, they have limited access to social welfare and other citizen rights, which are strongly tied to Hukou origin. Among the 53.7% urbanization rate in 2013 only 36% of the urban population owned local Hukou, which means 16.7% of the total population, around 234 million migrants are living under an exploited "floating" condition.

Shanghai, the largest city in China by population, has witnessed a rapidly increasing floating population. From 2000 to 2014, its percentage of floating population increased from 26.2% to 41.1%. In order to evaluate the situation of migrant communities in Shanghai, 7 migrant communities (with over 80% floating population) and 7 local communities (with over 80% of local Hukou residents) are chosen as cases. Mobile phone signal data, Baidu (a Chinese internet search engine) online map and interviews are analyzed to generate comprehensive statistics, demonstrating the low social-economic status and spatial deprivation of the vulnerable group.

Besides the apparent institutional limit of Hukou system, deprivation also results from missing fiscal allocation and lack of inclusive planning. Local governments have no extra fiscal resource to improve the living of a floating population; current urban planning practice in China is also more interested in building a splendid city image than improving the situation of a vulnerable group.

It should be noted that the government has taken notice of the exploited status of the migrant workers. Since July 2011, according to China's new social insurance law, migrant workers are included in the social welfare system; both employers and full-time employees should contribute to social insurance programs. Hukou is also put on a national reform agenda since July 2014, aiming to abolish the distinction between rural and urban residence, as well as to gradually step away from Hukou system. Although it is hard to imagine Shanghai opening its door towards a vast number of citizen candidates, smaller cities are carrying out trials to abandon Hukou. It is foreseeable that small to middle-sized cities might finally become real homes for migrants.

The political agenda would surely bring about economic and spatial consequences. With a more inclusive social insurance system, cheap labor behind the 'Made in China'-phenomenon might become history. Furthermore, the settling of a floating population might change China's urban landscape significantly. Britain's garden city, America's extensive suburb, HongKong's super density, or something characteristically Chinese? Migrant's footprint will be decisive in China's next new spatial character.

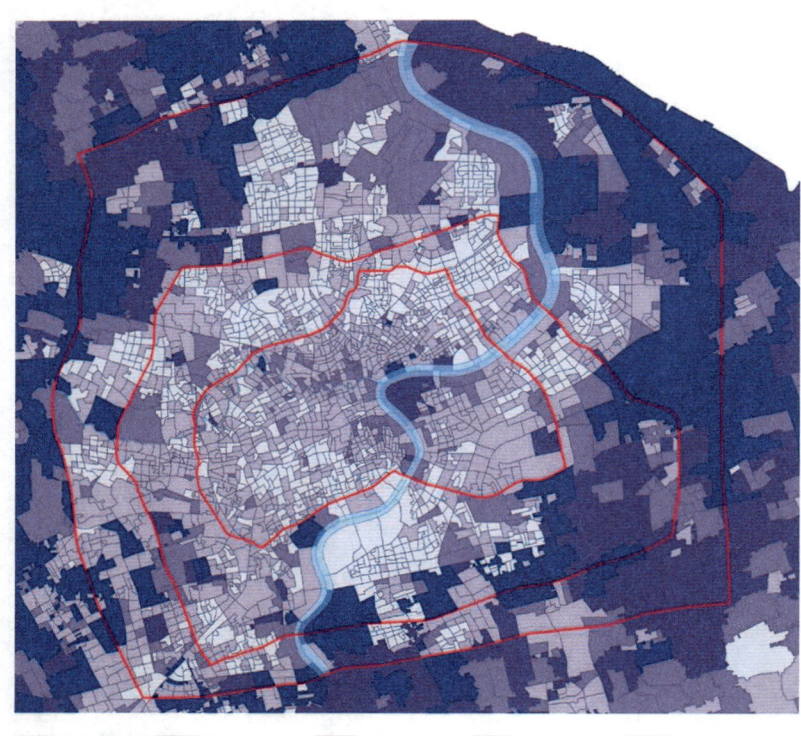

0%-20% 20%-40% 40%-60% 60%-80% 80%-100%

Percentage of migrant population in Shanghai in 2010

Social and economic information

● **Education**

Unkown 4.7% / 6.0% | Illiterate 1.6% / 5.3% | Primary school 16.2% / 7.1% | Junior School 64.1% / 19.9% | High School 10.4% / 26.1% | College 2.1% / 17.0% | Undergraduate 0.8% / 20.2% | Graduate 0.0% / 3.3%

■ Migrant community ■ Local community

● **Income**

<2000yuan 16.7% / 10.5% | 2000-5000yuan 58.9% / 14.7% | 5000-8000yuan 16.3% / 28.4% | >8000yuan 8.1% / 46.3%

■ Migrant community ■ Local community

● **Occupation**

Unkown 23.1% / 54.0% | Government employees 1.4% / 5.0% | Professionals 2.4% / 13.6% | Private companies staff 4.4% / 10.4% | Commerce 33.6% / 12.0% | Primary industry 0.3% / 0.2% | Manufacturing and transportation 34.8% / 4.9% | Others 0.0% / 0.0%

■ Migrant community ■ Local community

Comparison of the socio-economic status between migrants and local communities.

Deprivation of educational facilities

We use average distance to schools and the number of schools per 1,000 people to evaluate the deprivation level of educational facilities.

Average distance to schools

The average distance from migrant communities to schools is much longer than that from local communities to schools. The mean distance for migrant children to get to their corresponding primary school is 2.29km, while it is 0.76km for local children. Furthermore, the mean distance from migrant communities to the corresponding junior school is 2.5km, while it is 1.36km for local students.

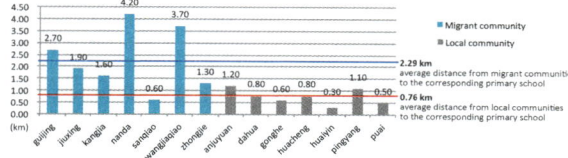

- Migrant community
- Local community

2.29 km average distance from migrant communities to the corresponding primary school

0.76 km average distance from local communities to the corresponding primary school

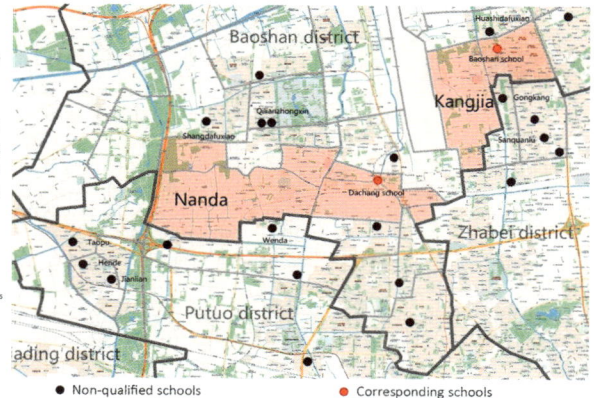

- Non-qualified schools
- Corresponding schools

In migrant communities, availability of schooling is limited due to unreasonable school district zoning.

migrant's children

Income disparity / City / Village

Housing deprivation

We use housing ownership structure, floor space per person, and quality of houses to evaluate housing deprivation.

Housing ownership structure

Only 10 percent of people in migrant communities live in a house purchased by themselves while 90% live in rental houses.

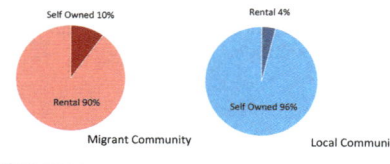

Self Owned 10% / Rental 90% — Migrant Community

Rental 4% / Self Owned 96% — Local Community

Quality of houses

Housing quality is evaluated on the basis of housing facilities. The scores of migrant communities are most often rated at 1 to 5 points, while the local communities nearly reach a full score of 7.

Facilities	Indicator	Score
Running Water	No	0
	Yes	1
Kitchen	No	0
	Public	1
	Private	2
Toilet	No	0
	Public	1
	Private	2
Bathroom	No	0
	Public	1
	Private	2

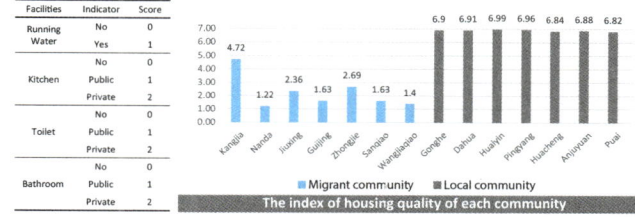

- Migrant community
- Local community

The index of housing quality of each community

Floor space per person

People living in the migrant community have an average floor space of 8 to 12 m² per capita, while this number is 45 m² in the local community.

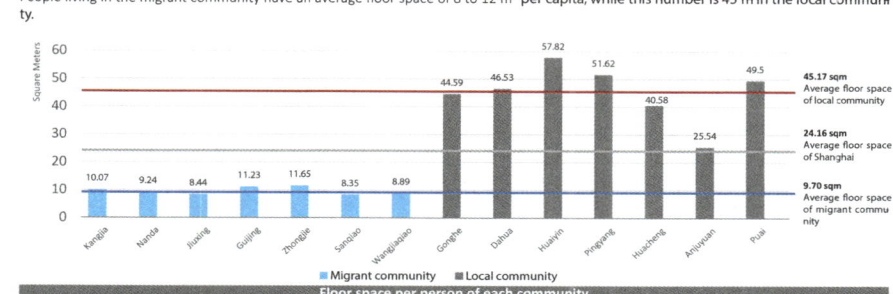

45.17 sqm Average floor space of local community

24.16 sqm Average floor space of Shanghai

9.70 sqm Average floor space of migrant community

- Migrant community
- Local community

Floor space per person of each community

Summary

The evaluation results demonstrate that deprivation is common in migrant communities. Ranking from highest to lowest, the deprivation levels are education, shopping, health and postal services, public transit, sports and cultural services. The spatial deprivation is characterized by a lack of sufficient facilities and poor accessibility.

"(Sozialer) Raum ist ein (soziales) Produkt … der solcherart produzierte Raum dient auch als ein Instrument des Denkens und des Handelns … er ist nicht nur ein Produktionsmittel, sondern auch ein Kontrollmittel und somit ein Mittel der Herrschaft, der Macht."
Henri Lefebvre, "Die Produktion von Raum"

Der Heimat den Rücken zu kehren und auf der Suche nach einem besseren Leben in eine größere Stadt zu ziehen, ist, historisch betrachtet, kein neues Phänomen. Das gab es schon zur Zeit der Industriellen Revolution in England, als die überschüssigen ländlichen Arbeitskräfte in die Großstädte abwanderten. Chinas Migrantenproblem hat jedoch eine besondere institutionelle Voraussetzung, nämlich das "Hukou"-System – ein Haushaltsregistrierungssystem, das 1958 landesweit eingeführt wurde. Während das System in der einstigen Planwirtschaft dazu diente, die Zuteilung von Ressourcen sicherzustellen, die Binnenwanderung zu regulieren und die soziale Sicherheit zu verbessern, stellt es heute für eine Vielzahl von Migranten eher einen Hemmschuh dar. Weit entfernt vom Ort ihrer Registrie-

rung und in einer fremden Stadt lebend, haben sie nur einen eingeschränkten Zugang zur Sozialfürsorge und zu anderen Bürgerrechten, die eng an ihren Hukou-Ursprung gebunden sind. Unter der 2013 ermittelten Urbanisierungsrate von 53,7 % verfügten nur 36 % der Stadtbevölkerung über eine örtliche Hukou-Registrierung, und das bedeutet, dass 16,7 % der Gesamtbevölkerung oder rund 234 Millionen Migranten ein ausgebeutetes, "wanderndes" Dasein führen.

Schanghai, die hinsichtlich der Bevölkerungszahl größte chinesische Stadt, hat eine rapide Zunahme seiner wandernden Bevölkerung erlebt. Von 2000 bis 2014 stieg deren Prozentsatz von 26,2 % auf 41,1 %. Um die Situation der Migrantengemeinden von Schanghai zu evaluieren, wurden sieben Migrantengemeinden (mit einer wandernden Bevölkerung von über 80 %) und sieben örtliche Gemeinden (mit über 80 % örtlich registrierten Hukou-Anwohnern) als Fälle ausgewählt. Signaldaten von Mobiltelefonen und über Baidu (eine chinesische Internet-Suchmaschine) bezogene Online-Karten und -Interviews werden analysiert, um umfassende Statistiken zu erstellen, die den niedrigen sozioökonomischen Status und die räumliche Deprivation der

schutzbedürftigen Bevölkerungsgruppe belegen. Neben den offenkundigen institutionellen Grenzen des Hukou-Systems resultiert die Deprivation auch aus der fehlenden Zuteilung fiskalischer Mittel und dem Nichtvorhandensein einer inklusiven Planung. Den örtlichen Behörden fehlen zusätzliche fiskalische Ressourcen zur Verbesserung der Lebensbedingungen der wandernden Bevölkerung; die gegenwärtige Stadtplanungspraxis in China ist eher an der Produktion eines prächtigen Stadtbilds interessiert als an der Verbesserung der Situation einer schutzbedürftigen Bevölkerungsgruppe.

An dieser Stelle muss darauf hingewiesen werden, dass die Regierung vom ausgebeuteten Dasein der Wanderarbeiter Notiz genommen hat. Seit Juli 2011 sind Wanderarbeiter gemäß dem neuen chinesischen Sozialversicherungsgesetz in das System der Sozialfürsorge einbezogen; Arbeitgeber und Vollzeitarbeitskräfte sollen in Zukunft Beiträge zu Sozialversicherungsprogrammen zahlen. Seit dem Juli 2014 steht auch das Hukou-System auf einer nationalen Reform-Agenda; die

Regierung möchte die Unterscheidung zwischen ländlichem und städtischem Wohnsitz abschaffen und sich schrittweise vom Hukou-System verabschieden. Obwohl es schwer vorstellbar ist, dass Schanghai seine Tore für ein Heer von Neubürgern öffnen wird, unternehmen kleinere Städte den Versuch, das Hukou-System aufzugeben. Es ist absehbar, dass kleine und mittelgroße Städte für Migranten schließlich zu einer echten Heimstatt werden können.

Die politische Agenda dürfte ökonomische und räumliche Konsequenzen haben. Mit einem inklusiveren Sozialversicherungssystem könnten die Tage des von billigen Arbeitskräften ermöglichten "Made in China"-Phänomens gezählt sein. Und die Eingemeindung der wandernden Bevölkerung könnte Chinas städtische Landschaft auf signifikante Weise verändern. Englands Gartenstadt, Amerikas weitläufige Vororte, Hongkongs Superdichte oder etwas spezifisch Chinesisches? Der Fußabdruck der Migranten dürfte für Chinas nächsten neuen räumlichen Charakter von maßgeblicher Bedeutung sein.
Text: Zhen Zhang

List of References

I. LOCAL EFFECTS OF GLOBALISATION

p. 42
The Kings Giants
1 Krüger, Lutz: Die Giganten des Königs. 150 Jahre Wellingtonien in Württemberg. Ebook: BookRix 2014.
2 Projekt Mammutbaum e.V. (2015), URL: http://projekt-mammutbaum.de
3 Schutzgemeinschaft Deutscher Wald, Landesverband Baden-Württemberg e.V. (2011), URL: http://www.sdw-bw.de
4 Manz, Eva-Maria: Der Trost der Wälder (16.06.2014), URL: http://www.stuttgarter-zeitung.de

p. 44
The Promised Land
1 Sime Darby Plantation: Palm Oil Facts and Figures (2014), URL: http://www.simedarby.com
2 Hansen, M. C. et al.: High-Resolution Global Maps of 21st-Century Forest Cover Change. In: Science 342, Nov 2013, p. 850-853, URL: http://earthenginepartners.appspot.com/
3 Boveland, J. F.: Auswirkungen der Palmöl-Produktion auf die abiotischen und biotischen Ressourcen tropischer Länder. Oldenburg, Deutschland: Carl-von-Ossietzky Universität 2010, p. 26 ff.
4 Schrier-Uijl, A. P. et al.: Environmental Impacts of Oil Palm Cultivation on Tropical Peat. Kuala Lumpur, Malaysia: Roundtable on Sustainable Palm Oil (RSPO) 2013.

p. 48
New Tribal Territories
1 Barik, Ratnaprava: Globalisation, Dispossessed and Displaced. A Theoretical Perspective on Tribal Issues in Odisha. In: Online International Interdisciplinary Research Journal, Sept 2014 (Volume IV), p. 202-206.
2 Gadgil, Madhav: Forest Management, Deforestation, and People's Impoverishment. In: Social Action, Oct-Dec 1989 (Volume 39), p. 357-383.
3 Orissa has a lion share of the country's mineral reserves. The chromite, nickel, bauxite, iron ore and coal resources of the state respectively stand at a staggering 83, 92, 55, 38 and 26 percent of India's total reserves. URL: http://orissaminerals.gov.in/Download/Geology_Mineral_Resources.pdf
3 Orissa hat den Löwenanteil der Mineralvorkommen des Landes. Die Chromit, Nickel, Bauxit, Eisenerz und Kohlevorkommen des Bundesstaates machen erstaunliche 83, 92, 55, 38 und 26 Prozent der Gesamtreserven Indiens aus.
4 The peak of Orissa's steel-production boom coincided with the 2008 Beijing Olympics.
4 Der Höhepunkt des Stahlproduktionsbooms in Orissa fiel mit den Olympischen Spielen in Peking 2008 zusammen.
5 The Kalinga Nagar Tata Steel Protest in 2006 lead to the death of at least 12 Adivasi and one policeman. Dummet, Mark: Battle over Indian Steel Mills (26.02.2006), URL: http://news.bbc.co.uk
5 Der Kalinga Nagar Tata Stahl Protest im Jahr 2006 führte zum Tod von mindestens 12 Adivasi und einem Polizisten.

p. 52
Pilbara – Country, Colony and Urbanisation
1 Brenner, Neil; Schmid, Christian: Towards a new epistemology of the urban? In: City 2-3, 2015 (Volume 19), p. 151-182.
2 Harvey, David: A Brief History of Neoliberalism. Oxford, UK: University Press 2005.
3 Department of Mines and Petroleum Western Australia: Mineral Information (2014), URL: http://www.dmp.wa.gov.au

p. 57
New Orleans: Port City to Global Hinterland
1 Keddy, P.A.: Wetland Ecology. Principles and Conservation. 2nd Edition. Cambridge, UK: University Press 2010. p. 497.
2 Reuss, M.: Designing the Bayous. The Control of Water in the Atchafalaya Basin 1800-1995. Alexandria, VA: U.S. Army Corps of Engineers, Office of History 1998.
3 Warrick, Joby; Grunwald, Michael: Investigators Link Levee Failures to Design Flaws (24.10.2005), URL: http://www.washingtonpost.com

p. 60
Urbanism of Disassembly
1 Terao, Tadayoshi: From Shipbreaking to Ship Recycling. The Relocation of Recycling Sites and the Expanding International Approach. In: Economic Integration and Recycling in Asia. An Interim Report. Chosa kenkyu Hoko Kusho Institute of Developing Economies 2011.
2 Demaria, Federico: Shipbreaking at Alang-Sosiya, India. An Ecological Distribution Conflict. In: Ecological Economics 2, Dec 2010 (Volume 70), p. 250-260.

p. 64
Global Urban Culture
1 McNeill, Donald: The Bilbao Effect. In: Fainstein, Susan S.; Campbell, Scott (Ed.): Readings in Urban Theory. New York City, NY: Wiley-Blackwell 2011. p. 303-318.
2 Kahn, Joseph; Landler, Mark: China Grabs West's Smoke-Spewing Factories (21.12.2007), URL: http://www.nytimes.com
3 Lian, Ruby; Stanway, David: China orders two local governments to punish polluting steel mills (02.03.2015), URL: http://www.reuters.com
4 Brown, Luke; Randall, Nicholas: Fifa corruption. Morocco won 2010 World Cup vote - not South Africa - as it happened (07.06.2015), URL: http://www.telegraph.co.uk
5 Hong, Jae C.: Olympic challenge. How do host cities fare after the games? (24.02.2014), URL: http://www.cbsnews.com
6 Fourie, Bronwyn; Dardagan, Colleen: Moses Mabhida down but not out, says city (03.02.2014), URL: http://www.iol.co.za
7 Haywood, Meredith: It's Official! Moses Mabhida Stadium will integrate with The Durban ICC (24.11.2015), URL: http://www.5stardurban.co.za
8 Dearden, Lizzie: Paris attacks. French Muslim council proposes 'licence to preach' for imams to stop Islamist extremism (25.11.2015), URL: http://www.independent.co.uk
9 Elbagir, Nima: New front line against ISIS: the classroom (28.11.2015), URL: http://edition.cnn.com

p. 68
The Rush on Foreign Land
- The Land Matrix Global Observatory (01.02.2016), URL: http://landmatrix.org/en
- FAO Food Price Index (07.01.2016), URL: http://www.fao.org/worldfoodsituation/foodpricesindex/en

II. THE INTERCONNECTED CITY

p. 74
City Update
1 Dax, Patrick: Der große 'Smart City'-Schwindel (13.06.14), URL: http://futurezone.at
2 Adam Greenfield: Against the Smart City. New York City, NY: Do Projects 2013.

p. 76
E-Commerce in Rural China
1 Zhejiang Investigation Team of Information Advocacy Group, Ministry of Agriculture: Zhejiang Suichang. "Ganjie" model – let farmers enjoy the profits as E-Commerce enters China's countryside (07.05.2015), URL: http://www.moa.gov.cn/ (Chinese)
2 E-Commerce Public Service Center in Suichang County: A brief introduction into the rural E-Commerce Ganjie Model of Suichang County, Lishui City (22.05.2015), URL: http://www.apclc.com/ (Chinese)
3 Shengjie, Ji: Suichang: Ganjie out of the mountains, facing the outer world (28.04.2015), URL: http://society.people.com.cn (Chinese)
4 NPC and CPPCC proposals focusing in rural E-Commerce: Ganjie-model to be nationwide implemented in 20,000 villages (16.03.2015), URL: http://www.cctime.com/ (Chinese)
5 Ganjie Offical, URL: http://info.51ganjie.com (Chinese)

p. 78
Anti-Pack-Aging
1 Benrath, Bastian: Die Macht der Marktplätze (08.05.2014), URL: http://www.handelsblatt.com
2 Forschungsgruppe Retourenmanagement (2015), URL: http://www.retourenforschung.de

p. 81
Manila – Ground Constellations
- Mercurio, Richmond: Traffic can make Metro Manila uninhabitable in 4 years (04.01.2016), URL: http://www.philstar.com
- Whaley, Floyd: Strained Infrastructure in Philippines Erodes the Nation's Growth Prospects (03.08.2014), URL: http://www.nytimes.com

p. 84
Syrbia
1 "Syrbia" is the portmanteau of Serbia and Syria.
1 "Syrbia" ist eine Wortkreuzung aus Serbien und Syrien.
2 Ito, Toyoo; Torres-Nadal, José María: Escritos. Colegio oficial de aparejadores y arquitectos tecnicos. Murcia, España: Libreria Yerba Cajamurcia 2000.
3 Turkle, S.: Alone Together. Why do we expect more from technology and less from each other? New York City, NY: Basic Books 2013.
4 Panel 1: left diagram "Earth Default". Original geography of the planet as we know it.
4 Tafel 1: linkes Diagramm "Earth Default". Typische Geographie des Planeten, wie wir ihn kennen.
5 Panel 1: diagram "Earth Plural". Alternate cartographies of Earth's not-so similar doppelgängers. Countries are reshuffled by changing their latitude and longitude based on how they score when it comes to a particular online activity. The ones with higher scores are moved towards the equator and conversely those with a lower score gravitate towards the poles, while retaining their original geographic hemisphere.
5 Tafel 1: Diagramm "Earth Plural". Alternative Kartographie eines nicht besonders ähnlichen Doppelgängers der Erde. Die Nationen sind durch Änderung ihrer Längen- und Breitengrade neu positioniert, basierend darauf, wie sie in Bezug auf eine bestimmte

Online-Aktivität punkten. Länder mit einer höheren Bewertung bewegen sich hin zum Äquator und die mit einer niedrigeren Punktzahl gravitieren im Gegenzug hin zu den Polen, während sie ihre ursprüngliche geographische Hemisphäre beibehalten.
6 Panel 4: diagram "Syrbia". Assumptions about changes in the urban matrix are based on the utter presence of the immaterial.
6 Tafel 4: Diagramm "Syrbia". Vermutungen über Veränderungen des städtischen Gefüges basieren auf der äußersten Präsenz des Immateriellen.

p. 88
Subversive Tehran
1 Calvino, Italo: Die unsichtbaren Städte. 2te Auflage. München: Carl Hanser Verlag 2007.
2 Bayat, Asef: Tehran – Paradox City. In: New Left Review, Nov-Dec 2010 (Volume 66), p. 99-122.
3 Habermas, Jürgen: The Structural Transformation of the Public Sphere. An Inquiry into a Category of Bourgeois Society. Cambridge: Polity 1989.
4 Harvey, David: The Right to the City. In: New Left Review Sept-Dec 2008 (Volume 53), p. 23-40.
5 Fraser, Nancy: Rethinking the Public Sphere. A Contribution to the Critique of Actually Existing Democracy. In: Robbins, Bruce (Ed.): The Phantom Public Sphere, Minneapolis, MN: Minnesota University Press 1993.
6 Sassen, Saskia: Open Source Urbanism. In: New City Reader, 2010 (Volume 15).
7 Till, Jeremy: Architecture depends. Cambridge, MA: MIT press, 2009.
8 Castells, Manuel: The Information Age. Vol. 1: the Rise of the Work Society. 2nd Edition. Oxford, UK: Wiley Blackwell 2010.
9 Revolution Decoded. Iran's Digital Landscape (2014), URL: http://smallmedia.org.uk/
10 http://smallmedia.org.uk/lgbtrepublic.pdf
11 http://smallmedia.org.uk/knowledge.pdf
12 Planetary Urbanism. Critique of the Present in the Medium of Information Design (2014), URL: http://www.archplus.net/home/planetaryurbanism
13 Castells, M.: An Introduction to the Information Age. In: Bridge, Gary; Watson, Sophie (Ed.): The Blackwell City Reader. 2nd Edition. Malden, MA: Wiley-Blackwell 2010.
14 Sieverts, Thomas: Mastering the city. Rotterdam: Exhibition Netherlands Architecture Institute 1998.

p. 92
Just Trust Us – Or Take This
- Kant, Immanuel: Beantwortung der Frage: Was ist Aufklärung? In: Bahr, Erhard (Ed.): Was ist Aufklärung? Thesen und Definitionen. Stuttgart: Reclam 1996, p. 9-17.
- Welche der folgenden Sicherheitsprogramme nutzen Sie auf Ihrem privaten Computer? (2014), URL: http://de.statista.com
- Facebook Terms of Use (Germany 2015), URL: https://de-de.facebook.com/legal/terms?locale=de_DE
- Google Terms of Use (Germany 2015), URL: https://www.google.de/intl/de/policies/terms/regional.html
- German Federal Data Protection Act (2015), URL: http://www.gesetze-im-internet.de
- Hamburg Data Protection Laws (2015), URL: https://www.datenschutz-hamburg.de

p. 96
The Architecture of the Grid
- ENTSO-E (2014), URL: https://www.entsoe.eu
- GeoProRegio (2015), URL: http://www.geoproregio.ch
- Hichey, Robert: Electrical Engineer's Portable Handbook. Chicago, IL: Mac-Graw Hill 1999.
- Itten, René; Frischknecht, Rolf; Stucki, Matthias: Life Cycle Inventories of Electricity Mixes and Grid. Uster, Switzerland: Paul Scherrer Institut (PSI) 2014.
- Swissgrid (2010), URL: http://www.raonline.ch

p. 100
United Regions of Europe
- Sudjic, Deyan: Laboratorien des Postnationalismus. Der multiethnische Kosmopolitismus der Megastädte ist wegweisend für die Menschheit (01.11.2006), URL: https://zeitschrift-ip.dgap.org
- Haffner, Dorothée: Europa der Regionen. Wenn Wirtschaft unabhängig macht (15.09.2014), URL: info.arte.tv
- Berlininstitut für Bevölkerungsentwicklung: Die demografische Zukunft Europas. Wie sich Regionen verändern (2008), URL: www.berlin-institut.org
- Demographia: World Urban Areas. Population Projections. The 6th Edition of World Urban Areas (2010), URL: www.demographia.com/db-wuaproject.pdf
- ESPON: Territorial Dynamics in Europe. Evidence for a European Urban Agenda. Territorial Observation No. 13, November 2014. Luxemburg: ESPON Programme 2013.
- EUROSTAT: Primary income of private households by NUTS 2 regions (28.09.2015), URL: http://ec.europa.eu
- Menasse, Robert: Der Europäische Landbote. Die Wut der Bürger und der Friede Europas. 9th Edition, Wien, Österreich: Paul Zsolnay Verlag 2012.
- Menasse, Robert: Heimat ist die schönste Utopie. Reden (wir) über Europa. Berlin, Deutschland: Suhrkamp Verlag 2014.
- Committee of the Regions: Division of Powers between the European Union, the Member States and Regional and Local Authorities. EIPA, ECR, European Union, December 2012.
- Mann, Thomas; Hoffschulte, Martina: "Deutsche Hörer!". Thomas Manns Rundfunkreden (1940 bis 1945) im Werkkontext. Münster, Deutschland: Telos 2003.

III. INFORMAL VERSUS REGULATED

p. 110
On the Myth of Informal Settlement: Karail Basti, Dhaka
1 Until today, Karail is an empty spot on Dhaka's official city maps. The project carried out by Habitat Forum Berlin was presented in detail in the previous pages.
1 Auf Dhakas offiziellen Stadtplänen wird Karail bis heute nicht angezeigt. Das Projekt des Habitat Forum Berlin wurde auf den vorhergehenden Seiten eingehend dargestellt.
2 Burri, Anja: Dhaka's biggest slum to finally get legal water supply (27.02.2013), URL: http://archive.thedailystar.net
The maintenance works – the construction of water tanks and the introduction of water pumps, which generally serve eight to ten families – were carried out by the inhabitants with logistical support from the NGO Dushtha Shasthya Kendra (DSK) and start-up financing from WaterAid and UNICEF, which supplemented the funds raised by the residents themselves. Today the residents pay themselves for both the water and the maintenance of the infrastructure.
2 Die Instandsetzungsarbeiten – der Bau von Wassertanks und die Einbringung von Wasserpumpen, die in der Regel acht bis zehn Familien bedienen – wurden von den Bewohnern mit logistischer Unterstützung der NGO Dushtha Shasthya Kendra (DSK) durchgeführt und dank einer Anschubfinanzierung von WaterAid und UNICEF ermöglicht, welche die von den Bewohnern selbst aufgetriebenen Beiträge ergänzte. Heute bezahlen die Bewohner selbst, sowohl für das Wasser als auch für die Instandhaltung der Infrastruktur.
3 CBO = Community Based Organisation. These organisations for local self-management have been established in many of the bastis in Dhaka – and elsewhere – with the aid of NGOs.
3 CBO = Community Based Organisation. Diese Organisationen zum Zweck der lokalen Selbstverwaltung sind in vielen Basti von Dhaka – ähnlich wie in anderen Städten – mit der Hilfe von NGOs etabliert worden.
4 bhai = brother: in Bangladesh, men are commonly referred to as brothers.
4 bhai = Bruder: In Bangladesch werden Männer geläufig als Brüder angesprochen.
5 According to UN-Habitat, approx. 60 per cent of Dhaka's inner-city unauthorised settlements have no sewage or drainage systems, even though they are more susceptible to flooding than the dwellings on "legal" land.
5 Von Dhakas innerstädtischen nicht-autorisierten Siedlungen haben laut UN-Habitat etwa 60 Prozent keine Ableitungskanäle und Entwässerungsanlagen, obwohl sie einer höheren Überschwemmungsgefahr ausgesetzt sind als die Behausungen auf "legalem" Land.
6 In late 2012, the local traders sold on the tapped electricity, for which they paid 5 Taka per unit to the regular suppliers, at a price by 33 per cent higher; after the legalisation of water supply in Karail, the monthly bill amounts to less than half of the sum that was due in the days of "informal" supply (data from the mentioned HFB study, see FN 2).
6 Ende 2012 verkauften lokale Anbieter den abgezapften Strom, für den sie 5 Taka pro Einheit an den Stromlieferer bezahlten, zu einem Aufpreis von 33 Prozent weiter; nach der Legalisierung der Wasserversorgung in Karail beträgt die monatliche Rechnung nur noch weniger als die Hälfte der Summe, die zu Selbstversorgungszeiten fällig wurde (Daten aus der genannten HFB-Studie, siehe FN 2).
7 mallik = Bengali for chief, boss or owner.
7 mallik = Bengali für Boss, Chef oder Besitzer.

p. 118
Cidade de Deus
1 Turner, John F.C.: Habitação de Baixa Renda no Brasil. Políticas a tuais e oportunidades futuras. In: Architetura. Revista do Instituto do Architetos do Brasil, Feb 1968, p.17.
2 Kennedy, John F.: Ansprache auf einem Empfang für lateinamerikanische Diplomaten, 13. März 1961, zitiert nach Gardner, John W. (Ed.): John F. Kennedy. Dämme gegen die Flut – Reden und Erklärungen 1962, aus dem Amerikanischen von Karl Mönch. Frankfurt a. M.: Fischer Bücherei 1964, p. 131.
3 Dimitriadou, Stella et al.: CDD history. In: Angélil, Marc; Hehl, Rainer (Eds.): Cidade de Deus. City of God. Working with Informalized Mass Housing in Brazil. Berlin: Ruby Press 2013. ISBN 978-3-944074-02-3. p. 112-129.
4 Hehl, Rainer: Standardized mass housing in Brazil. In: Angélil, Marc; Hehl Rainer (Eds.): Cidade de Deus. City of God. Working with Informalized Mass Housing in Brazil. Berlin: Ruby Press 2013. ISBN 978-3-944074-02-3. p. 130-137.
5 Bowater, Donna: City of God, 10 years on (06.08.2013), URL: http://www.bbc.com
6 Steele, Francesca: Brazil property. Buyers target homes in Rio's 'pacified' favelas (13.09.2013), URL: http://www.ft.com
7 Associated Press: Brazil pledges to cut carbon emissions 37% by 2025 (28.09.2015), URL: http://www.theguardian.com
8 Koumantou, Chrysoula: Our city, our life. In: Angélil, Marc; Hehl Rainer (Eds.): Cidade de Deus. City of God. Working with Informalized Mass Housing in Brazil. Berlin: Ruby Press 2013. ISBN 978-3-944074-02-3. p. 144-149.
9 Theodorakatou, Antonella: Advocating the compact city. In: Angélil, Marc; Hehl Rainer (Eds.): Cidade de Deus. City of God. Working with Informalized Mass Housing in Brazil. Berlin: Ruby Press 2013. ISBN 978-3-944074-02-3. p. 166-169.

p. 123
Lima: Co-produced City
1 Kapstein-Lopez, Paula; Aranda-Dioses, Edith: Inner Peripheries of Lima. Location and identification of vulnerability – generating neighborhoods. The case of San Cosme. In: revista invi, Nov 2014 (Volume 29) p. 19-62.
2 Riofrío, Gustavo: Urban Slums Reports. The case of Lima, Peru. In: UN-Habitat Global Report on Human Settlements 2003. The Challenge of Slums. London: Earthscan 2003, p. 195-228.

p. 126
Artificial Reef

1 Ungers, Oswald M.: Großformen im Wohnungsbau. Berlin: TU Berlin Lehrstuhl für Entwerfen und Gebäudelehre 1966, p. 15.
2 Metrolog(ue) Conference Mumbai. Jointly organised by CRIT, Mumbai and SARAI-CSDS (27 - 29.12.2006), URL: http://crit.in/initiatives/emerging-urbanism/metrologue/
3 Stallmeyer, John: New Silicon Valleys. Tradition, Globalization, and Information-Technology Development in Bangalore, India. In: TDSR, Spring 2008 (Volume 19), p. 21-36.
4 Benjamin, Salon: The Aesthetics of 'The Ground Up' City. Some Insights from Bangalore. In: Karnataka. Vignettes. A symposium on emerging trends in contemporary Karnataka. Seminar 612, 2010.
5 Ong, Aihwa: Introduction. Worlding Cities. The Art of Being Global. In: Roy, Ananya; Ong, Aihwa (Ed.): Worlding Cities. Asian Experiments and the Art of Being Global. Hoboken, NJ: Wiley-Blackwell 2011, p. 6.
6 Moustafa, Amer: Between Global and Local. The Global-Local Nexus and the New Urban Order. In: Urban Transformation. Berlin: Ruby Press 2008, p. 85.
7 Guha, R.: On some aspects of the historiography of colonial India (1988), quoted from Roy, Anaya: Slumdog Cities. Rethinking Subaltern Urbanism. In: International Journal of Urban and Regional Research, 2011 (Volume 35.2), p. 226.
8 Hosagrahar, Jyoti: Indigenous Modernities. Negotiating Architecture and Urbanism. Hove, UK: Psychology Press 2005, p. 7.
9 Ong, Aihwa: Introduction. Worlding Cities. The Art of Being Global. In: Roy, Ananya; Ong, Aihwa (Ed.): Worlding Cities. Asian Experiments and the Art of Being Global. Hoboken: Wiley-Blackwell 2011, p. 9.
10 Benjamin, Salon: The aesthetics of 'The Ground Up' City. Some Insights from Bangalore. In: Karnataka. Vignettes. A symposium on emerging trends in contemporary Karnataka. Seminar 612, 2010, p. 4.
11 Definition of Artificial reef, URL: https://en.wikipedia.org/wiki/Artificial_reef
12 Schrijver, Lara: The Archipelago City. Piecing together Collectivities. In: Avermaete et al. (Eds.): OASE 71. Urban Formation and Collective Spaces. Rotterdam: NAI Publishers 2006, p. 26.
13 Koolhaas, Rem: Bigness and the problem of Large. In: Koolhaas, Rem et al.: S, M, L, XL. Office for Metropolitan Architecture. Cologne, Germany: Benedikt Taschen Verlag 1997, p. 512.
14 Appadurai, Arjun: The production of Locality. In: Appadurai, Arjun (Ed.): Modernity at Large. Cultural Dimensions of Globalization. Public Worlds, Vol. 1. Minneapolis, MN: University of Minnesota Press 1996, p. 187.

IV. NEOLIBERAL URBAN POLICY

p. 132
Medellín – Human Right on Water

1 EPM (Empresas Públicas de Medellín): Consolidated financial statement. Medellín: Grupo EPM 2011.
2 EPM (Empresas Públicas de Medellín): Una Mirada el pasado. Una vision de futuro. Medellín: Grupo EPM 2000.
3 Kessides, I. N.: Reforming infrastructure. Privatization, regulation, and competition. Washington, DC: World Bank Group and Oxford University Press 2004.
4 The World Bank: Making services work for the poor. World Development Report 2004. Washington, DC: The World Bank Group 2004.
5 Linton, J.: What is Water? The history of a modern abstraction. Vancouver, Canada: University of British Columbia Press 2010.
6 Swyngedouw, E.: The political economy and political ecology of the hydro-social cycle. In: Journal of Contemporary Water Research & Education, August 2009 (Volume 142), p. 56-60.

p. 136
Berlin for Sale

- openBerlin e.V. (2015), URL: http://www.openberlin.org
- freespace Berlin (2015), URL: http://www.freespaceberlin.org
- Liegenschaftsfonds Berlin GmbH & Co. KG (2015), URL: http://www.liegenschafts-fonds.de

p. 138
Dwellings

- Welzer, Harald; Giesecke, Dana; Tremel, Luise (Hg.): FUTURZWEI Zukunftsalmanach 2015/16. Geschichten vom guten Umgang mit der Welt. Frankfurt a. M., Deutschland: Fischer 2014.
- Jeinic, Ana; Wagner, Anselm (Hg.): Is There (Anti-)Neoliberal Architecture. Berlin, Deutschland: Jovis 2013.
- id22. Institut für kreative Nachhaltigkeit Berlin (Hg.): Co Housing Cultures. Handbuch für selbstorganisiertes und nachhaltiges Wohnen. Berlin: Jovis 2012.
- Dreysse, Dietrich-W. (Hg.): Ernst May. Das neue Frankfurt. Fünf Jahre Wohnungsbau in Frankfurt am Main. Faksimile der Doppelhefte 2/3 und 4/5 von 1930. Frankfurt, Deutschland: Heinrich 2011.
- Nagler, Mike: Ursachen und Auswirkungen von Entstaatlichung öffentlicher Einrichtungen auf die Stadtentwicklung im Kontext einer gesamtgesellschaftspolitischen Entwicklung am Beispiel der Privatisierung der WOBA Dresden. Dissertation M. Nagler 2007.

p. 142
Buy Buy Berlin

- Amt für Statistik Berlin Brandenburg: Wanderungen Berlin (2010), URL: https://www.statistik-berlin-brandenburg.de
- Amt für Statistik Berlin Brandenburg: Ergebnisse des Mikrozensus im Land Berlin (2010), URL: https://www.statistik-berlin-brandenburg.de
- Berner, L. et al.: Zwangsräumungen und die Krise des Hilfesystem. Eine Fallstudie in Berlin. Berlin, Deutschland: Humboldt-Universität zu Berlin, Institut für Sozialwissenschaften 2015.
- Breckner, I.: Gentrifizierung im 21. Jahrhundert (20.04.2010), URL: http://www.bpb.de

p. 144
Istanbul – Great City Life

1 İslam, Tolga: Tarlabaşı (Nov 2009), URL: https://lsecities.net
2 Nurtsch, Ceyda: Gentrifizierung auf Türkisch (15.09.2015), URL: http://www.deutschlandradiokultur.de
3 Bourque, Jessica: Poor but Proud Istanbul Neighbourhood Faces Gentrification (04.07.2012), URL: http://nyti.ms/1Qyjkx3
4 Watson, Ivan: Istanbul's Tarlabasi under Constant Transformation (15.07.2007), URL: http://www.npr.org

p. 146
Citizens Right in Planning

1 Koolhaas, Rem; Mau, Bruce: S, M, L, XL. New York City, NY: Monacelli Press 1995.
2 Huynh, D.: The misuse of urban planning in Ho Chi Minh City. In: Habitat International, 2015 (Volume 48), p. 11-19.
3 Kim, A.M.: Accessed land takings in the private interest. Comparisons of urban land development controversies in the United States, China, and Vietnam. In: Cityscapes, 2009 (Volume 11/1), p. 19-32.
- Bitexco Group: Bitexco chosen to zone Binh Quoi - Thanh Da urban area (17.05.2014), URL: http://bitexco.com.vn
- saigon-gpdaily: HCMC approves two bridges in Thanh Da Island (11.10.2015), URL: http://www.talkvietnam.com
- Nam, Van: City okays investor selection plan for Binh Quoi-Thanh Da urban area (04.11.2015), URL: http://english.thesaigontimes.vn

p. 148
Gated Communities

- Glasze, G.: Privatisierung öffentlicher Räume? Einkaufszentren, Business Improvement Districts und geschlossene Wohnkomplexe. In: Berichte zur deutschen Landeskunde 2001 (Volume 75/2-3), p. 160-177.
- Füller, Henning; Glasze, Georg: Gated communities und andere Formen abgegrenzten Wohnens (13.01.2014), URL: http://www.bpb.de
- Arrighi, Ryan: City of Walls. The Motivation and Desire behind Gated Communities. Jupiter, Florida: Florida Atlantic University 2013.
- Statistics South Africa: The City of Cape Town. Census 2011, URL: http://www.statssa.gov.za
- Seethaler, Karin: Disney-Planstadt Celebration. Zu schön, um schön zu sein (18.07.2011), URL: http://www.spiegel.de

p. 152
Urban Exile

- Musterd, Sako; Murie, Alan (Eds.): The Spatial Dimensions of Urban Social Exclusion and Integration. A European Comparison. Comparative Statistical Analysis at National, Metropolitan, Local and Neighbourhood Level. URBEX-Series, No. 4. Amsterdam: TSER 2000.
- Mead, Derek: A New Look at Kowloon Walled City, the Internet's Favorite Cyberpunk Slum (03.04.2014), URL: http://motherboard.vice.com
- Semuels, Alana: Suburbs and the New American Poverty (07.01.2015), URL: http://www.theatlantic.com

p. 154
Motion Poster: Angry 99

- United for a Fair Economy (2013), URL: www.faireconomy.org
- Afferent Input: Fiorina's 2 min hate on the public sector (04.02.2013), URL: http://afferentinput.blogspot.de
- US Department of Commerce: Bureau of Economic Analysis (2013), URL: www.bls.gov/ces
- US Bureau of Labour statistics, Current Employment Statistics (2013), URL: www.bls.gov/ces
- Kopczuk, Wojciech; Saez Emmanuel; Song, Jae: Uncovering the American Dream. Inequality and Mobility in Social Security Earnings Data since 1937. NBER Working Paper No. 13345. Cambridge, MA: National Bureau of Economic Research 2007.

p. 156
World Metropols: About Wages and Prices

- UBS AG CIO Wealth Management Research (Hg.): Preise und Löhne 2012 (14.09.2012), URL: https://www.ubs.com
- The World Bank: GDP per capita (current US$), URL: http://data.worldbank.org/indicator/NY.GDP.PCAP.CD

V. URBAN METABOLISM

p. 162
Where there is Light, there is Shadow
- Posch, Thomas; Holker, Franz; Uhlmann, Thomas; Freyhoff, Anja (Eds.): Das Ende der Nacht. Lichtsmog. Gefahren – Perspektiven – Lösungen. 2nd Edition. Weinheim, Deutschland: Wiley VCH 2014.
- Eisenbeis, Gerhard: Lichtverschmutzung und ihre fatalen Folgen für Tiere. Heidelberg, Deutschland: Spektrum Akademischer Verlag 2001.
- Steinlein, Christina: Insektensterben treibt Lebensmittelpreise in die Höhe (02.05.2012), URL: http://www.focus.de
- Vadav, Anand: Guidelines Energy Efficient Street Lighting. US Aid India 2010.
- Wählervereinigung Pro-Hattersheim e. V.: Straßenbeleuchtung modernisieren (2015), URL: http://www.pro-hattersheim.de

p. 165
Diagnosis City
1 Rother, Richard: Feinstaub und Ozon. Krank durch dicke Luft (15.10.2013), URL: www.taz.de
2 WHO prognostiziert. Krebs, COPD, Schlaganfall. Sieben Millionen Tote durch Luftverschmutzung (25.03.2014), URL: www.focus.de
3 Krank durch Lärm. Stressreaktionen im Körper kaum vermeidbar (28.04.2015), URL: www.zdf.de
4 Hörlabor HTW Berlin: Lärmpegel (2013), URL: https://hoerlabor.wordpress.com/2013/04/
5 Statistica 2016: Häufigkeit ausgewählter Grunderkrankungen nach Ausprägungsgrad von Schlafstörungen 2009, URL: http://de.statista.com
6 Gesundheitsreport der Techniker Krankenkasse: Immer mehr Fehltage wegen psychischer Erkrankungen (2015), URL: https://www.tk.de
7 Bertelsmann Stiftung (Hg.): Faktencheck Gesundheit. Depression (2015), URL: http://faktencheck-gesundheit.de
8 Brzoska, Ina: Stress in the City. Große Stadt, kranke Seele (10.11.12), URL: www.n-tv.de

p. 168
Urban Mining
- Jensen, Anette: Ökonomie ohne Abfall. In: Le Monde Diplomatique (Hg.): Atlas der Globalisierung. Weniger wird Mehr. Berlin, Deutschland: taz Entwicklungs GmbH 2015.
- Statistica 2016 (Hg.): Zusammensetzung des Elektronikschrotts nach Materialien in Deutschland, URL: http://de.statista.com
- Diekmann, Florian; Kröger, Michael; Reimann, Anna: Desaster bei öffentlichen Großprojekten. Wie die Politik die Bürger täuscht (09.01.2013), URL: http://www.spiegel.de
- Phosphor-Recycling. Kostbarer Nährstoff aus Klärschlamm und Abwasser (26.09.2012), URL: http://www.handelsblatt.com

p. 172
Securing Water for Food
- Libbe, J.; Beckmann, K.: Infrastruktur und Stadtentwicklung. Technische und soziale Infrastrukturen. Herausforderungen und Handlungsoptionen für Infrastruktur- und Stadtplanung. Berlin, Deutschland: Deutsches Institut für Urbanistik 2010.
- Million, A.; Bürgow, G.; Steglich, A.; Raber, W.: ROOF WATER-FARM. Participatory and Multifunctional Infrastructures for Urban Neighborhoods. In: Roggema, R.; Keffe, G. (Eds.): Proceedings – 6th AESOP Food Planning Conference Leuuwarden, Netherlands 05.- 07.11.2014, p. 659-678.
- Bürgow, G.: Urban Aquaculture. Water-sensitive transformation of cityscapes via blue-green infrastructures. Dissertation Technische Universität Berlin. Schriftenreihe der Reiner-Lemoine-Stiftung. Herzogenrath, Deutschland: Shaker Verlag 2014.
- AECOM (Ed.): Water sensitive Urban Design in the UK. Ideas for Built Environment Practitioners. London, UK: CIRIA 2013.
- Hoyer, J.; Dickhaut, W.; Kronawitter, L.; Weber, B.: Water Sensitive Urban Design. Principles and Inspiration for Sustainable Stormwater Management in the City of the Future. Berlin, Deutschland: Jovis 2011.
- Verbücheln, M.; Grabow, B.; Uttke, A.; Schwausch, M.; Gassner, R.: Szenarien für eine integrierte Nachhaltigkeitspolitik. Am Beispiel. Die nachhaltige Stadt 2030. Band 2: Teilbericht Kreislaufstadt 2030. Dessau-Rosslau, Deutschland: Umweltbundesamt 2013.
- BMBF Federal Ministry of Education and Research (Ed.): Funding priority "Sustainable Water Management" (NaWaM) and Smart and Multifunctional Infrastructures (INIS) (2011), URL: http://www.bmbf.nawam-inis.de/en

p. 174
The Water Issues of Accra
1 Swyngedouw E.: Social power and the urbanization of water. Flows of power. Oxford, UK: Oxford University Press 2004.
2 Grimm, N.B. et al.: Global change and the ecology of cities. In: Science 319/5864, 2008, p. 756-760.
3 Bruns, A.; Frick, F.: Coastal Cities at Multiple Risks. The Case of Accra. In: Mainzer Geographische Studien 55, 2013, p. 59-77.
4 Stoler, J. et al.: When urban taps run dry. Sachet water consumption and health effects in low income neighborhoods of Accra, Ghana. In: Health & Place 18/2, 2012, p. 250-262.
5 The GIS Company Ghana (Hg.): Study on the drinking water distribution network of the Greater Accra Metropolitan Area (GAMA). Ghana 2012.
6 Swyngedouw, E.: Kaika, M.; Castro, E.: Urban Water. A Political-Ecology Perspective. Built Environment 28 (Volume 2), 2002, p. 124-137.
7 Adank, M. et al.: Towards integrated urban water management in the Greater Accra Metropolitan Area. Current status and strategic directions for the future. Accra, Ghana: SWITCH and Resource Centre Network 2011.
8 Peloso, M.; Morinville, C.: Chasing for Water. Everyday Practices of Water Access in Peri-Urban Ashaiman, Ghana. In: Water Alternatives 7/1, 2014, p. 121-139.

p. 176
Sanitation in India
1,2 Gardiner, Harris: Poor Sanitation in India May Afflict Well-Fed Children With Malnutrition (13.07.2014), URL: http://www.nytimes.com
3 The UNICEF/WHO Joint Monitoring Programme for Water Supply and Sanitation estimate for 2008 is based on the 2006 Demographic and Health Survey, the 2001 census, other data and the extrapolation of previous trends to 2010.
4 The World Bank: Punjab Rural Water Supply and Sanitation Project. Annex 1. Project Appraisal Document 2006.
5 Raghupathi, P. et al.: National Institute of Urban Affairs. Status of Water Supply. Sanitation and Solid Waste Management. New Dheli, India: National Institute of Urban Affairs 2005, p. xix-xxvi.
6 Center for Study of Science, Technology and Policy (CSTEP): San Tool (2014), URL: http://cstep.in/projects/santool

p. 178
Climate Change Adaptation in Tobago
1 Nicholls, R. J.; Hoozemans Frank M. J.; Marchand, Marcel: Increasing flood risk and wetland losses due to global sea-level rise. Regional and global analyses. In: Global Environmental Change 9, 1999, p. 69-87.
2 Mimura, N. et al.: Small islands. In: Parry M. L. et al. (Eds.): Climate Change 2007. Impacts, Adaptation and Vulnerability. Contribution of Working Group II to the Fourth Assessment Report of the Intergovernmental Panel on Climate Change. Cambridge, UK: Cambridge University Press 2007, p. 687-716.
3 Baban, Serwan M. J. et al.: Mapping and detecting land use/cover change in Tobago using remote sensing and GIS. In: Caribbean Journal of Earth Science 40, 2009, p. 3-13.
4 IPCC Summary for policymakers. In: Field, C. B. et al. (Eds.): Climate Change 2014. Impacts, Adaptation, and Vulnerability. Part A. Global and Sectoral Aspects. Contribution of Working Group II to the Fifth Assessment Report of the Intergovernmental Panel on Climate Change. Cambridge, UK: Cambridge University Press 2014.
5 For more information of the ParCA project please see: http://parca.uwaterloo.ca.
6 Pizarro, Rafael E.; Blakely, Edward; Dee, John: Urban Planning and Policy Faces Climate Change. In: Built Environment 32/4, 2006, p. 400-412.
7 Sheppard, Stephen R. J. et al.: Future visioning of local climate change. A framework for community engagement and planning with scenarios and visualisation. In: Futures 43, 2011, p. 400-412.
8 Hogarth, Peter J.: The biology of mangroves and seagrasses. Biology of Habitats Series. 2nd Edition. Oxford, UK: Oxford University Press 2007.

p. 182
Re-Generator
- United Nations: World Population Prospects. The 2012 Revision. New York, NY: Department of Economic and Social Affairs, Population Division 2013.
- Wang, Chun-ye; Zhu, Wei-ping: Analysis of the Impact of Urban Wetland on Urban Temperature Based on Remote Sensing Technology. In: 3rd International Conference on Environmental Science and Information Application Technology ESIAT, 2011.
- Qiao, Shuna; Pan, Delu; Xianqiang, He; Qianfang, Cui: Numerical Study of the Influence of Donghai Bridge on Sediment Transport in the Mouth of Hangzhou Bay. In: 3rd International Conference on Environmental Science and Information Application Technology ESIAT, 2011.
- "New Babylon" is an anti-capitalist city, perceived and designed in Amsterdam from 1959 to 1974 by Constant Nieuwenhuys.
- Diller Scofidio + Renfro: "Blur Building". Exposition Pavilion. Yverdon-Les-Bains, Switzerland: Swiss Expo 2002.
- City Mayors Foundation: The world's fastest growing cities and urban areas from 2006 to 2020, URL: http://www.citymayors.com
- Google Earth Engine: Landsat Annual Time-lapse, URL: https://earthengine.google.org/#intro/LasVegas

p. 194
Tehran: Green meeting Blue
- Sennett, Richard: Democratic Spaces. In: Hunch 9, The Berlage Center for Advanced Studies in Architecture and Urban Design, Delft University of Technology, 2005, p. 40-47.
- Gehl, J.: Life between Buildings. Using Public Space. 6th Edition. Washington, DC: Island Press 2011.
- Iran Water Resources Management Company (2015), URL: http://www.wrm.ir. (Persisch).
- Statistical Center of Iran: Tehran Statistical Yearbook, 2006. (Persisch).

p. 196
Ecology without Nature
- Ro, Charlton: Fundamentals of Fluvial Geomorphology. London: Routledge 2008.
- Hooimeijer Fransje et al.: Settlements in river regions. In: Hooimeijer Fransje et al.: Atlas of Dutch water cities. Amsterdam, Netherlands: Sun Publishers 2005.
- Huang, H.; Nanson, G. C.: Why some alluvial rivers develop an an abranching pattern. In: Water Resources Research 07441 (Volume 43), 2007, p. 1-12.
- Rijkswaterstaat Oost-Nederland (Ed.): Space for River, Nature and People: Sustainable Floodplains along the Rhine. Arnhem, Netherlands: Rijkswaterstaat Oost-Nederland 2008.

- Rink, Dieter et al.: Urban shrinkage in Leipzig and Halle. The Leipzig-Halle urban region, Germany. Shrink Smart EU Research Report. Leipzig, Deutschland: Helmholtz-Zentrum für Umweltforschung UFZ 2010.
- Haase, Dagmar: Urban ecology of shrinking cities. An unrecognized opportunity? In: Nature and Culture 1, (Volume 3), 2008, p. 1-8.
- Van Dijk, W. M.: Meandering rivers. Feedbacks between channel dynamics, floodplain and vegetation. PhD Thesis. Utrecht, Netherlands: Utrecht Studies in Earth Sciences 2013.
- WWF European fresh water programme: Wise use of floodplains. Policy and economic analysis of floodplain restoration in Europe. EU Life Environment 2000.
- Žižek, Slavoj: Nature and its discontents. In: SubStance 117/3 (Volume 37), 2008, p. 37-72.

p. 202
About Migrating Species and Human Happiness
1 Smil, V.: Making the modern world. Materials and dematerialization. Chichester, UK: John Wiley & Sons 2013.
2 Bundesministerium für Umwelt, Naturschutz, Bau und Reaktorsicherheit (BMUB): Flächenverbrauch. Worum geht es? Bonn, Deutschland: BMUB 2014.
3 Streit, B.: Verlust der biologischen Vielfalt. Über spekulative Zahlen und realisierbare Ziele. In: Forschung und Lehre 8, 2010, p. 240-243.
4 Fuller, R.A. et al.: Psychological benefits of greenspace increase with biodiversity. In: Biology Letters 3, 2007, p. 390-394.
5 Kowarik, I.: Novel urban ecosystems, biodiversity, and conservation. In: Environmental Pollution 159, 2011, p. 1974-1983.
6 Senatsverwaltung für Stadtentwicklung und Umwelt Berlin (SenStadt): Flächenverbrauch und Versiegelung. Berlin, Deutschland: SenStadt 2015.
7 Seitz, B. et al.: Der Berliner Florenatlas. Rangsdorf, Deutschland: Natur+Text 2012.

VI. MIGRATION

p. 206
Out of Proportions
1 UNHCR: Worldwide displacement hits all-time high as war and persecution increase (18.06.2015), URL: http://www.unhcr.org
2 Mullen, Jethro: Tony Blair says he's sorry for Iraq War 'mistakes', but not for ousting Saddam (26.10.2015), URL: http://edition.cnn.com
3 Helberg, Kristin: Westlicher Militäreinsatz in Syrien. Weniger Bomben, nicht mehr! (07.12.2015), URL: https://de.qantara.de

p. 210
States of Refuge
1 Asylkoordination Österreich: Information on the asylum procedure (09.05.2015), URL: http://www.asyl.at
2 Bundesministerium für Inneres: Asylwesen (2015), URL: http://www.bmi.gv.at
3 Plattform Rechtsberatung für Menschen Rechte: Videowegweiser (2015), URL: http://www.plattform-rechtsberatung.at
4 Google Maps: Deportation Centres in Austria (2015), URL: https://www.google.com/maps
5 Dialogue on Mediterranean Transit Migration (MTM): MTM I-map. Map on Mixed Migration Routes (2014), URL: http://www.imapmigration.org
6 UNHCR: Mid-Year Trends 2014 (2015), URL: http://www.unhcr.at/
7 Meeting with Djadi on April 10, 2015, Innsbruck, Tyrol. Meeting with Kalil, on April, 9, 2015, Weitensfeld, Carinthia. Names have been changed by the authors.
8 Five meetings with Mrs. H. (refugee from Palestine, has been waiting for her decision for three years), May 8 to May 16, 2015, Karwan Haus (Caritas Wien), Vienna.
9 Florian Stolz of Flüchtlingskoordination Tirol, e-mail message to the author, May 19, 2015.
10 SOS Mitmensch: Fragen & Antworten, Zugang zum Arbeitsmarkt für Asylsuchende (2015), URL: http://www.sosmitmensch.at
11-13 Arbeitsmarktservice (AMS): Asyl in Tirol. Arbeit (2015), URL: http://asyl-in-tirol.at/arbeit
14 Fr. Mag. Sylvia Zumtobel, AMS Imst, e-mail to the author, May 15, 2015.
15 Arbeitsmarktservice (AMS): Asyl in Tirol. Gemeinnützige Arbeit (2015), URL: http://asyl-in-tirol.at/arbeit/gemeinnuetzige-arbeit
16 Arbeitsmarktzugang.prekär.at: Arbeitsmarktzugang für Asylbewerber*innen (2013), URL: http://arbeitsmarktzugang.prekaer.at

p. 216
Borders and Movements
1 Meeting with Djadi on 10 April 2015, Innsbruck, Tyrol. The names of individuals have been changed by the author.
1 Treffen mit Djadi, am 10. April 2015, Innsbruck, Tirol. Der Name der befragten Person wurde von den Autoren geändert.
2 Meeting with Kalil on 9 April 2015, Weitensfeld, Carinthia. The names of individuals have been changed by the author.
2 Treffen mit Kalil, am 09. April 2015, Weitensfeld, Kärnten. Der Name der befragten Person wurde von den Autoren geändert.
3 De Certeau, Michel: Kunst des Handelns. Berlin, Deutschland: Merve Verlag 1988, p. 85-92.
4 Telser, Dietmar; Stöss, Benjamin: Der Zaun. Sofia, Bulgarien. Die Landesverteidigung (2014), URL: http://www.der-zaun.net
5 Neuhold, Clemens: Bundesheer gegen Flüchtlingsstrom (2.07.2015), URL: http://www.wienerzeitung.at
6 Baumann, Zygmunt: Flüchtige Moderne. Frankfurt a.M., edition suhrkamp, 2003, p. 113.

7 Ibid., p. 110.
8 Telser, Dietmar; Stöss, Benjamin: Der Zaun. Melilla, Spanien. Das Ghetto (2014), URL: http://www.der-zaun.net
9 Kalil, 9 June 2015.
10 Djadi speaks of Antep in the meeting. He is probably referring to the city or the region around Gaziantep, which is situated close to the rest of his route.
10 Djadi spricht im Gespräch von Antep. Vermutlich handelt es sich dabei um die Stadt oder Region rundum Gaziantep, die sich in geographischer Nähe zum Rest des Verlaufes seiner Route befindet.
11,12 Letsch, Constanze: Turkish border guards sweep up fuel smugglers and Isis fighters alike (25.09.2014), URL: http://www.theguardian.com
13 Syrische Flüchtlinge überwinden Grenze zur Türkei (15.06.2015), URL: http://www.sueddeutsche.de
14 Wohlwender, Mark: Syrian refugees cross into Turkey (15.06.2015), URL: http://www.theguardian.com
15 Gruhnwald, Sylke; Kohli, Alice: Die Toten vor Europas Toren (02.04.2014), URL: http://www.nzz.ch
16 Kalil was speaking here of the Turkish police when we met. PRO ASYL however also reports of violations of international law in push-back operations by Greek authorities on the sea and land boundaries between Greece and Turkey. "Masked special forces are accused of ill-treating refugees on pick-up, illegally interning them on Greek territory and returning them to Turkey in violation of international law." PRO ASYL: Pushed Back. Systematic human rights violations against refugees in the Aegean Sea and at the greek-turkish land border (07.11.2013), URL: www.proasyl.de
16 Kalil sprach im Gespräch von der türkischen Polizei. PRO ASYL berichtet aber auch von völkerrechtswidrigen Push-Back-Operationen durch griechische Behörden an den griechisch-türkischen See- und Landgrenzen. "Maskierten Sonderkommandos wird vorgeworfen, Flüchtlinge beim Aufgriff zu misshandeln, rechtswidrig auf griechischem Territorium zu inhaftieren und dann völkerrechtswidrig in die Türkei zurückzuweisen." PRO ASYL: Pushed Back. Systematische Menschenrechtsverletzungen an den griechisch-türkischen See- und Landgrenzen (07.11.2013), URL: www.proasyl.de
17 According to Kalil crossing by rubber dinghy costs 1,100 euro and with a faster "jet boat" 2,200 euro, which is first paid on successful arrival in Greece.
17 Eine Überfahrt mit einem Gummiboot kostet laut Kalil 1.100 Euro, ein schnelleres "Jetboot" 2.200 Euro, die erst bei erfolgreicher Ankunft in Griechenland bezahlt werden.
18,19 Telser, Dietmar; Stöss, Benjamin: Der Zaun. Ägäis, Griechenland. Inseln der Hoffnung (2014), URL: http://www.der-zaun.net
20 Giorgio Agamben: Mittel ohne Zweck. Noten zur Politik. 2nd Edition. Zurich, Switzerland: diaphanes 2006, p. 40.
21 Verschwiegen und vergessen? Flüchtlinge auf der ägäischen Urlaubsinsel Samos (22.08.2014), URL: http://www.zdf.de/aspekte
22 General Assembly of the United Nations: Article 3 of the Universal Declaration of Human Rights (A/RES/217, UN-Doc. 217/A-(III)), 10 December 1948.
23 General Assembly of the United Nations: Article 13.2 of the Universal Declaration of Human Rights (A/RES/217, UN-Doc. 217/A-(III)), 10 December 1948.
24 Kingsley, Patrick: Migrant's on Hungary's border fence. 'This wall, we will not accept it' (22.06.2015), URL: www.theguardian.com

p. 219
A Stranger at Home
- London School of Economics and Political Sciences (Hg.): The Impact of Recent Immigration on the London Economy (2007), URL: http://eprints.lse.ac.uk/
- ESRC Centre on Migration, Policy and Society: An evidence base on migration and integration in London. Oxford, UK: University of Oxford 2010.
- Statista 2016: Ausländeranteil in verschiedenen Berufsgruppen in Deutschland am 30. Juni 2014, URL: http://de.statista.com/
- Institut der deutschen Wirtschaft Köln 2016: Migranten in Deutschland: Zahlen und Fakten, URL: http://www.wirtschaftundschule.de

p. 222
City Pixels
1 Bai, Tianliang: Migrant workers gaining a sense of achievement (01.02.2016), URL: http://politics.people.com.cn/n1/2016/0201/c1001-28099260.html (chinese)
2 Xia, Xiongfei (Eds.): Can "real-name system" management fundamentally solve the problem of wage arrears of migrant workers? (21.01.2016), URL: http://hlj.rednet.cn/c/2016/01/21/3892961.htm (chinese)
3 Chan, Kam Wing: China: Internal Migration. Vol. 2: Ness, Immanuel; Bellwood, Peter (Eds.): The Encyclopedia of Global Human Migration. 1st Edition. Oxford, UK: Wiley-Blackwell 2013

p. 228
Migrant Communities in China
- Huang, Y.; Yi, C.: Invisible migrant enclaves in Chinese cities. Underground living in Beijing, China. In: Urban Studies 15 (Volume 52), Nov 2015, p. 2948-2973.
- The State Council of the People's Republic of China (2014), URL: http://www.gov.cn
- Zhang, L.: Strangers in the City. Reconfigurations of Space, Power and the Social Networks with Chinas Floating Population. Stanford, CA: Stanford University Press 2001.
- Ligorner, Lesli; Feng, Gordon; Mosvick, Mitchell: The New PRC Social Insurance Law and Expatriate Employees (01.01.2012), URL: http://www.chinabusinessreview.com
- http://www.12333sh.gov.cn
- Shanghai Municipal Human Resources and Social Security Bureau, URL: http://www.12333sh.gov.cn (Chinese)

The Last Page: Baking a Cake Together

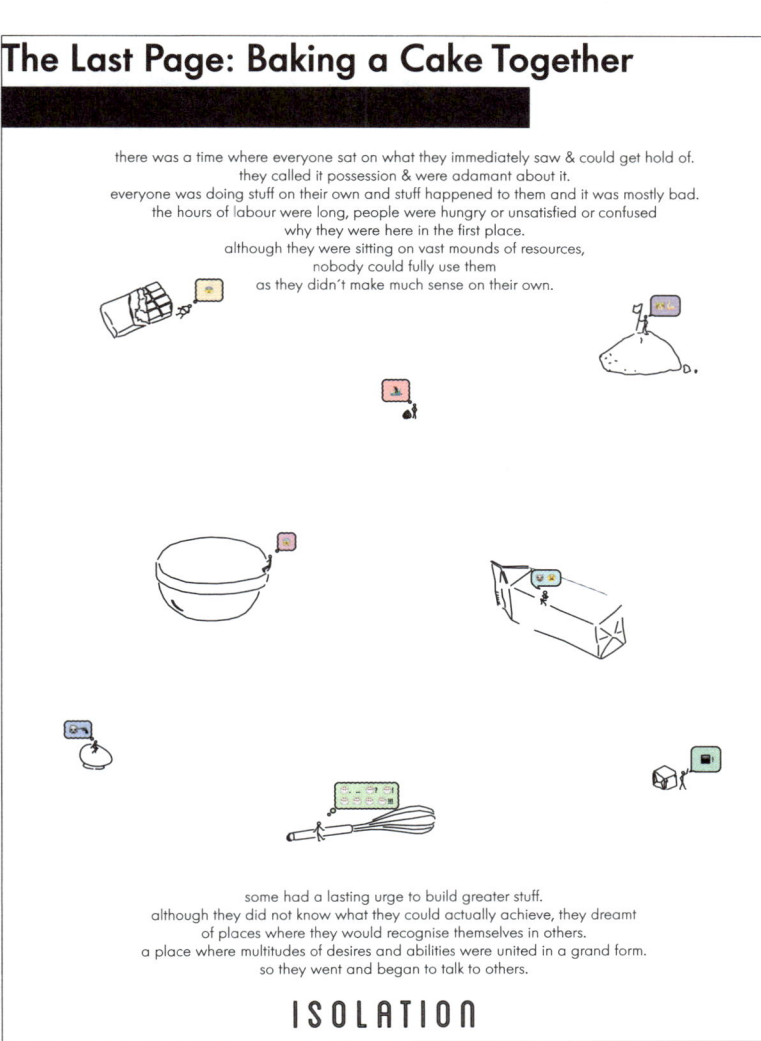

there was a time where everyone sat on what they immediately saw & could get hold of.
they called it possession & were adamant about it.
everyone was doing stuff on their own and stuff happened to them and it was mostly bad.
the hours of labour were long, people were hungry or unsatisfied or confused
why they were here in the first place.
although they were sitting on vast mounds of resources,
nobody could fully use them
as they didn't make much sense on their own.

some had a lasting urge to build greater stuff.
although they did not know what they could actually achieve, they dreamt
of places where they would recognise themselves in others.
a place where multitudes of desires and abilities were united in a grand form.
so they went and began to talk to others.

ISOLATION

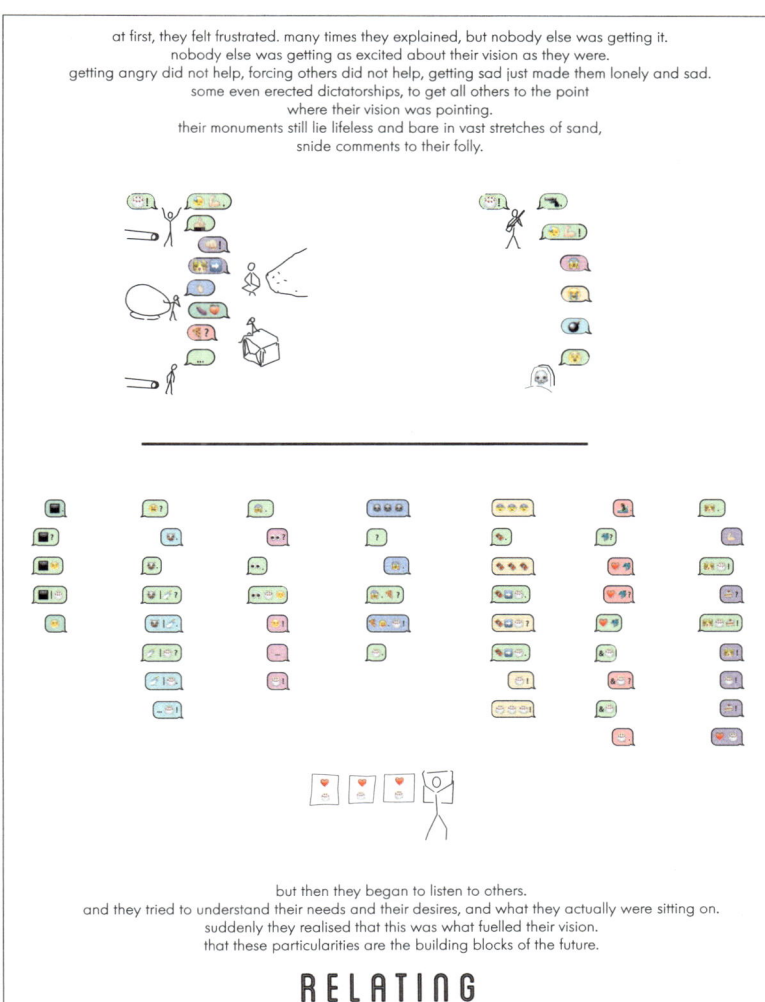

at first, they felt frustrated. many times they explained, but nobody else was getting it.
nobody else was getting as excited about their vision as they were.
getting angry did not help, forcing others did not help, getting sad just made them lonely and sad.
some even erected dictatorships, to get all others to the point
where their vision was pointing.
their monuments still lie lifeless and bare in vast stretches of sand,
snide comments to their folly.

but then they began to listen to others.
and they tried to understand their needs and their desires, and what they actually were sitting on.
suddenly they realised that this was what fuelled their vision.
that these particularities are the building blocks of the future.

RELATING

so they went on to tell everyone.
that they have an important part to play, and their participation made everyone richer.
and that it would be very sad if everyone was just sitting o
n their own mound of treasure they happened to find.
they used language that was very alive, and most importantly, they found an unique place for everyone.
soon enough, everyone was abuzz with the grandeur of the vision
and shared their excitement.

it didn't take long for the first ones to step forward and make actual plans.
some plans did not work out, because important bits of reality were missing.
everyone got continually better with sharing plans and improving upon the plans of others.
and so it came that everyone knew how to work towards the shared vision.

IDENTIFICATION

and then they baked their cake.

and it was delicious.

COOPERATION

Ruya Yuksel, Grégoire Farquet, Florian Schweizer

Colophon / Impressum

ARCH+
Zeitschrift für Architektur
und Städtebau
49. Jahrgang

Herausgeber
ARCH+ Verlag GmbH, Sabine Kraft,
Nikolaus Kuhnert, Günther Uhlig

ARCH+ Verlag GmbH
Kurbrunnenstr. 22, 52066 Aachen
Internet: www.archplus.net
eMail: verlag@archplus.net

Redaktionsadressen
ARCH+ Aachen (Verlagsadresse)
Fon: 0241–50 83 02
Fax: 0241–548 31
eMail: aachen@archplus.net

ARCH+ Berlin
Bergengruenstr. 35
14129 Berlin
Fon: 030–802 69 86,
030–80 90 31 34
Fax: 030–802 81 20
eMail: berlin@archplus.net

Redakteure
Sabine Kraft, Nikolaus Kuhnert,
Anh-Linh Ngo

Redaktionsassistenz
Anna Aichinger, Tobias Gruber, Zhen Zhang

Redaktionsgruppe dieser Ausgabe
Anna Aichinger, Sabine Kraft, Zhen Zhang,
Simone Hüttenberend,
Mitarbeit: Tatjana Wist

Redaktionelle Mitarbeiter
Sara Lusic-Alavanja, Rob Madole,
Stephan Redeker, Achim Reese,
Christine Rüb, Simone Hüttenberend

Stipendiaten der Sto-Stiftung
und des ARCH+ Fördervereins e.V.
Mirko Gatti, Katharina Kaufmann,
Quang Tuan Ta

Stipendiat der Hans-Sauer-Stiftung
Max Kaldenhoff

CvD
Christine Rüb

Online-Redaktion
Anh-Linh Ngo, Christine Rüb

ARCH+ features
Kurator Anh-Linh Ngo

Design
Anne Bissels,
Sabine Kraft

Titel
Anne Bissels,
Sabine Kraft

Lektorat
Gabriele Lauscher-Dreess

Übersetzungen der Projekttexte
aus dem Englischen ins Deutsche:
Fritz Schneider (S. 52-67, 76-77, 81-87,
92-99, 118-129, 132-135, 146-147, 178-186,
196-201)
Anna Aichinger (S. 48-51, 168-173, 194-195)
aus dem Deutschen ins Englische:
Rebecca Williams (S. 40, 72, 104, 110-117,
130, 136-137, 156-160, 204, 210-218)
Anna Aichinger (S. 4)

Ständige Mitarbeiter
Florian Böhm, Michael Hensel,
Joachim Krausse, Arno Löbbecke,
Martin Luce, Julia von Mende,
Achim Menges, Philipp Oswalt,
Philipp Schneider, Angelika Schnell,
Stephan Trüby

Vertrieb
Ute Stauch
Fon: 0241–50 83 29
Fax: 0241–548 31
eMail: vertrieb@archplus.net

Anzeigenverwaltung
Gabriele Lauscher-Dreess
Fon: 0241–50 83 03
Fax: 0241–548 31
eMail: anzeigen@archplus.net

Aboverwaltung
AVZ GmbH
Storkower Straße 127a
10407 Berlin
Fon: 030–42 80 40 40
Fax: 030–42 80 40 42
aboservice@avz-berlin.de
Konto: Postbank München
IBAN: DE32 7001 0080 0221 5608 08
BIC: PBNKDEFF

Einzelbestellungen
ARCH+ Verlag GmbH
Konto: Deutsche Bank Aachen
IBAN: DE80 3907 0024 0252 5426 00
BIC: DEUTDEDB390

Heftpreis
20 Euro

Katalogpreis
24 Euro

Abonnement
Inland 54 Euro, Ausland 63 Euro
(Ausland nur gegen Vorauszahlung),
Ermäßigtes Abonnement für Studenten,
Absolventen, Arbeitslose gegen
Bescheinigung: Inland 36 Euro,
Ausland 43 Euro

Abonnementbedingungen
Das Abonnement kann auch bis zu
max. drei Heften rückwirkend begonnen
werden. Ein Jahresabonnement umfasst
vier Hefte. Das Abonnement verlängert
sich automatisch um ein weiteres Jahr,
wenn es nicht bis sechs Wochen vor Ablauf
der Abonnementfrist gekündigt wird.
Bestellungen können innerhalb von
vierzehn Tagen widerrufen werden.

Umzug
Bitte teilen Sie dem Verlag unverzüglich
eine etwaige Adressenänderung mit,
da Zeitschriften leider vom Nachsende-
auftrag ausgeschlossen sind.

Rechte
Die Redaktion behält sich alle Rechte,
einschließlich der Übersetzung und der
fotomechanischen Wiedergabe vor.
Auszugsweiser Nachdruck mit Quellen-
angabe ist gestattet, sofern die Redaktion
davon informiert wird. Für unverlangt
eingesandte Manuskripte wird keine
Gewähr übernommen. Ein Autorenhonorar
kann nicht gezahlt werden.

Bildnachweis
ARCH+ hat sich bis Produktionsschluss
bemüht, alle Inhaber von Abbildungsrechten
ausfindig zu machen. Personen und
Institutionen, die möglicherweise Rechte
an verwendeten Abbildungen beanspruchen,
werden gebeten, sich mit der Redaktion
in Verbindung zu setzen.

Druck
Medialis Offsetdruck GmbH, Berlin

Lithografie
max-color, Berlin

ISSN: 0587-3452
ISBN: 978-3-931435-33-2

Dank
Wir danken dem Auswärtige Amt der
Bundesrepublik Deutschland für die
Förderung des Wettbewerbs- und
Ausstellungsprojekts "Planetary Urbanism –
Critique of the Present in the Medium of
Information Design".
Wir danken dem Wissenschaftlichen Beirat
der Bundesregierung Globale Umwelt-
veränderungen (WBGU) für die kollegiale
Unterstützung und Zusammenarbeit.
www.auswaertiges-amt.de
www.wbgu.de

Auswärtiges Amt

Wissenschaftlicher Beirat der Bundesregierung
Globale Umweltveränderungen

Kooperationen
Wir danken der Hans Sauer Stiftung, der
Sto-Stiftung und dem ARCH+ Verein zur
Förderung des Architektur- und
Stadtdiskurses e.V. für die Kooperation im
Rahmen des Stipendienprogramms zur
Förderung des Architektur- und
Stadtdiskurses.
www.hanssauerstiftung.de
www.sto-stiftung.de
www.archplusverein.de

Hans Sauer Stiftung

ARCH+ Displays

Sto Stiftung

ARCH+ VEREIN ZUR FOERDERUNG DES ARCHITEKTUR- UND STADTDISKURSES E.V.

in Kooperation mit ARCH+ Förderverein e.V

ARCH+ DISPLAYS

ARCH+ features wird ermöglicht durch
Siedle (Initiativpartner)
sowie Dornbracht und Euroboden

SSS SIEDLE

DORNBRACHT

EUROBODEN
ARCHITEKTURKULTUR